REDISCOVERING
RUSSIA IN ASIA

A publication of the Northeast Asia Seminar

Editors: Stephen Kotkin and David Wolff

REDISCOVERING RUSSIA IN ASIA

Siberia and the Russian Far East

Edited by
Stephen Kotkin and David Wolff

M.E. Sharpe
Armonk, New York
London, England

Library of Congress Cataloging-in-Publication Data

Rediscovering Russia in Asia : Siberia and the Russian Far East /
edited by Stephen Kotkin and David Wolff.
p.   cm.
Includes bibliographical references and index.
ISBN 1-56324-546-9. — ISBN 1-56324-547-7 (pbk.)
1. Siberia (Russia)—History. 2. Russian Far East (Russia)—History.
I. Kotkin, Stephen. II. Wolff, David.
DK761.R43 1995
957—dc20   95-1849
CIP

Printed in the United States of America

The paper used in this publication meets the minimum requirements of
American National Standard for Information Sciences—
Permanence of Paper for Printed Library Materials,
ANSI Z 39.48-1984.

♾

BM (c) 10   9   8   7   6   5   4   3   2   1
BM (p) 10   9   8   7   6   5   4   3   2   1

For Frank Golder (1877–1929)
and Robert Kerner (1887–1956),
pioneers

Contents

About the Editors and Contributors   xi

Acknowledgments   xv

Note on Transliteration   xvi

Maps   xvii

Introduction: Rediscovering Russia in Asia
   Stephen Kotkin   3

I. Overlapping Peripheries, Antagonistic Centers   17

   Photos 1–7 (following page 22)

   Conquering the Great East: Kulomzin, Peasant Resettlement,
   and the Creation of Modern Siberia
      Steven G. Marks   23

   Russia Finds Its Limits: Crossing Borders into Manchuria
      David Wolff   40

   Japan Moves North: The Japanese Occupation of
   Northern Sakhalin (1920s)
      Hara Teruyuki   55

II. Siberian Identities: Autonomy, Science, and Redemption   69

   Moscow and Siberia: Center–Periphery Relations, 1917–30
      Vladimir I. Shishkin   75

New Atlantis Revisited: Akademgorodok, Siberian City of Science
Paul R. Josephson   89

Village Prose Writers and the Question of Siberian Cultural Identity
Kathleen Parthé   108

Contemporary Siberian Regionalism
Vladimir A. Zhdanov   120

III. Far Eastern Identities: Settlement, Natives, and Borders   133

Photos 8–17 (following page 137)

A State Within a State: The Sakha Republic (Yakutia)
Marjorie Mandelstam Balzer   139

Nivkhi, Russians, and Others: The Politics of Indigenism
on Sakhalin Island
Bruce Grant   160

The Russian Far East: From a Colonial to a Borderland Economy
Pavel A. Minakir   172

**IV. After Communism: Resources for Cooperation
or Confrontation**   187

Photos 18–22 (following page 192)

Siberian Crude: Moscow, Tiumen, and Political Decentralization
Bruce Kellison   193

Property Free-For-All: Regionalism, "Democratization," and
the Politics of Economic Control in the Kuzbas, 1989–93
Paul T. Christensen   207

Back to the Collective: Production and Consumption on
a Siberian Collective Farm
Cynthia J. Buckley   224

Water Wars: Siberian Rivers, Central Asian Deserts, and
the Structural Sources of a Policy Debate
Michael L. Bressler   240

Whose Environment? A Case Study of Forestry Policy
in Russia's Maritime Province
Elizabeth Wishnick   256

V. Northeast Asia: Re-emergence of a Transnational Region   269

Photos 23–34 (following page 274)

Spontaneity and Direction Along the Russo-Chinese Border
Gilbert Rozman   275

"Yellow Peril" Again? The Chinese and the Russian Far East
Viktor Larin   290

The Emergence of Siberia and the Russian Far East as
a "New Frontier" for Koreans
Kim Hakjoon   302

The Future of Northeast Asia: Southeast Asia?
Hamashita Takeshi   312

Epilogue: Regionalism, Russia, and Northeast Asia—An Agenda
David Wolff   323

Selected Bibliography   331

Index   349

About the Editors and Contributors

Stephen Kotkin teaches in the history department at Princeton University. Author of *Steeltown, USSR: Soviet Society in the Gorbachev Era* (1991) and *Magnetic Mountain: Stalinism as a Civilization* (1995), he is writing a book on Siberia in the twentieth century. He completed the introduction to this volume while a visiting fellow at Tokyo University's Institute of Social Science.

David Wolff is assistant professor in the sociology department at Princeton University, where he teaches comparative history. He is the author of *To the Harbin Station: The Liberal Alternative in Russian Manchuria, 1898–1914* (forthcoming), and is now working on a sequel, *From the Harbin Station: Regional Development and International Conflict in Northeast Asia, 1895–1945*.

Marjorie Mandelstam Balzer teaches in the sociology and Russian Studies departments of Georgetown University. She is the editor of the journal *Anthropology and Archaeology of Eurasia*, and of the books *Shamanism: Soviet Studies of Traditional Religion in Siberia and Central Asia* (1990); *Russian Traditional Culture: Religion, Gender, and Customary Law* (1992); and *Culture Incarnate: Native Anthropology from Russia* (1995). She has two forthcoming studies: *The Tenacity of Ethnicity* and *Siberian Women's Lives: Autobiographies from the Sakha Republic (Yakutia)*.

Michael L. Bressler is assistant professor of political science at Furman University. He recently completed his graduate work at the University of Michigan, writing a dissertation examining the politics of environmental transformation and degradation in the Soviet Union during the Brezhnev and Gorbachev eras.

Cynthia J. Buckley is assistant professor of sociology and a member of the Population Research Center at the University of Texas, Austin. She has written on rural social and economic change. Her current project is a study of demographic and social issues related to rural population aging in the Russian Federation.

Paul T. Christensen is assistant professor of political science at Syracuse University. A specialist on Russian labor politics, he has published articles in several journals, including *Social Text* and *Economics and Trade Unions* (in Russia). He is currently working on a project entitled *Industrial Russia Under the New Regimes.*

Bruce Grant is assistant professor of anthropology at Swarthmore College. His book *In the Soviet House of Culture* (1995) explores the cultural history of an indigenous people of the Russian Far East, the Nivkhi of Sakhalin Island. He is currently at work on a study of the transition between late imperial and early Soviet anthropologies.

Hamashita Takeshi is professor at the Institute of Oriental Culture, Tokyo University. He is the co-editor of a seven-volume series, *Asian Perspectives* (1993–95), and the author of *Modern China's International Treaty System* (1990), all in Japanese. His current research focuses on Asian identities and regionalism.

Hara Teruyuki is professor of history at the Slavic Research Center, Hokkaido University, in Sapporo, Japan. He is the author of *The Indigirka Incident* (1993) and *The Siberian Intervention* (1988), both in Japanese. He is currently working on the Far Eastern Republic (1920–1922) and Russo-Japanese relations.

Paul R. Josephson teaches in the Science, Technology, and Society Department at Sarah Lawrence College. He is the author of *Physics and Politics in Revolutionary Russia* (1991), and a forthcoming history of Akademgorodok, *New Atlantis Revisited.* He is currently working on a political and cultural history of the Soviet atomic age.

Bruce Kellison is a candidate for the Ph.D. in political science at the University of Texas, Austin. His dissertation examines the politics of the West Siberian oil industry in the late- and post-Soviet era as well as the relationships among regionalism, economic reform, and political decentralization in Russia.

Kim Hakjoon is Chair of the Board of Trustees, Dankook University, Seoul, Korea. He has been an Alexander von Humboldt Foundation Fellow at the Universities of Munich and Vienna. The essay in this volume was completed while he was a Visiting Scholar at the Woodrow Wilson Center for Scholars, Washington, D.C.

Viktor Larin is director of the Far Eastern Institute of History, Russian Academy of Sciences, in Vladivostok. He has just completed a study of the relations between China and Southeast Asia in the nineteenth century. His current research focuses on relations between China and the Russian Far East.

Steven G. Marks is associate professor of history at Clemson University. Author of *Road to Power: The Trans-Siberian Railroad and the Colonization of Asian Russia, 1850–1917* (1991), he has participated in various joint projects with Siberian colleagues. He is currently writing a synthetic work on the reception of Russian ideas in the world during the twentieth century.

Pavel A. Minakir is director of the Far Eastern Institute of Economic Research, Russian Academy of Sciences, in Khabarovsk. Between 1991 and 1993 he was first deputy governor of Khabarovsk krai. He is the author or editor of numerous articles and books, including *Dal'nii Vostok: Ekonomicheskoe obozrenie*, 2 vols. (1993), and, in English, *The Russian Far East: An Economic Handbook* (1994). He is involved in various research projects on the contemporary economy of the Russian Far East.

Kathleen Parthé is associate professor of Russian at the University of Rochester. She is the author of *Russian Village Prose: The Radiant Past* (Princeton, 1992) and two dozen articles on Russian literature. She is working on two monographs, one on the politicization of the literary process in Russia, and the other on national identity in the post-Soviet period.

Gilbert Rozman is Musgrave Professor of Sociology and director of the Council on Regional Studies at Princeton University. He has written several studies on urbanization as well as mutual perceptions among China, Japan, and Russia. He is currently writing about views of Northeast Asian regionalism in these countries.

Vladimir I. Shishkin, former deputy director and current section chief at the Siberian Institute of History, Russian Academy of Sciences, in Novosibirsk, is the department chair for Russian and Soviet history at Novosibirsk University. He is the author of two books, *Sotsialisticheskoe stroitel'stvo v Sibirskoi derevne* (1985) and *Revoliutsionnye komitety Sibiri v gody grazhdanskoi voine* (1978), and the editor of two others: *Sovetskaia istoriia* (1992) and *Aktual'nye problemy istorii Sovetskoi Sibiri* (1990). He has written a forthcoming comprehensive study on Siberia during the Russian Civil War.

Elizabeth Wishnick is an independent scholar in Washington, D.C. She has published articles on Soviet and post-Soviet foreign policy and is the author of the forthcoming study, *Mending Fences with China: The Evolution of Moscow's China Policy, 1969–94.* She has been a visiting scholar at the Hoover Institution on War, Revolution, and Peace, and at the Harvard Russian Research Center. She is currently at work on environmental and educational issues of the former Soviet Union.

Vladimir A. Zhdanov is deputy director of the Siberian International Center of Regional Studies in Novosibirsk. Author of a study on Western perceptions of Soviet agricultural policy (1987), he has been a visiting researcher at the University of Massachusetts. He is now working on a joint British-Russian project on Siberian regionalism.

Acknowledgments

Financial support for the conference on which this volume is based was furnished by the Social Science Research Council; the Center for Global Partnership; and Princeton University's Woodrow Wilson School, Council on Regional Studies, Center for International Studies, Department of History, and Department of East Asian Studies. The editors gratefully acknowledge the assistance of Henry Bienen, John Waterbury, Martin Colcutt, Daniel Rodgers, and Gilbert Rozman. Lois Ornstein and Joyce Slack helped with organization and logistics. Tony Prather assisted in the translation of Vladimir Shishkin's essay. Julian Dierkes prepared the bibliography and index. Cynthia Buckley invested a great deal of her own time creating the maps.

Patricia Kolb of M.E. Sharpe showed keen interest in the project from the start. Ana Erlić offered expert editorial assistance. John Stephan has been exceptionally generous with his unsurpassed knowledge and his files of published and unpublished materials. The editors are also grateful to all who granted their permission for the reproduction of photographs.

The greatest debt remains that to the conference participants, including those whose papers could not be included in this volume, for exhibiting infectious enthusiasm and a collectivist spirit.

Note on Transliteration

Except for the names of a handful of famous individuals, Russian-language materials have been rendered using the Library of Congress transliteration system. For Chinese language we have used the *pinyin;* for Japanese language, the Modified Hepburn system. In the case of Chinese, Japanese, and Koreans the family name is placed first.

Maps

1. Northeast Asia   xviii

2. The Expansion of Imperial Russia into Northeast Asia   xix

3. Administrative Regions of Siberia and the Russian Far East   xx

4. Railways   xxi

5. Energy Resources of Siberia and the Russian Far East   xxii

6. Land Resources of Siberia and the Russian Far East   xxiii

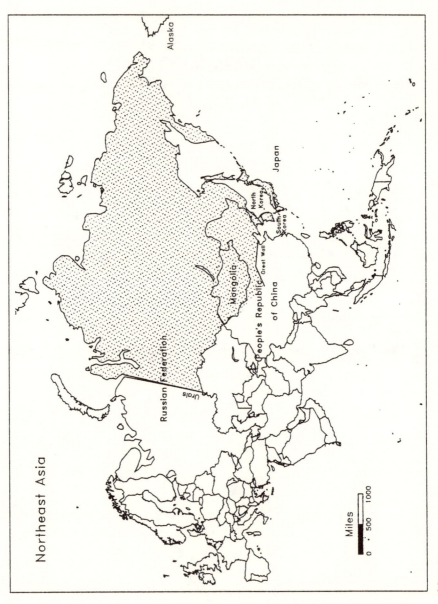

Northeast Asia

Map 1

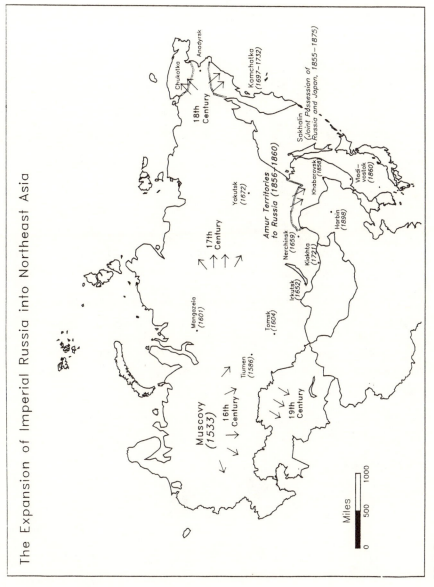

The Expansion of Imperial Russia into Northeast Asia

Chukotka

Anadyrsk

Kamchatka
(1697–1732)

18th
Century

Sakhalin
(Joint Possession of
Russia and Japan, 1855–1875)

Yakutsk
(1672)

Amur Territories
to Russia (1856/1860)

Khabarovsk
(1858)

Vladi-
vostok
(1860)

17th
Century

Harbin
(1898)

Nerchinsk
(1659)

Kiakhta
(1721)

Irkutsk
(1652)

Mangazeia
(1601)

Tomsk
(1604)

Tiumen
(1586)

Muscovy
(1533)

16th
Century

19th
Century

Miles

0   500   1000

Map 2

xx

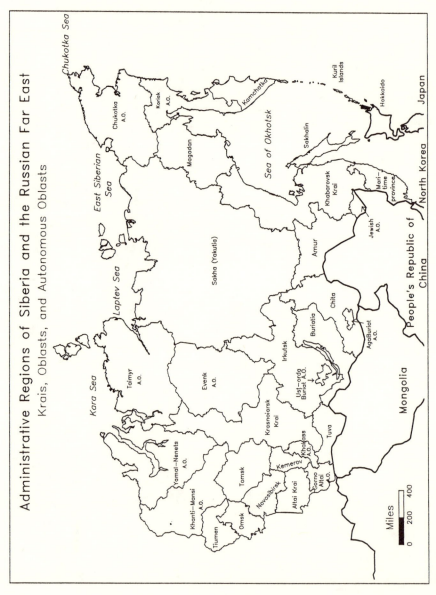

Administrative Regions of Siberia and the Russian Far East
Krais, Oblasts, and Autonomous Oblasts

Map 3

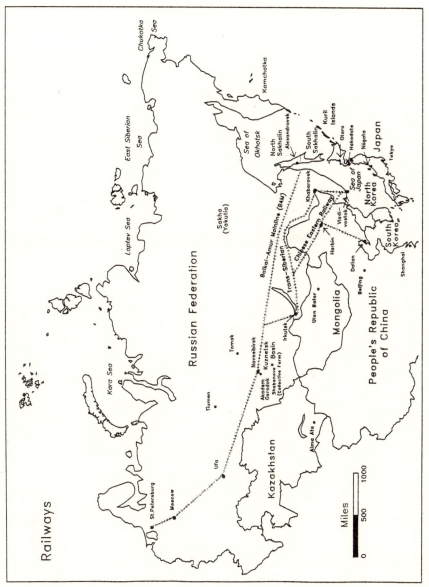

Map 4

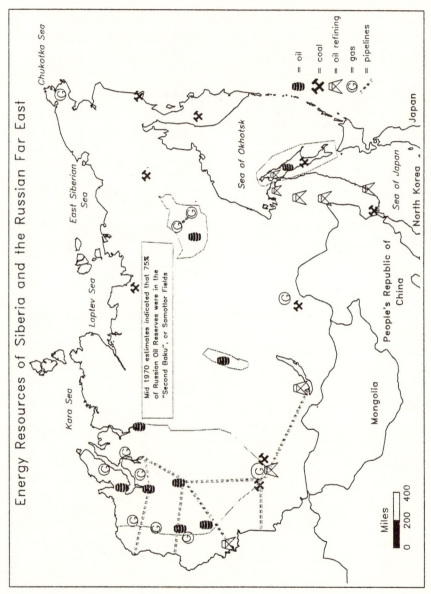

Energy Resources of Siberia and the Russian Far East

Mid 1970 estimates indicated that 75% of Russian Oil Reserves were in the "Second Baku", or Samotlor Fields

= oil
= coal
= oil refining
= gas
= pipelines

Map 5

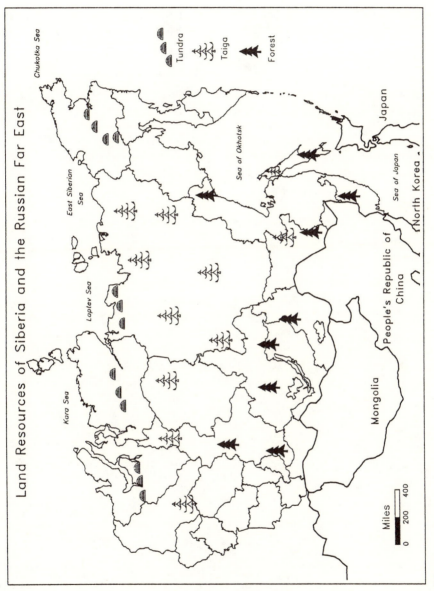

Land Resources of Siberia and the Russian Far East

Map 6

REDISCOVERING
RUSSIA IN ASIA

INTRODUCTION
Rediscovering Russia in Asia

Stephen Kotkin

In 1581, the Russian raider Yermak Timofeev crossed the Ural Mountains, plundering and claiming for the tsar the land called *Sibir* (Siberia) by its Tatar inhabitants. Within fifty-odd years another adventurer, Ivan Moskvitin, reached the Sea of Okhotsk by overland route, advancing Russia's claims (and the coverage of the term Siberia) well beyond the Tatar boundaries to a distance of almost 6,000 miles from Moscow. In the interval, Russians built a series of forts in these newly "discovered" eastern territories, subjugating or decimating scores of native peoples along the way. By the 1720s, when Peter the Great commissioned the Dane Vitus Bering to explore the straits leading to yet another continent, Russia was on the Pacific to stay.[1]

Despite official sponsorship of Bering's voyages, the Russian push from the Urals to the Pacific, and then briefly across the Pacific to America, was not primarily a state-sponsored endeavor. Rather, it was carried out by conquistadors, enterprising local administrators, and to a lesser extent, merchants and scholars. Preoccupied with events in Europe and the Near East, successive tsarist governments showed only intermittent interest in their eastern territories until the second half of the nineteenth century. By that time, however, what had begun as predominately an individually driven pursuit of lucre and renown had evolved into an officially encouraged colonization effort and a web of new strategic relationships with China, Manchuria, Mongolia, Korea, and a rising power, Japan.[2]

During the twentieth century, these strategic relationships have been intensified by the industrial-development schemes launched in the Russian east by the Soviet regime; by the imperial ambitions aggressively pursued by Japan on the Asian mainland, leading to the Russo-Japanese War (1904–5) and subsequent border clashes throughout the 1930s; by another Russo-Japanese war in August 1945; by the Chinese Communist revolution of 1949, a short-lived Sino-Soviet alliance, and the Sino-Soviet rift; by the division of Korea and the Korean War

(1950–53); by the transformation of Japan into a peaceful economic colossus; and now, by the collapse of Communism in the USSR. This last turn of events has imparted new significance to the internal re-examinations already under way in an evolving Japan, a rapidly changing China, a now self-governing Mongolia, and a divided Korea, as well as to Russia's own search for a new role in Asia.

That Russia has long been not simply a European but also an Asian country—with a huge economic, cultural, and military presence on the Asian landmass—is a cliché often stated but rarely given the attention it deserves. Each generation, it seems, is fated to rediscover Russia in Asia. What differentiates the current conjuncture, however, is that the collapse of the Soviet regime has brought about a revival of relationships across previously closed political borders and a sense of belonging to the transnational region of Northeast Asia. At the same time, large parts of Asia have been transformed by an economic boom that has compelled a reassessment of traditional divisions between a developed West and an underdeveloped East, as well as of the relative merits of military force and industrial productivity in notions of state security. This cluster of changes challenges no Asian power more than Russia.

Russia in Asia: The Views from Within

We know of Russia's presence in Asia first of all from the self-appointed conquerors themselves, who wrote with pride as well as exaggeration about their rapacious endeavors, and from the administrators Moscow sent east. The varying tales of these adventurers and officials, expressed in the language of patriotic service to the tsar and the Slavs' civilizing mission among benighted Asiatics, have helped to make many famous, at least within Russia. From Yermak and Moskvitin to Yerofei Khabarov, the initial explorer of the Amur basin; Gennadii Nevelskoi, the cartographer of Sakhalin; Ivan Kruzenshtern, the first Russian to circumnavigate the globe, Nikolai Rezanov, head of the Russian American Company; and Nikolai Murav'ev, governor-general of eastern Siberia and eventual conqueror of the Amur, Russia's pioneers in the east have left behind written records and oral legends that have contributed significantly to the story of Russia's rise in Asia.[3]

To the accounts by these men were added those of another renowned group, the political exiles sent east by the autocracy as punishment and for the purpose of aiding colonization. Beginning with the archpriest Avvakum in the seventeenth century, and continuing in the eighteenth century with Aleksandr Radishchev, in the nineteenth century with the Decembrists, Aleksandr Herzen, and Bronislaw Pilsudski (the brother of the future leader of Poland), and in the twentieth century with Aleksandr Solzhenitsyn and Varlam Shalamov, among many others, deportees have generated rich and varied accounts of eastern Russia and its inhabitants.[4] These writings were enhanced by outstanding individuals who followed in the exiles' footsteps, people such as Anton Chekhov and the American George Kennan.[5]

Articulate exiles condemned the transformation of eastern Russia into a vast prison as well as the malfeasance and corruption they encountered at every step. But they also expressed wonder at the natural environment and future possibilities of the east and provided a treasure trove of information on the geological and human history of remote areas. Some cultivated an interest in the native peoples, undertaking the first studies of Siberian native languages and culture. Were it not for the conscientious work of some of these exiles, the perspective of native peoples on the arrival of the Slavs would have been limited to otherwise unrecorded oral testimony and the mute evidence provided by northward migration and enlarged burial grounds.[6]

Slavs born in Siberia began to make a noticeable contribution to the understanding of their region in the early nineteenth century. By the 1860s, a group of self-proclaimed Siberian patriots took shape, inspired by the early nineteenth-century efforts of Siberia's first professional historian, Petr Slovtsov (1767–1843), and a handful of Irkutsk-born writers.[7] The two outstanding representatives of Siberian patriotism, Nikolai Iadrintsev (1842–1894) and Grigorii Potanin (1835–1920), argued that Siberians—Sibiriaki, meaning Slavs—possessed special qualities distinguishing them as a people and that these qualities could be fully developed only through autonomy, given central Russia's long mistreatment of its Siberian "colony." (These arguments would be taken up in the second half of the twentieth century by a subsequent generation of Siberian-born novelists.[8])

By the time Iadrintsev wrote his inspired polemic Siberia as a Colony (St. Petersburg, 1882) in commemoration of the three-hundred-year anniversary of Yermak's exploits, Siberia was on the way to acquiring its own educational and cultural institutions. In 1888, a university was founded in Tomsk. This first university in northern Asia had a library donated by a European Russian nobleman (with books transported across the frozen expanse on sleds). Construction on the Trans-Siberian Railroad began in 1891 and was mostly complete by 1903. Celebrations of Russia's east were soon echoed by foreign travelers, such as the Norwegian Fridtjof Nansen, who in 1914 published an enthusiastic account of what he called the "land of the future."[9]

After the revolutions of 1917, Siberian patriotism, arguments for the existence of a distinct Siberian people, and the celebration of Russia's east were taken a step further by a group of young Russian intellectuals living in foreign exile. Calling themselves Eurasianists, they published a manifesto in Sofia in 1921 arguing that "Russians and those who belong to the peoples of the Russian world are neither Europeans nor Asiatics," but having merged with native cultures formed a new race, "the Eurasians"—something analogous to the notion of "Americans."[10] The idea that because of its transcontinentality, among other reasons, Russia could be compared with America also became widespread among the new Bolshevik rulers of Moscow.

Of course, neither Russia nor the Soviet Union developed into an enduring new nation-state on the model of the United States, but the Eurasianists' post-facto defense of the Russian empire, by denying its existence as such, helped advance the notion that Russia had a powerful presence in Asia. The idea also achieved a certain popularity among the large community of Russian émigrés, many of whom lived in Harbin, Shanghai, and Kobe, as well as Prague, Berlin, and Paris. Eventually, the authorities in Moscow hit upon the formula of presenting the USSR as Europe to the Europeans and Asia to the Asians. Such were the many-sided reverberations two centuries later of Ivan Moskvitin's land odyssey to the shores of the Sea of Okhotsk.

Views from Abroad

For the Siberian patriots, later called regionalists (*oblastniki*), "Siberia" meant the narrow southern belt of Slavic settlement, or ecumene of the steppes, roughly from the Urals to Lake Baikal. Writing later, the Eurasianists showed a keener appreciation of the distinct area east of Baikal and north of the Amur River, but they took little notice of Russia's far north, let alone the territories south and east of Slav settlement that were claimed by foreign powers. For both the regionalists and the Eurasianists, the conquest and development of the eastern lands known collectively as Siberia was fundamentally an internal affair.

By the late nineteenth century, however, the outside world could not help but take notice, since Russia's spread across northern Asia impinged on the interests of several countries and seemed to increase Russia's might, as the Norwegian Nansen observed. The founding in 1860 of Russia's window on the east, Vladivostok, may have seemed to Russia a natural corollary to the founding in 1703 of its window in the west, St. Petersburg. Yet the name of the eastern outpost ("rule the east") gave evidence not of a desire to study and join what was considered a superior civilization, but to exert influence and domination over a supposedly inferior one. Further testimony to that effect was furnished by Russia's drive into Manchuria in the late nineteenth and early twentieth centuries.

Predictably, the assumption of destiny built into the largely uplifting stories of Russia's rise in the east as propagated by Russian explorers and officials, Siberian patriots, and émigré Eurasianists found little echo in Chinese or Japanese treatments. Early Chinese and Japanese internal communications of meetings and negotiations with Slavs set a continuing pattern of curiosity mixed with fear—understandable enough, given the sometimes bellicose nature of these encounters.[11] Russian involvement in northern China and Japanese intervention in Korea, among other episodes, helped create the legacy of mistrust in an emerging triangle connecting the competing Russian, Japanese, and Chinese empires.

When it came to expressions of hostility toward the rise of Russia in Asia, however, the Chinese and Japanese were outdone by the British. Locked in what they saw as a struggle with the Russians for mastery of the entire Asian continent, the British perceived the rise of Russia in Asia as a direct threat. British-

Russian rivalry over Asia crystallized in the Crimean War (1853–56)—fought in the Far East (albeit without significant military engagements) as well as the Near East—and in the unexpected Russian conquest at China's expense of the Amur basin not long thereafter.[12] Further alarmed by the construction of the Trans-Siberian Railway, the British generated a considerable public outcry on the subject of Russian expansion and the "Far Eastern Question" (a complement to the "[Near] Eastern Question"), an outcry that was marked by the application to Russians of condescending attitudes normally reserved for "Asiatics." Some British accounts even hinted at a Russo-Chinese alliance, or a Russo-Japanese alliance, or even a German-Russian-Chinese-Japanese alliance.[13]

Germans, for their part, exhibited strong interest in Russia's role in Asia, for much the same reason as the British, given the Germans' own ambitions in China.[14] But the official alarm in the late nineteenth century sparked by Russian expansion became by the 1920s an approving fascination among scholars with the developmentalism of the "Soviet experiment" in the context of the enormous *Lebensraum* of the east.[15] More than their counterparts elsewhere, German researchers focused attention on Siberia, a territory whose riches they had studied for the Russian Academy of Sciences in the eighteenth century.[16]

Some German specialists, such as Otto Hoetzsch, encouraged integration of the study of eastern Russia into that of Asia in order to expand upon the bridge Russia had established between the cultures of Europe and the Orient.[17] By the time Hoetzsch was active (the interwar period), Russia had essentially won its competition in the Far East with Britain, while Germany's narrowly colonialist aims had given way to active economic pursuits. The development of Russia's east loomed, a prospect that also aroused the Japanese, and later the Chinese, and one that until recently has remained mostly a matter of contention rather than cooperation.

Historiography in the United States

In the United States, the historical study of Russia in Asia began with Frank Golder (1877–1929), a student of Harvard's Archibald Cary Coolidge, the founder of Russian history study in America. In 1914, Golder published an expanded version of his Ph.D. dissertation on Russian expansion to the Pacific, echoing the story of America's westward expansion and drawing upon his three years' experience teaching native Alaskan school children before he entered Harvard.[18] American study of Russia and of Russia in Asia thus began more or less simultaneously.

Born to German parents in Odessa in 1877, Golder came to the United States in 1885, but he soon returned to his native land as a researcher, book collector, and administrator of famine-relief efforts. He took several trips across Eurasia on the Trans-Siberian and witnessed the February revolution in St. Petersburg before settling on America's Pacific coast in a dual position in 1920 as history professor at Stanford University and curator of the Russian collection of the newly formed Hoover War Library on the Stanford campus.[19] After Golder died in 1929, however, the tradition of studying Asian Russia at Stanford was not continued to the same degree by his replacements.[20]

Golder's role in championing U.S. study of Russia in Asia was taken up at another Pacific-coast institution, the University of California at Berkeley, by another Coolidge student, the son of Bohemian immigrants, Robert Kerner (1887–1956). Kerner gained a position at Berkeley in 1928, where he was active until his death in 1956. Through his inspirational teaching and dedication to the building of the university library, he established Berkeley as one of the country's premier institutions for Russian studies and as *the* place for the study of Russia in Asia, directing a substantial number of Ph.D. students in the field who later assumed professional posts.[21]

Critical to Kerner's influence was his broad approach. For him, Russia's eastward expansion was part of its transformation into an Asian power, which in turn formed part of a larger story involving the expansion of China and Japan.[22] In 1931, Kerner organized an interdisciplinary seminar on Northeast Asia that brought together specialists on China, Japan, and Russia and was a catalyst in solidifying Asian studies at Berkeley.[23] Kerner also successfully lobbied his colleagues in 1947 to appoint one of his students on Asian Russia, George Lantzeff (1892–1955), to the faculty. Lantzeff's research sought to show that seventeenth-century Russian colonization of northern Asia was comparable in scope and importance to the better-known cases of Spanish, Portuguese, English, and Dutch overseas colonization.[24] Regrettably, after Lantzeff died unexpectedly in 1955, followed by Kerner the next year, Berkeley's nearly three-decade tradition of studying Russia in Asia came to an abrupt end.[25]

During the 1930s, a parallel effort in the study of Russia in Asia was undertaken at yet another Pacific-coast institution, the University of California at Los Angeles, by the Russian émigré Prince Andrei Lobanov-Rostovsky, the son of a tsarist diplomat who had served in Beijing and Yokohama. In 1933 Lobanov-Rostovsky (1892–1979) published his lectures, which long served as a basic English-language textbook on Russia and Asia.[26] In 1942, however, the prince abruptly departed UCLA to avoid what he imagined was an impending Japanese invasion of California, moving to Wyoming and the safety of the interior.[27] He was replaced at UCLA by Raymond Fisher, a Kerner student and the author of a study demonstrating that in the seventeenth century the Siberian fur trade accounted for perhaps as much as one-third of Russian state revenues.[28]

Beyond Los Angeles, out in the Pacific at the University of Hawaii, Klaus Mehnert (1906–1984), a Moscow-born German, unknowingly began in 1937 what would become, after Berkeley's, the longest continuing U.S. program on Russia in Asia. That such a fate fell to Hawaii made historic sense. A century and a quarter earlier, Hawaii had almost become a Russian possession during the desperate search to locate a permanent food supply for Russia's North American colony in Alaska.[29] In 1859, the Hawaiian Kingdom and Russia established consular representation in Nikolaevsk-na-Amure and Honolulu, respectively. And even after its absorption into the United States, Hawaii's closest neighbor in Asia remained Russia; the city of Petropavlovsk-Kamchatskii is nearer to Hawaii than Guam or Tokyo and not much farther from Hawaii than Seattle or Anchorage.[30]

Equally propitious for the future of Hawaii was the fact that the task of establishing its program for the study of Russia in Asia fell to the German cosmopolitan Mehnert. After spending the 1928/29 academic year as an exchange student at Berkeley, where he studied with the newly arrived Kerner, Mehnert was trained in Oriental Studies in Berlin by Otto Hoetzsch. He shared his German mentor's fascination with the juxtaposition of Europe and Asia, as well as the long-standing German appreciation of Russia's continental character.[31] Ironically, however, having been assaulted by SA brownshirts while giving a lecture in 1932 and denied the opportunity to pursue his journalistic livelihood by the Nazi regime in 1936—an episode that helped bring him to Hawaii— Mehnert encountered difficulties in Honolulu because of his refusal to renounce his German citizenship or to condemn the Nazis publicly. He resigned and left the University of Hawaii in June 1941, subsequently traveling through Asia as a journalist and returning to West Germany after the war.[32]

After a hiatus, Mehnert's position at Hawaii was assumed in 1947 by John White, who as an undergraduate at UCLA heard Lobanov-Rostovsky's lectures and as a graduate student at Stanford made use of the Hoover Library resources accumulated by Golder to write a study of the American and Japanese intervention in Siberia (1918–22). White taught at the University of Hawaii for thirty years, and prior to retirement was joined by one of his students, John Stephan, now the leading scholar active in the field. Stephan continues to work along the path developed by White, Mehnert, and Kerner (who taught at Hawaii briefly in the summer of 1935), focusing on the international implications of Russia's expansion into Asia, particularly Russo-Japanese interaction.[33]

During the postwar period, other American-based scholars continued the study of Russia in Asia, notably Donald Treadgold at the University of Washington (Seattle), the Kerner student Basil Dmytryshyn at the University of Oregon (Portland), and the Berlin-born George Lensen (1923–1979) at the Florida State University (Tallahassee).[34] But the onset of the cold war created a seemingly immutable political division in Northeast Asia, much like the one in Europe, that served to conceal and discourage inquiry into the region's common past. Travel and contacts became difficult; access to important libraries and archives was restricted. Even Robert Kerner at Berkeley, in the years before his death, diverted attention from his beloved Northeast Asia seminar to fight what he viewed as the spread of the Communist menace.

By the 1960s (and into the 1980s), the historical study of Northeast Asia as a problem of the many-sided interaction among Russia, China, and Japan had largely given way to comparative Communist studies and to military security studies, both of which were frequently policy-inspired.[35] Such pursuits tended to shorten the time frame of analysis to the recent past, thereby magnifying the historical presence of the United States in Northeast Asia, and to define the ultimate subject of inquiry as U.S. relations with Moscow, Beijing, and Tokyo. The high quality of some of this scholarship aside, its narrowly political orientation and acceptance of cold war–imposed boundaries is striking.

Restoring Historical Ties

The collapse of Communism marked a breakthrough in Northeast Asia, revealing the "archaeological" layers of common history that are now being rediscovered and extended, albeit not without difficulties. Much the same could be said of efforts to follow these developments.

In Japan, the lone Slavic Research Institute is located on Hokkaido, in close proximity to Russia, but Japanese specialists on Russia still tend to concentrate overwhelmingly on European Russia and Moscow. Much the same can be said for the large community of Chinese scholars of Russia, as well as the smaller Korean cohort.[36] But interest in studying eastern Russia has been growing in northern China, Korea, and the area of Japan along the Japan Sea coast. As for Russian scholars from eastern regions, they have often aspired to the study of national issues, focusing on St. Petersburg and Moscow. But this, too, is changing. In any case, even in the depths of the Soviet period there was an enormous quantity of useful scholarship produced on Russia's eastern regions as well as other Asian countries.

In Russia, the prerevolutionary beginnings of Oriental Studies (*Vostokovedenie*), centered in Kazan, St. Petersburg, Moscow, and Vladivostok, were interrupted, and to an extent displaced abroad, by the upheavals of the revolutionary years; however, they were re-established by the 1930s, producing a significant body of scholarship in the postwar period.[37] Intensive study of Siberia and the Russian Far East, also within the Soviet Marxist framework, has been conducted at the Academy of Sciences Institute of History Siberian Division in Novosibirsk and Far Eastern Division in Vladivostok. These Institute divisions were founded in the postwar period, but Irkutsk University, a pioneer in Siberian studies, was established on the basis of a history faculty in 1918, joining Tomsk. And the Society for the Study of the Amur Region in Vladivostok traces a continuous existence back to the prerevolutionary epoch, through all the difficult times.[38] It is important to build upon these foundations in, and new initiatives from, eastern Russia and elsewhere around the region.

Such has been and remains the role of the University of Hawaii, and before it, Berkeley. Both institutionalized dialogue between otherwise segregated Russian and East Asian specialists in the United States and brought both groups together with their counterparts from China, Japan, and Russia. Berkeley and Hawaii also set a high standard of painstaking research in original source materials in numerous languages. It is this tradition that the present volume, based on an international conference held at Princeton University in December 1993, seeks to emulate as a step toward the revival of Robert Kerner's Russia-inclusive seminar on Northeast Asia.[39]

As befits the subject, the Princeton conference on Russia and Northeast Asia in the twentieth century was interdisciplinary, gathering anthropologists, sociologists, historians, political scientists, and a literary critic. Scholars were invited to participate on the basis of recent, hands-on research experience in the archives, libraries, villages, and cities of Siberia, the Russian Far East, China, Korea, and Japan. This is new research by new people, the fruits of a considerable investment in developmental scholarships provided by major funding agencies. In many cases, the conference papers represent the first substantial installments by recent Ph.D.'s on what promises to be a series of exciting new monographs.

The precise topic of each contribution was left entirely to the individual, with the understanding that a certain cohesion would be imposed by the history of the region itself. The papers have been divided into sections, each of which has been provided with its own brief introduction. Since original research was valued over comprehensiveness, however, lacunae inevitably arose. Future endeavors of the seminar may provide the opportunity to fill them in.

Notes

1. On Yermak and the legends that grew around him, see Terence Armstrong, ed., *Yermak's Campaign in Siberia* (London: Hakluyt Society, 1975).

2. Basil Dmytryshyn has argued that Russian government interest in its eastern territories increased in the eighteenth century. I would maintain that there was a qualitative leap in the second half of the nineteenth century. See the introduction to Basil Dmytryshyn et al., eds., *To Siberia and Russian America: Three Centuries of Russian Eastward Expansion, 1558–1867,* 3 vols. (Portland: Oregon Historical Society, 1985–89), vol. 1, pp. xxxv–lxx.

3. An overview is provided by Patricia Polansky, "The Russians and Soviets in Asia," *International Library Review,* 14, 1982, pp. 217–62.

4. For an introduction to the extensive literature by and about Siberian exiles, see the essays by Alan Wood, "Avvakum's Siberian Exile: 1653–64," in Wood and R.A. French, eds., *The Development of Siberia: Peoples and Resources* (New York: St. Martin's, 1989), pp. 11–34; and idem, "Siberian Exile in the Eighteenth Century," *Sibirica,* 1 (1), 1990, pp. 38–63.

5. Chekhov, *Ostrov Sakhalin (iz putevykh zapisok)* (Moscow, 1895), translated as *A Journey to Sakhalin* (Cambridge: Ian Faulkner, 1993); Kennan, *Siberia and the Exile System,* 2 vols. (New York: Century, 1891).

6. James Forsyth, *A History of the Peoples of Siberia: Russia's North Asian Colony, 1581–1990* (Cambridge: Cambridge University Press, 1992). As Forsyth has written, "the recorded history of Siberia begins (apart from some references in early Chinese works) with its invasion by the Russians in the late sixteenth century." Forsyth, "The Siberian Native Peoples Before and After the Russian Conquest," in Alan Wood, ed., *The History of Siberia: From Russian Conquest to Revolution* (New York: Routledge, 1991), pp. 69–91; quote from p. 69.

7. S.G. Sviatikov, *Rossiia i sibir' (K istorii Sibirskogo oblastnichestva v XIX veke)*

(Prague: Obshchestvo Sibiriakov v ChSR, 1930); I.I. Serebrennikov, "The Siberian Autonomous Movement and Its Future," *Pacific Historical Review,* 3 (3), September 1934, pp. 400–415; Wolfgang Faust, *Russlands goldener Boden: Der sibirische Regionalismus zweiten Hälftes des 19. Jahrhunderts* (Cologne, Vienna: Bohlau, 1980); Stephen Watrous, "Russia's Land of the Future: Regionalism and the Awakening of Siberia," Ph.D. dissertation, University of Washington, 1970; idem, "The Regionalist Conception of Siberia, 1860–1920," in Galya Diment and Yuri Slezkine, eds., *Between Heaven and Hell: The Myth of Siberia in Russian Culture* (New York: St. Martin's, 1993), pp. 112–33; Galya Diment, "Exiled from Siberia: The Construction of Siberian Experience by Early-Nineteenth-Century Irkutsk Writers," in Diment and Slezkine, pp. 47–65; and Norman Pereira, "Regional Consciousness in Siberia Before and After October 1917," *Canadian Slavonic Papers,* 30 (1), 1988, pp. 112–33.

8. Examples available in English include Viktor Astaf′ev, *Siberian Polonaise* (1970); Georgii Markov, *Siberia* (1972); Vasilii Shukshin, *Snowball Berry Red and Other Stories* (1979); and Valentin Rasputin, *Farewell to Matera* (1979), *Live and Remember* (1978), and *Siberia on Fire* (1989).

9. Fridtjof Nansen, *Through Siberia, the Land of the Future* (New York: Frederick Stokes, 1914). This tradition continues today, viz. Frederick Kempe, *Siberian Odyssey: A Voyage into the Russian Soul* (New York: Putnam, 1992). Nansen's enthusiasm can be compared with the practical experience of the American Washington Vanderlip, *In Search of a Siberian Klondike* (New York: Century and Co., 1903).

10. *Iskhod k vostoku* (Sofia, 1921). See the analysis by a member of the Harbin emigration, Nicholas V. Riasanovsky, "The Emergence of Eurasianism," *California Slavic Studies,* 4, 1967, pp. 39–72; idem, "Asia Through Russian Eyes," in Wayne Vucinich, ed., *Russia and Asia: Essays on the Influence of Russia on the Asian Peoples* (Stanford: Hoover Institute, 1972), pp. 3–29; and Otto Böss, *Die Lehre der Eurasier: Ein Beitrag zur russischen Ideengeschichte des 20. Jahrhunderts* (Wiesbaden: O. Harrassowitz, 1961).

11. George Lensen, *The Russian Push Toward Japan: Russo-Japanese Relations, 1697–1875* (Princeton: Princeton University Press, 1959), ch. 6; idem, "The Russian Impact on Japan," in Vucinich, *Russia in Asia,* pp. 338–68; and Michael Pavlovsky, *Chinese-Russian Relations* (New York: Philosophical Library, 1949). Lensen has pointed out that until 1875, Russo-Japanese relations were largely congenial.

12. John J. Stephan, "The Crimean War in the Far East," *Modern Asian Studies,* 3 (3), 1969, pp. 257–77. See also the comments in the preface of the first English-language study devoted to the Russian conquest of the Amur, E.G. Ravenstein, *The Russians on the Amur: Its Discovery, Conquest, and Colonisation* (London: Trübner, 1861), p. vii.

13. Alexis Krausse, *Russia in Asia: A Record and a Study, 1588–1899* (London: G. Richards, 1899); Vladimir [Zenone Volpicelli], *Russia on the Pacific and the Siberian Railway* (London: S. Low, Marston, 1899); F.H. Skrine, *The Expansion of Russia, 1815–1900* (Cambridge: Cambridge University Press, 1903); and Alexander Ular, *A Russo-Chinese Empire* (Westminster: A. Constable, 1904; French edition 1902). One British geographer put forth a startling and influential geohistorical argument about the supposed superiority of land to sea power, and hence of the Russian Empire to that of the British. See Harold MacKinder, "The Geographical Pivot of History," *The Geographical Journal,* 23 (4), 1904, pp. 421–44. The immense subject of turn-of-the-century Russo-British geopolitical competition, from the Baltics through Central Asia to the Far East, is treated by John White, *Transition to Global Rivalry: Alliance Diplomacy and the Quadruple Entente, 1895–1907* (Cambridge: Cambridge University Press, forthcoming 1996).

14. Exemplary is the multivolume series, *Russland in Asien,* written primarily by Gustav Krahmer and published in Leipzig (Verlag von Zuckschwerdt, 1899–1904). See

also Rudolf Martin, *Die Zukunft Russlands und Japans* (Berlin: C. Heymann, 1905); and Franz Quadflieg, *Russische Expansionspolitik von 1774 bis 1914* (Berlin: F. Dummler, 1914). Commentary on German aims is provided by N. Kassianow, *La Sibérie et la poussée allemande vers l'Orient* (Bern: P. Haupt, 1918). One Englishman advocated Japanese intervention in Siberia to save foreign investment there and the people of Siberia from "the Hun." Frederic Coleman, *Japan or Germany: The Inside Story of the Struggle in Siberia* (New York: G.H. Doran, 1918).

15. P.W. Danckwortt, *Sibirien und seine wirtschaftliche Zukunft; ein Rückblick und Ausblick auf Handel und Industrie Sibiriens* (Leipzig: Teubner, 1921); Rudolf Albert August Wilhelm Asmis, *Als Wirtschaftspionier in Russisch-Asien* (Berlin: G. Stilke, ca. 1924); Georg Cleinow (1873–1936), *Neu-Sibirien (Sibkrai): eine Studie zum Aufmarsch der Sowjetmacht in Asien* (Berlin: Hobbing, 1928); Michael Rosenberg, *Die Schwerindustrie in Russisch-Asien: eine Studie über das Ural-Kusnezker-Kombinat* (Berlin: Volk und Reich, 1938), with bibliography pp. 252–60. Hitler seems to have been aware of Siberia's riches but displayed only passing interest in them, being more enamored of the Caucasus, Afghanistan, and Central Asia as a gateway to India. See Mikhail Geller and Aleksandr Nekrich, *Utopiia u vlasti: Istoriia Sovetskogo Soiuza s 1917 goda do nashikh dnei,* 2d ed. (London: Overseas Publications Exchange, 1986), p. 327; and Milan Hauner, *What Is Asia to Us? Russia's Asian Heartland Yesterday and Today* (Boston: Unwin Hyman, 1990), pp. 165–90.

16. J.L. Black, "J.-G. Gmelin and G.-F. Mueller in Siberia, 1733–43: A Comparison of Their Reports," Wood and French, *The Development of Siberia,* pp. 35–49.

17. Hoetzsch lost his Berlin position in 1935 for refusing to desist from directing the dissertation of a Polish Jew. Michael Burleigh, *Germany Turns Eastward: A Study of Ostforschung in the Third Reich* (Cambridge: Cambridge University Press, 1988). A text by Hoetzsch, completed just prior to his death in 1946, was published posthumously: *Russland in Asien: Geschichte einer Expansion* (Stuttgart: Deutsche Verlags-Anstalt, 1966), with a foreword by Klaus Mehnert.

18. Frank Golder, *Russian Expansion on the Pacific 1641–1850* (Cleveland: A. Clark, 1914).

19. Golder taught for almost a decade at Washington State University, Pullman, before moving to Stanford. See Allen Glen Wachold, "Frank A. Golder: An Adventure in Russian History," Ph.D. dissertation, University of California, Santa Barbara, 1984; published under the name Alain Dubie, *Frank A. Golder: An Adventure of a Historian in Quest of Russian History* (Boulder, CO: East European Monographs, 1989); Harold A. Fisher, "Frank A. Golder, 1877–1929," *Journal of Modern History,* 1 (2), June 1929, pp. 253–55; and Golder's diaries, *War, Revolution, and Peace in Russia: The Passages of Frank Golder, 1914–1927,* ed. Terrence Emmons and Bertrand Patenaude (Stanford: Hoover Institute, 1992).

20. Anatole Mazour and Wayne Vucinich, both students of Berkeley's Robert Kerner, did work intermittently on eastern Russia; Harold Fisher trained John White; and in 1967, a conference was held at Stanford on Russia and Asia (and published in 1972). See Wayne Vucinich, ed., *Russia and Asia.*

21. Kerner's principal publications were *The Urge to the Sea: The Course of Russian History—The Role of Rivers, Portages, Ostrogs, Monasteries, and Furs* (Berkeley: University of California Press, 1942); and the collaborative *Northeastern Asia, A Selected Bibliography,* 2 vols. (Berkeley: University of California Press, 1939).

22. Robert Kerner, "The Russian Eastward Movement: Some Observations on Its Historical Significance," *Pacific Historical Review,* 17, May 1948, pp. 135–48.

23. "A Northeastern Asia Seminar," *Pacific Affairs,* vol. 5, December 1932, pp. 1069–71; Robert Kerner Papers, University of California, Bancroft Library, boxes 6, 10,

26. See also John Harrison, *The Founding of the Russian Empire in Asia and America* (Coral Gables: University of Miami Press, 1971), p. 15. A Russianist, Kerner was instrumental in establishing Asian studies at Berkeley.

24. George V. Lantzeff, *Siberia in the Seventeenth Century* (Berkeley: University of California, 1943). Another work, *Eastward to Empire* (Berkeley: University of California, 1973), was published posthumously thanks to the efforts of Richard Pierce, a student of Lanzteff and Kerner.

25. Kerner's demanding personality played a role in the decision by the Berkeley department not to continue this kind of historical study after he and Lantzeff died. Basil Dmytryshyn, "Russian Expansion to the Pacific, 1580–1700: A Historiographical Review," *Siberica*, 1 (1), Summer 1990, pp. 4–37.

26. Lobanov-Rostovsky, *Russia and Asia* (New York: Macmillan, 1933). Another émigré work was published in English around the same time, Victor Yakhtonoff, *Russia and the Soviet Union in the Far East* (New York: Coward-McCann, 1931).

27. According to John White, the prince remarked rather colorfully that he had lived through one revolution and did not want to experience another. John White, interviewed by the author, Manoa, Hawaii, May 1994. Lobanov-Rostovsky moved to the University of Michigan in 1944.

28. Raymond H. Fisher, *The Russian Fur Trade 1550–1700* (Berkeley: University of California, 1943). A comparable study has yet to be undertaken of the Siberian oil industry and its contribution in the second half of the twentieth century to the foreign currency reserves of the Soviet state budget. Fisher subsequently wrote a study of Russian exploration in the Pacific that took issue with both Golder and Kerner. Fisher, *Bering's Voyages: Whither and Why?* (Seattle: University of Washington Press, 1977). Canadians have also shown keen interest in eastern Russia. Examples include James Gibson, *Feeding the Russian Fur Trade* (Madison: University of Wisconsin Press, 1969); and idem, *Imperial Russia in Frontier America* (New York: Oxford University Press, 1976).

29. Mehnert, "The Russians in Hawaii, 1804–1819," University of Hawaii, Occasional papers, no. 38, Honolulu, 1939; Richard Pierce, *Russia's Hawaii Adventure, 1815–1817* (Berkeley: University of California Press, 1965).

30. As has been pointed out by John J. Stephan, "Hawaii's Russian Connection in Asian and Pacific Studies: Tradition and Prospects," *Center for Asian and Pacific Studies (CAPS) Newsletter*, 1 (4), October–December 1982, pp. 1–2.

31. Mehnert, *Ein Deutscher in der Welt: Erinnerungen 1906–1981* (Stuttgart: Deutsche-Verlags-Anstalt, 1981), pp. 210–54. Hawaii seems to have had a long-standing interest in Russian Asia, evidenced by its invitation to Golder to deliver a paper in 1928 and to Kerner to teach the summer session in 1935.

32. Mehnert was hounded by unfounded accusations of disloyalty, spying, anti-Semitism, and even of having provided the Japanese with the idea to attack Pearl Harbor—accusations that catapulted him into *Time* magazine (26 August 1949) and that were later expanded and repeated worldwide by United Press. In 1941, FBI investigations of Mehnert were discontinued for lack of any evidence to the charges, and in 1946 Mehnert was cleared definitively by an American tribunal in Germany of any Nazi affiliations. He returned to Hawaii in 1955 and thereafter several times until 1982. He continued to be hounded by insinuations. At a public lecture delivered during his final visit, a reporter challenged him to explain why he had not publicly denounced the Nazis. Burleigh, *Germany Turns Eastward*, p. 36; *Honolulu Star Bulletin*, 3 and 5 June 1941, 27 October 1947, 25 November and 10 December 1982, and 10 January 1984; "Seine Leidenschaft war der Osten," *Frankfurter Allgemeine Zeitung*, 5 January 1984. These references were supplied by John Stephan.

33. John White, *The Siberian Intervention* (Princeton: Princeton University Press,

1950); and idem, *The Diplomacy of the Russo-Japanese War* (Princeton: Princeton University Press, 1964); Stephan, *Sakhalin: A History* (Oxford: The Clarendon Press, 1971); idem, *The Kuril Islands: Russo-Japanese Frontier in the Pacific* (Oxford: The Clarendon Press, 1974); idem, *The Russian Far East: A History* (Stanford: Stanford University Press, 1994). Mention should be made of Hawaii's SUPAR (now CeRA) Report, edited by Robert Valliant and published since 1986.

34. Lensen's parents were Russian émigrés to Germany; they emigrated again, in 1939, to the United States. For a discussion of Lensen's career and voluminous publications, see the foreword by John Stephan to Lensen, *Balance of Intrigue: International Rivalry in Korea and Manchuria, 1884–1899*, vol. 1 (Tallahassee: University Presses of Florida, 1982), pp. ix–xiv.

35. Some outstanding examples include Donald Treadgold, *Soviet and Chinese Communism: Similarities and Differences* (Seattle: University of Washington Press, 1967); Allen Whiting, *Siberia and East Asia: Threat or Promise?* (Stanford: Stanford University Press, 1981); and Rodger Swearingen, ed., *The Soviet Far East: Strategic Dimensions in Multinational Perspective* (Stanford: Hoover Institute, 1987).

36. Gilbert Rozman, *The Chinese Debate About Soviet Socialism, 1978–1985* (Princeton: Princeton University Press, 1987); and idem., *Japan's Response to the Gorbachev Era, 1985–1991: A Rising Superpower Views a Declining One* (Princeton: Princeton University Press, 1991). Both MITI and the Keidanren, the private umbrella organization for Japanese businesses, have their own Russia specialists.

37. Richard Frye, "Oriental Studies in Russia," and Wayne Vucinich, "The Structure of Soviet Orientology: Fifty Years of Change and Accomplishment," in Vucinich, *Russia in Asia*, pp. 30–51, 52–134. See also, E. Stuart Kirby, *Russian Studies of China: Progress and Problems of Soviet Sinology* (London: Macmillan, 1975); idem., *Russia Studies of Japan: An Exploratory Survey* (New York: St. Martin's, 1981).

38. Amir Khisamutdinov, *The Russian Far East: Historical Essays* (Honolulu: Center for Russia in Asia, 1993), pp. 35–79.

39. A parallel can be drawn with the important British Siberian studies seminar organized by Alan Wood in the early 1980s, which has published the results of several conferences and founded a journal, *Sibirica* (1982–89). The journal moved to Portland and changed its name to *Siberica* (1990–91), before returning to Britain and its former name. Another important publication of the seminar is the bibliography by David Collins, *Siberia and the Soviet Far East* (Santa Barbara, CA: Clio Press, 1991).

Part I

Overlapping Peripheries, Antagonistic Centers

Russia's conquest of Siberia, David Dallin has written, "was the most easily accomplished phase of [its] expansion."[1] The rapidity with which Russians traversed the lands between the Urals and the Pacific seems to have startled the Russians no less than the disparate native peoples, whose sometimes fierce but uncoordinated resistance was easily overcome. Beyond conquest, exercising effective sovereignty over the eastern territories was another matter. One key to Russian control would become the construction of a railroad, as Steven G. Marks has re-emphasized in the first comprehensive English-language study of the Trans-Siberian.[2] Another key was migration and settlement.

Siberia is infamous as a land of exile, but the exiles never formed more than a small fraction of the population. Rather, settlement was carried out by Cossack soldiers and, above all, peasants, in a process that was sponsored, albeit bureaucratically, by the tsarist authorities.[3] The leading official responsible for coordinating settlement was Anatolii Kulomzin (1838–1924). In the essay that opens this section, Marks re-examines Russia's colonization drive in Siberia, arguing that Kulomzin's role there can be compared with the much better appreciated exploits of Britain's Lord Curzon in India and Cecil Rhodes in Africa.

* * *

Russia's *Drang nach Osten* was carried forward by true believers, one of whom, Esper Ukhtomskii, wrote in 1900 that "essentially there are not and cannot be any frontiers for us in Asia."[4] Despite Ukhtomskii's assertion, Russian expansion had at that time already experienced several setbacks, such as the unsuccessful attempt to penetrate the Amur basin in the late seventeenth century, an episode that brought the Russians into contact with the China of the Manchus, as well as the Mongols, both of whom offered far greater resistance than Siberia's native peoples.[5] Further setbacks were in the offing.

In the eighteenth century, Russia set its sights on North America, founding a colony in Alaska overseen by the Russian-America Company, chartered in 1799. Feeling the burden of carrying supplies from the Baltic Sea halfway around the world, representatives of the company searched for a nearby food supply, reaching northern California in 1812 and not long thereafter making what may have been an abortive attempt to claim the Hawaiian Islands. But Russian settlement in America never exceeded a few hundred people, and after a second drive was launched to gain control over the Amur in the 1850s, more or less simultaneously with the bid for a sphere in Central Asia, the Russian-America Company was dissolved. In 1867, Alaska was sold to the westward—expanding United States. Many of the employees of the Russian-America Company went to work for the newly established Amur Company.[6]

It was the Amur basin that became the centerpiece of Russia's eastern sphere of influence, under the energetic leadership of the governor-general of eastern Siberia, Nikolai Murav'ev (1809–1881). At the time that Russian control of the Amur was sealed by two treaties with China (Aigun in 1858 and Peking in 1860), this vast territory, the size of France and Germany combined, had only about 15,000 inhabitants, most of whom were native peoples. Russian settlement faced uncertain prospects, for land travel from European Russia to the banks of the great river could take as much as a year. Only visionaries such as Murav'ev could look beyond the daunting obstacles, especially since Russian expansionism did not go unchallenged by other powers seeking to profit from China's weakness, above all the British.

With Murav'ev's departure in 1861, Russia temporarily lost the initiative, but his work was placed in a new light in 1891, when work commenced on the stretch of the Trans-Siberian between Vladivostok and Khabarovsk, and the next year, from Cheliabinsk to Lake Baikal. Moreover, after supporting the Chinese in the wake of the Sino-Japanese war of 1894–95, Russia secured the right to link Lake Baikal with Vladivostok through Manchuria, Vladivostok's "natural" hinterland. Thus opened the second great episode in Russian eastward expansion connected with the railroad, but this time inside the borders of another country.[7] In this section's second essay, David Wolff, author of a study on Harbin, the Russian colony in China that developed in connection with the Chinese Eastern Railway, examines the story of the Russian presence in Manchuria, demonstrating that echoes of activities in far-off northern China resounded in St. Petersburg.[8]

It was in Manchuria in the early part of the twentieth century that Russian expansion found its ultimate limits. With the construction of the Chinese Eastern Railway, Russia seemed at the peak of its power in the Far East, particularly since Russia's search for a warm-water port on the Pacific was fulfilled when as a result of the German occupation in 1897 of Jiaozhou Bay (across the Yellow Sea from Manchuria), Russia obtained a lease on the Liadong Peninsula as well as permission to extend the railroad south from Harbin to Port Arthur and Dairen. Yet Russia only gradually, and in the end incompletely, embraced the idea of incorporating Port Arthur and then the whole of Manchuria into the empire. Wolff shows why.

* * *

At the place where the Amur River empties into the Pacific sits the island of Sakhalin, a reminder that Russia's conquest of the Amur and further advance brought it into contact with Japan. In fact, Commodore Perry's fame notwithstanding, it was Russia that earliest and most persistently sought to pry open Japan for trade.[9] With the Russians in Sakhalin, Japan encountered a land frontier with a foreign country (rather than a native tribe) for the first time. Delineation of the Russo-Japanese frontier took place over an extended period of time, and like the Sino-Russian border, remains in dispute. Both Sakhalin, the "Alsace-Lorraine" of East Asia, and the 800-mile chain of volcanic islands called the Kuriles by the Russians have changed hands several times.[10]

Russian exploration of Sakhalin was roughly simultaneous with that of the Japanese (the Chinese had reached the island at least four centuries before, exerting a loose dominion but failing to incorporate it into their empire).[11] In 1855, Sakahlin was made a joint possession of Russia and Japan but not partitioned; in 1875, in exchange for recognition of Japanese sovereignty over the Kuriles, Russian sovereignty was recognized over Sakhalin, after which the Russians promptly turned it into a vast penal colony. With the 1905 Russo-Japanese war, however, the island was again divided, and this time officially partitioned along a non-natural frontier.

During the Russian Civil War, when the Japanese as well as the Americans intervened militarily in eastern Siberia, the Japanese occupied the northern Russian half of Sakhalin. They made no moves toward annexation, and in 1925, not long after they ended their occupation of the Russian Far East, the Japanese relinquished control of northern Sakhalin, retreating to the southern half of the island. Hara Teruyuki, a leading Japanese scholar on the Russian Far East, takes up the story of the Japanese occupation (1920–25) of northern Sakhalin in the third essay of this volume's opening section.

In the 1870s, the Japanese, prompted by encounters with the Russians, called in American experts to assist in a major colonization drive on the island of Ezo, which they renamed Hokkaido (the northern sea route).[12] Japanese activities on Sakhalin after 1905 form a part of that story and are linked to their interventions in Formosa and Korea, Siberia and the Russian Far East, and eventually all of China and most of Southeast Asia in the 1930s and 1940s. In the end, although the Japanese colonization of Hokkaido proved successful, Japanese expansion onto the Asian mainland turned out to be no more long-lasting than the Russia experiment in Manchuria. Hara examines both the reasons behind Japan's thrust into northern Sakhalin and the legacy of its presence there.

* * *

Such, in bare-bones outline, is the early story of overlapping "peripheries" and antagonistic "centers" that have been the continuing experience of Northeast Asia and which group the three essays in this section. Many people have noted the turn-of-the-century transformation of Northeast Asia from a "backwater" to a site of intense geopolitical rivalry, lamenting China's weakness and chastising either Russia or Japan, sometimes both, for imperial ambition.[13] But fewer have shown an appreciation for the immense investment necessary for Russia to develop its eastern lands and defend its exposed position in Asia.[14]

By 1900, immigrants accounted for more than 80 percent of the population of the Russian territories east of the Urals, and this number would grow in subsequent years. But no matter how many people were encouraged to resettle east— indeed despite the considerable boost provided by the importation of prison labor during the Stalin period—the contrast between the vastness of Siberia and the sparseness of its population persists as one of the defining characteristics of Asian Russia. Distance and foreign ambitions have heightened Russia's vulnerability.

It should come as no surprise that it was in Outer Mongolia in 1921, not in eastern Europe, where Soviet Russia established its first protective satellite state.[15] This was 340 years after Yermak crossed the Urals, but only a generation removed from the accelerated colonization efforts under Anatolii Kulomzin and the failed push into Manchuria, and right in the middle of the Japanese occupation of northern Sakhalin. The incomparable scope yet enduring incompleteness of Russian eastward expansion and colonization, and its collision with Chinese and Japanese northward expansion, form the unifying threads for this section's essays.

Notes

1. David Dallin, *The Rise of Russia in Asia* (New Haven: Yale University Press, 1949), p. 6. For pertinent documents see Basil Dmytryshyn, ed., *Russia's Conquest of Siberia (1558–1700): A Documentary Record* (Portland, OR: Western Imprints, the Press of the Oregon Historical Society, 1985). See also David Collins, "Russia's Conquest of Siberia: Evolving Russian and Soviet Historical Interpretations," *European Studies Review*, 12 (1), 1982, pp. 17–44. An important new contribution is James Forsyth, *A History of the Peoples of Siberia: Russia's North Asian Colony, 1581–1990* (Cambridge: Cambridge University Press, 1992).

2. Steven Marks, *Road to Power: The Trans-Siberian Railroad and the Colonization of Asian Russia, 1850–1917* (Ithaca, NY: Cornell University Press, 1991). More special-

ized is the work by Robert Valliant, "Japan and the Trans-Siberian Railroad, 1885–1905," Ph.D. dissertation, University of Hawaii, 1974.

3. Donald Treadgold, *The Great Siberian Migration* (Princeton: Princeton University Press, 1957); Francois-Xavier Coquin, *La Sibérie: Peuplement et immigration paysanne au XIXe siècle* (Paris: Institut d'études slaves, 1969).

4. Esper Ukhtomskii, *K sobytiaam v Kitae* (1900), p. 84, as cited in Dallin, *The Rise of Russia*, p. 54.

5. The English-language scholarship on the long history of Russo-Chinese interaction is extensive, beginning with John F. Baddeley, *Russia, Mongolia, and China, Being Some Record of the Relations Between Them from the Beginning of the XVIIth Century to the Death of the Tsar Alexei Mikhailovitch* A.D. 1602–1672 . . . (London: Macmillan, 1919). See also Michael Pavlovsky, *Chinese-Russian Relations* (New York: Philosophical Library, 1949); Tien-fang Cheng, *A History of Sino-Russian Relations* (Washington, D.C. Public Affairs Press, 1957); W.A. Douglas Jackson, *The Russo-Chinese Borderlands* (Princeton: D. Van Nostrand, 1962); Dennis J. Doolin, *Territorial Claims in the Sino-Soviet Conflict: Documents and Analysis* (Stanford: Hoover Institution Press, 1965); George Lensen, *The Russo-Chinese War* (Tallahassee: Diplomatic Press, 1967); Mark Mancall, *China and Russia: Their Diplomatic Relations to 1728* (Cambridge, MA: Harvard University Press, 1971); O. Edmund Clubb, *China and Russia: The "Great Game"* (New York: Columbia University Press, 1971); R.K.I. Quested, *Sino-Russian Relations: A Short History* (Boston: Allen and Unwin, 1984); S.L. Tikhvinsky, *Chapters from the History of Russo-Chinese Relations* (Moscow: Progress Publishers, 1985).

6. English-language literature on Russian America is also extensive, beginning with P.N. Golovnin, *The End of Russian America: Captain P.N. Golovnin's Last Report*, trans. Basil Dmytryshyn and E.A.P. Crownhart-Vaugan (Portland: Oregon Historical Society, 1979); and S.B. Okun, *The Russian-American Company*, ed. B.D. Grekov, trans. Carl Ginsburg (Cambridge, MA: Harvard University Press, 1951). See also Anatole Mazour, "Dmitrii Zavalishin: Dreamer of a Russian-American Empire," *Pacific Historical Review*, 5 (1), 1936, pp. 26–37; Robert Mosse, ed., *The Soviet Far East and Pacific Northwest* (Seattle: University of Washington Press, 1944); Hector Chevigny, *Russian America: The Great Alaskan Venture, 1764-1867* (New York: Viking, 1965); Richard Pierce, *Russia's Hawaii Adventure, 1815–1817* (Berkeley: University of California Press, 1965); Howard I. Kushner, *Conflict on the Northwest Coast: American-Russian Rivalry in the Pacific Northwest, 1790–1867* (Westport, CT: Greenwood Press, 1975); James Gibson, *Imperial Russia in Frontier America* (New York: Oxford University Press, 1976); Glynn Barratt, *Russia in Pacific Waters, 1715–1825* (Vancouver: University of British Columbia Press, 1981); Frederick Starr, ed., *Russia's American Colony* (Durham, NC: Duke University Press, 1987); John J. Stephan and V.P. Chichkanov, eds., *Soviet-American Horizons on the Pacific* (Honolulu: University of Hawaii Press, 1986).

7. For information and bibliography on the Chinese Eastern Railroad see Peter S.H. Tang, *Russian and Soviet Policy in Manchuria and Outer Mongolia, 1911–1931* (Durham, NC: Duke University Press, 1959).

8. David Wolff, *To the Harbin Station: The Liberal Alternative in Russian Manchuria, 1898–1914* (Berkeley: University of California Press, forthcoming).

9. George Lensen, *The Russian Push for Japan: Russo-Japanese Relations, 1697–1875* (Princeton: Princeton University Press, 1959); idem, "Japan and Tsarist Russia: The Changing Relationships, 1875–1917," *Jahrbücher für Geschichte Osteuropas*, 10, October 1962, pp. 337–49; and Kurt Krupinski, *Japan und Russland: Ihre Beziehungen bis zum Frieden von Portsmouth* (Königsberg and Berlin: Ost-Europa, 1940).

10. John J. Stephan, *Sakhalin: A History* (Oxford: Clarendon, 1971); idem, *The Kuril Islands: Russo-Japanese Frontier in the Pacific* (Oxford: Clarendon, 1974). That a few

islands in the sparsely populated archipelago have been made into the principal matter in Russo-Japanese relations boggles the mind. Without a sense of an ancestral homeland and with fishing rights negotiable, the Japanese irredentist crusade seems primarily aimed at confirming Russian guilt and Japanese victimization in a war in which the Japanese are otherwise seen as aggressors.

11. As Stephan points out, the ideographs used by Japanese for the island (pronounced Karafuto) originally designated "Chinese people" (i.e., people of the Tang Dynasty). Stephan, *Sakhalin,* p. 25. The term used by the Russians appears to have been taken over from the native Nivkhi (Giliaks) and means the dark island at the end of the river. See K.M. Braslavets, *Istoriia v nazvaniiakh na karte Sakhalinskoi oblasti* (Iuzhno-Sakhalinsk, 1983), pp. 93–94. Recently, some Yakuts have claimed that the name of the island comes from their language and means the forward part of Yakutia (Sakha-lin). Although Yakut did serve as a kind of lingua franca for the native peoples of eastern Siberia, the Yakuts remained quite a distance from Sakhalin.

12. Alfons Scheinpflug, *Die japanische Kolonisation in Hokkaido* (Leipzig: F. Hirt und Sohn, 1935); John Harrison, *Japan's Northern Frontier: A Preliminary Study in Colonization and Expansion with Special Reference to the Relations of Japan and Russia* (Gainesville: University of Florida Press, 1953); Yoshi Kuno, *Japanese Expansion on the Asiatic Continent: A Study in the History of Japan with Special Reference to Her International Relations with China, Korea, and Russia,* 2 vols. (Berkeley: University of California Press, 1937–40).

13. There is an enormous scholarly literature in English on Russian diplomacy in the Far East. Some key works not already cited in notes above include David Dallin, *Soviet Russia and the Far East* (New Haven: Yale University Press, 1948); Harold Ford, "Russian Far Eastern Diplomacy, Count Witte, and the Penetration of China, 1895–1904," Ph.D. dissertation, University of Chicago, 1950; Andrew Malozemoff, *Russian Far Eastern Policy, 1881–1904, with Special Emphasis on the Causes of the Russo-Japanese War* (Berkeley: University of California Press, 1958); George Lensen, *Korea and Manchuria Between Russia and Japan* (Tallahassee: Diplomatic Press, 1966); Ernest Mason Satow, *Korea and Manchuria Between Russia and Japan, 1895–1904* (Tallahassee: Diplomatic Press, 1966); Seung Kwon Syun, *The Russo-Japanese Rivalry over Korea, 1876–1914* (Seoul: Yuk Phub SA, 1981); and George Lensen, *Balance of Intrigue: International Rivalry in Korea and Manchuria, 1884–1899,* 2 vols. (Tallahassee: University Presses of Florida, 1982).

14. An exception is John Erickson, "Military and Strategic Factors," in Alan Wood, ed., *Siberia: Problems and Prospects for Regional Development* (New York: Croom Helm, 1987), pp. 171–92.

15. George Murphy, *Soviet Mongolia: A Study of the Oldest Political Satellite* (Berkeley: University of California Press, 1966); Robert A. Rupen, *Mongols of the Twentieth Century,* 2 vols. (Bloomington: Indiana University Press, 1969).

1. A. N. Kulomzin (1838-1924), from his seat on the Trans-Siberian Railway Committee, organized the resettlement of more than five million peasants in southern Siberia. *Source: Aziatskaia Rossiia* (St. Petersburg, 1914).

2. Peasant migrants and state-supplied yurts near Bogotil station on the Trans-Siberian. *Source: Velikii put': Vidy Sibiri i ee zheleznykh dorog* (Krasnoiarsk, 1899).

3. Settlers going down the Shilka River, an Amur tributary. *Source: Das Russland der Zaren: Photographien von 1839 bis zur Oktoberrevolution* (Moscow, 1989).

4. Imported locomotives being assembled at the Chinese Eastern Railway's private port, alongside Vladivostok. *Source: Le transsibérien* (Paris: Herscher, 1980), Charles Daney.

5. Russians and Chinese on a railway platform in Trans-Baikalia. *Source:* Wirt Gerrare, *Greater Russia: The Continental Empire of the Old World* (New York, 1903).

6. The green art-deco facade of the Harbin station, Manchuria. *Source: Al'bom Kharbina* (Harbin, 1930).

7. As part of the rapprochement that made enemies into allies after the Russo-Japanese war, Japan erected a monument to fallen Russian heroes of the Port Arthur siege. Russian troops were invited to the unveiling ceremony. *Source: Arthur Judson Brown, The Mystery of the Far East (New York, 1918).*

Conquering the Great East

Kulomzin, Peasant Resettlement, and the Creation of Modern Siberia

Steven G. Marks

The nineteenth and early twentieth centuries were an age of robust European expansion overseas and territorial consolidation in the frontiers of the United States, Canada, South Africa, and Asian Russia. Historians often neglect to consider Russia's involvement in this arena, yet of all the examples of colonization in modern world history, few compared in extent with Russia's effort in Siberia, the destination of approximately five million peasant migrants between 1891 and 1914.

Asian Russia before the demise of the Soviet Union encompassed more than six million square miles, nearly double the size of the continental United States. Within the borders of this Siberian subcontinent, extensive stretches of fertile land were to be found, most notably in the Black Earth Zone of western Siberia, central Siberia, and northern Kazakhstan, and in the subtropical Maritime province of the Russian Far East. These regions were potentially well suited to agricultural life but were only sparsely populated before the 1890s. In addition, the state showed little interest in Siberia, the largest territorial entity under one flag on the face of the earth. But by the 1880s, the Russian government came to see colonization—extensive rural settlement and economic development—as vital.

Domestic political and strategic circumstances after the 1870s compelled the Russian government to shed the benign neglect of its immense Asian colony. No longer could it continue to maintain Siberia as an isolated "forest cordon," holding at bay outside influences by means of lack of development. Internally, the loyalty of Siberia's natives seemed at issue, and a flourishing Siberian regionalist movement was feared to be stirring up separatist and revolutionary sentiment. In foreign affairs, the Russians were faced with the vigorous activity of the English and Americans in the Pacific, imputed revanchist territorial designs on the part of the Chinese, and after 1894–95, Japanese aggression on the Asian mainland. While these powers appeared strong and active, Siberia and especially the Russian Far East were poorly defended owing to their size, poor means of communication, low population density, and distance from the center—all of which made it difficult to transport or maintain troops there. The Far East region seemed ripe for the picking by any of the above-mentioned interested parties. Military and civilian officials came to believe that construction of the Trans-Siberian Railroad would solve their logistical problems at a single stroke and give the government the means to reassert its authority.[1]

The shift in the government's Siberian policy can also be explained by the emergence of a new attitude on the part of the Russian elite toward the governance of the empire on the whole after the 1860s. At that time, the empire came to be perceived as unitary Russian instead of multinational, a belief shaped by the strong currents of contemporary politics. In brief, such a view was in keeping with the spirit of an age in which monolithic national, as opposed to federalist, principles gained prevalence around the world in the wake of the Union victory in the American Civil War, the unifications of Germany and Italy, and the start of Germanization and Magyarization campaigns in the multiethnic Austro-Hungarian empire. Within Russia, the new unitarism was a natural culmination of bureaucratic reformers' endeavors to create a *Rechtsstaat* on the European model and introduce legal and social systematization as the precondition to a smoothly functioning government. It was also a reaction to rising ethnic nationalist agitation, which heightened the "demographic fear" of the Great Russians stemming from their realization that they no longer made up the majority in their own empire.[2]

Modernizing reformism and the Russifying aspirations of Pan-Slavs and reactionary officials thus converged to produce by the late nineteenth century a more assertive, less tolerant imperial policy that sought to compensate for the perceived weakness of the Russian state and nation. In Siberia this added up to a compulsion to solidify governmental control and expedite the unambiguous Russian occupation of the territory by means of railroad construction, peasant resettlement, and Russification. Out of a polyethnic empire with far-flung borders, the Russian government was trying to create something of a single-ethnic nation of the Western European variety.

The inspiration behind Russia's fin de siècle drive to colonize Siberia was Sergei Witte.[3] But if Witte provided the inspiration, the man responsible for bringing Witte's vision to fruition and accomplishing the colonization of Siberia was Anatolii Kulomzin. The latter's exploits in the age of imperialism have largely gone unsung, but Kulomzin should rank among the greatest of colonizers, equaled only by Lord Curzon, viceroy of India, and overshadowed by Rhodes in South Africa, whose early accomplishments are all the more impressive for having been done as a young man without government connections.[4] Outside of Siberia, nowhere else, except perhaps in South Africa and India, was so much accomplished in so little time by one individual.[5] What Kulomzin did in Siberia set the stage for all subsequent development in Russia's eastern territories in the twentieth century; his work gives an indication of both the strengths and the weaknesses of late-tsarist Russia's management of its empire.

Kulomzin

Anatolii Nikolaevich Kulomzin (1838–1924) was born into an old, but undistinguished, provincial noble family. According to Dominic Lieven, he owed his self-discipline and intellectual curiosity to the upbringing given him by his Calvinist mother.[6] His penchant for hard work, as well as his intellectual and political talents, brought him to the attention of the highest bureaucratic officials. He remained at the very center of power in Russia for decades, holding one of the most important positions in the realm, the post of administrative secretary of the Committee of Ministers, from 1883 to 1902.[7]

In 1892, Witte tapped Kulomzin to manage the Committee of the Siberian Railroad, the "temporary supreme organ" chaired by Nicholas II that was established to organize construction of Russia's transcontinental railroad. Kulomzin was also placed in charge of the "auxiliary enterprises" associated with the Trans-Siberian: the improvement of Siberian water transport, the expansion of Siberian industry, and the coordination of peasant resettlement. In this capacity, Kulomzin came to dominate all matters of colonization in Siberia.[8]

By dint of his experience, personality, and official responsibilities, Kulomzin was especially well suited for the task. Not only did he have the ear of the tsar, he was considered to be one of the government's leading authorities on the peasantry. He was an exception among his aristocratic peers, running an innovative and profitable agricultural estate in the north of Russia. He had been a peace arbitrator in his home Kineshma district, a Deputy Minister of State Domains, and a member of major governmental commissions on the rural economy.[9] Because of his intimate familiarity with the theoretical and practical dimensions of Russian rural reality, in his own estimation he was well suited to foster successful peasant agriculture in Siberia.[10]

Although an "extremely obsequious" courtier and a consummate politician, Kulomzin disliked politics.[11] He came into his own in Siberia, away from the formalized rigidity of St. Petersburg's tradition-laden, corrupt bureaucracy. Lieven calls him a "Russian Victorian" and ascribes to him Western liberal ideas. Certainly Kulomzin remained committed to the legacy of Alexander II, but he came into prominence only under the reactionary tsar Alexander III, whose government sanctioned economic and administrative modernization to enhance autocratic rule. As will be evident, in Siberia Kulomzin's policies were by no means liberal—if that is defined as supportive of unregulated market capitalism and popular rule—but they do indicate realism and an openness to innovation. He acted with the dual goals of strengthening Russian political control over its territory and improving the condition of the Russian countryside. Insofar as he was engaged in colonizing activities on a grand scale, the label Victorian does indeed suit Kulomzin.

In another sense, too, the Victorian label suits this energetic Russian. Like many of his English contemporaries, Kulomzin was dedicated to serving the community and to applying his personal energies to improve society.[12] In Victorian England was the ethos of the middle class, which barely existed in Russia. But similar ideas could be expected to appear there among benevolent bureaucrats and enlightened noblemen. The closest parallel to the British example is to be found in the *zemstvo,* or rural local-government, movement, of which Kulomzin was a lifelong advocate. Kulomzin saw the peasants as savages who needed the guidance of the zemstvo, and he urged noblemen to involve themselves in rural life so as to uplift the peasants and forestall revolution.[13]

Kulomzin brought these notions to Siberia, which he saw, in his words, as a "tabula rasa," fertile ground for social experimentation.[14] "How much one would wish to go there and work for Russia's good," he wrote in 1875.[15] This was the function served by the periphery for many of Russia's bureaucratic rulers, who sought to apply controlled political, economic, and social reforms here as a prelude to introducing them in Russia proper.[16] Unfortunately, the same spirit was never able to take hold in the Russian heartland, where entrenched autocratic and elite interests combined to hinder substantive change.

Centrifugal Siberia

As Kulomzin and others lamented, the Russian North had been neglected for centuries and allowed to sink into poverty since it became undisputed Russian territory. By contrast, South Russia and the western borderlands had been the focus of the government's development efforts since the eighteenth-century drive to bring them under full Russian control.[17] In the late nineteenth century, it became Kulomzin's task to do the same in Siberia, where colonizing activities aimed to make the construction of the Trans-Siberian Railroad a successful extension of government power through economic development. The government's goal in building the railroad and, ancillary to that, in controlling Russian peasant resettlement and stimulating local industry was primarily to bind vast, remote Siberia to the center.

Russia's rulers hoped thereby to counter the supposed designs of foreign powers on Russia's Pacific littoral and reverse the seemingly dangerous tendencies evidenced by suspected Siberian separatists and potentially disloyal natives.[18] If these forces were to combine, the possibility existed that "the entire country [east of] the Enisei would inevitably form a government independent of Russia."[19] Kulomzin intended to apply strong measures there "to counteract the increasing centrifugal tendencies."[20]

For Kulomzin and his contemporaries, sinophobia caused equally great concern and required the urgent attention of officialdom. Fear of the "Yellow Peril" afflicted other imperialist nations,[21] but the strength and persistence of the Russian strain are worthy of note, for it remained a periodically active element in policy formulation for the Russian Far East from the 1880s into the 1990s.[22]

Although St. Petersburg was aware of its strategic weakness on the Chinese border, in the late nineteenth century the belief that hordes of Orientals might sweep across Siberia and even into European Russia was largely based on the demographic disparity between China and the Russian Far East. A severe population imbalance of this sort was undesirable given the importance contemporaries placed on both homogeneous nation-states and the availability of manpower as sources of political and military strength. According to the official census, in 1897 the number of Russians living in the Amur and Maritime provinces totaled 213,287. In the same year, there were 43,000 Chinese and 26,000 Koreans residing in those two regions, making up 32 percent of the total population and 25 percent of the urban population. Just across the border, of course, were the remaining 300 million Chinese, who in the eyes of Russian strategists posed a direct threat to Russian security. Even a sober-minded official such as Kulomzin showed alarm: "With the object of strengthening our bulwark in the Far East against the waves of the yellow race," he urged that the tsar make increased amounts of land available to peasants in the Far East and encourage anyone possible to settle there.[23]

Kulomzin reveals in his memoirs the most glaring deficiencies of Russian dominion in Siberia. To start with there were weak communications, including what he found to be "hellish" roads and a minuscule number of postal stations serving one of the largest landmasses on the globe.[24] Low population density also served to weaken Russia's presence. The South Ussuri krai, for instance, was the size of Portugal; but whereas the latter had a population of 5 million, the population of the former—a strategic region located between Manchuria and the Sea of Japan—amounted to a mere 70,000 in 1893.[25]

For the preceding, Kulomzin blamed a deficient bureaucratic apparatus, which constituted a formidable obstacle to the "flourishing" of Siberia: There were very few bureaucrats capable of administering such an immense, ethnically diverse region. Tens of thousands of peasants were making their way to Siberia and setting up villages wherever they pleased without regard for the government's needs. Each uezd was the size of a large Western nation—Ishim uezd was the size of Sweden, for instance—and within each were but two or three officials to supervise peasant affairs. In the Transbaikal, administrative chaos reigned—a complete "kasha" in Kulomzin's view. Russian peasants, mining settlements, Cossack hosts, and native Buriats lived side by side, each governed by an inadequate administrative body. Many knew nothing about civil affairs. In its most extreme form, the most paradoxical feature of the Russian state was thus evident in Siberia: overgovernment at the center and underadministration in the provinces.[26]

An earlier attempt to contend with these problems had failed. Far Eastern Cossack hosts had been established under N.N. Murav'ev-Amurskii to settle the region by forming a military-agricultural colony. By the 1890s, the Cossacks, for the most part, were not doing well in this harsh land—many families had lost their land and were going hungry. Those who retained their holdings as often as not did so only by renting them out to Koreans or Chinese farmers. And some ended up moving to Manchuria, where they were exploited as cheap laborers by the Chinese population. Thus the presence of Asians was stronger, Russia's presence was weaker, and the provisioning necessary to sustain local settlements remained inadequate.[27]

Although Kulomzin did find many of the old settlers in western Siberia to be prosperous, he deemed the cultural level of *Sibiriaki* dangerously wanting. Siberia's large criminal exile population (according to Kulomzin between 13 and 34 percent of the various regions' inhabitants) often terrorized residents, perpetrating all manner of violent crimes, such as the daily armed robbery of central Siberian freight trains.[28] A near complete lack of schools and churches, distance from the sources of Russian culture and governmental authority, and proximity to native and criminal populations all combined to rip away the bonds of civilization and allow the Russian Siberian to go wild (*odichat'*).[29] The Sibiriaki had "forgotten [their] origins in European Russia, the place of [their] ancestry," and they no longer considered themselves "people of the Russian empire."[30] Kulomzin had no romantic image of the Sibiriak as noble savage. Rather, this barbarous creature was to be the beneficiary of a civilizing mission the Russian government would undertake in its own land: "The Siberian railroad committee appeared as the first ray of sun in the kingdom of darkness."[31]

Peasant Resettlement

The underlying purpose of Kulomzin's civilizing mission was to strengthen the Russian state's political control over its territory. Reflecting its modernizing impulse, the autocratic regime applied a technological solution—the construction of the Trans-Siberian Railroad—to its political and cultural predicament in Siberia. With its extensive auxiliary enterprises, the railroad was supposed to allow the government to guide the mass, spontaneous migration of Russian peasants into Siberia and thereby assist the government in reversing Siberia's centrifugal tendencies.

Kulomzin's inspiration for his specific program came from many different foreign and domestic sources, indicating the extent to which he saw himself as fulfilling the role of contemporary colonizers. He constantly referred to the United States, Canada, Germany, and Europe's overseas colonies in discussing precedents for his actions. He wanted the experience of Western European outmigration studied for the lessons it might yield. He believed Russia would do well to give Siberian officials the type of training European colonial administrators received. He took note of potential "little Americas" on his 1896 and 1897 trips beyond the Urals, readily acknowledging his aspiration to re-create the thriving grain centers of North America in the Siberian Black Earth Zone. Similar recognition was given to Berlin's attempt to move German peasants into its Polish provinces, which he cited as the model of internal colonization he would apply in Siberia.[32]

Kulomzin, to a lesser extent, relied on Russian precedent, following in the footsteps of those rulers who sought to strengthen the empire through the coordinated movement of settler populations. Catherine the Great had followed the Prussian absolutist example and undertook planned colonization by inviting groups of Germans, Georgians, Armenians, and Jews to settle in designated regions.[33] Kulomzin expressed admiration for K. Kaufmann, governor-general of Turkestan, and N. Kaznakov, Western Siberian governor-general, both of whom he asserted were the only Russian officials before his time to augment the Russian presence in native territories.[34] None of his predecessors, though, attempted anything on the scale of what he did. Moreover, he was moving Russia away from its traditional patterns of military administration and into line with contemporary Western practices in order to transform the empire into a modern and efficiently run political entity.

Witte and Kulomzin hoped their endeavors would extend the authority of the tsarist regime and simultaneously help alleviate the agricultural crisis in European Russia without resorting to socially disruptive measures, such as dismantling the repartitional communes. Although Siberia ultimately failed to absorb enough of the Russian peasant population to ease the problems of overpopulation and land hunger in the center, these efforts are worthy of note since the perception of Witte and the tsarist government before the turn of the century is one of all-consuming concentration on industrialization and disregard for the plight of Russian agriculture. Such a view could not be further from the truth: Witte and Kulomzin expected Siberia to fulfill for European Russia the same function America had for the overpopulated rural nations of Western Europe.[35] Peasant resettlement in Siberia might thus solve two problems at once: Siberian separatism and Russian rural poverty.

Unlike some of the ministers of the interior, Kulomzin and Witte recognized early on that trying to stop the mass migration of peasants seeking a better life was impossible and undesirable. But it was thought possible to "control and direct" this spontaneous wave of humanity in Siberia in accord with the state's political interests.[36] Insofar as they were successful in accomplishing this goal, one can assert that the Siberian frontier bore little resemblance to the individualistic, democratic prototype of the American West championed by Frederick Jackson Turner.

In principle, Kulomzin, as a representative of the Russian autocracy, stood for exerting control over the spontaneous movement of the lower classes, but there were certain practical reasons involved in his aims as well. For one, the government was losing tax revenues. Hundreds of villages were built deep in state forests where treasury officials could not find them.[37] Also, Kulomzin recognized that Russia's peasant migrants were destitute, worlds away from farmers on the American prairies. As the number of settlers grew larger, he feared they would not survive without the government's help.[38] Their poverty and independence would undermine government efforts to strengthen its control over Siberia with the construction of the Trans-Siberian Railroad.

One of Kulomzin's major responsibilities within the Committee of the Siberian Railroad was to sustain newly arriving peasants in Siberia, whose problems he investigated on his three-month-long inspection tour of western and central Siberia in 1896. To this end, Kulomzin involved the government in as many aspects of their lives as possible—before they arrived, en route to their new villages, and once settled. For peasants considering migration, Kulomzin had millions of brochures published to identify available lands in the Black Earth Zone and to generally counter the rumors about Siberia floated by old settlers who wanted to attract cheap, exploitable labor. Kulomzin found that many settlers did not realize until it was too late how difficult conditions were, having been duped by reports that in Siberia each *desiatin* (2.7 acres) of land yielded 300 *puds* of rye and 250 *puds* of oats; that anyone could claim possession of fifty desiatins of land; and that the hills were all rich in gold and silver.[39]

Safeguarding the health of migrants en route became Kulomzin's most persistent concern. This required the provision of barges, rafts, and horses for transport from railroad stations and adequate shelter in the form of barracks or yurts at designated resettlement points. Here he established the distribution of free food and medical care, with the result that rates of death and disease fell dramatically. He asserted, with only slight exaggeration, that this was the first time doctors or medicine were made available in Siberia's history. Peasants may have been disappointed not to be greeted in Cheliabinsk by Empress Mariia Feodorovna handing out bowls of kasha, as rumor had her doing, but they kept coming.[40]

The Committee of the Siberian Railroad arranged the surveying of more than twenty million acres of farmland on either side of the railroad, as well as in the taiga of Tobol'sk and Tomsk provinces and in the Irkutsk general-governorship. Once surveyed, the distribution of plots commenced. According to Kulomzin, land was distributed not at random but in agreement with representatives of old settler communities and an expanding cadre of local resettlement officials. Individual peasant households received a standard plot of 15 desiatins (40.5 acres). Roughly one hundred households formed a village. For every 200 desiatins settled by peasants, a certain amount of land was to be set aside for construction of a school and a church. The government reserved to itself large plots of land for possible future factory construction, as well as stretches of forest land. The latter were needed to guarantee a fuel supply to the railroad at a time when vast stretches of western and central Siberia were being deforested to supply the railroad and colonists with building materials.[41]

The land-use arrangements implemented in Siberia reveal much about Kulomzin and contemporary official thinking with regard to Russia's agrarian problems. The vast majority of migrants were leaving repartitional communes in European Russia. Kulomzin's research showed that many of them had wanted to will land to their children, but found it impossible to do so when it was subject to subdivision and redistribution. This, as well as landlessness, compelled peasants to migrate to Siberia.[42] Kulomzin thus recognized some of the deficiencies of Russian communal agriculture, anticipating Stolypin's critique in the years ahead.

As Lieven has pointed out, in the midst of the 1905 revolution Kulomzin saw that the commune's time was up, but it is clear from his memoirs that even earlier he had perceived the shortcomings of the commune and tried to foster change. In the 1890s it was for practical reasons that he did not consider it possible to make a sudden shift to individual farming and abandon the commune. Although he would allow peasants to make their own choice, he rejected the suggestion made by some reform-minded officials that all plots in Siberia be distributed as *khutors,* or non-communal, individual homesteads. Even though he agreed that that was desirable in the long run, for the time being he felt the government could not simply place peasants on their own and expect a new rural culture to develop overnight. He saw it as first necessary to raise the technical and educational levels of Russian peasants; only then might the attempt be made to experiment with different forms of landholding.[43]

He was also wary of dismantling the commune system for reasons of security in the vulnerable Far East. He and other officials were convinced that even if beneficial in theory, in the short term the khutor would disrupt farming among peasants who were not used to it. Russia simply could not take that risk in a region facing the certain "pressure of the yellow race." The only means of maintaining Russian nationality here was in group cohesion, and that was best achieved with the commune.[44]

Although cautious about the commune, Kulomzin was the most active advocate of introducing private property in landholding into Siberia, in this way also anticipating the spirit of the Stolypin reforms. Heretofore all property in Siberia had been owned by the government, but Kulomzin argued that this hindered agricultural and industrial productivity and prevented high-caliber officials from sinking roots in the region. The law that was put into effect allowing for private property was written by Kulomzin and was designed to prevent foreigners and Siberian natives from owning land. It maintained real-estate speculation at low levels by imposing a cap on the amount of land individuals might hold and by requiring that buyers work through licensed agents, invest a certain amount in land improvements, and have the necessary financial backing. The government preserved its exclusive rights to mining and forests and gave special privileges to the nobility.[45] This law demonstrates Kulomzin's doubts about the old ways and also indicates another major difference between the Russian and American frontiers, the latter depended heavily on land speculation and private exploitation of mineral and forest wealth.[46]

Once peasants were settled on plots, the government provided aid and assistance to sustain farming and cattle rearing. Kulomzin's subcommittee arranged to make loans available for home construction and agricultural needs. It provided an array of veterinary services, built grain storage facilities, and sold lumber and farm implements and machinery at fixed prices. The last was one of the few profitable ventures associated with the Trans-Siberian project, bringing in gross revenues of 4,393,956 rubles between 1898 and 1903 alone.[47]

Of course, much of the success of the committee was in western and central Siberia. Efforts were also made in the Far East, but it remained for Stolypin to undertake a more concerted program of resettlement in that region far from the desired destinations of most migrants. For now, Kulomzin and Witte urged the relaxation of restrictions on Old Believers residing in the Amur and Ussuri regions to attract their coreligionists there en masse. As a hard-working and relatively prosperous segment of the population, they could be expected to make great strides in reversing the stagnation of these strategically vital areas. But K.P. Pobedonostsev, procurator of the Holy Synod and reactionary ideologist of the regime, vigorously fought and defeated their proposal.[48]

Pobedonostsev would have no reason to object, however, to the major emphasis Kulomzin placed on education and religion to strengthen the Russian element and check the strength of native culture in Siberia. Kulomzin gained repute separate from his work on the Trans-Siberian as an advocate of education for the masses—in the hopes of bringing prosperity and preventing revolution.[49] In the Committee of the Siberian Railroad he constantly emphasized the need to give peasants knowledge of Russian history alongside technological training, hoping to make them patriotic citizens as well as productive farmers. For Siberian merchants he suggested a course in Asian and European languages, and for natives he urged training in the Russian language.[50] He felt his recommendations would be beneficial for the entire realm and lamented the government's failure to act on them. "There was no spirit [within the government]," he wrote, "stimulating [it] to attend to the needs of the people."[51]

Via school and church, the political and linguistic Russification of Siberia forms a theme that runs throughout Kulomzin's papers, as it does throughout the utterances of Sergei Witte and the deliberations of the Committee of the Siberian Railroad. Kulomzin's irritation with the fact that Siberia was a "motley mixture" of nationalities and religions—Orthodox, sectarians, Muslims, Buddhists, and pagans—implies a desire for a homogeneous empire.[52] The attempt to foster homogeneity represents a transition from an earlier style of imperial rule that accommodated itself to heterogeneity. Economic and administrative modernization in Russia, as in Europe, required a level of uniformity to facilitate the smooth operation of the state.[53]

Furthermore, now that the state was open to the adoption of Western industrial technologies, it acquired the capability of projecting the political reach of the government and creating a more perfectly centralized and integrated realm. Not only did this aspiration entail discrimination against minorities, and thus generate new ethnic tensions, it also proved impossible to achieve without a willingness to resort to extensive coercive measures of a type later applied under the Stalinist regime.

Siberian Natives

In 1905, Kulomzin criticized the government for its insensitivity in attempting to Russify ethnic groups with established cultures, such as the Poles, Finns, and Armenians. But he did not hold the Kazakhs or Buriats of Siberia in such high esteem. He himself bore a large measure of responsibility for Russification among them and for speeding up the transfer of their lands into Russian hands. Although he desired to protect these indigenous peoples from economic ruin, there is no doubt he was ready to sacrifice their interests to benefit Russian settlers. After all, in his mistaken view, the territory of western and central Siberia could be considered Russia's ancestral homeland, having possibly once belonged to the ancient Scythians, whom he, like many, believed to be the forebears of the Slavs.[54]

Kulomzin wrote frequently of his "dream" of settling Russian peasants on the Kazakh steppe lands south of the Trans-Siberian. Time and again he referred to these territories as a "Resettlement Eldorado," requiring only drainage, irrigation, and the removal of the Kazakhs before Russians might move in. He felt the colonization and exploitation of this fertile expanse should go forward, even at the risk of forsaking Kazakh goodwill toward the Russian government.[55]

Kulomzin recognized that paying or forcing Kazakhs to give up land to Russian settlers might undermine their traditional nomadic lifestyle and disrupt their cattle-herding patterns, but he convinced himself that the Russian government could nonetheless settle "millions" here and at the same time avoid inflicting much pain on the Kazakhs. One study he relied on found that Kazakhs occupied 5,352,425 desiatins of land, but that this far exceeded what their 597,736 head of cattle required for grazing. The government could take 2,384,214 desiatins away from them and still guarantee that their minimum dietary and economic needs would be met! Kulomzin's response to a study of the Kazakh diet showing healthy consumption of bread, meat, kumys, and milk was that if Russian peasants ate so well there would be no agricultural crisis. He implied that the Kazakh lifestyle was not as fragile as assumed and could tolerate the loss of more grazing land.[56] In preparing the way for the settlement of thousands of Russian peasants in Kazakh territory, Kulomzin laid the foundation for the devastation of the traditional Kazakh existence and the establishment of the region as a Russian settler colony with many similarities to Europe's overseas possessions.

Kulomzin had a slightly different perspective on the Buriats, although in essence it amounted to the same mistrust and desire for their land.[57] On his official tour of the Transbaikal region in 1897, Kulomzin found the Buriats to be an "undoubtedly likable and attractive population," superior to Russia's other natives, but he felt Russian influence among them was too weak and should be strengthened. Here all government business was done in Mongolian, and the beauty and appeal of the elaborate Buddhist temples put the crude wooden Orthodox churches to shame, as the educated lamas did the drunken, half-literate Russian clergy. In dismay he wondered whether "Mongolian civilization would prove sturdier than Slavic."[58]

Kulomzin's battle plan in this struggle between cultures was to urge a concerted effort to revive church missions in the Transbaikal. He expected that conversion of Buriats by Mongolian-speaking Orthodox clergy and then intermarriage of these natives with Russians would produce a population with blond hair and blue eyes within a few generations.[59] He gave equal emphasis to educating Buriats in Russian-language schools, believing that "the more the natives educate themselves the stronger the spirit of separatism becomes."[60] Better to supervise their education and encourage them in the use of Russian than leave them in the hands of their own religious authorities.

As for the Buriats' territory, Kulomzin assumed they occupied "far more . . . than they need" and that only a stepped-up Russian presence would block their claim to half of the Transbaikal. He wanted to reform landholding arrangements in order to dispossess the Buriat elite, the heads of clans who controlled land distribution. This, though, was a sign not of his concern for Buriat welfare, but of his desire to replace traditional Russian reliance on co-opted local ethnic elites with more direct rule by the Russian government, in line with modernizing reforms implemented elsewhere in the empire at this time.[61]

Kulomzin admitted that his goal was to whittle away at native lands, and his policies helped Russia do just that, even if he was concerned enough to impose some limits on Russian settlement to prevent the full impoverishment of native communities.[62] He thus epitomizes Russian imperial policy as a whole at the end of the tsarist era, and even in much of the pre- and post-Stalin periods, with its striving for uniformity but simultaneous forced compromise in the face of ethnic diversity.

Conclusion

Despite his best efforts, in one respect Kulomzin made little headway in achieving his goals. Siberia remained, like the Russian Empire, a heterogeneous society composed of diverse ethnicities and traditions. In one typical village in Tobol'sk province, for instance, Russians, Ukrainians, Belorussians, Maris, Komis, and Chuvash all lived and worked side by side. After one of his fact-finding missions Kulomzin called Siberian villages a "veritable ethnographic exhibition" of the peoples of the empire. In his opinion, the coexistence of so many different agricultural traditions within the confines of individual communes was undesirable. It was hard enough to find consensus among Russians; with so many others added to the mix, the result was endless quarreling and economic inefficiencies. But he accepted the inevitable and gave up trying to influence who came to Siberia. Russians were preferred and formed the majority, but it was impossible to prevent others from coming too.[63]

In all other respects, though, Kulomzin's efforts were successful. More than any other person, it was he who made possible the settlement of five million migrants in the wide fertile corridor of southern Siberia in the two decades preceding World War I. By 1907, all land lying in close proximity to the railroad had been parceled out.[64] Agriculture was booming, especially in western Siberia. In twenty years land under cultivation rose from 14 million to 31 million acres, a 122 percent increase. The amount of livestock more than tripled to over 38 million head, and wheat and rye harvests each approached a million tons per year.[65] The Siberian butter-making industry raised its annual production from 400 puds in 1894 to 2 million puds in 1904 and continued to grow thereafter, gaining large export markets in England, Denmark, and Germany.[66] Geographical research, essential for the assertion of the government's control over its territory, received sharp stimulus as well. For the first time, systematic, government-sponsored surveying of water routes and geological conditions took place on an extensive scale, setting the pattern for future Soviet scientific research in Siberia.[67]

Kulomzin was naturally pleased that so much had been done so quickly out of nothing and in such difficult conditions. Although the Trans-Siberian in other respects was a costly disappointment, no one disputed that at a price of 32 million rubles, his auxiliary enterprises, especially peasant resettlement, were a spectacular achievement.[68]

Above all, Kulomzin could be said to have laid the foundation for the subsequent Soviet development of Siberia. His work in the Committee of the Siberian Railroad made possible the continued mass movement of people and the future relocation of heavy industry east of the Urals. And his activities set a precedent for further encroachments on native lands. For better or worse, his was thus a vital contribution to the making of modern Siberia.

Few scholars see the tsarist regime as effective or even competent, but the colonization of Siberia should gain that regime more credit, thanks largely to its talented, dedicated servant Kulomzin. Kulomzin was one of the great colonizers of world history. He singly helped guide what occurred in piecemeal fashion at the hands of many hundreds of individuals on the American and Canadian frontiers.

Paradoxically, however, his success in remaking Siberia enhanced the underlying weaknesses of the Russian Empire. The tsarist government gave its viziers like Kulomzin room to experiment with social and economic reform in the borderlands, if only to extend central authority. The same opportunities were rarely to be had in Russia proper, which was firmly under the government's control and where conservative forces staunchly resisted alterations to the status quo. Exceptions were made only in times of crisis, for instance after 1902, when the government was forced by famine and peasant unrest to consider extensive agrarian reforms; even then many important proposals, such as Kulomzin's regarding education, failed to survive bureaucratic inertia.

Kulomzin might rival other European colonizers, but the nation he represented was not like theirs. For the most part, European imperialism was an expression of economic and military strength. Russian colonization in Siberia was an expression of geopolitical weakness. The whole venture was a push for homogeneity that, flying in the face of the empire's diversity, only intensified ethnic tensions and required the redirection of scarce financial and intellectual resources away from the heartland. Ultimately, these misdirected priorities contributed to the collapse of the regime, and with it the empire on which so much energy and wealth had been expended.

Notes

I would like to express my gratitude to the following people for assisting my research in St. Petersburg: Vladimir V. Lapin, director of the Russian State Historical Archives (RGIA); Serafima I. Varekhova, manager of the archive reading room; and Boris V. Anan'ich and Sergei K. Lebedev, both of the Institute of History. I cannot thank Alexander, Zhanna, and Sergei Turgaev enough for their hospitality. Research for this article was supported in part by a grant from the International Research and Exchanges Board (IREX), with funds provided by the National Endowment for the Humanities, the United States Information Agency, and the U.S. Department of State, which administers the Russian, Eurasian, and East European Research Program (Title VIII).

1. See Steven G. Marks, *Road to Power: The Trans-Siberian Railroad and the Colonization of Asian Russia, 1850–1917* (Ithaca, NY: Cornell University Press, 1991).

2. The quote is from Hans Rogger in *Russia in the Age of Modernisation and Revolution, 1881–1917* (London: Longman, 1983), p. 182. For diverse elements of these phenomena, see also S. Frederick Starr, *Decentralization and Self-Government in Russia, 1830–1870* (Princeton: Princeton University Press, 1972), pp. 58–109, 336–47; Hugh Seton-Watson, *The Russian Empire, 1801–1917* (Oxford: Clarendon, 1967), pp. 412–13, 486–87; and Andreas Kappeler, *Russland als Vielvölkerreich* (Munich: C.H. Beck, 1992), pp. 203, 207–15, 224–29. For an overview of the functioning of the tsarist empire, see S. Frederick Starr, "Tsarist Government: The Imperial Dimension," in *Soviet Nationality Policies and Practices*, ed. Jeremy Azrael (New York: Praeger, 1978), pp. 3–38.

3. On Witte, see Marks, *Road to Power,* passim.

4. On Rhodes, see Robert I. Rotberg, *The Founder: Cecil Rhodes and the Pursuit of Power* (New York: Oxford University Press, 1988); on Curzon, see David Dilks, *Curzon in India,* 2 vols. (New York: Taplinger, 1969).

5. Kulomzin's 4,000-page memoir with its integration of state papers is to be found in the Russian State Historical Archive in St. Petersburg, fond 1642, opis' 1. The memoir was written mostly after 1905, but it closely follows the extensive documentation compiled by Kulomzin over the course of his life in government. Over half of this rich, largely unexplored source is devoted to Siberia and yields ample material with which to judge Kulomzin's activities and the Russian government's intentions in promoting Siberian peasant resettlement. The latter is a topic that has not yet received the attention it deserves.

For an overview, see Marks, *Road to Power,* chs. 7–10 and passim. Donald W. Treadgold's classic, *The Great Siberian Migration* (Princeton: Princeton University Press, 1957), is still of great use, but misapplies the Turner thesis to Russia. François-Xavier Coquin, *La Sibérie: Peuplement et immigration paysanne au XIXe siècle* (Paris: Institut d'études slaves, 1969), is concerned largely with settlement before construction of the Trans-Siberian Railroad. Above all, further research in Siberian local archives is necessary to test the assertions of the preceding three works.

6. Dominic Lieven, *Russia's Rulers Under the Old Regime* (New Haven: Yale University Press, 1989), p. 234.

7. Erik Amburger, *Geschichte der Behördenorganisation Russlands von Peter dem Grossen bis 1917* (Leiden: E.J. Brill, 1966), p. 125. Lieven incorrectly states that Kulomzin was secretary of the Committee of Ministers until 1904 (*Russia's Rulers,* p. 231); rather, Kulomzin had resigned to concentrate on Siberia.

8. See Marks, *Road to Power,* pp. 131–33, 144–45. Kulomzin later implied that he saw Witte as a manipulator with too much power (see his quote in Lieven, *Russia's Rulers,* p. 249).

9. Lieven, *Russia's Rulers,* pp. 236–42.

10. Rossiiskii gosudarstvennyi istoricheskii arkhiv (RGIA), f. 1642, op. 1, d. 185, l. 20.

11. The quote is by A.A. Polovtsov, cited in Lieven, *Russia's Rulers,* p. 243.

12. For the English parallel, see J.F.C. Harrison, "The Victorian Gospel of Success," in *Victorian Studies,* vol. I, no. 2, December 1957, pp. 155–64. For Kulomzin's close observation of English life, see Lieven, *Russia's Rulers,* pp. 234–37.

13. Lieven, *Russia's Rulers,* pp. 238–39.

14. For the quote, see RGIA, f. 1642, op. 1, d. 185, ll. 12–13.

15. Lieven, *Russia's Rulers,* p. 244. Along with his attachment to Siberia for its physical beauty, these were sentiments Kulomzin shared with all past and future Siberian administrative reformers and regionalist intellectuals, including the contemporary "village writer" Valentin Rasputin. See RGIA, f. 1642, op. 1, d. 201, l. 75; on Rasputin, see the chapter below by Kathleen Parthé. On similarities with the views of Solzhenitsyn and earlier Russian thinkers, see Mark Bassin, "Inventing Siberia: Visions of the Russian East in the Early Nineteenth Century," *American Historical Review,* vol. 96, no. 3 (June 1991), pp. 778, 793–94.

16. See, e.g., Kappeler, *Russland als Vielvölkerreich,* p. 57 and passim.

17. RGIA, f. 1642, op. 1, d. 197, l. 31.

18. For these and other motives behind construction of the Trans-Siberian Railroad, see Marks, *Road to Power.* For evolving administrative arrangements in Siberia, see A.V. Remnev, *Upravlenie Sibir'iu i Dal'nim Vostokom v XIX-nachale XX vv.: Uchebnoe posobie* (Omsk, 1991).

19. RGIA, f. 1642, op. 1, d. 204, l. 107.

20. Ibid., d. 204, l. 111.

21. See Heinz Gollwitzer, *Europe in the Age of Imperialism, 1880–1914,* trans. David Adam and Stanley Baron (New York: Harcourt, Brace and World, 1969).

22. See the chapters below by Gilbert Rozman and Viktor Larin, as well as Allen S. Whiting, *Siberian Development and East Asia: Threat or Promise?* (Stanford: Stanford University Press, 1981), p. 93.

23. RGIA, f. 1642, op. 1, d. 205, l. 25; d. 211, ll. 59–60. The same concern was evidenced later in Stolypin's Committee for the Colonization of the Far East. See RGIA, f. 394, op. 1, d. 7; d. 13; d. 48. For the population statistics, see *Aziatskaia Rossiia,* vol. 1 (St. Petersburg, 1914), pp. 72, 80, 82.

24. RGIA, f. 1642, op. 1, d. 204, l. 28; d. 197, l. 28.

25. Ibid., d. 185, ll. 41–42.

26. Ibid., d. 198, l. 28; d. 185, ll. 12–13, 24–26; d. 204, ll. 40–41, 46–47. On Russia as an underadministered nation, see Rogger, *Russia in the Age of Modernisation,* p. 48.

27. RGIA, f. 1642, op. 1, d. 204, ll. 49–50; d. 197, ll. 4–5.

28. Ibid., d. 198, l. 8; d. 190, l. 41; d. 204, ll. 21–22.

29. Ibid., d. 201, l. 14. For analogous complaints made by Rome about Italian colonists in Ethiopia, see Haile M. Larebo, *The Building of an Empire: Italian Land Policy and Practice in Ethiopia, 1935–1941* (Oxford: Clarendon, 1994), p. 117.

30. RGIA, f. 1642, op. 1, d. 204, l. 107.

31. Ibid., d. 198, l. 75.

32. Ibid., d. 206, l. 16; d. 198, l. 28; d. 186, l. 13; d. 202, l. 50; d. 191, ll. 1–3; and *passim.*

33. See Marc Raeff, *The Well-Ordered Police State: Social and Institutional Change Through Law in the Germanies and Russia, 1600–1800* (New Haven: Yale University Press, 1983), pp. 230–32; Ingeborg Fleischhauer, *Die Deutschen in Zarenreich* (Stuttgart: Deutsche Verlags-Anstalt, 1986), pp. 97–119; and Kappeler, *Russland als Vielvölkerreich,* pp. 117–21.

34. RGIA, f. 1642, op. 1, d. 207, ll. 17–18.

35. A notable exception to the traditional portrayal of Witte's agricultural policies is to be found in David A.J. Macey, *Government and Peasant in Russia, 1861–1906: The Prehistory of the Stolypin Reforms* (DeKalb, IL: University of Northern Illinois Press, 1987), pp. 35–36, although without mention of Siberia.

36. RGIA, f. 1642, op. 1, d. 208, l. 11; d. 191, l. 7; see also d. 213, l. 63.

37. Ibid., d. 185, l. 14.

38. Ibid., d. 201, ll. 23–24.

39. Ibid., d. 185, ll. 13, 28–29; d. 198, ll. 76–77; d. 202, ll. 107–8, 115–16. For Kulomzin's official report of this tour, see *Vsepoddaneishii otchet Stats-Sekretaria Kulomzina po poezdke v Sibir' dlia oznakomleniia s polozheniem pereselencheskogo dela,* 2 vols. (St. Petersburg, 1896).

40. RGIA, f. 1642, op. 1, d. 190, l. 40; d. 198, l. 75. Establishment of resettlement stations en route reduced illness by three to four times and cut the death rate among the sick from 50 percent to 20 percent.

41. Ibid., d. 185, ll. 20–23, 28–29, 34. On deforestation, see "Izvlechenie iz vsepoddaneishego doklada ministra finansov," *Vestnik finansov, promyshlennosti i torgovli,* no. 8, 23 February, 1903, p. 312; S.K. Fitingov, "Perspektivy ugol'noi promyshlennosti v zapadnoi Sibiri," *Zhurnal obshchestva sibirskikh inzhenerov,* April 1915, no. 4, p. 98.

42. RGIA, f. 1642, op. 1, d. 201, ll. 23–24.

43. Ibid., d. 208, ll. 4–5.

44. Ibid., d. 208, l. 5.

45. Ibid., d. 211, *passim; Polnoe sobranie zakonov rossiiskoi imperii,* sobranie tret'e, vol. XXI, 1901 (St. Petersburg, 1903), no. 20338.

46. See Frederick Merk, *History of the Westward Movement* (New York: Alfred A. Knopf, 1978).

47. RGIA, f. 1642, op. 1, d. 208, ll. 11–12.

48. Ibid., d. 204, ll. 75–77; d. 213, ll. 39–40.

49. Lieven, *Russia's Rulers,* 246–48.

50. RGIA, f. 1642, op. 1, *passim.*

51. Ibid., d. 207, l. 19.

52. Ibid., d. 190, l. 41.

53. See Kappeler, *Russland als Vielvölkerreich,* ch. 7–8.

54. RGIA, f. 1642, op. 1, d. 201, l. 75. See Lieven, *Russia's Rulers,* p. 251, for Kulomzin's critique of Russification.

55. RGIA, f. 1642, op. 1, d. 198, l. 77; d. 206, ll. 18–19. For the fate of the Kazakhs in general in this period, see Martha Brill Olcott, *The Kazakhs* (Stanford: Hoover Institution Press, 1987), pp. 83–126.

56. RGIA, f. 1642, op. 1, d. 198, l. 27; d. 201, l. 19; d. 202, ll. 83–84. For the two studies, see d. 197, ll. 57–58 and d. 204, ll. 20–21.

57. On the Buriats in this period, see James Forsyth, *A History of the Peoples of Siberia: Russia's North Asian Colony, 1581–1990* (Cambridge: Cambridge University Press, 1992), pp. 168–74.

58. RGIA, f. 1642, op. 1, d. 204, ll. 27–28, 30–32, 59–60.

59. Ibid., d. 204, ll. 28, 61–62.

60. Ibid., d. 204, ll. 30–31, 37, 63.

61. Ibid., d. 204, ll. 49, 96–100; and Kappeler, *Russland als Vielvölkerreich,* pp. 262–63, on movement away from the government's traditional reliance on local elites.

62. RGIA, f. 1642, op. 1, d. 207, ll. 17–18.

63. RGIA, f. 1642, op. 1, d. 198, ll. 77, 103–4; d. 201, l. 21.

64. Ibid., d. 185, l. 33.

65. See Marks, *Road to Power,* pp. 207–8; and N.D. Kondrat'ev, *Rynok khlebov i ego regulirovanie vo vremia voiny i revoliutsii* (Moscow: 1991), pp. 330 ff.

66. *Aziatskaia Rossiia,* vol. 2, pp. 331–38.

67. See Marks, *Road to Power,* pp. 145–48, 151–53; and V.A. Esakov, *Geografiia v Rossii v XIX-nachale XX veka* (Moscow, 1978), pp. 188–205.

68. RGIA, f. 1642, op. 1, d. 198, l. 77; Marks, *Road to Power,* pp. 144n12, 153–54n41.

Russia Finds Its Limits

Crossing Borders into Manchuria

David Wolff

From the 1890s until the present, Russians have lived and died, worked and played, built and destroyed in the Chinese Northeast, a region known in all languages—but Chinese—as Manchuria. Beginning with the survey for and subsequent construction of the Chinese Eastern Railway, Russian money and migrants poured into a location on the Amur tributary, the Sungari (*Songhuajiang*), where the "instant city" of Harbin soon rose. In fifteen years, an unprepossessing fishing village with a population under 100 metamorphosed into an urban conglomerate with more than 100,000 inhabitants. After 1917, émigré Harbin became the only Russian city outside the Soviet Union, and as such played a special role in Sino-Soviet bilateral relations, the delayed reassertion of Moscow's rule over the Russian Far East, and Northeast Asia's perception of Russia, both old and new.[1]

The importance of the Russian presence in Manchuria varies with the context into which it is placed. The angle from which most Russian historians and historians of Russia would approach Russian Manchuria identifies the Chinese Eastern Railway as a key rail connection in the fragile communications infrastructure built in the final decades of the tsarist regime to link the Russian Far East together and to European Russia. Harbin, in this view, becomes one of several multiethnic—but Russian-dominated—cities in the Far East, including Blagoveshchensk, Khabarovsk, Nikolaevsk-na-Amure, Nikolsk-Ussuriisk, and Vladivostok. In the narrative that follows, I will highlight the value of this conceptualization for examining the mechanism by which affairs of Russia's domestic frontier, particularly civil–military rivalry, jumped the border to influence life on the other side.[2] Such an interpretation incorporates the history of Russian Manchuria into that of the Russian Far East.

In many ways, however, analyzing Russian Manchuria as integral to the rest of the empire excludes much that was fascinating and important about the place.[3] A second approach would emphasize that the Manchurian experience represents a unique historical vein, one that should also be mined in search of alternatives to our center-dominated views of Russian history. If studies of Siberia and the Russian Far East help us to debunk monolithic visions of national history and validate local perspectives, studies of Russian Manchuria can take us one step further in that direction. Moreover, historical trends do not merely flow outward from the center. The relative administrative and ideological freedom of the frontier often made it Russia's laboratory for social experiments unwelcome in St. Petersburg and Moscow. The periphery can also take the initiative, transmitting its experience back to the center.[4]

A third perspective would place emphasis on Russian Manchuria's regional context. Such a view complements the first approach, which posited the essential unity of the subnational region we call the Russian Far East with Russian Manchuria included. But by focusing on the shared social histories of the countries and parts of countries that make up the transnational region of Northeast Asia, we begin to see the correlations between the broader and narrower versions of regionalism. After all, *dal'nii vostok* (Far East) without context could be either the Russian or the international unit. Once we acknowledge the socially constructed nature of state borders and their limited value in analyzing transnational phenomena, the path is open toward a regional history integrating the shared aspects of several national histories. Here, comparative methods help to reconstruct the international competition at the core of Northeast Asian identity.

All three perspectives were available to contemporaries and are thus essential in our efforts to comprehend the multidimensional history of a border region into which the Russian Empire extended itself, only to come up against its limits.

Civil–Military Tension in the Russian Far East

Until the late nineteenth century, much of eastern Siberia was little more than an armed camp where military personnel and methods were employed to keep a tenuous grip on large expanses of wilderness. Since relay time for communications to St. Petersburg was counted in months, governors-general wielded broad discretionary powers encompassing activities generally delegated to different specialized organs in the center. Since Siberian satraps commanded the army units in their territories, they were of necessity all military men with field-campaign experience. After 1884, the Amur governor-general, headquartered in Khabarovsk, ruled the entire Russian Far East, where the possibility of armed conflict with either China or Japan favored continuing militarization.[5]

Although life within the constraints of strategic thinking could be burdensome for the victims, in the Far East most of the inhabitants were used to living under *diktat.* Until the 1880s, the majority of Russian settlers in both the Amur and Maritime provinces were subordinate to military authorities, whether as Cossacks, regular troops, or exiles. Many more were retired reservists who might be called to arms at any time. This tendency on the part of the government to see regional demography through a strategic prism persisted into the twentieth century. In 1901, the fallout from the Boxer Uprising included a plan to quadruple the Amur Cossack population and sextuple their Ussuri counterparts.[6]

Into this zone of garrison towns and Cossack settlements came the railroad, bringing with it an alternative to the military monolith. The opening of the Suez Canal (1869), the declaration of the Vladivostok free port (1872), the establishment of regular service from Odessa to Vladivostok by the Volunteer Fleet (1879), and the Amur "gold rush" of the late 1880s had gradually increased the civilian presence among the population and vital affairs of the Russian Far East. Already in the surveying stage, Alexander III's 1887 order to the Siberian governors-general to report all matters concerning the Trans-Siberian to the Ministry of Transport, instead of through the normal chain of command to the War Ministry, portended the wave of the future. Nonetheless, it was the Tsarevich Nicholas's ceremonial shovelful when breaking ground on the Ussuri Railway in 1891 that heralded irreversible change and divided authority.[7]

Railroad construction set off an economic boom. Between 1897 and 1902, 1.1 billion rubles in government funds were lavished upon the Russian Far East. With such backing, the colonization plans attached to the Trans-Siberian flourished. Between 1892 and 1911, the population of the Amur province tripled, while the Maritime province's quintupled. Urban growth was particularly striking, as the cities in the latter province grew by a factor of seven. An elevenfold increase in Russo-Chinese land trade between 1892 and 1902 helped populate biracial cities on both sides of the border.[8]

The Chinese played several important roles in these far-reaching changes, since high growth rates could only be sustained by integrating productive factors across the Amur and Ussuri borders. In his report for 1896–97, the Priamur governor-general, S.M. Dukhovskoi, noted that recent developments have "multiplied our contacts with Manchuria." The Far Eastern Military District's mobilization in 1895 (in conjunction with the Triple Intervention) and the ban on livestock exports imposed by Chinese officials in 1897 highlighted the Russian Far East's increasing dependence on border trade. The military presence and railroad construction could not be provisioned otherwise; imports of grain and cattle rose.

Chinese workers also moved freely back and forth across the border rivers. The completion of the Ussuri Railway was hastened by the participation of 17,000 Chinese migrants. Many of them remained in Russian territory after the termination of the project. The 1912 Vladivostok census revealed a multiracial city in which Russians constituted a majority of just 58 percent. In 1910, a partial survey of the Amur province's most important employer of unskilled labor, the gold mines, found that 83 percent of the diggers were Chinese. "Yellow labor," as it was called by contemporaries, became even more essential after 1914, when all able-bodied Russian men were called to arms.[9]

Increasing social stratification and ethnic variety in the Russian Far East greatly complicated the administrative tasks of the Priamur commander in chief. Railroad engineers and management demanded operational autonomy in the name of technocratic rationality. Civilians, especially influential merchants, tended to see commercial and industrial tasks as primary. The Chinese, Japanese, and Korean communities were also viewed as aggressive entities, threatening to stain the map of eastern Russia an indelible yellow. Since effective countermeasures to these challenges lay outside the military sphere, civilian affairs occupied ever more of the local government's attention. In 1910, the governorship of the Maritime province was converted to a civil appointment.

Occasionally, these new social components might reinforce strategic needs. For example, in 1895, the Chinese merchant Tifontai (né Ji Fengtai), a recent convert to Russian Orthodoxy and citizenship, played a pioneering role in the inclusion of Russian shipping interests in a trade-route expansion that followed the Sungari River into the Manchurian heartland. The use of Russian transportation for importing provisions was an important step toward liberation from the whims and avarice of local Chinese officials in Jilin and Heilongjiang provinces. Tifontai, however, is probably best considered the exception that proves the rule. Other Chinese who petitioned successfully for admission into the Russian merchant guilds have thus far eluded historical detection.[10]

More common for the military authorities were misunderstandings with the Chinese population and its consul, disagreements with local civilians and their representative bodies, and administrative conflicts with the local branches of Petersburg ministries interested in the railroads and corollary enterprises. On his appointment as manager of the Ussuri Railway in 1895, Colonel D.L. Khorvat was granted an imperial audience at which Nicholas II commanded him to "set in order the relations between the local civil and military elements which as was often the case in Russia, left much to be desired."[11]

Of course, regardless of the threat to entrenched local interests, there could not be any question of opposing the tsar's orders or railroad construction. The Siberian military authorities were responsible for defending the empire's eastern borders, and in the long run, this could only be accomplished by a rail connection to the west, where the main forces of the Russian army were located. On the domestic front, the nonpassage of the railroad through a given area meant condemnation to stagnation. The Siberian metropolis of Tomsk, for example, sank to the second tier when bypassed by the trunk-line. Likewise, the upper and middle stretches of the Amur languished for an additional fifteen years when the decision was made to lay the final stretch of transcontinental tracks across Manchuria as an ostensibly joint Russo-Chinese venture called the Chinese Eastern Railway (CER).

Since Priamur Governor-General Dukhovskoi also answered for the economic well-being of his region, the fate of Tomsk must have been on his mind when in an 1896 recommendation to the throne he argued against the Manchurian variant, not only on strategic grounds, but also in the interests of development along the Amur:

> It will be an extremely heavy blow for the Priamur'e if the ray of light which shone upon it is extinguished. Colonization, gold mining and the powerful rise of Russian life will all suffer a reverse. . . . Will it not be an historic error to continue the Great Siberian Railway for two thousand versts through a region that will long be foreign to us?

Here, the tsar penned "no" in the margin, and that was that.[12]

Crossing the Border: The Harbin Difference

The short period of Russian predominance in Manchuria that lasted from 1897 until 1904 can be interpreted as the culmination of a centuries-long eastward drive. An emphasis on continuity, though, obscures some of the more compelling aspects of this imperialist venture. In any case, from wherever the underlying impulse emanated, the railway, not the army, would lead the Russian forces into China. The mastermind of the advance was Finance Minister Sergei Iu. Witte, who had been a railroad manager. Since entering government service, he had acquired an international reputation as a brilliant financier and enlightened administrator.

Not surprisingly, the railroad assumed a central significance in Witte's empirewide schemes. In his 1894 budget report he called the Russian rail network "a very powerful weapon . . . for the direction of the economic development of the country." If the jewel in his iron crown was the great Siberian trunk line, the Chinese Eastern Railway would be the last link in that historic undertaking, which Witte claimed would give Russia "control over the entire movement of international commerce in Pacific waters." Witte ascribed almost mystical powers to technology as an agent of civilization, writing that

> the railroad is like a leaven, which creates a cultural fermentation among the population. Even if it passed through an absolutely wild people along its way, it would raise them in a short time to the level prerequisite for its operation.

His modernizing zeal was aimed at comparatively modest advances by targeting neither the Siberian nor Manchurian aborigines, nor even the Chinese coolies, but the Russian educated public, whose lack of understanding for his Promethean projects he dismissed as social immaturity.[13]

In contrast to eastern Siberia, in Manchuria the railroad and its Finance Ministry backers arrived before the military. The 1896 Russo-Chinese defense treaty and CER construction contract provided the legal basis for a predominantly civilian presence. Funding, much of it from France and Belgium, was channeled through the multinational Russo-Chinese Bank, but the controlling shares of the

Chinese Eastern Railway Company rested securely in the vaults of Witte's ministry. The appointment of Colonel D.L. Khorvat as general manager of the railroad guaranteed expert guidance through shoals of civil–military conflict right up until his forced retirement in 1920. As in the case of the Siberian trunk line, the construction plan for the CER included the formation of a community along the railway.[14]

The center point of this colonization effort was the "instant city" of Harbin. Since the CER construction contract had pledged that the Russians would avoid settlements of the Chinese (both living and dead), the route chosen for the Trans-Manchurian line only rarely emerged from the wilderness. Just upstream from the point where the railroad's longest bridge would have to span the Songhua River (Sungari), a few cottages stood. A few miles inland from the south bank, the engineers bought an abandoned distillery for lodging. Chinese and Russian maps predating the railroad label both the riverbank and *hanxing* factory as "Haerbin" or "Khaobin."[15]

To accelerate completion of the project, the Russian builders decided to float materials upriver from Khabarovsk and lay tracks in both directions (from Harbin as well as from the Ussuri and Transbaikal borders). To avoid conflicts (and associated delays and distractions) with other ministries' minions in Vladivostok, Chief Engineer Iugovich moved his headquarters to Harbin in 1898. Within fifteen years, a transportation hub with more than 100,000 inhabitants had sprung up. Its size and importance were commensurate with its de facto role as the provincial capital of Russian Manchuria.

In 1913, a one-day census that excluded Harbin's Chinese sister city, Fujiadian, recorded a population of 68,549. Of these, 34.5 percent were Chinese nationals (compared to 28.7 percent in Vladivostok the previous year), many living in the crowded, unsanitary blocks around the Pristan, or dock's, central market. As if to protect their fellow countrymen, the legations of the local diplomatic representatives (*Jiaosheju*) from Fengtian and Jilin provinces stood opposite the marketplace. The Heilongjiang legation could be found one block over. Since this riverside section of Harbin was also the main commercial area, however, many well-off Chinese merchants also lived at prestigious addresses along the main avenues. The Russian administrative center in New Town had a smaller Chinese population of 17 percent (compared to Pristan's 43 percent). Almost all of New Town's Chinese were employed as "boys," cooks, or unskilled labor.

Because the Chinese authorities feared further Russian encroachments, the census committee's request to poll Fujiadian was refused. Harbin's municipal statistician, V.V. Soldatov, suggested 45,000 as a conservative population estimate. Fujiadian was born of the magnetism exerted by the large masses of Russian gold invested in the CER and Harbin. In December 1901, slightly more than 30 percent of Fujiadian's permanent residents were innkeepers. This suggests that the city's original function was to house Harbin's Chinese workforce. Fujiadian was also the distribution center for laborers on their way to construction sites elsewhere along the railway.

In 1911, a study of mobility between various parts of Harbin revealed that on average 29,346 crossings between Pristan and Fujiadian were made daily. Assuming that most of this traffic consisted of local commuters—a hypothesis given plausibility by the nearly equal numbers moving in both directions—then a third of Fujiadian's populace spent its days on the Russian side of the tracks. Harbin's well-being, in other words, was becoming ever more dependent on the symbiotic relationship of its constituent parts, Russian and Chinese.

In fact, on closer examination the "Russianness" of Harbin's 44,000 Russian citizens becomes questionable. A total of 5,032 Jewish residents gave Harbin the second largest Jewish population in eastern Siberia (after Irkutsk). By 1913, the Jews of Harbin had established a full complement of communal institutions, including a synagogue, primary school, burial brotherhood, Hebrew school, cemetery, *mikvah,* old age home, Talmud Torah, Jewish Women's Charity Committee, and library. Commercial activity was the economic backbone of the Jewish community, so it comes as no surprise that 90 percent lived in the bustling Pristan district.

There are several reasons why Jews flocked to Harbin. Most importantly, they were allowed to do so. Ostensibly to protect Slavic peasants from the Jewish "bloodsucker," Jews had been officially excluded from Siberian migration in 1899. In March 1902, however, Witte visited Harbin and argued that since Manchurian colonization would take place under "exceptional" conditions of competition with the Chinese, what was needed most was

> private initiative. Then, desirable individuals will come here—the most energetic, steadfast and adaptable; namely those of the trade and industrial class, searching for enrichment at their own risk.

After the large-scale pogroms of 1903 and 1905, many Jews in the European part of the empire were eager to move elsewhere. A good number of future Jewish in-migrants had their first exposure to Harbin either on the way to or from the Manchurian front as soldiers in the Russian army. Harbin, they realized, was far enough away to escape persecution and institutionalized prejudice and yet remain in a Russian cultural environment. Almost two-thirds of the Jews of Harbin claimed Russian, rather than Yiddish, as their native tongue. For them, Harbin possessed clear linguistic advantages over other popular out-migration destinations, such as New York.

Educational restrictions on Jews were also removed. After 1908, the administrative rules defining the *numerus clausus* for secondary and higher education hardened into law. Within the empire, the percentage of Jewish students allowed in state secondary schools was limited to 5 percent in the capitals, 15 percent in the Pale of Settlement, and 10 percent elsewhere. In Harbin, 20.1 percent of secondary school students were Jewish. Since the 402 students enrolled represented most of the Jewish cohort of high school age, we can safely assume that education was available on meritorious demand. In privileged Harbin, dire tidings of legal restrictions and blood libel cases occasioned no more than long-distance commiseration and secret relief.

In December 1897, the landing of a Russian detachment at Port Arthur successfully expanded Russian influence from northern to southern Manchuria. The following March, a lease for the tip of the Liaodong peninsula would provide the military with an ice-free port, a beachhead in China, and a base for civil–military conflict throughout Manchuria. Dal'nii (Dalian, Dairen), the new commercial port at the Siberian railway's ice-free terminus, immediately presented jurisdictional problems by being a CER project within the army-administered leasehold. Witte's attempt to keep the military out of North Manchuria by establishing railway guards subordinate to himself only provoked the generals further, since guard duty was one of the functions that the army staff considered particularly detrimental to the cultivation of soldiery.[16]

Artificial separation between the civilian and military could only be maintained in peacetime, however. When hostilities broke out in 1900 and again in 1904, guards proved to be insufficient protection for the railroad tracks and appended settlements. In the course of the Russo-Japanese War, the army and the CER carried their earlier enmity to new heights. The generals complained that the railway's inability to deliver vital matériel made victory impossible, while the CER argued that ignorant spearchuckers had abused their rank to interfere with orderly and efficient technical operations. As the location of both the rear headquarters and CER headquarters, Harbin stood at the center of these conflicts.

When a general railroad strike broke out in European Russia in October 1905, the CER and army perceived it quite differently. For the high-ranking railway officials who joined the CER Employee Strike Committee, this was an opportunity to mobilize social forces for the task of transporting the stranded army back to Russia. In fact, during the course of the strike, the Strike Committee oversaw increased utilization of the railroad. Local Social Democrats and other radicals found this apparent contradiction quite suspicious. These fine points, however, were lost on the military men. Proclamations rolling off the army printing presses played on "stab in the back" sentiment and homesickness to call for a violent settling of accounts with the railwaymen, revolutionaries, Jews, and other Harbinites.

One of the more virulent tirades was delivered by General M.I. Bat'ianov, commander of the Third Manchurian Army, during a military review of the Order of St. George:

> Gentlemen, listen to the words of a man who has served fifty years and has little [time] left to live. I have served four tsars and I tell you that Russia became rich and powerful thanks to the tsars, not the people. . . . We are sitting here and waiting to depart for Russia, I myself have ten children and we're all

> bursting to get home, and yet we are held here. The reason for this is the
> railway strike; the employees demand a raise: they don't have enough. What
> does the peasant get? Now railway battalions are being formed, and when we
> occupy the railway, then we'll drive the employees and their families and
> children into the cold.

Bat´ianov went on to suggest that the matter be handled as at Tomsk, where
about 600 employees of the Siberian railway had died in a pogrom on 3 November 1905.[17]

An evaluation of the revolutionary movement as disruption, rather than as a
path to a more cooperative state–society relationship, reflected not only an army-
Finance divergence but also a basic disagreement regarding the future of Russian
Manchuria. Since the military men considered annexation the most desirable
solution, policies that brought the would-be new addition into greater harmony
with the rest of Russia made sense.[18] This implied, among other things, political
conservatism and anti-Semitism, for no Jews were allowed to settle in the
Liaodong leasehold.

For the Finance Ministry and the CER, economic and demographic penetration was enough, at least for the immediate future. Both Witte and his successors
exhibited pragmatism and flexibility in employing tolerance and laissez-faire as
the guiding principles of their experiment in social engineering. The Russo-Chinese
border shielded these policies from conservative opposition. After all, it was
argued, Manchuria was not Russia. In its treatment of ethnic political and religious variety, Harbin became Russia's most progressive city precisely because it
was outside the empire's borders.

But Russian Manchuria was not only different, it was also influential. Outside
the empire, a free discussion of unorthodox approaches could be pursued unimpeded by the taboos of autocracy. The fact that many of the novel migration
policies either implemented or merely discussed in connection with Manchuria
were later extended to Siberia and even European Russia suggests that "Manchuria" may, in fact, have played an Aesopian role. In any case, both the Manchurian search for "private initiative" and the Siberian version passed as the law of 6
June 1904, adumbrate the basic thrust of the Stolypin reforms. A clear line of
transmission runs through the two men most responsible for carrying out
Stolypin's "wager on the strong," A.V. Krivoshein and A.A. Rittikh. Prior to
Stolypin's ministry, both had been intimately involved in the formulation and
execution of Far Eastern colonization policy.[19]

Regional History, Comparative History:
Competition and Convergence

By 1905, victorious Japanese armies had transferred the image of Northeast
Asian overachiever from the Russians to themselves. The world was compelled

to re-evaluate the power, character, and potential of what was quickly diagnosed as the most Western of Eastern countries. The short-lived "Russian miracle" in the Far East was quickly forgotten even by the Russians themselves. The tsar's government in St. Petersburg would henceforth premise eastern policy on the fear of Japanese land and sea forces continuing as far as Harbin and Vladivostok, respectively, the campaign that had been cut short at Portsmouth. This dire apparition would indeed come to pass, but only when Petersburg had become Petrograd and the tsar a prisoner of the Bolsheviks.

We should, however, keep in mind that regional primacy was not the sole quality transmitted across "no man's land" in 1904–5. The first major conflict of the twentieth century acquainted almost two million men with trenches, saturation artillery bombardments, machine guns, and other grim novelties of modern warfare. Additionally, a year of armed conflict on the soil of Manchuria encouraged millions of Chinese either to flee the scene of battle or fleece the assembled armies. On the home front, increasing popular perception of the gap between official propaganda versions of the war and the darker realities fueled both the Russian Revolution of 1905 and Japan's Hibiya riots of the same year. The grim harvest of corpses and cripples, the fruit of modern medicine's limited powers, repatriated to the East and West an enduring sense of loss for entire national populations. As a landmark in the shaping of the region's modern memory, Northeast Asia's shared experience in the Russo-Japanese War deserves the same attention paid to similar transnational phenomena in Europe in the wake of World War I.

Article Five of the Portsmouth Treaty ceded Russian "rights, privileges and concessions" in southern Manchuria to the Japanese. These included the Liaodong leasehold and the railway leading from it northward as far as Changchun. Although Japan would steadily expand both her de facto and de jure powers on the Chinese mainland, the essential juridical equivalence of Russian and Japanese claims in Manchuria in 1905 set the stage for parallel, easily comparable imperialist initiatives. On a broader scale, we could argue that the history of Northeast Asia from 1894 to 1945 amounts to a tale of competitive colonialism. By different means, with additional players, this tug-of-war continues even today. Historically, however, comparison of the measures and countermeasures taken by Russia, China, and Japan will not only contrast the national interests and concerns that led to incessant triangular conflict but will also bring out the degree to which coexistence and competition in the disputed area combined with increasing regional knowledge to produce a convergence of colonial and anticolonial strategies. As an illustration, we can turn to the question of local administration in the years preceding and following the Russo-Japanese War.

That the Russian presence in the Far East was characterized by a basic divergence between civil and military forces had become by the turn of the century common knowledge among both Chinese and Japanese observers. The former, forced to deal with the Russian occupation force from 1900 until 1902, attempted to provoke internal dissension by complaining to the CER and Witte about army behavior. This classic barbarian management technique was aimed not only at enlisting support for the return of usurped authority and firepower to Chinese local government but also at dividing and weakening the general thrust of Russian aggression. In late 1903, as fruitless negotiations and accelerated railroad construction cornered Tokyo into a decision to wage war, the fall of Witte and the rise of Admiral Alekseev were correctly interpreted as a further sign of Russian intransigence. For the Japanese, the Russian drift along a civil–military spectrum translated into a corresponding shift along a parallel peace–war scale.[20]

The failure of the Russian military in Manchuria may also have played a role in the 1907 conversion of the Chinese administration of the three eastern provinces to a civilian structure. The Chinese colonization, finance, and railroad initiatives that followed can also be seen as a competitive imitation of the CER's antebellum policies, although a lack of funds crippled the Chinese moves right from the start. The elimination of the Manchu-dominated military government should, however, also be viewed as administrative unification at the regional level.[21] With the end of the Qing mandate, what was originally intended to coordinate and centralize control of the Northeast provinces became a structural factor favoring local autonomy.

The *pas de trois* framework works well to describe rapidly changing circumstances and resultant historical ironies. For example, the first recorded proposal for downgrading the Manchu military role in Manchuria's overall administration came from Prince Konoe Atsumaro, the speaker of the Japanese House of Peers, in a 1901 letter addressed to the Chinese senior officials, Zhang Zhidong and Liu Kunyi. This plan, together with the suggestion to open Manchuria to international trade, development, and residence, was transparently intended to eject the Russian occupation force from the Chinese northeast.[22] By 1907, when these ideas were enacted, however, their main target had become the Japanese themselves in southern Manchuria.

In 1904, Cheng Dequan became the deputy military governor of Qiqihar, the highest rank ever bestowed on a nonbanner Chinese in Manchuria. His memorials both preceding and following this appointment called for the abolition of the banner-dominated military government in the Northeast provinces. Despite strong resistance to Cheng's perceived anti-Manchu bias, the Qing court felt itself constrained to approve the proposed reforms when they were taken up by Xu Shichang, minister of the Board of Civil Affairs, and his mentor, Yuan Shikai.[23] Thus, to counteract foreign encroachment, the Qing had taken measures that would dilute the symbolism of the northeast as the dynastic homeland. Within a few years, the place-name "Manchuria" would be outlawed by public opinion both for the recognition it offered the fading dynasty and for the implication that these rich lands were not part of the age-old patrimony of China. In a sense, the Manchus had been projected back to the periphery, where they could occupy their original place beside the foreigners as an object of "frontier defence."

The specter of effective Chinese administration raised by the 1907 reform and personified by the powerful new governor-general of the Three Eastern Provinces combined with the crescendo of the Rights Recovery Movement to produce Japanese and Russian responses, both separately and in tandem. Goto Shimpei, president of the South Manchurian Railway, argued in biological terms consonant with his medical training for closer coordination of the railway, the Guandong government-general (headed by an army general), and consular authorities. Japan in Manchuria, he warned, "is destined to lose a struggle against a better administration that has a unified nervous system like that of a higher vertebrate."

Although Foreign Ministry resistance frustrated the streamlining Goto had in mind, his policy for administering the leasehold and railway zone was adopted. Generally speaking, "military preparedness in civilian garb" (*bunsoteki bubi*) ran parallel to the Chinese civilian approach for countering foreign aggression. Modernization, which Goto considered an integral part of his plan, was aimed at disarming third-party complaints about Japanese activities in Manchuria by presenting a tally of incontestable benefits newly enjoyed by the Chinese population. Since civilization was best promoted and exhibited in an urban showcase, southern Manchuria's cities became the locus for hospitals, schools, industry, stock exchanges, and Japanese immigration. The role of Korean petty bourgeois migrants awaits further exploration, but it at least superficially resembles the Jewish presence in Harbin. Goto's resettlement policies, it seems, produced similar results to those of Witte.

The Russians, too, spent 1906 and 1907 in search of the appropriate administrative structure under which to consolidate their presence in Manchuria. As in the Japanese case, the main contenders were the army, the railway (CER), and the foreign ministry. General Grodekov, previously Priamur governor-general, was about to evacuate the last regular army forces from Manchuria. Rather than turn over his responsibilities as rear commander to the railway, he suggested a new division of authority that would increase the War Ministry's and the Priamur governor-general's control of "technical" railway management. Purely civilian affairs would still fall under the CER's jurisdiction. Fear of foreign scrutiny and objections was cited by the foreign and finance ministries in batting down this proposal. In addition, this Harbin conference produced new guidelines for the municipal self-government of the Russian urban presence in Manchuria. The Russians had also decided to wager on the staying power of civilian institutions.[24]

A final momentous event that took place in 1907 was the signing of the first Russo-Japanese treaty. The suddenness with which battlefield enemies became cooperative neighbors virtually upon the evacuation of their opposing armies greatly surprised diplomatic observers. The most logical explanation lies in shared concerns regarding the new Chinese administration in the northeast and the fear of Western powers' protests regarding the coercive measures with which Russia and especially Japan would soon answer a revived Chinese nationalism.

With the clear statement of spheres of influence that they had not been able to make prior to the war, Japan and Russia insured themselves against diplomatic isolation on Manchurian issues. When the Russians, tired of delays caused by China's moving the negotiations back and forth from Harbin to Peking, unilaterally issued Harbin's municipal regulations in 1909, only the Japanese recognized their validity. When the Japanese presented the Twenty-One Demands to Peking in 1915, Yuan Shikai did not even bother to petition the Russians for countervailing support.[25]

This case should serve to underscore the driving force of these triangular influences in connecting the national histories of Northeast Asia. A similar analysis could be employed to illuminate the connections among participants in the Siberian intervention of 1918–25, as well as the parallel experiences of the separate Soviet Far Eastern Army, Chinese warlords Zhang Zuolin and Zhang Xueliang, and the Guandong Army, in the later 1920s and 1930s. Ultimately, it is to the local level that we must look to solve many of the national and international historical puzzles in which this region has been involved as we search for solutions to long-term problems of coexistence imposed by geography.

Notes

1. Until recently, historical research on this topic was hindered by the triple taboo placed by Soviet archival authorities on Russo-Chinese relations, the Russian émigré diaspora, and all matters pertaining to disputed borders. This situation has now improved, at least for the pre–World War II period. Since I am currently exploring the pertinent Soviet-era archives, I will limit my comments here to a discussion of prerevolutionary Russian Manchuria, with an emphasis on its demographic center of gravity, Harbin.

2. Although a number of recent works have treated interministerial rivalry in late Imperial Russia, the only work to focus specifically on civil–military tensions is William C. Fuller, *Civil–Military Conflict in Late Imperial Russia, 1881–1914* (Princeton: Princeton University Press, 1985).

3. Harbin has generally been treated as vestigial both geographically and temporally. John Stephan has written that "like excised tissue preserved in formaldehyde long after the parent body has perished, the émigrés of Harbin persisted, a lifelike fragment of the prerevolutionary era." Stephan, *The Russian Fascists: Tragedy and Farce in Exile, 1925–45* (New York: Harper and Row, 1978), p. 43.

4. S.F. Starr, "Tsarist Government: The Imperial Dimension," in J. Azrael, ed., *Soviet Nationality Policies and Practices* (New York: Praeger, 1978), pp. 29–30. In a somewhat different context, a similar point has been made by Henry Reichman, *Railwaymen and Revolution: Russia, 1905* (Berkeley: University of California Press, 1987), p. 10.

5. The Russian word for governor-general, *general-gubernator,* has shades of meaning slightly different from its English equivalent. In English, the "general" refers to breadth of function; in Russian, a stronger hint of military rank is present. Both Ushakov's and the Soviet Academy of Sciences's dictionary (but not Dal') give the term "*voenno-administrativnyi*" to describe the *general-gubernator*'s role. Fuller points out that in the Caucasus and Central Asia, as well as the Far East, "vast territories were under direct military rule." Fuller, *Civil–Military,* p. xxii. For more on administrative reshuffling in Siberia and the Russian Far East, see Erik Amburger,

Geschichte der Behordenorganisation Russlands von Peter dem Grossen bis 1917 (Leiden: E.J. Brill, 1966), pp. 407–8.

6. V.M. Kabuzan, *Dal'nevostochnyi krai v XVII–nachale XX vv., 1640–1917* (Moscow, 1985), pp. 162–64; *Priamur'e: fakty, tsifry, nabliudeniia* (Moscow, 1909), p. 90.

7. *Vladivostok: Sbornik istoricheskikh dokumentov, 1860–1907 gg.* (Vladivostok, 1960), pp. 53–54.

8. Dietrich Geyer, *Russian Imperialism* (New Haven: Yale University Press, 1987), pp. 209–10. Although Geyer correctly points out that the 1902 *overall* Russo-Chinese trade results contradict Witte's grandiose visions of the rapid, "peaceful penetration" of China, the increase in local cross-border trade was impressive. And besides, how can the ultimate commercial viability of a railroad be judged before construction is even completed? Kabuzan, appended tables 3, 12, 13; G.N. Romanova, *Ekonomicheskoe otnoshenie Rossii i Kitaia na Dal'nem Vostoke: XIX–nachalo XX v.* (Moscow, 1987), appended tables 6, 11.

9. Kabuzan, p. 224; S.M. Dukhovskoi, *Vsepoddaneishii otchet priamurskogo general-gubernatora Generala-Leitenanta Dukhovskogo, 1896–1897* (St. Petersburg, 1898), pp. 5, 92–95; Lewis Siegelbaum, "Another 'Yellow Peril': Chinese Migrants in the Russian Far East and the Russian Reaction Before 1917," *Modern Asian Studies*, vol. 12, no. 2, April 1978. Estimates of the number of Chinese laborers in Russia by 1917 range as high as 200,000 to 300,000, although the Chinese Eastern Railway, the main avenue for "coolies," reported a total of only 67,121 transported through 1 September 1917. TRGIA (Russian State Historical Archive, St. Petersburg), f. 323, op. 1, d. 835, ll. 44–45.

10. On Maritime governorship, see John Stephan, *The Russian Far East* (Stanford: Stanford University Press, 1994), p. 311. Details on Tifontai can be found in R.K.I. Quested, *"Matey" Imperialists?* (Hong Kong: Hong Kong University Press, 1982), p. 134; D.I. Shreider, *Nash Dal'nii Vostok: Tri goda v Ussuriiskom krae* (St. Petersburg, 1897); and TRGIA, f. 1343 (Heraldry Department), op. 40, d. 5077.

11. D.L. Khorvat, "Memoirs," ch. 2, p. 6 (manuscript held in the Hoover Institute Archives).

12. "Pervye shagi russkogo imperializma na Dal'nem Vostoke," *Krasnyi arkhiv*, no. 52, 1932, pp. 85, 87–88. As a compromise measure, Dukhovskoi suggested a 500-verst detour through northernmost Manchuria from Sretensk to Blagoveshchensk via Mergen.

13. B.A. Romanov, *Rossiia v Man'churhii* (Leningrad, 1928), p. 4; "Pervye shagi," pp. 115, 118; Theodore von Laue, *Sergei Witte and the Industrialization of Russia* (New York: Columbia University Press, 1963), pp. 188–92, citing Witte's *Lectures on the Economy and State Finance* (1900); TRGIA, f. 1273, op. 1, d. 271, ll. 4–43.

14. On the ties between railroad building and colonization in Siberia and the Russian Far East, see Steven Marks's contribution to this volume and his *Road to Power*, cited therein.

15. For a more extensive treatment of Harbin and Russian Manchuria in the prerevolutionary period, see David Wolff, *To the Harbin Station: The Liberal Alternative in Russian Manchuria, 1898–1914* (Berkeley: University of California Press, forthcoming).

16. Fuller, *Civil–Military Conflict*, pp. 15, 95–96, 104, 110.

17. V. Lembergskaia, ed., "Dvizhenie v voiskakh na Dal'nem Vostoke," *Krasnyi arkhiv*, nos. 11–12, 1925, p. 299.

18. Several times, notably in 1903 and 1910, military men had forced a "decision in principle" for annexation of at least part of Manchuria, but civilian ministers always argued successfully that the moment was not yet ripe. See Andrew Malozemoff, *Russian Far Eastern Policy, 1881–1904* (Berkeley: University of California Press, 1958), p. 207; and Peter Tang, *Russian and Soviet Policy in Manchuria and Outer Mongolia, 1911–1931* (Durham, NC: Duke University Press, 1959), pp. 102–3.

19. Rittikh had been slated to manage the Russian colonization of Manchuria when the Russo-Japanese War broke out.

20. Ian Nish, *The Origins of the Russo-Japanese War* (London: Longman, 1985), p. 190, citing Nihongaikobunsho 36/I, nos. 13 and 22.

21. Robert H.G. Lee, *The Manchurian Frontier in Ch'ing History* (Cambridge, MA: Harvard University Press, 1970), ch. 7.

22. Ibid., pp. 138–39.

23. Cheng and Xu memorials on Manchurian reform can be found in *Cheng zhongcheng zoukao* and *Dongsansheng zhenglue,* respectively (Changchun: Jilin wenshi chubanshe, 1989).

24. The 1910 appointment of a civilian governor in the Maritime province is another illustration of the "trickle-back" process. E.Kh. Nilus, "Upravlenie dorogi kak tsentral'nyi organ tekhnicheskogo i administrativnogo nadzora" (manuscript held in Hoover Institute Archives), pp. 16–18.

25. Ernest Price, *The Russo-Japanese Treaties of 1907–16 Concerning Manchuria and Mongolia* (Baltimore: The Johns Hopkins Press, 1933).

Japan Moves North

The Japanese Occupation of
Northern Sakhalin (1920s)

Hara Teruyuki

"Twenty years from the Japanese invasion of Sakhalin in 1905 to the Soviet-Japanese Convention in 1925 witnessed more turbulent change than any comparable period of the island's history."
—John J. Stephan

Hokkaido, the Japanese island closest to the Russian Far East, retains several traces of Russo-Japanese contact. Perhaps the best-known example is the first Russian Orthodox church constructed in Japan, at the port city of Hakodate in 1872. While Hakodate served as an entryway to Russian culture,[1] another port city on Hokkaido, Otaru, became one of the principal advance bases for reaching Sakhalin, especially in the years prior to the extension of the railroad to the northernmost Japanese settlement of Wakkanai in 1922.

In Otaru there are at least two historic spots worthy of note from the viewpoint of Russo-Japanese relations. One is the former Otaru branch of the Nippon Yusen Company, where in November 1906, in the aftermath of the Russo-Japanese War, a diplomatic meeting was held. Delegations on both sides discussed questions concerning border demarcation along the fiftieth parallel on Sakhalin Island, in accordance with the Treaty of Portsmouth concluded on 5 September 1905. To this day, the original furniture and chandeliers of the conference hall recall the atmosphere of those negotiations.

The other historic location in Otaru can be found on a hill overlooking the harbor. It consists of a charnel for the victims of the Nikolaevsk incident, a bloodletting that took place in March and May 1920. For most of the Japanese occupation of northern Sakhalin (1920–25), the victims' ashes were temporarily kept at the Japanese Expeditionary Army headquarters in Aleksandrovsk. On 17 October 1924, the ashes were moved to a Buddhist temple back on Hokkaido. Otaru was chosen as the site for such a commemoration because it had served as the chief gateway through which the expeditionary forces traveled back and forth from Japan to Nikolaevsk and Aleksandrovsk.

These two historic sites on Otaru frame the various stages of Japan's brief advance northward. That advance was closely connected to the fact that the northern half of the island had abundant natural resources, especially oil. With oil as the centerpiece, Japanese interest in northern Sakhalin can be divided into three phases: the period of surveying of the oil fields by Japanese engineers and a special consortium (1912–19); the period when drilling for oil commenced under the auspices of the Japanese navy (1920–25); and the period of continued exploitation of the oil reserves by a state-run oil company (1926–44).

The problem of Sakhalin's oil reserves was well studied in Japan before and during World War II.[2] By contrast, in the postwar period, little attention was devoted to this problem until the appearance in 1973 of a Japanese translation of John Stephan's book, *Sakhalin: A History* (1971). Since then, two articles devoted to northern Sakhalin and its oil have been published, as well as an official history of Japan's Northern Sakhalin Oil Company written by former employees.[3] This essay aims to build on these studies, re-examining the reasons behind and the consequences deriving from the short-lived Japanese occupation of the Soviet-half of Sakhalin in the early 1920s.

Targeting Northern Sakhalin

Following its victory in the Russo-Japanese War, Japan converted Korea into a protectorate, gained a foothold on the Chinese continent, and continued to explore opportunities for further expansion. Along with the southern stump of the Chinese Eastern Railway (CER) in Manchuria, northern Sakhalin remained a key unrealized Japanese objective following the Treaty of Portsmouth.

Despite a rapprochement with Russia, the Japanese high command formulated a naval policy in 1907 that envisioned Russia as the principal adversary and assumed that the Japanese army would commit troops to two possible fields of battle with Russia: northern Manchuria and the Ussuri region of Russia's Maritime province. In accordance with this strategy, the city of Harbin was a prime target. When Russia sought Japanese weapons and ammunition during World War I, the Japanese government demanded as payment the stretch of the CER from Changchun to Harbin and made inquiries about the territory of northern Sakhalin. The Russian government was naturally disinclined to relinquish its half of the island in exchange for two or three hundred thousand rifles.[4]

Compared with Japan's demand for the CER, which became a matter of official negotiation in 1916, the idea of pursuing oil concessions on northern Sakhalin remained vague. This was true even though the Japanese navy had eyed

Sakhalin for fuel purposes at least since Ishikawa Sadaharu, an engineer, completed a survey of the oil fields in the Chaivo district in 1915.[5] Even the conclusion of a Russo-Japanese Treaty of Alliance in July 1916, coming only eleven years after a bitter war, did little to further commercial relations between the two countries on the question of Sakhalin oil.

Following the February Revolution in 1917, Aleksandr Kerensky's Provisional Government adopted a pro-American foreign policy. At the same time, the new government hoped for foreign investment in its ailing mining and extraction industries, including the oil of northern Sakhalin. Combining these two goals, S.F. Maliavkin, director of the Mining Department, stated publicly on 21 June 1917 that "it might be extremely profitable to introduce Americans to Sakhalin as a counterbalance to Japanese influence."[6] In Tokyo, Japanese Foreign Minister Motono Ichiro, a former ambassador to Russia, expressed disapproval of such an openly pro-American policy to the Russian ambassador, urging instead a pro-Japanese policy in matters of natural resource development. Ambassador Vasilii N. Krupenskii, for his part, saw in Motono's words a symptom of "pretensions to create a Japanese sphere of influence inside our border."[7] The brief era of Russo-Japanese alliance was clearly at an end.

The Soviet government formed after the October Revolution not only continued the démarche of the Provisional Government, welcoming American investment as a "counterbalance" to Japanese influence, but also exploited U.S.-Japanese differences. When the Japanese marine landing at Vladivostok was followed by a British, but not an American force, an official of the People's Commissariat of Foreign Affairs called a consular attaché in Moscow and stated that the Soviet government had previously rejected American applications for concessions in deference to Japan but would now conclude an agreement for concessions in Sakhalin and Kamchatka with the United States.[8]

Japan seemed to be well behind the United States in the race to acquire oil concessions on Sakhalin. A proposal submitted by the Naval Ministry to the Foreign Ministry on 30 May 1918 implored that it was advisable for Japan to secure access to the oil resources on Russian Sakhalin "at the first suitable opportunity, in one way or another."[9] But Japanese business circles showed more initiative than the government, and on 21 May 1918, the Kuhara Mining Company signed an agreement with Ivan Stakheev and Company to operate jointly in the latter's mining areas.

Kuhara, a newly risen *zaibatsu* (financial group), had several branches throughout the Russian Far East and engaged in business ventures as well as political maneuvering behind the scenes. In Blagoveshchensk, for example, the management of the Kuhara branch, together with officers of the Japanese General Staff, organized Japanese residents into a "voluntary" unit that supported an anti-Bolshevik uprising in March 1918 (the so-called *Gamovskii miatezh*).

Stakheev, for his part, was one of the largest concerns in Russia prior to World War I, with operations in metallurgy, oil, textiles, flour milling, railroads, forestry, fishing, and other endeavors.[10] Stakheev's contract with Kuhara became a critical step in the Japanese advance to northern Sakhalin.

Admiral Kolchak and the Japanese Navy

When the Allies began their intervention in the Russian Far East in August 1918, Japan's Terauchi cabinet decided to dispatch the Twelfth Division to Russia's Maritime and Amur provinces and the Seventh and Third Divisions to northern Manchuria and the Transbaikal region. By 4 November 1918, the Japanese intervention force was more than 72,000 strong. But at this time, no detachment was sent to northern Sakhalin, for the Japanese were adhering to their own imperial national defense policy laid down in 1907.

On 18 November 1918, Admiral Aleksandr V. Kolchak carried out a coup d'état in the Russian east and declared himself to be "supreme ruler." Virtually all of Siberia and the Russian Far East fell under his rule. In Japan, the Hara cabinet, which had been formed at the end of September, gradually shifted its Siberian policy from one of backing local Cossack groups headed by the Atamans Semenov and Kalmykov to the support of Kolchak's "All-Russian" government. The Japanese navy, however, was anxious about Kolchak's stiff attitude toward Japan, for beginning on 7 February 1919, the admiral's government, located in Omsk, turned away all new applications for prospecting and drilling on Russian territory. Kuhara, too, could not help but feel uneasy about the future of its business interests.

Simultaneous with military intervention, the Japanese government created a Special Commission for Siberian Economic Aid (*Rinji Shiberia Keizai Enjo Iinkai*) in Tokyo "to establish a basis for Japanese economic activities in opposition to the acquisition of concessions by the United States and other countries." On 18 January 1919, the commission organized consortiums to coordinate the interests of participating enterprises. In this vein, five companies involved in Sakhalin oil were brought together into the Polar Star Association (*Hokushinkai*), under the auspices of the Japanese navy.

On 1 April 1919, the Hara cabinet adopted a resolution presented by Kato Tomosaburo, the Navy Minister, emphasizing the need to exclude all capital other than Russian and Japanese from northern Sakhalin. In response, Kolchak's cabinet deemed it undesirable to grant concessions exclusively to Japan in violation of the "open-door" principle.[11] Kolchak also sent General Romanovskii to Japan to "sound out Japanese military authorities on the possibility of negotiations for technical and military support."[12] The Japanese Navy Ministry, for its part, viewed Romanovskii's visit as a golden opportunity "to solve the northern Sakhalin oil question."[13]

In this context, on 16 May 1919 the Hara cabinet decided to recognize Kolchak's government in Omsk and four days later issued a resolution emphasizing the need to "prioritize the pursuit of oil fields and coal mines in Russian

Sakhalin for the Empire and its subjects."[14] But Japanese recognition of Kolchak did not lead to the granting of any concessions. One reason may have been that although the Omsk government persistently urged the Japanese to send troops west of Baikal, the Japanese stubbornly refused to do so. Romanovskii surmised that Japan's hesitancy in committing troops far west was related to the problem of "the lingering anti-Japanese movements in China and Korea."[15]

Tokyo sent Rear Admiral Tanaka Kotaro, an authority on Russian affairs, to Omsk. Having met Kolchak in Sevastopol' in 1916 and in Tokyo in 1918, Tanaka was well acquainted with the "supreme ruler." For Japan, the purpose of this visit may well have been to secure northern Sakhalin oil concessions.[16] But Tanaka's unpublished memoirs indicate that during his stay in Omsk from February to July 1919, he was occupied trying to settle disputes between Kolchak and the Cossack leader Semenov.[17]

It is true that the Japanese navy made an attempt to send a special envoy to Omsk specifically to negotiate the oil question. Rear Admiral Yamaguchi Ei, a specialist on fuels for naval vessels, was nominated to go at the end of October 1919.[18] But his mission began too late, for by that time Kolchak's forces had been routed on every front. Japan's indecisive efforts to negotiate with Kolchak had come to nought.

Leonid Grigor'ev: A Japanese Protégé?

By the time Kolchak was executed in Irkutsk on 7 February 1920, in numerous cities of the Russian Far East either executive committees of soviets (as in Blagoveshchensk) or zemstvo provincial boards (as in Vladivostok) had come to power. In Aleksandrovsk, Bolsheviks had seized power on 14 January 1920, although by February they had entered into a local coalition with representatives of the zemtsvo to form a Revolutionary Committee (revkom).

News about the Bolshevik insurrection caused a scare among Japanese engineers and workers of the Japanese navy's Polar Star Association. Formed on 1 May 1919, the association had inherited the rights specified in the old Kuhara–Stakheev contracts and had dispatched about two hundred engineers and workers to the Chaivo district. They conducted surveys of the oil fields throughout the summer of 1919, but with the January 1920 political turnabout they decided to evacuate. It took a month for them to cross on foot to southern Sakhalin.

Having received word of the situation in Aleksandrovsk, the Japanese navy dispatched two vessels there "to protect residents." A. Tsapko, the chairman of the revkom, and G. Voitinskii, the vice-chairman, reassured a Japanese commanding officer that the new authorities would protect Japanese residents. The Japanese vessels were ordered to return to Otaru.[19] According to a newspaper report from Toyohara of southern Sakhalin, the Japanese inhabitants of Aleksandrovsk, said to number more than forty, "suffered no casualties."[20]

Meanwhile, Nikolaevsk, near the mouth of the Amur, was surrounded by more than two thousand "partisans." On 6 February, with the fall of the Chnyrrakh fortress, communications with the Japanese garrison in Nikolaevsk were cut off. The partisans, after concluding a peace agreement with the Japanese, entered the town on 29 February. Two weeks later, Japanese detachments under the command of Major Ishikawa launched a sudden attack on the headquarters of the partisans. Most Japanese residents and civilian personnel, including Consul General Ishida, were involved in the battle, but a partisan counterattack gave the Russians the upper hand. Surviving Japanese troops were forced to capitulate and were incarcerated. This episode constituted the first part of the Nikolaevsk tragedy.

Events continued to churn in a confused swirl. A group of partisans crossed the Tatar Straits and landed at Aleksandrovsk. In mid-March 1920, they proclaimed the liquidation of the Aleksandrovsk coalition revkom, dominated by Bolsheviks, and the formation of a soviet executive committee to rule Sakhalin Island. The Japanese government dispatched a relief force. On 18–19 April, two thousand troops left Otaru for Aleksandrovsk, but ostensibly because a sheet of ice "prohibited" them from landing at Nikolaevsk, they docked instead at Aleksandrovsk on 22 April. This appears to have been a calculated ploy to gain control over all of Sakhalin, not just to protect the Japanese southern half, in retaliation for the annihilation of the Japanese garrison at Nikolaevsk. With the Japanese landing, the executive committee of the soviet for Sakhalin Island collapsed. Surviving Bolshevik loyalists fled to Nikolaevsk.

Met by A. Tsapko, along with other moderate Russian leaders who had been released from jail, Japanese troops proceeded to occupy the telegraph office and the post office, confiscate weapons from local inhabitants, and search Tsapko's house. This was, in effect, the beginning of the Japanese occupation of northern Sakhalin, accomplished without announcement by the central government in Tokyo. Colonel Tamon, commander in chief of the landing forces, explained the onset of the de facto occupation by declaring that the aim of his mission was to establish the truth about the "Nikolaevsk incident."

To Aleksandrovsk the Japanese army officers secretly brought with them the ex-governor of Sakhalin, Leonid Grigor'ev, to install as titular provincial chief, but the plan failed. Because this stratagem has been either ignored (in Japanese historiography) or characterized tendentiously (in Soviet historiography), a careful examination of the available evidence would seem warranted. Who precisely was Grigor'ev? And why did the Japanese bring him along?

At one time Grigor'ev served as an executive of the Russian Far East Industrial Company, which operated with another oil enterprise called Sakhalin Oil Field Limited (established in 1912 in London by a Belgian baron).[21] Both the Japanese army and navy seem to have been unaware of Grigor'ev's background as a businessman. In any case, he was dismissed from the governorship in 1916. Remaining in Petrograd during the revolutionary events, Grigor'ev fled to London before finally making his way to Japan, where he met a number of businessmen, including Shimada Gentaro, the owner of the Shimada Company of Nikolaevsk and a man known as "the king of Nikolaevsk."

Making the most of such a contact, Grigor'ev seems to have waxed enthusiastically to Shimada about an "independent" Sakhalin, while a certain Sakurai, a member of the Polar Star Association, reported what he heard from Shimada to General Tanaka Giichi, Japanese Army Minister, and General Fukuda Masataro, vice-chief of the General Staff. Although Sakurai commented on the unsuitableness of Grigor'ev's plan, the generals appear to have been very interested in it and ordered that reinforcements be sent to Nikolaevsk and that Grigor'ev be brought to Aleksandrovsk to form a new government there.[22]

In 1918, when the Terauchi cabinet launched the military intervention in the Russian Far East, the General Staff and Tanaka, then its vice-chief, undertook every effort to set up a puppet government headed by the Cossack Ataman Semenov. The ensuing civil war forced the abandonment of these plans, but the incident indicates that two years later, in the spring of 1920, General Tanaka had not completely abandoned the notion of creating an "independent" puppet state.

Just as it had appointed Captain Kuroki Chikayoshi an advisor to Semenov in 1918, the General Staff appointed Major Mike Kazuo an advisor to Grigor'ev. Having disguised himself as a merchant and changed his name to Miyake, Mike kept his mission secret even from rank-and-file naval colleagues. The Japanese navy was in fact reluctant to exploit a puppet, and Captain Kondo Nobutake, a navy staff officer, urged Mike to refrain from carrying out the plan.[23]

Soviet commentators have argued that Grigor'ev's attempt to set up an "autonomous Sakhalin state" or "Kingdom of Sakhalin" was so fiercely resisted by "the people" that the Japanese were compelled to remove him.[24] This view is unsatisfactory, for although Grigor'ev was indeed unpopular among Russians, the reason for his removal by the Japanese was his critical attitude toward Japanese policies. Grigor'ev publicly stated that in the Russian Far East Belgian capital would be more welcome than Japanese. He criticized Stakheev's incompetence and urged that Stakheev's oil fields be divided among their former proprietors. Uchida Yasuya, the Japanese foreign minister, pointed out that such views constituted "obstruction of the activities of the Polar Star Association," adding that the Japanese government "should take the matter seriously."[25] In such circumstances, the General Staff ordered the abandonment of the plan for a puppet state under Grigor'ev, who departed Aleksandrovsk on 22 May 1920, only a month after his arrival with the Japanese forces.

Meanwhile, the Japanese interfered in the elections to the Aleksandrovsk municipal *duma,* or council, held on 20 May. Radicals (mostly incumbents) contended for the twenty seats with moderates (mostly former members). A certain Takamura, a leader among Japanese residents in Aleksandrovsk, backed by the Polar Star Association, aided the campaign of the moderates, who won seventeen seats.[26]

According to local newspaper reports monitored by the Japanese, Colonel Tamon was considered "somewhat of a liberal," whereas his successor, Major

Yonekura, was said to have "introduced a rigorous regime" accompanied by "general oppression."[27] Tsapko, the key figure among radicals, was arrested and taken to a Japanese cruiser. He disappeared. The Japanese no doubt surmised that as the director of the telegraph office, Tsapko was privy to the unvarnished truth regarding the initial Nikolaevsk incident. His abduction formed part of the general bloodletting on both sides.

Japanese Military Administration

On 3 June 1920, when Japanese reinforcements finally arrived at Nikolaevsk, they found the city reduced to ashes. It was then discovered that in May, the partisans, having learned of the imminent approach by Japanese forces, murdered all Japanese and Russian prisoners they held, set the city on fire, and fled. This episode constitutes the second part of the Nikolaevsk tragedy.

Japanese victims of both parts of the Nikolaevsk tragedy numbered nearly 700. Some 122 people, including 108 soldiers, 2 sailors, and 12 civilians, were among those held in prison, victims of a partisan massacre conducted by Ia.I. Trapitsyn, a leader of the Anarchist-Communists. But the greater number of victims died in a suicidal attack against the partisans carried out on the night of 12–13 March. It should be noted that Japanese commentators often fail to distinguish between these separate groups of victims, as if everyone who died had been massacred without provocation by the Russians.

Word of the "Nikolaevsk massacre" brought forth an outpouring of nationalistic and anti-Bolshevik sentiments among the Japanese people, who appear to have rallied around a policy of retaliation. On 29 June, the cabinet met and decided formally to occupy Sakhalin in its entirety as an indemnity, "until a satisfactory settlement of the Nikolaevsk affair could be obtained from a government Japan recognized." This decision was announced on 3 July; a week later, another cabinet resolution ordered that army units be sent to support the exploitation of oil fields. A subsequent interministerial memorandum dated 16 July specified that supervision of oil extraction be carried out by the Navy Ministry.

On 28 July, the Japanese Expeditionary Army for Sakhalin province was established; it arrived at Aleksandrovsk on 8–10 August, raising to 4,600 the number of Japanese troops. At the same time, a Military-Administrative Board (*gunseibo*), with branch offices (*gunseishu*), was founded. General Tsuno Kazusuke, chief of the Expeditionary Army and, as such, head of the Military Board, announced on 26 August that with the July declaration of occupation by the Japanese cabinet, Russian administration on the island had effectively been abolished.[28] The unofficial occupation of northern Sakhalin in effect since April had now become official. The Expeditionary Army headquarters and the Military Board proceeded to issue a number of regulations, including a decree on civil and criminal cases, on courts, and others.[29]

One order governing town and village "elders" (*starshiny*) specified that they were to be appointed or removed only by the branch offices of the Military Board, with the latter's sanction, bringing Japanese authority down to the grass roots. A regulation governing certificates for "foreigners" arriving from Japan explicitly referred to Russians, who were thereby turned into visitors on their own soil. Matters of speech and assembly, meanwhile, were regulated by a strict set of rules on public order issued in September 1920.[30] Directives for the mining industry, issued on 31 August 1920, forbade any new applications for the acquisition of rights and gave the Military Board broad powers to "limit" existing operations governed by unexpired contracts.[31]

An agent for Stakheev, Kuhara's Russian partner in Sakhalin oil, traveled to Japan seeking to have the army minister clarify the meaning of the mining industry directives, which seemed to transfer all Sakhalin coal mines and oil fields to the Japanese government. General Tanaka assured the Stakheev representative that his firm's applications for further exploitation rights would be "received after a governmental instruction is issued."[32] True to the minister's word, on 28 September, a cabinet meeting adopted a resolution stating that "Stakheev's mining areas should be exploited in a joint Russo-Japanese undertaking with the Polar Star Association." The joint operation obtained monopoly rights.[33]

Japanese rule in northern Sakhalin brought a broad-based Japanization. Settlers, particularly from southern Sakhalin but also from the main Japanese islands, began arriving in large numbers, so that by late October 1920, in the town of Aleksandrovsk alone the population of Japanese reached 1,650, including some 150 entrepreneurs.[34] An Aleksandrovsk branch of the Chosen Ginko (Bank of Korea), the principal colonial bank of Japan, opened for business on 24 September 1920. And streets were renamed in Japanese style.

Prospecting for oil, meanwhile, progressed at Okha, Katangli, and other fields. Daily output at Okha soon exceeded 200 *koku* (approximately 227 barrels).[35] The Expeditionary Army also embarked on a program to build much-needed infrastructure. Railroad and engineering detachments arrived from Japan to lay a narrow-gauge line from Aleksandrovsk to Rykovskoe and a trunk line from Aleksandrovsk to the Japanese border.

Northern Sakhalin's construction boom and corresponding Japanization, however, did not last. With the Washington Conference of 1921–22 and the Goto–Ioffe talks of 1923, the Japanese mood of eager anticipation of eventual annexation turned into one of despair over the impossibility of such an outcome. This shift, in turn, brought about a change in the Japanese attitude toward their Russian subjects.[36] In the spring of 1923, the occupation army was reduced from 3,883 to 2,713 troops, and the number of Japanese inhabitants also declined (see Table 4.1).

Conclusion

Japan's interest in northern Sakhalin, as John Stephan pointed out, was slow in developing. When a member of the border demarcation commission of 1906–7

Table 4.1

Population of Northern Sakhalin

	Japanese	Koreans	Chinese	Russians	Aborigines	Total
June 1922	4,377	1,063	950	5,880	2,857	15,127
April 1923	3,595	1,321	1,344	6,347	2,362	14,969
Dec. 1923	3,466	1,730	1,754	8,125*	—	15,165
May 1924	3,304	1,477	2,258	7,496	2,165	16,700
Aug. 1924	2,863	1,017	1,330	8,987*	—	14,197
Dec. 1924	1,727	1,078	1,000	7,877*	—	11,682

Sources: *A History of the Occupation of Sakhalin Province, 1923–1925*, ed. Japanese General Staff [in Japanese] (Tokyo, 1926), p. 154; Ota Shinokichi, *A War Correspondent's Observation of Sakhalin* [in Japanese] (Toyohashi, 1923).
*includes aborigines

learned of the rich oil deposits to the north and informed Tokyo, the government showed itself to be remarkably unresponsive.[37] With the passage of time and the general substitution worldwide of oil for coal as the principal ship fuel, however, the Japanese government came to realize the importance of Sakhalin oil. Yet even at its height, Japanese interest remained vague.

Governments in Petrograd and then Omsk sought Japanese military support, providing the Japanese government with considerable leverage on a range of matters, including Russian natural resources. This circumstance did in fact spark Tokyo's interest in Sakhalin's oil, especially at the Navy Ministry, whose Admiral Kato Tomosaburo envisioned either outright takeover or at the very least oil concessions.[38] But there is no evidence to indicate that such stirrings went beyond expressions of enthusiasm to serious negotiations with either Petrograd or Omsk.

All this changed in the spring of 1920 with the "Nikolaevsk massacre," as it became known. The deaths of around seven hundred Japanese provided the government with a cause and galvanized it into action, led by the military. Troops were landed at Aleksandrovsk, an occupation begun, and oil drilling intensified under the auspices of the navy. But rhetoric about the need, in the words of General Tanaka, "not to withdraw from northern Sakhalin in the future," clashed with the pretext of the entire operation, "a satisfactory settlement of the Nikolaevsk affair"—by definition, a finite enterprise.[39] Moreover, as the United States pointed out in protest, the connection between the Nikolaevsk incident and the question of northern Sakhalin was dubious.

Already by February 1923, just prior to the Goto–Ioffe talks on normalization of diplomatic relations, the Navy Ministry came to view the occupation's continuation as ill-advised.[40] But the oil retained its value. At the Dairen and

Changchun conferences with the government of the Far Eastern republic in Chita, and at the Tokyo and Beijing talks with the Soviet government, Japanese diplomats harped on the Nikolaevsk affair, no doubt as a pretext for a favorable settlement of the Sakhalin oil question.

At preliminary meetings prior to the Goto–Ioffe negotiations, a Japanese envoy, Kawakami Toshitsune, offered 150 million yen for the purchase of Sakhalin Island. Ioffe countered with an asking price of one billion gold rubles (later raised to a billion and a half), on the basis of instructions from the Politburo in Moscow on the willingness to sell provided the price were high enough.[41] Unable to reach an understanding on a sale price, the two sides turned instead to negotiations on a long-term concession for the development of coal mines and oil fields.

On 25 January 1925, with the conclusion of the Soviet-Japanese Basic Convention, Japan recognized the USSR. Here is not the place for an extended discussion of this important event, except to say that access to northern Sakhalin's natural resources was one of the principal goals guiding Japanese actions.[42] The Japanese army completed its evacuation of northern Sakhalin by 15 May 1925, in exchange for oil and coal concessions. Most Japanese residents left with the army, although 220 people stayed (including 80 each in Okha and Due, and 60 in Aleksandrovsk). "The bourgeoisie, intellectuals, and pro-Japanese Russians" also departed.[43]

On the basis of concession contracts signed on 14 December 1925, the Northern Sakhalin Oil Company, headed by retired Admiral Nakasato Shigetsugu, was established. Activities of the company peaked in 1933, slowly declining thereafter, but it remained in operation until 1944. Examination of the history of Sakhalin Island after 1925 must await another occasion, but it deserves to be pointed out that beginning at the turn of the nineteenth century with the sale of coal, timber, and fish to purchase steel for the Trans-Siberian Railroad, and continuing through the joint development of Sakhalin oil in the 1920s and 1930s, there has been extensive economic activity between Russia and Japan.[44]

By the 1970s, the Japanese were second only to the Germans in their interest and investment in Russia, even showing a desire to develop port, rail, and air-transport facilities. True, there has not been nearly as much economic interaction as there seems to be potential. For example, a project to renew the joint development of Sakhalin oil, now thirty years old, languishes—to say nothing of far more ambitious proposals for the construction of oil and gas pipelines from West Siberia to Japan.[45] But as the episode covered in this paper demonstrates, Soviet-Japanese economic cooperation has been achieved in the most difficult of circumstances, even directly following a military occupation.

Notes

1. George Lensen, *Report from Hokkaido: The Remains of Russian Culture in Northern Japan* (Hakodate: Municipal Library of Hakodate, 1954).

2. Ota Saburo, *Nichiro Karafuto Gaikōsen* (A History of the Russo-Japanese Diplomatic War in Sakhalin) (Tokyo, 1941); Oka Sakae, *Kita Karafuto* (Northern Sakhalin) (Tokyo, 1942).

3. Yoshimura Michio, "Nihongunno Kitakarafuto senryo to Nisso Kokkōmondai" ("The Japanese Occupation of Northern Sakhalin and Diplomatic Relations with the Soviets"), *Seiji Keizai Shigaku*, no. 132, 1977; Hosoya Chihiro, "Kitasaharinno sekiyu shigen o meguru nichi-bei-ei no Keizai Funsō" ("Japan-U.S.-U.K. Conflicts Over Northern Sakhalin's Oil Resources") in Hosoya, ed. *(The History of International Economic Conflicts in Pacific-Asian Regions)* (Tokyo, 1983); Kidosaki Masutaka et al., *Kitakarafutoni sekiyu o motomeru* (In Search of Oil in Northern Sakhalin) (Yokohama, 1983).

4. *Mezhdunarodnye otnosheniia v epokhu imperializma: Dokumenty iz arkhivov tsarskogo i vremmennogo pravitel'stv, 1878–1917 gg.* (Moscow, 1931–38), series III, vol. 8, part 2, p. 236 (Sazonov communication to Polivanov, 24 August/6 September 1915).

5. Japanese Foreign Ministry Archives (hereafter JFMA), 1.7.6.4–1, vol. 1 (Ishikawa's report, 25 July 1912).

6. *Ekonomicheskoe polozhenie Rossii nakanune velikoi Oktiabr'skoi sotsialisticheskoi revoliutsii* (Moscow-Leningrad, 1967), vol. 2, 462.

7. A.V. Ignat'ev, *Vneshniaia politika vremennogo pravitel'stva* (Moscow, 1974), p. 346.

8. JFMA, 1.6.3.24–5 (Kumasaki Communication to Motono, 6 April 1918).

9. Yoshimura, p. 4.

10. T.M. Kitanina, "Russko-Aziatskii bank i kontsern I. Stakheev," in M.P. Viatkin, ed., *Monopolii i inostrannyi kapital v Rossii* (Moscow-Leningrad, 1962), pp. 428–30; Elena Varneck and H.H. Fisher, eds., *The Testimony of Kolchak and Other Siberian Materials* (Stanford: Hoover Institute, 1935), p. 325. John Stephan has described Stakheev as a "shadowy concern" of "dubious connections," but this judgment is unsound. Stephan, *Sakhalin: A History* (Oxford: Clarendon, 1971), pp. 94, 98.

11. *Pobeda Sovetskoi vlasti na Severnom Sakhaline, 1917–1925: Sbornik dokumentov i materialov* (Iuzhno-Sakhalinsk, 1959), document no. 96 (Sukin communication to Sazonov, 29 March 1919).

12. Gosudarstvennyi arkhiv Rossiiskoi Federatsii (GARF), f. 200, d. 119, l. 16 (Sukin communication to Krupenskii, 2 May 1919).

13. JFMA, 1.6.3.24-13-63 (Tochinai communication to Hanihara, 10 May 1919).

14. JFMA, 1.7.6.4-2-1 (the Navy Ministry's report, July 1924).

15. GARF, f. 200, d. 120, l. 22 (General Romanovskii communication to Sukin, 29 July 1919).

16. Hosoya, p. 186.

17. JFMA, SP 22 (Tanaka, "The Siberian Government Under Admiral Kolchak, the Supreme Ruler").

18. JFMA, 1.7.6.4-1, vol. 1 (report by Shimada Gentaro).

19. JFMA, 5.2.6.33 (report by the General Staff Intelligence on Russia, no. 60, 2 July 1920).

20. *Karafuto Nichinichi Shimbun*, 5 March 1920.

21. JFMA, 1.7.6.4-2-1 (report of the Department of Supply, Navy Ministry, April 1923).

22. Japanese Defense Ministry Archives (JDAA), Nichidoku sensho, T–3–171/628 (report by Captain Kondo).

23. JDAA, Nichidoku Sensho, T-3—169-626 (Captain Kondo communication to the vice-chief of the navy staff, 20 April 1920).

24. *Pobeda Sovetskoi vlasti na Severnom Sakhaline,* document no. 153; Iu. Osnos, "Iaponskaia okkupatsiia Severnogo Sakhalina," *Bor'ba klassov,* 1935, no. 10, p. 66.

25. JFMA, 5.3.2.153 (Uchida communication to Hanaoka, received 12 May 1920).

26. JDAA, Nichidoku sensho, T-3—171/628 (report by Captain Kondo).

27. JDAA, Nichidoku sensho, T-3—169/626 (Captain Kondo communication to the vice-chief of the navy staff, 20 April 1920).

28. *Deistviia Iaponii v Priamurskom krae: Sbornik dokumentov, otnosiashchikhsia k interventsii derzhav v predelakh Priamur'ia* (Vladivostok, 1921), pp. 67–68.

29. JFMA, 5.2.6.33-1 (official gazette of the Military-Administrative Board). A Russian-language edition of a selection of Japanese regulations was published immediately upon the end of the Japanese occupation: *Sbornik rasporiazhenii, opublikovannykh Voenno-administrativnym upravleniem ekspeditsionnoi armii v Sakhalinskoi oblasti* (Aleksandrovsk, 1925).

30. *Sbornik rasporiazhenii*, pp. 18, 42, 162.

31. Ibid., p. 94; *Japanese Intervention in the Russian Far East* (Washington, DC: Special Delegation of the Far Eastern Republic to the USA, 1922), pp. 77–78. John Stephan has written that apart from the Soviet government in Moscow and the Far Eastern Republic in Chita, the United States was the only country to lodge a protest against the Japanese occupation of northern Sakhalin. But along with his Russian counterpart, the British ambassador to Japan protested the above order on the mining industry. Stephan, *Sakhalin*, p. 100; JDAA, Siemitsuju dainikki, November–December 1921 (British ambassador communication to Japanese foreign minister, 16 November 1920; Russian ambassador communication to same, 25 October 1920).

32. JFMA, 1.7.6.4-2-1 (report by the Navy Ministry, July 1924).

33. JFMA, 1.7.6.4-1, vol. 1 (report by the Foreign Ministry, 16 February 1925).

34. JDAA, Seiju dainikki, September 1921, vol. 1 (report by Tsuno); *Shiberia Shuppeishi* (A History of the Siberian Expedition, 1918–1922), ed. The General Staff (Tokyo, 1924), vol. 3, p. 969.

35. Oka, pp. 59–60.

36. *Pobeda Sovetskoi vlasti na Severnom Sakhaline*, document no. 172.

37. Stephan, *Sakhalin*, p. 94.

38. Hosoya, p. 185, citing Kato communication to Motono, 26 September 1917.

39. Nakasato Shigetsugu, "Sekiyumondai nikansuru kaikoroku" ("Reflections on the Oil Problem") *Yushu*, vol. 28, no. 6, pp. 142–43.

40. *Nihon gaikō bunsho* (Documents on the Diplomacy of Japan, 1923) (Tokyo, 1980), vol. 1, p. 274.

41. "Prodazha Sakhalina Iapontsam! Kommunisty prosili miliard nalichnymi," *Moskovskii komsomolets*, 31 July 1992 (extracts from the protocol of the Politburo meeting on 3 May 1923).

42. George Lensen, *Japanese Recognition of the USSR: Soviet-Japanese Relations, 1921–1930* (Tokyo: Sophia University, 1970).

43. *A History of the Occupation of Sakhalin Province, 1923–1926*, ed. The General Staff (Tokyo, 1926), p. 154.

44. Russo-Japanese trade even continued on a large scale throughout the Russian Civil War and the Japanese military intervention in Siberia. George Lensen, "The Russian Impact on Japan," in Wayne Vucinich, ed., *Russia and Asia: Essays on the Influence of Russia on the Asian People* (Stanford: Hoover Institute, 1972), p. 346.

45. Raymond Mathieson, *Japan's Role in Soviet Economic Growth: Transfer of Technology Since 1965* (New York: Praeger, 1979); Kiichi Saeki, "Towards Japanese Cooperation in Siberian Develpment," *Problems of Communism*, 21 (3), May–June 1972, pp. 1–11; John J. Stephan, "The Political and Economic Landscape of the Russian Far East," in Tsuyoshi Hasegawa et al., eds., *Russia and Japan: An Unresolved Dilemma Between Distant Neighbors* (Berkeley: Berkeley-Stanford Program in Soviet and Post-Soviet Studies, 1993), pp. 279–98.

Part II

Siberian Identities:
Autonomy, Science, and Redemption

Except for the Amur basin, incorporated in 1858, the Russian conquest of Siberia was completed by the middle of the seventeenth century, making Siberia a part of the empire longer than the Baltic territories, the Crimea, the Caucasus, or Central Asia. With its permafrost, arctic winds, and forbidding winters, Siberia helped give Russia the reputation of a harsh land. But as the Canadian James Gibson has written, "the grand scale of Siberia's own features—its great rivers, immense marshes, enormous taiga, and boundless steppe—contributed to the Russian sense of bigness."[1] So vast were the distances, that to travel overland from one end of the empire to another meant something akin to circumnavigating the earth.

Siberia also contributed grandly to the Russian Empire's treasury. By the eve of the 1917 revolutions, Siberia enjoyed a measure of relative prosperity rooted in its villages. A vigorous agriculture was complemented by the manufacture of agricultural implements, a modest metallurgical industry, plus some coal, copper, and gold mining. The gold was hoarded (although much was lost) by the bumbling state, while grain, along with high-quality Siberian butter, was exported in large quantities.[2] Yet Siberia was known less for its productivity than for its remoteness and utter subordination to Moscow, a paradoxical combination exemplified by Siberia's being used as the place of banishment for undesirables.

Deportation as well as distance have helped maintain the view of Siberia as a place apart, despite the contiguousness of its land connection with European Russia and the massive immigration that made Siberia's population overwhelmingly Slav.[3] Some have feared that because of this separateness Siberia invites comparison with the New World, which was "discovered" and settled by Europeans at around the same time and later rejected its colonial status, broke away, and became independent.[4] Others have hoped that as part of a continental landmass and as having been incorporated into a greater fatherland by pioneering settlers (who pushed aside native peoples), Siberia might be compared with the American West— and therefore granted a similar degree of self-rule.[5] This enduring ambiguity of Siberia as a place apart, yet one not in charge of its own destiny, forms the subject of this section's first essay, written by Vladimir I. Shishkin of Novosibirsk, a leading Russian historian of Siberia in the interwar period.

Shishkin traces the story of the establishment of Soviet power in Siberia, focusing on the revival of local hopes for autonomy and the centralizing policies pursued indefatigably by Moscow's new rulers. The imposition of extreme centralization was greatly facilitated by the need to fight the Russian Civil War, but Shishkin argues that the Red victory presented an opportunity to retire revolutionary administrative organs in favor of a system of democratically elected and self-governing soviets. Such a reorientation to nondictatorial, local rule was rejected by Bolshevik authorities in Moscow, who made Siberia into even more of a colony than it had been in the tsarist period. Shishkin analyzes this process from within, placing considerable emphasis on the intentions and actions of individuals.

* * *

Moscow's "colonial" rule over Siberia brought extensive industrialization. As Siberia prepares to enter the twenty-first century, its once largely agricultural landscape is flecked with hundreds of gigantic factories making steel, heavy machinery, fighter planes, bombs, and myriad other industrial products. In addition, networks of hydroelectric plants, oil rigs, natural gas fields, coal and other mines, logging stations, and canneries, not to mention unseen nuclear weapons silos, secluded military bases, and sophisticated radar installations, distinguish Siberia as a land of predominantly heavy industry.[6] This formerly rural region is now three-quarters urban, boasting three cities with a population of more than 1 million, nine of more than 500,000, twenty-two of at least 200,000, and almost forty of 100,000.[7]

Siberia's extraordinary urban and industrial transformation for a long time served as the basis of the Soviets' self-understanding of their great eastern territory and as an important source of legitimacy for the Soviet regime. Soviet authorities could never seem to get enough development, promoting improbable projects so enormous even sober-minded individuals became enthused about them. A key element in the strategy and ideology of developmentalism was the rise of a class of scientists, a process particularly visible in Siberia, which was home to a new city of science, Akademgorodok, built just outside Novosibirsk. Science in Siberia forms the second theme in this section.

Paul R. Josephson, author of a study of Soviet physicists and a forthcoming work on Akademgorodok, which he calls the New Atlantis, recaptures much of the hope surrounding the decision wrung from Moscow to commit substantial investment to the development of science in Siberia in the 1950s.[8] He argues that the vision of a better world achieved through science that was held by scientists in Siberia, many of whom were young, was simultaneously a wish for a more humane form of socialism to be achieved through de-Stalinization. It was not to be. Indispensable as science proved to be for their developmental schemes, it remained a double-edged proposition for Soviet authorities intent on preserving the integrity of orthodoxy, which remained the uneasy complement to progress and developmentalism in their legitimacy. In his paean to Akademgorodok, Josephson explores the dynamics of this awkward combination.

Science has survived even if its patron, the Communist Party, has not. Yet it was Communism's collapse that has definitively revealed the extent to which scientists formed a privileged caste in Soviet society, notwithstanding the censorship, travel restrictions, and entanglements with Marxist-Leninist dogma. Cutbacks in the state's patronage have brought a reduction in the number of scientists, as well as in the standard of living of those remaining vis-à-vis the rest of the population. Faced with the possible closing of entire research institutes and a much-feared brain drain, "native" scientific traditions in Siberia are fighting to avoid the fate of the Communist Party, calling on much of the hope that inspired the creation of Akademgorodok, which Josephson seems to share. Whether there is cause for such optimism remains to be seen.

* * *

In hindsight, it has become commonplace to point out that important processes of change were under way inside the USSR well before its implosion—particularly the awakening of the country's many regions and the reconsideration of its industrial nature. Nowhere was the general shift toward regionalism, and the search for a rural past somehow more genuine and fulfilling than the depersonalized urban present, more visible than in the literature produced by Siberians since the 1960s.[9] Siberian writers seemed to discover in their native land the roots of a way of life that could "save" all of Russia. The putative existence of a separate Siberian culture, constituting the underlying layer of true "Russianness," forms the next theme of this section.

Kathleen Parthé, a literary critic and author of the principal monograph on the Village Prose writers (from Siberia and elsewhere), takes us through the varying images of Siberia in these writers.[10] She notes the contrasts among them, as well as the tensions within their work, singling out for extended review the writings of the Irkutsk-born Valentin Rasputin, usually seen as the quintessential Village Prose writer and the one most preoccupied with Siberia. For Rasputin, Siberia, as a source of renewal for Russian identity, promises redemption. For others, the great landmass has become fundamental to the kind of intolerant nationalism that threatens to succeed Communism. Siberia is home to dreamers of many types.

* * *

In the last essay of this section, we return to where we began, the question of Siberian autonomy. Vladimir A. Zhdanov, a political scientist from Novosibirsk, picks up the story of Siberia's relations with Moscow in the period after 1985. Under perestroika, the Siberian economy lost most of Moscow's regionally directed investment (at least for western Siberia), yet failed to obtain the freedom to manage its own affairs. The result was indignation, which because of glasnost could be expressed publicly. Their antipathy toward Moscow bound representatives of the diverse regions of Siberia together into an association, the Siberian Agreement, dedicated to the pursuit of "Siberian interests."

The great dream of Siberian autonomy was revived, but it soon became enmeshed in the political struggles in Moscow. After the forcible dispersal of the Russian parliament in October 1993 by Boris Yeltsin, national elections dealt a blow to the self-styled reformers. As Zhdanov shows, Pan-Siberian regionalism and talk of autonomy gave way to the time-honored tradition of competition among Siberian localities for Moscow's attention. Siberia may still be seen as a place apart from Russia proper, but its many regions are divided. If some measure of genuine autonomy is to come, it will come province by province, not for a unified entity. Meanwhile, the basis of the Soviet-era elite's power, the heavy industrial enterprises, remains more or less intact. How long that situation will persist is hard to say.

Notes

1. James Gibson, "The Significance of Siberia to Tsarist Russia," *Canadian Slavonic Papers*, 14 (3), 1972, pp. 442–53.

2. Nikolaus Poppe, "The Economic and Cultural Development of Siberia," in Erwin Oberlaender et al., eds., *Russia Enters the Twentieth Century, 1894–1917* (London: Temple Smith, 1971), pp. 138–51; Victor Mote, "The Cheliabinsk Grain Tariff and the Rise of the Siberian Butter Industry," *Slavic Review*, 35 (2), 1976, pp. 304–17; Richard Lonsdale, "Siberian Industry Before 1917: The Example of Tomsk Guberniya," *Annals of the Association of American Geographers*, 53, 1963, pp. 479–93. Siberia's urban workforce in 1913 numbered perhaps 250,000, much of this formed in the years 1900–1912. *Statisticheskii ezhegodnik Rossii 1913 g.* (St. Petersburg, 1914), pp. 53–55. Siberia's manufacturing base, even more than the rest of the tsarist empire, consisted of crafts and peasant light industry, what Nikolai Iadrintsev aptly called the "grand peasant workshop [*ogromnaia muzhichnaia fabrika*]," as cited in Leonid Goriushkin, "Migration, Settlement, and the Rural Economy of Siberia, 1861–1914," in Alan Wood, ed., *The History of Siberia: From Russian Conquest to Revolution* (New York: Routledge, 1991), pp. 140–57. See also *Aziatskaia Rossia*, vol. 2 (St. Petersburg, 1914), pp. 413–46; and *Istoriia Sibiri*, vol. 3 (Leningrad, 1968), pp. 340–48. As late as 1927, Siberian manufacturing accounted for less than 2 percent of USSR output.

3. Alan Wood, "Siberia's Role in Russian History," in *The History of Siberia*, pp. 1–16.

4. Such were the views of Baron Meyendorff, the head of the government's Siberia Committee around the time of Russia's Great Reforms in 1861, as cited in Mark Bassin, "Inventing Siberia: Visions of the Russian East in the Early Nineteenth Century," *American Historical Review*, 96 (3), 1991, pp. 763–94. Even after tsarist officials accepted the need to industrialize, they remained wary of Siberia. After a visit there in 1910, Stolypin wrote to the tsar of "an enormous, rudely democratic country, which will soon throttle European Russia." *Krasnyi arkhiv*, no. 30, 1928, pp. 82–83, as cited in Treadgold, *The Great Siberian Migration* (Princeton: Princeton University Press, 1947), p. 159.

5. Fridtjof Nansen, for example, took the latter view in *Through Siberia, the Land of the Future* (New York: Frederick Stokes, 1914), p. 303. The absence of an ocean separating Siberia from the empire's Muscovite core has meant that Siberia can rightly be seen as both a "New World" colony and as a frontier society integral to Russia's original territories—a dual legacy that may or may not suggest that the possibilities for Siberia breaking away, like the New World colonies, and becoming a self-sustaining, independent unit are perhaps less strong than sometimes assumed. See the remarks by Bassin, "Inventing Siberia," pp. 763–94.

6. As detailed in *Razvitie narodnogo khoziaistva Sibiri* (Novosibirsk, 1978).

7. *Chislennost', sostav i dvizheniie naseleniia v RSFSR* (Moscow, 1990); E.N. Pertsik, *Gorod v Sibiri* (Moscow, 1980); Gary Hausladen, "Recent Trends in Siberian Urban Growth," *Soviet Geography,* 28 (2), 1987, pp. 231–46; V.V. Alekseev, ed., *Urbanizatsiia Sovetskoi Sibiri* (Novosibirsk, 1987). Before 1917, Siberia's designated "urban settlements," except for a few medium-sized commercial centers along the newly built railroad, were rural-like administrative outposts or rustic regional markets.

8. Paul Josephson, *Physics and Politics in Revolutionary Russia* (Berkeley: University of California, 1991).

9. David Gillespie, "A Paradise Lost? Siberia and Its Writers, 1960–1990," in Diment and Slezkine, *Between Heaven and Hell: The Myth of Siberian Russian Culture* (New York: St. Martin's, 1993), pp. 255–73.

10. Kathleen Parthé, *Russian Village Prose: The Radiant Past* (Princeton: Princeton University Press, 1992).

Moscow and Siberia

Center–Periphery Relations, 1917–30

Vladimir I. Shishkin

Since the fall of the Soviet Union in late 1991, provincial historians, no longer pining to investigate the problems of the entire Russian republic or the USSR, have begun to focus on local themes. The names of Russia's regions appear more and more frequently in the titles of scholarly conferences and on the covers of new historical monographs, essay collections, and memoirs. Such expanded interest in local history has important repercussions for the debates over the structure of the Russian Federation. To understand the present and future relations between the "center" and the provinces that make up the federation, and which may have their own interests, a knowledge of the past is essential.

This article will investigate the interrelations between Moscow and Siberia from 1917 to 1930.[1] Not all aspects of Moscow-Siberian relations can be considered in the space of a short essay. Rather than focus on specific issues such as the place and role of regions in national budgets or the development of government policy in respect to regions, this article will concentrate on the broad parameters of the relationship between central governmental organs (first the RSFSR, then the USSR) and Siberian governmental organs.

Among the multitude of regional partners which Moscow had to deal with between 1912 and 1930, Siberia was given priority for a number of reasons. It occupied the largest territory, yet had the lowest population density, and was poorly studied. The poor condition of internal means of communication was exacerbated by weak ties with capitals and adjacent regions. Its economy was based largely on agriculture, and peasants were dominant in the social structure of the population. Siberia was in the position of an economic colony of Russia and had been used by the tsarist government as a place for political and criminal exile; at the same time, due to the presence in Siberia of strong regional tendencies (*oblastnichestvo*), it had the reputation of a province leaning toward separatism.

During the more than seventy years of Soviet power, Siberia changed its appearance substantially and simultaneously made an enormous contribution to the Soviet treasury. It will suffice to mention that from the mid-1970s onward the western Siberian petroleum complex was the USSR's primary source of hard currency. In the 1990s, Siberia made its sociopolitical presence strongly, albeit ambiguously, felt. It became the nurturing ground for the independent workers' movement, which played a prominent role in the fall of the Communist regime. During the late September–early October 1993 conflict between the president and parliament, however, the economic and political elite of Siberia took an openly pro-Communist position.

Until recently, it was assumed that there were no significant contradictions between national and local interests in the Soviet era, and consequently nothing to study. This does not mean, however, that factual material shedding light on this subject is totally absent in the existing literature, which has, for example, treated central policies regarding food provision, industrialization, and the nationality problem. The great bulk of this factual material must be sought in widely dispersed archives, periodicals, and official publications of the period, a circumstance that complicates significantly the analysis of the problem. Furthermore, one often encounters only fragmentary information on local reactions to measures carried out in Siberia under orders from the center. Therefore, this article should be considered an initial, very imperfect attempt to outline the basic direction of research and to formulate conclusions that will later be subject to confirmation or contradiction.

Tsentrosibir': The Establishment of Soviet Power in Siberia

One of the peculiarities of the revolutionary process in Siberia was the emergence there of a transregional Soviet organ two days before the Bolshevik coup in Petrograd. On 23 October 1917 in Irkutsk, the First All-Siberian Congress of Soviets met and elected a Central Executive Committee of the Soviets of Siberia (Tsentrosibir'). Participants at the congress, which was attended by 184 delegates from seventy Siberian regional soviets, for the most part expressed the interests and views of workers and soldiers sympathetic to the revolution. Representatives of only three soviets of peasant deputies attended.[2] In short, in predominantly peasant Siberia the First All-Siberian Congress of Soviets, which proclaimed itself the government of the people, did not represent the principal group of the Siberian population.

Elected by only a slim majority of the congress delegates and consisting of little more than a dozen members, Tsentrosibir' took an active role in supporting the Petrograd armed uprising, carrying out the decisions of the Second All-Russian Congress of Soviets which met in Moscow, and establishing the rule of soviets in Siberia. Owing to the persistence and efforts of Tsentrosibir', during the period from late November 1917 to the first half of February 1918, Soviet rule was established in a majority of major administrative centers of eastern Siberia and the Baikal region, the armed resistance of officers and cadets in Irkutsk was suppressed, and the Siberian duma in Tomsk was disbanded. The authority of Tsentrosibir' among radicals was evidenced by its recognition as a ruling organ by the Bolshevik-dominated soviets of western Siberia and by the regional krai-level Executive Committee of the Soviets of the Far East, as well as by its convocation of the Second All-Siberian Congress of Soviets, held in Irkutsk 16–26 February 1918.

After this Second All-Siberian Congress of Soviets, the functions of Tsentrosibir' changed from revolutionary agitation to government. In the process, it tripled the number of its members and established various departments (commissariats) for coordination among the local soviets, including defense; the battle with counter-revolution; food provision; labor and industry; transport and communication; agricultural, financial, and social welfare; education; justice; postal and telegraph operations; and foreign affairs. Tsentrosibir' strove, both directly and through its departments, to subordinate and control the activity of those Siberian soviets that already existed as well as those being established.[3]

In 1918, while almost all the time and effort of both central and local Soviet organs were consumed by the consolidation of their own power, the contacts between central and regional organs were of a sporadic nature and consisted chiefly of the exchange of information. According to the first chairman of Tsentrosibir', B.Z. Shumiatskii, the only request made by the Bolshevik leaders to their Siberian party comrades was to support the armed coup in the capitals "not only with a series of local uprisings, but also with an uninterrupted food supply."[4]

During the course of Tsentrosibir''s existence, no legal documents were drawn up to determine its jurisdiction or its relation to central authorities.[5] In principle, a model of federalism was put forth, for although local soviets were supposed to "work in coordination with the central executive power," they were to "remain autonomous and maintain their right to social and revolutionary initiatives."[6] In practice, however, conflicts over jurisdiction were frequent.

On 21 February 1918, for example, the Second All-Siberian Congress of Soviets unanimously voiced its disapproval of the proposed Treaty of Brest-Litovsk with the Germans, asserting that the congress would not be bound by it.[7] Not surprisingly, when a vacancy arose in the post of Tsentrosibir' chairman (as a result of the congress's selection of B.Z. Shumiatskii as chairman of the Sovnarkom, or government, of Siberia), the Bolshevik Central Committee (CC) recommended a firm supporter of Lenin, N.N. Iakovlev. Iakovlev had earlier headed the executive committee of the West Siberian regional soviet and was a decisive opponent of Siberian autonomy. Under his direction, the executive committee branded Siberian autonomy "a liberal-bourgeois trick."[8]

But, the designation of Iakovlev as chairman of Tsentrosibir', far from putting an end to the opposition of the majority of the leadership of the regional soviets to the Treaty of Brest-Litovsk, heightened the conflict. A conference of representatives of the soviets of the Enisei gubernia and the Baikal Regional Executive Committee adopted a decision, the essence of which was that the directives of higher organs had no power and must not be adopted without the approval of local soviets.[9] One of the possible variants considered in continuing the battle with German imperialism was that of uniting the oblasts and gubernias of Siberia and the Far East into a federation of soviets, which would be independent and rely on the support of the United States. In newspapers and official documents of the period, such terms as "The Siberian Soviet Republic" and "The Siberian Worker-Peasant Army" appeared more and more frequently.[10]

In early April 1918, the deputy chairman of Tsentrosibir', Ia.D. Yanson, sent Lenin a note informing him of the mood for Siberian independence and the establishment of a commissariat of foreign affairs within Tsentrosibir'. Lenin sent an express government telegram, diplomatically urging against such an action.[11] Iakovlev demonstrated his loyalty, sending the executive committee of the Enisei soviets, distinguished by the most pronounced separatist tendencies in Siberia, a note recommending the unconditional fulfillment of the decrees and decisions of the central governmental authority.[12] On 20 April 1918 the Irkutsk newspaper *Vlast' truda* printed a programmatic announcement of Iakovlev (paraphrased five days later in the Moscow paper *Pravda*) announcing that "the thought of independence and autonomy in the battle with international imperialism is not only absurd, but criminal."

During the battles with Siberian soviets against separatist moods, the central Sovnarkom under Lenin's initiative named A.G. Shlikhter to the newly created position of special commissar for food provision in Siberia, making directives by Shlikhter obligatory for all corresponding Siberian government bodies.[13] It is difficult to explain this action as anything other than an effort by Moscow to curtail the jurisdiction of regional soviets, for Siberian soviets already had an effective food provision apparatus (after December 1917, but before the appointment of Shlikhter, Siberia was the exclusive reliable source of grain for Moscow, Petrograd, the front, and the Central–Industrial and North–West districts). The reaction in Siberia to Shlikhter's appointment was marked by confusion, to put it mildly.[14]

After a lengthy and emotional debate, Tsentrosibir' resolved to protest to the Sovnarkom against the granting of special jurisdiction to Shlikhter and to invite him to join Tsentrosibir' and its food provision organs as a representative of the center and an equal partner. Lenin rejected such a move, writing that Shlikhter's appointment reflected the central government's "aim of strengthening regional power through the authority of the center in instances which require speedy and responsible resolution of matters."[15] The next day, Sovnarkom enhanced the scope of Shlikhter's authority. Due to the pressure exerted by higher government organs and the recognition of the need to maintain a hold on power locally, Siberian soviets offered no objections to this latest action in Moscow's relentless pursuit of centralism.[16]

The rebellion of the Czech legion that broke out in late May 1918 along the Trans-Siberian Railroad brought about the rapid decline of the soviets of Siberia and cut off contacts between Tsentrosibir' and Moscow. During the subsequent civil war and foreign intervention, Tsentrosibir' tried without support from higher organs to control the battle of Siberian soviets against the counter-revolution for another three months (until late August 1918). Thus, centralizing tendencies in Tsentrosibir''s own behavior, evident already in spring 1918, reached their furthest development at the moment of decline.[17]

Sibrevkom: The Civil War

In Siberia no less than in European Russia, the period from late spring through summer 1918 witnessed the replacement of the rule of local soviets, containing elements of limited democracy, by centralized "Soviet power" (*Sovetskaia vlast'*), based on the dictatorship model. But in Siberia, the subordination of lower organs to those above them and of local interests to federal interests proceeded more slowly and was interrupted as a result of the victory in Siberia of the White armies.

The Bolshevik leadership in Moscow looked at Siberia with hope and alarm: With hope, inasmuch as they intended to utilize Siberia's rich human resources and stores of food as a means of strengthening their rule. With alarm, inasmuch as Siberians had from the outset failed to inspire confidence, owing to the limited size of the proletarian segment of the population and the fact that the peasantry, not to mention the Cossacks, was distinguished by its comfortable standard of living and love of freedom. Siberian partisans, meanwhile, remained a largely uncertain and enigmatic force. Furthermore, Moscow had not forgotten the "transgressions" of Siberian soviets in the first half of 1918, when they opposed the center on certain policies, displaying streaks of independence yet failing on their own to control the forces of counter-revolution.

In August 1919, Moscow established a powerful governmental apparatus dedicated to reinstituting Soviet power in Siberia, strengthening the region's attachment to the RSFSR, and restoring, in the meantime, the flow of grain. This organ was the Siberian Revolutionary Committee (Sibrevkom). All local organs and most national organs of civil authority in the territory of Siberia were to be subordinated to it.[18] Each of the three individuals named to Sibrevkom—I.N. Smirnov (chairman), V.M. Kosarev and M.I. Frumkin (members)—knew Siberia both from exile and work with the soviets; they also each held a high post in the central party and government hierarchy.[19]

The emergence of this powerful unelected organ established to regain and govern the Siberian region stood in opposition to the constitution of the RSFSR and cannot be said to have expressed the will of the people of Siberia. Even from an administrative viewpoint it was a curious creation, for the resolution establishing Sibrevkom said little about its jurisdiction, structure, or term of existence, creating confusion and conflicts with military organs as well as central civilian authorities and their representatives in Siberia.[20] The Sibrevkom itself tried to work out rules governing its structure and responsibilities, setting the terms of its existence until the expulsion of the Whites and the organization of normal Soviet organs in Siberia.[21] Preoccupied as it was, Moscow made no response to these proposals.

In early September 1919, Sibrevkom's leadership and a small group of staff left Moscow for Cheliabinsk, but in November the liberation of Omsk from Kolchak's forces allowed Sibrevkom to relocate there. As more territory was regained, the establishment of Soviet power in Siberia meant not the formation of constitutional organs (elected soviets), but the appointment of revolutionary committees (revkoms) by higher authorities that were staffed mostly by Bolsheviks, a circumstance that permitted the reincorporation of Siberia into Moscow's control. Not long after moving to Omsk, the Sibrevkom sent about two hundred trainloads and dozens of rail convoys with food, weapons, and military equipment to European Russia. Siberian partisan units, meanwhile, instead of continuing to pose a threat (as in the reoccupied Ukraine), were incorporated into the Red Army and the People's Revolutionary Army of the Far East Republic, which was then being formed.[22]

In March 1920, with Kolchak defeated, the leadership of Sibrevkom addressed Moscow with a new proposal to codify its organizational structure and responsibilities. This new plan, which envisioned an expansion of Sibrevkom's prerogatives, was received sympathetically by Moscow. Furthermore, the plan coincided with the desires of the Revolutionary Military Soviet of the Republic, which had earlier proposed the creation of a military department within Sibrevkom.[23] Sibrevkom would thereby be confirmed as both a civilian and a military organ, a state of affairs made official by the Central Committee (CC) at its plenum held in April 1920. Sibrevkom set about creating departments for food provision, the military, and economic management. Sibrevkom also granted itself rights over its subordinate organs analogous to the rights exercised by the central Sovnarkom.[24]

Sibrevkom pursued its own aggrandizement. In May 1920, Sibrevkom adopted a resolution forbidding gubernia-level organs from bypassing it and dealing directly with central commissariats, defending this action not only on technical grounds (dealing directly with the commissariats would overload the telegraph system) but also on legal ones ("Sibrevkom is the supreme Soviet organ in Siberia").[25] A complaint brought the next month by the Moscow Commissariat of Internal Affairs (NKVD) to the CC's Organizational Bureau resulted in a decision that commissariats deal with Sibrevkom on all local matters and with the gubernia-level authorities only in extraordinary instances, notifying Sibrevkom with a copy of its correspondence. This was confirmed on 10 June 1920 by the Presidium of the All-Union Central Executive Committee (VTsIK), which also annulled Sibrevkom's resolution preventing gubernia-level organs of Siberia from dealing directly with the center.[26]

In late June 1920, Sibrevkom members A.G. Goikhbarg and A.V. Shotman met in Moscow with Lenin to discuss the status of Sibrevkom. Lenin expressed doubts about granting Sibrevkom the same powers as Sovnarkom and recommended the matter be referred to the Politburo. On 22 June, the Politburo discussed the status of Sibrevkom and also examined a report of the bureau of the Enisei Gubernia party committee, which had been received in the spring of 1920 and proposed that Sibrevkom be abolished as unnecessary. A commission consisting of representatives of the CC, the VTsIK, and the NKVD was formed to examine this question.[27]

In summer 1920, revolutionary committees were replaced by elected soviets in a large portion of the territory of Siberia. Sibrevkom's principal mission, the one for which it had been created, had been basically resolved. The opponents of Sibrevkom's existence became especially active at this time—the eve of the Second Siberian Party Conference, which was held in Omsk from late July to early August 1920. Countering proposals from the Enisei party gubkom, the highest party organ of the region, the Siberian Bureau of the Central Committee, decided to have the further existence of Sibrevkom voted on by participants of the party conference.[28] Before the vote a report was heard on the activities of the Sibrevkom, said to include maintaining Siberia as a source of food and raw materials for the central regions of Soviet Russia. The conference came out in favor of the preservation of Sibrevkom and called on party organizations to fully cooperate with its work.[29]

Having attained such authoritative local support, the leadership of Sibrevkom once again addressed Lenin with a request to assist them in the adoption of a new project on the status of Sibrevkom. On 5 and 12 October 1920, this matter was examined at the Sovnarkom, and at the second session, after taking into account the corrections of the representatives of the commissariats, the project was passed, formally legalizing the Sibrevkom's existence for the first time and determining its strategic mission, rights, and duties, as well as its internal structure, for the remaining years of its existence.[30]

Commissariats were, as a rule, obliged to issue all directives for the Soviet organs of Siberia through their representatives in Sibrevkom, that is, through the departments of Sibrevkom. Direct contacts between commissariats and local soviet authorities were allowed only in extraordinary circumstances and required a simultaneous notification of these contacts to Sibrevkom. The departments of Sibrevkom were subordinated to both Sibrevkom and their corresponding commissariats.[31]

On 4 December 1920, with the major battles of the civil war won, Sibrevkom adopted a resolution ending martial law in Siberia. Owing to this circumstance, some officials of the Enisei, Irkutsk, and Omsk gubkoms had come around to the position of abolishing Sibrevkom.[32] A rather heated discussion of Sibrevkom's status broke out on the eve of and during the period of the Third Siberian Party Conference, held in February 1921.[33] Its defenders argued that Sibrevkom was necessary "as a battle organ possessing total power in the territory of Siberia," an argument that carried some weight since in January 1921 a large anti-Communist uprising had broken out in the enormous territory spanning the Tiumen, Omsk, Ekaterinburg, Cheliabinsk, and Semipalatinsk gubernias. Although quickly liquidated, the uprising provided a firm basis for the arguments supporting the continued existence of the Sibrevkom for the foreseeable future. The continued defeat of the efforts to abolish the Sibrevkom demonstrate that it was completely a child of the center. Sibrevkom was a regional organ in only one respect: in the scope of its governing activity. Most illustrative of its character was the policy Sibrevkom carried out in Siberia on Moscow's instructions. This policy was clearly oriented to the resolution of overall Russian problems, most often at the expense and even the harm of the interests of the region.

Sibrevkom's Moscow-oriented position appeared most blatantly in food provision as well as tax and budget matters. During the period from 1920 to 1923, Siberia, possessing about 6 percent of the country's arable land, accounted for approximately 25 percent of the country's grain and feed. Furthermore, a large part of the food produced within Siberia was exported beyond its borders, whereas in other regions food was consumed locally. The predictable result was a severe agricultural crisis in Siberia. Although 1923 generally saw a tendency toward improvement in the Russian agricultural sector, Siberia experienced a reduction in the area of cultivated land and the quantity of livestock. This was a direct consequence of the continued grain requisitions in Siberia well after the establishment of the New Economic Policy in European Russia.

The belated substitution in Siberia of a tax for requisitions did not help matters much, since the tax was high. Only in the middle of 1923, when it became apparent that the quotas Moscow had set for the agricultural tax were incapable of being endured and could lead to catastrophe, did the Siberian party and soviet leadership dare to address Moscow with a request for a reduction. As a result of this intervention, the amount of the tax was lowered by about 30 percent! With regard to other forms of taxation, however, including the harsh general civilian and transport taxes, Siberia still contributed more than the countrywide average. In fact, Siberia's overall share of taxation was higher in the crisis year of 1923 than it had been in the prosperous year of 1913. In 1924 and 1925, the tendency toward growth in the region's share of taxation continued.

A similarly striking picture emerges from a consideration of Siberia's place in the federal budget. The rate of growth of expenditures from the federal budget directed toward Siberia's needs lagged behind the overall Soviet indicators, and the region's share of federal expenditures even shrank, from 3.9 percent in fiscal year 1923/24 to 2.9 percent in fiscal year 1924/25.[34] Sibrevkom chairman M.M. Lashevich, in response to proposals by gubernia- and uezd-level representatives to appeal to Moscow for an increase in Siberia's share of the national budget, remarked, "I can guarantee that Sibrevkom will make its case in Moscow, but this will produce almost no results."[35]

Perhaps the most compelling testimony regarding Sibrevkom's inability to defend the interests of its region from the center was that during the period it held power Siberia underwent a loss of territory. In April 1920, a VTsIK resolution removed Tiumen (Tobol) gubernia, as well as the Ishim uezd of Omsk gubernia, from Sibrevkom's jurisdiction and placed them under the Revolutionary Soviet of the First Workers' Army. In the middle of 1921, the Akmolinsk and Semi-palatinsk gubernias were given to the Kirghiz (Kazakh) ASSR (after earlier reso-lutions on such a transfer by the VTsIK in July 1919 and Sovnarkom in August 1920). Sibrevkom did make several attempts to regain the Ishim uezd and the Bukhtarma region of the Ust-Kamenogorsk uezd (which was neither ethnically nor economically tied to the Kirghiz ASSR), but these efforts were in vain.

Sibkraiispolkom: Centralization Institutionalized

From 1923 at the latest, there ceased to be an urgent military or economic need for the continued existence of Sibrevkom. "Soviet power" was firmly in place and the remnants of the major White armies, deployed in the area immediately adjacent to Siberia, had been crushed along with any significant armed resistance by the Siberian population to Communist rule. With the victory of neighboring Mongolia's "popular-democratic" revolution, a pro-Soviet puppet government was formed there; the nominally independent Far Eastern Republic, for almost three years a worrisome headache for Moscow, was liquidated. Control over regional soviets was firmly in the hands of party organizations. Even Sibrev-kom's chairman, Lashevich, admitted that the existence of Sibrevkom in the ninth year of Soviet power was "somewhat of an anachronism."[36] Officially, the justification for prolonging the existence of the Sibrevkom was said to be the administrative and territorial reorganization of Siberia (the abolition of gub-ernias, uezds, and volosts and their replacement by okrugs and raions). In reality, Moscow was motivated by the need to retain unimpeded access to grain, butter, fur, gold, and the other resources of Siberia. The existence of Sibrevkom allowed the center to receive the resources of the region without significant problems and delays.

In May 1925, VTsIK announced the formation of the Siberian krai. In De-cember of the same year, the first krai-level conference of soviets—the highest organ of local power according to the constitution of the RSFSR—took place. At the conference, Sibrevkom for the first time made an accounting to the Siberian population of the work it had done. To take its place in leading the krai during the period between krai-level conferences of soviets, a new government body was formed: the Siberian krai-level Executive Committee of Soviets (Sibkraii-spolkom). Three plans for determining the structure of the Sibkraiispolkom were drawn up, one by the Sibrevkom, one by the VTsIK commission on territorial reorganization, and one by the new agency itself. In March 1927, the agency's plan was adopted by the presidium of Sibkraiispolkom and became a binding legal document.[37]

Sibkraiispolkom and its presidium were granted a wide range of rights. They were able to appeal to the legislative organs of the Russian Federation for the alteration of existing laws. In special instances they had the right to delay the execution of the directives of the individual commissariats of the RSFSR, provided they informed Sovnarkom of the question under discussion. They were even able to make a complaint on a decision of Sovnarkom to the VTsIK (although they were unable to stop a decision's implementation). They were granted the right to control and inspect all government bodies and institutions immediately subordinated to the center and not among the departments of Sibkraiispolkom, with the exception of military organs and branches of the Commissariat of Foreign Affairs, and to dismiss with due cause officials assigned by the central authorities to work in Siberia. Despite these impressive-sounding rights, however, Sibkraiispolkom seems to have believed that the governing of the krai remained excessively centralized and that a widening of its rights was necessary.[38]

To be sure, the new system of governance for Siberia was more democratic than during the period of Sibrevkom's dominance. Krai-level conferences of soviets in Siberia could pass public judgment on the government of the USSR, and the local soviets did have a legal basis with which to defend the interests of the region against Moscow. It would, however, be extremely naive to mistake the formal and visible side of the Soviet system for its essence. The fact of the matter is that the Bolshevik party, especially the plenums of its CC, not the soviets, determined the strategy and priorities for the development of the country as a whole as well as for its individual regions. The executive committees of soviets at all levels were given the role of executors of the party's decisions. Conferences of soviets, in theory all-powerful to make policy, acquired a ritualistic and decorative character.

There was no countering Moscow's drive for central control, which was enforced by the administrative structure. At the conclusion of discussion at the first krai-level conference of the soviets of Siberia in 1925, Moscow was presented with two demands: to cover the deficit of the krai budget with the resources of the center and to allot the financial resources necessary for a fundamental reorganization of Siberia's economy on an industrial basis.[39] But in remarks to the conference, A.S. Enukidze, the Secretary of the VTsIK, spoke in the name of the government of the USSR and declared that although Siberia had "done an extremely great amount for the Soviet Union" and that "the accomplishments of the Siberian krai were great," the government could not help Siberia at the present time to the degree that the krai deserved.[40] Siberia was compelled not only to deal with its problems alone for several years but also to act, just as before, as a benefactor for the other regions of the Soviet Union.

In the 1924/25 fiscal year, the overall sum of receipts entering the federal budget from Siberia comprised 63.3 million rubles. Conversely, the sum of funds received from the center during the same year was 18.5 million rubles less.

Given such a balance, the first conference of the soviets of the Siberian krai confirmed a krai-level budget for the fiscal year 1925/26 of 36.7 million rubles in receipts and 44.9 million rubles in expenditures and assumed that it would be compensated by the center for the 8.2 million ruble deficit. Nothing of the sort occurred. In the end, the Commissariat of Finances contributed only 3 million rubles to cover the deficit. Actual per capita expenditures to satisfy administrative, economic, social, and cultural needs in Siberia were only 65 to 72 percent of what they were for the RSFSR as a whole.[41]

In the same 1925/26 fiscal year, Siberia's share of Soviet exports, for which it received no compensation, was 7.2 percent. The share of Siberian krai industry subordinated to the center and the Russian republic (for which Moscow, and not the region, received income) comprised 17.6 percent of all production produced by the government-owned industry of Siberia.[42] If Siberia had received this income, it would have had no budget deficit.

The leadership of Sibkraiispolkom continually beseeched Moscow to get the center to strengthen the local budget through a more fair redistribution of income, increase Siberia's receipt of federal revenues, and grant the region assistance from central financial sources, but Moscow made only minor concessions. At the same time, the Sibkraiispolkom continued to address the center with the matter of the industrialization of Siberia, arguing that only industrialization would allow the region to fundamentally revive its economy and finances as well as make progress in the social and cultural spheres. Until the middle of 1930, however, these efforts brought virtually no results; Moscow had other priorities, in Ukraine, in European Russia, and elsewhere.

In advancing their calls for industrialization, the Siberian authorities felt the need to defend themselves against accusations of regional separatism and "autonomism." In a report delivered to the Siberian krai scientific-research conference, A.M. Pevzner, the director of the Novosibirsk office of the National Bank, stated that "we do not propose to develop tendencies toward either economic or cultural autonomy; our mission is not to consolidate the Siberian economy into a unified economic unit but to try to raise the share of the Siberian economy."[43] But Moscow, rebuffing the pleas to invest in Siberia, did not always shrink from employing arguments that resembled political accusations.[44]

On 15 May 1930, the CC adopted a resolution on the metallurgy industry of the Urals that determined the development of the Siberian economy for an entire decade. The resolution established that the country could no longer rely only on the southern coal and metallurgy base (in the Ukraine) and announced the goal of creating a second coal and metallurgy base in the east, using the rich deposits of coal and ore in the Urals and Siberia.[45] The center's adoption of a new strategy for Siberian development can be considered a belated victory for the leadership of the Siberian region. It must be stated, however, that the victory was Pyrrhic.

Grouping Siberia with the regions of rapid industrialization led to a change in its administrative and territorial structure and a reorganization of its government apparatus. VTsIK's resolution of 30 July 1930 liquidated the unified Siberian krai and formed in its place two units, a West Siberia and an East Siberia krai. This is not the place to analyze the purported and actual motives for the adoption of such a resolution. But we cannot help remarking on the destruction of Siberia as a unified geographic, administrative, and economic whole, the organic quality of which was not doubted by the major authorities of the theory and practice of governing and economic management.

The possibility of defending the interests of Siberia against Moscow—which did exist on paper, even if never fully realized in practice during the second half of the 1920s—was lost. The absence of effective Trans-Siberian government institutions and mechanisms for coordinating and defending the interests of the region from the center was one of the main reasons that industrial Siberia remained an economic colony of the USSR. The inhabitants of Siberia derived little benefit from its vastly increased wealth and scientific achievements.

Notes

1. The chronological framework of this article is somewhat untraditional. Its starting point, the end of 1917, marks the consolidation of Soviet rule in both Siberia and Russia as a whole, as well as the establishment of the first contacts between central and regional Soviet organs. The end date marks the abolition of the last administrative-territorial unit to encompass the entire region, the Siberian krai.

2. A large number of the 184 delegates belonged to revolutionary parties: 64 were Bolsheviks, 35 were Leftist Socialist Revolutionaries, 10 Internationalist Social Democrats, and 2 Anarchists. A. Abov, "Oktiabr' v Vostochnoi Sibiri (otryvki vospominanii)," *Sibirskie ogni,* 1924, no. 4, p. 114; V.T. Agalakov, *Podvig Tsentrosibir'i* (Irkutsk, 1968), p. 29.

3. For more detailed information on the formation and activities of Tsentrosibir'' see V.V. Riabikov, *Tsentrosibir' (Novosibirsk, 1949), pp. 3–134;* Agalakov, *Podvig Tsentrosibir'i;* and *Podvig Tsentrosibir'i (1917–1918): Sbornik dokumentov* (Irkutsk, 1986).

4. B.Z. Shumiatskii, *Sibir' na putiakh k Oktiabriu: Vospominaniia pervogo predsedatelia Tsentrosibir'i* (Irkutsk, 1989), p. 343.

5. This matter was not mentioned at all in the "Project for the Organization of Soviet Rule in Siberia," which was adopted by the Second All-Siberian Conference of Soviets and touted by the Bolsheviks as the Siberian constitution (although initially the matter of the organization of Soviet rule in the center and the localities was supposed to be discussed at this conference). *Bor'ba za vlast' sovetov v Irkutskoi gubernii: Sbornik dokumentov* (Irkutsk, 1957), pp. 117–18, 241–62.

6. Ibid., pp. 64–66. See also the resolution of the Third All-Russian Congress of Soviets (January 1918), "On Federal Organizations of the Russian Republic," in *S''ezdy Sovetov Soiuza SSR, Soiuznykh i Avtonomnykh Sovetskikh Sotsialisticheskikh Respublik: Sbornik dokumentov v trekh tomakh (1917–1936 gg.),* vol. 1 (Moscow, 1959), p. 31.

7. *Bor'ba za vlast' sovetov v Irkutskoi gubernii,* pp. 214–15. The military department of Tsentrosibir' even announced the mobilization of Red Army reserves for the defense of the revolution from the German occupying force, and several soviets initiated the formation of volunteer detachments.

8. *Bol'sheviki Zapadnoi Sibiri v bor'be za sotsialisticheskuiu revoliutsiiu (mart 1917–mai 1918g.): Sbornik dokumentov i materialov* (Novosibirsk, 1957), p. 290; V.S.

Poznanskii. *V.I. Lenin i sovety Sibiri (1917–1918): Rukovodstvo voenno-politicheskoi deiatel'nost'iu sovetov v bor'be s kontrrevoliutsiei* (Novosibirsk, 1977), pp. 175–77.

9. V.T. Agalakov, *Sovety Sibiri (1917–1918 gg.)* (Novosibirsk, 1978), pp. 236–37.

10. Ibid., p. 232; *Vlast' truda* [Irkutsk], 2 March, 4, 18, and 20 April 1918; *Dal'nevostochnye izvestiia* [Khabarovsk], 2 and 9 April 1918; *Bor'ba za vlast' sovetov v Irkutskoi gubernii*, p. 311; P.M. Nikiforov, *Zapiski prem'era DVR: Pobeda leninskoi politiki v bor'be s interventsiei na Dal'nem Vostoke (1917–1922 gg.)* (Moscow, 1963), p. 65.

11. V.I. Lenin, *Polnoe sobranie sochinenii*, 5th ed. (Moscow, 1965), vol. 50, p. 366.

12. V.S. Poznanskii, *V.I. Lenin i sovety Sibiri*, p. 4.

13. *Dekrety Sovetskoi vlasti*, vol. 2 (Moscow, 1959), p. 4.

14. See the comments by the head of the Siberian Commissariat of Supplies and Food Provision, V.D. Vilenskii-Sibiriakov, in an appearance on 1 April 1918 at the plenary session of Tsentrosibir', in *Podvig Tsentrosibir'i*, p. 135.

15. *Dekrety Sovetskoi vlasti*, vol. 2, p. 595.

16. On 28 March 1918, Tsentrosibir' declared that all commissars and emissaries named by national government organs to work in Siberia had to receive confirmation for their mandates in local soviets. But Sovnarkom adopted a different decision on this same question. On 5 April, Lenin signed a decree obligating local soviets of all levels to carry out all orders and to support all special and other commissars named by Sovnarkom. *Podvig Tsentrosibiri*, pp. 128–30; *Dekrety Sovetskoi vlasti*, vol. 2, p. 59. See also the 27 April 1918 telegram stressing discipline sent by the commissar of soviet leadership of Tsentrosibir', F.M. Lytkin, to the localities of Siberia. *Zapadnaia Sibir'* [Omsk], 1918, no. 8, p. 8.

17. In contrast to the Far East Sovnarkom, Tsentrosibir' called for the unification of military and diplomatic efforts of all soviets in Siberia to oppose the Whites and interventionists. See the declaration in *Podvig Tsentrosibiri*, p. 373.

18. Local representatives of the majority of national commissariats came under the full subordination of Sibrevkom, although some of them had special status ensuring them autonomy from Sibrevkom (for example, the Siberian Expedition of the National Commissariat of Transport, headed by the deputy Sovnarkom chairman V.M. Sverdlov).

19. *Izvestiia VTsIK* [Moscow], 3 and 4 September 1919; *Dekrety Sovetskoi vlasti*, pp. 73–74. Smirnov was a candidate-member of the Central Committee and a member of the Revolutionary Military Soviet of the Fifth Army of the Eastern Front; Frumkin was a member of the collegium of the National Commissariat of Food Production; Kosarev directed one of the regional committees of the party in Moscow.

20. See the November 1919 letter from Smirnov to Lenin: RTsKhIDNI (Rossiiskii tsentr khraneniia i izucheniia dokumentov noveishei istorii), f. 17, op. 65, d. 362, l. 1.

21. RGVA (Rossiiskii gosudarstvennyi voennyi arkhiv), f. 185, op. 1, d. 134, l. 72.

22. For more details, see V.I. Shishkin, *Revoliutsionnye komitety Sibiri v gody grazhdanskoi voiny (avgust 1919-mart 1921)* (Novosibirsk, 1978). Siberia turned out to be the only region of the RSFSR in which revolutionary committees were created on all levels of government: gubernia, uezd, volost, and selo (poselok).

23. GANO, f. R-1, op. 2, d. 23, l. 71; and f. R-1, op. 1, d. 116, ll. 148–49, 181; RTsKhIDNI, f. 17, op. 12, d. 499, l. 61.

24. GANO (Gosudarstvennyi arkhiv Novosibirskoi oblasti), f. R-1, op. 1, d. 2264a, l. 90.

25. As an exception, local gubernia-level organs were allowed to turn to the commissariats only in the event that they were not in agreement with resolutions of Sibrevkom and intended to make a complaint to the central authorities. *Izvestiia Sibirskogo revoliutsionnogo komiteta* [Omsk], 1920, no. 2, p. 4.

26. GANO, f. R-1, op. 1, d. 180, l. 77; *Vlast' sovetov* (Moscow, 1920), no. 8, p. 16.

27. GANO, f. R-1, op. 1, d. 269, l. 51; GARF, f. 130, op. 4, d. 498, ll. 49–51, 53.

28. Tsentr khraneniia dokumentatsii noveishei istorii Krasnoiarskogo kraia (TsKhDNIKK), f. 1, op. 1, d. 3, 1.75; GANO, f. p. 1, op. 3, d. 5, ll. 27, 29.

29. *Izvestiia Sibirskogo biuro TsK RKP(b)* [Novosibirsk], 1 August 1920; *Sovetskaia Sibir'*, 4 August 1920.

30. RTsKhIDNI, f. 19, op. 1, d. 390, ll. 4–6. The only major change was an amendment of Sovnarkom dated 1 August 1921 that granted Sibrevkom the right to economic consultation for matters affecting Siberia. *Izvestiia VTsIK,* 10 August 1921.

31. *Sibirskii revoliutsionnyi komitet (avgust 1919–dekabr' 1925 g.)* (Novosibirsk, 1959), pp. 53–54.

32. Tsentr khraneniia dokumentatsii noveishei istorii Irkutskoi oblasti, f. 1, op. 1, d. 531, l. 4; TsKhDNIKK, f. 1, op. 1, d. 3, l. 176; GANO, f. p. 1, op. 1, d. 840, l. 467; Omskii oblastnoi tsentr dokumentatsii noveishego vremeni, f. 1, op. 2, d. 30, l. 8; *Izvestiia Eniseiskogo gubkoma RKP(b)* [Krasnoiarsk], 1921, no. 1–2, pp. 1–2; no. 3–4, pp. 2–3, 22.

33. *Izvestiia Sibirskogo biuro TsKRKP (b),* 5 March 1921.

34. GANO, f. p. 1, op. 2, d. 241, ll. 220–27; *Otchet piatogo Sibirskogo ekonomicheskogo soveshchaniia s predstaviteliami gubernii i uezdov (4–7 ianvaria 1924 g.)* (Novonikolaevsk, 1924), pp. 15, 43, 116; *Kratkii otchet Sibirskogo revoliutsionnogo komiteta (mai 1924 g.)* (Novonikolaevsk, 1924), pp. 23, 25; *Kratkii otchet Sibirskogo revoliutsionnogo komiteta pervomu kraevomu s''ezdu sovetov* (Novonikolaevsk, 1925), pp. 60–61.

35. *Otchet piatogo Sibirskogo ekonomicheskogo soveshchaniia s predstaviteliami gubernii i uezdov,* p. 44.

36. *Pervyi kraevoi s''ezd sovetov Sibiri (3–9 dekabria 1925 g.): Stenograficheskii otchet* (Novosibirsk, 1993), part 1, p. 55.

37. *Proekt polozheniia o Sib[irskom] krae v redaktsii Sibrevkoma: Polozhenie o Sib[irskom] krae v redaktsii komissii pri VTsIK po raionirovaniiu t. Priadchenko* (Novonikolaevsk, 1925); *Proekt polozheniia o Sibirskom krae, utverzhdennyi prezidiumom Sibkraiispolkoma 4-ogo marta 1927 g.* (Novosibirsk, 1927).

38. *Otchet Sibirskogo kraevogo ispolnitel'nogo komiteta sovietov rabotnikh, krestianskikh i krasnoarmeiskikh deputatov vtoromu Sibirskomu kraevomu s''ezdu sovietov* (Novosibirsk, 1927), pp. 2–3.

39. *Pervyi kraevoi s''ezd sovietov Sibiri (3–9 dekabria 1925 g.)* (Novosibirsk, 1993), part 2, pp. 209–11, 223–25.

40. *Pravitel'stvo SSSR otchityvaetsia pered rabochimi i krestianami Sibiri: Doklad sekretaria Tsentral'nogo ispolnitel'nogo komiteta SSSR tov. Enukidze na pervom Vsesibirskom s''ezde sovietov* (Novosibirsk, 1925), p. 2.

41. *Doklad Sibirskogo kraevogo finansovogo otdela 4-mu plenumu Sibkraiispolkoma 1-ogo sozyva po ispolneniiu mestnogo biudzheta kraia za 1925/1926 g. i po proektu mestnogo biudzheta kraia na 1926/1927 g.* (Novosibirsk, 1926), pp. 3, 9, 24; *Otchet 2-mu kraevomu s''ezdu sovietov po ispolneniiu mestnykh biudzhetov Sibirskogo kraia za 1925/1926 g.* (Novosibirsk, 1927), p. 28.

42. *Narodnoe khoziaistvo Sibirskogo kraia (po kontrol'nym tsifram na 1926/1927 g).* (Novosibirsk, 1926), pp. 33, 65–67.

43. A.M. Pevzner, "Sovremennoe sostoianie narodnogo Sibirskogo khoziaistva i perspektivy ego razvitiia," in *Pervyi Sibirskii kraevoi nauchno-issledovatel'skii s''ezd* (Novosibirsk, 1928), vol. 5, pp. 5, 20.

44. In arguing for industrialization, Siberians also stressed that this was their goal not just for their region but for the whole country. See, for example, *Otchet Sibirskogo kraevogo ispolnitel'nogo komiteta sovietov Sovnarkomu RSFSR* (Novosibirsk, 1927), pp. 4, 80.

45. The Sixteenth Party Conference, held 26 June–13 July 1930, approved the forced construction of the Ural-Siberian coal and metallurgy base. *KPSS v rezoliutsiiakh i resheniiakh s''ezdov, konferentsii i plenumov TsK* vol. 4 (Moscow, 1970), pp. 398, 441–42.

New Atlantis Revisited

Akademgorodok, Siberian City of Science

Paul R. Josephson

"From the integral to metal!"
—One of the founding slogans for Akademgorodok

In December 1956, the mathematician Mikhail A. Lavrent'ev journeyed to the Siberian industrial center of Novosibirsk, where he met with T.F. Gorbachev, a geologist and chairman of the West Siberian Affiliate of the Soviet Academy of Sciences. They walked through the Golden Valley, a hilly, forested region, twenty-five miles south of the city and 2,500 miles east of Moscow, on the western shore of the Ob River. They agreed it would be a fine place to build Akademgorodok, the Siberian city of science.[1] They decided that the scientific institutes of Akademgorodok would be located somewhat to the north of the Golden Valley itself, which would be preserved for a handful of cottages for the leading scientists, several orchards connected with the Biology Institute, and trails used for hiking, cross-country skiing, and gathering mushrooms. Construction began in 1958. A mere seven years later, fifteen scientific research institutes opened. Tens of thousands of scientists and administrators, accompanied by their families, moved to Siberia to begin new lives.

While visionaries have long imagined the creation of a scientific utopia, Akademgorodok may be the only case where scientists, officials, and society as a whole had the opportunity to try to realize such an endeavor. From the moment it was built, Akademgorodok became a symbol not only of science and progress but of the development of rich Siberian resources and of the freedom associated with Khrushchevian de-Stalinization, including the democratization and decentralization of science (as an institution).

Under Stalin, science had been concentrated in Moscow and Leningrad, where research was dominated by individuals or their institutes, sometimes thwarting the growth of entire fields and leading in some cases, such as genetics, to pseudoscience. But the founders of Akademgorodok intended to create world-class scientific research institutes divorced from the typical pressures of Soviet politics and the economy. Many of the first scientists were young, recent recruits, the so-called children of the Twentieth Party Congress (1956), at which Khrushchev denounced Stalin's "cult of the personality." It helped, too, that Akademgorodok was far from Moscow, the central party apparatus, and strict ideological control. Akademgorodok had its own party organization that was not nearly as vigilant as Moscow came to desire, especially at the level of the primary party organizations in the institutes.

Scientists in Siberia came to accept intellectual freedom as a given, exploring fields previously closed to them, either because of philosophical prohibitions owing to the alleged idealism of a particular field or because of political centralization, which discouraged innovation. In Akademgorodok, Gersh Budker employed new techniques for colliding beam accelerators to achieve new luminosities in high energy physics. Other scientists used research in animal husbandry and plant hybridization to commence study of genetics even before the condemnation of T.D. Lysenko in 1965. Tatiana Zaslavskaia freed Soviet sociology from increasingly metaphysical Marxian concepts of class conflict to study labor migration and worker (dis)satisfaction, studies that revealed all was not well in the Soviet countryside. Abel Aganbegian accelerated the rebirth of interest in linear programming and Taylorist scientific organization of labor. Owing in part to a relatively open atmosphere, significant results were achieved in various fields, and research in Siberia soon became distinct from that produced by the rest of the Soviet scientific establishment.

And yet, the utopian designs of scientists and Communist Party leaders to build a city of science were subject to the same handicaps that hindered Soviet science in general. Ideological constructs, political desiderata, and economic constraints impinged on the efforts of Akademgorodok's founders to create a unique scientific community in the West Siberian forest. Moreover, as in other societies, the power of the purse shaped the face of research. In the USSR the state pressured scientists to abandon basic research to take up projects dedicated to the economic development of Siberia.

Tremendous pressures were exerted by the widely accepted view in the USSR that science constituted a branch of the economy. Siberian science had to compete with other branches to secure funding, manpower, machinery, and equipment. After initially garnering sufficient favor and resources, Akademgorodok came to be seen by Moscow policy makers as no different from any other scientific organization. As such, it was expected to produce applied science in the service of the economy and military.

With time, the shortfalls of rubles, hard currency, machinery, and equipment, as well as building supplies, that had plagued construction from the start only multiplied. More than that, the ruling Communist Party apparatus grew increasingly conservative under Brezhnev. Local and regional party officials had come to fear the apparent autonomy scientists developed under the influence of Western science and ideological precepts. The response among some scientists to the Soviet invasion of Czechoslovakia in 1968, as well as to other events described below, furnished the authorities with a pretext for tightening their grip on the scientific community.

Yet a uniquely Siberian science emerged in Akademgorodok. It was Siberian in terms of personnel, for many of the young recruits came from Siberia and eventually became laboratory directors. It was Siberian in terms of novel research approaches, for in addition to the exploration of previously closed fields of study, Akademgorodok scientists were directly involved in the study of Siberian natural resources. And it was Siberian in consciousness, for in cases such as the fight to preserve Lake Baikal and to derail the costly, environmentally destructive project to divert Siberian river flow to Central Asia, Siberian scientists publicly opposed policies emanating from Moscow.

In the utopian early days of Akademgorodok, scientists believed they were more free than their colleagues in the center. From the corridors of scientific research institutes in Akademgorodok to the social clubs and cafés, where scientists read poetry, saw art exhibitions, and listened to itinerant bards, there was greater openness and freedom in Akademgorodok than in the center. This openness was political, but it was also generational and cultural, rooted in the informal exchange of ideas explicitly intended by Akademgorodok's founders to foster the creative impulse among researchers.

The Soviet New Atlantis

In 1608, Sir Francis Bacon, British statesman, philosopher, and the father of the modern inductive method of reasoning, composed his *New Atlantis,* one of the major utopian works of Western literature. Bacon's book described the activities of Salomon's House, a learned society and city of science—which served as the model for the British Royal Society—in which scholars searched for knowledge of and power over nature, using laboratories laden with modern equipment and instrumentation and libraries to facilitate research in the cause of "enlarging the bounds of human empire" and "the effecting of all things possible."[2] For Bacon, as for both his contemporaries and many social commentators since, "science" meant the acquisition of objective knowledge freed from the pressures of day-to-day life.

Akademgorodok was part of this Western utopian scientific tradition. It was also the logical outcome of decades of Soviet political, economic, and ideological developments. On the eve of the Russian revolution, the biogeophysicist V.I. Vernadskii and the writer Maxim Gorky, among others, advanced ideas of the creation of something akin to Salomon's House to raise the cultural level of

Russia and bring the backward nation into the twentieth century. Throughout Soviet history, leading party representatives, economic planners, and members of the scientific intelligentsia hoped to achieve a higher form of civilization—socialism—on the basis of science and technology. Scientists would uncover the secrets of nature, and the Soviet state would master them, building a modern industrial power. As in Salomon's House, the success of Akademgorodok in facilitating these ends would be secured through a series of organizational, architectural, and scientific innovations intended to protect science from broader social forces, economic inefficiencies, and the vagaries of political life.

The organizational structure of Akademgorodok was derived from three principles, often referred to as "Lavrent'ev's triangle." The first was an emphasis on an interdisciplinary approach to fundamental research. Through the broad application of mathematics and cybernetics, scientific productivity would grow by means of healthy feedback among the various branches of the sciences. The second principle was the creation of strong ties between science and production—something always emphasized in the USSR, but in Akademgorodok it was to be achieved by the formation of industrial research institutes and design bureaus with close physical and scientific connections to the city, forming a so-called innovation beltway. The third principle involved new ways to identify and train young scientists. In an exception to the Soviet norm, research and teaching were to be joined together under one roof, in something akin to the university setting familiar in the United States and parts of Europe.

Beyond these basic principles, the administration of Akademgorodok was intended to be more decentralized, if not democratic, than the status quo in the USSR Academy of Sciences in Moscow. Lavrent'ev intended institute directors to talk freely and informally with each other and their staffs and made himself accessible. In reality, of course, administrative style differed from institute to institute. Some directors, such as the biologist D.K. Belieav, were imperious and diffident. But many, including the physicist Gersh Budker and Lavrent'ev himself, welcomed open discussion of issues scientific and social, and occasionally even those of art and politics.

It is important to keep in mind that although ideology and politics eventually came to obstruct the normal operation of Akademgorodok, they were crucial for getting it off the ground. The idea for the new community was first proposed by Mikhail Lavrent'ev while Stalin was still alive, but conditions became right for the endeavor only during de-Stalinization, by which time many leading scientists came to recognize the importance of "decentralizing" science from Moscow and Leningrad. At an open meeting of the Academy of Sciences in November 1957, when Lavrent'ev called for "the development of science in Siberia and the [Soviet] Far East," such leading scientists as Igor Kurchatov, head of the atomic bomb project; Nikolai Semenov, a Nobel Prize–winning chemist; Lev Artsimovich, the head of the fusion research program; and Petr Kapitsa, a low-temperature specialist and future Nobel Prize winner, urged unconditional support.[3]

Kapitsa, in particular, noting the heavy favoritism accorded to Muscovite scientists, petitioned his colleagues to avoid personal biases in the awarding of Lenin Prizes and in the elections to the posts of academician and corresponding member, editorial boards, and the VAK, or higher-degree attestation committee. He implored scientists to treat the Siberians with respect, "not as outcasts, but as beloved sons who are fulfilling a great undertaking," and concluded that "we must create the moral climate for scientists to move to Siberia."[4]

Akademgorodok also benefited from the view, more and more prevalent among Soviet officials, that modern science and technology were the keys to moving from socialism to Communism, and in surpassing the economic production of the capitalist world. Equally as important, Akademgorodok seemed to have a strategic component. The great human and material costs of the Nazi invasion and occupation underscored the importance of developing Siberian wealth far from Russia's European borders.[5] Such a strategy would, moreover, enable Akademgorodok to achieve a slogan promulgated back in the 1920s: "Science to the Provinces!" To become more than a slogan, though, forces of localism, openness, and freedom would have to counter those of centralization in the Soviet economic and political system.

Officials believed that Akademgorodok would reinvigorate science. The Soviet scientific enterprise had made remarkable strides since the revolution in the numbers of researchers, institutes, publications, and other quantitative indices of performance. During Khrushchev's rule, the rate of growth of each of these categories increased more rapidly. But from a qualitative perspective, Soviet science lagged. Whether by such indices as Nobel prizes and scientific citations, or by more subjective evaluations such as those offered by the Western peers of Soviet scholars, Soviet science did not fare as well. In many areas of biology, chemistry, the new field of computers, in fields both fundamental and applied, Soviet science had stumbled. What was more, the Soviet economy only grudgingly introduced the achievements of scientific research and development into the production process. The question was how best to wed the advantages of the Soviet system with the power of science to accelerate economic development, promote social welfare, and compete with capitalism. Scientists and officials alike believed that Akademgorodok, like the development of nuclear power, would serve as a symbol of the innate advantages of the Soviet social system.

Most important, Khrushchev himself personally endorsed the plan for a Siberian city of science. His triumph in the succession struggle following Stalin's death in 1953 was critical to the emergence of Akademgorodok. Khrushchev had come from a peasant family and made his career as a party boss in agriculturally rich Ukraine. Now, in addition to the modernization of Soviet agriculture, he would show himself to be a twentieth-century man whose visions extended beyond the farm to the city and laboratory.[6] Khrushchev had promoted nuclear power, recognizing its value both for Soviet economic and his own purposes. Sputnik, the first satellite sent into space, also became important to Khrushchev's career when he discovered that he could use the achievements of Soviet science and technology to solidify his position as party leader.[7]

Khrushchev took the lead in encouraging Russia's scientists to accelerate the pace of the construction of communism. Convinced that cities of science already existed in America; that they had secured its technological leadership; and that they were the epitome of scientific achievement, he supported the construction of a series of scientific cities around Moscow—the physics centers at Troitsk and Dubna, biology in Pushchino—ordering party, government, and economic organs to facilitate their realization. On Siberia's Akademgorodok, the Soviet leader placed a personal stamp of approval, twice visiting during its construction.

A Unique Scientific Center

Much of the hope for Akademgorodok lay in choosing the right mix of architecture and forest; of science, commerce, family, leisure, and nature. But here the reality of Soviet poverty intruded from the start. On 10 May 1957, after hearing Lavrent'ev's report on the proposed Siberian city of science, the Presidium of the Soviet Academy of Sciences ordered a committee under his direction consisting of the mathematician Sergei Sobolev, the physicist Lev Artsimovich, the geologist Andrei Trofimuk, and several other leading scientists to prepare a proposal for the Council of Ministers. It was submitted and approved only eight days later.[8] Within another week, Lavrent'ev returned to the Golden Valley, met with the organizational committee in a pine forest, and surrounded by fields of berries, fruits, and medicinal herbs and grasses, selected a site for Akademgorodok about two thousand meters from the shore of the Ob River reservoir, not far from the nearly complete Ob Hydroelectrical Power Station and near the rights-of-way for a soon-to-be-built commuter train and highways.

Within a month, the first ten institutes had been named, their directors selected, and scientists' internal visas authorized. By the end of the summer, all the governing and academic bodies had been appointed. The Siberian Division (*Sibirskoe otdelenie*) of Academy of the Sciences had come into existence—on paper. It received the right to publish a series of new, but as yet unestablished, journals and limited runs of mimeographed reports with minimal prepublication restrictions. As an indication of the importance of the division the USSR Academy designated Lavrent'ev one of the Academy's handful of vice presidents.

Akademgorodok's visionaries wanted to design institutes, apartments, luxury cottages, and other buildings in styles intended to encourage open communication among scientists and to preserve the beauty of the Golden Valley. Problems of material and equipment supply, however, as well as construction delays, poor labor discipline, cost overruns, and the vagaries of the Soviet planning system, combined with the harsh Siberian winter to impede the project at every step. Construction started somewhat later than anticipated, moved along slowly, rapidly depleted the budget, and essentially failed to attract the necessary equipment or manpower until the late 1960s.

A new construction trust, Sibakademstroi, until recently a "closed" organization involved in the construction of ICBM missile silos, was made responsible for the massive undertaking of building Akademgorodok. Of the more than five square miles initially allotted to Akademgorodok, about one-fifth was designated as built "greenery"—parks, gardens, and playgrounds—and apartment buildings. There were six microregions for the 43,000 residents, with between 84 and 110 square feet per resident, but only 40 to 60 square feet for student dormitory rooms (although there were 180 square feet, large by Soviet standards, for scientists). Each microregion had identical rudimentary shops ("Meat," "Milk," "Bakery"), dining halls, schools, and kindergartens. Institutes were built on another one-fifth or so of the land; the rest was preserved as forest and trails. The major book and department stores, the "Moscow" movie theater with 800 seats, and the scholars' club (begun in 1963) were located near the center, equally accessible to all. A university was built just to the northeast of town center. The proximity to natural resources and an industrial center, the siting in the midst of beautiful forests, and the use of modern architecture and city planning were intended to attract scientists from Moscow and Leningrad.[9]

The building of Akademgorodok required nearly superhuman effort, yet it was hampered at every step. The Novosibirsk regional economic organization (Sovnarkhoz) had to create a construction industry from scratch. Labor brigades materialized only slowly out of the taiga, and often they consisted of young, untested volunteers and conscripts. Supplies and equipment were shipped by trains that grew to be several kilometers long. When buildings were finished, the laboratories and institutes that would fill them, often still in Moscow or Leningrad, also had to be loaded onto trains for the journey to Siberia. In spite of support from all sides—party, scientific, and Sovnarkhoz organizations—the tasks proved to be daunting and were made more so by the bottlenecks and deficiencies endemic to the centralized Soviet economy. Severe problems also arose from the effort to force the pace of construction in the Siberian climate.

Khrushchev's personal interest had a varied impact on Akademgorodok. On 10 October 1959, on his way back to Moscow from China, the Soviet leader showed up to criticize the construction. Standing before a mock-up of the science city, Khrushchev dressed down Akademgorodok architects for the design of the twelve-story hotel, calling its height "unreasonable and uneconomical." "Don't you have any extra land out here?" he chided. "Why are you trying to imitate New York skyscrapers?" Four-story buildings were said to be cheaper, especially if they could be put together from the prefabricated concrete forms that were then the rage of the Soviet leader's apartment-construction campaign. Concluding his harangue, Khrushchev leaned forward and snipped away the top floors of the hotel, imitating scissors with his fingers. "That's what I think about this skyscraper."[10] The building came in at eight stories.

Fascinated in his own way with Taylorism, Americanism, and modern mass production techniques, Khrushchev demanded a general change from bricks to prefabricated forms, in keeping with what was called the "high culture" of construction. Accordingly, the largest factory in the USSR for the production of prefabricated reinforced concrete forms, the Novosibirsk Factory of Large Panel Apartment Construction, was to be built, producing enough slabs to build 280,000 square meters of living space annually (enough for 5,500 500-square-foot apartments—by 1961 the plan was cut to one-fifth of this target). The occasion of the first large panel being laid was a moment of great celebration, "Our Victory," the local newspaper *Akademstroevets* announced.[11]

Poor construction practices characteristic of the USSR as a whole were in evidence. Plans were rarely fulfilled on time, so researchers often had to remain under the wing of some laboratory in Moscow or Leningrad, move to poorly appointed furnishings in downtown Novosibirsk while waiting for building to commence or double or triple up in shared facilities, and then jockey to be given the next completed building. In 1958, only six miles of roads, forty miles of communications, and roughly 600 apartments were completed. Gosstroi, the state construction committee, roundly criticized Sibakademstroi and local party officials and construction organizations for the adherence to "non-industrial methods"[12]—manual labor by hand and shovel, rather than jackhammer and crane; bricks and mortar, in place of prefabricated concrete blocks. Plans, designs, and materials, meanwhile, originated in Soviet bureaucracies, thousands of miles away.

The result was meeting after meeting of Sibakademstroi employees to raise "construction culture" to a higher level. Workers were admonished, "Faster, Cheaper, Better!" and "Always Economize, Reserves Into Action!" Such exhortations fell short of producing the desired results. Part of the problem were the cottages built for the scientific elite, which the class-conscious workers resented, especially since they lived in barracks and their food was spartan and bland. But the workers got on with the task of building, some no doubt believing in the glory of their struggle, others simply worn out by the constant exhortation to achieve ever higher targets during construction carried out in frigid weather with inadequate equipment and supplies.

As machines took over all aspects of work, as excavators, cranes, and dump trucks, and the "furthest development of complex mechanization" became the rule, and as concrete blocks replaced bricks, problems of aesthetics came to rival those of quality. Periodic inspection commissions revealed numerous examples of the use of low-quality reinforced concrete. Poured concrete was often distorted and failed to meet clearances. Finishing work was poor. Spaces between panels caused them to freeze all the way through. To be fair, crews battled the harsh deep freezes of the Siberian winter, permafrost, and the mud and mosquitoes of the spring thaws and summer rains, and they were given equipment designed for less severe climates. In any case, eventually even the scientific research institutes had to be built by the "high culture" industrial methods, which affected their individuality (or lack thereof).[13]

Problems only multiplied. The celebration for the opening of the skating rink gave way to the realization that cracks and bumps destroyed the skates. As for the local beach on the banks of the Ob, built at a cost of two million rubles, a cyclone in October 1959 with winds gusting to ninety miles per hour destroyed much of the shoreline, forcing the substitution of an artificial beach as protection against future acts of nature.[14] Few apartments had both warm and cold water on a regular basis until the mid-1960s. Electric and gas service were subject to similar disruptions. Some apartment buildings leaked both from the roof and basement. Over thirty kinds of mushrooms were discovered to be growing in freshly painted hallways.[15]

For all this, Akademgorodok remained far more attractive than most postwar Soviet cities. Nature and city did coexist. A mixture of architectural styles provided a quaintness to the town, enhanced by the presence of parks, some with illuminated cross-country ski trails to permit skiing in the dark, long, cold continental Siberian climate with snow cover almost half the year. The designers succeeded in preserving green space. The Ob reservoir provided for boating and fishing. Children could play freely in parks right near their apartments; most inhabitants could walk to work. The crush and filth of Moscow and Leningrad were noticeably absent, making for an environment where good science could be and was practiced. Academician Andrei Ershov, a key figure in the history of Soviet computing, summed up the widely shared warm feelings for Akademgorodok in a 1983 poem celebrating "the path in Akademgorodok," along which he walked to work free of worries and enamored of "the living things/ Birds, squirrels, grass, trees/ . . . and the passerby encountered not by coincidence/ Who makes his way on this path of mine."[16]

Cadres Decide Everything!

From the point of view of staffing, things went much better. Akademgorodok attracted first-rate young minds in a variety of fields. At the moment of the creation of the Siberian Division, however, in all academic scientific institutions of Siberia and the Far East there were less than one thousand "scientists," of whom nearly five hundred had no academic degree, and no academicians or corresponding members of the Academy.[17] Most of the initial scientists, in other words, came from outside Siberia.

A pattern for staffing new research centers was established by the father of Soviet physics, Abram F. Ioffe. Beginning in the late 1920s and 1930s, Ioffe created "spin-offs" of his Leningrad Physical Technical Institute in Kharkov (the Ukrainian Physico-Technical Institute, a world leader in nuclear physics); in Sverdlovsk (the Siberian Physico-Technical Institute, important in the physics of metallurgy); and in Moscow (the Kurchatov Institute for Atomic Energy). For Akademgorodok, Lavrent'ev's Hydrodynamics Institute was first formed within the Moscow Physical Technical Institute with recent graduates and students from upper division courses before its transfer between 1958 and 1965 to Siberia. Gersh Budker's Institute of Nuclear Physics existed as a laboratory of high energy collisions within the Kurchatov Institute in Moscow until its move to Akademgorodok in 1961. The Institute of Automation and Electrometry was formed from laboratories of the Lvov Polytechnical Institute and Institute of Machine Building and Automation of the Ukrainian Academy of Sciences. Others were created from scratch in Novosibirsk, although their directors, often Moscow scholars, attracted other Muscovite colleagues to the newly established institutes.

Another path for staffing institutes in Akademgorodok was to encourage young scientists, many of whom had yet to finish their schooling, to join the utopian endeavor. In December 1957, the party's Central Committee gave Akademgorodok first choice of young scholars who had finished at the leading universities and institutes in recent years and instructed interested ministries to facilitate the transfer of established scholars.[18] In its early years, as many as two-thirds of the country's promising specialists declared an interest in moving to Akademgorodok.

To be sure, a number of scientific and ministerial organizations in Moscow and Leningrad objected to Akademgorodok's favored position. Some "categorically refused" to permit their students to leave for Siberia.[19] Many scientists in the center resented what they alleged was the awarding of honorific titles and positions as laboratory and institute directors on the basis of geography rather than merit. But in spite of this resentment, and a lag in dissertation defenses that persisted throughout its first decade, the staff of Akademgorodok grew quite rapidly in the early years, primarily by adding young scientists. The average age of scientists was lower than the country's average age of thirty-nine by five years, with almost 40 percent younger than thirty as of July 1, 1963.[20] Most important, the formative events in the lives of these scientists were the Khrushchev thaw and de-Stalinization. They shared hope for the future and the belief that societywide reform would be followed by the construction of communism within their lifetimes. Their predominance in institutes shaped the openness of scientific and political life in Akademgorodok.

Both established and younger scientists were motivated to move to Siberia for the freedom to do research away from scientists who dominated entire institutes and fields; the possibility of more rapid advancement to the honored titles of "academician" or "corresponding member" of the Academy; perhaps faster achievement of the doctor or candidate of science degrees; and the lure of larger apartments and marginally higher salaries. The mathematician Iurii G. Reshetniak jumped at the opportunity to move to Novosibirsk from Leningrad. His father, although a well-connected military man, commanded an apartment of only 86 square feet for a family of four. Reshetniak's wife, an astronomer, had access to larger quarters at the Pulkovo Observatory outside Leningrad (at nearly 200 square feet for a family of four, it seemed positively palatial). But in Akademgorodok Reshetniak received a two-room, 600-square-foot apartment. And when he became an academician, he received one of the spacious cottages in the Golden Valley.

In Siberia, an impressive group of scholars rapidly achieved the status of academician or corresponding member of the USSR Academy of Sciences. Lavrent'ev wrote Khrushchev personally with requests to authorize increased numbers of Siberian seats for membership in the Academy. In one such letter in 1961, he reminded Khrushchev how rapidly the Siberian Division had grown in terms of laboratories and institutions. Opening vacancies in the Academy, Lavrent'ev argued, would help overcome the poverty in personnel.[21] Through biannual elections in the 1960s the number of academicians and corresponding members swelled rapidly, especially in the physical and mathematical sciences.[22] By 1 May 1964, Akademgorodok maintained fifteen institutes, with 7,300 employees, including 2,200 scientists, of whom 14 were academicians, 31 corresponding members, 49 doctors of science, and 551 candidates of science. (As of 1991, there were 77 full and corresponding members of the Siberian Division of the Academy of Sciences, more than 450 doctors of science, and around 4,000 candidates of science, spread out among twenty-two institutes.[23])

Several innovations were introduced to increase the pool of future scientists. Knowing that Soviet universities and institutes were isolated by wide gulfs of ministerial jurisdiction and that teaching was divorced from the laboratory, Lavrent'ev encouraged a series of measures designed to reduce these divisions. Scientists in Akademgorodok set up a boarding school for junior high school children, the Physics-Mathematics School, which had a rigorous two-year curriculum.[24] Beginning in 1962, "olympiads" were used to identify talented young people throughout Siberia, provide them with first-rate instruction from academicians and professors, and channel them into the university. Novosibirsk State University, for its part, grew rapidly in size and reputation, becoming the third leading higher educational institution in the USSR. To this day, most of its graduates stay on in Akademgorodok to study and work at the Academy.[25]

In spite, or perhaps because of the novice staff, Akademgorodok thrived in its first decade. In fields as diverse as biology, sociology, physics, and computer science, researchers completed original studies that attracted an international audience. Paradoxically, it may have been the lag in construction and equipping institutes that facilitated great achievements, for researchers were required to focus on theoretical endeavors rather than experimental ones and were freed from the typical requirement to tie their work to the practical needs of the economy. Once Akademgorodok was established, however, and conservative Brezhnevite administrators began to insist that scientists adhere to Soviet ideological pronouncements, researchers began to abandon some of the novel approaches of earlier years. At the same time, the atmosphere of Akademgorodok also changed.

Brezhnevism and the Crisis in Akademgorodok

After a decade of academic freedom not seen since the 1920s, the Communist Party put an end to the golden years in the Golden Valley. The central apparatus in Moscow and its agents in Novosibirsk had grudgingly tolerated the vibrant, critical atmosphere in Akademgorodok. But from the first days, the party apparatus strived to place loyal members in the scientific, construction, and social organizations in Akademgorodok. In a way, it was inevitable that "socialist competitions," "socialist obligations," and other forms of ideological scrutiny would have an impact on scientific life.

Initially, the scientists had maintained a modicum of independence, for they had their own party committee. The existence of the Siberian Division "partkom," which was dominated by scientists, meant that the Novosibirsk provincial party organization (obkom) kept its distance. Indeed, the activities of the national, regional, and local party and economic organizations were concerned at first with facilitating the construction of Akademgorodok, not in establishing party control. But in 1965, the Siberian Division partkom was subordinated to the Novosibirsk obkom. And at about the same time, the central party apparatus grew impatient with the lag between scientific research in Akademgorodok and applications in regional industry and economy. The party mandated renewed emphasis on applied research at the expense of basic science programs. Most important, the central party apparatus grew increasingly conservative once Brezhnev replaced Khrushchev.

As part of a general clampdown on all sorts of literary, artistic, and political freedoms achieved during the de-Stalinization policies of the Khrushchev years, the party campaigned against the autonomy of the scientists. They required devotion to the ideological precepts of the Brezhnev era, including warnings against becoming "tainted" by Western scientific or philosophical thought. Especially after the Soviet invasion of Czechoslovakia in 1968, the party grew more vigilant against perceived ideological deviations, shutting down the social clubs that to the scientists had signified the freedoms characteristic of Akademgorodok.

Officials in the regional party apparatus followed changes in the policies and instructions sent from Moscow and introduced changes on the local level. Local officials had long envied the favor Lavrent'ev enjoyed at the top of the party, including his personal acquaintance with Khrushchev (which dated to the 1940s in Ukraine) and his admittance pass to the Kremlin, so important for enabling scientists to expedite orders, free up personnel, and take occasional procedural liberties. Apparatchiks also resented the scientists' unusual access to goods and services and their intellectual freedom. Actions spurred by these feelings, in conjunction with the redirection of research to topics with immediate economic impact, signified that the glory days of rapid construction, scientific achievement, and intellectual freedom had come to an end.

Whereas Khrushchev had shaken the party apparatus and undermined the authority of central party cadres to make economic policy, his replacement, Leonid Brezhnev, intended to re-establish the supremacy of the apparatus. Brezhnev called for "trust in (party) cadres," meaning reliance on the apparatus and "management techniques" imposed from above to ensure homogeneity in decision making. Brezhnev also called for the "perfection" of existing mechanisms rather than reform. Science and technology came to be seen not as areas of innovation and experimentation, but as instruments to achieve higher industrial production and military parity with the United States. The "bulldozer" science of river diversion, schemes for development around Lake Baikal, and the BAM (Baikal-Amur Mainline) were seen as more important than fundamental research. All of these changes took their toll upon Academy science, and on Akademgorodok in particular.

One could argue that Akademgorodok had, by Soviet standards, managed to avoid kowtowing to central authority in Moscow, but the consequences of policy shifts under Brezhnev were fast in coming. Basic science lost its esteemed status, and as an adjunct to "trust in cadres" the party apparatus exerted more control over Akademgorodok life through the incorporation of the Siberian Division partkom into the local party apparatus and the subordinated party organizations in each research institute. The latter exercised authority over the conduct of research, the hiring and firing of individuals, and the political and philosophical discussions that took place in the institutes.

Furthermore, there was a direct effort to end Akademgorodok's special status. As symbols of the Khrushchev years, of the thaw, of academic freedom, and of free thought on a wide variety of subjects, Akademgorodok's institutes had virtually open doors; few paid attention to the standard identification cards required to gain entry. Leading personnel made themselves accessible. Most colleagues were on a first-name basis. There was even a close relationship between students and academicians, since the latter taught willingly in the university and boarding school. But this, too, gave way to the more formal styles of Iurii Marchuk and later, Valentin Koptiug, a chemist (and reactionary). For these men, the city of science was seen as too international, if not in terms of personal acquaintances then often in terms of world outlook. The existence of hierarchy in Akademgorodok, which up to this time was not crucial to its political, cultural, and scientific life, became the basis of management style, just as elsewhere in the USSR.

Akademgorodok was well known for its informality and its sometimes open satires on Soviet life. The Scholars' Club held exhibitions of the works of such painters as Pavel N. Filonov, and there was even talk of showing some Chagalls. At the social clubs—"Under the Integral" and "Grenada"—the scientists played cards, drank, and sang into the wee hours. There were rumors of prostitutes. For the gerontocrats who ran the USSR, whose formative years occurred during the Stalin period, Akademgorodok was too young, both in terms of age and in its great faith in the de-Stalinization thaw. In a word, Akademgorodok represented generational, ideological, stylistic, and academic freedoms that were anathema to the conservative leadership of the Brezhnev regime.

Academic, cultural, and political freedom in the Siberian oasis ended in 1968 as the result of three events: open protest over the show trial for "anti-Soviet activity" of the writers Siniavskii and Daniel, who called for an amnesty for all political prisoners and abolition of the death penalty; the appearance of singing bards whose lyrics challenged Communist Party dogma; and the Soviet invasion of Czechoslovakia.

In March 1968, after Aleksandr Ginzburg and Iuri Galanskov sent the transcripts from the trial of Siniavskii and Daniel to England for publication and were themselves arrested as a result, forty-six Akademgorodok scientists, teachers, and students signed a letter of protest. What was most troubling to the authorities was the fact that a large number of young people had signed the letter, the party's efforts at political education notwithstanding. On 27 March, the letter of the forty-six was broadcast over Voice of America and then published in the *New York Times*. The publication abroad seems also certainly to have been the KGB's doing, giving the authorities a pretext for clamping down on Akademgorodok. The Novosibirsk obkom secretary, V.P. Mozhin, and the directors of the institutes were given instructions to hold meetings to discuss the signatories' treason and mete out punishment.

At the "Under the Integral" and "Grenada" social clubs, "unprincipled ideological behavior, pursuits of pleasure, and now and again amorality" were said to be in evidence. Examples cited included beauty contests, where scientists took and advertised the measurements of young ladies, and the presence of prostitutes, as well as intemperate political discussions and seditious songs, whose lyrics were typed and disseminated. Even the Komsomol and the Council of Young Scholars were said to be filled with "politically unhealthy" elements. "To raise the level of Communist conviction, feelings of Soviet patriotism, and proletarian internationalism," the raikom in Akademgorodok instructed institute directors and party officials to be more careful in hiring employees and to pay more attention to instilling class and party consciousness in science. The rector and party secretary of the university were ordered to replace teachers in the humanities departments and boarding school, where so many of the signatories had worked.[26] There was even talk of transferring the entire humanities department of the university—long "considered the main breeding ground for sedition"—to isolated and closed Krasnoiarsk, although the party stopped short of this action.[27]

Each Akademgorodok institute held a meeting in concert with the raikom's instructions. The meetings were usually closed to all but party members and leading scientists. The physicists and economists tried to keep matters from getting out of hand, that is, from giving party officials any reason for significant crackdowns. They approved censure of the signatories but avoided dismissal of employees. At the Institute of Cytology and Genetics, however, there was an uproar, owing to the presence there of Raisa Berg, a respected scientist and open-mouthed critic of the regime and the ghost of Lysenko. The last thing geneticists wanted was renewed political interference only three years after the official rebirth of their field, and they responded with particular venom. Berg eventually had to leave Akademgorodok.[28]

At the Scholars' Club, Makarenko, director of the art gallery, had organized shows of Falk, Neizvestny, Chemiakin, and the Spaniard Goya. In earlier years, a raikom commission would come and look at the paintings, their hair would stand on end, and the matter would blow over. But when Pavel Filonov's paintings were hung in May 1968, the exhibit was closed by the obkom before most people got a chance to see it. When Makarenko decided to respond with an exhibition of Chagall, the authorities arranged for two photographs to be stolen from the club, then sent in local party bigwigs and police. Makarenko threatened to send a telegram to the Minister of Culture, and within an hour the police found the stolen photographs (Makarenko had taken the precaution of putting the real ones in the safe). Within two weeks, however, Makarenko was removed as director and moved to Moscow. Shortly thereafter, he was arrested for speculation in icons and other artistic treasures and received an eight-year prison term.[29] He died in emigration.

The festival of the bards was bolder still. Folk singers had passed through Akademgorodok on many occasions. Now it seemed as if they were holding annual pilgrimages. Galich arrived in May 1968 with more than two dozen others. The letter of the forty-six had already been sent and punishment meted out, yet the festival went on. It was nearly impossible to get tickets. People waited for hours to hear Galich sing his well-known "Ballad on Surplus Value," "Clouds," and "Ode to Pasternak," the last referring to the announcement of the great author's death—not by the prestigious Union of Writers to which he belonged, but by the Literary Fund (Litfund), a second-class official organization of writers, since Pasternak had been expelled from the Union after winning the Nobel Prize in literature in 1958. Galich's performance in the Scholars' Club received a standing ovation. He was escorted back to the hotel after a banquet around midnight, but the students from the university and the physics-mathematics boarding school got word and insisted upon hearing him perform as well. He obliged, giving another show at 2:00 A.M. in the movie theater.[30]

The Prague Spring had the greatest impact on Akademgorodok, but the invasion of Czechoslovakia revealed just how intolerant the Brezhnev regime had become. There was protest throughout the USSR that frightened the KGB into action. This included the campaign to end academic freedom in Akademgorodok. Galich responded to the invasion with a poem that included the lines, "Citizens, the Fatherland is in danger. Our tanks are on alien soil!" This provoked a number of Akademgorodok young people to put up banners and slogans throughout Akademgorodok: "Freedom for Socialist Czechoslovakia!" and "Invaders, Hands Off Czechoslovakia." The authors were hunted down but never identified.

The "Under the Integral" social club opened again a few times when Western scientists came to Akademgorodok for conferences. In August 1968, for example, at the Third International Congress on Plasma Physics, the club hosted some Western scientists. But as soon as the conference was over, the authorities closed it again. In any event, the social clubs now lacked the spontaneity and ambience of the earlier years. In their place, Marchuk directed scientists to create a plan developing social services and cultural organizations, a move that further contributed to the stultification of the cultural life in Akademgorodok.[31] In was becoming ever more difficult to attract talented young scientists to Siberia. And for the older residents, now that the social clubs were closed, the intense intellectual excitement that carried them through the first hard years gave way to a feeling that Akademgorodok was no different from the rest of Russia.

Conclusions

Some observers believe that the decline of the city of science from its vibrant founding years was the natural result of aging. Akademgorodok leaders were no longer able to attract the best young people to Siberia. Housing starts lagged. Under Marchuk and Koptiug, leadership and administration had become conservative. Formal channels had to be followed. Then there was the natural aging of the infrastructure. The town was becoming run-down; budgets provided far more for new construction than for repair. The creative impulse that Lavrent'ev gave to Siberian science had run its course. Scientists no longer felt the need to relocate to Siberia to develop new research programs. Colliding beam accelerators, genetics, and mathematical models had become standard fare. And maybe the scientists had gotten fat since they knew their funding was fairly stable, if too low, year after year.

But was it only a matter of aging? I think not. Party controls were crucial in changing the face of scientific and social life in Akademgorodok. Scientists were able to ignore many of them. Discussions about foreign policy or the recent directives of the Central Committee rarely had a direct impact on research. Methodological seminars had lost the vigilance of the Stalin years. Scientists had sufficient autonomy to select research topics within the constraints of finance and manpower. Yet ideological controls were insidious. The party apparatus had grown enormously, with representatives in every research group and laboratory, the "eyes and ears" of conformity with central directives. Moscow required that Akademgorodok science reflect Soviet norms of practice, collectivism, and conformity. Faceless bureaucrats "administered" science; before they had "supported" its development. Akademgorodok had grown out of a Russian tradition of excellence in fundamental research. Now accountability to state development programs was the rule.

In spite of the organizational, political, and ideological impediments to its creation, Akademgorodok had thrived by Soviet standards. The farsightedness of its organizers; its geographical, political, and ideological distance from Moscow; its centrality to Soviet postwar economic development programs; and its creation during the height of the Khrushchev thaw helped create an atmosphere of freedom and independence conducive to scientific research. In a number of fields, from high energy physics to economics and sociology, this fostered alternative ways of thinking. These alternative views were important both with respect to those regions of science themselves and with regard to undercurrents of criticism concerning how the Soviet Union had evolved and where it was going. An increasingly well-educated Soviet "middle class" began to question fundamental assumptions about Soviet politics and society. Ultimately, this element in Akademgorodok contributed actively to Mikhail Gorbachev's policy of perestroika.

The political and economic crises enveloping Russia today notwithstanding, Akademgorodok remains a center of scientific excellence with future promise. If centralization ultimately damaged the scientific and social life of Akademgorodok, then decentralization may provide a key to future accomplishment. Market forces will enable researchers to pursue new ventures in biotechnology, computers, and other specialties to establish independent firms whose excellence and novelty result from competition with traditional centers of research. In addition, since Russian government funding for science has been cut substantially or eroded by rampant inflation, the big science projects of the Soviet past may give way to more efficient, productive, and cheaper small science. In this environment, distinctly Siberian science stands a chance to prosper in the way Akademgorodok's founders envisaged.

Notes

I would like to thank the International Research and Exchanges Board, the National Endowment for the Humanities, the National Council for Soviet and East European Research, and the Fulbright-Hays Programs for supporting research important to this chapter.

1. Mikhail A. Lavrent'ev, "Tak nachinalsia Akademgorodok ... " *Komsomol'skaia pravda,* 14 May 1977, p. 4.

2. Sir Francis Bacon, *Essays and New Atlantis,* ed. Gordon S. Haight (Toronto: D. Van Nostrand, 1942), p. 288.

3. L.A. Artsimovich, "Sibirskii nauchnyi tsentr budet odnim iz krupneishikh nauchykh tsentrov strany," *Tekhnika-molodezhi,* 1958, no. 2, p. 3; "Novyi nauchnyi tsentr v Sibiri," *Pravda,* 3 November 1957, p. 2; and *Khronika. 1957–1982 gg. Akademiia Nauk SSSR. Sibirskoe otdelenie,* ed. V.L. Makarov (Novosibirsk, 1982), pp. 14–18.

4. P.L. Kapitsa, "Osnovnuiu stavku delat' na molodezh'," *Tekhnika-molodezhi,* 1958, no. 2, pp. 2–3.

5. On the prehistory and formation of Akademgorodok, see E.T. Artemov, *Formirovanie i razvitie seti nauchnykh uchrezhdenii AN SSSR v Sibiri, 1944–1980 gg.* (Novosibirsk, 1990). See also Z. Ibragimova and N. Pritvits, *"Treugol'nik" Lavrent'eva* (Moscow, 1989), pp. 9–24.

6. See N.S. Khrushchev, *Khrushchev Remembers,* trans. Strobe Talbott (Boston: Lit-

tle, Brown, 1974), pp. 58–71, for a discussion of Khrushchev's relationship with the scientific intelligentsia.

7. On space culture, see Paul Josephson, "Rockets, Reactors and Soviet Culture," in Loren Graham, ed., *Science and the Soviet Social Order* (Cambridge, MA: Harvard University Press, 1990), pp. 168–91.

8. Ibragimova and Pritvits, *"Treugol'nik" Lavrent'eva*, pp. 24–25.

9. A.M. Veksman et al., *Stroitel'stvo goroda nauki* (Novosibirsk, 1963), pp. 9–13.

10. "N.S. Khrushchev v gostiakh u Akademstroevtsev," *Akademstroevets*, no. 77 (99), 13 October 1959, p. 1.

11. Veksman, *Stroitel'stvo*, p. 14; I. Ivanov and A. Veksman, "Akademiia sibirskikh stroitelei," *Izvestiia*, 12 September 1963, p. 3; I. Pribytko, "Otsenka: khorosho!" *Akademstroevets*, no. 86 (108), 17 November 1959, p. 1; and "Svershilos'!" ibid., no. 2 (233), 6 January 1961, p. 1.

12. Nauchnyi arkhiv Sibirskogo otdeleniia AN SSSR (hereafter NASO), f. 10, op. 3, d. 157, l. 3.

13. "Za vysokuiu stroitel'nuiu kul'tury!" *Akademstroevets*, no. 20 (42), 13 March 1959, p. 1; C. Glushchenko, "Za dal'neishee sovershenstvovanie upravleniia stroitel'stvom," ibid., no. 21 (140), 15 March 1960, p. 2; A. Leskov, "Zadachi stroitel'noi industrii," ibid., no. 16 (237), 24 February 1961, p. 2; M. Chemodanov, "Postanovlenie . . . o ser'eznykh nedostatkakh i o merakh po uluchsheniiu ekspluatatsii zhilishchno-kommunal'nogo fonda nauchnogo gorodka," ibid., no. 17 (238), 28 February 1961, p. 2; N. Ivanov, "Po puti industrializatsii," ibid., no. 61 (282), 4 August 1961, p. 2; and *Za nauku v Sibiri*, no. 13 (38), 27 March 1962, p. 3.

14. NASO, f. 10, op. 3, d. 241, ll. 20–22, 50–57, and ibid., d. 157, ll. 84–86; Partiinyi arkhiv Novosibirskoi oblasti (hereafter PANO), f. 384, op. 1, d. 2, l. 21; A. Kulikov, "Gorod bol'shoi nauki," *Sibirskie ogni*, 1958, no. 3, pp. 163–64; *Za nauku v Sibiri*, no. 8 (85), 21 February 1963, p. 4; ibid., no. 13 (90), 28 March 1963, p. 4; and no. 28 (53), 11 July 1962, p. 3.

15. *Za nauku v Sibiri*, no. 32 (57), 8 August 1962, p. 3; no. 11 (36), 13 March 1962, pp. 2–3; no. 15 (92), 11 April 1963, p. 1; no. 38 (63), 19 September 1962, p. 4; and no. 28 (105), 22 July 1963, p. 4. See also M. Nozdrenko, "Domovye griby," *Za nauku v Sibiri*, no. 17 (94), 28 April 1963, p. 4.

16. A.P. Ershov, *Stikhi* (Akademgorodok, 1991), p. 28.

17. PANO, f. 10, op. 4, d. 849, l. 1.

18. NASO, f. 4, op. 1, d. 7, l. 6; and *Khronika AN SSSR SO*, p. 20.

19. *Za nauku v Sibiri*, no. 41 (118), 21 October 1963, p. 3.

20. A successful defense was the cause for great pride, as the front-page photograph of the young Roald Sagdeev, a specialist in plasma physics, in *Za nauku v Sibiri* attests. See *Za nauku v Sibiri*, no. 34 (59), 22 August 1962, p. 1. See also *Za nauku v Sibiri*, no. 20 (45), 16 May 1962, p. 1; and N.A. Dediushina and A.I. Shcherbakov, "O formirovanii nauchnykh kadrov sibirskogo otdeleniia AN SSSR," in *Voprosy istorii nauki i professional'nogo obrazovaniia v Sibiri*, vol. 1, ed. A.P. Okladnikov (Novosibirsk, 1968), p. 236.

21. NASO, f. 10, op. 1, d. 84, ll. 1–4.

22. These included the mathematicians A.D. Aleksandrov and L.V. Kantorovich; the physicists G.I. Budker, Spartak Beliaev, Roald Sagdeev, V.A. Sidorov, and A.N. Skrinskii; the biologist Dmitrii Beliaev; the economist Abel Aganbegian; the sociologist Tatiana Zaslavskaia; the mathematics-computer specialists Andrei Ershov and Gurii Marchuk; and others.

23. NASO, f. 10, op. 4, d. 849, ll. 52–53; G.S. Migirenko, ed., *Novosibirskii nauchnyi tsentr* (Novosibirsk, 1962), pp. 197–202; *Khronika AN SSSR SO*, pp. 76, 92–93, 114–15, 135; and Dediushina and Shcherbakov, "O formirovanii," pp. 232–35.

24. In 1963–64, 93 students completed this program, of whom 12 were girls. In all, by 1965 there were over 600 students in residence in three grades (11 percent were girls). See *Nauka i prosveshchenie* (Novosibirsk, 1965), pp. 10–19; and Dediushina and Shcherbakov, "O formirovanii," p. 242.

25. On the founding of Novosibirsk State University, see M. Lavrent'ev and S. Khristianovich, "Vazhnoe uslovie razvitiia nauki," *Pravda*, 2 April 1957, p. 3; N.I. Vekua, "Universitet novogo tipa," *Pravda*, 19 June 1959, p. 2; S. Zalygin, "Novosibirsk gosudarstvennyi," *Izvestiia*, 4 September 1959, p. 2; Vladimir Vinogradov, "Sibirskii tsentr nauki," *Sibirskie ogni*, 1967, no. 5, p. 128; *Za nauku v Sibiri*, no. 21, 28 November 1961, p. 3; ibid., no. 49 (74), 3 December 1962, p. 3; and I.A. Moletotov, "Problema kadrov sibirskogo nauchnogo tsentra i ee reshenie (1957–1964 gg.)," in B.M. Shchereshevskii, ed., *Voprosy istorii Sovetskoi Sibiri* (Novosibirsk, 1967), p. 342.

26. PANO, f. 269, op. 7, d. 9, ll. 134–38.

27. Raisa Berg, *Acquired Traits,* trans. David Lowe (New York: Viking, 1988), p. 382.

28. PANO, f. 5434, op. 1, d. 8, ll. 6–13, 27; and Berg, pp. 457, 459–62, 467.

29. Interview with artificial intelligence specialist A.S. Narin'iani (Akademgorodok, 14 December 1991).

30. For the lyrics to "Ode to Pasternak," see Aleksandr Galich, *General'naia repetitsiia* (Moscow, 1991), pp. 57–59. Galich himself was expelled from the writers' union in December 1971 for anti-Soviet activity. He emigrated in the summer of 1974 and died three years later.

31. PANO, f. 269, op. 12, d. 27, ll. 30–32.

Village Prose Writers
and the Question of
Siberian Cultural Identity

Kathleen Parthé

Siberian writers, settings, themes, and regional identity were the driving forces behind Russian Village Prose (*derevenskaia proza*), the largest and most coherent body of ideologically and aesthetically significant literature published in the Soviet Union during the three decades between Stalin's death and the beginning of glasnost. Village Prose is often simply identified as a fiercely patriotic and aggressively provincial literature from and about Siberia. Although this definition both misses and exaggerates a great deal, it does reflect something of the essence of derevenskaia proza, where it came from in the thaw period, and what it evolved into after 1985.

Village Prose offers an insider's view of village life from the 1920s through the Brezhnev era. Its voices are lyrical, historical, and at least potentially ideological, as writers contemplate the past with a mixture of nostalgia and pain, the present with confusion, and the future with anxiety. The core properties of Village Prose include: an emphasis on a specific *rodnaia derevnia* (native village); a rural childhood; the peasant home; nature, whose rules the peasant must accept and whose riches he must protect for succeeding generations; memory; a sense of time in which the cyclical is suffused with a sense of impending loss; and the rich linguistic resources of peasant Russia that are seen as a *lesnaia gramota* (forest literacy) specific to each village and region. The colorful names of villages tell something of the history of each settlement, provide continuity with the pre–collective farm (kolkhoz) past, and contribute to a sense of local and national identity. The names of villages that no longer exist are used as one indication of the linguistic and spiritual wealth of the past and are contrasted to kolkhoz names such as "The Path to Socialism" and "The First of May," which demonstrate to the *derevenshchiki* (Village Prose writers) the bombast and spiritual poverty of the Soviet period. In Valentin Rasputin's "Downstream" (1972), the writer-hero realizes as he travels along the Angara River to his native realm that the islands like Khlebnik and Berezovik he knew as a boy are gone forever. "There are no more islands, and their names . . . are receding into the distance from which they are not fated to return."[1] Village Prose used the loss of colorfully named villages and the weakening of regional linguistic variation (because of radio and television) to approach—during the years of stagnation—questions that had a deep cultural, spiritual, and political resonance. The core properties of Village Prose make a contrast at almost every point to those of the kolkhoz novel; indeed, contrast is an important structural principle for both types of rural literature: old/new, endings/beginnings, old age/youth, submitting to nature/ruling nature, preservation/destruction, local/national, spiritual/material, continuity/revolution, past/present, and hand/machine.[2]

What is most relevant to the theme of Siberian identity in Village Prose are this literary movement's exhaustively documented claims that a richly layered, traditional Russian life existed in a microcosm in each village, and that the farther one travels from Moscow the more one can see that the roots of village Russia have not been entirely destroyed even by collectivization and postwar abandonment of *besperspektivnye derevni* (villages with no future). Writers believed that there remained a chance to form a Russian state that would protect and preserve the Russian people, their land, their culture, and their proud history. Village Prose was not born of the cultural-ideological myth of Siberia, but it fed off and in turn strengthened that myth and the much broader and more significant myth of a "Russianness" (i.e., a strong, unadulterated Russian identity) whose continued existence is guaranteed by Siberia.

There were at least three distinct cultural-political images of Siberia by the mid-1950s. It had for centuries been a place of exploration and development, a manifestation of the power of a growing state, an image that socialist-realist writers used to full advantage. Siberia was also a place to temper—if not extinguish—the rebellious instincts of many of those who questioned the expanding center. It was the temporary residence of Avvakum and Dostoevsky as well as the Decembrists and Chernyshevsky, in other words, of people all along the ideological spectrum. People fled to Siberia not only from oppression but also from innovation. What filtered through a number of prerevolutionary narratives of journeys eastward was that Siberia was a land not only of suffering but also of *priroda* (nature), *prostor* (a great expanse), and *volia* (a sense of personal—as opposed to civic—freedom), a place of healing and renewal. The epilogue to *Crime and Punishment* begins with the word "Siberia"; it is there that Raskolnikov experiences intimations of a New Jerusalem, a spiritual, if not physical, utopia, where his role model will no longer be Napoleon, but Lazarus. The final entry of Dostoevsky's *Diary of a Writer* (January 1881) suggests that Asian Russia may be the place where the old European Russia will be restored and resurrected.

These images of Siberia formed part of the background against which Village

Prose writers worked. At the same time, socialist-realist sagas of the conquest of virgin land and politicized family epics (Georgii Markov) were still being written and published. More importantly, prison memoirs based in Siberia and other areas of Russia began to surface in the wake of Solzhenitsyn's *One Day in the Life of Ivan Denisovich,* some of them in officially sanctioned publications, many others in samizdat and tamizdat, including Andrei Amalrik's caustic *Involuntary Journey to Siberia.* And, while the theme of "suffering" is as important to Village Prose as it has been to many other literary movements throughout Russian history, the derevenshchiki and other conservative nationalists did not fully embrace the Stalinist and post-Stalinist prison narratives. They have made clear distinctions between those who suffered *for* Russia (e.g., practicing Christians and monarchists) and those who suffered because of the harm they tried to do *to* the great Russian state (e.g., avant-garde writers, Jewish activists, urban intellectuals).

The appearance of Anatolii Rybakov's novel *Deti Arbata* (*Children of the Arbat,* 1987) and Vasilii Grossman's epic *Zhizn' i sud'ba* (*Life and Fate,* 1988) and novella *Vse techet* (*Forever Flowing,* 1989) greatly angered Siberian writers. Grossman was accused of attacking Russians and their history as a whole; his offenses were compared to those of Andrei Siniavskii, whose *Progulki s Pushkinym* (*Strolls with Pushkin,* 1989) was seen as deeply and deliberately Russophobic. Rybakov's work, which focused on the tribulations of what conservatives call a narrow group or caste—the well-fed children of the urban and party elite, many of whom were Jewish—was read specifically as an insult to Siberians.

> There is a reason why the novel's Siberian pages are being read as a direct attack on Siberia and Siberians, as Valentin Rasputin has stated very clearly. After all, we live in the region that has been described as "hell," and yet we are even proud to be called Siberians. Why then is life here such a punishment for the "children of the Arbat"?! . . . Russia's real children do not recognize the "children of the Arbat" as their contemporaries or fellow countrymen.[3]

The "children of Russia" are pitted against the "children of the Arbat" when they both try to occupy the same Siberian chronotope (i.e., combined time and space). When the former suffer, they do so without denouncing their homeland; the latter are accused of causing most of Russia's suffering, and sometimes they get their "just deserts." Siberian patriots have resisted the efforts of urban writers to turn their *rodina* (homeland) into nothing more than a gulag; they seek to restore an image badly tarnished by the seemingly endless reams of *lagernaia proza* (prison-camp literature).

If Village Prose includes more than literature about Siberia, Siberian literature since the early 1950s has boasted of more than just a rural branch. There are, in addition: Vladimir Chivilikhin's historical novels; Viktor Astaf'ev's environmental prose; Valentin Rasputin's ethnographic essays, some entertaining detective stories by Vil Lipatov, Boris Mozhaev, and Mikhail Chernenok; stories set in provincial cities and settlements by Astaf´ev and Rasputin, plays by Aleksandr Vampilov, Leonid Borodin's Christian prose; and dreadful and long-winded poetry from Yevtushenko about the Bratsk hydroelectric project and some of his less dreadful lyrical essays.

Although Siberian writers from the post-Stalinist to the post-Soviet years can be found mostly in the nationalist camp, their ideological profiles include extreme, conservative, moderate, and liberal forms of regional and national identity and range from those who are comfortable with the alliance between far-right nationalism and old-guard Communism to the most internationally minded and democratic of Siberians. And ideological positions can, of course, evolve. Viktor Astaf´ev, for instance, was seen as one of the most chauvinistic of Siberian writers in 1986–87 because of his exchange of letters with the literary scholar Natan Eidelman and several stories of the same period. By the early 1990s, Astaf'ev had retreated to his native Krasnoiarsk to write, having firmly rejected the campaign to "cleanse" Russian literature of "aliens" by saying that as much as he disliked the work of Aksenov, Voinovich, and a number of other writers (who all happen to be at least partly Jewish), there was only one Russian canon and nothing would—or should—change that. The 6 October 1993 issue of *Literaturnaia gazeta* carried a letter that Astaf´ev dictated from Siberia, in which he stated his support for the suppression of the Russian parliament and his abhorrence—as a patriot and disabled veteran—of any coalition between Russian nationalists, Communists, and fascists. Other Siberian writers reacted to the October 1993 crisis differently, Rasputin with a virtual silence, and Yevtushenko with the promise of a poem.

Village Prose came from primarily three areas: Central Russia (Vladimir, Orel, Ryazan), the North (Vologda, Arkhangelsk), and Siberia (Irkutsk, Krasnoiarsk, Altai). During the first decade after Stalin's death, the new rural *ocherki* (essays on the borderline between journalism and literature) and stories came mostly from central and northern Russia. The Siberian contribution to this literary movement became significant only in the mid-1960s, but it grew in importance with each new work of Sergei Zalygin, Viktor Astaf´ev, Vasilii Shukshin, Valentin Rasputin, and other Siberians. Writers from Siberia and northern Russia saw their areas as sharing many similar qualities, attitudes, and concerns: the sense of remoteness (from Europe and European Russia, constituting a non-European Russia), ruggedness, conservatism, the respect for religious dissent (especially Old Believers), the belief that their culture was popular and patriotic as opposed to the culture of the urban elite, and an anxious pride in their pristine and yet endangered natural surroundings. They also shared a sense of living in a place of expulsion or escape from the center, of being at the empire's frontier, which serves as a last refuge of the essential, undiluted Russianness irrevocably weakened in the capitals by a long series of "cosmopolitan" Western influences from Peter the Great to the post-modernists. Because of this natural affinity and because so many talented and productive rural writers came from these two regions (Abramov, Belov, Rubtsov, Tendriakov, Yashin, Kazakov—one generation removed—Lichutin, and Krupin are from the North; Soloukhin is from the center, and Mozhaev is from the center but has lived in and written about a number of regions), the combined Siberian-northern voice dominated rural prose from the mid-1960s to the late 1970s, when this movement was at its height. The two most important provincial centers for the derevenshchiki were the Siberian city of Irkutsk and the northern city of Vologda, which was attractive to rural writers from all over because of its relatively rich native cultural tradition as well as its proximity to the literary life in Moscow.

Siberia has a distinctive presence in literature but also claims to represent the whole of Russia (as New Englanders, Southerners, or Midwesterners might combine a strong regional patriotism with a claim to be the "real Americans"). And it is Siberia that figures most prominently in the *russkost'* (Russianness) debate of the early 1990s. Siberian writers, backed up by the northern literary contingent and like-minded writers and critics in Moscow and Petersburg have launched a serious "Russification" campaign to intensify the national content of Russian literature by artificial means, by exclusion as much as inclusion.[4]

One aspect of the search for a stable national-cultural identity—for "native soil"—in Russia today is the attempt to distinguish genuine *russkie pisateli* (ethnically Russian writers) from those who are merely *russkoiazychnye* (Russian-language writers, mostly Russian Jews), or—even worse—from the *lzhe-russkie pisateli* (literally, false/pseudo-Russian writers, i.e., ethnic Russians like Yevtushenko who have betrayed the Russian cause).[5] On the pages of such publications as *Den'* (and its successor *Zavtra*), *Moskovskii literator, Sovetskaia Rossiia, Nash sovremennik,* and *Molodaia gvardiia,* writers and critics have drawn up specific criteria for the model Russian writer. They have also elaborated theories about the deaths of famous literary figures such as Pushkin, Lermontov, Gumilev, Blok, Esenin, and Mayakovsky, transforming these writers into symbols of the Russian nation whose martyrdom at the hands of *chuzhie* (aliens) has earned them the status of saints who can intercede with God on Russia's behalf. Siberian writers have gone beyond the idea of an informal saintly status and have proposed that Fedor Dostoevsky, whose chauvinistic *Diary of a Writer* has become one of their sacred texts, be seriously considered for formal canonization. A crucial element of the Dostoevsky myth is that—like Raskolnikov—he was healed from his Western "sickness" by a long stay in Siberia, taking on, as it were, a true Russian (i.e., Siberian) identity.

The nationalists envision their model writer as ethnically Russian, at least nominally Orthodox, inflexibly righteous, politically conservative—favoring a strong national state and strong military—nostalgic for the empire, loyal to his orthodox Slavic brothers but wary of foreigners in general, and a proud archaist who in his art adheres to the best traditions of Russian civic and moral realism. The model *literator* (literary figure) is based in part on the strongly articulated self-image of the derevenshchiki who saw themselves as witnesses, chroniclers, Old Believers, and the righteous sons of dying mothers. While the Russification campaign in the literary world draws on some very old Russian myths—like the writer as a *pravednik* (righteous person) and the literary text as a *podvig* (glorious, heroic deed)—the tone of the recent discussion is much more aggressive than in times past, matching the strident rhetorical style of far-right nationalist writing on politics. The nationalist right wants to control what it still feels to be an important ideological tool, to be the imperial bards of a Russia that once again classifies its writers as pro- or anti-state and rewards or punishes them accordingly. With no sense of irony, Stanislav Kunaev published a poem in the March 1993 (20) issue of *Den'* that begins with the exclamation "Oh empire! I am your bard!"

This *russkost'* movement has the express purpose of combating "Russophobia" and "cultural genocide" and thereby saving what they call an "occupied" culture by a reverse *cordon sanitaire.* The "real" Russia must draw its borders precisely and then withdraw to the interior to restore the Russian Empire and the Russian soul. What could only be broadly suggested in published work from the mid-fifties to the mid-eighties has been openly discussed since 1985.[6]

There have been numerous responses from Russian writers and critics who find this cultural-ideological agenda offensive, ludicrous, and potentially dangerous. The roots of this agenda in the chauvinism allowed to surface in such periodicals as *Molodaia gvardiia* in the late 1960s stimulated a response—with a Siberian angle—by Feliks Roziner (who now lives in emigration). In his novel *Nekto Finkel'maier* (*A Certain Finkelmeyer*), his unmistakably Jewish hero is a gifted poet who works for the Ministry of Fisheries because anti-Semitism prevents him from advancing in the literary world. When he hears that editors are looking for poetry from the indigenous Siberian population, he comes up with the idea of publishing his work as a "translation" from Tongor, the language of an obscure and rapidly dwindling tribe. He uses as his cover the name of a hunter whom he heard singing a drunken, mournful song in the Siberian night. Although much of the novel is comic in tone, eventually Finkelmeyer is destroyed by Sergei Prebylov, a Russian nationalist poet whose mediocre verse praises out-of-the-way villages and denounces the "rot of the Arbat mold"; when sent into exile, the hapless Finkelmeyer is killed by his Siberian alter ego.[7]

When the newspaper *Den'* proposed that the Russian capital be moved from Moscow to Siberia (Omsk), it was emphasizing the perception on the nationalist right that the center of Russia has been moving steadily eastward, from the *pra-pra-rodina* (ancient homeland) in Kievan Rus' to the *pra-rodina* (homeland) in Muscovy to the Siberian taiga. According to this line of thinking, "Russia" is not simply or necessarily centered in a particular region; the parameters of Russianness are set, while the center of Russia can shift to a more remote and defensible place.[8] This is a move generally expressed not in terms of an advance, but of a strategic, nation-preserving withdrawal, like Kutuzov before the French advance on Moscow in 1812. Siberia is the ideal choice for the new Russian center because it is demonstrably non-European Russia, relatively untouched by the influences that have flowed into European Russia since the eighteenth century. And, despite mismanagement of its resources and damage to the environment during the Soviet period, it is still seen as a land of great natural beauty that could become self-sufficient if not stripped of its wealth by foreigners and their unscrupulous Russian partners.

There are many actors in the contemporary Siberian drama, but the most prominent among them has been Valentin Rasputin, whose career covers a broad spectrum of approaches to Siberia's place in Russia and Russia's place in the world. In his youth on the banks of the Angara River, he was exposed to nature and peasant culture, to the tribulations of Stalinist injustice (his father was unfairly imprisoned), wartime privation, and postwar development that destroyed much more than it created. He went from village youth to urban university student, to journalist, essayist, fiction writer, environmental activist, ethnographer, passionate defender of Russia's culture and traditions, member of Gorbachev's council, and an anguished voice for the conservative nationalist opposition. Along the way, he helped to make Lake Baikal, Siberia, and Siberia-as-Russia a "paraliterary space": "the space of debate, quotation, partisanship, betrayal, reconciliation . . . not the space of unity, coherence, or resolution that we think of as constituting a work of literature."[9] His work has emphasized the spiritually rich, sacred space of Baikal, Siberia, and Russia in which everything is divided into pure and impure, *svoi i chuzhie* (one's own people and aliens), *sviatye i besy* (saints and demons). Siberia was important to the writers of Socialist Realism as a *tabula rasa*, a place where the energies and achievements of the new society could best show up against a primitive, underdeveloped background. For Rasputin, this land of centuries-old settlements—which served as outposts of the Russian Empire—is now ready to take a more crucial and more abstract role as the center of post-Soviet (also post-glasnost and post-perestroika) Russia, and a last stand for "Russianness."

The idea of Lake Baikal as a nature preserve has been extended by Rasputin and other conservative nationalists to be a metaphor for Russian culture and for the entire Russian people, who are said to be in need of the status of a precious—and endangered—species.

> To Rasputin the struggle for the protection of Lake Baikal becomes a final struggle for the soul of Siberia, and even the soul of Russia itself, a struggle to which he now [the early 1990s] devotes all his energies. . . . Siberia is the last Russian paradise still with a purity of spirit that can offer hope and salvation to Russia whose European *materik* [mainland] is perceived as having lost its morality and its spiritual identity.[10]

We should not overestimate Rasputin's status as a conservative or right-wing nationalist role model, but his literary and nonliterary activities do demonstrate the essence of the Siberian-writer myth. He is of village background, was educated at a provincial university, has mostly lived and worked around Irkutsk and Baikal, and only reluctantly spends time in Moscow and abroad when duty calls. He was first noticed by Russian historical novelist and Siberian patriot Vladimir Chivilikhin (1928–1984) at a 1965 seminar for young writers in Chita (where Vampilov was also identified as a major talent).[11] During the same week that the Russian Writers' Union was working in Siberia to influence Russian literature's future, back in Moscow Solzhenitsyn's archive was seized, and in a separate incident, Siniavskii and Daniel were arrested after they were discovered to be the authors of works published abroad under the pseudonyms of Tertz and Arzhak, respectively.

Siberia is the subject of virtually everything Rasputin has written; he has a strong attachment to his *malaia rodina* (local region) and is not easily seduced by intellectual life outside of Siberia. In general, he is devoted to making Russians once more a *narod* (a people, nation), not just a *naselenie* (a population), and to developing in his fellow Russians a regional and national identity and a feeling of patriotism, not just for large divisions like Siberia, the North, or Central Russia, but specifically for Irkutsk, Tomsk, Vologda, Vladimir, and Riazan, all the way down to each person's own native village or hometown. His stories and essays both celebrate the values and traditions of his native Siberia and mourn the loss of traditional rural culture, where every village had its own lexicon and its own identity. He has returned periodically to his village to listen to the older inhabitants, mostly women, and record their colorful phrases, lest he forget them in his more urban existence in Irkutsk or Moscow.

Rasputin's best works—*Money for Maria* (1967), *The Final Bow* (1970), *Live and Remember* (1974), and *Farewell to Matyora* (1976)—demonstrate that there is nothing primitive about the writing of the most talented village-born authors, at least when they write about what they know best, growing up in rural Russia. According to Rasputin, the source of his artistic inspiration and his patriotism was a childhood spent on the shores of the Angara next to his native village of Atalanka, "with the islands across the water from me and the sun setting on the opposite shore. I've seen many objects of beauty both natural and man-made, but I will die with that picture before me which is dearer to me than anything else in the world. . . . It is how I see my homeland."[12] Rasputin is devoted to his homeland, virtually to the exclusion of all else, and he is abnormally sensitive to its pain. He watches over it zealously and sees his fate as irrevocably linked to its continuing existence and spiritual well-being.

Canonical Village Prose flourished for more than two decades, until the latter part of the 1970s. Rasputin's *Farewell to Matyora,* which appeared in 1976, is by common consent the single most important work in this movement and the one that seemed to both its author and the critics to "logically complete the village theme."[13] The apocalyptic finale of the work was the strongest possible image for expressing the sense that the traditional village had reached the end of its history, and that the literary movement that had tracked its final years was itself coming to a close. When new movements in Soviet Russian literature began to take shape in the mid-1980s, once again it was Valentin Rasputin (who had by then recovered from the severe beating he received at the hands of thieves in 1980) whose writing proved to be seminal. His 1980 story "The Fire" was the first major work of the Gorbachev era; it was also the last major fictional work by Rasputin, who like many a Russian writer before him, decided that the demands of the times forced him to directly address the "burning questions."[14] Two of the best-known new literary works of the glasnost years, "The Fire" and Viktor Astaf'ev's "A Sad Detective" (1986), are set in Siberia, while a third, Vasilii Belov's *The Best Is Yet To Come* (1986), is not only closely linked in spirit to the first two but also features a hero who is saved—like a character in as Dostoevsky novel—by his years in prison far away from Moscow.

In 1976, the end of *Farewell to Matyora* was read as an affectionate if apocalyptic leave-taking of thousand-year-old rural Russia. The Siberian island village of Matyora would sink beneath the waves of the hydroelectric project's reservoir, and Dasha Pinigina and other villagers who chose not to leave would perish along with the remains of their ancestors (the houses having already been burned down by those sent to clear the island). But Rasputin left the ending ambiguous, and a reading in the 1990s leaves one with the feeling that possibly it is her son Pavel and the other men in the boat adrift in the foggy Angara who will perish because they have lost their roots, their sense of a homeland, and they have found nothing to replace it.

Matyora can easily be read as a latter-day Kitezh, the Russian city that legend says "sank uncorrupted to the bottom of a trans-Volga lake at the time of the first Mongol invasion" and which cannot be discerned by any foreigner.[15] Kitezh, too, was saved by a protective mist—a sort of natural *pokrov* (sacred covering) in answer to the prayer for divine intercession—that hid it as the enemy approached.[16] It was believed that the very retelling of the Kitezh legend would help it to rise again.[17] The fate of Kitezh provides—like the seventeenth-century schism in Russian Orthodoxy—what Nikolai Berdiaev calls "a way out of history . . . the orthodox Tsardom went underground. The true Kingdom is the City of Kitezh which is to be found at the bottom of a lake."[18] This true kingdom is not lost, but exists in a state of suspended animation, awaiting *svetoprestavlenie* (the end of time), when it will just as magically appear to the righteous, that is, to genuine Russians. Rasputin's vision of the Siberian island of Matyora—which best symbolizes the traditional and rapidly disappearing Russian village—fits onto the plane of "spiritual geography" alongside the sacred, hidden space of *Grad Kitezh* and Jerusalem (the city of sacred return), as well as Atlantis (another term used in connection with the loss of village Russia).[19] There are not only links between Matyora, Kitezh, Jerusalem, and Atlantis but, more importantly, between all of these and Russia as a whole, for which each serves as an emblem both of past suffering and of future opportunity. The spiritual categories that dominate Russian culture often get mixed up with ideological and political concepts and agendas.[20]

Is it in fact Rasputin's reader—rather than the inhabitants of Matyora—who is in greater danger of perishing? The rich ambivalence of the ending, and the evolution (or revelation) of the author's ideological-cultural stand, lends itself to an interpretation that equates Matyora with Siberia and with the real, eternal Russia. At the end of Rasputin's story "The Fire," the hero Yegorov walks into the forest, away from the still-burning logging settlement in which he has lived since his own village was flooded by the Bratsk dam.

> [H]is steps were light, free . . . as if he'd finally been carried off down the right road. . . . He saw himself from a long way off: a little man who'd gotten lost was walking across the spring earth despairing of ever finding his home, and now he'd disappear behind a thicket and vanish forever. Half meeting him, half seeing him off, the earth was silent.[21]

To save itself—the Siberian writers imply—Russia should retreat to its Kitezh, to a self-sufficient and self-contained place, impervious to a foreigner's glance and influence; this is a retreat not from oppression but from a demonically inspired anti-Russian innovation. The provincial cities of Siberia—so beautifully described in Rasputin's book *Siberia, Siberia*—the still-vast forests, and the mysterious, mystical, immeasurably deep, injured-but-eternal Lake Baikal seem indeed to be resonant metaphors for Rasputin's view of Siberia and the Russian people. In his work we find an extension of what the Village Prose writers saw in this grand expanse—a place to save what is left of Russian identity, what remains of Russia's sacred native soil. To the nonpluralistic nationalists on the far right, a Siberian-based society and culture is not the *best* choice for Russia, it is the *only* choice.

Notes

1. Valentin Rasputin, "Vniz i vverkh po techeniiu," in *Vniz i vverkh po techeniiu* (Moscow, 1972), p. 260; "Downstream," trans. Valentina Brougher and Helen Poot, in *Contemporary Russian Prose,* ed. C. Proffer and E. Proffer (Ann Arbor, MI: Ardis, 1982), p. 393.

2. For the fullest discussion of this literary movement, see my book *Russian Village Prose: The Radiant Past* (Princeton: Princeton University Press, 1992).

3. Boris Lapin, in Lapin and Nadezhda Tenditnik, "Deti Arbata ili Deti Rossii? Dialog pisatelia i kritika o massovoi kul'ture v sovremennoi proze," *Sibir',* 1989, no. 3, pp. 117–21.

4. See, for instance, an article by the ultranationalist Petersburg theater critic Mark Liubomudrov, who stated that "Russian culture today is very much in need of . . . 'Russification' "; in "Izvlechem li uroki? O russkom teatre i ne tol'ko o nem," *Nash sovremennik,* 1989, no. 2, p. 181.

5. The discussion of the "Russification" campaign is based on my unpublished paper "What Makes a Writer 'Russian'? (The 'Russification' of Russian Literature After 1985),"

which I presented at the Kennan Institute for Advanced Russian Studies, Washington, D.C., 7 October 1993. For an abstract of this paper, see the KIARS *Meeting Report*, vol. XI, no. 2 (November 1993), or *The Woodrow Wilson Center Report*, vol. 5, no. 3 (November 1993).

6. The violent events of early October 1993 led to the banning of the most extreme right-wing and "red-brown" newspapers, like *Den'* and *Sovetskaia Rossiia*, and the call by some liberal democratic writers and critics to extend the ban to conservative nationalist publications like *Nash sovremennik* and *Literaturnaia Rossiia*. *Den'* was reconstituted in rapid order under *Soglasie, Zavtra*, and other names, with the words "Editor—Aleksandr Prokhanov" in enormous letters on the front of each issue to signal the publication's true identity and direction.

7. Feliks Roziner, *Nekto Finkel'maier* (London: Overseas Publication Interchange, 1981), pp. 254–56; *A Certain Finkelmeyer*, trans. Michael Heim (New York: W.W. Norton, 1991), p.164. The events of the novel take place in the 1960s; it was written between 1971 and 1975, when Roziner still lived in the Soviet Union. The novel was published in Russia shortly before the English translation came out.

8. This is, of course, reminiscent of Solzhenitsyn's suggestion in 1974 that the Russian state retreat from the center to the Northeast and Siberia, which he calls "our hope and our reservoir." See Aleksandr Solzhenitsyn, *Letter to the Soviet Leaders*, trans. Hilary Sternberg (New York: Harper and Row, 1975).

9. Rosalind Krauss, "Poststructuralism and the Paraliterary," in *The Originality of the Avant-Garde and Other Modernist Myths* (Cambridge, MA: MIT Press, 1985), pp. 292–93.

10. David Gillespie, "A Paradise Lost? Siberia and Its Writers, 1960 to 1990," in *Between Heaven and Hell: The Myth of Siberia in Russian Culture*, ed. Galya Diment and Yuri Slezkine (New York: St. Martin's Press, 1993), pp. 263, 271. This anthology contains many other interesting articles on Siberia's cultural and historical role. On Valentin Rasputin and Lake Baikal, see Peter Matthiessen, "The Blue Pearl of Siberia," *The New York Review of Books*, 14 February 1991, pp. 37–47.

11. For reminiscences about this gathering, see Vladimir Chivilikhin, "I.N. Zhukov," in *Doroga: Iz arkhiva pisatelia* (Moscow, 1989), pp. 394–406.

12. Valentin Rasputin, "Nuzhno vzvolnovannoe slovo," *Sovetskaia kul'tura*, 19 March 1985.

13. Liliia Vil'chek, "Vniz po techeniiu derevenskoi prozy," *Voprosy literatury*, 1985, no. 6, p. 72.

14. "The Fire" has been called an "emblem" of the Gorbachev years. See Gerald Mikkelson and Margaret Winchell, "Valentin Rasputin and His Siberia," introduction to *Siberia on Fire, Stories and Essays by Valentin Rasputin* (Dekalb, IL: Illinois University Press, 1989), p. xvii.

15. James Billington, *The Icon and the Axe, An Interpretive History of Russian Culture* (New York: Vintage, 1970), pp. 369, 540.

16. *Proshchanie* (Farewell), Elem Klimov's 1982 film of the Rasputin story, makes the Matyora–Kitezh connection much more explicit, especially in the opening scene—not present in the text—in which a boat full of hooded figures crosses a sun-dappled expanse of water toward an island rising out of the mist.

17. Munin Nederlander, *Kitezh: The Russian Grail Legends*, trans. Tony Langham (London: Aquarian Press, 1991), p. 110.

18. Nikolas Berdyaev, *The Russian Idea*, trans. R.M. French (Boston: Beacon Press, 1962), p. 13.

19. See Igor' Zolotusskii, "Tropa Fedora Abramova. K 70-letiiu so dnia rozhdeniia," *Literaturnaia gazeta*, 28 February 1990, p. 3.

20. The term "spiritual geography" (*dukhovnaia geografiia*) comes from the review of a historical novel by Vladimir Lichutin about nineteenth-century Old Believers; see Valentin Kurbatov, "Plamia iskaniia," *Literaturnaia Rossiia,* 1987, no. 39, p. 8. In *The Russian Idea,* Berdiaev discusses how Jerusalem is equated with Rus and Kitezh as the places where "true belief" still exists (pp. 9, 13). The contemporary nationalist poet Iurii Kuznetsov presents the image of a self-contained homeland, impenetrable to the alien eye: "It is Kitezh, rising up from the watery depths,/ Whose crosses we see shining from the future." As quoted in Aleksandr Ageev, "Varvarskaia lira," *Znamia,* 1991, no. 2, p. 225.

21. Valentin Rasputin, "The Fire," trans. Gerald Mikkelson and Margaret Winchell, in *Siberia on Fire,* pp. 159–60.

Contemporary Siberian Regionalism

Vladimir A. Zhdanov

A century has passed since the 1894 death of Nikolai M. Iadrintsev, the champion of Siberian autonomy and the author of the well-known classic, *Siberia as a Colony* (St. Petersburg, 1882). Although these hundred years drastically changed the world, they did not alter the subordinate position of Siberia vis-à-vis European Russia as it emerged from the very beginning of Siberia's colonization by ethnic Slavs. The persistence of a colonial relationship between Moscow and Siberia is rooted in the nature of economic development in Siberia. This colonialism has, if anything, been reinforced by the efforts to transform the country's economy and the corresponding political struggles under way since 1985. The present essay examines the recent re-emergence of a Siberian regionalism in the context of the region's continued economic subordination to Moscow.

Political Consequences of Economic Development in Siberia

Immense as the riches extracted from Siberia by Moscow through the fur trade of the seventeenth century and the gold rush of the eighteenth and early nineteenth centuries proved to be, they were exceeded by the gains from the construction of the Trans-Siberian Railroad at the end of the nineteenth century. Moscow's goal for the Trans-Siberian Railroad was to increase its control over territories to the east; but from the viewpoint of Siberian patriots, the railroad promised something altogether different. Siberian patriots looked forward to an alternative economic strategy whereby Siberia would be oriented away from Moscow toward the Asia–Pacific region. Siberia would become a dynamic economic and cultural crossroads, a link between Europe and Asia.

In actuality, the Trans-Siberian Railroad failed to serve as a link between Western Europe and the Asia–Pacific region (to have met such expectations the Trans-Siberian would have to have been ten times more powerful than it was projected to be). Rather, the railroad served more or less to further the colonial goals of Moscow. Moreover, after the October Revolution of 1917, political constraints buried even the vague expectations for a Siberian bridge between Europe and Asia. Instead, Siberia served as a proving ground for the methods of forced collectivization (the so-called Ural-Siberian method), an epoch that also saw the first steps in the creation of Siberian heavy industry. During World War II, the dramatic evacuation of industry to the east facilitated the transformation of Siberia into one of the main military-industrial centers of the Soviet Union.[1]

From the second half of the 1960s until the late 1980s, West Siberia (mainly the area of Tiumen province) became the basic source of oil and gas for the USSR—and oil and gas, of course, served as the basic sources of valuable foreign currency. During the two decades following discovery, more than 6 billion tons of oil and more than 5 trillion cubic meters of gas were extracted from the Tiumen fields. Almost all of this "black gold" went to fill coffers in Moscow, underwriting the USSR's arms buildup, as well as the ill-fated war in Afghanistan.[2] Siberia saw relatively little benefit from its own oil and gas boom. Until recently, Siberia formed part of the centralized command economy, whereby all wealth produced was funneled through Moscow.[3]

In typical Soviet fashion, the reform package known as perestroika targeted industrial sectors rather than regions. And because perestroika emphasized the modernization of existing industrial plant, there was almost no attention paid to new investment—a turn of events that struck regions requiring heavy investment disproportionately hard. "At the same time," wrote the British geographer Michael Bradshaw, "an increased emphasis on efficiency and self-financing, in the absence of price reforms, discriminated against resource industries in high-cost locations such as Siberia."[4] In short, perestroika, whatever its other shortcomings, was not a policy geared toward Siberia.

Under perestroika, the Siberian economy lost the advantages of the centralized economic system, including preferential investment and the supply of fixed capital stock, yet did not benefit from the promised relative freedom, owing to the large share of industries that remained under the direct control of central authorities. The Siberian economy was further jolted by the social forces unleashed, notably the miners' strikes. But no one was prepared for the blow struck by the program of economic liberalization that began in 1992 and provoked a sharp decline in industrial production.[5]

In Siberia, "shock therapy" caused not only the decline of industrial production but also the further differentiation among regions because of the much higher rates of decline in manufacturing industries than in the extracting ones and the growth of prices in the fuel complex. The share of Tiumen province in the gross output of Russian industry, for example, increased from 3.6 percent in 1991 to 10.1 percent by the end of 1992. Kemerovo province also improved its economic position due to the pressure of miners' strikes, which led to increases in the price of coal. But Novosibirsk province, with its high-tech military industry, saw its share of Russian industrial production decline from 1.54 percent to

0.91 percent. Provinces outside the oil and gas complex entered a period of intense narrow reproduction of their fixed capital.[6] As living standards declined across Russia, Siberian provinces remained among the country's poorest.[7]

Paradoxically, the economic policy of Russian reformers, more oriented to solve the urgent tasks of financial stabilization, adversely affected the social basis for the further development of political democracy and economic liberalism. The historical experience of the most advanced countries of Western Europe and North America, as well as that of new industrial countries, shows that the main social bearer of economic modernization and political democracy is the middle class. In Russia, expectations that the directors of state and joint-stock enterprises would become the core of a future Russian middle class proved unfulfilled, for although many managers and functionaries have made financial fortunes, these fortunes have been invested not in manufacturing but in real estate, banking, hard currency, and speculations. The lack of the stabilizing influence of a middle class upon the economic and political processes, argues one analyst, "accounts for ... the dashes from one extreme to another, the emergence of conservatism not in reasonable but in aggressively archaic forms, and the preference for a revolutionary way of solving problems to an evolutionary one."[8]

All of this might seem fertile ground for the re-emergence of a powerful Siberian separatism, but the enormous social and economic instability caused by Moscow's policies has given rise instead to a fierce Russian nationalism, no less in Siberia than in the rest of the country.[9] And yet, the realization of market reforms will be impossible without the kind of political reform that includes the expansion of regional sovereignty and the transformation of the so-called Russian Federation from a unitary state into a real federation of lands with constitutionally guaranteed rights. The solution of the problems facing the country is a vital task for Siberian local elites.[10] Within the whirlwind, there have in fact been some efforts to coordinate economic and political activity on a regional basis, a development to which we now turn.

A Movement for Regional Autonomy

The crash of the old regime meant the abrupt end of the vertical integration achieved through Communist Party committees and industrial ministries. Moscow was left to contemplate a new basis upon which to carry out effective control of the country's far-flung regions. For a long time after 1991, the Russian government tried to ensure the support of local elites in the political struggle du jour: first, against the All-Union government (before the August coup of 1991), then against the Russian parliament (after the August coup). Moscow further sought to pit one group of territories against the others, in a classic policy of *divide et impera*—a policy not well suited to achieving either reintegration or economic redevelopment.

In place of a strategic regional policy, Moscow seemed to prefer grand imperial visits. Of course, decisions made during such visits, often under considerable local pressures, could not be well-thought out. And representatives of Moscow had a lot of regions to placate yet scarce resources to do so, meaning they left behind a plethora of unfulfilled promises. Moscow's regional policy—or more precisely, its lack of one—bred cynicism, but it also contributed to the stimulation of local activity.

In November 1990, during a meeting of the chairmen of the regional soviets of Kemerovo, Novosibirsk, Tomsk, Tiumen, Altai, and Krasnoiarsk, a new organization for uniting Siberian territories was announced. The Siberian Agreement (*Sibirskoe soglashenie*), as the association formed in Kemerovo was called, pledged to coordinate economic reforms at the regional level, regulate the exploration and use of Siberian natural resources, and help facilitate "social adjustments" during the reform process.

The early appearance of an inter-regional body in Siberia was the result of a unique combination of socioeconomic circumstances: the specialization of Siberia's regions in extracting and developing industries, and their general sparseness on the vast territories. Coordination was essential, especially given the absence of a state regional policy. Siberian local elites had long participated in pitched battles with Moscow over the allocation of resources. Each provincial leader fought to secure both as much local investment and as much control over local resources as possible, while minimizing taxes. Often, local elites found common cause in their haggling with Moscow. Now they were taking these experiences one step further.

Within a few months of the initial pronouncement of the Siberian Agreement, other Siberian regions joined. By 1994, membership included nineteen Siberian constituent parts (*sub''ekty*)—republics, territories (krai), and provinces (oblasts)—of the Russian Federation.[11] The association formed a Council (the so-called Greater Council), consisting of the governors and the chairmen of provincial soviets, as its supreme representative body. The meetings of the Council were to be held not less than once every half year. The future governor of the Novosibirsk province (then chairman of the Novosibirsk provincial soviet), Vitalii Mukha, was elected chairman of the Association Council.[12]

Below the Association Council, a number of coordinating councils were created. These were small bodies that included authorities, experts, a working group, and a secretariat. All coordinating councils were headed by a member of the Greater Council. In 1994, coordinating councils handled the activities of the Association in the spheres of economic contacts with foreign countries; conversion of military industry and industrial politics; law; ecology; the exploration of natural resources (rent payments and tenders); the struggle against criminal structures; social and cultural programs; and so on.

Work between meetings of the Association was to be carried out by the Executive Directorate (located in Novosibirsk), headed by the executive director.

Starting in February 1992, this post was held by Vladimir Ivankov.[13] The Executive Directorate was in charge of insuring contacts among Siberian provinces, as well as between the provinces and possible partners, informing all members of the Siberian Agreement about current affairs and problems, and promoting adopted decisions. According to the charter of the agreement, its main goal was to attain the stable development of regional economies under market conditions. This meant encouraging the economic cooperation of Siberian enterprises to turn out the commodities demanded by the Siberian market, as well as the more general economic integration of the many provinces—worthy aims, indeed.[14]

The latter goal inevitably carried the Association beyond the bounds of economic integration into the arena of political activities. In fact, during 1992 the authorities of Siberian provinces acquired some functions of the central government. They began to regulate the transfer of commodities and resources (including transit) on their territories by the procedures of licensing of export; to regulate prices by establishing maximum limits; to regulate the rate of the value-added tax; and to regulate the money in circulation by the determination of the order of payments. Regional authorities also announced their right of control over the federal property situated in their territories.[15]

Thus, despite the widely proclaimed economic character of the Siberian Agreement, it did not restrict its activities to economic tasks; it also acted as a political association aimed at securing the interests of the local elites. Even at the first meeting of the Association in Novosibirsk (November 1990), its Greater Council adopted a decision criticizing the work of the Constitutional Committee for supposed violations of the Declaration of State Sovereignty of the RSFSR. It condemned the Constitutional Committee for the decision to abandon the term "socialist" in the text of the Constitution, for failing to mention that the Russian Federation was a part of the Soviet Union, and for the replacement of the "soviet" form of government with a presidential or parliamentary form of republic.[16]

These political statements were reinforced at the Association's next meeting (February 1991), when the need for the Association to become involved in political tasks was openly proclaimed. At this meeting it was decided to create a Political Council consisting of the chairmen of provincial soviets.[17] But the time was not yet ripe for such open political claims, and the creation of the Political Council was found inconsistent with the charter of the Siberian Agreement. It was subsequently abolished at a meeting of the Association in Ulan-Ude in July 1992.[18]

Simply by gathering together into an inter-regional association, however, local elites had raised their own political status. They also created a mechanism for their own protection vis-à-vis the central government. In April 1993, when President Yeltsin dismissed the governors of Irkutsk (Yurii Nozhikov) and Novosibirsk provinces (Vitalii Mukha) from their positions, the Siberian Agreement voted unanimously not to carry out this decision. The Russian president was obliged to withdraw his order, with apologies to the governors. Thus, in spite of the increasing differentiation among Siberian provinces—a tendency that might engender a desire on the part of "richer" provinces to insulate themselves from their less fortunate neighbors—the necessity of securing their positions in the bargaining process with Moscow tempered provincial egoism.

The political character of the Siberian Agreement was further revealed by its activities in 1993. In February of that year, the Association received official status from the Russian Ministry of Justice. That same month in Tomsk, a meeting of the Siberian Agreement was held, attended by an impressive group of Russian ministers and high-ranking officials, led by the premier, Viktor Chernomyrdin. Regional interests were on full display, as the chairman of the Siberian Agreement suggested proclaiming Siberia a priority sphere, which meant added state investment in Siberian defense conversion and Siberian industry as a whole, helping to attract foreign capital and bolstering Siberian science. The Association chairman was supported by Viacheslav Novikov, chairman of the Krasnoiarsk krai soviet and of the coordinating council for foreign economic activity of the Siberian Agreement. Novikov demanded the abolition of the system whereby Moscow determined the share of export from Siberian provinces.[19]

Chernomyrdin reacted negatively to these demands. He compared the slogan "Strong Russia—Strong Regions" with the slogan that had been proclaimed by the Baltic republics and had helped to destroy the USSR ("Strong Republics—Strong Union"). The Russian premier rejected the proposal that the determination of the export share of Siberian natural resources should be the prerogative of provincial authorities, although he allowed for regional participation in this process.[20] As compensation for this rejection, the Russian premier accepted the idea of including representatives of the Siberian Agreement onto the boards of some government ministries.[21] The Association, for its part, continued to beseech Moscow, appealing not just to the government but also to the president and the Supreme Soviet, using increasingly alarmist language.

At the next meeting of the Siberian Agreement in Saianogorsk in July 1993, Sergei Shakhrai, a vice-premier of the Russian government, headed a delegation of central authorities and showed himself to be much more receptive to the idea of regional integration. "It is becoming evident that an inter-regional association is not only a form of inter-regional economic cooperation," Shakhrai remarked, "but perhaps the most important element of the future state system of the Russian Federation, or an element that will have a strong influence on this system." Such an apparent change in the government's attitude to the existence of the Siberian Agreement may be regarded as an attempt to obtain the support of the regions in the clash with the Russian parliament.[22] Nonetheless, the lack of an adequate response by the government to the growing problems of the Siberian economy induced the members of the Siberian Agreement to launch a public appeal to the president, Supreme Soviet, and Russian government.[23]

On 24 October 1993—three days after the infamous decree of the Russian president effectively abolishing the Russian parliament—another meeting of the

Association was held (in Novosibirsk). It was devoted to the concrete economic problems of Siberian territories, such as a common agricultural policy in Siberia, the preparation for the winter, and the chronic underpayment to the territories from the state budget. Delivering a report about the last problem, the first deputy of the Novosibirsk governor, Vasilii Kiselev, mentioned that the tax contributions to the state budget by Siberian provinces, and the allocations from the state back to the provinces, were the biggest secrets in Russia. This secrecy led to the situation whereby some provinces gave much more to the state budget than they received back.[24] Such discrepancies culminated in the infamous "budget war against the center," whereby provinces detained payments to the state budget, using these monies for their own purposes. It was, in other words, the central government that proved to be the true "separatist" in Russia.[25]

Branding the central government as the main separatist in Russia was typical for the leaders of the Siberian Agreement, who also called for much slower market reforms. Vladimir Ivankov, executive director of the Association, supported the ideas of Sergei Baburin (one of the most active opponents of Yeltsin from the left wing) that to obtain political stabilization in Russia it was necessary to elect a new president and a new parliament and to create a new government where regional elites would have their representatives.[26] This growing assertiveness by regional elites may have figured into Yeltsin's calculations in October 1993, when he moved against the parliament. But Yeltsin's victory was temporary, and the price he paid exceeded his gains.

The Regional Impact of the October 1993 Showdown

On 22 September 1993, the day after the president announced his decree disbanding the Russian parliament, the "little soviet" of the Novosibirsk provincial soviet adopted a resolution pronouncing the actions of Yeltsin a coup d'état. The soviet deputies decided to terminate the responsibilities of the president's representative in Novosibirsk province, Anatolii Manokhin. They informed all the members of the Siberian Agreement of their action, and requested support. Mukha's rhetoric became especially impassioned.[27] Support was forthcoming from a variety of Russian political associations and parties, including the Russian Salvation Front, the Communist Party of Russia, the Liberal-Democratic Party of Russia, the Democratic Party of Russia, the "Pamiat" society, and others.

On 29 September 1993, an All-Siberian Conference of representatives of the supreme soviets of "republics," as well as krai and provincial soviets, was held in Novosibirsk. Delegations from fourteen territorial units of the Siberian Agreement took part. The resolutions of the conference were shockingly harsh, threatening a variety of actions if the siege of the Russian parliament was not lifted, including offering a Siberian city as a meeting place for the Russian Congress of People's Deputies and holding a referendum on the possibility of forming a separatist Siberian republic.[28]

The threat of a Siberian republic was far from credible, since it was said to be only a tactical slogan and in any case was long opposed by top Siberian leaders, among them Vitalii Mukha.[29] This time, however, rather than directly counter the proposals for a Siberian republic, Mukha commented that "it is only a slogan to proclaim a republic or not. I am making a concrete suggestion: all bodies of the representative power of the Federation's constituent parts that are the members of Siberian Agreement should immediately examine the question of amalgamating their budgets in one consolidated budget." This proposal received a positive reaction from the audience, with one exception: The chairman of the Krasnoiarsk krai soviet, Viacheslav Novikov, added that his province was self-sufficient and thus could achieve the status of a republic by itself.

On 1 October 1993, an extraordinary meeting of the Siberian Agreement convened in Novosibirsk at the request of the Russian government. It was attended by Vice-Premier Sergei Shakhrai, who was then in charge of regional politics. Answering questions at a press conference after the meeting, Shakhrai stressed that it was only a rumor that the Russian president intended to remove the chairman of the Siberian Agreement from office, adding that if such a rumor were true, the government would never have asked to hold the meeting. At the same press conference, Vitalii Mukha told the journalists that despite the fact that the Siberian Agreement was an economic association, the government requested the leaders of the Agreement to formulate their point of view about the political situation in the country. They did so, unanimously endorsing a set of resolutions aimed at settling the dispute between President Yeltsin and the parliament without parliament's abolition. The representatives also recommended that the central government pay more attention to economic questions and avoid political confrontation, and they assigned the governor of Krasnoiarsk krai, Valerii Zubov, the task of elaborating a program for the amalgamation of the budgets of Siberian provinces.[30]

When asked about the idea of amalgamated budgets at the press conference, Shakhrai answered that he had done everything to prevent this course of events. Mukha then interceded to say that they intended only an effort to create a special united budget to finance the contemplated plans of the territories' development. He was supported by Vladimir Ivankov, who added that there never had been and never would be a joint Siberian budget. The readiness of the Siberian Agreement's leaders to seek consent was immediately grasped by Shakhrai, who pointed out that there had been no speeches at the meeting about the creation of a Siberian republic. Moreover, by this time the government had come to regard the establishment of regional agreements as an active form of Russia's development, issuing a special decision on 16 September 1993 formulating the rules governing relations between the central government and regional associations.[31]

Despite this apparent rapprochement, the tragic events in Moscow of 3–4 October 1993, when the parliament was bombed and its supporters arrested, drastically altered the situation. In Novosibirsk there was an official announcement that Vitalii Mukha was "ill." On 4 October, Vladimir Ivankov held a press conference during which he tried to rescue the political position of the Siberian Agreement and its chairman, Mukha. "The winners must be generous," Ivankov remarked. "They should understand quite clearly that reform is very hard and a complicated process and the reformers must be prepared for long work and should not try to reform Russia in one jerk. . . . The victory today does not mean that everybody will take the side of the government and the reformers." Ivankov alluded to the need to consult public opinion and appealed to the "generosity [that] has always been a virtue of the Russian politician and Russian character."[32]

The events of the next day showed that Vladimir Ivankov was optimistic in his evaluation of Russian political habits. On 5 October, Yeltsin's decree to dismiss Vitalii Mukha as Novosibirsk governor was announced.[33] On 6 October, Mukha held his last press conference as the governor of Novosibirsk province. He said that his dismissal had been a logical culmination of events, but he had not changed his ideas: It was impossible to create a civilized state by the violation of the Constitution. He remained an opponent of the shock method of economic reform. And although he admitted that former vice-president Aleksandr Rutskoi and former parliament speaker Ruslan Khasbulatov were criminals, he claimed that "we did not support Khasbulatov and the armed uprising but we supported his words that he would defend the Constitution."[34]

As Mukha pointed out, the tasks of the Siberian Agreement were very important and it would be very bad if the Association ceased to exist. It was decided to carry out elections for a new chairman of the Siberian Agreement at a forthcoming meeting of the Association, scheduled for 15 November 1993 (but soon postponed until January 1994). Yeltsin telephoned Ivankov to indicate that he had no claims against the continued activity of the Siberian Agreement.[35]

A Balance Sheet

Following their military victory over the old parliament headed by Khasbulatov, self-styled reformers were dealt a blow in the 1993 elections to the new Russian parliament. Even before the elections, the president was obliged to satisfy the demands of the Russian military as payment for their loyalty in the days of confrontation. These developments culminated in the coming to power of the industrial and agricultural lobbies, whose representatives assumed a leading role in the government. The new political situation in Russia was welcomed by the leaders of the Siberian Agreement. With the exodus of radical reformers from the government, the obstacles to the cooperation of local elites with central officials were eliminated.

On 10 January 1994, a meeting of the Siberian Agreement was held in Moscow. It was decided to elect a chairman of the Association from the leaders of Siberian provinces for one year only. For 1994 it would be the governor of Omsk province, Leonid Polezhaev. The meeting also nominated Vladimir Ivankov as the permanent associate chairman of the Association (with retention of his position as executive director). Speaking about the results of this meeting, Ivankov remarked that it was high time to move away from confrontation with the president and the government, because neither regarded the Siberian Agreement as a prototype for a Siberian republic.[36] According to Ivankov, the government fully comprehended the importance of the Association as a coordinating center and link for Siberia. His words were echoed by Vice-Premier Aleksandr Shokhin and Minister of Regional Politics Sergei Shakhrai (soon to become vice-premier).[37]

In the Federal Assembly, the leaders of the Siberian Agreement actively supported the election of Vladimir Shumeiko to the post of chairman of the Council of Federation. In response, Shumeiko suggested that the Executive Directorate of the Siberian Agreement work for him as an expert consultant. By this time, top Russian officials were actively supporting the transfer of some powers from the center to regional associations. Although such a turn of affairs was not envisaged in the statutes of the Siberian Agreement, its leaders welcomed the idea. It was even announced that the Russian president would take part in the next meeting of the Siberian Agreement (probably in the late spring of 1994), which was to be devoted to the problems of the socioeconomic development of Siberia.[38] Predictably, however, the leaders of the Association failed to establish a united Siberian faction in the new Russian parliament—for the same reason that prevented them from organizing this kind of faction in the former one: the members of parliament preferred loyalty to their national parties above any feelings of Siberian patriotism.

Ironically, although the activities of the radical reformers in the central government were regarded by the local Siberian elites as the principal threat facing Siberia, the activities of the radical reformers were the key unifying factor for the members of the Siberian Agreement in their efforts to achieve a kind of Siberian centralism to replace Moscow's. The withdrawal of Gaidar and his party from the government eliminated this "unifying threat" and thus might well give rise to a revival of the patron–client relations between central officials and their provincial counterparts, relations that were typical for Soviet political culture. One need only recall that within Siberia provinces are very different, and becoming more so. In the battle for scarce resources, what counts is making a lot of noise and having friends in high places, especially friends from your region who will favor it over others.

It seems that the Siberian Agreement's Directorate, whose members reside in Novosibirsk province, understand this pending realignment, for they have revived the idea of a unified Siberian budget.[39] But the outlook for such a budget remains less than encouraging.[40] Siberia desperately needs a higher level of inter-regional integration and greater involvement in the world market. But its future development seems more dependent on the careers of its local elites and their relations to national political trends than on expanded relations among Siberian regions, let alone the integration of Siberia into the world economy. As long as Moscow controls Siberian resources and commands the loyalties of Siberian elites, it seems doubtful that an alternative vision of economic development for Siberia can be realized.

Notes

1. By the end of 1990, 10 percent of all enterprises of the Russian defense industry and 18 percent of the Russian industrial labor force were in the Siberian military-industrial complex. See E. Amosenok and V. Bazhanov, "Oboronnyi kompleks regiona," *EKO* [Novosibirsk], no. 9, 1993, p. 17.

2. It might even be argued that the discovery of West Siberian oil postponed the crash of the Communist system for twenty years. At the same time, however, more than 200 billion cubic meters of oil related gas were burned in torches, more than 50 million tons of oil were spilt on the ground, more than 80 thousand hectares of land were destroyed for the construction of boring wells and the pipelines, and more than 17 million cubic meters of timber were lost. V. Kriukov and A. Sevastianova, "Tiumenskaia oblast' v perekhodnyi period," in *Vserossiiskaia konferentsiia po ekonomicheskomu razvitiiu Sibiri* (Novosibirsk, 1993), pp. 3–4.

3. True, the command economy appeared to foster a slightly pro-Siberian tilt in that the rates of industrial growth there had become higher than the ones in Russia in general, while the standard of living of the Siberian population was approaching the all-Russian level. But these averages hid huge disproportions in the Siberian economy. Despite the fact that as early as the beginning of the 1980s western Siberia passed all other economic regions of Russia in the share of investment and fixed capital stock (more than 15 percent of the all-Russian capital stock), 50 percent of this investment and capital stock was concentrated in a single province (Tiumen). Outside of its oil and gas complex, Siberia's share of investment and capital stock was in fact declining. For the USSR economy as a whole, the lack of integrated development for the Siberian economy brought some short-term advantages (e.g., an economy of investment), but in the long run it preserved the existing disproportions and thus lowered the efficiency of the national economy, as the academicians Abel Aganbegian and Aleksandr Granberg have long maintained. Their calls for the integrated development of Siberia fell on deaf ears.

4. M. Bradshaw, "Siberia Poses a Challenge to Russian Federalism," RFE/RL Research Report, vol. 1, no. 41, 16 October 1992, p. 11.

5. The methods of monetary regulation, although appropriate in a developed market economy, caused many unexpected problems in the Russian economy, which lost its centralized command character but did not change its monopolized nature. Russia would have benefited from a different method of transformation to the market. See, for example, the excellent book by Ronald McKinnon, *The Order of Economic Liberalization: Financial Control of the Transition to a Market Economy* (Baltimore: The Johns Hopkins Press, 1991).

6. Iu. Ershov, "Noveishaia ekonomicheskaia istoriia: Kratkaia kharakteristika ekonomicheskoi dinamiki na obshcherespublikanskom fone," *EKO*, no. 9, 1993, pp. 8, 11.

7. "Sotsial'nye problemy sovremennoi Sibiri," in *Vserossiiskaia konferentsiia po ekonomicheskomu razvitiiu Sibiri*, p. 15.

8. V. Umov, "Rossiiskii srednii klass: Sotsial'naia real'nost' i politicheskii fantom," *Polis (Politicheskie issledovaniia)*, no. 4, 1993, pp. 32–33.

9. The success of the Liberal-Democratic Party, led by Vladimir Zhirinovsky, was very pronounced in Siberia. Zhirinovsky's party took first place in Novosibirsk oblast (24 percent of the vote), Kemerovo oblast, Tomsk oblast, Krasnoiarsk krai (including the

Taimyr and Evenk okrugs), and Irkutsk and Chita oblasts. In Chita, Zhirinovsky's success was particularly striking: his party received 85 percent of the vote. By contrast, the party Russia's Choice, led by Egor Gaidar, won only in Tiumen and Omsk oblasts. The republics of Tuva and Buriatia gave first place to the party of Sergei Shakhrai. The Agrarian Party prevailed only in the Altai region. *Sibirskaia gazeta,* no. 50, November 1993, p. 3.

10. The emergence of local elites is a problem for separate analysis. Briefly, it may be said here that the Brezhnev period of "stagnation" was a time when local elites acquired a strong sense of their role as local officials, rather than as commissars of the center. For an analysis of regional elites by experts from the Institute of Geography of the Russian Academy of Sciences, see *Nezavisimaia gazeta,* 11 June 1993.

11. Among the nineteen parts, those with the status of "republics" included Tuva and Khakasia; those designated "territories" (*krai*) included Altai and Krasnoiarsk; "provinces" (*oblasti*) included Tiumen, Omsk, Tomsk, Kemerovo, Novosibirsk, Chita, and Irkutsk; and "autonomous territories" included Khanty-Mansi, Yamal-Nenets, Evenk, Taimyr, Ust-Ordynsk, and Aginsk Buriat. Most, but not all, of these are in West Siberia.

12. Mukha had been the first secretary of the Novosibirsk oblast Communist Party committee, or *obkom;* prior to this, he served many years as director of a large factory in Novosibirsk.

13. Ivankov's accession to power was marked by a total change of personnel. He dismissed the entire staff of the Executive Directorate of the Association because of their activities in private business under the cover of the Siberian Agreement. Author's interview with Alexander Patlai, first deputy of the executive director, 23 August 1993. (Materials from interviews with Siberian officials are used with the permission of Dr. James Hughes, who is a co-owner of the copyright.)

14. Under the supervision of the Siberian Agreement, several corporations were organized through Siberian enterprises. The biggest of them were the Siberian agroindustrial corporation Agrosib and the Siberian production corporation Sibagromash, which produced agricultural machinery. Despite the support of the Siberian Agreement, these corporations suffer from the same kind of troubles as other Siberian machine-building enterprises.

15. These developments may be regarded only as emergency measures called forth by the necessity to alleviate the results of economic crisis, for the realization of true integration will inevitably require huge investment, which is lacking. Sergei Pavlenko, "Tsentr i regiony: Kto kogo?" *Mezhdunarodnaia zhizn',* no. 4, 1993, p. 91.

16. "Reshenie Sibirskogo Soglasheniia," no. 11, 16 November 1990, typescript, chancellery of the Directorate of the Siberian Agreement, Novosibirsk.

17. "Reshenie Sibirskogo Soglasheniia," no. 1, 8 February 1991, typescript, chancellery of the Directorate of the Siberian Agreement, Novosibirsk.

18. "Reshenie Sibirskogo Soglasheniia," no. 15, 10 July 1992, typescript, chancellery of the Directorate of the Siberian Agreement, Novosibirsk.

19. "Reshenie Sibirskogo Soglasheniia," Tomsk, 16 February 1993, typescript, chancellery of the Directorate of the Siberian Agreement, Novosibirsk, pp. 5–7, 18.

20. Ibid., pp. 26–27.

21. Ibid., pp. 30–31.

22. "Protokol Soveshchaniia Mezhregional'noi Assotsiatsii, Sibirskoe Soglashenie," Saianogorsk, 9–10 July 1993, typescript, chancellery of the Directorate of the Siberian Agreement, Novosibirsk, p. 48. The political ambitions of Shakhrai, who seems to have been trying to secure the support of regional elites for his future career, might also have contributed to this apparent softening of the government's position.

23. See *Materialy Soveshchaniia Mezhregional'noi Assotsiatsii, Sibirskoe Soglashenie: Saianogorsk Iiul' 1993 g.* (Novosibirsk, 1993), p. 75.

24. For example, during the first eight months of 1993, Novosibirsk oblast collected 85.5 percent of the territory's income but received from the Ministry of Finance only 37.7 percent; Omsk oblast collected 77 percent and received 39 percent; the Altai region collected 81 percent but received 47 percent; and, Tiumen oblast collected 92 percent but received 46 percent. "Protokol Soveshchaniia Mezhregional'noi Assotsiatsii, Sibirskoe Soglashenie, Novosibirsk," 24 September 1993, typescript, chancellery of the Directorate of the Siberian Agreement, Novosibirsk, p. 36.

25. According to Kiselev, these actions of the Ministry of Finance were a reflection of a more general tendency in the state's policy to reduce the independence of regions and the scope of their decision making. He pointed out that "the position of central organs hurts Russia much more than the clamor of separatist aspirations, if any political bodies or social groups actually have such aspirations." Ibid., p. 39.

26. Author's interview with Ivankov, 24 August 1993.

27. *Vedomosti Novosibirskogo oblastnogo soveta narodnykh deputatov*, no. 39, September 1993, p. 3.

28. *Sibirskaia gazeta*, no. 39, October 1993, p. 2.

29. Ibid., p. 1. Even on 28 September 1993, the idea of a Siberian republic was again rejected by Mukha and Ivankov. Ivankov said that the next day Aman Tuleev (chairman of the Kemerovo oblast soviet and a candidate for the Russian presidency in 1991) would call for the creation of a Siberian republic, but it would be his personal point of view. At the 29 September meeting of the All-Siberian Conference, Tuleev did appeal for the creation of a Siberian republic uniting Tomsk, Novosibirsk, Kemerovo, and the Altai.

30. According to reports on the evening news, Novosibirsk Television, 1 October 1993.

31. In 1994 there were eight such regional associations in Russia.

32. *Sibirskaia gazeta*, no. 40, October 1993, p. 1.

33. *Vedomosti Novosibirskogo oblastnogo soveta narodnykh deputatov*, no. 42, October 1993, p. 1.

34. *Novosibirskie novosti*, no. 74, October 1993, p. 1.

35. *Sibirskaia gazeta*, no. 40, October 1993, p. 3.

36. Ivankov suggested that the notion of a Siberian republic was a fanciful invention by journalists. He pointed out that such an idea had never been proclaimed in any documents of the Siberian Agreement and warned that mere mention of a Siberian republic would bring a court action and heavy fine. *Novosibirskie novosti*, no. 3, January 1994, p. 3.

37. Interview with Vladimir Ivankov on Novosibirsk Radio, 2 February 1994.

38. Boris Yeltsin did not attend the next meeting of the Association, held on 4 March 1994 in Moscow. Central authorities were represented by First Vice-Premier Oleg Soskovets. *Sibirskaia gazeta*, no. 10, March 1994, p. 1.

39. *Vek*, no. 3, January 1994, p. 2.

40. Valerii Zubov, the governor of Krasnoiarsk krai (which faces a less severe economic situation than Novosibirsk oblast), characterized the idea of a possible unified budget as "absolutely needless." *Sibirskaia gazeta*, no. 1, January 1994, p. 3.

Part III

Far Eastern Identities:
Settlement, Natives, and Borders

If Russian settlement of its eastern territories, although much studied, remains poorly integrated into general narratives on Russian state and society, this is even more true of the history of native peoples who inhabited Siberia for thousands of years (before the arrival of the Russians in the late sixteenth century) and fell under Russian suzerainty. These native peoples, some of whom appear to have crossed over to the North American continent, had an impact on Russian state and society in some ways more enduring than the engagement with the Chinese or Japanese.

Estimates place the number of different language communities in Northern Asia encountered by the Russians at about 120, ranging from the various Tatar peoples of western Siberia and the nomadic Tungus tribes of central Siberia to the Buriats, Yakuts, and Nivkhi east of Lake Baikal. Already by the end of the seventeenth century, however, the Slavic population equaled that of the widely dispersed and differing natives. In the eighteenth and especially nineteenth centuries, immigration from European Russia increased substantially. Greatly outnumbered, subjected to tribute payments and Russification, frequently maltreated and occasionally slaughtered, many indigenous communities nonetheless managed to grow in size. Others have largely or completely died out. Today, perhaps thirty-five native-peoples groups remain.[1]

With the exception of some nomadic peoples without fixed homelands, most of the extant Siberian peoples were granted an ostensibly self-governing ethnopolitical territorial unit within the Russian Federation by the Soviet regime. Some natives in sensitive areas, such as the Buriat-Mongols on the border with

China, received a measure of autonomy even under the tsars, partly in exchange for service in special border detachments. For the most part, however, promises of autonomy went unfulfilled. This comes as no surprise, given Moscow's abiding penchant for centralized control, heightened in the Russian Far East by the abundance of gold and other riches, as well as contested borders with formidable neighbors. With an eye to the presence of natural resources and the proximity of foreign powers, Slavic settlement was viewed as an all-purpose solution, both for control in eastern Russia and, until 1914, for overpopulation in western Russia. Although disagreements as to the nature of the ideal colonists, be they Cossacks, merchants, criminals, or Jews, continued, so did state-sponsored migration.

Russian eastern settlement has already been treated in Part I by Marks and Wolff. The essays in this section discuss Russian relations with native peoples, as well as the permeability of borders, factors crucial to the understanding of Russian Far Eastern identities. A discussion of the largest of the Siberian native peoples, the Yakuts, begins the section.

* * *

To evade the Russian colonial regime, the Yakuts, who call themselves the Sakha (Yakut is a variation of the name applied to them by the Tungus), spread considerably beyond their ancestral lands on the Lena River. Partly by migration and partly by adaptation, they withstood the Slavic onslaught. Yakut, which is derived from Turkish, became the only native Siberian language to gain a foothold in Russian town society, even serving as something of a lingua franca among native peoples throughout eastern Siberia. Yakutian society developed its own nobility, intellectuals, and revolutionaries with a strong national consciousness.[2]

In 1905, amid the war with Japan and revolutionary events in far-off St. Petersburg, a Yakut Union aimed at bringing about national autonomy arose, although in the face of tsarist repression it made little progress toward that goal. After the 1917 revolutions, a declaration of autonomy made during the confusion of the civil war proved short-lived. Notwithstanding a series of rebellions in the 1920s and the establishment of a Yakutian Autonomous Republic, Moscow successfully imposed central rule, showing particular interest in local gold fields and diamond mines. Yakutia originally comprised a territory as large as the Indian subcontinent, but in a demonstration of its control, Moscow lopped off various sections containing underground riches.

Since the collapse of the Soviet Union in 1991, however, Yakut autonomy within the Russian Federation has become more of a reality.[3] Marjorie Mandelstam Balzer, an anthropologist and specialist on Siberian peoples, analyzes the struggle to realize the dream of a true Sakha Republic. She shows that Sakha's bilateral ties with successor states to the USSR have expanded, as have direct links with ethnopolitical units within eastern Siberia (for example, Buriatia). But as Balzer argues, the desire for full-fledged autonomy does not signify political separatism. Not only do Russians remain a majority even in the Sakha capital of Yakutsk, but an ever growing economic integration in the east necessitates cooperation rather than confrontation. A state within a state and in possession of vast resources, Sakha remains an important test case for Russia's federalist structure.

* *. *

Indigenous populations of the Russian Far East vary considerably in size. The Yakuts have a relatively large population (about 400,000). By contrast, the Nivkhi, also known as the Giliaks, are far fewer in number (under 10,000). But the two primary ancestral homes of the Nivkhi, the Amur basin and the northern end of Sakhalin (across from the Amur's estuary), make them no less an apt subject than the Yakuts for understanding the past and future of Northeast Asia.

When the first Russian sailor landed on Sakhalin in 1783, he thought that the island belonged to Japan; he discovered, however, that the natives, including the Nivkhi, were paying tribute to the Chinese. A system of Russian tribute was substituted, although many natives in the Far East, especially those who migrated seasonally, had no choice but to pay both the Russians and the Chinese. After 1875, Sakhalin became a Russian penal colony; the natives had to make way.[4] Russian occupation was followed by Japanese occupation, and then the return of the Russians. In the interim, the October Revolution brought party officials and ethnographers, who organized missionarylike expeditions to proselytize the natives, set up medical facilities and schools, and gather artifacts for museum exhibitions.[5] In this section's next essay, Bruce Grant, an anthropologist, investigates this process of Sovietization and its legacy for the Sakhalin Nivkhi in the longer context of their relations with the outside world.[6]

Living as fishermen and hunters, Nivkhi pursued trade contacts widely throughout Northeast Asia. Despite being subject to Russian governors, they appear for a long time to have been much better known to the Japanese and the Manchus. Many Nivkhi spoke the languages of their Asian neighbors. But as Grant shows, Nivkhi are today hesitant to recognize themselves as Asians, given the pejorative connotations attached to that word in the Soviet vocabulary. Neither do they identify themselves as Europeans, far off in London or Moscow. Grant suggests that this Northeast Asian cosmopolitanism of the Nivkhi, ironically nurtured by the experience of Soviet rule, shows signs of strengthening.[7]

* * *

Sakhalin's shift from Russian penal colony to incipient cosmopolitan periphery is an important indicator of the direction of regional change in eastern Russia. But the past will not be overcome so easily. Not only has the gulag system left its mark on the Russian Far East as much as on Siberia (no less than the latter, the

Far East's gulag awaits its archival rather than literary exposé), but the Russian Far East's economic and social character have been tied more closely to the armed forces than any other part of Russia or the Soviet Union.

The military has had and will continue to have a decisive impact on center–region relations. It was the military presence that served as the rationalization for closing much of Siberia and the Far East not only to foreigners but also to Soviet citizens without special permits. Only recently have critically important episodes related to the military and gulag been open to exploration, such as the use of Russian Asia as a prisoner-of-war detention area for Germans, Czechs, Chinese, and Japanese. With much of the Russian Pacific fleet idly rusting for lack of fuel, though, military influence seems to have lost its vise grip on the region. Openness, internal and external, together with hopes for international cooperation are in ascendance.

The belated opening of the border and the possible internationalization of the economy of the Russian Far East form the subject of this section's final essay by Pavel A. Minakir, director of the Far Eastern Institute of Economic Research in Khabarovsk. Drawing on years of research as well as recent experience in provincial administration, Minakir offers an overview of the regional economy, from the legacy of planning to prospects for future development.[8] He argues that if the Russian Far East is to overcome its status as one of Moscow's many "colonies" in the formerly centralized system, it can do so only through integration with its Asian neighbors. In contrast to Russian nationalists, Minakir emphasizes the indispensability of foreign capital and technology for long-term development.

Minakir sounds a note of cautious optimism, striking a balance between the region's huge potential and its many challenges, including those of infrastructure. Whether central authorities and the still-powerful Far Eastern military establishment will permit an opening up of the economy is perhaps less critical than whether substantial foreign investment will be forthcoming. Property rights remain ambiguous, and investment opportunities elsewhere beckon, most notably in China and Southeast Asia. Meanwhile, native peoples are actively pursuing claims to mineral, forest, and fishing resources, and even gung-ho local administrators worry about whether the opening up of the economy will simply mean the transformation of Russia's Far East into a supplier of raw materials. To throw off "colonial" servitude to Moscow only to kowtow to an even more foreign (if closer) metropole would be an ironic victory indeed.

Notes

1. James Forsyth, *A History of the Peoples of Siberia: Russia's North Asian Colony, 1581–1990* (Cambridge: Cambridge University Press, 1992). Other relevant studies in English include Waldemar Jochelson [Vladimir Iokhelson], *Peoples of Asiatic Russia* (New York: Museum of Natural History, 1928); Walter Kolarz, *The Peoples of the Soviet*

Far East (New York: Praeger, 1954); and M.G. Levin and L.P. Potapov, eds., *The Peoples of Siberia* (Chicago: University of Chicago Press, 1964), Russian-language edition, 1956.

2. Forsyth, *A History of the Peoples of Siberia*, pp. 163–67.

3. A very real sign of Sakha autonomy was the right to retain and sell a small percentage of the annual diamond harvest. However, since DeBeers has a monopoly position in that market, Sakha has experienced difficulties in finding an alternative buyer less open to suasion by Moscow, according to diamond merchants interviewed in Moscow.

4. Hokkaido was also the main zone of deportation in Japan. Harrison, *Japan's Northern Frontier: A Preliminary Study in Colonization and Expansion with Special Reference to the Relations of Japan and Russia* (Gainesville: University of South Florida Press, 1953), pp. 75–76.

5. Yuri Slezkine, *Arctic Mirrors: Russia and the Small Peoples of the North* (Ithaca, NY: Cornell University Press, 1994).

6. Grant and Balzer can be compared with Caroline Humphrey, "Population Trends, Ethnicity, and Religion Among the Buryats," in Alan Wood and R.A. French, eds., *The Development of Siberia: Peoples and Resources* (New York: St. Martin's Press, 1989), pp. 147–76. Another interesting comparison, an exercise in triangulation, would match the ethnographic observations of the early-nineteenth-century Japanese explorer of Sakhalin Rinzo Mamiya to those of his Russian counterparts.

7. Russia's best-known "native" is Dersu Uzala, a member of the Gold tribe. Although Dersu was a legend-worthy hunter, the Gold were mainly fishermen, especially after the elimination of the annual sable tribute in 1880. They lived along the Amur, near the junctions with the Ussuri and Sungari, and were visited in 1930 by Owen Lattimore, who wrote of "a few families living on islands in the Amur who hardly know whether they belong to the Chinese or the Russians." Lattimore, "The Gold Tribe, 'Fishskin Tatars' of the Lower Sungari," in *Studies in Frontier History: Collected Papers, 1929–58* (London: Oxford University Press, 1962), p. 342. Although Dersu was made famous early in this century by the writings of V.K. Arsen'ev, a 1975 film by Kurosawa Akira brought him worldwide recognition. There is a certain irony in that this people, long resident in the Russo-Chinese borderland, came to public view via a Russo-Japanese joint production. An earlier view of the Golds and their service as border guards in Imperial China—parallel to the statements regarding Buriat-Mongols, above—can be found in Dmitrii Pozdneev, *Opisanie Man'chzhurii* (St. Petersburg, 1897), pp. 229–32.

8. The Institute of Economic Research is also the most important repository of economic data on the Russian Far East since the 1970s. Its recent two-volume publication *Dal'nii vostok Rossii: ekonomicheskoe obozrenie* (Moscow, 1993) contains the most complete picture available of the socioeconomic status of and trends in the region. Of particular interest are the 253 tables in the statistical overview that makes up the second volume.

8. Troops of the Allied Intervention marching in Vladivostok, 1918. *Source: Grazhdanskaia voina na Dal'nem Vostoke (1918-1922): Vospominania veteranov (Moscow, 1973).*

9. The Red Army enters Irkutsk, 1920, victorious in the Russian Civil War. *Source: Sibir'* (Moscow, 1985).

10. The Far Eastern Republic and the Japanese Army negotiate the latter's withdrawal from Siberia at Gongota station, 1920. *Source: Grazhdanskaia voina na Dal'nem Vostoke (1918-1922): Vospominania veteranov* (Moscow, 1973).

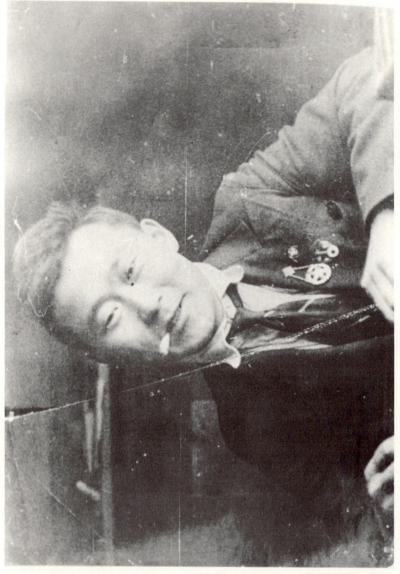

11. A Nivkh soviet official, northwest Sakhalin, 1940s. *Source:* Sakhalin Regional Museum.

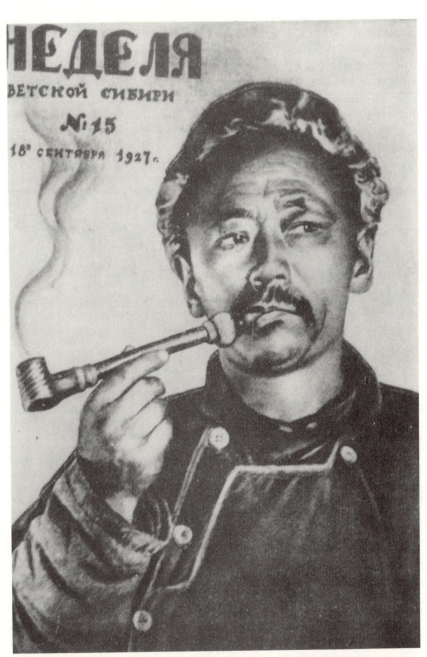

12. 1927 cover of the weekly supplement to the journal *Soviet Siberia* depicting the anticipated modernization of native peoples. *Source: Strokoi otmechennoe vremia* (Novosibirsk, 1970).

13. A Nivkh "Soldier of Culture" learns to read in the 1930s. *Source:* Sakhalin Regional Museum.

14. The Congress of the Peoples of the North in Vladivostok, 1937. *Source: Istoriia Sibiri,* vol. 4 (Leningrad, 1968).

15. Noted Soviet ethnographer V. K. Arsen'ev in the dress of the Udekhe people, Khabarovsk Museum, 1920s. *Source:* V.K. Arsen'ev, *Dersu Uzala* (Moscow, 1972).

16. G. G. Khodzher, an author and representative of the Ul'chi people (who live along the Amur), meets with local admirers. *Source: Amurskie dali* (Khabarovsk, 1973).

17. M. A. Lavrent'ev inspecting the construction of his brainchild, Akademgorodok, the city of science just outside Novosibirsk. *Source: Sibir'* (Moscow, 1985).

A State Within a State

The Sakha Republic (Yakutia)

Marjorie Mandelstam Balzer

In late 1993, a Sakha (Yakut) sociologist, one of the authors of the Sakha Republic constitution, related a metaphorical tale that she used to explain the paradox of pain yet potential that characterizes Sakha approaches to their future. In the story, a young orphan finally achieves prosperity, a white horse, and the leadership of his forest people, but only after the sacrifice of his hunter father and much suffering. The tale was told in the context of criticizing the Russian Federation constitution for its sharp reduction of republic sovereignty. "We may have to wait a generation before the freedoms we thought we had won, even within the federation, are realized," the sociologist lamented.[1]

Some Russian Federation republics, such as Chechnia, proclaimed themselves ready to chase an elusive independence from Russia without waiting another generation. Within the federation, non-Russian populations have moved in the past decade from mildly politicized ethnic consciousness to various forms of nationalism. But this hardly means each republic or group is demanding the same degree of autonomy. Even the most radical cases—Chechnia, Tatarstan, and Tyva (Tuva)—are not neatly falling nation-state dominoes, but rather examples of varied responses to changing conditions and crises. Indeed, Tatarstan's and Bashkortostan's spring 1994 agreements with Moscow indicate attempts to negotiate relative sovereignties within the Russian Federation. At the same time, polarizing conditions have helped to foster the crystallization of national identities, the use of nationalist idioms to express a range of differences, the exploration of new sources of influence, and a return to historical regional interconnections.

Tentative, cautious sociopolitical activism has begun among the Sakha urban intelligentsia and is spreading to more rural areas. Informal political-group activity has escalated within the past several years, recently becoming more organized. At the same time, mass enthusiasm has waned as initial excitement over "sovereignty" declarations gives way to depression over economic conditions.

The Sakha Republic represents a case in which some of the internal tensions between the Russian center and its republic periphery may be managed on the basis of a greater regional sharing of local resources newly wrenched from central control. Although living standards are notoriously poor for indigenous residents, the Sakha Republic nonetheless has come into a position of strength with central authorities because of its vast and underexploited mineral and energy wealth. The republic's predominantly Sakha leadership has been alternately cautious and assertive in its relations with Yeltsin's Moscow government. Sakha President Nikolaev supported President Yeltsin in the December 1993 elections but signed the March 1992 Russian Federation Treaty only after winning some separate economic concessions.[2]

New opportunities for relative sovereignty are by no means assured. Much depends on the flexible political savvy of republic leaders and people, as well as on Moscow policy makers, whose inconsistency has wreaked havoc with the creation of political and economic alliances and the evolution of trust based on goodwill. Much also depends on the extent to which the Sakha will be able and permitted to take advantage of new or renewed relationships with peoples and countries to their east.

Sakha political and cultural "consciousness-raising," along with economic conditions, has led to a widespread exploration of Sakha identity and the (re)invention of tradition. Sakha cultural revival and spiritual vitalization began before the Gorbachev era, but it intensified in the late 1980s, leading to a campaign for the rebirth of Sakha language and literature. A more highly politicized period began with elections to the All-Union Congress in 1989 and with the birth of several movements encompassing cultural, ecological, economic, and constitutional demands. Party formation is nascent, and growing haltingly.

My approach to this chaotic and fluid situation is to avoid assumptions that all "nationalism" must be negative or chauvinist and instead to explore various platforms, claims, and activities of specific groups and leaders.[3] Their resonance in an ethnically mixed republic, where the Sakha themselves are less than half of the population, is probed, despite the difficulties in measuring changing political attitudes.

The Sakha Republic, the largest of the Russia Federation's republics, is pivotal in setting an example for other ethnically defined areas in Siberia and the Far East. Sakha's location between the mass of Siberia and the Pacific Rim historically has made it a broker of trade and influence in the region. The use of its capital, Yakutsk, as an airport "hub" is indicative of this today. Central within Siberia and the Far East, the republic remains geographically peripheral to Moscow. It is argued here that the Sakha Republic is nonetheless politically and economically central to the survival of the Russian Federation.

Of the more than thirty non-Russian ethnically based political entities recog-

Table 9.1

Russian Federal Structure: Ethnonational and Siberian Dimensions

Republics Signing the Federation Treaty, or Negotiating Bilateral Treaties	Ethnically Based Regions, Districts
Adigei	Aga (Buriat)*
Altai (Altai-Kizhi)*	Ust-Orda (Buriat)*
Balkaria	Chukotsk (Chukchi)*
Bashkortostan	
Buriatia*	Evenk*
Chechnia [asserting independence]	Eveno-Bytantaisk (in Sakha Republic)*
Chuvash (Chavash)	Evrei (Birobidzhan)*
Dagestan	Gorno-Altai
Ingushetia	Khanty-Mansi*
Kabarda	Komi-Permiak
Kalmykia (Khalmg Tangch)	Koriak*
Karachai-Cherkessia	Nenets*
Karelia	Yamalo-Nenets*
Khakasia*	Dolgan-Nenets*
Komi*	Taimyr (Nganasan)*
Mari-El (Mari)	
Mordva	
North Ossetia	
Sakha (Yakutia)*	
Tatarstan	
Tyva (Tuva)*	
Udmurtia	

Sources: "Federativnyi dogovor," *ITAR-TASS International Service,* 14 March 1992; Ann Sheehy, "The Republics of the Russian Federation," *Radio Free Europe/Radio Liberty Research Report,* 5 June 1992, p. 14.
  *Siberian and Far Eastern areas are starred

nized as viable for parliamentary representation within Russia, seventeen are within Siberia and the Far East (see Table 9.1). Most of these are only regions or districts within the hierarchically organized matrioshkalike structure of Russia, but four—the Sakha, Tyva, Buriat, and Komi republics (former misnamed "autonomies")—have higher status. The framework, an adapted legacy from the Soviet period, makes the large territory in Siberia and the Far East that is ethnically defined far more significant than is commonly recognized.[4] The rights and obligations of Siberian and Far Eastern indigenous peoples, as well as of the increasingly discontented Slavic peoples, are being redefined within federal and constitutional struggles. Examination of messy and oscillating center–periphery relations from the perspective of a republic that is at once peripheral and central can tell us much about the changing sociopolitical dynamics of Russia and the role of Siberia and the Far East within the federation.

The Politics of Geography, Demography, and Ethnicity

On declaring sovereignty in 1990, the Sakha Republic signaled a willingness to compromise with Russia by hyphenating its name to "Yakut-Sakha Republic." "Yakut" is an outsider's name, a Russian corruption of an Evenk appellation for the northernmost Turkic-language speakers who call themselves the Sakha. By March 1992, the elected Sakha president, Mikhail Nikolaev, accepted the Federation Treaty, signing in the name of "The Sakha Republic (Yakutia)." The name change marked a determination to negotiate a more independent path, yet one still within the framework of Russia—a strategy employed in the adoption of a Sakha constitution by a relatively reformist republic legislature before Russia itself and many of its other republics had managed to ratify constitutions.[5]

For many residents of the republic, the Sakha constitution symbolizes a new pride and an unaccustomed chance to orient themselves in multiple cultural and political directions. When it was passed, people poured into the streets of the capital, Yakutsk, cheering, celebrating, and even hugging strangers. Many of those on the streets were Sakha, but some were members of other republic nationalities—Russians, Ukrainians, and indigenous peoples of the North, including the Yukagir, Even, and Evenk. The constitution is based on the principle of territorial (multiethnic), not national Sakha, sovereignty.

The Sakha Republic encompasses territory four times the size of Texas, but in 1989 the Sakha population numbered only 381,922, or 33 percent of the republic's population, while Russians comprised 50 percent. By 1994, the Sakha portion was closer to 40 percent, but still a minority. In contrast, the Sakha constituted 82.3 percent of the republic's population in 1926, before massive influxes of Russian settlers.[6] Recently, some Sakha cultural leaders have suggested that Sakha youth should hurry to marry and have more children as a way to improve the demographic balance. This has caused discussion among the Sakha intelligentsia as to whether such advocacy is too nationalistic and discriminatory. Most Sakha leaders have not emulated some other republics in agitating for Russians to leave.

The Sakha, like many of the other nationalities within Russia, could claim land lost when they became a Soviet autonomous republic in 1922. In the Sakha case, this amounts to hundreds of square kilometers reaching to the Okhotsk Sea. Sakha interest in ferreting out kin who now live in this region, or who left traces of themselves in toponyms, has grown. Jokes are even made about the conflict between Sakha and Japanese claims to Sakhalin.[7] But boundary disputes have not been the focus of ethnic politics. Rather, since 1990 groups, often resurrecting the names of 1920s organizations such as *Sakha Keskile* (Sakha Perspective) and *Sakha Omuk* (Sakha People), have sponsored cultural, ecological, political, and economic rights campaigns.

Despite the high ideals of the Sakha constitution, interethnic tension within the republic has a long history and has been growing. Tensions usually have simmered beneath the surface of calm ethnic relations, but occasionally have burst onto the surface of republic social life. Tensions exist predominantly between the indigenous Sakha and the newcomer Slavic workers, mostly Russians but also Ukrainians and Belarusians. Some conflicts have historically also been part of the complex Sakha and northern native relationships, given the concerns of the numerically smaller nationalities over dual dangers of "Yakutization" as well as "Russification." The Sakha in turn are trying to reverse Russification and promote "Sakhazation" among both rural and urban Sakha. This is viewed as an urgent, though not impossible, task. Some recall with pride that in the nineteenth century, "Yakutization" of Russians was prevalent throughout northeastern Siberia.

The cool interethnic climate between Russians and Sakha is exacerbated by Sakha perceptions that the workers who have poured into their republic since World War II are better paid and are given better housing, as well as access to privileges such as cars. Available data confirm at least some of these perceptions. In 1992, workers in agriculture, 87 percent of whom are Sakha, received pay averaging 16 percent of what those in the highly subsidized, mostly Slavic, energy sector earned.[8] Perhaps even more destructive to the social fabric are the emotional underpinnings of resentment, a belief that newcomers of whatever nationality have little sense of moral responsibility or respect, either for Siberian lands or for indigenous peoples. Russian epithets against natives, such as "wood chip," "slit eyes," and worse, are merely symptoms of this. Especially serious are Sakha accusations, notably in northern areas, that Russian male workers, who often come without stable families, are corrupt and exploit Sakha women.

Urban tensions between Sakha university students and Russian toughs erupted in spring 1986 in the capital of Yakutsk. Police mishandling of the fighting, which reputedly landed several Sakha girls in a hospital, led to a street demonstration three days later by several hundred Sakha students. It became the first of a long line of demonstrations in the Soviet Union in the Gorbachev period, preceding youth–police clashes in Kazakhstan in December 1986. In the Yakutsk case, many students explained the demonstration as an attempt to bring perestroika to their lagging republic. They resented the lack of arrests of Russians involved in the fighting and hoped to call attention to what they perceived as unequal treatment of Russians and Sakha. The republic Communist Party leader, Iu.N. Prokop'ev, himself Sakha, resorted to a traditional technique, accusing the Sakha students of improper internationalist upbringing. He also organized a commission that included Moscow officials, who, in fine materialist fashion, concluded that the students would be quieter if they had hot water in their dorms. A quota system was introduced in the university, allowing for greater numbers of Slavic students than had been the case previously; several student leaders were arrested, but the Russian instigators of the fighting were, by most accounts, never punished. Students were officially exonerated only in 1990.[9]

While the 1986 Yakutsk incident became famous—categorized as "nationalist" in the Russian-language press—other cases of sporadic interethnic conflict going back at least to the 1960s and continuing through the 1980s are also well known within the republic. In the 1960s, a minor university student protest was quelled quietly and quickly with the expulsion of a few Sakha. A brawl in the town of Niurbe resulted in the arrest of Sakha accused of perpetrating it as an expression of nationalism, when they tried to defend a Sakha man they thought was unjustly apprehended. In the late 1970s, the Ukrainian exile Chernovil reported on the inadvisability of Slavic residents violating the Sakha "ghettos" in some villages and towns.[10]

The preponderance of publicity in these cases singles out Sakha as instigators, but Sakha have also been acknowledged as targets. The shooting of a Sakha youth by an angry Russian in summer 1979 resulted in a street riot by hundreds near the university that was quickly hushed up at the time. Some interpret a street fight in early 1990 in which two Sakha students were shot, and which was followed by a demonstration, as a product of interethnic tension. It may have been more a reflection of the growing alcoholism and crime in Yakutsk, although in a more general sense, crime, alcoholism, and interethnic tensions can be seen as manifestations of inter-related social volatility.[11]

A further manifestation of interethnic tensions involves the issue of "marginals"—people of mixed ethnic background who feel increasingly uncomfortable if they do not decide to "fit in" to one ethnic group or another. Both Sakha and Russians express annoyance at people who "try to play their ethnic identity both ways." Some complain they are compelled to choose, both unofficially and officially, one dominant ethnic loyalty, although this certainly does not mean they cannot maintain friendships with people of other groups. In the Soviet period, the internal passport requirement that children of mixed marriages choose an ethnic identity at age sixteen meant that many potential Sakha, but not necessarily the majority, became Russian. The trend has turned the other way, with more Russified, well-educated Sakha rediscovering their roots.[12]

The Politics of Culture, History, and Memory

Many Sakha are aware of their Turkic linguistic and cultural roots and are fascinated by ethnographic and archaeological evidence of a mixed ethnic background that includes local northern hunting, fishing, and reindeer-breeding peoples (Evenk, Even, Yukagir) plus ancestors who may have come from the area around Lake Baikal, having been driven north by kin of the Mongol-Buriat.[13] The Sakha traditionally were cattle and horse breeders, living on large, far-flung homesteads (*alaas*) throughout Yakutia by the sixteenth century. Some still consider this an ideal today and are gradually using post-Soviet opportunities to wean themselves from collectives. For such people, cultural revival is a way of life wedded to private households rather than a public manifestation of protest or democracy. But some of these families follow urban cultural and political events through newspapers and the valued reports of relatives and friends. Sakha social networks are highly interconnected.

Sakha religion has evolved into a complex blend of Russian Orthodoxy, Turkic cosmology, animism, and shamanism, with a focus on sacred sites and trees associated with traditional patrilineal kinship-based territories. Though shamanism, as elsewhere, was driven underground in the Soviet period, it was not entirely destroyed. It has become one aspect of a Sakha cultural revival, symbolized by the presidential sponsorship of an international conference on shamanism in Yakutsk in 1992 and by the founding of an Association of Folk Medicine. A smaller group, *Kut-Siur* (roughly glossed as Soul-Reason), has led a campaign for more general awareness of Sakha ritual and philosophical traditions of "folk wisdom."[14] Its leaders include a linguist, a filmmaker, an ethnographer, and an artist. Its ideals, expressed through articles in the Sakha-language paper *Sakhaada,* were perhaps more widely discussed and admired just after the 1990 sovereignty declaration, when they were fresh. Some critics have called their reconstructions of tradition banal or ersatz. While important for recovery of personal and communal senses of moral, ritual, and spiritual well-being, the revival of religion usually has not taken mass, official forms, nor does shamanism seem likely to become a "state religion," as some have suggested.

The widely revered annual *yhyak* festival, evolved from Turkic spring fertility traditions, has taken various regional forms since World War II, after a hiatus due to Stalinist repression. Its popularity represents a resurgence of cultural awareness more than a deeply religious ritual, although for some it has religious aspects. One of the key elements of this two- or three-day celebration of seasonal renewal and creativity is the revival of a popular form of improvisational poetry that is chanted and danced. While it has religious roots, it is performed today not only at festivals and weddings but in a weekly Yakutsk social club. Its revival, after Stalinist repression, has been spurred by the personal efforts of a former Communist linguist.

Sakha cultural and spiritual revival began before the Gorbachev era and intensified in the late 1980s and early 1990s. Focus has been on the campaign for rebirth of the Sakha language and literature. While only 5 percent of the Sakha listed their primary language as Russian in 1989, fear of linguistic Russification, especially in the capital Yakutsk, has led to sharp monitoring of politicians' language abilities, to language legislation mandating more Sakha training in the schools, and to joint "state language" status for Sakha and Russian. In practice, this means encouraging but not forcing Russians to learn Sakha, especially since only about 2 percent knew it in the final years of the Soviet period. Efforts to adapt the previous unbalanced bilingualism (most Sakha knew Russian, but not vice versa) are being made through new "national" school programs in both rural and urban areas. The programs are specially designed to help Sakha children learn, and in some cases recover, their heritage. They were instituted by a dynamic, young Minister of Education, Egor Zhirkov.[15]

Historical memory recovery has been stimulated by a revision of the Soviet propaganda that stressed the peaceful incorporation of Yakutia into the Russian Empire in the sixteenth century and belittled the degree of economic efficiency and literacy among prerevolutionary Sakha. Leaders of this revision are intellectuals at the Institute of Languages, Literature and History, such as the toponym specialist Mikhail Ivanov (pen name Bogdaryn Siulbe) and the historian Egor Alekseev, who heads the Sakha branch of the All-Russian group Memorial, formed to honor victims of Soviet repression. The most passionate revisions, in theater and writing sponsored by the Ministry of Culture, have focused on figures such as Platon Sleptsov—pseudonym Oiunsky (from the Sakha word for shaman)—revolutionary, folklorist, and founder of the Institute of Languages, Literature and History, who died in Stalin's jails in 1937.[16] The existence of such revered Sakha intelligentsia of the period spanning the revolution, many of whom were punished for nationalism in the Stalin era, belies current Russian allegations that Sakha ethnic consciousness is simply a figment of Soviet-period political organization.

The most radical Sakha nationalism is that associated with groups calling for further cultural and political ties with Turkey and better contacts with other Turkic peoples, including non-Islamic Siberian peoples such as the Tyvans and Khakas. In its most extreme form, represented in the chauvinist writings of the newspaper journalist Uqqan (a pseudonym meaning "great"), this includes denigration of Slavic peoples as well as celebration of Turkic culture. Uqqan has admitted that mixtures of Turkic "blood" with non-Turkic make him uncomfortable. He has traveled to Turkey for a Pan-Turkic congress and associated himself with the reputedly fascist Turkic revival group the Gray Wolves. More benevolent aspects of his platform include the advocacy of a Latin alphabet for the Sakha, based on the Turkish model.[17]

Given Sakha cultural and spiritual roots, it is logical that many Sakha intellectuals are attracted to further cultural, political, and economic ties with Turkic peoples. But the more chauvinist aspects of Uqqan's writings are often condemned as extreme and seem to have little resonance in rural areas. Furthermore, most of the Turkic peoples of the former Soviet Union and the Russian Federation are themselves in such serious political and economic straits that they are hardly in a position to actively influence the Sakha. Turkey itself is far enough away, both geographically and culturally (including in religious orientation), to be investing only minimally in Sakha regeneration. A Turkey–Sakha Friendship Society has been established, an educational exchange is under way, and a few businessmen are exploring trade possibilities. Turkic congresses in Ankara, Almaty, Baku, and Kazan have included delegates from the Sakha Republic.

Another direction for Sakha cultural orientation is toward the north, with a new solidarity developing among at least some Sakha and minority indigenous peoples of the north. This is based on a sense not only of shared roots but also of shared responsibility for the fate of minorities who have in the past suffered from

Yakutization as well as Russification. New activism involves the establishment of the Association of Northern Minorities of the Sakha Republic and the founding of a new Institute of the Problems of the Northern Minority Peoples, headed by Vladimir Robbek. Both of these institutions include Sakha members. A related development has been the attempt to establish both governmental-level and informal contacts with a wide range of groups who share northern circumpolar civilization. Thus, the republic government has a program entitled "The Cooperation of the Sakha Republic (Yakutia) with Northern States" and has already signed a number of international cultural agreements. President Nikolaev has become vice president of the new Organization of Northern States, which has a branch office in Yakutsk. Official and unofficial ties with Alaska, Canada, Greenland, Denmark, Iceland, Norway, Sweden, and Finland have increased in the last several years.

A third, still weak but growing, orientation is toward Russia's eastern neighbors—Mongolia, China, the Koreas, and Japan. This marks a return to the regional cosmopolitanism that characterized prerevolutionary Yakutia, and indeed all of the Russian Far East. Workers, traders, and businessmen, especially from China and Korea, now have cultural and certainly economic, if not political, influence. Intermarriage cases and possibilities are discussed in the Sakha press and among the Sakha with the fascination of the previously forbidden and without the racism of some local Russians. President Nikolaev touts competition among Eastern businessmen, some of whom (especially the Japanese) try to keep a low profile regarding activities that may run counter to their own governments' policy of cautious investments. Nonetheless, a Japanese–Sakha Friendship Society has blossomed, leading to some cultural exchanges. Sakha students are in Mongolia, and conferences in all of the eastern states have become fashionable. A 1993 delegation to northern China found Sakha and Evenk kin Sinocized but hungry for further contacts.[18] Throughout the century, many Sakha have revered Eastern (especially Tibetan and Chinese) medicine and have sought correlations to their culture in the East. In 1990, a sophisticated filmmaker confessed an emotional and aesthetic kinship with Eastern cultures that was far stronger than with the West or with Russia.

While orientation toward other states is growing popular, most Sakha are especially concerned with finding their own path to cultural and political development, on the basis of adapted, or newly defined, "traditional" values. One group in the vanguard of this movement is *Sakha Keskile* (Sakha Perspective). Begun before the breakup of the Soviet Union, one of the group's first goals was Union status within the former USSR. The group was among the first to produce materials for public consumption on historical demography (Russification), colonialism, and "our sharp politics against those in power," according to one of the founders, the linguist Lazar Afanaseev. Both the group's leadership and following have reached beyond the elite intellectuals of Yakutsk to a broad cross section of Sakha. *Sakha Keskile* was itself a spin-off from the less successful multiethnic Popular Front, headed by Demitri Petrov, an electrician who also taught at the university. *Sakha Keskile*'s most active period was during the campaign to support the republic's 1990 sovereignty declaration. Members also were strong supporters of Yeltsin during the August 1991 putsch. In its aftermath, despite Yeltsin's triumph in Moscow, some former Communist Party members tried to block the group's growing influence by having members fired from their jobs in provincial cities such as Viliuisk. In speeches and news articles, Lazar Afanaseev has appealed to the Sakha to "behave as if we have a real republic: to grow up. The republic is rich. We can handle our own future. . . . If the republic is really ours, then it should be for the Yakut and the small minorities of the north. Why name it Yakutia if it is not our own?"[19]

While *Sakha Keskile* is not a political party, it has the potential to become one if electoral conditions within the republic become conducive to its organization. This has not occurred, partly due to the strength of its nemesis, the Communist Party, which has enjoyed a small comeback among some of the population, including elite Sakha rallied around the newspaper *Kyym*. Cleverly co-opting some of *Sakha Keskile*'s platform, former and current Communists, regional economic leaders, and some of the Sakha intelligentsia met in a much hyped "Sakha Congress" in December 1992. Some participants argue that it was more democratic than a typical Communist congress, for it had representatives from all regions, including some who felt free to criticize Yakutsk social and political policies. Such criticism included concern over the slow pace of land reform, coupled with a desire to ensure that foreigners would not monopolize land purchases or business privatization. Another significant aspect of the congress was its inclusion of representatives from Memorial (who was nonetheless booed off the stage) and the popular movement *Sakha Omuk*.

Sakha Omuk (Sakha People) is led by the Minister of Culture, Andrei Borisov. Since 1989, it has functioned as an umbrella organization, bringing diverse groups together, including at certain strategic moments even its rival *Sakha Keskile*. It has been active in the election of reformist deputies to various levels of legislatures, the passing of sovereignty legislation, the formulation of the republic constitution, and the election of the moderate and popular Sakha president Mikhail Nikolaev. Its main journalistic outlet is the magazine *Ilin* (glossed Forward), which includes exciting fiction, satire, and poetry as well as political commentary. Other more radical or shrill political groups, including some calling themselves Popular Fronts (e.g., the local Mirny Popular Front) or parties (e.g., *Il*, meaning Solidarity), have been less effective in a republic with a majority Slavic population and a high interethnic marriage rate.[20]

The most successful reform leaders, including President Nikolaev and Andrei Borisov, have stressed unifying, not polarizing, the republic population. Members of *Sakha Omuk* especially respond to the group's propaganda against ecological degradation, its concerns for the deteriorated psychological and physical health of a demoralized people, the stress on language revival, privatization, and legally defined sovereign rights vis-à-vis Moscow. Andrei Borisov explained in 1991, "*Sakha Omuk* was formed in response to Gorbachev's call for new ideas. It is not a Party. Perhaps only now are people ready for another Party. Earlier, people were too afraid."[21] Indeed, while more than ten "parties" were listed when the first opportunities for party registration legally emerged, they have faded fast in most people's consciousness for lack of charismatic leaders, organization, funds, or broad popular platforms. In December 1993 elections for a newly revamped and smaller republic parliament, deputies won more on the basis of personal reputation and networks than any party affiliation.

As *Sakha Omuk* has evolved, it has struggled, and by some accounts floundered, over its role as a quasi-party based primarily on Sakha membership. By 1993, *Sakha Omuk* vice president Vladimir Nikolaev justified Sakha leadership in the republic as based on the mixed ethnic nature of the dominant Sakha indigenous nationality: "The Sakha people formed from a synthesis of Yukagir, Even-Evenk, Rus and Sakh tribes and clans, thus governance by the Sakha People is a general governance for all northern nations." He also expressed disappointment that the republic had not yet reached a "second stage" of truly effective multiethnic sovereignty: "We are neither a real state nor a colony, but something unclear in-between."[22]

The Politics of Economics

The Sakha Republic, like other Siberian and Far Eastern areas, is among the poorest in per capita living standards in Russia. But republic authorities have developed positions of strength with the central government because they have learned to bargain over the vast and underexploited mineral and energy wealth of the republic. Not only have oil, gas, and coal been discovered (in large yet hard-to-reach quantities), but gold, silver, tin, copper, and nearly every precious gem valued by "civilization" exist in the republic, especially diamonds and emeralds. These resources are paradoxically both a blessing and a curse for the indigenous population, which in the past has not been able to reap many of their benefits.[23] Rumors abound of parts of the republic where local people try to hide the presence of rich mineral discoveries, so as not to draw more outsiders into their areas. Sakha concern that newcomers, whether Russian or foreign, will monopolize major resources has led to protests over particular business deals, for example, the agreement that gave exploration and sale rights of *charoit*, a semi-precious purple stone held sacred by the Sakha, to a Russian.[24]

The republic depends on negotiations with Moscow to provide many of its critically needed supplies, especially foodstuffs, to survive the harsh Siberian winter. In summer 1993, when less than half the normal supplies had arrived and credits for buying them elsewhere were not forthcoming, republic leaders decided to withhold taxes. This was a strategy born of frustration and anger rather than a protest secession drive calculated to take advantage of chaos, as some central authorities claimed. The Sakha leadership under President Nikolaev promised eventual renewal of tax payments (as they had in a similar previous incident) and also vowed to "eat the diamonds," if necessary. This extracted a promise from the center to allow the republic to keep some taxes for federal expenditures within the republic. Ability to use some resource wealth in sales directly to foreign bidders, or as collateral, has also only recently been negotiated and is highly controversial in Moscow. Before 1990, the republic kept none of its extracted wealth for direct sale. Its gold supplies amounted to over 60 percent of the yearly total for Russia, and its diamonds were 98 percent.[25]

Insistence on resource sharing resulted in a 1992 agreement that the Sakha Republic and the Moscow government each control 32 percent of the diamond profits, with the labor collective controlling 23 percent, eight regions getting a 1 percent cut, and the rest for administration and economic development. The republic has the right to buy at a fixed wholesale price 20 percent of the gem-quality diamonds for stimulation of its fledgling gem industry, dealing directly with foreign bidders like DeBeers. A joint-stock company, Almaz-Rossiia-Sakha, was established in 1992 to administer the diamond industry, and a new factory has begun turning out finished gems, something never permitted under Soviet rule. The changes have been painful for both sides, with some Russians accusing naive Siberian natives of making bad (less profitable than possible) deals with DeBeers and some Sakha close to President Nikolaev arguing (unofficially, with some defensiveness) that they should be allowed to make their own mistakes and learn from them.[26]

As Moscow has loosened its colonial-style economic grip on natural resources, the Sakha have been able to quickly turn toward direct, potentially profitable international contacts, especially in the Pacific Rim.[27] The South Korean firm Hyundai has signed an agreement involving the Elgin coal deposits and a branchline off the Baikal–Amur railway. Japanese firms have negotiated for republic lumber and other possible investments. The danger for the rural Sakha, uneasily collectivized yet hesitant about privatization, is that they will trade economic and ecological exploitation by Moscow for similar exploitation by foreigners. The railway is particularly controversial, for it will split an already decimated Evenk reindeer-herding group and create the potential for more industrialization than the delicate northern ecology can withstand. Yet ironically, given the history of Russification through Trans-Siberian rail colonization, one of the arguments winning over some members of the Sakha intelligentsia is that the new rail line will provide a solid communication and transport link with Eastern countries, making the Sakha less beholden on Moscow. The Sakha already rely heavily on Pacific Rim trade, especially in foreign cars.

Both political and economic concerns in turn have led some of the Slavic population to leave the republic in the early 1990s, although not in enormous numbers and often for purposes of claiming citizenship in other newly independent states. As in many areas of Siberia, most of these came to "Yakutia" as temporary workers, to make a "long ruble" and then return to their homelands. Incoming northern workers have been paid considerably more than their normal salaries in Russia as compensation for hardship conditions, but this policy of attracting workers is now bitterly resented. Precisely these workers are often blamed by Siberians, of both Slavic and indigenous backgrounds, for creating a psychology of immediate gratification that has led to terrible ecological destruction in mining and lumbering areas and to the ethnic tensions described above.

The issue of interethnic tensions is intertwined with that of economic politics, for the Slavic newcomer population has dominated the energy and mining industries, while the Sakha remain preeminent in the poorer agricultural sector. In contrast, Sakha Communist Party leaders dominated traditional Soviet administrative positions, and Sakha deputies in the parliament occupied and still occupy more than their demographic share of seats. Thus an imbalance developed between economic and political power brokers, partially marked by ethnic differences, albeit with some notable exceptions.[28] Some of the former power holders formed an uneasy conservative alliance that welcomed the August 1991 putsch and supported parliament speaker Khasbulatov in October 1993. After the 1991 putsch, they were only partially discredited, remaining, as in many areas of Russia, a force blocking privatization of land and limiting reform. Cautiously reformist President Nikolaev has needed to battle these conservative elements, as well as demands for economic rights that reached strike proportions in predominantly Slavic subregions of the republic. Nikolaev's compelling argument to stave off strikes has been that all will benefit if local Russian and Sakha Republic leaders together can negotiate successfully with the center for a greater share of the republic's phenomenal wealth, while still maintaining the ties that provide food subsidies.[29]

The resource-sharing argument has also moderated threats of some minority Slavic regionalists to split the republic in a north–south divide. The basis for this proposal, deeply frightening to the Sakha, is the claim that most of the Slavic population lives in southern, relatively industrialized regions, while more of the Sakha and other indigenous groups are in central and northern areas. But both Slavs and natives are too intermixed for this demographic description to be valid.[30]

Russian leaders have shown some sensitivity to the political implications of the Sakha Republic's wealth. Visitors from Moscow have acknowledged that workers in diamond mines should not have to live in wooden barracks. Central authorities conceded to some Sakha tax demands during negotiations over the Federal Treaty, and they have continued other economic negotiations. Despite internal republic debate over the degree to which the center merely throws the republic a few bones, President Yeltsin has been particularly attentive to President Nikolaev, whose leadership role in two incarnations of the Russian Federation Council and overtures to other Russian and former republics have helped give the Sakha Republic a high profile. During October 1993, Nikolaev openly supported Yeltsin. The republic's parliament was less enthusiastic and was quickly dissolved by Nikolaev, who welcomed the opportunity to eliminate members holding back reform.

A State Within a State: Center–Periphery Relations

The Sakha case can be placed roughly midway on a scale of republic comparisons stretching from secession-mindedness to mere turmoil. Within Siberia and the Far East, it is a pivotal player in striving toward regional political and economic decision making. Given republic geography (without outside state borders except in the Arctic), the demographic minority status of the Sakha indigenous nationality, the predominantly peaceful historical relationship of Russians and Sakha, and the compromise orientation of most ethnic politics, most Sakha are far from radical and secessionist. But their case is significant precisely because of its contingent, swing-vote nature. As elsewhere, ethnic politics within the republic have evolved from a focus on cultural and ecological issues toward a more politicized, not necessarily chauvinist, nationalism. The potential for interethnic polarization is very real, yet ethnic politics have not hardened into the rhetoric or actions of uncompromising antagonism.

The Sakha relationship with the Russian administrative center is not only critical and dynamic but also dangerously misunderstood on all sides. President Nikolaev and the republic itself are engaged in a delicate balancing act. The 1992 Sakha constitution places republic laws above Russian federal ones and has a controversial provision for the republic's "right to leave the Russian Federation." Many Sakha say they would prefer not to exercise that right unless a major upheaval in the center pushes them into it. Sakha Republic demands for sovereignty are limited, with no pretense of establishing a full range of independence attributes, such as a national currency, a banking system, a separate defense strategy, or an army. The goal of many activists, for what is hoped to be a long-term peaceful post-Soviet transition period, is to carve out new political and legal territory in creative, negotiated federal relations.

Part of the republic's negotiated status involves relationships with other republics within the Russian Federation and with countries of the Commonwealth of Independent States. Whereas previously the hierarchically organized Soviet Union was geared to channel communication between republics through Moscow, since the Soviet breakup (and for a short time before it) cross-republic and cross-state contacts have flourished in a plethora of barter deals and cultural agreements. Within Siberia and the Far East, Sakha ties with Buriatia, for example, have increased, and the main highway to the Okhotsk Sea has been reinforced to support greater truck traffic. Toward the west, direct contacts with Ukraine and Latvia have been publicized. In addition, the presidents of Tatarstan, Bashkortostan, and Sakha gave notice in 1992 that they would join in monitoring Russian compliance with federal agreements. Such ties have had diverse effects on the Sakha economy and politics, but they can be viewed as a step away from unilateral dependencies on the Russian center toward multilateral, mutually beneficial arrangements.

At the same time, the Sakha are leery of regionalist secession moves. For example, Far Eastern economic separatism, led by Slavic Siberians often of Communist Party backgrounds, has provoked concern regarding selfish economic policies and violations of indigenous minority rights. While many Sakha express solidarity with general regional claims that argue against the inefficiencies of an overcentralized economy, they are alarmed that conditions could become so bad that a Russian nationalist government might form in Vladivostok, recapitulating in a new context the 1920s Far Eastern Republic.[31] In this sense, most Sakha claim very little political identity with the whole Far Eastern region, despite growing economic interdependencies.

Different Sakha political and cultural groups view the various orientations now available to them for exploration in different ways and in terms of priorities that sometimes are compatible and sometimes clash. This has become an aspect of unaccustomed debate within the republic over economic and political direction as well as over the need to increasingly involve the whole republic populace in the politics of a fledgling democracy. To make this debate productive, rather than destructive, people are only beginning to develop a psychology of self-governance and self-determination.[32]

A self-conscious Sakha ethnicity, along with regional and extended kinship identities, was present well before the Soviet period, but it did not evolve into a state-oriented nationalism until the twentieth century. A mild, nonchauvinist nationalism grew in the cultural and economic climate of the 1920s, but was then officially repressed in the Soviet period. As in other republics, conditions for nationalism were present from the outset of Soviet rule, given the ethnically based republic hierarchical structure that created specific, often contested, "autonomous republic" boundaries and supported educated, ethnic (albeit mostly puppet) elites. These conditions were compounded by repressions of political and cultural leaders, as well as whole groups of economic elites who had formed the backbone of republic prosperity. Cultural and political life was squelched only temporarily and unevenly. Nationalism was even exacerbated by relatively tolerant policies of paternalism that chafed as non-Russian elites of so-called "autonomous" republics came to know more about other peoples' human-rights struggles both within and outside the Soviet empire. All of this nourished a potential for multiple expressions of ethnic identity, multiple manifestations of political activism, and by 1990, new constitutions for "sovereign" republics.

The 1990s explosion of ethnic and nationalist expression came not simply out of newly created post-Soviet societal chaos, a power vacuum, or a thawing of frozen, pre-Soviet identities, but more as the result of a cumulative series of dynamic interethnic encounters that evolved throughout the twentieth century. Crucial to this dynamic, not only was intended policy fostered from the center but also unintended consequences. Demographic changes illustrate both planning pretensions and subsequent problems, as many of the chapters in this volume reveal. The Russians constitute more than 80 percent of Russia, with most of the ethnically based republics, like that of the Sakha, coping with a Soviet legacy that has turned their primary (titular) ethnic groups into minorities in their own lands. This is particularly relevant in Siberia and the Far East, with the exception of Tyva.

Like many experiments in social planning, the Communist version of melting-pot ideology scalded its cooks. The ironic consequence of Soviet ethnic policies was a heightened awareness of ethnicity, including establishment of conditions that led eventually, in the case of Chechnia, to separatism and invasion. In the Sakha Republic, however, neither extremists nor nostalgic de-ethnicized Soviet patriots have become the norm. This is illustrated symbolically by the continued multiethnic nature of the capital, Yakutsk (where the Sakha are less than 30 percent), and the lack of agitation to change its name to Sakhask.

None of the republics or regions in Siberia and the Far East began the post-Soviet period from positions of equality in relation to the center: economic conditions varied, the degree of geopolitical boundary and ethnic-group correlation varied, and legacies of "punishment" before, during, and after Stalin varied, to name only a few of the most salient dimensions.[33] These differences meant that ethnic groups, and individuals within them, experienced different degrees of radicalization. Given Pan-Soviet problems, similar kinds of formal and informal opposition groups evolved, yet nuances are significant here too. Ecological activism, for example, has been more correlated with nationalism in the Sakha Republic than in Buriatia, where the movement to save Lake Baikal became international and mainly Russian-led.

When analyzing interethnic relations, it is important to make a distinction between minor tensions manifest on the streets and the really serious violence that erupts when outside troops are brought in to quell a disturbance. In such cases, relations between indigenous populations and Russians deteriorate rapidly, crystallizing nationalism into its more virulent forms. This occurred in Chechnia and Tyva, but thus far has not happened in the Sakha Republic. Nonetheless, specially trained Ministry of Internal Affairs troops (OMON) patrol the streets of the capital, and their visibility is resented by local peoples. A Moscow-directed over-reaction to interethnic disturbances could be tragic for the republic.

Diverse views within Sakha society show the shakiness of generalizations about the meaning of culture, history, economics, and center–periphery politics itself. Even such "solid" aspects of data as demography and geography are up for interpretive grabs in a politically destabilized context. In a world where political and geographic fault lines are changing daily, one lesson is that "Western" models, "Soviet" legacies, and renewed "Eastern" orientations are all adapted and adaptable in unexpected ways by sometimes desperately creative people. Although the word "democracy" may be discredited due to overuse by people who behave undemocratically, the mechanism of electoral politics in the Sakha Republic has resulted in the election of a popular (former Communist reformist) president and a criticized, but functioning, post-Soviet two-house parliament. While "Westernization" is often eschewed in favor of fascination with the East, some mix between East and West, themselves shifting concepts, is emerging in Sakha nationalist approaches to economic and diplomatic relations. Inside the republic, crude Soviet stereotypes of either noble or ignoble herders and hunters have long been replaced by a complex awareness of multiple identities. Yet the power of the Sakha language, with its metaphorical tales about forest people, has not been lost. The immediate fear of reprisals by angry Russian nationalists, unaccustomed to internal hemorrhaging, has made many Sakha postpone dreams of independent white horses racing eastward.

Notes

Data for this essay were collected during fieldwork in the Sakha Republic in February–July 1986; and the summers of 1991–94. I am indebted to the International Research and Exchanges Board (IREX), the Social Science Research Council (SSRC), the Kennan Institute of the Smithsonian's Wilson Center, Leningrad University, Yakutsk University, the Academy of Sciences Institute of Languages, Literature and History in Yakutsk (IaLI), and the Sakha Ministry of Culture for fieldwork and/or research support. I am deeply thankful to my Sakha language teacher, Klara Belkin, and to numerous Sakha friends who have opened their homes to me in the republic and have visited me in Washington, including I. Alekseev, A. Gogolev, V. and Z. Ivanov, A. Reshetnikova, A. Tomtosov, and U. and P. Vinokurova.

1. I am grateful to Uliana Vinokurova, elected deputy to the Upper House of the Sakha parliament, for this story and for many insights into Sakha culture and politics, and to the John D. and Catherine T. MacArthur Foundation for making work with her in the United States possible in November 1993.

2. See the speech by M. Nikolaev in *Literaturnaia gazeta*, December 1, 1993, p. 11. Eighteen ethnically based republics signed the March 1992 Russian Federation Treaty, consolidating a status upgrade for several republics. The Chechen and Tatar republics held back from signing and from participating in the December 1993 elections. For a comparison of Chechnia, Tatarstan, Tyva, Buryatia, and Sakha, see Marjorie Mandelstam Balzer, "From Ethnicity to Nationalism: Turmoil in the Russian Mini-Empire," in James Millar and Sharon Wolchik, eds., *The Social Legacy of Communism* (Cambridge: Cambridge University Press, 1994).

3. My approach to nationalism syncretizes Fredrik Barth, *Ethnic Groups and Boundaries* (Boston: Little, Brown, 1969); Anthony D. Smith, *The Ethnic Origins of Nations* (London: Blackwell, 1986); Benedict Anderson, *Imagined Communities* (London: Verso, 1983); Yael Tamir, *Liberal Nationalism* (Princeton: Princeton University Press, 1993); and Gisli Palsson, *Beyond Boundaries: Understanding, Translation and Anthropological Discourse* (London: Berg, 1993). For relevant cases, see Caroline Humphrey, *Karl Marx Collective: Economy, Society and Religion in a Siberian Collective Farm* (Cambridge: Cambridge University Press, 1983); Ronald Grigor Suny, *The Making of the Georgian Nation* (Bloomington: Indiana University Press, 1988); and Katherine Verdery, *National Ideology Under Socialism: Identity and Cultural Politics in Ceauşescu's Romania* (Berkeley: University of California Press, 1991). See also Marjorie Mandelstam Balzer, "Nation-

alism in the Soviet Union: One Anthropological View," *Journal of Soviet Nationalities,* vol. 1, Fall 1990, pp. 4–22.

4. The significance lies in the ethnically based nature of much of the political structure rather than in population figures. But non-Russian ethnic groups within Russia are considerably more numerous than is recognized in the formal political structure. The 1989 census recorded 126 non-Russian indigenous groups in Russia; some researchers have revised this to about 160. See L.M. Drobizheva, "Kazhdomu—svoi," *Rodina* 1991, pp. 19–22; Irina Krasnopol'skaia interview with Solomon Bruk, "128 ili 500?" *Soiuz,* no. 16, April 1991, p. 14. Statistics here and below are from *Natsional'nyi sostav naseleniia SSSR* (Moscow, 1991), unless otherwise noted. Depending on how they are counted, approximately thirty-four groups are Siberian or Far Eastern (including twenty-nine "small nationalities of the North, Siberia and the Far East" and the four larger groups, Sakha, Tyvans, Buriat, and Komi). The non-Russian population in Russia, based on the 1989 census, is approximately 30 million, or about 20 percent of the population of Russia (147 million). Of these, less than 2 million are non-Russian indigenous Siberians and Far Easterners.

5. "Deklaratsiia," *Sotsialisticheskaia Iakutiia,* 28 September 1990, p. 1.; "Konstitutsia," *Iakutskie vedomosti,* 27 February 1992, pp. 1–8. President Nikolaev, a former Communist Party reformer, has a mixed ethnic background but declares his nationality as Sakha and speaks fluent Sakha as well as Russian.

6. For both statistics and excellent analysis, see P.S. Maksimov, *Mezhnatsional'nye otnosheniia v regione (po materialam Iakutskoi ASSR)* (Yakutsk: Academy of Sciences, 1990). He confirmed the Sakha increase from 1989 to 1993 in a July 1993 personal communication.

7. "Sakha-lin" may have a root in common with the ethnonym "Sakha" and the Sakha word "ilin," which means "forward." For derivation of various toponyms, see the work of Bogdarin Siulbe, *Toponimika Iakutii* (Yakutsk: Academy of Sciences, 1985).

8. Uliana A. Vinokurova, *Skaz o Narode Sakha* (Yakutsk: Bichk, 1994), pp. 98–111. In 1989, pay for a state-farm worker averaged 377 rubles a month, and in industry, 619. In 1992, average pay was 9,002 rubles for an agricultural worker and 56,000 for an energy worker. About 74 percent of the Sakha population was rural in 1989, while Sakha constituted only 13 percent of the republic's urban population. See also Maksimov, *Mezhnatsional'nye otnosheniia,* p. 8.

9. The 1986 incidents coincided with my residence in a Yakutsk university dorm. I was falsely accused of being an outside agitator of the demonstrations and narrowly avoided being deported. As with all incidents of this kind, various participants and analysts see the "same" events in different ways. A full analysis requires a Rashomon-like telling of many stories in many different voices. For statements by the republic Communist Party leader, Iu.N. Prokop'ev, see "Internatsional'noe vospitanie—delo vsei oblastnoi partiinoi organizatsii," *Sotsialisticheskaia Iakutia,* 18 May 1986, pp. 2–4.

10. Viacheslav Chernovil's allegations appeared as "Zaiavlenie ministru vnutrennikh del IaASSR o mezhnatsional'nykh konfliktov v Iakutii," 30 August 1979; and in print in *Svoboda,* 22 February 1980. A Russian manuscript version circulated abroad, depicting sexual graffiti insults exchanged by Sakha and Russians of Niurbe, plus stereotypes voiced to Chernovil by both sides. On the Russian side, Sakha were called "monkeys," "slit-eyes," and blamed as "terrible nationalists" who would still "be in furs" on the edge of starvation if it were not for Russians. On the Sakha side, Russians were termed exploiting, racist louts, although Chernovil notes this was not everyone's opinion about every Russian. After several threatening personal incidents, mostly with drunken Sakha youths, the unprejudiced Chernovil felt he had "become a victim of local inter-nationality tensions" and requested transfer.

11. A short report on the 1990 incident appeared from the Siberian Information Agency, in *Express Khronika*, no. 2, 9 January 1990. Information comes mainly from witnesses. On worsening crime statistics in the republic from 1985–89, see *Sibir' i Dal'nyi Vostok: Sotsial'noe razvitie* (Moscow: Goskomizdat, 1990), p. 141. Sakha sociologists bemoan a general breakdown in morals begun well before the Gorbachev period, encouraged through the discrepancies between Soviet social ideals and practice, exacerbated by the breakdown of family values, and expressed through ethnic scapegoating. See Uliana A. Vinokurova, *Tsennostnye orientatsii Iakutov v usloviiakh urbanizatsii* (Novosibirsk: Nauka, 1992); *Bihigi Sakhalar* (Yakutsk: Sakha sirineehi, 1992); and Maksimov, *Mezhnatsional'nye otnosheniia.*

12. Daria G. Bragina, *Sovremennye etnicheskie protsessy v Tsentral'noi Iakutii* (Yakutsk: Academy of Sciences, 1985); B.N. Popov, "Mezhnatsional'nye braki i ikh osobennosti v regione," in *Mezhnatsional'nye otnosheniia*, pp. 73–95; and E.N. Fedorova, "Dynamika sotsial'no-demograficheskoi struktury naseleniia Iakutskoi ASSR," in ibid., pp. 105–13.

13. On ethnic history, see A.I. Gogolev, *Istoricheskaia etnografiia Iakutov* (Yakutsk: University Press, 1986); "Cultural History of the Yakut (Sakha) People: The Work of A.I. Gogolev," *Anthropology and Archeology of Eurasia*, vol. 31, no. 2, Fall 1992, pp. 1–84. Other Turkic peoples of Siberia include the Tyvans, Khakas, Altai-Kizhi, Teleut, Kumandin, Shor, and Tofalar.

14. *Kut-Siur* ideas are expressed in L. Afanas'ev et al., *Aiyy yorehe* (Yakutsk: Sakha keskile, 1990). Uliana A. Vinokurova begins her book *Bihigi Sakhalar* with a poem by Eiduo: "I wish the ideas and *kut-siur* of the Sakha to be as joined and strengthened as in a strong cyclone, and raised up to the sky." See also Marjorie Mandelstam Balzer, "Dilemmas of the Spirit: Religion and Atheism in the Yakut-Sakha Republic," in *Religious Policy in the Soviet Union* (Cambridge: Cambridge University Press, 1992), pp. 231–51; and Marjorie Mandelstam Balzer, "Shamanism and the Politics of Culture," *Shamanism*, vol. 1, no. 2, 1993.

15. Egor P. Zhirkov, the Minister of Education, organized a 1993 international conference on the development of national school programs: Zhirkov, "Obrazovanie i razvitie: natsional'naia strategiia na podstupakh k XXI veku," *Mezhdunarodnaia konferentsiia natsional'naia shkola: kontseptsiia i tekhnologiia razvitiia* (Yakutsk: UNESCO, 1993). President M. Nikolaev's presidential decree "Ukaz prezidenta respubliki Sakha (Yakutiia) o merakh po razvitiiu obrazovaniia" (Yakutsk, 1993) supports the reforms, also described by G.N. Volkov, "Etnopedagogicheskaia kontseptsiia natsional'noi shkoly," in ibid. Some Russians have already enrolled in kindergarten programs to learn Sakha at an early age. See also the language sections of the Declaration of Sovereignty and the Sakha constitution, cited above. Cf. M. Muchin, "Nuzhen li zakon o iazykakh?" *Sovety Iakutii*, 18 March 1992, p. 6. Sakha-language newspapers have blossomed, for example, *Keskil, Sakha sire,* and *Sakhaada; Kyym,* the old Communist Party paper, has adapted. In 1989, 15 percent of the urban Sakha did not know the Sakha language, according to E.N. Fedorova, "Dinamika sotsial'no-demograficheskoi struktury naseleniia Iakutskoi ASSR," in *Mezhnatsional'nye otnosheniia*, p. 112.

16. Other revered Sakha intelligentsia of the period spanning the revolution include the writer and ethnographer A.E. Kulakovsky, the ethnographer and activist P.V. Ksenofontov, the dramatist and reformist A.I. Sofronov, the writer N.D. Neustroev, and the jurist-dramatist-politician V.V. Nikiforov, all of whom were punished for nationalism in the Stalin era. See I.I. Nikolaev and I.P. Ushnitskii, *Tsentral'noe delo: Khronika Stalinskikh repressii v Iakutii* (Yakutsk: Yakutsk Press, 1990); and the journal *Ilin*, vol. 1, nos. 1–3, 1991, especially Uliana A. Vinokurova, "Natsional'naia pamiat'," *Ilin*, no. 1, pp. 22–23. For a sense of the talent lost, see A.E. Kulakovsky, *Nauchnye trudy* (Yakutsk: Institute of Languages, Literature and History, 1979).

17. See, for example, Uqqan, "Qaan tara'ta," *Sakhaada,* 9 December 1992, no. 49, pp. 3–4, in which he said, "Just as my organism is not comfortable with other blood groups, so I am not comfortable with alien truth, and the sincerity of alien blood." An angry rebuttal against his chauvinism was written by the historian Egor Alekseev, "Chabylanyy, tylga tiihii abyrya suokha," *Kyym,* 19 January 1993, no. 101, p. 3. I am grateful to Egor Alekseev, who is head of the Sakha branch of Memorial, for directing my attention to this debate.

18. See, for example, Lia Vinokurova, "V poiska soroichei," *Yakutiia,* 3 June 1993, p. 3. She concludes by emphasizing that further exchange programs with Northern China (Inner Mongolia Autonomous Region) "will raise prestige and morally enrich state sovereignty."

19. Lazar Afanas'ev interview, August 1992. He fell into the old habit of calling the republic Yakutia, although more recently he is careful to say "Sakha."

20. "*Il*" glosses as "agreement," "solidarity," and "peace," but the party had fared badly as of November 1993, according to sociologist Uliana Vinokurova.

21. Andrei S. Borisov interview, June 1991. See "Ustav Sakha Omuk," 10 August 1990, manuscript.

22. Vladimir T. Nikolaev, in a March 1993 letter to M.M. Balzer describing *Sakha Omuk* group meetings and positions. Followers complain that not enough meetings were called, nor enough leadership initiatives taken. A new stage may not emerge until political parties with slates of candidates develop.

23. See, for example, D. Fedorov, "Tablitsa mendeleeva 'uletuchivaetsia'," *Afto nom,* 1 November 1991, p. 8. Living standards vary widely, being lower for indigenous, rural populations. The republic was overall better off than poor regions of the North Caucasus, according to *Izvestiia,* 13 February 1993, p. 1. See also Maksimov, *Mezhnatsional'nyi otnosheniia,* pp. 8–10.

24. One such protester is Lazar Afanas'ev, head of the group *Sakha Keskile* (interview, August 1993).

25. The "eat the diamonds" phrase was reported by Uliana Vinokurova, personal communication, October 1993. Compare this concern with those raised by Pavel Minakir in this volume. Accurate statistics on diamond resources are more available than on gold. See the pamphlet by President Mikhail Nikolaev, *Nuzhen li Rossii sever?* (Yakutsk: Presidential administration, 1993), pp. 6–14. Tax policy has been widely debated; see comments by the chairman of the Sakha supreme soviet, Kliment Ivanov, "Ne boikott . . ." *Rossiiskaia gazeta,* 19 August 1992, p. 2.

26. The diamond deal has been misunderstood and misreported. Data come from an interview with President Mikhail Nikolaev, "Period trudnostei nada skoree proiti," *Literaturnaia gazeta,* 1 December 1993, p. 11. See also "Need for Drastic Action," *FBIS,* 28 January 1992, from "Misfortunes of the Diamond Storehouse," *Rossiiskaia gazeta,* 27 January 1992, p. 1.

27. See Ivan Nikolaev, *Zagadka Mikhaila Nikolaeva* (Yakutsk, 1992), especially p. 9, for a claim that the republic expects a $646 million investment in 1992–94.

28. One exception was the head of Yakut Gold (*Yakutzoloto*) in the 1980s, who was Sakha. Sakha remain in leadership positions there. The administrative and parliamentary disproportion in Sakha favor is well known in the republic and is pointed out in the document written under then Goskomnats minister Valery Tishkov, "O sostoianii i merakh po razresheniiu pervoocheredykh neotlozhnykh problem v sfere mezhnatsional'nykh otnoshenii," *Gosudarstvennyi komitet Rossiiskoi Federatsii po natsional'noi politike,* 7 September 1992, p. 13. The Yakutsk city council is dominated by Russians, and this may be one reason why Yakutsk has been slow to change street names, much less change the name of the republic capital.

29. Mikhail E. Nikolaev, "Nuzhen li Rossii sever?" *Nezavisimaia gazeta,* 23 June

1992, p. 5; P. Shinkarenko interview with M. Nikolaev, "Almaznyi moi venets," *Rossiiskie vesti,* 2 June 1992, p. 2.; and the interview with him by Radik Batyrshin in *Nezavisimaia gazeta,* 18 February 1993, pp. 1–3. For background on Nikolaev, see *Lider reforma* (Yakutsk: Ilin, 1991). In 1992, a group of forty-two conservative supreme soviet deputies signed a petition protesting the direction the "sovereign" republic was taking "toward the destruction of the Russian state." See *Zaiavlenie gruppy narodnykh deputatov Verkhovnogo Soveta Respubliki Sakha (Iakutia),* 6 February 1992. The group included both Slavic and Sakha politicians, with the former in preponderance.

30. Little about these threats has appeared in print. For one hint, see Nikolaev, *Zagadka* (Yakutsk, 1992), p. 17. It was only in these southern, and relatively more Slavic regions, that Zhirinovsky did well in the December 1993 elections. The use of the demographic argument is particularly ironic, given the ill-conceived colonial-style settlement policies of nearby regions described in this volume by Steven Marks (along the Trans-Siberian). The displacement and driving north of indigenous populations, however, is a familiar pattern in the history of Europe, Russia, and North America and to some extent has also occurred in Yakutia. Compare Eric Wolf, *Europe and the People Without History* (Berkeley: University of California Press, 1982).

31. For historical perspective, see John J. Stephan, "Far Eastern Conspiracies? Russian Separatism on the Pacific," *Australian Slavonic and East European Studies,* vol. 4, nos. 1–2, 1990, pp. 135–52.

32. This idea is more fully developed in Vinokurova, *Bihigi Sakhalar,* p. 93. See also Mikhail Nikolaev's speech, as recorded in *Literaturnaia gazeta,* 1 December 1993, p. 11.

33. Ethnologists acknowledge these variable legacies, stressing the "irretrievable" problems caused by the 1922 national–state hierarchical administrative system. Greater rights of republics over Russian "oblasts" have been criticized. Conflicts are seen as: over status; territorial; and internal political. See A.N. Iamskov, ed., *Sovremennye problemy i veroiatnye napravleniia razvitiia natsional'no-gosudarstvennogo ustroistva Rossiiskoi Federatsii* (Moscow: Academy of Sciences, 1992), pp. 7, 11–19.

Nivkhi, Russians, and Others

The Politics of Indigenism on Sakhalin Island

Bruce Grant

> *"Overcoming the past is a prerequisite for full membership in the family of nations of the USSR."*
> —from the masthead of the Sakhalin newspaper
> *Bolshevik Fish Run*, 1930s

In Murmansk in the late 1980s, Mikhail Gorbachev proclaimed the Soviet Union's commitment to the "common European home," yet earlier in Vladivostok he had declared the USSR to be "an Asian country." However convenient it may have been for the Soviet authorities to adjust these allegiances, for the indigenous peoples of the Soviet Far East neither side of this duality quite captured their experience.

On Sakhalin Island in 1990, I often asked indigenous Nivkhi whether they thought of themselves as Asians or Europeans. "Europeans?" came the usual first reply. Europe was London, Paris, maybe Moscow, but certainly not Sakhalin Island. Asia then? Only fifty kilometers north of Japan, the Nivkhi, Paleoasiatics of scholarly lore, rarely showed much enthusiasm for being known as Asians. Asia had long represented the dark side of Russia's character, and Nivkhi shared in this unease. To speak of Asians on Sakhalin was also to invoke the widely held conviction that the Chinese and Japanese who once held the island did little but pillage its resources. "We're Soviets," came the most common reply. And after seventy years of Soviet rule, this answer made sense. Yet the question came up again and again, since, for the current generations whose parents and grandparents had routinely intermarried with and spoke the languages of their northeast Asian neighbors, perestroika was making them heirs to a long forgotten past.

A small group of some four and a half thousand people living on northern

Sakhalin Island and the banks of the Amur, Nivkhi, or Giliaks as they were known until roughly the 1930s, made their debut in Russian lore in 1859 as a result of the journeys of the German naturalist Leopold von Schrenk, who was commissioned to study the Far East by the Imperial Academy of Sciences. In the next decade, Nivkhi became the subjects of protracted investigation by the exiled revolutionary turned anthropologist Lev Shternberg. From that time on, they became one of the most studied of Siberia's native peoples, with major contributions being made by exiled Polish scholar Bronislaw Pilsudski (elder brother of the Polish leader Józef Pilsudski), Shternberg's graduate student Erukhim Kreinovich, the Russian ethnographer Anna Smoliak, the Nivkh ethnographer Chuner Taksami, and the Sakhalin Regional Museum.

Yet our knowledge of Nivkh history is nonetheless a selective one. We know a great deal, for example, about the prerevolutionary ways of life of Nivkhi *within* their own communities, such as kinship relations, belief systems, and material culture, yet we find little if anything on relations *between* Nivkhi and other groups. We know much about the early achievements of Sovietization, but learning how the Soviet vision was implemented and received in Nivkh communities requires a certain amount of piecing together.

My objectives in this essay are twofold: first, to briefly survey the tumultuous and contradictory state policies aimed at the Sovietization of Nivkh life; and second, to see how this reconfigured Nivkh identity in relation to their Northeast Asian neighbors. What emerges is a paradox faced by many other Far Eastern nationalities in the former Soviet fold: The Soviet period would make Nivkhi more "international"; it would also make them much less "Asian."

Nivkhi Before Sovietization

Although the October Revolution echoed around the world in 1917, the news took some time to reach Nivkhi living along the Amur and on Sakhalin. It was a full eight years before the Soviets were able to establish a unified government across to the Pacific, and a few years still before they fully made themselves known in the remotest corners of the former tsarist empire. Russian accounts of Nivkh life in the nineteenth and early twentieth centuries roughly conjured Nivkhi as heirs to Sakhalin's reputation as the "island of the damned." Anton Chekhov's curt summary of Nivkhi as "intelligent, gentle and naively attentive," though "dirty, repulsive and prone to lying" did much to sum up late nineteenth-century Russian perceptions of Nivkh life.[1]

Up until this time, however, the Nivkh population had been better known to their North Asian neighbors than their Russian governors. Throughout the nineteenth century, living primarily as fishermen and secondarily as hunters, increasing numbers of Nivkhi had cause to travel throughout the North Asian Pacific Rim in the interests of trade. The most traveled among these figured in descriptions by the Japanese explorer Rinzo Mamiya, who, writing of Nivkhi in 1808, reported that they wore Manchurian-made cotton clothes, washed their mouths and faces every day "to keep their looks clean and handsome," and were amiable to strangers.[2]

In a sense, both Chekhov and Rinzo tell us about different groups from different parts of the region. Nivkhi who were most active in trade with the Manchu administration, those along the Amur valley and Sakhalin's northwest coast, traveled widely between the mainland and Sakhalin by dogsled in winter, and through a system of seven ferries traversing the Tatar Strait. Their more isolated kinsmen, particularly those living on Sakhalin's eastern shores along the Sea of Okhotsk, had less outside contact, apart from the neighboring Orok Ul'ta reindeer herders. What all Nivkhi did share, however, was a complex language (divided into three regional dialects, but roughly intelligible to each other), a way of life based on small fishing communities often no larger than fifty persons, and a triangulated system of clan relations governing trade relations and marriage.

Though Nivkhi were without their own written script on the eve of the Soviet period and few were literate, many spoke the languages of their Asian neighbors, as older Nivkhi with whom I worked on Sakhalin in 1990 looked back and recounted:

> My father was born in 1892. He used to talk about all the Japanese that used to be on Sakhalin and the Amur. . . . There were Chinese too; one of our relatives was married to a Chinese man. . . . My grandfather, . . . an Ainu and very famous hunter, used to tell us about how they kept horses, and used the horses to go across to Manchuria. . . . They traded furs for Chinese silks and brocades. My father spoke a little Evenk, and a little Chinese. He spoke Japanese best of all.[3]

Russians were by no means unknown to Nivkhi, however. They were the formal proprietors of all and then half of Sakhalin from the treaties of Petersburg in 1875 and Portsmouth in 1905. But the Russian interest in the native population extended little beyond the occasional hiring of Nivkh bounty hunters for pursuing fugitives from Sakhalin's notorious prisons.

The Japanese presence may have been most keenly felt by Nivkhi in the period 1920–25, when Japan, which had been governing the southern half of Sakhalin (then known as Karafuto) from 1905 onward, took control of the remaining northern half of the island. After the USSR recovered the former Russian territory in 1925, Communist Party organizers set out to eradicate loyalties to the Japanese and cultivate party membership, especially among youth. But party officials were advised not even "to think about working among the Giliaks."[4] That task would be left to specialists.

By the time Soviet administration was being established on northern Sakhalin, Moscow had already commissioned a group of politically inspired ethnographers, historians, and activists to guide the Siberian indigenous population through the new order. The newly founded Committee for the Assistance to

Peoples of the Northern Borderlands, or Committee of the North, had a threefold mandate: to facilitate native self-government, to reorganize the economic base of northern life, and to undertake programs of social enlightenment sensitive to local cultures.[5]

In the Far East, early reforms followed much of the groundwork earlier laid by Karl Ianovich Luks, who had worked as the Minister of Nationalities during the short-lived Far Eastern Republic based in Chita (1920–22). Luks developed a plan for native autonomy and encouraged activist ethnographers such as Erukhim Kreinovich, who studied under Shternberg in Leningrad and accepted a posting to Sakhalin in 1926 at the age of twenty. From 1926 to 1928, Kreinovich worked on the presidium of the Sakhalin Revolutionary Committee in Aleksandrovsk, first as an assistant to the Commissioner for Native Affairs and later as the Commissioner himself.

Kreinovich traveled widely during his tenure on the Sakhalin Revolutionary Committee, looking to eradicate survivals of debt servitude, organize financial credit for the natives, train native village chairmen, help develop hunting and fishing cooperatives, and compose a native dictionary.[6] Traversing an island frontier that was home mainly to convicted criminals or newcomers looking to make fast money off of the fish and fur supplies, Kreinovich encountered a long litany of Russian and Chinese exploiters who had outlasted the transition to the infant Soviet system on Sakhalin: the director of the state trading station was found to be working for the Japanese; the head of a group of Chinese traders claimed to be poor, but all of the Nivkhi were in debt to him.[7] Kreinovich's supervisor, Aleksandr Il'in, made his own expedition to the Rybnovsk district on the island's northwestern shore in 1925 and expressed many of the same frustrations.[8]

The problem that the new missionaries Luks, Kreinovich, and Il'in had in implementing reforms stemmed not only from the prerevolutionary legacy but also from the nature of the nationality policy being drawn up. The Bolshevik agenda for cultural development called for a drawing together of all the nationalities of the new Union. Some specialists, such as the Russian ethnographer Vladimir Bogoraz, rejected this view, insisting instead that the Northern peoples live apart so that they might avoid the inevitable devastation of Russianization.[9] Bogoraz argued in favor of the North American and Scandinavian experiences of creating territorial reservations, but his proposal was rejected as non-Marxist and nonprogressive by Narkomnats, the People's Commissariat on Nationalities.[10]

Despite contrasting visions for attaining their goals, reformers such as Kreinovich, Il'in, and Bogoraz were united in the presumption that Nivkh cultural autonomy—extending to freedom of language, dress, food and, in limited circumstances, shamanic practice—should flourish under Soviet direction. But by the close of the 1920s, a shift toward cultural revolution narrowed the parameters of social behavior throughout the country. The new emphasis fell on "cultural construction," where the culture in question was expressly Soviet rather than indigenous. For Nivkhi, the late 1920s marked a momentous change in their relations with the new state. Whereas Russian Orthodox missionaries on pre-revolutionary Sakhalin had hounded the Nivkhi for their pagan ways, Lenin praised them. Yet by 1930, only five years into their membership in the Soviet system, Nivkh icons of native life were again being subject to Russian censure.

This narrowing of the committee's mandate, and the conflation of cultures local and Soviet that it entailed, represented the start of a balancing act in Stalin's nationality policy. Languages and cultures of individual nationalities would be promoted, so long as they contributed to the flourishing of a Pan-Soviet community. In the native context, this formula was mapped onto the supposed dialectic between modernity and tradition. Embracing a Comtean brand of evolutionism, the state supported indigenous traditions in order that native peoples themselves would recognize the errors of their ways and eventually join the cause of "development." It was a familiar theme now gaining greater currency. As the nationalities' ideologist S.I. Dimanshtein had argued in 1919, the overt distinctiveness of peoples like the Nivkhi would gradually diminish but, like salt, would lend flavor to the Soviet character.[11]

The shift to Soviet cultural construction of the early 1930s did not reduce Nivkhi to mere ornamentation or "flavoring," but it did begin a process whereby the state appropriated control over the definition of what "Nivkh" meant. On 10 February 1930, when the Nivkhi, Oroki, and Evenki of Sakhalin held their first District Clan Congress in Nogliki, some natives, such as the Nivkh Pimka, began to display evidence of having mastered a new Soviet idiom:

> We—we are a dark and uneducated people. Before Soviet power, people thought of the natives as there to be trod upon and said, why not let them die off? The Japanese gave us vodka and little else. Under the Japanese, everyone died off because the Japanese didn't pay us. The Soviet authorities prohibited the sale of vodka and paid us wages. We are grateful. . . . We have become farmers. . . . [But] natives need credit for building, cattle and equipment. We are all poor hired hands [*batraki*].[12]

Such conspicuous nods to Soviet rule became characteristic of the increasingly effusive public discourse of the day, but it was not characteristic of Pimka, who had been described in a 1928 expedition to Chir-Unvd as uncooperative and recalcitrant.[13]

Around this time, a new type of organization, the so-called culture base, appeared. An all-purpose social service center designed by the Committee of the North for implementing state programs and collecting information on the local populations, Sakhalin's first such base, in Nogliki, opened in 1929. Within a few years, it comprised a hospital, a two-story boarding school, a reading room (*izba-chital'nia*), three houses for the staff, a storage wing, an icehouse, a dog stable, trade workshops, and administrative offices for the district clan council, the Communist Party, the Youth League, and a newspaper. Other buildings, such as a veterinary unit, were planned.[14]

In addition to the culture base, the committee set up a House of the Native (*Dom Tuzemtsa*). In prefatory remarks in a 1931 *Bolshevik Fish Run* article on the house, one correspondent imagined that "natives passing through Nogliki" would be able "to warm up, have something to eat, and stay overnight." He added that "representatives of the district council will tell the natives in their own language about Soviet cultural construction, about how Soviet power is improving the lives of the natives through the culture base," while "doctors will read lessons about the human body, about epidemic diseases" and "teachers will organize discussion groups with the magical flashlight about cultural construction." Natives could even expect to be advised on "how to best build their house, dog houses and yukola racks," and "how to help their dogs and reindeer."[15]

Such images of the "magical flashlight" predominate in the literature on Sakhalin Nivkhi during the years of Sovietization. Culture volunteers in the form of "red delegates" taught Nivkhi to make bread, "and soon Nivkh women were comparing bread and competing." Nivkhi were taught to plant potatoes, "and soon they were harvesting bushels."[16] Sakhalin Nivkhi who were shown motion pictures in 1926 "had virtually no idea what precisely a movie was, or how it was that living people, horses, moving cars, ships and crowded battles could take shape on the screen." Naturally, "some ran away in fear that there really were armed crowds, that it was not simply a picture, but something sent by an invisible power," but "little by little they began to request certain films such as . . . 'Battleship Potemkin' and other revolutionary works."[17] These accounts took for granted the natives' childlike fear of and fascination with Russian visions of modernity and elided many of the difficulties that arose in implementing the Soviet agenda.

The state may have tightened its control over the presentation of native identity, but the new rigor did not mean that there was any shortage of idealism. As the years advanced, the process of cultural construction became more standardized, assuming in some instances an almost paramilitary quality. Typical of the new mass emphasis on cultural transformation throughout the Soviet Union was a 1931 "culture relay race" organized jointly by students of the Khabarovsk Polytechnical Institute for Peoples of the North and the Communist Youth League. The idea was to "relay" or "bring culture to the taiga and tundra."[18] The race began with the liquidation of illiteracy among native adults; next, these new "soldiers of cultural enlightenment," as the graduates of the literacy courses were called, would pass their training on to their compatriots, who could in turn set an example to others.[19]

In the town of Viskovo on Sakhalin's northwestern shore, spirits were high among the twenty student-relay participants, who proclaimed their "readiness in the battle to reconstruct the semi-primitive North along a new socialist line." Guided by "the spirit of the Communist Youth League and the Bolshevik way," the students collectively pledged to "fight hard for culture, for a new way of life, for the collectivization of the native economy, for the liquidation of exploitation [*kulachestvo*], for the correct implementation of the Leninist nationality policy, and for the general line of the party."[20]

Armed with a quote from Lenin—"The illiterate man stands outside of politics, so first one must teach him to read"[21]—the students arrived in Viskovo in July 1931 to discover that 86 percent of the local Nivkh population was illiterate, but the existing infrastructure of native affairs programs enabled the students to move quickly. Viskovo itself already had a district native bureau, while three villages, Viskvi, Iuk, and Vas'kvo, had corresponding branch units, permitting soldier-of-culture courses to be established in all four places. Twenty-four Nivkhi enrolled in the course in Viskvi, for example, where classes were held in the fishery. Shamans reputedly attempted to disrupt the courses, spreading rumors that participants would be charged for the literacy lessons. A number of women were reluctant at first to participate, until two Nivkh mothers completed the first course and "began to enjoy the respect of others."[22]

The Khabarovsk students wrote with particular pride of the forty-nine-year-old Nivkh chairman of the Viskovo district committee, Mikhail P. Kul'pin. Although almost completely illiterate at the start of the cultural relay race, Kul'pin had done much to distinguish himself as a leader among Nivkhi in the new order. As chairman of the Viskovo *tuzraikom* since the start of 1931, he was commended in a number of Sakhalin newspapers and state documents for having initiated special sanitation measures among Nivkhi—the digging of garbage ditches outside homes, the daily cleaning of benches and floors, and the construction of a bathhouse and special fish-drying areas. His commitment to social hygiene was said to extend with equal diligence to suspect collective farmers, many of whom he purged from the fishery.

Kul'pin himself could not write, so V. Kim, the Korean secretary of the native council, had to prepare the dismissal notices for the farmers (such as the Russian Plamskovskii, who was said to have propagated antinative sentiment and "messed up the artel finances like a Black Hundreds element"[23]). Despite his educational handicaps, Kul'pin vowed to become a literacy shock-worker. For that purpose he entered into competition with Ugnun, the Nivkh chairman of the village collective farm, and reported spending all his free time with a pen and paper. "To help the collectives produce qualified cadres—this is the task before us," wrote the Khabarovsk coordinator. "The Kul'pins and the Ugnuns represent the start of this work."[24]

Pasts Revised, Culture Reified

If early reforms sought to reformulate Nivkh pasts by recasting non-Russian foreign influences as villainous, the onset of collectivization in the early 1930s made this campaign far more explicit. On the heels of Japanese, Chinese, and Korean communities' forcible expulsion from the island to Siberia or Central Asia, the personal biographies of scores of leading Nivkhi were revised to legitimate the "foreigners'" removal from the island community. Nivkhi, too, were subjected to mass arrests and retroactive revisionism. NKVD reports indicate that in the year 1937–38 alone, 36 percent of the adult Nivkh population in the Rybnovsk region of northwest Sakhalin was "liquidated."[25] Even Kul'pin became an "enemy of the people," only six years after being hailed as an exemplary soldier of culture, charged with sabotage against the state (he owned a Japanese watch, his granddaughter recounted in 1990, perhaps taken as proof of foreign ties).[26]

The same predilection for refiguring the past would surface again in the 1960s with the advent of a dramatic resettlement program aimed at improving rural efficiency through a reduction in the number of rural communities. This series of relocations was not the first for Nivkhi in the Soviet period, but it was by far the most sweeping. In a twenty-four-year period from 1962 to 1986, the program reduced the number of communities on Sakhalin as a whole from slightly more than 1,000 to 329, while along the island's northwest shore alone, the number of Nivkh communities was reduced from 82 to 13.[27]

Having been initiated under the slightly more relaxed political climate of the Khrushchev administration, the rural consolidation plan was met with widespread resistance among both Nivkhi and Russians and at times had to be forcibly implemented. As one incredulous Nivkh fishing brigadier remarked in 1990 on the closing of his collective farm on Sakhalin's east coast, "none of us could believe the news when we first heard it. The town had grown to about 700 people, about 300 of us, Nivkhi. The government had spent so many years building us up! There was a school, a laboratory, two clubs, a farm. . . . They had only just finished a whole new set of houses and a two-story hospital on the edge of the village. A new rail line too." But a meeting of the whole village had been called, and an official explained that "small settlements were no longer profitable for the country, that they were too broadly spread out and maybe even dangerous."

An added scourge of the resettlements was wrought by the absurdity that in the areas to which Nivkhi were relocated, the main criterion for site selection appeared to be ease of administration by the regional center. Walter Benjamin once wrote that "ruins are where history merges into the setting." In the Nivkh case, the ruins left behind by scores of empty villages testified to the history of social engineering in a way that the relatives lost to mass arrests could not. The enormous transformations wrought during the early Stalinist period and the resettlements of the 1960s constitute the more obvious examples of the restructuring of Nivkh pasts by the state. But these were only two moments in a series of transformations in Nivkh life over the twentieth century that altered fundamentally not only the content of Nivkh culture but the very manner in which that culture was objectified and perceived.

In 1990, on a rainy afternoon after lunch at the home of an elderly Nivkh woman in the North Sakhalin town of Moskal'vo, my hostess brought out a Manchurian dress once owned by her mother, a floor-length gown in a blinding silk brocade, the likes of which I had never seen in any museum. As she attended to some of the Chinese coins sewn around the hem, she said, "It's in pretty good condition, considering how long it was buried in the ground." The woman's mother had buried the dress, along with other outward trappings of premodern Nivkh life, in a box in the sand in 1937, to be unearthed only in the years of Khrushchev's political reprieves, some twenty years later.

The woman's comment at first struck me as singular, but it did not take long to realize that the dress was only one in a series of icons of Nivkh life that survived a dramatic roller coaster of state policy shifts over the century. From before the October Revolution, when Russian Orthodox missionaries hounded Nivkhi to convert to Christianity, we can follow a trajectory of Nivkh culture being discouraged (Nicholas II) and then encouraged (Lenin), repressed (Stalin) and then revived (Khrushchev), ignored (Brezhnev) and then revived again (Gorbachev).

In the wake of perestroika, Nivkhi, often left behind in faltering towns and villages that the new government has little interest in supporting, are routinely told that they are finally free to live according to their age-old traditions. But after so many years of cultural management, there remain few Nivkh traditions which can be seen outside the sphere of the broader Soviet rubric.

The reinvention of the past may be germane to modernity itself, as Freud and Nietzsche have both argued.[28] Indeed, the Soviet case gives us one of the most compelling visions of what modernity's taste for reinvention could bring, through the reification of culture as an object to be constructed, reconstructed, and dismantled at will. In the twilight of perestroika, Nivkhi on Sakhalin I knew often talked about having "traded in" their culture for a Pan-Soviet one, conscious of having taken a path which had not led them to where they had intended. Like an automobile, culture seemed to be an object which could be repaired, upgraded, and if necessary, exchanged. The idea of culture as a thing subject to willful transformation reminds us of what anthropologists Virginia Dominguez and Richard Handler both have referred to as "cultural objectification."[29] Yet what obtains in the process of such objectification often elides much of what is lost: here the Soviet materials present a case in the extreme, since the dramatic policy shifts also meant the systematic elision of documents, ideas, and persons from the preceding periods on which each step forward was predicated. By destabilizing the physical bases for knowing the past in such a fundamental way, the state had a far greater capacity for managing the identities of each of the nationalities under its aegis, the smaller ones in particular.

Throughout the Soviet ethnographic corpus, the titles of countless monographs on Siberian indigenous peoples testified to one aspect or another of native life such as kinship systems, material resources, or economic modes of production, followed by the trailer, "from the late nineteenth to early twentieth century." Greatly outnumbering studies of the Soviet period, the predilection for nineteenth century studies demonstrated the state investment in counterposing national ways of life gone by to the internationalism of Soviet modernity. In the internationalism of the Soviet present, Nivkhi's Asian alliances were a curio of the past.

To think of Sakhalin at both ends of the Soviet period, at the turn of the twentieth century and now at its close, there are signs that the former cosmopolitanism of the island is resurgent. With the return of Japanese fishing interests, American oil developers, Korean foresters, and Chinese consumer goods, and with an indigenous population increasingly aware of the political rights of what being "indigenous" means elsewhere, the face of the island is poised for change. Yet if Nivkhi look upon their future as not quite Asian, their passage through the Soviet period may help us understand why.

Notes

1. Anton Chekhov, *The Island: A Journey to Sakhalin* (New York: Washington Square Press, 1967), p. 146; Cathy Popkin, "Chekhov as Ethnographer: Epistemological Crisis on Sakhalin Island," *Slavic Review,* 1992, 51(1), p. 47.

2. John A. Harrison, *"Kito Yezo Zusetsu* or a Description of the Island of Northern Yezo by Mamiya Rinzo," *Proceedings of the American Philosophical Society,* 1955, vol. 99, no. 2, pp. 111–13.

3. All field quotations are taken from interviews I conducted in the North Sakhalin villages of Nogliki, Chir-Unvd, Okha, Moskal'vo, Nekrasovka, Rybnoe, Rybnovsk, and Romanovka between April and November of 1990 and between June and August of 1992.

4. Sakhalinskii Tsentr Dokumentatsii Noveishei Istorii (formerly the archive of the Communist Party of the Sakhalin Oblast', Iuzhno-Sakhalinsk) [hereafter STsDNI], f. 2, op. 1, d. 1*zh* (1925). See also Gosudarstvennyi Arkhiv Sakhalinskoi Oblasti [hereafter GASO], f. 267, op. 2, d. 10, "Po Rykovskomu Raionu" [Report by Abramenko], l. 56. For a Soviet assessment of the Japanese administration of North Sakhalin from 1920 to 1925, see A.I. Krushanov, ed., *Stranitsy istorii rybnoi promyshlennosti Sakhalinskoi oblasti (1925–1987 gg.)* (Iuzhno-Sakhalinsk, 1989), p. 24; and STsDNI, f. 13, op. 1, d. 2 (1926), l. 52.

5. The main source of information on the Committee of the North is fond 3977 at the State Archive of the Russian Federation, or GARF (formerly TsGAOR). For an analysis, see Yuri Slezkine, "Russia's Small Peoples: The Policies and Attitudes Towards the Native Northerners, 17th Century–1938," Ph.D. dissertation, Department of History, University of Texas at Austin, May 1989, pp. 278–334; and Adele Weiser, *Die Völker Nordsibiriens: Unter Sowjetische Herrschaft von 1917 bis 1936* (Munich: Klaus Renner, 1989).

6. STsDNI, f. 2, op. 1, d. 89 (1928) "Materialy po rabote sredi tuzemtsev," ll. 1–6.

7. Tsentral'yi Gosudarstvennyi Arkhiv Dal'nego Vostoka (Tomsk) [hereafter TsGADV], f. R4560, op. 1, d. 3 (1926–27), ll. 16, 76

8. Ibid., ll. 17–19

9. W. Bogoras [V. Bogoraz], *The Chukchee* (New York: Stechert, 1909), p. 732; ibid., "O pervobytnykh plemenakh," *Zhizn' natsional'nostei,* 1922 (1). Bogoraz was an influential player in the early development of aboriginal policy in Soviet Siberia and the Far East. Having been exiled to Kolyma in 1890, he had impeccable political credentials. His monumental monograph on the Chukchee, a result of his internment, made him one of the foremost ethnographers (along with Lev Shternberg) to lead the new field of Soviet ethnography. See also V. Bogoraz, "Ob izuchenii i okhrane okrainnykh narodov," *Zhizn' natsional'nostei,* 1923, nos. 3–4, pp. 168–80.

10. See the critical comments by M.A. Sergeev, *Nekapitalisticheskii put' razvitiia malykh narodnostei Severa [Trudy Instituta Etnografii, Novaia Seriia, Tom XXVII]* (Moscow-Leningrad, 1955), p. 216. Other criticisms of Bogoraz's proposal can be found in I.S. Gurvich, *Etnicheskoe razvitie narodnostei severa v Sovetskii period* (Moscow, 1987), p. 15.

11. S.I. Dimanshtein, "Sovetskaia vlast' i mel'kie natsional'nosti," *Zhizn' natsional'nostei, no.* 46 (1919).

12. From M. Mel'nikov, quoted in Sergeev, *Nekapitalisticheskii put'*, p. 304. A second congress was held in Nogliki the following October, but fewer natives attended because of the fishing season. Viskovo held its first district congress in December of the same year. For more on the congresses, see GARF, f. 3977, op. 1, d. 117–1 (1931), ll. 71–74.

13. Lev Alpatov, *Sakhalin (putevye zapiski etnografa)* (Moscow, 1930), p. 58. Having been rehabilitated for political advantage during the Nogliki native congress of 1930, Pimka was denounced in 1931 as "a quasi-kulak," an exploiter of others, in the words of the local Nogliki newspaper, *Bolshevik Fish Run.* The immediate pretext was the collectivization campaign, which he had evidently opposed. He was accused of "spreading the rumor that those who enter the kolkhoz would be sent to prison" and of "trying to prevent people from sending their children to school." "Stavka kulakov bita," *Za Bolshevistskuiu putinu* [Nogliki], 1 February 1931.

14. For more material on culture bases in general, see A.K. L'vov, "Kul'turnye bazy na severe," *Sovetskaia Aziia* (1926) 3:28–36; and P. Ustiugov, "Zadachi natsional'noi raboty na krainem severe," *Revoliutsiia i natsional'nosti* (1931) 1:40–49, esp. 46.

15. GARF, f. 3977, op. 1, d. 940, l. 7.

16. Ibid., d. 117–1 (1928–31), ll. 22–24.

17. Ibid., d. 1117, ll. 153–54.

18. P. Skorik, "Kul'turnyi shturm taigi i tundry," *Prosveshchenie natsional'nostei,* no. 10 (1932), pp. 32–39.

19. For more on this and other related terms of the mass culture movement of the 1920s, see Barry Crowe, *Concise Dictionary of Soviet Terminology, Institutions and Abbreviations* (London: Pergamon, 1969).

20. Skorik, "Kul'turnyi shturm," p. 35.

21. Ibid., p. 33.

22. Ibid., p. 36.

23. The Kul'pin quotation is from GASO, f. 513, op. 1, d. 1, "Protokoly prezidiuma Zapadno-Sakhalinskogo natsional'nogo RIKa za 1931 g." (1931), p. 20. The same file documents the extensive assistance that Kul'pin extended to the Khabarovsk contingent, pp. 36–38.

24. Ibid., p. 37.

25. Medvedev, "Politiko-ekonomicheskaia kharakteristika Rybnovskogo raiona Sakhalinskoi oblasti," ll. 4o–5o, 6. The figures are comparable with those from Chukotka in Aleksandr Pika, "Malye narody severa: iz pervobytnogo kommunizma v real'nyi sotsializm," in *Perestroika, glasnost', demokratiia, sotsializm: V chelivecheskom izmerenieo (Moscow, 1989), p. 320.*

26. STsDNI, f. 13, op. 1, d. 29 (1937), l. 70. Orders for Kul'pin's arrest are listed on l. 93.

27. A.I. Gladyshev, ed., *Administrativno-territorial'noe delenie Sakhalinskoi oblasti* (Iuzhno-Sakhalinsk, 1986), pp. 79–106, 125. Gurvich estimated that as a result of the kolkhoz-strengthening plan, the number of enterprises in northern regions was reduced by more than 60 percent. For example, on Chukotka between 1953 and 1966, the government reduced the number of *selkhozarteli* from 1,444 to 300, and the number of fishing artels

from 600 to 250. Inversely, the number of state farms in the area, considered by the state to be a more developed form of socialist industry, rose from 50 to 200. I.S. Gurvich, *Etnicheskoe razvitie* . . . , p. 94. See also "Osushchestvlenie leninskoi natsional'noi politiki u narodov Krainego Severa SSSR," *Sovetskaia etnografiia*, 1970, no. 1, p. 26. These figures are comparable to those on the Khanty-Mansiiskii okrug in Kerstin Kuoljok, *Revolution in the North* (Stockholm: Almqvist and Wikseu, 1985), p. 128.

28. Sigmund Freud, *Civilization and Its Discontents* (New York: Norton, 1989); Friedrich Nietzsche, *On the Genealogy of Morals* (New York: Vintage, 1989), pp. 57–58.

29. Virginia Dominguez, *People as Subject, People as Object: Selfhood and Peoplehood in Contemporary Israel* (Madison: University of Wisconsin Press, 1989); Richard Handler, *Nationalism and the Politics of Culture in Quebec* (Madision: University of Wisconsin Press, 1988).

The Russian Far East

From a Colonial to a Borderland Economy

Pavel A. Minakir

The Russian Far East (RFE) stretches from Arctic seas in the north to the Chinese border in the south, and from the Pacific Ocean in the east to Siberia in the west. Thus defined, the total territory amounts to 6.2 million square kilometers, a full 42 percent of the Russian Federation. The RFE can be broken down into many administrative divisions, but economically the most important distinction is between north and south.

The south includes the Maritime province (*Primorskii krai*) and Khabarovsk krai, the Amur province (oblast), the Jewish autonomous oblast of Birobidzhan, and Sakhalin oblast. Most of the RFE's population lives in these areas because of their comparatively favorable climatic, transportation, and agricultural conditions. The south also holds more than 70 percent of the region's economic potential, including 90 percent of agricultural production, heavy industry, consumer goods production, and food processing enterprises. The northern part of the RFE includes Magadan and Kamchatka oblasts and the Sakha (Yakut) republic. In contrast to the south, these territories in large part live off extractive industries, with the emphasis on nonferrous metals in Magadan and Sakha and on the fishing industry in Kamchatka. In a sense, by supplying food, materials, and transportation, the southern part of the region serves as the "base" for the north.

This essay will offer a description and analysis of the Russian Far East, beginning with economic development in the decade from 1980 to 1990 and continuing through to the reforms of the early 1990s.[1] Emphasis will be placed on pinpointing not simply negative but also positive trends, with the hope of showing the way toward an accentuation of the latter. A concluding section will offer prescriptions for encouraging the kind of international development strategy that the Russian Far East needs.

Table 11.1

Industrial Structure of the Far Eastern Economy (in percentages)

	1990*	1991**	1992***
All industries, including:	100.0	100.0	100.0
Energy	4.5	3.6	4.5
Fuels	5.5	3.8	3.9
Ferrous metals	0.9	1.1	0.8
Nonferrous metals	15.2	19.2	20.2
Chemicals and petrochemicals	1.7	1.8	1.6
Machinery	18.7	15.3	16.3
Wood and paper products	9.8	9.2	10.0
Construction materials	6.6	6.8	5.7
Light industry	4.1	4.2	4.6
Food processing	31.4	33.7	31.9

Sources: Economic Reform in Regions of the Russian Federation. (Moscow: State Statistical Bureau, November 1993).

    *in 1982 prices

    **current prices

    ***calculation based on the physical index of industrial production for the first half of 1992

Economic Development 1980–90

The goals and conditions of Soviet central planning set the stage for the developmental tendencies exhibited by the RFE in the 1980s. For the RFE, this meant strict adherence to its place in All-Union considerations regarding natural resources and the territorial division of labor. Central planning prioritized the development of the RFE's extractive sector. Large-scale state investment promoted a sufficiently stable economic structure connected to the national economy by very strict links. Underlying this structure was the extraction of natural resources and related industries. Other types of economic activity were auxiliary. (See Table 11.1.) Although these overall characteristics hold true for the whole decade, a number of important trends make possible a subperiodization within the decade.

The period from 1981 to 1987 saw the region increasingly focused on raw materials. State concern regarding this sector of the economy grew as production rates fell. These negative trends were most visible in the nonferrous metal sector, where production decreased absolutely in some years. By the early 1980s, it became clear that sources of cheap raw materials were nearly exhausted. As a consequence, since the growth rate of state investments was decreasing, a high rate of regional economic growth based on the extensive development of new natural resources could no longer be supported.

The decrease in the share of forest and paper industry and nonferrous metals in the total volume of regional industrial production illustrates this tendency. Among all the specialized sectors, only fishing and related processing industries developed in stable fashion during this period. Another exception to the generally downward trend was the increased share of industrial production occupied by machine building. This was caused not only by the growth of military orders but by the development of consumer goods output within the framework of military industry.

By the end of 1985–86, the structure of the RFE's economy was even more strongly oriented toward extractive production, the primary sector of the economy. The extractive sector produced more than 30 percent of the gross regional product during this time. In 1985, the Far East's share of the USSR's fish and marine products reached 40 percent, while timber was at 13 percent. Although tungsten only stood at 14 percent, almost 50 percent of gold, 80 percent of tin, 90 percent of raw boron, and 100 percent of the USSR's diamonds came from the Far East.

It was in this period, however, that symptoms of stagnation began to appear. Growth rates decreased, production efficiency fell, and state investment became less profitable. In this context, the idea of a shift in the RFE's development strategy took hold among scientists and economic leaders during the mid-1980s. Because of the complexity and increasingly erratic nature of financial inter-relations between Moscow and various regions, as well as the large transportation costs that made Far Eastern products inherently more expensive in comparison with other regions, an attempt to alter the nature of Far Eastern economic development was undertaken.

The main goal of this program was the formation in the RFE of an economic complex that would depend for its development not only on state investments but on its own financial resources as well. The key goals became modernization of the primary sector of the economy and the creation of new manufacturing enterprises that could effectively supplement the mining and primary production of natural resources. The development of the manufacturing sector with a view toward increasing the share of products with a high degree of value added was supposed to reinforce the financial independence of the RFE.

In actuality, this program was implemented for only two years. Despite certain structural shifts, the character of regional development did not change substantially. Together with some increases in the production of ferrous metals and energy resources, a slight increase appeared in the specialized sectors. This, however, was too short a time to realize the preconditions for effective structural change in the Far Eastern economy.

A second subperiod, from 1988 to 1991, when separate attempts to reform the planned economy were carried out, reflected appreciably on Far Eastern development. After the decrease in the growth rate in 1985–88, an increase in industrial growth of 5.1 percent was recorded, according to the official data. But, in fact, production decreased in almost all industrial sectors, except light industry and the chemical and food industries. Nonferrous metallurgy and the energy sector also bucked the trend. By 1990, a crisis overcame practically all sectors.

The years 1991 and 1992 saw this crisis deepen. Although as early as the middle of the 1980s experts had pointed out some disturbing trends in the economic development of the country and the region, conjunctural events brought them into the open with spectacularly deleterious effects. Among the sources of the approaching crisis one should mention the changing situation in world markets, the sluggish development of science and technology in the USSR, the chronic growth of the hidden deficits in the state budget, the lagging development of modern infrastructure, and the constricting effect of the monopolistic economy in the sphere of production.

Hand in hand with economic collapse went social-political factors, which were both a cause and a symptom of economic problems. By the beginning of 1991, these problems had taken several forms, ranging from political clashes between the central authorities and the republics, as well as interethnic conflicts in the republics and regions, to the spreading of a nihilistic attitude among enterprises toward the fulfillment of state economic plans influenced by the prevailing view—declared and supported by the government—of the need for unlimited freedoms and self-financing for all enterprises. There was at the same time a deepening erosion of state control over price formation. All these factors brought about the disintegration of long-established economic linkages in the country, resulting in decreased industrial production as early as the first quarter of 1991.

Producers adopted policies that proved to be quite successful under the conditions of economic disintegration and the inflationary price discrepancies between consumers and the capital goods markets. They embarked on reductions in production on terms that enabled them to minimize the risks arising from the unreliability of supplies and suppliers. Prices rose to compensate for the decline in production and the use of increasing financial resources for consumption purposes. As a result, the share of consumption rose from 73.6 percent in 1985 to 79.6 percent in the beginning of the 1990s. Actual accumulation became negative. By 1991, it was quite clear that a process known as the "eating out" of fixed capital was under way.

Beginning in 1988, the so-called "non-market, non-plan" economic system was in full-scale operation throughout the country. The drop in production and the rise in prices provoked an onset of stagflation. Consumers and producers lost confidence in the national currency. Faced with growing shortages of everything, the enterprises instinctively resorted to a system of protection against the depreciation of money and the outflow of commodities from local markets. Under this system, monetary relations were quickly replaced by simple commodity or barter transactions.

The rising deficits on the consumer and foodstuffs markets, together with uncertainty about future opportunities for material supplies from state funds and other producers, forced the regions and the republics to implement some urgent measures to protect regional consumer markets. As a result, different types of coupons and consumer goods rationing were introduced on the territorial level. Moreover, amid the deepening crisis in the state economy, the nonstate sector simply was not yet able to be a real alternative to the ailing state social and economic mechanisms because of its small size and the lack of credit from the population. So at that stage, the activities of the private sector were not sufficient to compensate for the breakup of the state economy.

As for the Russian Far East, it would be correct to assert that the disintegration of the economy began not with the reform of 1992 but earlier. The year 1991 was a turning point in the economic development of the region. It was then that the last chance to develop a proper understanding of the situation and to stabilize the economy was thrown away. A certain euphoria connected with momentary, relatively good financial results was only a prelude to the hidden transformation of the regional economy from one characterized by state support of production and consumption, however insufficient, to an economy with uncompetitive production, low export potential—counting commodity flows to other regions of the country also as exports—and a high level of import dependency.

Price liberalization was the most painful step in the process of economic reform. It covered practically every commodity (only the prices for fuels and grain as well as some transportation fares remained under state control). The new price proportions drastically changed the industrial structure of the regional economy in value terms, increasing significantly the nominal share of the primary sector in total production. But the real changes in industrial structure were not too significant, although judging by the dynamics of separate economic indicators, there was some reinforcement of the specialization of the RFE in extractive industries.

In fact, the consequences of implementing anti-inflationary measures, alternating with recurrent inflational stimulation, were almost the same in the RFE as in the rest of Russia. Galloping increases in all retail and wholesale prices in the region had the effect of squeezing the consumer market due to depreciation of the population's income and savings. This in turn led to the rapid curtailment of production in the consumer sector of the economy (light industry and particularly the food industry, public catering, retail trade, services). Simultaneously, there was also a depreciation in the fixed and current capital in all industries, resulting in a paralysis of the financial and credit systems. Added to this was a steep increase in demand for loan capital, with the subsequent rise in interest rates and the emergence of financial speculation as the main sphere of business activity. Yet another result involved a decline in investment activities as the result of depreciation in functioning capital and an enormous rise in discount rates, as well as a reorientation of capital flows from production toward the trade and financial spheres. Finally, the balance between commodity and financial flows,

Table 11.2

Main Economic Indicators (in millions of rubles)

	1991	1992	1993	1993/1991
Industrial production	580,838.7	491,384.5	412,762.9	71.1%
Production of consumer goods	264,236.4	229,130.9	—	—
Capital investments	266,058.7	172,188.1	138,350.5	51.9%

Sources: Information on Social and Economic Development of the Far Eastern Economic Region in 1992. Representative Office of the Ministry of Economy of the Russian Federation in the Far Eastern Economic Region. *Economic Reform in Regions of the Russian Federation* Moscow: State Statistical Bureau, November 1993).

which was barely maintained in 1991, began to fall. Under such conditions, the main reason for the decline in production was not the squeezing of demand, but the sharp outflow of financial capital to the sphere of inflationary accumulation.

By 1992, the scale of economic activities was declining in all sectors of the economy. Almost every economic indicator was going down (see Table 11.2); production of the most important items was practically stopped. To take only a few examples, production of crude oil decreased by 8 percent, coal by 10 percent, timber by 22 percent, paper by 27.5 percent, prefabricated ferroconcrete items by 26.3 percent, and fish and sea products by 21.8 percent. Agricultural production also experienced a steep decrease: meat by 27.5 percent; milk, 28 percent; eggs, 36 percent; potatoes and vegetables, 36 percent.

The situation of deep economic crisis has had a very limited influence on the labor market. There has been no corresponding reduction in the number of the employed, during the first stage of the reform. In 1994 the unemployment level increased by 30 percent. The main causes of unemployment continue to be financial crises on the microlevel of the economy. Total debts of enterprises by September 1994 amounted to 5,000 billion rubles (roughly $2 billion). Because of this situation, many enterprises (both governmental and nongovernmental) pushed their workers into taking administrative vacations. And many people have been working part time. By 1 August 1993, the number of job vacancies appeared to exceed the number of workers officially registered as unemployed. But by 1 July 1994 this proportion was completely reversed.

With the beginning of radical economic reform, inflation rates in the consumer market became one of the most important indicators of the population's living standards. It should be noted that inflation rates are presented by the official statistics as the growth rates for retail prices. It is inflation that corrects the nominal growth of the population's income and thereby presents an accurate picture of living standards. Money incomes in the Far East have been growing more quickly than in Russia. By December 1992, they had increased between 10.9 and 24.7 times (figures differ for separate territories of the Far East), while the corresponding figure for Russia in general was only 12.3. So in 1991, money incomes in the Far East exceeded that of Russia by 30 percent, in the middle of 1992 by 62 percent, and in October 1993 by 50 percent.

According to official statistics, the desperate situation in the Far East does not differ much from that in the rest of Russia. The retail trade turnover in the first half of 1992 decreased by 38.6 percent compared with the same period in 1991, but this figure is also marginally lower than that for Russia (39.7). Compared with the first half of 1991, the value of chargeable services for the population decreased by 60 percent (in constant prices). Therefore, although the general deterioration of the social situation in the region is quite apparent, it is no worse than elsewhere in Russia.

This means that changes in the RFE population's behavior, namely, growing out-migration, cannot be explained by developments in the social sphere alone. (The general living standards in the region were always lower than in the European part of the country.) This is not a novel situation arising from reform. Rather, the main changes have been psychological. For many years the local population believed in and counted on the support of the state, which was interested in attracting and settling new immigrants in the region. To some extent, everyone in the Far East has experienced this support. But with the beginning of the reform, the central authorities declared and began to implement policies of "self-reliance" for the population of the Far East. Many, especially first-generation Far Easterners, felt themselves abandoned and isolated. They responded by re-emigrating westward.

In general, the year 1992 saw hidden destabilization mechanisms put down roots in the Far East. If there are no significant changes in the economic situation within and outside the region (e.g., resumption of state support), the current developments may ultimately bring about a situation whereby the process of getting out of the regional crisis would proceed even more slowly than the earlier "creeping in" of the crisis. And the costs of that recovery process for the Russian Far East could be even higher than for Russia as a whole. These harmful processes have been accompanied by the reinforcement of the traditional specialization among the territories of the RFE. The production share of northern areas in primary industries is increasing. Manufacturing, as before, is concentrated in the southern parts of the region. But now, under the conditions of economic crisis, there is a discernible move toward economic autarky among the particular territories.

The pressures of economic reform have produced both negative and positive results and tendencies for Far Eastern development. Among the negative are the appearance of a real "regional self-financing" situation for the Russian Far East as well as for many other regions in Russia. Regions and enterprises have to solve their financial and supply problems by themselves without any support from the central government. The present system of dividing taxes between the central budget and local budgets continues to leave the region in a state of dependence. For many regions in the Far East (except the Sakha Republic) taxes collected do not cover social and infrastructure expenses. In this situation, regions have to look for additional sources of income or ask central authorities for subsidies. Unfortunately, additional income, usually in the form of new local taxes, impacts negatively on regional economic activities.

A second negative development is the noncompetitiveness of the majority part of goods produced in the Far East due to a general change in the price system structure, high transportation costs, and high wage levels. Previously, production costs and social expenses that were much higher in the Far East than in the European part of the USSR and Russia had been variously compensated by the central government (e.g., special prices for Far Eastern products, building social infrastructure costs into weapon prices, budget subsidies). The central government, however, has rejected these burdens of compensation. In a situation where prices are free and state orders very limited, regions must find a new way.

There has also been a disinvestment trend throughout the economy. Since the beginning of 1992, the role of the federal budget as an investment source has been drastically reduced. At present, about three-fourths of investment needs must be covered by four possible sources: corporate profit and amortization funds, bank loans, local budget investments, and foreign investments. But all of these are very limited at the moment. For all practical purposes, the region is bereft of investment capital. As a result, the construction of houses and social facilities (hospitals, kindergartens, schools, etc.) has fallen off drastically, and equipment retooling has ground to a halt.

Also on the negative side, there has been a disintegration in the economic life in the Far East growing out of a disconnectedness, whereby territorial administrations try to solve their problems by themselves. The reasons for this trend are complex. In November–December 1991, new managerial bodies were formed in Russian regions by presidential decree. Accordingly, the heads of these administrations are nominated by the president. Their functions and prerogatives are parallel to those held by Communist Party provincial first secretaries in the past. This was the first reason why all local administrative heads dealt bilaterally with the center, while conducting "hard-line" policies toward their neighbors. A second reason was the central government's decision not to carry out the Long-Term State Program on the Economic Development of the Far Eastern Economic Region until the Year 2000, a plan premised on intraregional integration. Since 1992, local territories have been on their own in their relations with the center.

But there are also positive tendencies. Since 1992, the economic ties of the region have begun to be reoriented from the European part of Russia and other previous Soviet republics to the Pacific Rim countries. The liberalization of foreign economic relations since 1992 has promoted an increase in exports to Pacific countries and imports from them. The volume of exports in 1992–94 increased by 38 percent in comparison with 1990–91. The volume of imports increased more than threefold. Approximately 80 percent of RFE export-import operations are connected with Pacific countries, chiefly China, Japan, the United States, and South Korea.

Moreover, although the situation in regional industry since the very beginning of the radical economic reform has been very hard because of general non-competitiveness, the liberalization of foreign economic relations has furnished a new opportunity for the region in the form of transit services through the Far Eastern territory from the rest of Russia and other CIS (Commonwealth of Independent States) countries.

At the same time, the orientation of public opinion is changing. Because of quick privatization and a strong propaganda campaign in favor of private property, most of the population has accepted privatization and market development. And yet, for many people private business is equivalent to "dirty money," criminal activity, and the "black market." The reason for this is that the economic and financial situations do not encourage investment in productive capacity. The most popular and profitable spheres of business are trade, banking, and the securities market. For these sectors, high inflation, a bane for most people, represents a welcome opportunity. Be that as it may, overall in the RFE, private business and privatization are very active. One sign of this is that over 68 percent of governmental property has been transformed into private or stock companies.

The near future of the Russian Far East will depend on the possibility of encouraging the positive tendencies and eliminating the negative ones.

Perspectives on RFE Economic Development: Northeast Asia

Because of the uncertainty and instability in the economic and political situations in Russia, it is impossible to make a real forecast of the Russian Far East's economic development. What follows is only a general estimation of potential economic development, highlighting some prospects for economic cooperation in the Northeast Asian region.

From a long-range standpoint there are two feasible paths to development for the region. The first supposes an open model of development oriented toward integration of the Russian Far East into the Pacific community. This model is practicable under the assumption that internal and external political and economic factors remain favorable. The second model calls for self-reliance and a primary orientation toward Moscow and the Russian market.

The realization of the open model relies heavily on the raw materials sector (tourism, services, etc.). The preferred market type is the world one, although ties with the domestic market must be maintained in order to stabilize fluctuations in demand. It is especially important to take note of the fact that even this extroverted plan depends on cooperation with the central government in two crucial areas. First of all, the central government must take upon itself some expenditures in the nonproductive sphere and that portion of social programs that cannot be financed through local taxation. In addition, the central government should establish tax privileges for the region to help accumulate local capital.

The second model proceeds from the assumption that conditions will not permit the development of the "open model." In this case, although market relations are developing, the region will have to orient toward development at the expense of the production resources. This means the creation of a regional productive structure involving industries that can provide the required financial resources. The midterm objective is a strategy of exploitation of the region's natural resources. Such a wager on the past is unlikely to raise production to any significant degree. Development would take the form of increased efficiency attained by modernizing the raw materials sector. This would allow for limited cooperation between the RFE and Northeast Asia, probably in traditional forms exhibited by the status quo.

It is an incontrovertible fact that Russia is linked to the Pacific Rim by its most sparsely populated and economically least developed part. Moreover, despite the fact that Russia recognizes the Pacific Rim as a region of great future importance and understands the necessity for playing a more active role, there are still no clear foreign-policy and foreign-trade doctrines for relations with the Pacific Rim and the Northeast Asian countries. And Russia is also far from becoming a large-scale trade partner in the region. The turnover of CIS trade with the Pacific Rim countries totaled about 19 billion rubles in 1990, but the CIS share in the total amount of foreign trade of these countries was less than 1 percent.

Ongoing market transformation in Russia brings us nearer to the day when full-scale long-term cooperation will be possible, yet even now the largest portion of joint ventures with Northeast Asian countries have chosen their field of action in Russia's eastern part, especially the Russian Far East. This is a hopeful sign. Countries of the Sea of Japan basin have a positive approach toward the Far East's participation in international economic cooperation. The Far East itself is no less interested in that, because external factors can significantly influence its development.

Reorientation of Far Eastern trade relations to international markets will increase competitiveness by reducing transportation costs. Full-scale development of the Far East's natural resources is possible only on the basis of access to foreign capital and technologies because of the central government's budget deficit and of the poor development of local capital goods industries. Under present conditions, the Far East should develop an externally oriented economy as an incentive to investment and a source of economic growth. Structural change and the establishment of an efficient market with close economic ties among its areas might well be the outcome.

In this context, it is worth noting that foreign economic relations of Russia's Far Eastern areas already have a strong orientation toward the Asia–Pacific market, which accounts for about 85 percent of the territory's exports. Over the last twenty years, Far Eastern exports have grown steadily. During that period exports grew by 3.5 times, with the most remarkable progress attained in the late 1970s and early 1980s, when the Far East significantly strengthened its role in the Soviet export trade. The major export items are fish at 48.8 percent, wood at 40 percent, and cement at 10 percent.

Since the early 1990s exports have almost doubled. This means that openness is becoming a reality for the Far Eastern economy, but in a context where national export is increasing while national production is decreasing. Recently, the role of international private capital has become more active. More than five hundred joint ventures are reported to have been established in the Russian Far East. Their activities to a large extent promote the expansion of the territory's exports.

Nevertheless, the influence of external factors on the economic development of the Far East is far from adequate, since only about 5 percent of output goes to export markets. In fact, it could be said that the RFE's transport–transit role is more significant for Russia's foreign economic relations in the Asia–Pacific zone than the region's own exports. According to some estimates, in 1990 RFE's share in the former Soviet Union's trade with Asian-Pacific countries did not exceed 20 percent. The share of raw materials in Far East exports was over 70 percent. Its commodity structure has not changed much to date.

Opportunities for international cooperation in economic development remain unrealized because of the lack of effective foreign economic policy, investment and trade promotion, and financial support from the central government. During the past two years, after the city of Nakhodka and Sakhalin province became free economic zones, their development has been dependent on their own efforts only. Lack of an import policy that targets technology imports is also a drawback. Actually, by importing large amounts of food and consumer goods, the Far East is consuming its own future and losing an opportunity for development. To conclude, it should be noted that at present the pattern of international economic cooperation is determined more by the intentions of foreign partners than by the long-term interests of the region.

A Few Suggestions

Three general directions seem most promising for cooperation between the Russian Far East and Northeast Asian countries. The first is the development and use of natural resources on the basis of modern technology. The second is to foster the development of the transport–transit function of the region using practically all types of transport (land, sea, and air). The third direction concerns the use and development of the scientific base of the RFE, that is, organization of a cooperative technology exchange with the participation of other regions of Russia and the CIS.

Under these three rubrics are a large number of concrete proposals, among which are seven that seem worth emphasizing:

1. The use of modern technology in the timber- and fish-processing sectors, which are the foundations of the RFE export economy, could increase the quality standards of timber and fish products and also the assortment available for export. The construction of new fish-processing facilities equipped with modern machinery would increase production and the quality of products. Expansion of both the domestic and export markets could be the prospective goal of cooperation.
2. Modernization of the ship-building and ship-repairing industries could improve the qualitative parameters of fishing, passenger, and merchant ships, including the updating of equipment with modern machinery and appliances and utilizing ships with smaller tonnage for coastal fishing.
3. Construction of installations for raw materials processing demands large investments in order to provide the most efficient use of mineral deposits. The iron ore, oil and gas, coal, and nonferrous metal deposits can be the objects of cooperation to expand the production and technical level of ferrous and nonferrous metallurgy and to construct chemical and petrochemical complexes.
4. Modernization of existing construction-material production enterprises and the creation of new ventures along with the development of the construction industry dealing with housing and industrial facilities can be a cooperative effort.
5. Military enterprises can be converted for fish and timber processing and for mining industries.
6. Modernization of the food industry and agricultural business should enrich the domestic market.
7. Tourist centers should be built. The geographically favorable position, picturesque surroundings, and opportunity to provide some special recreation services (e.g., fishing, hunting) create favorable conditions for the construction and cooperative use of hotels, motels, and recreation zones for foreign tourists.

The Russian Far East, due to its geographical position, has all the requisite conditions to become a large-scale transit center for Northeast Asia. New projects dealing with the transportation and processing of goods in Far Eastern ports, as well as with providing transit opportunities while en route, have been launched, and more are being prepared. These projects could serve the mutual interests of the RFE and the countries of Northeast Asia.

An orientation toward expansion and improvement of the economic, scientific, and technical connections of the Russian Far East in Northeast Asia may lead to the creation in the Far East of special information and consulting centers to provide detailed information about the direction of and conditions for cooperation. A system for training and strengthening the proficiency qualifications of specialists must be organized. The exchange of information through contacts between scientists and businessmen should also be expanded.

Integration of Russia's Far East with Asian-Pacific countries, especially with Northeast Asia's constituent economies, requires an increasing openness of its economy to foreign capital, goods, and technologies in order to form industries that will favor a well-balanced development of the territory. The results of policies promoting independent economic exchange with foreign countries will depend to a great extent on a clear understanding of long-term goals for development, which in turn will determine the Far East's approach to international economic cooperation. Therefore, the approach should be based on the premise that natural resources should become strategic goods for Far East development. This approach also implies developing all sectors of the industrial and social base rather than individual industrial projects.

To create a well-balanced industrial structure closely tied to the international division of labor, the Far East ought to pursue a stage-by-stage policy, choosing various ways to provide outside stimuli to the local economy. As a first stage, creation of a basic infrastructural system and resource-oriented export processing should become the main goals. Within these guidelines, emphasis should be placed on quality of primary products and their utilization, as well as on investments to strengthen infrastructural competitiveness, especially in such areas as railroading, sea transportation, and communication. It is also important to start redirecting the Far East's trade toward the markets of neighboring countries.

To attract foreign capital and technology, the highest priority at this stage should be assigned to the development of tourism, the construction materials industry, and industries based on the region's traditional specialties (e.g., nonferrous metallurgy, forestry, and fishery), which are highly dependent on exchanges with the western territories of the country. If promotion policies for the technological development of these industries are adopted, the opportunities for international economic cooperation are more likely to bear fruit.

Growth of foreign currency earnings as a result of strengthening natural resource–based exports would make it possible later on to pay more attention to import substitution and serious structural changes, to extend the area of naturalresource exploration on the basis of advanced technologies, and to improve the infrastructural system of the Far East's northern areas. At this stage, the conversion of military industries, the development of machine building, and the infusion of foreign capital and technologies to serve the needs of fish, forest, and mining industries may be accelerated. Finally, the goal of the third stage, which continues beyond the limits of the present century, is a transition to more advanced and diversified production for domestic and export markets.

The successful achievement of the above-mentioned goals would make a significant contribution to Far Eastern development, but there are underlying issues that must be considered. The most important factors in a long-term vision of development are capital, technology, and infrastructure. At the same time, these seem to be precisely the areas in which the Russian Far East could benefit most from international economic cooperation with its Northeast Asian neighbors. To support priorities in improving industrial structure, it may be possible to attract advanced foreign technologies that could be exchanged for access by foreign partners to the domestic market and to natural resources.

But here lies a potentially crippling paradox. If the Russian Far East gets the necessary foreign capital for infrastructural, industrial, and technological development, it will without doubt undergo rapid economic growth supported by increasing trade openness and strengthening market forces. Yet it is difficult to attract private industrialists without already having a proper infrastructure, because private international capital usually requires infrastructure as part of a favorable investment climate.

This brings to the fore the importance of multinational and national lenders. The World Bank and the Asian Development Bank, as well as the national banks of Japan and South Korea, will only supply funds for RFE development if they are used to facilitate international cooperation and development in Northeast Asia, and only if the projects are strongly supported by the Russian central government and local authorities. This means that serious steps should be taken to promote investment and trade in order to inspire confidence in private, national, and international business circles. To achieve success in pursuing preferential policies and the creation of special economic zones, however, will require considerable cooperation and coordination among all the Far East territories.

Note

1. This essay is based on many years of research at the Far Eastern Institute of Economic Research as well as on hands-on managerial experience gained as first deputy governor of Khabarovsk krai (1991–1993). Elaboration of the material can be found in P.A. Minakir, ed., *Dal'nii Vostok Rossii: Ekonomicheskoe obozrenie,* 2 vols. (Moscow, 1993). An earlier English-language analysis can be found in V.P. Chichkanov and P.A. Minakir, "Economic Development of the Soviet Far East," in John J. Stephan and V.P. Chichkanov, eds., *Soviet-American Horizons on the Pacific* (Honolulu: University of Hawaii Press, 1986). For an American perspective on the issues discussed, see John J. Stephan, "The Political and Economic Landscape of the Russian Far East," in Tsuyoshi Hasegawa et al., eds., *Russia and Japan: An Unresolved Dilemma Between Distant Neighbors* (Berkeley: University of California Center for International and Area Studies, 1993), pp. 279–98.

Part IV

After Communism:
Resources for Cooperation
or Confrontation

Debate within the USSR on economic policies for Siberia and the Russian Far East revolved around two basic approaches: extract resources to supply and advance the European part of the country; or, try to bring about comprehensive development and make the eastern territories self-sufficient. During the Stalin period, the latter, more ambitious vision captured the imaginations of high officials and regional loyalists.[1] Following the dismantling of the gulag labor force after 1953, however, an inability to carry out even the first alternative led the Soviet authorities in the 1960s to invite the Japanese to supply capital and technology and the Chinese, as well as the North Koreans, to supply labor power.[2]

The 1965 Joint Soviet-Japanese Development Scheme produced what one scholar has called "very substantial results," including construction of a port at Wrangel (Vostochnyi), progress in the joint development of Sakhalin oil and Yakut natural gas, and a brisk trade in fish, timber, wood chips, and coal.[3] Although this activity was marred by periodic misunderstandings, by 1970 Japan had become the Soviet Union's largest trade partner, and remained the second largest (after West Germany) for the rest of the decade.[4] By the 1980s, though, economic cooperation between the USSR and Japan was faltering. Moreover, at no point did the USSR account for more than 2 percent of the total volume of Japan's trade, a reflection of inherent geographic and economic difficulties and of a Japanese unwillingness either to strengthen Soviet military capabilities or to become dependent on imports from the USSR.[5]

At the same time, within Russia there has been a marked decline in investment in large-scale projects.[6] Remaining cautious about the prospects for western Siberia, many scholars are fatalistic about developing eastern Siberia.[7] The leading study asks whether the region should be seen as a bonanza or a quagmire, answering that it is neither, but reinforcing doubts simply by posing such a question.[8] Development seems highly unlikely without substantial foreign participation. From such a vantage point, the economic future of Russia's eastern territories looms as the transregional issue with the greatest potential for cooperation.[9] Some notion about what is happening to the resources of Asian Russia during the transition away from Communism is provided by the five papers in this section.

* * *

Located under marshy wetlands, the Tiumen oil fields were discovered in the late 1950s. Exploration and development began in the 1960s. By the 1980s, West Siberian oil accounted for 80 percent of Soviet foreign currency earnings, underwriting the Brezhnev arms buildup and the war in Afghanistan. Today, the West Siberian basin remains the world's largest known storehouse of hydrocarbons.[10] Bruce Kellison, a young political scientist from Texas, investigates the rise of local economic and political structures that are challenging Moscow's exclusive hold over the management of these resources—a set of developments fraught with international implications.

A complementary picture of hesitant but potentially fateful decentralization emerges in the story of West Siberian coal, as told by Paul T. Christensen, also a young political scientist. Christensen shows that what normally goes by the name of democratization more accurately could be called a property free-for-all involving local officials at all levels, as well as enterprise managers, but rarely worker collectives. Christensen's window into the process of privatization in the coal industry reveals a world of aspirations turned into naked opportunism and a lingering dependency on central authorities.

* * *

Post-Communism has brought its share of surprises, not the least of which has been the near complete failure of private family farming to take root even when traditional obstacles have been reduced or removed. Cynthia J. Buckley, a young sociologist, examines the prospects for another key resource—land—that has been at the center of most of the decisive episodes in Russian history. Nowhere perhaps is the contrast between abundant land and persistent low agricultural output more evident than in western Siberia, where Buckley conducted fieldwork on a collective farm that undertook a sincere attempt to decollectivize.

Aided by outside experts, the members of the collective farm Zaria (Dawn) surged ahead of national reform efforts in 1990, implementing a well-thought-out program of de facto privatization through the distribution of specific assets to those who worked them. Under the new "cooperative system," agricultural output rose and theft declined, but many old problems remained and new ones appeared, including inequities in access to tools or other formerly common resources and the near total decline of social welfare services. In 1992, disillusioned villagers assembled and voted to reinstitute the collective. Buckley examines this turn of events from the inside, emphasizing how in the area of agricultural reform, the case of West Siberia provides a marked contrast with the experience of Chinese neighbors across the southern border.

* * *

One of the most important and much-lamented facts about Siberia is that its numerous rivers all flow north, draining into the Arctic Sea, rather than south toward the densely populated but exceedingly dry regions of Central Asia. In such a context was born the scheme to reverse the flow of Siberian rivers. This project reflected not only the deeply held Soviet view that nature could be mastered, but also the intense lobbying within the centralized system by local interests and the resourcefulness of Siberian researchers in search of government funding. Much of the well-funded research for the river-diversion scheme was carried out at the Institute of Economics in Novosibirsk under Abel Aganbegian, the same institute that produced the heralded 1983 "Novosibirsk Report," said to have been a catalyst to the onset of perestroika.

During the public debate over the proposed diversion, references to "Siberian" water became commonplace. Regional interests came to the fore as various groups sought to influence central policy—the subject of the next paper in this section, written by yet another young political scientist, Michael L. Bressler. Bressler uses the Siberian river project to gain access to the policy-making process under Brezhnev, determine the effects of glasnost on that process, and identify the significance of its legacy for today's post-Communist planners.

A key role in the struggle for control over resources has been played by environmental concerns, which became a vehicle for nongovernmental political activity among scientists in Siberia seeking to defend Lake Baikal and among protonationalists in Kazakhstan opposed to the use of Semipalatinsk for nuclear testing.[11] Since the collapse of Communism, efforts to protect the environment in eastern Russia have become entangled with export get-rich-quick schemes, center–periphery relations, and the larger problem of Russian federalism. Elizabeth Wishnick, a consultant in Washington, D.C., and the author of a forthcoming study of Moscow's China policy since the 1969 border clashes, examines these issues by focusing on forestry policy in the Maritime province.[12]

As Wishnick shows, struggles for control over the resources of Asian Russia have intensified, exacerbating an already sobering legacy of environmental degradation. Privatization and chaotic decentralization have further weakened the effect of feeble safeguards. Only newly activist native peoples seem to be exerting a counterpressure. Wishnick concludes with a report on a joint venture between the provincial timber trust and the Korean multinational Hyundai Corporation, focusing on the conflicting goals pursued by a host of actors, from federal and local officials to Russian managers, native Siberian tribes, and foreign investors. Asian Russia's forests, no less than its water, land, coal, and oil, will continue to attract attention at home and throughout the wider Northeast Asian region.

Notes

1. Jonathan Schiffer, *Soviet Regional Economic Policy: East–West Debate on Pacific-Siberian Development* (Basingstoke, England: Macmillan, 1989); Michael Bradshaw, "Trade and High Technology," in Rodger Swearingen, ed., *Siberia and the Soviet Far East: Strategic Dimensions in Multinational Perspective* (Stanford: Hoover Institution Press, 1987); Theodore Shabad, "Economic Resources," in Alan Wood, ed., *Siberia: Problems and Prospects for Regional Development* (New York: Croom Helm, 1987), pp. 62–95. A brief overview of some of the literature is provided by Peter de Souza, "Siberian Futures? Economic Perspectives," *Siberica*, 1 (3), 1990, pp. 170–83.

2. Nikita Khrushchev, *Khrushchev Remembers: The Last Testament* (Boston: Little, Brown, 1974), pp. 248–50; Paul Dibb, *Siberia and the Pacific: A Study of Economic Development and Trade Prospects* (New York: Praeger, 1972), p. 122.

3. Stuart Kirby, "Siberia and Its Far Eastern Neighbors," in Wood, *Siberia: Problems and Prospects,* pp. 193–212; Allen Whiting, *Siberian Development and East Asia: Threat or Promise?* (Stanford: Stanford University Press, 1981).

4. Kazuo Ogawa, "Economic Relations with Japan," in Swearingen, *Siberia and the Soviet Far East,* pp. 158–78; Richard Louis Edmonds, "Siberian Resource Development and the Japanese Economy: The Japanese Perspective," in Robert Jensen et al., eds., *Soviet Natural Resources in the World Economy* (Chicago: University of Chicago Press, 1983), pp. 214–31.

5. Raymond Mathieson, *Japan's Role in Soviet Economic Growth: Transfer of Technology Since 1965* (New York: Praeger, 1979); Kiichi Saeki, "Towards Japanese Cooperation in Siberian Development," *Problems of Communism,* 21 (3), May–June 1972, pp. 1–11.

6. Theodore Shabad, "The Gorbachev Economic Policy: Is the USSR Turning Away from Siberian Development?" in Alan Wood and L.A. French, eds., *The Development of Siberia: People and Resources* (Basingstoke, England: Macmillan, 1989), pp. 256–60.

7. Leslie Dienes, "A Comment on the New Development Program for the Far Eastern Economic Region," *Soviet Geography,* 19 (4), 1988, p. 495; and idem, *Soviet Asia: Economic Development and National Policy Choices* (Boulder, CO: Westview Press, 1987). See also Boris Rumer, "Current Problems in the Industrialization of Siberia," *Berichte des Bundesinstituts für Ostwissenschaftliche und Internationale Studien,* no. 48 (Cologne, 1984); and "Panel on Siberia: Economic and Territorial Issues," *Soviet Geography,* 32 (6), 1991, pp. 363–432.

8. Whiting, *Siberian Development and East Asia,* ch. 2.

9. John Stephan, "Siberia and the World Economy: Incentives and Constraints to Involvement," in Wood, *Siberia: Problems and Prospects,* pp. 213–30.

10. David Wilson, "The Siberian Oil and Gas Industry," in Wood, *Siberia: Problems*

and Prospects, pp. 96–129. East Siberia may contain equally vast riches, but runaway military spending has eclipsed investment in adequate exploration, let alone development. John Hardt, "Soviet Siberia: A Power to Be?" in Swearingen, *Siberia and the Soviet Far East,* pp. xxi–xxx.

11. Boris Komarov [pseudonym], *The Destruction of Nature in the Soviet Union* (White Plains, NY: M.E. Sharpe, 1980), Russian-language edition 1978; Martha Olcott, *The Kazakhs* (Stanford: Hoover Institution Press, 1987); and Geoffrey Hosking, *The Awakening of the Soviet Union* (Cambridge, MA: Harvard University Press, 1990). For general background on environmental problems in Russia, see Marshall I. Goldman, *The Spoils of Progress: Environmental Pollution in the Soviet Union* (Cambridge, MA: MIT Press, 1972); Philip R. Pryde, *Environmental Management in the Soviet Union* (Cambridge: Cambridge University Press, 1991); and Murray Feshbach and Alfred Friendly, Jr., *Ecocide in the USSR: Health and Nature Under Siege* (New York: Basic, 1992).

12. Elizabeth Wishnick, *Mending Fences with China: The Evolution of Moscow's China Policy, 1969–1992* (forthcoming).

18. West Siberian oil fields of Samotlor. *Source: Sibir'* (Moscow, 1985).

19. Siberian pipeline traverses the frozen earth.
Sibir' (Moscow, 1985).

20. A harvest of logs transported down the Angara. *Source: Violet Conolly, Siberia: Today and Tomorrow* (New York: Taplinger, 1976).

21. Striking coalminers of the Kuznetsk basin ordered to return to work by then Moscow Coal Minister M.I. Shchadov, July 1989. *Source:* Viktor Kostiukovskii, *Kuzbass: Zharkoe leto 89-go* (Moscow, 1990).

22. Boxcars of Siberian coal awaiting departure. *Source: Sibir'* (Moscow, 1985).

Siberian Crude

Moscow, Tiumen, and Political Decentralization

Bruce Kellison

The role that western Siberia's vast oil resources will play in the development of Russia, Siberia, the Far East, and the Northeast Asian region puzzles Russian policy makers as well as analysts of Russian affairs. Unquestionably, Siberia's oil and gas deposits are world class in size; they powered Soviet postwar economic expansion and provided much-needed hard currency for Soviet purchases of Western agricultural and manufactured goods. Since 1988, however, the Soviet (and then Russian) government's budget could no longer sustain the enormous investment required to keep the fields producing. Furthermore, local governmental bodies in western Siberia increasingly demanded the authority to direct investment and tax oil and gas production associations, at Moscow's expense.

Local control of resource development and use is a source of political conflict not only at the national level but also, perhaps surprisingly, at the local level. This is because the collapse of the ministries, the Communist Party, and the Union have presented local leaders, including those in Siberia, with both opportunities and challenges. To be able to exploit an enormous oil resource largely without Moscow's control excites provincial leaders, many of whom have Kuwait on their minds. The trouble for local legislatures, however, is deciding *which* local level will have the most authority to direct production.

Conflict on a variety of issues, from taxes to labor, among oblast, okrug, and city elected bodies is in many ways more important for the future of Siberia than the center–periphery struggle often referred to by analysts of Russian affairs. Moscow still commands many tools for control over the Siberian oil resources, as we will see. But as in so many areas of the economy, Moscow's will far exceeds its abilities of late.

This essay addresses the development of economic and political structures that are gradually challenging Moscow's traditional role as "manager" of the vast oil resources of western Siberia. The term "Moscow," or the center, will be used throughout to refer to the Energy Ministry and the Yeltsin government. Most attention will be paid to politics in the Tiumen oblast in western Siberia, a typical "periphery," and the ways in which local governments are using new-found authority to take control of natural resources.[1] Mention, too, will be made of the role of oil in the Northeast Asian region more broadly and the potential for trade among the nations of the area.

Previous work by Bahry[2] and Gustafson[3] has shown that while regional political elites may have been effective in lobbying the center for a share of invest-ment in the periphery, they have been far less able to alter the direction of policy itself to balance uneven economic development patterns. The success of pro-grams initiated from Moscow turned on the cooperation of local political lead-ers—but this is hardly a recent or novel phenomenon in Soviet politics. Now it appears that local economic leaders are using their recently acquired economic might to strike back against the inefficiency and distorted incentives characteris-tic of the centralized economy. In so doing, economic elites are replacing politi-cal elites as "transmission belts" for periphery demands on the center, a turn of events fraught with consequences for the future of Russian politics. Market-oriented reform is empowering a new class of economic elites that is using different structures to wield power, even though in many cases they are hold-overs from the old nomenklatura system.

The provinces are much more politically autonomous now than they have been at any time since 1917, a development that has been brought about as a result of the economic reform undertaken first by Gorbachev after 1985 and continued by Yeltsin after 1991. This is not to say that devolution of political power to the provinces has been intentional. To the contrary, much of the politi-cal decentralization has been unintentional and unwanted, both under Gorbachev and Yeltsin. I hope to illustrate the process of decentralization with a study of the recent politics of the western Siberian oil region and suggest that movement away from the command economic system toward some type of market system has its own political implications for the relations between Moscow and the provinces. The provinces have taken much more control over the resources in their geographical jurisdiction since economic reform began. I conclude, though, that political decentralization is by no means unidirectional; that is, the devolu-tion of political authority is not proceeding solely away from the center (Mos-cow) toward the periphery (western Siberia, in this instance). Rather, the provinces themselves are grappling with an altered political and economic land-scape that is blurring and eroding old lines of regional authority.

Geographers have long studied the destructive and exploitative impact of the metropolis as it has integrated the hinterlands into its political and economic sphere without significant regard for indigenous societies.[4] The interests of local-ities were usually secondary to Moscow's economic and military priorities. Not surprisingly, this situation led to extreme economic dependence of the periphery on the center and heightened competition among all regions of the Soviet Union for an ever-decreasing amount of available social infrastructure and capital investment from the center.

A.G. Granberg, director of the Institute of Economics and Organization of Industrial Production (EIOPP) of the Siberian Division of the Russian Academy of Sciences, remarked in an interview that Siberia might be imagined as a colony of Moscow, because raw materials are exported at "larcenist" prices, while all social, economic, and political problems are decided at the center. "The richest [Siberian] krai under normal economic conditions," he observed, "could have a quality of life no less than that of the oil emirates." The key question is how to restructure relations between the center and periphery, and he argues that local control over economic decision making is a necessary precondition for a stable future. Granberg demands that a "normal" budgeting system be established for enterprises and that competitive world oil prices be paid for fuel in Russia.[5] In other words, the manner in which the Russian periphery struggles for economic and political autonomy from the center and the way former nomenklatura elites in the periphery attempt to imitate capitalist consumption in the center but fail to incorporate lower social strata are reminiscent of development patterns elsewhere in the world economy.

Background to the Oil Crisis

The case of Russia's oil sector is particularly illustrative of the center–periphery development pattern. Oil production in the Soviet Union did not follow the worldwide pattern; the seven major transnational oil companies played little part in the Soviet oil industry after the Bolshevik Revolution.[6] The USSR itself found and developed oil in the Volga-Urals region in the 1930s and then discovered the world-class oil and gas fields of western Siberia in the 1960s. They developed them without the help, either financially or for the most part technologically, of the major Western oil companies. It was not until the mid-1970s that investment in the vast reserves of western Siberia became a priority area for the Brezhnev Politburo.

An oil emergency in 1977 resulted from declining output from the older oil-producing areas in the Caspian Sea and the so-called Second Baku in the Volga-Urals region, as well as from increasing costs of producing oil in western Siberia. Geologists failed to meet targets for identifying proven and probable fields, the number of new fields coming under production slowed, the flow rate of new wells decreased, and the overall growth rate of Siberian production began to drop.[7] The shortages, which continued until 1982, forced policy makers to increase output from Siberia radically.

The infrastructure was not yet in place, however, to enable western Siberian areas such as Samotlor in Tiumen oblast to raise production on the scale called for by Moscow. The result was huge increases in investment in Siberia: Between

1981 and 1985, energy investment grew by 50 percent, fully two-thirds of the total increase in industrial investment for the period.[8] This, of course, meant that other industrial sectors, often vital to energy production, made do with stagnant investment budgets over the same period, exacerbating the pressure on the Soviet industrial sector. Moreover, the new sums spent on the oil sector favored extraction over "upstream" investment in such areas as exploratory drilling and geological mapping. This was due, in large part, to the leadership's view of oil exports as a cash cow with which to finance imports of technology, grain, and consumer goods in the late 1970s.

To make matters worse, oil consumption continued to grow during the 1970s, and conservation and efficiency programs did not become priorities for the Brezhnev Politburo, which was unwilling to make the difficult political choices such programs would have required. Fuel switching (from oil to natural gas) *did* become possible in 1980–81 because of the increasing marginal cost of producing oil versus gas. This allowed the Soviet leadership some breathing room before the increased investment in the energy sector took effect.

Since 1988, oil production in Russia has fallen precipitously, from an average of 11.34 million barrels a day (mb/d) to 6.06 mb/d in 1994.[9] There are many contributing reasons for this, including those cited above, but the principal one is that the Soviet, and now Russian, government simply could not continue to invest the enormous sums to keep production up. The drop in oil output has meant a severe hard-currency deficit for the Russian government, as oil sales on world markets have dried up. It has also meant fewer ways of financing state petroleum orders other than printing rubles, which is highly inflationary.

At the same time, refineries and other purchasers of energy are not paying their bills, a situation that has gas workers in Nadym and coal miners in Vorkuta and the Kuznetsk basin ready to strike over nonpayment of wages.[10] Further contributing to the crisis in the oil sector is the artificially low price of oil within the domestic Russian market: Gasoline was selling in Moscow for 70 rubles per liter in May 1993, or roughly $4 per barrel, well below the world price of $16.50 per barrel.[11] It remains to inquire what the response has been to this crisis at various levels, beginning with Moscow authorities and proceeding downward to those in Tiumen oblast, the Khanti-Mansiisk and Yamal-Nenets autonomous okrugs, the city of Nizhnevartovsk, and the oil production associations and joint ventures.

Decentralization and Moscow's Control of the Oil Industry

Oil investment has always flowed out of Moscow and to the producing regions of Siberia. Gustafson has examined the periods of crisis in oil investment.[12] What is important here is that industrial investment in the oil sector began to decline in the late 1980s, and as a result, oil output peaked in 1988 and began declining after that. The ministries simply ran out of money to invest in the industry.

With the decline in investment has come a loss of control over oil production. Decisions are now made locally over how and where to produce and with whom to barter for materials. This brings a much greater amount of leverage to the side of the production associations in their negotiations with the Energy Ministry over the amount of oil to be allocated to Moscow instead of sold to suppliers, smuggled out of the country, or legally exported for hard currency.

There is a limit, however, to the autonomy of production associations and their relationship with Moscow, and here is where the ongoing process of decentralization becomes a bit murkier. One of the more interesting aspects of the role of the Energy Ministry is the seemingly dichotomous incentives the reform government has established by simultaneously encouraging new market institutions and decentralization of power, while retaining some of the residual coercive and bureaucratic power left over from the Soviet period.

The center remains equipped with an array of tools to maintain order in the energy sector. The largest is its power to declare that all mineral resources are state property and subject to its license requirements, as the state did when President Yeltsin signed the Law on Mineral Resources in March 1992. In addition, the Energy Ministry, with its four-tiered bureaucratic structure, oversees the entire Russian energy sector in much the same way that nine USSR ministries used to for the Soviet Union. The Ministry also retains some control over the four quasi-private oil corporations, Rosneft, Yukos, Lukoil, and Surgutneftegaz, although these structures are still being developed. The state has the ability to set export quotas and taxes on firms, both foreign and domestic, as well as to control profit and the expropriation of profit. There is little doubt that Moscow, through the Energy Ministry, wants continued control over the enormous energy resources in places like Siberia. It relies too heavily on energy exports to generate hard currency. But it no longer possesses the ability to dictate development and investment decisions that it used to.

The struggle over oil prices is among the most important points of contention between the center and periphery in the oil industry and is indicative of the different agendas of the two sides. Moscow wants production associations to continue supplying the state with oil and gas at prices far below market rates in exchange for maintaining the system of state-subsidized investment in the industry. Moscow is then able either to sell this oil on world markets for hard currency or to control its internal distribution to other industrial sectors. It retains the authority to set the price of oil at artificially low levels, arguing that the Russian economy remains too fragile to absorb the inflationary surge that an immediate jump to world oil prices would produce, not to mention how Russian consumers would fare. In January 1995, however, Yeltsin's cabinet yielded to pressure from the World Bank and the IMF and agreed to gradually reduce state quotas, thereby freeing production associations to charge market prices for domestic oil products.

Just before the coup in 1991, Russian president Boris Yeltsin declared that 10 percent of Russian Federation production could be sold directly by production associations on world markets, increasing to 30 percent by 1992. Siberian producers wanted 50 percent.[13] This did not happen, as the state continually forced production associations to renegotiate this share (in 1993 it stood at about 10 percent, depending on the deal arranged by the production association with Moscow). There has been growing evidence that oil and gas are increasingly among the array of minerals smuggled out of the country because of the disincentives of doing business with the state, and that the profits from such sales are deposited in foreign banks and kept in hard currency, not rubles.

The Russian government seems very aware of this problem. In early 1993, Prime Minister Viktor Chernomyrdin himself traveled to western Siberia to negotiate a production quota for producers, regional authorities, and the central government. The trip testified not only to Moscow's concern over the ability of producers to circumvent central decrees but to the fact that policy was still being set in the center, which was not ready to relinquish its powerful position in the management of the country's resources.[14]

Decentralization and Tiumen Oblast

Tiumen oblast, in western Siberia, is three times the size of Texas and produces two-thirds of Russia's oil. The city of Tiumen, located in the southwestern corner of the oblast, is the oblast capital and home to many of the Soviet planning bodies that previously directed all of the investment in the region's oil industry. In the 1990s, however, its roles as the center of the industry and the political and geographic capital of the region have been challenged on a number of fronts, as the decentralization of the political system proceeds in the wake of economic restructuring and reform.

The centrally planned oil industry was extraordinarily complex, with at least nine former ministries overseeing oil exploration, production, refining, and distribution. All of them had offices in Tiumen. The experience of one institute, the State Scientific Research and Design Institute of the Oil and Gas Industry (GIPRO), is indicative of what has happened to the bureaucracies that used to direct the industry.

Yuri Lukashkin, the current director of GIPRO, has been working there since the 1970s.[15] Lukashkin claimed in the summer of 1993 that of the six thousand employees and scientists who worked for the institute in the mid-1980s, only two hundred remained. He explained that this was mostly a result of the dramatic reduction in funds coming from Moscow for the industry. The research that scientists used to conduct at the institute, vital to the proper functioning of the industry, was then either not being performed or was being undertaken by production associations themselves. No matter how Lukashkin juggled the finances, the new reality of life in the industry meant that the most talented technicians, scientists, and workers were leaving the field altogether for work in commercial businesses unrelated to oil and gas production. At the same time, attracting young specialists had become impossible, so that the institute was slowly dissolving. Lukashkin added that no new oil-bearing areas in Tiumen oblast were being explored or exploited in connection with research carried out at the institute.

When asked about the role the center *should* play in future development of western Siberian oil reserves, Lukashkin said he did not think that the oblast, okrug, or city soviets could invest rubles in the industry on the scale needed to bring production back to 1988 levels. At the same time, he claimed to be unable to understand why Prime Minister Chernomyrdin and Energy Minister Shafranik did not support the industry more, given their backgrounds in gas (Chernomyrdin) and oil (Shafranik). Credit was unavailable from the Central Bank or the Ministry for his institute, and under inflationary conditions, Lukashkin could not continue to ratchet up employee salaries to keep pace with prices. He complained that the industry lacked direction, proper regulation, and institutional support. In short, the old system has broken down, and there was no effective program to replace it, a familiar refrain heard throughout most branches of industry.

Politically, the oblast has become much more autonomous now than it used to be under Soviet administration. Even before the formal collapse of the USSR after the coup in 1991, the Tiumen oblast soviet had reserved for itself the right to pass laws that could not be abrogated by Moscow, including the right to set prices on oil, gas, and wood products. The "transition to the market" was mentioned often in these declarations as a way of demonstrating the oblast soviet's commitment to reform.[16] The oblast's administrative head was appointed by Yeltsin—Leonid Roketsky was the "governor" as of the end of 1993—and theoretically might oppose the locally elected supreme soviet, which was tied to the disbanded Russian Supreme Soviet in Moscow. But in discussions with members from both the legislative and executive branches in Tiumen, the feeling seemed to be that the threat to local oblast-level control over resources and authority to tax lay not with Moscow but with the autonomous okrugs in Tiumen oblast— Khanti-Mansiisk and Yamal-Nenetsky.

Decentralization and the Autonomous Okrugs

The autonomous okrug known as Khanti-Mansiisk, located just north of the city of Tiumen, contains most of the oil-producing areas of the oblast. Its capital is the city of Khanti-Mansiisk, situated at the confluence of the Irtish and Ob rivers. Yamal-Nenetsky, located north of Khanti-Mansiisk and extending to the Kara Sea, contains most of the oblast's vast natural gas reserves. Its capital is the city of Salekhard.

These okrugs were given special authority under the old Soviet constitution because of the presence of ethnic minorities. In recent years, the okrugs have used these powers to create parallel structures in banking, budgeting, and taxation that compete directly with those of the oblast. For instance, when Khanti-Mansiisk drew up its budget for 1993, it went directly to Moscow for the funds, not through Tiumen, and it secured a sum of 680 billion rubles, the second largest budget of any region in all of Russia, behind only Moscow.[17] The entire budgeting process, which used to flow linearly from Moscow through Tiumen and on to the okrugs, now goes directly from Moscow to both Tiumen and the okrugs simultaneously.

With this authority, the okrugs began playing off Moscow and Tiumen to get the most out of their position as trustees of the vast oil and gas reserves of western Siberia. Such tactics frustrate oblast-level administrators, who realize that they will be shut out of a share of the revenue stream if they permit the okrugs any more freedom than they already have.

Decentralization and the City: Nizhnevartovsk

The responsibilities of city governments in Russia have mushroomed as a result of economic reform. No longer are enterprises required to build and maintain social infrastructure for their workers, so city governments have had to supply these services. But the money to pay for them has not been available. V.S. Grabovskii, First Deputy Head of Administration for the city of Nizhnevartovsk, when asked to name the largest problem facing the city, responded that it was paying for the budget.[18] He pointed out, moreover, that the tax system was complex enough without the added worry for city officials of competing with raion- and oblast-level administrators arranging their own tax deals with firms and enterprises.

For their part, officials in the financial department of the city administration complained that the existing tax laws were not clear enough to prevent joint ventures, for instance, from establishing separate tax-arrangement payments with the raion soviet and shutting out the city soviet. With 10 percent of the city's population living in boxcars at the railway yard because of a housing shortage, missing funds from city budgets loomed as a potentially explosive problem.

Decentralization at the Firm Level

The question of whether oil production association managers want privatization of their companies can be given no easy answer. On the one hand, it would be reasonable to expect them to favor the current arrangement, halfway between private and state ownership. This way, managers would be ensured maximum control over the activities of their firms. On the other hand, privatization would lead to more financial stability for production associations and for the managers who now run them. In the course of discussions with managers at Tiumen-neftegaz and Nizhnevartovskneftegaz, it became clear that all wanted to take the first step toward the second approach, privatization, by converting their firms into joint-stock companies along the lines agreed to by Yeltsin and the Energy Ministry.

Under the share-holding agreement, proposed in the privatization plan for the industry, 38 percent of shares in an oil production association would be retained by the state and would come with voting rights. Twenty-five percent of the shares would be sold to workers without voting rights, 22 percent sold to investors without voting rights, 10 percent would go to workers with voting rights, and the remaining 5 percent of the shares would be sold to managers with voting rights. In the end, the managers, on a per capita basis, would maintain considerable voting power in the company, as well as day-to-day control over operations.

At the same time, however, individual enterprises, especially the most financially successful ones, have sought economic independence from the production associations to which they belong. Former Russian Energy Minister Lopukhin already granted permission to "secede" to Chernogorneft, an oil enterprise attached to Nizhnevartovskneftegaz. Other production associations began actively pursuing privatization programs of their own, but the legality of such moves under the 1986 Law on Enterprises was questioned by former Prime Minister Yegor Gaidar and was then openly challenged by some production associations. Bolstering its position, Nizhnevartovskneftegaz received in 1993 the first loan to a Russian oil company from the European Bank for Reconstruction and Development (EBRD) to buy oil-field equipment to bolster production at the Samotlor field in Tiumen. Significantly, the entire loan goes directly to the production company—no money will pass through the Fuel and Energy Ministry.[19] The importance of such developments cannot be underestimated in the current struggle between center and periphery in Russia. Such spontaneous privatization directly challenges Moscow's political control of the industry through the development of market-driven incentive structures.

The Chernogorneft story is a fascinating one that sheds considerable light on the process of decentralization under way in Siberia. Nizhnevartovskneftegaz had five "NGDU," or oil and gas production companies, under its umbrella organization in 1988–89, all producing in and around the city of Nizhnevartovsk. In 1988, S. Volkov, a former party official with good connections in Moscow, was elected by the workers of Nizhnevartovskneftegaz to be the general director of the entire production association but was opposed by others at the top. The case went to arbitration, and the parties waited for a year before a decision was handed down. Volkov won but decided not to take the position at Nizhnevartovskneftegaz; rather, given a choice, he selected the general directorship of Chernogorneft, which he then managed, under the Law on Enterprises, to take completely private.

In the ensuing years, Chernogorneft has formed three separate joint ventures with foreign oil firms, including one with Occidental Petroleum (an enhanced oil-recovery operation) and one with Anderman-Smith (an exploration, drilling, and production agreement). By mid-1993, both were seeking financing from the

EBRD. These joint ventures were producing oil successfully in Nizhnevartovsk, albeit with the usual problems associated with doing business in Russia, such as arbitrary tax laws, whimsical enforcement of environmental regulations, and an inability to find bureaucrats who will make decisions regarding their operations.

Chernogorneft was taken private through the efforts of one entrepreneurial person with solid connections in Moscow. The risk that he took, and that his company Chernogorneft continues to take—by all accounts, some of which were confidential (there is still quite a bit of resentment toward Chernogorneft both in Moscow and in Nizhnevartovsk)—is indicative of the type of business activity in Russia directed at challenging old bureaucratic structures to take advantage of potentially enormous raw material resources. Ironically, however, the economic and political decentralization occurring in the Chernogorneft story could not have come about without the acquiescence of very highly placed people in Moscow. F.Kh. Galeev, the chief engineer for Nizhnevartovskneft (another NGDU of Nizhnevartovskneftegaz), said in response to a question about how Volkov's privatization of Chernogorneft in 1989 was perceived by other NGDUs that it would have been impossible to duplicate at the time. Volkov's Moscow connections were simply too good.[20]

That political and economic decentralization is not occurring without the cooperation of very well-placed bureaucrats in Moscow seems indisputable. Whether such cooperation is a sign of corruption is more difficult to tell. Without a doubt there is corruption in the Energy Ministry, just as there is oil being smuggled out of Russia to be sold on the world market. The problem is identifying and measuring it.

The presence of joint ventures in the oil industry is also fueling economic decentralization. The more contact that Russian oil industry workers and managers have with Western business practices, the sooner they move away from the confines of the command system. Anderman-Smith, for example, receives Russian work crews from its joint venture partner, Chernogorneft, and trains them to work their drilling sites with American equipment. But in an effort to expose as many of the Russians to American drilling techniques, Anderman-Smith executives have decided to rotate these crews back to the Russian partner and replace them with new Russian crews. The goal is to encourage more familiarity with American work habits, concepts of profit and loss, and problem-solving skills that eventually will result in greater entrepreneurial innovation. As of late 1993, both sides appeared satisfied with this arrangement.

And yet, there is a baseline of resentment toward the West and Western business in Russia that will take time to dissipate. This feeling is evident in the reaction among Russian media toward increased involvement by Western firms in the oil industry. On the one hand, there are those who are skeptical of the intense interest by Western investment bankers in Russia's principal natural resources, oil and gas, and who fear being taken advantage of, as if Russia were a naive third world state.[21] *Komsomol'skaia pravda* wrote of the "pillage" of Soviet oil fields by "commercial organizations" with the help of the Russian

Table 12.1

Yearly Oil Consumption (thousands of metric tons)

Year	China	N. Korea	S. Korea	Japan
1982	83,000	2,550	26,166	—
1983	85,000	2,713	27,387	—
1984	88,000	2,877	27,634	—
1985	93,500	3,042	27,862	—
1986	99,500	3,205	29,721	200,014
1987	106,000	3,235	31,204	202,087
1988	112,500	3,235	36,891	217,025
1989	117,000	3,495	42,470	225,467
1990	116,000	3,495	51,268	236,358
1991	125,000	3,565	61,648	240,047

Sources: Data for China, North Korea, and South Korea are from *Energy Statistics and Balances on Non-OECD Countries, 1990–1991.* Data for Japan are from *Oil and Gas Information 1992.*

state and implicated former Prime Minister Valentin Pavlov and Ivan Silaev, chairman of the Interstate Economic Committee, in a scheme to enrich the Communist Party.[22] On the other hand, there have been frank discussions of the Russian oil crisis and impassioned pleas for Western investment.[23] This ambivalence toward the outside world, characteristic of the country as a whole, has been one of many impediments to foreign investment.

Until there is some consensus between Russian oil production associations and Moscow on questions of taxation and expropriation of profits for Western companies, there is likely to be continued turmoil between Russia and the foreign companies seeking a share of its wealth. But perhaps what is most needed is time—time for both parties to become accustomed to doing business in Russia for the first time on this scale.

The Russian Far East and Northeast Asia

Internationally, the Northeast Asian region has quite a bit to gain from energy trade with Russia. Of the countries of the area, only Russia and China produce enough oil to satisfy domestic consumption, with the remainder being exported. South Korean oil consumption almost doubled in the four years between 1987 and 1991, and Japan's increased by almost 20 percent (see Table 12.1), as these economies enjoyed robust growth during the 1980s. Virtually all of North Korea, South Korea, and Japan's oil must be imported. For Japan, 70 percent of its oil comes from the Middle East, with the lion's share of the rest imported from Indonesia. Currently, Russia supplies only 2 percent of Japan's yearly oil imports.[24]

Table 12.2

Oil Production (thousands of metric tons)

Year	China	Russia
1982	102,120	—
1983	106,070	—
1984	114,610	—
1985	124,900	542,300
1986	130,690	561,180
1987	134,140	569,480
1988	137,050	568,780
1989	137,650	552,230
1990	138,310	516,400
1991	140,990	461,100
1992	142,000	395,800

Source: Energy Statistics and Balances of Non-OECD Countries, 1990–91.

China, for its part, appears unable to meet its own oil needs and will have to import more and more oil in the future if its economy continues to expand (Table 12.2). Coupled with South Korean economic growth, China's situation dem-onstrates that there exists in Northeast Asia a natural market for Russian oil exports. For Japan, though, Russia remains an unlikely source because of its ongoing energy crisis and its inability to decide whether or not it wants Western investment in its energy sector. In addition, the diplomatic impasse over the fate of Sakhalin Island is crucial to the future of Russo-Japanese relations.

Japan, for obvious reasons, is intensely interested in the enormous oil and gas reserves that exist on Sakhalin Island and offshore. The issue, however, is complicated by Japanese territorial claims on the island. Although Japan wants this matter resolved before committing to full-scale negotiations and development of resources on the island, talks, nevertheless, are under way. The potential for cooperation between the two countries is enormous: Japan has the market, the technology, the financial resources, and the energy need to invest heavily in Russia's Far Eastern energy resources, and because of Sakhalin's proximity to Japan, it is a most attractive source of energy. The West is ready to commit to investing in energy production and exploration on Sakhalin, but energy joint ventures there suffer from the same types of problems as elsewhere in Russia now, and progress has been slow.

Conclusion

An exploration of the process of economic and political decentralization under way in Russia, through the case of the western Siberian oil industry, has demonstrated that Moscow retains much of the authority it enjoyed during the Soviet period and is able to dictate to the provinces how resources will be extracted and consumed. As market mechanisms take hold in the industry, however, Moscow is finding it has less control than it would like. Strikes by oil-field workers over nonpayment of wages are a possibility that the industry has not experienced yet but might soon, if the strikes threatened by coal miners are any indication. But Moscow also retains the ability to sell licenses to explore and produce oil in Siberia. It still provides most of the industry's investment, although the amounts have dropped since the late 1980s. Economic elites in Siberia, many with former party affiliations, are being created in the transition to market principles, but these elites are still dependent on Moscow's authority to operate.

We have also seen that decentralization is producing tensions among levels of government within the periphery itself. Political elites in the periphery appear to want economic autonomy from Moscow for their krais, oblasts, and autonomous okrugs, without necessarily gaining complete independence.[25] But the prospect of autonomy from Moscow has set various-level local officials to fighting among themselves.

Oblast executives and oblast soviets compete with similar bodies in autonomous okrugs for funding and tax revenue. In Tiumen, the competition involves the authority to direct the revenue stream generated by enormous reserves of oil and gas. How this struggle will end is not clear. The December 1993 elections clarified little: President Yeltsin, Prime Minister Chernomyrdin, and Energy Minister Shafranik all emerged in place. The national constitution, ratified by a narrow margin, gave Yeltsin and his cabinet wide authority to direct industries, such as energy, deemed critical to the nation. Not surprisingly, a shift in the rhetoric from Moscow over the pace of national economic development has translated into more state funding for oil production. If it persists, this increase may mean less pressure on oil production association managers to take the risky step of privatizing their enterprises and less pressure on local governments to meet the social needs of the population in the oil-producing areas of western Siberia. Also, a slowdown in the transition to a market-based economy only reduces the potential for stimulating energy trade in the Northeast Asian region.

The tensions between center and periphery in Russia are likely to continue, especially in the crucial public policy arena of Siberian oil. Decentralization of the Russian economy encourages political regionalism, which in turn produces political turf battles among localities in Siberia over control of this enormous natural resource. The outcome of the struggle is far from certain, but one thing is sure—Russia must rejuvenate its oil industry if it is to have any hope of economic recovery in the short or long term.

Notes

1. I use the terms "center" and "periphery" to describe Moscow and Tiumen, respectively, because I believe that a center–periphery framework most adequately describes the

unbalanced, exploitative relationship between Moscow and Siberia. For a comprehensive treatment of this view, see Leslie Dienes, *Soviet Asia: Economic Development and National Policy Choices* (Boulder, CO: Westview Press, 1987).

2. Donna Bahry, *Outside Moscow: Power, Politics, and Budgetary Policy in the Soviet Republics* (New York: Columbia University Press, 1987).

3. Thane Gustafson, *Crisis Amid Plenty: The Politics of Soviet Energy Under Brezhnev and Gorbachev* (Princeton: Princeton University Press, 1989).

4. Dienes, 1987, *Soviet Asia.*

5. *Tiumenskie izvestiia,* 14 February 1991, p.1.

6. They *had* played a role, of course, in its development before the revolution. For a lively treatment of the involvement of the Rothschilds, the Nobels, and Royal/Dutch Shell in Russia, see Daniel Yergin, *The Prize: The Epic Quest for Oil, Money and Power* (New York: Simon and Schuster, 1991).

7. Gustafson, *Crisis Amid Plenty,* p. 27.

8. Ibid., p. 36.

9. *New York Times,* 6 January 1995, p. A3.

10. Radio Free Europe/Radio Liberty, Daily Report no. 226, 26 November 1993.

11. *Sibirskaia gazeta,* no. 22, June 1993, p. 4.

12. Gustafson, *Crisis Amid Plenty,* especially ch. 2.

13. *Oil and Gas Journal,* 26 August 1991, pp. 27–30.

14. *Petroleum Intelligence Weekly,* 15 February 1993.

15. Material taken from an interview with Lukashkin conducted by the author, July 1993, Tiumen.

16. See, for instance, "Polozhenie o statuse Tiumenskoi oblasti," *Tiumenskie izvestiia,* 5 January 1991, p. 5 (from the second session of the oblast soviet).

17. *Nashe vremia,* 7 July 1993.

18. Interview conducted by the author, July 1993, Nizhnevartovsk, with Grabovskii.

19. *Petroleum Intelligence Weekly,* 25 January 1993.

20. Interview by the author, August 1993, Nizhnevartovsk, with Galeev.

21. See, for example, Mikhail Berger's bitingly sarcastic "U korporatsii 'Rosneftigaz' —Inostrannye finansovie sovetniki," *Izvestiia,* 23 January 1992, in which he refers to advisors from Daiwa, the Japanese securities house, and Banker's Trust as "London bums from the City," or the furor in the liberal *Moscow News* in the spring of 1991 warning the Soviet government not to sign the Chevron deal because of its allegedly unfavorable terms. *Moscow News* later claimed that it was only warning Chevron and others that unless the terms for deals like this one in Kazakhstan were more favorable to the Russians, conservatives would surely use this huge joint venture as an example of how the Soviet Union was being exploited by a rapacious West. The deal almost collapsed before the coup, but Chevron's interest never flagged and the Kazakh government reopened negotiations in the coup's aftermath, albeit under harsher terms. See *Oil and Gas Journal,* 5 August 1991, pp. 14–18.

22. *BBC Summary of World Broadcasts,* 13 December 1991.

23. See, for example, Valerii Neverov and Alexander Igolkin, "Kon'iunkturnyi obzor," *Ekonomika i zhizn',* December 1991, special issue. They are very candid about Russia's inability to continue its astronomically high rate of investment in oil exploration and production without dramatically reducing the national standard of living.

24. *Oil and Gas Information 1992* (Paris: International Energy Agency, 1993), p. 360.

25. Vera Tolz, "Regionalism in Russia: The Case of Siberia," *Radio Free Europe/Radio Liberty Research Report,* vol. 2, no. 9, 26 February 1993.

Property Free-For-All

Regionalism, "Democratization," and the Politics of Economic Control in the Kuzbas, 1989–93

Paul T. Christensen

One of the many disputes that served to intensify the conflict between Boris Yeltsin's government and the Russian legislature prior to the abolition of the Russian parliament in October 1993 was the issue of how political and economic power was to be divided between the center and the constituent regions of the Russian Federation. Regional leaders argued that the rights of the regions were the final bulwark against the consolidation of presidential dictatorship. Yeltsin retorted that appeals to "the sovereignty of regions" were a mask behind which die-hard Communists and/or fascists were hiding. As mutually disingenuous as these arguments were, serious analytical issues about the role of regionalism in Russia do exist beneath the political posturing. It will be my contention that in Siberia at least, the conflict over the rights of regions versus the center has had little to do with democracy[1]—at least in the Schumpeterian sense of that term—and still less with defending some notion of "Siberian identity," and much more to do with the reconfiguration of property rights and the rearticulation of class interests that are now taking place in post-Communist Russia.

The struggle over property rights has been and remains the central focus of politics in all of the regions of Russia. Nowhere in Russia has this struggle been more visible or tendentious than in the southwestern Siberian region of the Kuznetsk basin, or Kuzbas. At the center of the struggle is the issue of control over the coalfields that cover more than one quarter of the region's ninety-five thousand square kilometers of territory. The Kuzbas produces more than 150 million tons of coal per year—over one-third of Russia's overall production[2]— and coke produced in the Kuzbas is used in the production of one-third of Russia's metal. The Kuzbas mines are among the most technically advanced in the former

Soviet Union, and compared to coal from other mining regions in Russia, Kuzbas coal is relatively inexpensive. The coal industry in the Kuzbas directly employs hundreds of thousands of people and directly or indirectly affects the lives of virtually everyone living in the Kuznetsk basin.

Given the importance of the coal industry in the Kuzbas both for the region and for Russia, it is not surprising that debates and conflicts over control of the coal, the mines, and the revenues generated by them have occupied a central place in the struggle over the reconfiguration of property rights in this part of Russia. These conflicts were fueled by the accelerating collapse of the centralized Soviet economy after 1989 and exacerbated by the potential for increased access to the global market held out to the regions by both Gorbachev and Yeltsin.

Although those who would control this resource see Kuzbas coal as the means to economic security and political power, the potential economic benefits to be derived from gaining control over Kuzbas coal differ markedly depending on the context. In the short term and within the CIS market, prospects are generally positive. Despite economic problems, control over coal production and marketing still provides a solid basis for economic security. Russia remains coal-dependent compared to most other industrialized nations, with per capita annual consumption in 1990 still approximately two and one-half times the world average.[3] Per capita consumption continued to rise moderately in the early 1990s, and current projections predict a steady increase in coal production levels until the end of the century.[4] These trends bode well for the Kuzbas, particularly given the fact that two other major coal production centers of the former Soviet Union—Karaganda and the Donbas—are now located in foreign countries, with all the attendant difficulties to which this situation can give rise: transportation difficulties, the possibility of tariffs, and the vagaries of CIS politics.

When viewed in the longer term and in the context of the world market for coal (particularly if the CIS countries fully join that market), however, the position of the Kuzbas appears much more tenuous. In 1990, world production of hard coal amounted to 3.56 billion metric tons, with Russia accounting for approximately one-fifth of that total. The most important aspect of the international profile of coal production and consumption, however, is that the overwhelming majority of coal produced in the world is consumed in the country of origin. Of the 3.56 billion metric tons produced in 1990, only 389 million tons were exported.[5] The USSR in 1990 ranked fifth among major coal exporters, behind Australia, the United States, Canada, and the South African Customs Union. The market for coal internationally is thus relatively limited, while the set of importers and exporters is highly concentrated. As of 1993, it remained unclear whether Russian producers, including those of the Kuzbas, would succeed in breaking into these exceedingly competitive markets.

Russian producers are handicapped by their lack of contacts, the absence of a track record for reliability, the high cost of transporting and shipping coal from the interior of Russia, and in the case of the Kuzbas, the low overall quality of the coal, which tends to disintegrate in the process of shipment. One must add to this picture the mixed blessing that the collapse of the East/West blocs represents for Russian coal producers. While the end of the cold war opened up new opportunities for Russian producers to sell in Western markets, the breakup of the Council for Mutual Economic Assistance (CMEA) also removed the one guaranteed market that Russian producers enjoyed.[6] The extent to which the former republics of the Soviet Union will provide new markets for Russian coal is a question mark, as is what currency those countries will use for payment.

At the same time, as in the rest of the industrialized world, coal has been losing out to oil and gas as a fuel source in Russia.[7] For the moment, this does not seem to figure in the calculations of those involved in the struggle for property. Coal is still vital to the Kuzbas, and Kuzbas coal is still vital to Russia, even if the potential for profitable expansion internationally appears limited. Indeed, if the potential for profits is limited and the future unsure, then the issue of who controls those profits and the property from which they are derived in the short term takes on an even greater urgency. Like their counterparts in other parts of Russia, participants in property struggles in the Kuzbas have raised the banner of regionalism and regional rights to legitimize their attempts to gain control over the coal industry. These battles in the name of regionalism have important implications for the transition from Soviet-style authoritarianism.

The increasingly insistent demands for political and economic sovereignty that began in earnest in the Soviet Union in 1987, and that have continued unabated in all the states of the former Soviet Union, were denounced by former President Gorbachev and continue to be denounced by President Yeltsin and his representatives as counterproductive and a threat to further democratization.[8] Although these leaders' views could not help but be conditioned by their political positions, Western political science theories of transitions from authoritarianism have echoed the view that devolution of authority during a transition ought to be avoided.

Over the past thirty years, research into the question of how transitions occur has demonstrated that there is no single, identifiable method for making a successful shift from an authoritarian system to a nonauthoritarian one. Every successful transition has reflected the particularities of its country's history, culture, economy, and social structure, just as the form of each country's authoritarian system reflected these same particularities. Yet in spite of this, studies of transitions have identified three basic requirements for making a transition work.[9]

First, a set of institutions guaranteeing all relevant sociopolitical groups the right to participate in a postauthoritarian system must be devised and agreed upon by both the regime leaders and the groups concerned.[10] Second, the institutions devised and the policies followed during the transition must not involve any kind of redistribution of property, wealth, or privilege vis-à-vis powerful societal interests, except for the diminution of political advantages that these interests agree to as part of the transition. And third, there must be social forces already in place independent from the regime that can provide the basis for participatory politics once the authoritarian regime begins to relinquish power.[11]

The one basic and defining characteristic shared by all the countries that have undertaken transitions is that they were both authoritarian and capitalist; markets and private property already existed. The key to success was the protection of the economic elites' property and power, the preservation of a market system, and the acquiescence of other social forces to such policies in exchange for political rights.

By contrast, in the Soviet/Russian case, the previous system was founded on state ownership and central planning; private property and market mechanisms did not, and for all practical purposes still do not, exist in Russia.[12] There were and are elements of an independent "civil society" in the sense theorists of transitions use the term, but even now these elements are only in the initial stages of development—as the pre-election political process in late 1993 clearly demonstrated.

Control over property and resources—be they collectively or privately owned—is the mechanism through which independent groups either allied with or opposed to a regime can retain or re-establish their place in a post-transitional system. In the case of the former Soviet Union, any program of democratization had to do—and still has to do—exactly what the Western theorists of democratization claim is fatal to transitions: that is, challenge and reformulate the existing structures of property and power in order to "create" politically and economically viable groups that support the transition and give such groups the resources necessary to make that support visible and effective.

To put this in specific terms, as long as the nomenklatura elites—be they members of the Communist Party, the economic ministries, or regional apparats—controlled the property and resources of the Soviet Union (and, I would add, as long as they control those of Russia), they possessed the lion's share of the political power to be had in the system and, therefore, could be the arbiters of the reform process. The story of perestroika from at least 1987 to the end of the Soviet Union and of the politics and economics of post-Communist Russia is the story of attempts from various quarters either to break this control or preserve it in diverse ways. This may go against the prescriptions of transition theory, but given the nature of the Soviet system, such a situation is unavoidable and necessary.

If the most basic traditional assumptions about what is and is not permissible for a transition to succeed, particularly those regarding redistributive programs, do not hold in the Soviet/Russian case, the question immediately arises whether subsequent assumptions remain valid. Two such assumptions, which are of particular interest for the case of the Kuzbas and Siberia more generally, are that any form of militancy on the part of labor is dangerous during a transitional period[13] and that the central authorities must allow regional leaders free play in the political arena, while regional leaders must agree to maintain the unity of the state and to compete for power within the institutions devised during the transition.[14] In other words, both regionalism and class politics are, at least during a transitional situation, antithetical to democratization.

Based on the political processes and conflicts that have taken place in the Kuzbas since 1989, and which continue, I want to argue that the preceding assumptions are misleading. Labor militancy and the assertion of the primacy of regional interests in Siberia, I would argue, have assisted the democratization process more than they have hindered it. Furthermore, the real struggle has been and remains not whether democratization will continue, but rather what form of "democracy" will emerge from the process and whose long-term interests it will serve. We must distinguish between the effects of regionalism and class politics on the *process* of democratization and the import of these forms of political action on the *content* of political praxis in post-Soviet Russia.

To analyze the effect of labor militancy in the Kuzbas on the democratization process, one must begin with the Law on the State Enterprise of 1987. The provisions of the law were designed to transfer control over industry from the central ministerial bureaucracies to the enterprises themselves and, in addition, to give workers some control over the enterprises and their managers. During the course of 1987–89, however, the growing economic crisis in the Soviet Union, combined with the basic flaws in provisions of the enterprise law concerning decentralization and self-management, translated into a lack of supplies, a disruption of work schedules necessitating longer hours or extra workdays, and a decrease in safety procedures owing to excess haste.

Three years of glasnost, much of it in the Kuzbas directed against the corruption, waste, and poor working and living conditions in and around Soviet factories, created an atmosphere of protest and expectation. At the same time, however, a long list of unresolved economic and social problems festered,[15] while the self-management institutions at the factory level proved to be incapable of forcing managers to respond to the grievances of workers. At the same time, the political leadership at the local, regional, and national levels, which either believed that the new perestroika-era institutions did in fact work or at least claimed to believe so, continued to view strike action as the result of either ignorance, hotheadedness, or irresponsibility on the part of the Soviet industrial worker.

The miners' strike of July 1989, like the others before it,[16] was not well planned or organized ahead of time. The strike spread quickly from one mine in Mezhdurechensk to other mines in the city and then other cities of the Kuzbas. The organizations at the level closest to the mine workers, the trade unions and the councils of the labor collectives, were conspicuous by their absence from the ranks of the strikers. Although individual leaders of union locals and enterprise councils of the mines did play a significant role in the strike on the side of the striking miners, the unions and councils as organizations not only did not lead the strikes, in most cases they ended up on the opposite side of the table in negotiations with the miners.[17]

The reaction of the Communist Party to the strike was notable in that it highlighted the growing schism and lack of coordination between the central party leadership and the leadership in the provinces. Although concerned by the implications of the strike, Gorbachev saw it as "evidence of grassroots worker support for reform."[18] Local party officials took a different view. A resolution of the oblast party committee of 10 July condemned the strike as a manifestation of "lack of discipline, illegality, and permissiveness."[19] The administrative hierarchy of the coal industry, from the scientific and technical workers to Coal Minister Shchadov, was seriously divided in its attitude toward the strike. In general, the technical workers, engineers, and shop-level managers were supportive.[20] Working as they did in close proximity to the mines, these groups were affected by the same increasing supply and safety problems as the coal face workers and were equally frustrated by continued control over their industry from Moscow.

The attitude of the local and regional administrators of the mines, namely mine directors and the bureaucracy of the mine associations, ran the gamut from support to vitriolic opposition. Many mine directors sympathized with the demands of the miners and said nothing against the strike, even though most were uncomfortable with the miners' methods. A few managers even took an active role in the strike.[21] Many other directors, however, sided with the association-level bureaucracies, which were uniformly hostile to the strike.[22]

The explanation for this division lies in the arcana of organizational jurisdiction within the Soviet coal industry. Virtually all coal mines were under the jurisdiction of regional production associations and therefore not considered "juridical persons" as far as the Law on the State Enterprise was concerned. This meant that the mines had no independence—even in legal terms—in making economic decisions. The miners, and many regional coal-industry officials, viewed this as the main cause of their difficulties and made granting the mines independence from the associations one of their central demands. Many other directors and association-level bureaucrats, whose power derived from their execution of *centrally generated commands,* saw such demands as a threat to their power and continued existence and so opposed the strike.

The attitude of individual directors was roughly dictated by the relative profitability and technological viability of their respective mines. The more that directors felt that the mines could survive and turn a profit on their own, without the support of the regional associations, the greater their support or sympathy for the strike. The associations, since the passage of the 1987 Law on State Enterprises, had been engaging in a process of the further "associationization" of the mines in most regions of the country in order to counter the ability of mines to exercise decision-making rights granted in the enterprise law. According to V. Shchebrakov, then president of the USSR State Committee on Labor, since the beginning of perestroika, "in the ministry of coal the number of independent mines had dropped 3.5 times." He also pointed out that in other sectors of industry the process was even worse, in some reaching the level of an elevenfold drop.[23]

With the enactment of the enterprise law, directors who feared they were accorded a lack of trust on the part of the collectives they led had all the more reason to agree to the subordination of their mines to the regional coal associations. Once the mines became part of the association, the labor collective of the mine lost the right to subject the director and other managers to an election process—at least under one interpretation of the enterprise law. This bound the directors to the association, and never more so during the strike. If the demands of the miners were met, the mine collectives would once again gain the right to elect managers and effectively use the mine Councils of Labor Collectives; this would fundamentally jeopardize the directors' positions—as many mine managers found out after the strike settlement was reached.

Such a bifurcation of the elite reached the highest levels of government. As noted above, Gorbachev was concerned about the effect of the strike action, but he saw the miners' demands as just and said so on more than one occasion during the strike. The attitude of the government's point man—Coal Minister M.I. Shchadov—was quite different. Although he was the person sent to the Kuzbas to negotiate an end to the strike, Shchadov exhibited no sympathy with the strikers whatsoever.[24]

One cause of the fissures within elite opinion was the nature of the demands and appeals made by the miners during the strike. Although the list of demands varied from region to region, reflecting the particular problems facing each one, the core demands in all of the mining areas were the same. The miners (and their supporters within the nomenklatura) demanded that they be given in fact what the enterprise law had given them in theory: economic independence from the Ministry and the association structure and greater control over the internal operations of their places of work. There were also wage demands, to be sure, including increases to offset inflation and supplemental pay for dangerous and night work,[25] but the essence of the demands was a call to implement Gorbachev's policy of industrial perestroika.

The emergence of rival power centers in the mining regions as a result of the strike reflected and encouraged a similar process that was taking place in the country as a whole in 1989. As the unity of the party/state system cracked in response to fundamental disputes within the ruling elites over the course and nature of reform, other social and political groups seized the opportunity to establish themselves as important players in the political process. The strike committees were one such group. They advanced slates of candidates for local, regional, and national elections in opposition to those nominated by the local and regional party and state organizations. Just as demands for regional control over the economy were central to the strike, so efforts to gain control over regional politics were central after the strike.

The effects of the strike on the local and regional party and governmental structures were harder to measure. In some parts of the Kuzbas, strike committees demanded early elections to replace the sitting members of city and oblast soviets in light of their failure to support or even respond to the miners' strike.

This demand was not met, but the strike committees continued to monitor the actions of these soviets and pressure their members to take effective action on the points of Resolution 608 that pertained to them.

The opposition of party committees located in the mining regions to the strike did a good deal of damage to the credibility of the party both in the regions and more generally. The most lasting effect of the conflicting positions taken by the local, regional, and central party organizations was that workers' organizations stopped viewing the party as a unified organization that was willing or able to carry out the policies of the leadership.

These efforts took on institutional form with the establishment of the Union of Workers of the Kuzbas, and the roundly negative official reaction to its founding worsened relations between the workers' movement and the local, regional, and national governments by the fall and early winter of 1989. The next event to compound this problem was the approach of the new year: 1 January 1990 was the deadline for the government to fulfill the major substantive points of the protocol concerning regional self-financing and economic independence from the central ministries.

As the deadline approached and the government failed to act, reaction in the mining regions was swift and harshly critical. Mikhail Kisliuk reminded readers in the newspaper *Stroitel'* on 20 December 1989 that the government's declaration on self-management and self-financing for the Kuzbas had "been returned to the USSR Council of Ministers, where it was already reviewed and signed." This, he argued, was "a maneuver that signified the practical burial of self-financing for the Kuzbas."[26] Soon thereafter, Prime Minister Nilokai Ryzhkov turned the draft resolutions on regional self-financing over to the republics' Councils of Ministers, which was not part of the protocol agreement. This was viewed as a delaying tactic and prompted even more strident responses.[27]

In early March 1990, a series of elections took place throughout the Soviet Union that fueled the growing confrontation between the workers' committees and the government by demonstrating the growing influence of the "democratic opposition groups" in many parts of the country. In the mining regions, the main focus of attention and conflict was the March elections to regional soviets. In the Kuzbas, the workers' committees put up their own slate of candidates, which in most cases did quite well.[28] The results of the elections led to a split in the soviets between the workers' committees' deputies and those supported by the party, state, and other social organizations.

At the end of June 1990, yet another meeting that proved crucial in changing the dynamic of the labor movement took place: On 23 June, a delegation from the workers' committees of the Kuzbas met with Boris Yeltsin, who had been elected chairman of the Russian Supreme Soviet less than a month before.[29] The dispute between the workers' movement and the Union government now became embroiled in the power struggle between the republics and the Union, and most particularly between Gorbachev and Yeltsin.

The increasing radicalization of the workers' movement was only one manifestation of the growing conflicts within the Soviet Union; since 1989, "nationalist" movements and ethnic conflicts had also been gathering force. The drive for republican "sovereignty" began later in Russia than elsewhere in the Union, but by the spring of 1990 it had gained considerable momentum. Yeltsin's program, presented in his campaign for the speaker's chair, reflected this drive and included demands for "ownership of all the republic's natural resources, an independent foreign policy, and the primacy of republican legislation over that of the USSR as a whole."[30]

Yeltsin's proposal for transferring ownership of Russia's natural resources to the Russian republic provided an opportunity for the workers' movement to adopt a new tactic in its struggle to obtain the implementation of Resolution 608. The Council of Workers of the Kuzbas and the Federation of Labor would support Yeltsin in his struggle to wrest power from Gorbachev in exchange for a promise from Yeltsin to enact Resolution 608. Yeltsin was all too willing to accede to this arrangement. At the 23 June meeting with the Kuzbas workers' representatives, Yeltsin stated that "as far as the agreement which the Union government has refused to sign—hand it over to us. . . . We are prepared to take the most radical steps."[31] With this declaration, a new triangular conflict began to develop, one that gathered strength in the coming months.

By 1991, the Soviet Union was in the grip of an unprecedented political and economic crisis. Since at least May of the preceding year, a "war of laws" between the Union government and the republics had contributed to a deepening of the country's economic problems and political disagreements. The question of economic control was part and parcel of the ongoing negotiations over a new Union treaty, which culminated 1991.[32] While Gorbachev appealed for maintaining strong republics and a strong center and warned against the "Lebanonization" of the Soviet Union, the republican elites were demanding extensive rights in both the economic and political spheres, with a very limited role for the central government.

This war of laws affected labor collectives directly, insofar as the different economic programs gave the republics, regions, and enterprises vastly different rights, yet it was unclear which laws were authoritative. The miners' committees of the Kuzbas had already sided with Yeltsin and the other republican elites on the question of sovereignty. The committees viewed the central government's economic program and position on the Union treaty as evidence of "a growing reactionary wave," with the "center strengthening the union structures which are blocking radical reform." By the beginning of March 1991, a number of factors had coalesced, leading once again to increasing calls for strike action by the Kuzbas miners. From the middle of February on, Yeltsin's opposition to Gorbachev had become increasingly uncompromising and the drive within the Russian parliament for full sovereignty ever more insistent.[33] Yeltsin's statements encouraged the miners' committees, which had been forcefully arguing this position for some time. All of this occurred in the context of the upcoming referendum on the future of the Soviet Union, and the miners' committees saw a strike as a means to counter the pro-Union appeals of the party and state institutions.

The strike of 1991 began in earnest on 4 March. Given the nature of the miners' demands—which included calls for the resignation of Gorbachev and the government—and the power struggles under way in the country, it was not surprising that the action was confrontational from the outset. By this time, *none* of the sides involved—the Union government, the Russian government, or the miners—was in any mood to compromise, and it was unclear whether they were in any position to do so had they wanted to. The strike continued, with varying degrees of intensity, for more than two months, as each side tried to outmaneuver the other.

Yeltsin and the Russian government were in the middle of this dispute from the very start, and it was Yeltsin who finally broke the impasse. On 1 May, Yeltsin arrived in Kemerovo and proposed to the miners' committees that they consider ending the strike if the Gorbachev government could be convinced to transfer all of the mines of Russia from the jurisdiction of the USSR Ministry of Coal to the jurisdiction of the Russian Federation.[34] The committees agreed, and on 6 May 1991, the Cabinet of Ministers of the USSR and the Council of Ministers of the Russian republic signed an agreement transferring control of the mines to Russia. As a result, on 10 May the miners' committees of the Kuzbas suspended the strike, pending the fulfillment of the provisions contained therein.[35]

In the 1991 strike, attention focused on the miners' demands that Gorbachev and the government resign, but the motivations behind those demands were fundamentally economic. The story of the radicalization of the labor movement from 1989 to 1991 was the story of a movement coming to the conclusion that its economic demands could not be fulfilled as long as the centralized Soviet economic system still existed and, equally important, as long as those who ran that system were in charge of dismantling it. The compromise that ended the strike, the transfer of jurisdiction, signified a transfer of political power from the center to the Russian republic, but the miners accepted the compromise *only because Yeltsin promised to cede greater control over the coal industry to the localities.* The central government's failure to cede this control in the two years since the first strike was the fundamental reason that the miners demanded the government's resignation and advocated a no vote during the referendum on the Union.

The results of the 1989 and 1991 strikes were also, among other things, a triumph of regionalism over centralism—not in regard to actual control over resources, although this did progress—in terms of organizational politics leading to the inclusion in the political process of previously disenfranchised social groups, including but not limited to the miners. The interplay between class politics and regional politics helped to undermine the control of the regime's central governing apparatuses. These apparatuses had served as a brake on democratization from the beginning, as President Gorbachev—who by that point was involved with republican leaders in the drafting of the Union Treaty—was well aware.

The abolition of the USSR in December 1991 and the establishment of an independent Russian state did little to alter the trend toward greater regionalization of politics and economics that had begun under Gorbachev. In large part, it was the crisis of the Russian economy that drove the continuing disintegration of the central political structures; the two in tandem drove the process of regionalization. As the structures of the command economy ceased to function effectively, production indicators for a series of "basic goods" began to fall with some rapidity, falling 13 percent in 1991 and another 18 percent in 1992.[36]

As a result of this crisis, regional elites—from enterprise directors to leaders of regional governments, and many within the miners' committees—began to see the benefits, if only as a means of defense against further collapse, of regional economic autarky. For Siberia, given the fact that its industry was in relatively better shape than much of the rest of Russia, the advantages of protecting its regional resources from the demands of the center were and remain substantial, at least in the short run.[37] This of course has resulted in a decline in economic exchange among the various regions of the Russian Federation, which has further intensified the economic slide of the Russian economy as a whole.

It is in this context that the growing strength of regionalism in the Russian political system must be understood. There are arguments to be made on both sides of the issue as to whether this economic regionalization is good or bad for the economy and society in the long run. Those who say no can point to the statistics noted above and the historical record of the ill effects of autarkic behavior. On the other hand, no one will deny that the overcentralization of the economy during the Soviet period was a major factor in the economic crisis that had developed by the 1980s. At present, however, regionalism serves the economic purposes of one sector of the old Soviet elite, just as it undermines the economic purposes of another, while at the same time having positive and negative effects on the process of democratization in post-Communist Russia.

In terms of the ongoing conflict between the central authorities and the regional authorities, there seems little to choose from as far as evidence of democratic political behavior is concerned. Both sides appear more concerned with consolidating or extending their power than with abiding by any "rules of the democratic game." Should one be more concerned by regional leader Aman Tuleev's machinations regarding the establishment of a Siberian republic and his call for a political strike to undermine Yeltsin in October of 1993,[38] or by the statement of Yeltsin's official in charge of territorial administration, Nikolai Medvedev, that "the last few years have demonstrated that the division of powers—given the Russian mentality—was a mistake"?[39] The important point is that given the obvious incompatibility not of their programs, but of their claims to power, regionalism has been a necessary counterweight to excessive control by the center. (The reverse, clearly, also holds).

In view of the fact that continued democratization depends in part on the agreement of all major power-holders to the establishment of equitable forms of contestation, as long as *none of the sides* can agree, the existence of more than one side—and therefore regionalism—serves a positive purpose. That Yeltsin's constitution virtually strips the regions of effective power and gives it to the President, and that the document has been criticized by friends and foes of Yeltsin alike, is testimony to the importance of (at least perceived) fair contestation and of agreed-upon distribution of powers for the continuation of the democratization process.

All of that having been said, what animates the debate over regionalism in Russia, including in the Kuzbas, more than issues of either identity or democratic procedure is the question of economic power. The issue now is not so much the relationship between regionalism and the *process* of democratization, but of regionalism and the *content* of Russian "democracy." As noted above, the particularities of the Soviet system meant that any form of democratization necessitated a redistribution of property and power, contrary to the prescriptions of transition theory. Since 1989, the debates on regional rights that deal with substantive issues have been focused on the issue of who is going to control that property.

As noted above, one of the central demands of the miners' strikes in 1989 and 1991 was that the Kuzbas be given greater control over its own resources. By September 1993, there was still a great deal of dissatisfaction in the region over the level of independent decision making permitted the enterprises in the Kuzbas.

In 1991, Mikhail Kisliuk, the administrative head of Kemerovo oblast, proposed the creation of a free economic zone in the Kuzbas, but by the fall of 1993 such a zone still did not exist. Significantly, Kisliuk agreed with the assessment of a journalist that "progress had been made, in spite of the decrees of the President and the government."[40] Kisliuk went on to argue that the fate of development in the Kuzbas hinged on "either foreign trade operations, or more simply stated, the export of coal, metal, chemical products, etc., or the distribution of foreign credits."[41] These operations could not proceed, however, because no law had been adopted giving the region the right to engage in such trade. While the Kuzbas has been pressing for the ability to engage in such activity since before the collapse of the Soviet Union, using the argument of regional rights, the Russian government in the guise of the constitution clearly reserves that right to itself.[42]

In a similar vein, a dispute erupted in late October 1993 over a steep increase in rates charged by the Russian Federation to ship goods on the railway system. Viacheslav Golikov, one of the leaders of the Council of Workers' Committees of the Kuzbas and usually a strong supporter of President Yeltsin, wrote an open letter to the president in which he declared that "the increase in the rail tariff makes it impossible not only to ship coal overseas, but also to trade inside Russia."[43] In the view of many organizations in the Kuzbas, the increases in transport costs would threaten the entire development program of the region.

According to *Izvestiia,* "the Independent Union of Mineworkers of the Kuzbas directly warned that such a situation could not but lead to the most serious social unrest, accompanied by demands for the resignation of the government."[44] In this case, the labor organizations sided with the regional administrators—a rare occurrence in the last four years—over the question of who controlled pricing and what rights the regions—especially regions like the Kuzbas, for which transportation links are the lifeblood—should have in making decisions of this type. The headline over the article in which this situation was described nicely, if unconsciously, exemplifies the sleight of hand that typifies the discourse of regionalism. Although the arguments in the letter demonstrated that actions by the government hurt individual economic interests, the headline read: "The Kuzbas Warns." The economic concerns of disparate groups, many with profoundly conflicting interests, are here represented as an issue of regional identity and solidarity.[45] The fact that warring factions of the regional and national elites were responsible for initiating the policies in question, and that the vast majority of society was not consulted by either side—as the letter from Golikov makes clear[46]—is obscured by the discourse of regionalism, federalism, and democracy.

Furthermore, in an article entitled "Siberia—Only for Russians?" what would appear to be a typical story of ethnic animosity long held in check by the precepts of Soviet nationalities policy suddenly loosed upon the world was quickly transformed into a discussion—indirectly, of course—of the economic foundations of Siberian versions of "ethnic cleansing." In this case, some members of the economic elite were found to be expelling "foreigners" from Siberian towns (this is itself a strange concept, given the historical nature of the Siberian population) to gain popularity among the newly unemployed and/or poor, while others were inviting them in because, in the words of one "local boss," "not only do [foreigners] not demand any special, European conditions, they don't even demand those conditions that are normal for us."[47]

The current debates surrounding regionalism, democratization, and the unity of Russia—not unlike the debates in this country about whether "free trade" will benefit Mexico and/or the United States—are only tangentially related to the issues that they purport to be about. The North American Free Trade Agreement (NAFTA) will not benefit "the United States" or "Mexico" as abstractions—it will benefit and it will hurt particular classes and sections of classes in diverse sectors of the political economy. In Siberia, too, the key issue is not the political rights of regions, but the economic interests of the newly emerging classes. Further, the form that the politics and economics of this transition have so far taken has made the debate more about which section of the old elite is going to have its ox gored than about democracy or societal empowerment.

The workers, about whose militancy so much concern was evinced from 1989 to 1991, for all practical purposes have been closed out of the debate over what the content of the post-transitional system of power relations in Russia will be. Their organizations are now primarily involved in rearguard actions to defend workers' jobs and social benefits or have descended into internal bickering, neither of which is likely to answer the long-term strategic goals of the Russian labor movement.[48] The strategy of workers' organizations since the collapse of the Soviet Union has been two-pronged: like regional elites, workers' groups appeal to regionalism as a means of protecting "class" interests; at the same time, they vie with competing workers' (and entrepreneurial) organizations in other economic sectors for the largesse of the increasingly corrupt central authorities.

Finally, the realities of politics in the Kuzbas, in Siberia, and for that matter in Russia generally since the collapse of Communism have demonstrated that Western assumptions about the nature of transitions are entirely inadequate. This is so not only in descriptive terms but also—and perhaps more importantly—in prescriptive terms. To put the best possible face on it, the West has responded to events in Russia, including disputes between Siberia and other regions and the central government, with dangerous policy positions and bad advice based on faulty assumptions about the nature of Russian politics, society, and economy on the one hand and the nature of post-Communist transitions on the other. Understanding the nature of regionalism, in Siberia and elsewhere, may not lead to the adoption of wiser policies in Russia or the West, but without such an understanding, the chances for any kind of democracy in Russia are very slim indeed.

Notes

1. This is not to say that the conflict has nothing to do with *democratization,* which is, however, a different issue, particularly in the Soviet and post-Soviet Russian context.

2. See *Russia and Eurasia Facts and Figures Annual,* (Gulf Breeze, FL: Academic International Press, 1993) pp. 55–56, 133; and V.E. Suslova, *Ugol' Kuzbassa* (Moscow, 1984), p. 7.

3. *1990 Energy Statistics Handbook* (New York: United Nations, 1992). The data are approximate, given that the statistics were given for world per capita consumption and per capita consumption for the Soviet Union. The numbers are 664 kilos and 1789 kilos, respectively.

4. See *Russia and Eurasia Facts and Figures Annual,* p. 55.

5. *1990 Energy Statistics,* pp. 160–61.

6. More than 40 percent of Russian coal exports were directed to the other member countries of the former Warsaw Pact. The other major importer of Russian coal was Japan; however, in 1990 Japan imported only 8.3 million tons of coal from the USSR, while it imported more than 54 million tons from Australia, 18 million from Canada, and 10 million from the United States.

7. As of 1992, coal provided slightly less than 14 percent of the fuels produced in Russia and approximately 18.5 percent of the fuel consumed in Russia.

8. President Yeltsin, of course, supported the concept of greater sovereignty for both Russia and its regions as long as it suited his political purposes in 1990 and 1991. For

later examples, see A. Lugovskaia, "Vsia vlast'—Kremliu?" *Izvestiia*, 19 October 1993, p. 1; "Rossiia primenit sanktsii k regionam, kotorye ne platiat nalogi," *Izvestiia*, 29 October 1993, p. 1; and A. Pashkov, "Ural'skaia respublika nachinaet zhit' po svoei konstitutsii," *Izvestiia*, 2 November 1993, p. 2.

9. We are concerned here, of course, with only one of the many forms of transitions: a transition from authoritarianism initiated and largely carried out by the regime itself. For greater detail, see Alfred Stepan, "Paths Toward Redemocratization: Theoretical and Comparative Considerations," in Guillermo O'Donnell et al., *Transitions from Authoritarian Rule* (Baltimore and London: The Johns Hopkins Press, 1986); Giuseppe Di Palma, *To Craft Democracies* (Berkeley: University of California Press, 1990); and Samuel Huntington, *The Third Wave* (Norman: University of Oklahoma Press, 1991), chs. 3 and 4.

10. This lowers the probability that any group will attempt to sabotage the process either at the transition phase or later. See Adam Przeworski, "Democracy as a Contingent Outcome of Conflicts," in Jon Elster and Rune Slagstad, *Constitutionalism and Democracy* (Cambridge: Cambridge University Press, 1988), p. 79.

11. It may well be the case that the regime co-opted or crushed the organizations representing these social forces; what is important is that the regime never claimed these organizations as its own and that the organizations retained roots in society beyond the compass of the regime itself.

12. I am referring here, of course, to large-scale private holdings of the basic components of the means of production, not to personal holdings or small-scale entrepreneurial ventures.

13. See O'Donnell, *Transitions,* pp. 52–53.

14. See Di Palma, *To Craft Democracies,* p. 65. His argument is based in large part on the experiences of Spain; for further analysis of that case, see Donald Share, *The Making of Spanish Democracy* (New York: Praeger, 1986).

15. See Aleksandr Susoev, "Komu nanosit ushcherb zabastovka," *V boi za ugol',* 16 January 1990, p. 6. The link between problems of social infrastructure and industrial action at the factory level is unique to Soviet-style systems. Unlike capitalist economies, where there is a well-defined separation between authorities responsible for public works, housing, and job-related issues, the Soviet system collapsed all of the above, with factory administrations and city governmental and party organizations equally responsible for the maintenance of working conditions and social infrastructure. See V. Andriianov, "Gornyi udar," *Dialog,* 1990, no. 1, p. 60. Also, see the remarks of Coal Minister Shchadov during his speech before a joint meeting of the Supreme Soviet prior to being confirmed as minister on 6 July 1989 (quoted in Kostiukovskii, *Kuzbass: Zharkoe leto, 89ogo goda* [Moscow, 1990], p. 14). From the workers' point of view, those responsible for the breakdown of the cities' infrastructures were the same ones responsible for the failure of perestroika to improve their conditions at the workplace. Therefore, the impetus to strike came from dissatisfaction with the state's performance both inside and outside the production sphere narrowly defined.

16. The most important case in this regard was the strike of 4 April in Noril'sk, involving approximately one thousand miners and mine workers. On the Noril'sk strike, see *Ekonomicheskaia gazeta* for April and May of 1989. For other cases of labor unrest, see Linda J. Cook, "Lessons of the Soviet Coal Miners' Strike of Summer 1989," *The Harriman Institute Forum,* vol. 4, no. 3, March 1991, pp. 2–3; *Ekonomicheskaia gazeta,* no. 27, 1989, p. 5; Elizabeth Teague, "Miners' Strike in Siberia Winds Down, Strike in Ukraine Spreads to Other Areas: A Status Report," *RL 334/89,* 20 July 1989, p. 4; V. Andriianov, "Gornyi udar," *Dialog,* no. 1, 1990, p. 61. The strikes were not limited to coal mines: see, for example, Iurii Tepliakov, "Chrezvychainoe proisshestvie," *Moskovskie novosti,* no. 42, 18 October 1987, pp. 8–9; Leonid Kapeliushnyi, "Predel neterpeniia," *Moskovskie novosti,* no. 27, 3 July 1988, p. 12.

17. Author's interviews with Makarov, co-chair of the Donetsk City Strike Committee, 13 April 1991; with A.V. Nenanigi, co-chair, Council of the Workers' Committees of the Kuzbas, 26 April 1991; and with Professor E.P. Torkanovskii, Institute of Economics, AN SSSR, 18 October 1990. See also V. Andriianov, "Gornyi udar," p. 62; Kostiukovskii, *Kuzbass: Zharkoe leto,* pp. 8, 10; "Dialogi vokrug sobytii," *Moskovskie novosti,* no. 32, 6 August 1989, p. 8; N. Chentsov, "Zabastovki moglo ne byt'," *Dialog,* 1, 1990, p. 69; and Elizabeth Teague, "Embryos of People's Power," *Radio Liberty Report on the USSR,* 11 August 1989, p. 1, particularly footnote 2.

18. Linda J. Cook, "Lessons of the Soviet Coal Miners' Strike," p. 5. See also his address to the Supreme Soviet of 19 July 1989, quoted in Kostiukovskii, *Kuzbass: Zharkoe leto,* pp. 101–6.

19. Quoted in Kostiukovskii, *Kuzbass: Zharkoe leto,* pp. 8–9.

20. Author's interviews with Makarov of the Donetsk strike committee and Nenanigi of the Kuzbas workers' council, 13 April 1991 and 26 April 1991, respectively.

21. Kostiukovskii, *Kuzbass: Zharkoe leto,* p. 45. M.I. Naidov was a representative example. Naidov, the former general director of the Lenin mine in Prokop'evsk and at the time of the strike head of a mining research association in the Kuzbas, was asked by a journalist if he had read the strikers' demands. The journalist reported that "Naidov smiled, lowered his voice, and said: 'I haven't read them; I wrote them.' "

22. For some interesting details, see Kostiukovskii, *Kuzbass: Zharkoe leto,* pp. 124–42.

23. *Izvestiia,* 17 October 1989, p. 2.

24. During a meeting with select members of the local Communist Party, Shchadov announced that he was going to issue an order the following day to all mines that striking workers were not to be paid and that they would be posted as "absent without reasonable cause." This latter formulation was grounds for dismissal under existing Soviet law.

25. See Kostiukovskii, *Kuzbass: Zharkoe leto,* pp. 20–21 and 92–98 for the final draft agreement.

26. M. Kisliuk, "Proshchai, regional'nyi khozraschet? Proshchai, protokol?" *Stroitel'—Soiuz trudiashchikhsia Kuzbassa,* 20 December 1989, p. 1.

27. See "Obrashchenie sovmestnogo soveshchaniia predstavitelei rabochikh komitetov, obkoma KPSS, oblispolkoma, oblsovprofa k pravitel'stvu SSSR i trudiashchimsia kuzbassa," *Zheleznodorozhnik Kuzbassa—Soiuz trudiashchikhsia Kuzbassa,* 30 December 1989, p. 3; "Predvybornaia platforma," *Za bol'shuiu khimiiu,* 10 January 1990, p. 3. "Pravitel'stvo SSSR otkazyvaetsia vypolniat' vziatye na sebia obiazatel'stva. Kakim budet otvet Kuzbassa?" *Zheleznodorozhnik Kuzbassa,* 30 December 1989, p. 3.

28. Author's interview with Makarov in Donetsk, where all forty-nine candidates were elected. In Vorkuta, Shchadov was defeated by Vikor Iakovlev, a miner from the Komsomolsk mine and a member of the local strike committee. In the Kuzbas, more than 40 percent of the candidates endorsed by the workers' committees were elected in the oblast as a whole, with a much higher percentage in the mining communities. "Ministr Shchadov proigral na vyborakh chlenu stachkoma Iakovlevu," *Nasha gazeta,* 27 March 1990, pp. 1–2.

29. On his election, see Stephen White, *Gorbachev and After (Cambridge: Cambridge University Press, 1992), p. 172.*

30. Ibid.

31. Yeltsin speaking during a meeting with representatives of the Council of Workers' Committees of the Kuzbas, 23 June 1990; the stenographic record of the meeting was reprinted in *Nasha gazeta,* 26 June 1990, p. 4.

32. Both Ryzhkov and Primakov, for example, spoke of the dangers of what the former termed "economic separatism" and the latter referred to as " 'economically absurd'

regional self-sufficiency" at the Twenty-eighth Party Congress in July 1990. See White, *Gorbachev and After,* p. 178.

33. See Yeltsin's speech to a meeting of "Democratic Russia" and other allied groups on 9 March 1991 in which he describes the course of events as he saw them in this period. The speech was reprinted in full in *Nasha gazeta* on 15 March 1991, p. 4.

34. See "Vystuplenie Borisa Yeltsina pered chlenami zabastovochnykh komitetov Kuzbassa," *Nasha gazeta,* 4 May 1991, pp. 2–4. An arrangement such as this had been worked out on 15 April for the Raspadskaia mine by the president of the RSFSR Council of Ministers Ivan Siliev; see the protocol in *Nasha gazeta,* 19 April 1991, p. 3.

35. The documents to this effect are in *Nasha gazeta,* 7 May 1991, p. 1, and 11 May 1991, p. 1, respectively.

36. V.I. Suslov, "Predotvratim li raspad?" *Eko,* no. 5, 1993, p. 17. The data indicate that the production of raw materials from the basic extractive industries did not decline at as rapid a rate as the production of foodstuffs and light industrial goods; as a consequence, the overall decline in production indices for most regions of Siberia was less than for the country as a whole. The rates of decline in the oblasts of western Siberia were as follows: Tomsk, 23 percent; Novosibirsk and Tiumen, 19 percent; Kemerovo, 17 percent; Omsk, 14 percent; and Altai krai, 19 percent.

37. Ibid., pp. 19–22. See also Richard Ericson, "Soviet Economic Structure and the National Question," in Alexander J. Motyl, ed., *The Post-Soviet Nations* (New York: Columbia University Press, 1992), ch. 10; Michael Burawoy and Pavel Krotov, "The Economic Basis of Russia's Political Crisis," *New Left Review,* no. 198, March/April, 1993, pp. 49–70.

38. See Viktor Kostiukovskii, "Kuzbass ne otvechaet na prizyvy k zabastovkam," *Izvestiia,* 2 October 1993, p. 1.

39. Aleksandra Lugovskaia, "Vsia vlast'—Kremliu?" *Izvestiia,* 19 October 1993, p. 1.

40. Viktor Kostiukovskii, "Chto meshaet kuzbassu stat' deistvitel'no svobodnoi ekonomicheskoi zonoi?" *Izvestiia,* 11 September 1993, p. 2.

41. Ibid.

42. See Article 71 of the draft, published in *Izvestiia,* 10 November 1993, pp. 3–5.

43. Viktor Kostiukovskii, "Kuzbass preduprezhdaet: proschety politikov opasny dlia zdorov'ia reform," *Izvestiia,* 21 October 1993, p. 1.

44. Ibid., p. 2.

45. A similar set of disputes has occurred in other industries. See, for example, Aleksei Tarasov, "Energeticheskii peredel v sibiri," *Izvestiia,* 22 September 1993, p. 4.

46. This being the case, it is surprising that the Kuzbas labor movement has remained so solidly behind Yeltsin, all the more so because this is not the only issue on which the government has made decisions detrimental to workers' interests.

47. Aleksei Tarasov, "Sibir'—tol'ko dlia russkikh?" *Izvestiia,* 2 November 1993, p. 5.

48. See Boris Kagarlitsky, *The Disintegration of the Monolith* (London: Verso, 1992), pp. 126–31, 163–64; and Simon Clarke et al., eds., *What About the Workers?* (London: Verso, 1993), especially chs. 8 and 9.

Back to the Collective

Production and Consumption on a Siberian Collective Farm

Cynthia J. Buckley

The dissolution of collective production in agriculture and the accompanying re-establishment of the peasant as master of the land have emerged as central issues in Russia's economic-reform process. Although decollectivization provides the perceived answer to the question of what is to be done, the crucial issue of how to do it inspires more controversy than consensus. The distribution of the material and natural resources associated with the Russian agricultural sector has proven even more difficult than in the industrial sector. In this essay I seek to examine difficulties inherent in both the division of collective agricultural assets and the socioeconomic conditions in which the division will take place. The success of private farming and concurrent marketization will not only be judged by measures of agricultural productivity and gross output but also by the way in which the shift to private farming and marketization can provide replacements for the full range of activities collective farms have performed in rural society and the perceptions of the agricultural labor force toward the legitimacy of asset distribution.

The continuing crisis in Russian agriculture has gained great attention. Only one-tenth of the collective farms in 1991 were expected to be operating profitably.[1] In 1992 alone, the amount of acreage sown for grain decreased by 10 million hectares.[2] As more power and authority move from the center to local and regional governments, the fact that "of the eighty-eight krai and oblasts in this country only twenty-eight can feed themselves" begins to look critical.[3] Increasingly, the central government has seen the answer to this agricultural crisis in the dismantling of state and collective farms.[4]

The irony of dismal agricultural output in spite of vast land resources is perhaps most clear in western Siberia. Often, the primarily Russian rural populations of Novosibirsk and Kemerovo oblasts need only trace back two or three generations to find the forefather who left the poverty of a village in European Russia to stake a claim in the area. Though soil quality was far from that found in the Black Earth regions of southern Russia, land was plentiful and settlement opportunities for Russians relatively hospitable. Tales of wealth and opportunity among these Siberian sodbusters may have been of questionable accuracy, but they nonetheless served to attract more migrants even in the face of severe weather and the isolation of settlements. Nearly sixty years of collective agricultural production have significantly dimmed the memory of peasant family farming.

The Chinese economic miracle has often been linked to a return to family responsibility for production.[5] The Chinese experience has been used to support arguments for decollectivization in Russia and other Soviet successor states. But analyses of the revitalization of the Chinese rural sector indicate that rural industry, not agriculture, was the primary engine of economic growth.[6] Trends in crop yields also raise questions regarding the relative efficacy of the new incentive structure. Yields fail to show the productive superiority of family-responsibility systems.[7] Recent investigations have indicated overestimations of the increase in labor productivity generated by the switch to family-responsibility systems.[8] Generally, the literature focusing on the effect of agricultural reorganization in China has been centered on measuring total output and sector productivity. Increasingly, the Chinese economic miracle is apparently less miraculous in the area of agriculture.

Even if early analysts of the shift to family responsibility are correct and China was successful in revitalizing the agrarian sector, the extent to which China can be used to inform the Russian case is less than clear. China has been fairly successful, thus far, at maintaining firm central political control and stable administrative control of the economy.[9] There are few indications that the Russian Federation will experience either in its transition period. Instability at the central level, in the case of the Russian Federation, places significant responsibility for social services at the local level.

Soviet-Era Collective Farms

Many villages in Russia strongly resemble the company towns found in America at the turn of the century. Collective farms throughout western Siberia have held direct and indirect control over nearly all aspects of rural life. The dependence of rural residents upon collective farms represents not only the extensive political and social control farms possessed but also the absence of alternative social institutions. This is due, in part, to low levels of government investment, severe restrictions on social organizations and movements, and state policies that through either conscious exploitation or simple neglect left rural areas to their own means of survival.[10]

Collective farms, no less than the peasant households they supplanted, failed to divide production and consumption—or social service—functions, making them poorly suited to traditional measurement techniques regarding efficiency, not to mention easy subdivision. To take the example of housing, collective farms have long relied on their own funds to support housing construction or have encouraged members to build their own houses with help from farm subsidies.[11] Between 1980 and 1988, 2.4 million square meters of rural housing were built entirely by farm funds.[12] More than 25 percent of the total rural housing to be privatized in 1991 belonged to collective farms (23,100 units).[13] In the absence of either state assistance or subsidiary markets, collective farms remained responsible both for utilizing the productive labor of the peasantry and for providing the social conditions needed to maintain a rural labor supply. And housing provision was only one of the services supplied.

Farm administrators assisted in numerous areas of social service provision, such as the acquisition of goods for village stores and the distribution of deficit items. Village infrastructure, including roads and water systems, depended upon subsidies from collective farm budgets.[14] Traditionally, crèches, canteens, and medical aid stations have been directly subsidized. Additionally, wages have routinely received indirect supplementation through the provision of housing for workers. Collective farms, like their industrial counterparts, have borne the double burden of having to operate as an economic entity oriented toward production and a service organization oriented toward distribution. This is especially true in sparsely populated areas of the Russian Federation, such as western Siberia, where climate, distance, and transportation combine to prevent rural residents from routinely accessing services provided in regional centers.

Collective farms have provided extremely important assistance to the rural elderly, both in monetary and in-kind subsidization.[15] In 1987, more than 9 million collective farmers were on old-age pensions, amounting to 23.18 percent of the entire rural population.[16] By the year 2000, more than 20 percent of the Russian population will be above the current retirement age, with many of the elderly living in rural areas.[17] According to a survey of 1,300 rural pensioner households (without any individuals employed), state and collective farms offered assistance such as garden tilling, private plot inputs, animal feed, heating materials, home repair, and transport.[18] Not all of the pensioners needing assistance received it, nor did all of those receiving help obtain all that they requested. Yet farms did deliver some level of assistance. Between an absence of alternative state agencies to extend benefits and the cumulative results of outmigration of the young, the rural elderly have had few alternative sources of support. As the rural population continues to age rapidly, the importance of these benefits increases.

Collective farms are intrinsically linked to the rural community as both an economic entity and a provider of expected social services. This double function served the central government of the Soviet Union well. It enabled the central government to devote little to the countryside in terms of social resources.[19] What has often been referred to as the "urban bias" of state socialism was facilitated by shifting responsibility for many aspects of social services from the central state to the state-owned farms.[20] In Siberia, collective farmers, in contrast to the early peasant settlers, grew accustomed to a social contract that included social services and benefits such as pensions, schools, and road systems.

A primary goal of collectivization was to gain state control over agricultural production and increase the amount of output marketed. State propaganda extolled the ideological virtues of collective, and especially state farms, through films, newspapers, and poster campaigns.[21] The benefits to the peasantry in terms of rural development were also highlighted. Collective agriculture was to be the basis for building socialism in the rural areas. From inception, collective agriculture in Russia has been not only responsible for agricultural output but also liable for rural development. As an economic organization, its priorities were to be oriented toward fulfilling production plans. As a social organization, it was to furnish services to village inhabitants and insure that the economic operations of the collective farm did not interfere with the social and political goals of equality and the construction of socialism.

The interaction between collective farm structures and the local and national community are multifaceted. Standard measures of output, labor hours used, or capital utilization cannot capture the value or importance of the transportation support, coal delivery, goods acquisition, or housing subsidization provided by collective farms. Focusing on one facet, such as total agricultural output, runs the risk of ignoring other important aspects of the collective farm entity.[22]

The boundaries between productive processes implemented by the state (associated with the state economy) and the provision of social services (associated with citizens' rights and the social contract with the state) were not clear in the Soviet case. They remain blurred in the Russian republic. Restructuring agricultural production will seriously change the nature and organization of social services, with ramifications throughout the rural community. When evaluating the potential success of private farming in Russia, an appreciation of both the productive and distributive functions of the collective farms is merited. A reevaluation of the economic, and most importantly social, contexts in which rural inhabitants find themselves is essential for understanding the effects of economic reorganization in rural Russia.

Decollectivization at Zaria

To illustrate the changes in organizational structure on collective farms and the concerns rural inhabitants, especially the elderly, associated with decollectivization, I have chosen to focus on one West Siberian farm, Zaria (Sunrise). Zaria is not representative—no one farm could be. Across areas of Russia and throughout various types of agricultural production, different issues will take on varying degrees of importance and urgency. But the effect decollectivization will have on the rural social structure, as seen on the collective farm Zaria, brings into focus two primary areas of importance: distributional equity and social service provision. Evaluating these concerns in the context of the general conditions in Siberian agriculture, indicates that the troubles of this specific farm apply far beyond its boundaries.[23]

The collective farm Zaria is located in the Lenin-Kuznetsk raion (district) of Kemerovo oblast in western Siberia. The farm is the primary employer for the nearly 1,900 residents of the village of Shabanova and the neighboring village, Toropova. Almost 700 people work on the farm full time, producing pork, oil seeds, milk, grain, and beef. Like many of the villages in western Siberia, Shabanova was subject to large-scale out-migration during the 1970s. This out-migration has slowed in recent years, but many of the young people still move out of the village. There are thirty-four households in the village in which pensioners live either alone or with a spouse also on pension.

The living conditions in Shabanova are somewhat better than in many of the villages in Kemerovo or neighboring Novosibirsk oblast. Only eight of the houses in the village were without running water in spring of 1992. Three of the primary streets in the village are paved. The village maintains a sports hall, children's garden, and newly expanded medical clinic. Wages, for 1989, were 13 percent above average for the raion. Evidence of increasing prosperity could be found in 1989 in three modern private homes constructed along the central street. By 1992, the number of these modern houses built had grown to twelve, with another five in progress at other locations in the village. These homes, along with three that have been remodeled, are the only homes in the village with indoor plumbing—a rarity in rural Russia, especially in Siberia.

Like many of the villages in western Siberia, Shabanova does not border on any other populated settlements. A markedly smaller settlement, Toropova, is eight kilometers away. The central village of the area and former Machine Tractor Station, Krasnai, is more than fifteen kilometers away. Travel to the urban centers of the region (Novosibirsk, Kemerovo, and Lenin-Kuznetsk) requires a day's round-trip by bus.

Shabanova enjoys a relatively privileged location in terms of transport, due to its proximity to the road linking Novosibirsk to Kemerovo. Yet, even to travel to the nearest city, Lenin-Kuznetsk, requires passing through long stretches of field. The abundance of uninhabited land that attracted migrants from central Russia at the turn of the century is still in evidence. Population density, even in this relatively populated region of western Siberia, remains far lower than in the rural areas of European Russia.

In the late 1980s, specialists employed at Zaria began working with an economist from the Siberian Academy of Sciences in Novosibirsk, V.D. Smirnov, who was involved in developing alternative plans for labor organization on collective farms. He found an interested and attentive audience at Zaria and mapped out a new system of organization for the kolkhoz that was presented to the workers at a general meeting in January 1989. It was proposed that each brigade operate as an independent cooperative, with administrative links to a common center.

The reorganization program attempted to reintroduce a direct relationship between work accomplished and pay received. Cooperatives were free to select leaders and determine the method of income distribution. Each cooperative was to work on the principle of *khozraschet* (self-financing), paying a portion of revenue to a board of cooperative representatives and distributing the rest as income. Decentralizing decision making would increase the flexibility of the brigades, better enabling them to deal with specific conditions and concerns. It was also hoped that self-accounting at the brigade level would help to stem pilfering from farm resources, as peasants would be in effect "taking from their own pockets."

The brigade system of asset distribution was an attempt to parcel out kolkhoz assets in an equitable fashion. Rather than a free-for-all privatization lottery, in which assets might be given to individuals lacking the knowledge to make them productive, turning the brigades into autonomous cooperatives gave each member of the kolkhoz control over his or her means of production. When the program, with much encouragement from the collective-farm specialists, was adopted by the workers at a general farm meeting, it struck observers as extremely progressive. This was especially true for the region, as both Kemerovo and Novosibirsk oblasts had been known for conservative voting patterns in their rural areas. Notices of the changes on the kolkhoz appeared in a positive light in the raion newspaper during 1989 and 1990.[24] As debate about reforming Soviet agriculture continued in Moscow, Zaria forged ahead in breaking down the old system, aided and empowered in part by its distance from central authorities.

The farm experienced an increase in productivity, helped in part by favorable weather conditions. Pay levels for most of the brigades (cooperatives) increased, most markedly for milkmaids and tractor drivers, who experienced minimum increases of 37 percent and 26 percent, respectively. One worker, reflecting the feeling of members of the cooperative, remarked that "before there were no incentives to push yourself, no rewards. I was the top tractorist in the raion a few years ago and won an award, met the party brass in Kemerovo and got my picture taken. But you can't buy a car with that. Of course it's better now."

For a few of the new cooperatives, their relative standing fell. Farm drivers, who still received their pay from the farm's central funds, saw their wages fall far behind the general pay level. Pig breeders, whose capital holdings were in dismal condition, also suffered. General work discipline among both these brigade members remained slack under the new system, with relatively high rates of alcohol abuse and absenteeism in spite of supposedly increased individual incentives. For specific brigades there appeared to be little opportunity for working harder and earning more through official channels.

On the farm, there was not a noticeable decrease in petty (or capital) pilfering, according to cooperative leaders, who held hope that such a decrease would come with time. Pilfering did not affect the brigades equally. The farm drivers were often found to be filching from the cars for spare parts or moonlighting with trucks for personal gain. The belief that workers would pilfer less because they would be stealing from their own pockets seems to have validity only for those brigades whose pockets were deepened under the new cooperative system.

Continued pilfering, or "sharing," of communal resources was not equally distributed among cooperatives. Local residents were more likely to "liberate" a piglet from the confines of the collective farm than to steal milk. Likewise, residents were more likely to "borrow" a carburetor from a farm car than to take a part from a tractor. By breaking the farm into collectives along brigade lines, the cost of pilfering was shifted disproportionately upon some of the cooperatives, as various types of informal appropriation came at different costs to the cooperatives involved.

Borrowing a small tractor "after hours" to till a private plot entailed little cost aside from fuel used and was typically done only twice a year. The effect on the assets of the tractorists was minimal. The vast majority of households in Shabanova (89 percent) kept a private cow, with hay continuing to be available for purchase at a subsidized rate from the board of cooperatives. As a result, the assets of the milkmaids were seldom pilfered. Piglets, on the other hand, provided a portable, consumable, and valuable asset that could fit easily in a large pocket. Similarly, spare auto parts were easily concealed and especially valuable. The filching of straw and hay, plentiful at subsidized prices, was low. In contrast, animal vaccines and medicines were also "shared," not only among cooperative members but also between the veterinarian technician and the other villagers.

The lines between perpetrator and victim in regard to petty filching were not clear. Most brigade members found themselves in a pilfering catch-22. They were resentful of the "sharing" of their assets, but to varying degrees they, too, were dependent upon the help of other cooperatives for their private plot. The tendency to pilfer to enhance private plots cut across almost all of the brigades but did not draw on all areas of the collective farm equally. Dividing the whole of the collective farm shifted the burden of subsidization, an important mechanism for private-plot subsidization, unequally upon the resulting sections. Low farm wages and poor working conditions were partially offset by the implicit allowance of petty filching. Since most rural areas suffered from underdeveloped service sectors, inhabitants had few alternatives for procuring private-plot inputs other than appropriating them from the collective farm. Farms paid low wages, knowing that workers would pilfer enough to restore their labor power. Elderly village residents, paid low pensions by the state, also figured the pilfering into their budgets. "The collective belongs to us," stated one pensioner in the village, "who can blame us for using what is ours?"[25]

One important reason for the high productivity of private plots are the inputs "borrowed" from the collective sector. Z.I. Kalugina notes that even official government figures for 1985 admit that the 20 to 25 percent of private production sold supplied 41 percent of all potatoes, 14 percent of all vegetables, and 13 percent of all the meat marketed.[26] The high productivity and low operational costs of private plots would be unsustainable without the state sector. Total agricultural output, from both the private and the state sectors, drew on inputs from the state sector.

The inequities caused by pilfering patterns were, in many cases, increased by capital stock differentials. Over the past two decades, Zaria's records indicated that the majority of capital investment funds had been funneled into the purchase of tractors and new combines. In most years, between 20 percent and 35 percent of the kolkhoz funds for investment went to these areas. Some funds had been invested in automatic milking machines, but as replacements, not upgrades, of equipment. The pigpens, large barns housing several hundred piglets, were eighteen years old, in serious need of irrigation repair, poorly ventilated, and poorly heated. The division of assets by brigade placed some cooperatives at an advantage relative to others, due not to the relative effort expended, but to their capital stock.

Such inequity led to anger among the cooperative members whose capital stock left them at a disadvantage. Adding to the inequities, the price schedules for intercooperative activities (such as manure removal) were established to reflect market cost of inputs such as technical equipment and fuel. This left some of the cooperatives, such as the drivers, with little opportunity to enhance their wages (in the face of rapidly rising gasoline prices). The pricing schedule was not completely fixed. Some brigades negotiated among themselves for nonscheduled prices. Nonetheless, the "exploitation" of the market led to price schedules that placed certain brigades at a disadvantage.

Differential pilfering, variations in capital stock, and difficulties in establishing pricing systems, then, resulted in structural inequities among the brigades. The intended reintroduction of a direct relationship between effort expended and pay received proved elusive. While changes in wages led to a system of occupational stratification in the village, changes in the organizational structure led to shifts in the balance of power. The power of the president of the kolkhoz diminished as brigade autonomy increased and the brigades negotiated with limited autonomy among themselves. The importance of the central specialists, as consultants and monitors, increased. As the wages of several of the cooperatives rose, their support for the chief economist, who introduced the program of reform to the farm, grew.

Throughout the reform process in Shabanova, the importance of personality over parliamentary process was evident. Areas far from Moscow are typically poorly integrated into policy discussions. In such conditions, the individual charisma of reformers has more local value than decrees from Moscow. In times of economic and political instability, trust becomes a valuable social commodity. Issues regarding local families' ties and knowledge of rural conditions were important to the residents of Shabanova, whose specialists and elected leaders were all from farm backgrounds and from villages in western Siberia. Trust in known local leaders, directly accountable to the village, has been and continues to be much stronger than the confidence in legal decrees from the distant central government.

During the next year, the new cooperative system continued to provide more benefits to some cooperatives than others, as well as to generate increasing intracooperative differentials in pay. Prior to the "new" system, wages within brigades did not vary more than 20 percent, according to the farm accountant. Under the new reforms, monthly intrabrigade differentials ran as high as 50 percent. Rather than inciting hostility, many workers seemed to accept this differentiation. Pay differentials were generally perceived as being related to effort and generated respect rather than envy among most residents of the village. The structural disadvantages of cooperatives such as the pig nurses were much more likely to be attributed to individual shortcomings. Far from being reluctant to shake off more than seventy years of collectivist indoctrination, village inhabitants seemed to display a preference for individual culpability as an explanation.

Difficulties in the village, however, were markedly evident by mid-February 1991, when a village meeting with the regional political committee (*raipolkom*) secretary was held. It was noted the school required capital repair, a music teacher was needed, and that several of the elderly were in want of assistance. Complaints regarding the lack of goods in the store (focusing on vodka, cigarettes, and fish) were also voiced. The recommendation of the secretary highlighted the implicit government reliance upon collective farms to satisfy needs in the social sphere. He encouraged the collective farm (declining to call them a cooperative) to strike bargaining agreements directly with other productive enterprises to secure goods for the village store. Such interfirm bartering was far from a new idea, but to be officially endorsed by a regional official while central government advocated dissolving the farm emphasized the conflict between the ideal of economic reform and the reality of day-to-day life in regions far from Moscow. It was becoming clear that reorganizing the collective farm as an economic organization left a void with regard to the other functions of the farm in the village.

Recollectivization

Life in Shabanova did improve during the summer of 1991 as supplies increased and wages continued to rise, but the gains seen by cooperative members in the previous year were not matched. Regional inflation, set in motion by the wage concessions gained by the miners in the neighboring Kuzbas coal region, eroded the earnings of most village inhabitants. Only one of the planned projects for social improvement in the community, the conversion of the local hostel to an inpatient care facility, was completed (bringing a level of health-care provision rare for a village of Shabanova's size). Other long-planned projects, such as road construction, had to be tabled due to a lack of funds.

The 1992 meeting of the board of the cooperatives in Shabanova was held in mid-April, after several delays. The specialists on the farm sought to continue what they saw as progress: the movement toward the dissolution of the collective farm. Plans were made to establish each of the cooperatives as a separate legal entity. Farm administrators made economic plans for the division of land and capital resources among the workers and pensioners. Shabanova planned to continue in the direction of dissolving the collective farm.

If in their initial stages the reforms in Shabanova were somewhat of a novelty, by spring 1992 they were accepted as something of a model.[27] Yet at this time, the residents of Shabanova reinstituted the collective farm, weakened the cooperatives (now renamed "brigades"), and shelved any plans for division of kolkhoz assets. Initially, the decision brought shock not only to several specialists and consultants but to many of the cooperatives. What prompted this seemingly surprising "recollectivization" in Shabanova?

Discussions of the difficulties of economic reform in agriculture have often focused on poor factor markets, the potential for manipulation and coercion on the part of local officials against change, and poor horizontal and vertical integration. Few have focused on the social context of the actors in rural society and why they might oppose the dissolution of collective farms, not simply from a psychological or economic perspective, but from a social standpoint. An examination of what transpired in Shabanova provides insight into precisely this aspect.

The meeting of the members of the cooperatives in 1992 took place in conditions dramatically different from those of the previous year. Shabanova found itself in a new country with a new government. The economic gains made in the initial stages of the change to the cooperatives had been eroded by rapid central and regional inflation. Funding for school equipment, subsidized transportation between the village and nearby cities, the new medical center, and the sports club were in jeopardy.

The villagers had understandably grown weary. As one of the former kolkhoz presidents stated, "we need to shovel out the barn but we can't find the door." Many of the residents, old as well as young, bemoaned the lack of a "clear leader." The miners in the area, well thought of last year by the residents during their strike for showing initiative, were now pariahs, responsible for the extreme inflation in the area. "Just give me a peaceful life" was the feeling of many, tired of change and looking for a return to normalcy.

This trend in public opinion was encouraged by several former members of the local apparatus. The president of the kolkhoz (chairman of the board of cooperatives) had called for more power late in 1991, acquiring the posts of local administrator and president of the *sel'sovet* (village government) in addition to his post with the cooperatives. "If each of the posts is weak itself, they should all be held together so one person can get things done," he stated, in an interesting twist of political wisdom. He had only narrowly retained his position as president the previous year, yet 1992 found him with a strong base of support. Much of this had to do with the selective, and perhaps distorted view of the past in the village. Inhabitants who earlier had spoken of the collective farms in disparaging terms began to look back longingly.

The president, with several former members of the raipolkom, was instrumental in delaying the meeting of the cooperatives. When the meeting was finally held in April, it was too late to talk about reform. The farm needed to get into the fields. During the delay (from February to April), the former raipolkom secretary often stopped in to talk to pensioners in the village, reportedly asking them how they would live if the collective farm did not assure coal delivery or provide a supplement to their pensions. Information went out to the social-service providers in the village, reminding them how much money they received from the kolkhoz. Agitation was subtle, but the point was clear: In an unstable situation, the kolkhoz represented village stability and a structural framework that was familiar.

The decision to recollectivize did not stem from simple peasant fear of the unknown, inability to orient toward the market, resentment for exclusion from decision making, or a supposed desire for economic equality. Simply put, the dissolution of the collective farm was not advantageous to the village. The reliance of the peasants on the collective farm was not limited to the sphere of economic production. Links to nearly every aspect of the village community ran through the kolkhoz. Changing the production process threatened to leave the community without other, central aspects of the old system. No subsidiary structures were suggested or explored. No alternative mechanisms for municipal funding were offered. No attempt to increase the equity of the distribution of assets was made. Indeed, due to the uneven nature of the various sectors of the farm, equity seemed elusive.

In Shabanova, as in many Siberian villages, the sel'soviet had a long history of selecting projects, not obtaining the funds to complete them, and handing them over to the kolkhoz to complete. This was the case with several road-paving projects, the construction of the kindergarten, renovation of the medical center, the music school, and others. The farm underwrote cost of coal delivery in the village. Monetary pension supplements from the farm constituted 17 percent of average pension payments. The farm had built over half of the housing in the village and controlled almost a third of the housing stock, despite repeated attempts at privatization.

In addition to paying for the construction of the school building in 1978, the collective farm provided all of the food for the school cafeteria, paid the salary of the gym teacher and the shop teacher, provided a car for the school director, and provided between 45 percent and 56 percent of all funds for textbooks for the school. Teachers purchased items through the kolkhoz at a discount and in high-profit years were given an appreciation bonus (in 1987 this bonus was equal to two months' official pay). Without the financial support of the collective farm, the local school was in danger of serious cutbacks.

The day-care center was also dependent upon the subsidies given by the kolkhoz. Although nominally under state direction, the collective farm played a significant role in providing housing for day-care workers, supplementing the toy budget, providing food for the kitchen, and funding capital repairs on the building. The fee paid by parents covered only 50 percent of the operating costs of the center. As the day-care director threatened, "We may have to close. I won't run a poor center like in some villages. I'd rather send the children home."

The kolkhoz provided 70 percent of the budget for the medical station in the village and 30 percent of staff salaries. And it provided most of the funds used for road construction between 1980 and 1990, independently negotiating with seasonal brigades. In short, the dissolution of the collective farm brought with it the collapse of social services as they had been. In a situation where the central government was viewed as insolvent, distant, and unstable, the choice whether or not to reform the collective farm could not be made with an exclusive focus on economic production and efficiency.

Pensioners were the group most threatened by the breakup of the collective farm. Their reaction to the dissolution of a farm they had struggled to build, far from being emotional, was largely financial. Government pensions for collective farmers were then set at 80 percent of the pension for workers, which the kolkhoz supplemented, both in cash and in kind. Pensioners were provided two tons of coal with no delivery charge and two wagons of hay each winter at no cost. They also received bonuses in years of high profit (in 1987 this was equal to three months' pension supplement). With the kolkhoz no longer in operation, the elderly faced severe cutbacks in their standard of living, which already held little room for luxury.

The people of Zaria who voted to return to the collective structure were not fearful of the market, unable to change old work habits, or unwilling to accept new patterns of economic stratification. For the majority, the old system was more beneficial, both in terms of service provision and of private-plot subsidization.

The Alternatives?

There were no alternative sources for funding social services in Shabanova. When increases in local taxes were suggested to generate funds for the village, the response from many was hostile. Each of the brigades had continued to pay central taxes throughout the period under discussion. There was simply not much perceived return of these tax funds to Shabanova. "We live as we live and the tsar sleeps in peace in Moscow," one of the women working in the village government was fond of saying, illustrating not only the physical but the social distance between the central government and the region, as well as the historical continuity of rule.

Shifting the responsibility of funding local social services to municipal taxes might offer the opportunity to separate production processes from service provision. It could potentially assist in the establishment of subsidiary institutions to fill the void left by the farm. But legislation poses obstacles. Farmers are currently exempt from paying land tax for at least five years.[28] Problems relating to farm procurement and payment may lead to difficulties in establishing rural income taxes. Yet, even if limited, these options, as well as others, must be explored if rural residents are to become supportive of decollectivization in the long term.

Continuing to ignore the multiple roles collective farm structures play in rural society may well lead to more collective farms changing their production organization in name only.[29] Or, as in the case of Zaria, the alternative may mean returning to old methods and forms. More ominously, it could lead to drastic decreases in rural services, already appallingly inadequate in western Siberia.[30]

The failure to recognize the noneconomic role of collective farms in rural society prevents adequate appreciation of the consequences of decollectivization. The situation is not devoid of historical irony. During and after the collectivization drive, policy makers failed to understand the influence of supposedly nonproductive kinship networks and self-exploitation in peasant production. As a result, the productivity gains from self-exploitation were relegated exclusively to subsidiary private plots instead of to the new central focus of production, the collective farm. The social aspects of household production had significant ties to its economic functioning. The push toward wide-scale and rapid decollectivization in Russia risks failing to appreciate the ties of the economic institutions (collective farms) to the social aspects of village life: The economic functioning of collective farms has significant ties to the social functioning of rural areas.

Failing to appreciate the difficulty of an equitable distribution of agricultural assets, be they natural or material, runs the risk of institutionalizing the stratification systems existent under collective production into new market relations. In this example, distributional equity raised more of a social justice problem than a practical one, at least in the short term. Still, the potential obstacles raised by questions of how to distribute assets will doubtless remain an issue of contention. Although the case study examined focuses upon a brigade-distribution procedure, difficulties in parceling out assets of varying value in an equitable fashion will exist regardless of the method employed.

The conditions at Zaria are specific, but the experience of this farm raises several important issues related to the viability of smaller family farms or even production cooperatives in replacement of Soviet collective farms. Especially in more remote regions of Russia with poor transportation, inferior social infrastructure, and low population density, such production organizations will not flourish in the absence of alternative centralized or local structures to provide basic services. Without such support, the success of economic reform of agriculture across Russia, not just in western Siberia, is called into serious question.

Will Zaria remain functioning for long? The large-scale, long-term transformation of Russia's rural areas may have passed the point of return. Yet, questions remain regarding the cost and precipitance of change. Careful consideration of the context in which privatization takes place in the emergent economies of the former Soviet empire is important generally and especially vital in the area of agricultural reform. Encouraging the simultaneous emergence of alternative structures to replace the noneconomic functions of collective farms may be one way to lessen the costs of transformation. If collective farms are to be restructured into smaller production-oriented economic units, the generation of replacements for their hidden (or unmeasured) functions of service provision and private-plot subsidization must be pursued.

In the rural areas of western Siberia, where alternative providers for social services are scarce, the long-term success of agrarian reform and marketization will be closely linked to the replacement of the full range of activities provided by collective farms.

Notes

This essay draws on a longer paper, "One Step Forward Two Steps Back: Decollectivization, Recollectivization and Social Change," presented at the conference "Collectivization and Its Alternatives," Budapest, 1992, sponsored by the MacArthur Foundation. Research was supported by The British Council and the Soros Foundation, under the project "The Social Structure of Soviet Agriculture," Professor T. Shanin, primary investigator.

1. V. Tikhonov, "Farmers ought to own land," *Moscow News,* 14 January 1990, p. 6. There are wide regional variations, with only one-third of all farms found insolvent in agriculturally rich regions such as Saratov, see V.N. Dem'ianenko, "Pravovye problemy 'razgosudarstvleniia' kolkhozov," *Gosudarstvo i pravo,* no. 2 (1993), pp. 54–63.

2. *Rossiiskaia gazeta,* 5 July 1993, p. 1.

3. V.N. Siniukov, "O forme federatsii v Rossiia," *Gosudarstvo i pravo,* no. 5, 1993, pp. 28–35.

4. Dem'ianenko, "Pravovye problemy," pp. 54–56.

5. C. Bramall, "The Role of Decollectivization in China's Agricultural Miracle, 1978–1990," *Journal of Peasant Studies,* vol. 20, no. 3, 1990.

6. W. Hinton, *The Privatization of China* (New York: Monthly Review Press, 1990).

7. Phillip Huang, *The Peasant Family and Rural Development in the Yangzi Delta, 1350–1988* (Stanford: Stanford University Press, 1990).

8. Xiao-yuan Dong and G. Dow, "Monitoring Costs in Chinese Agricultural Teams," *Journal of Political Economy,* vol. 101, no. 3, 1993.

9. Examples of the difficulties related to this sectorally bounded reform relating to agriculture can be found in S. Goldstein and A. Goldstein, "Population Mobility in the People's Republic of China," *Papers of the East–West Population Institute,* no. 95 (Honolulu: East–West Center, 1985).

10. A.A. Razymov, "Pomozhet li rynok vozrodit' derevniu?" *Sotsiologicheskie issledovaniia,* no. 3, 1991, pp. 58–63.

11. E.D. Azarkh et al., "Osnovnye printsipy i napravleniia perestroiki upravleniia sferoi obsluzhivaniia naseleniia i reshenie zhilishchnoi problemy na sele," *I.E.O.P.P. Preprint* (Novosibirsk, 1987).

12. Razymov, "Pomozhet li rynok vozrodit' derevniu?" p. 60.

13. *Vestnik statistiki,* no. 11, 1991, p. 66.

14. *Krest'ianskie vedomosti,* 31 March 1992, p. 6.

15. Some have argued that the supplements provided to pensioners were small and "therefore not much help in providing a decent retirement income." But such interpretations rely upon monetary income, which is a poor indicator of living levels in rural areas with high levels of household production. W. Moskoff, *Labour and Leisure in the Soviet Union: The Conflict Between Private and Public Decision Making in a Planned Economy* (London: Macmillan, 1984).

16. *Sel'skoe khoziastvo v SSSR* (Moscow, 1988), p. 481.

17. V. Velkoff and K. Kinsella, *Aging in Eastern Europe and the Former Soviet Union* (Washington, DC: Center for International Research, Bureau of the Census, 1993), report no. 93/1.

18. *Sel'skoe khoziastvo v SSSR,* p. 481

19. This expanded responsibility concerning social services was not limited to the collective farms. It does seem collective farms have borne a proportionately greater burden in terms of the administration and financing for social services. Rural sel'soviets generally held little financial power due to underfunding. This is especially true in western Siberia, where villages are often far from each other and whose economy is completely dominated by the collective farm, see E.E. Gorechenko, "Sotsial'nye problemy razvitiia malykh sel'skikh poselenii," *I.E.O.P.P. Preprint* (Novosibirsk, 1986).

20. Two main types of collective agricultural structures have been employed in the former Soviet Union. The first, collective farms, or kolkhozy, were communal in nature and based wages on the productivity of the farm. Individual wages were allotted by the number of labor days worked. Payment in kind was practiced through the mid-1960s for collective farm workers, who were not included in the official pension system until the mid-1960s. State farms, or sovkhozy, were seen as a higher level of socialist production. Workers on state farms were classified as workers, paid a set wage rate, and covered by the state pension and passport systems. This paper focuses on the difficulties faced by collective farms, although many of the arguments applied to state farms to varying degrees.

21. For an excellent collection of materials referring to the collectivization drive, see Victor Danilov and N.A. Ivanitskii, *Dokumenty svidetel'stvuiut: 1927–1929, 1929–1932* (Moscow, 1989).

22. A.V. Chayanov, *Theory of Peasant Economy* (Madison: University of Wisconsin Press, 1986). Recently, international aid–granting institutions have allowed for a re-evaluation of the methods used to calculate income and production levels, yielding significantly different levels of income and production. These differences are due in part to alterations in setting exchange rates and in part to a greater appreciation of nonmonetary remuneration (social guarantees).

23. Data on Zaria were gathered on the farm during the winter of 1989–90, fall 1990 through summer 1991, and spring 1992 by way of interviews, participant observation, local press, kolkhoz records, and village registries. Interviews with the officials of the collective farm were used to identify the attitudes and opinions of the local "power elite" toward the push for privatization. These interviews were complemented by a series of group discussions with two of the larger brigades of farm workers (the tractorists and the milkmaids) and excerpts from the life histories of the older inhabitants of the village.

24. See *Znamia truda,* various issues 1989–93 (Lenin-Kuznetsk).

25. It is possible to interpret the petty pilfering taking place as an example of a "weapon" the peasants of Shabanova used to defend themselves against their difficult position, or as a shielded protest against the collective farm. James Scott, *Weapons of the Weak* (New Haven: Yale University Press, 1985). Another interpretation comes from Liebow, who argued that in some cases employers and employees figure the costs and

benefits to pilfering, respectively, and consciously calculate it into the wage rate. E. Liebow, *Tally's Corner* (Boston: Little, Brown, 1967).

26. Z.I. Kalugina, *Lichnoe podsobnoe khoziaistvo v SSSR* (Novosibirsk, 1991), p. 168.

27. See "Zakon RSFSR o plate za zemliu ot oktiabria 1991 g.," in *Vedomosti s''ezda narodonykh deputatov Rossiiskoi Federatsii i Verkhovianogo Soveta Rossiiskoi Federatsii,* no. 44, 1991, p. 1424; and V.S. Ustinov and G.S. Shirokalova, "Krizis sel'skogo khoziaistva i sovremennoe agrarnoe zakonodatel'stvo," *Gosudarstvo i pravo,* 1993, no. 3, pp. 49–60.

28. "Zakon RSFSR o krest'ianskom (fermerskom) khoziaistve ot 22 novembre 1990 g.," in *Vedomosti s''ezda narodnykh deputatov Rossiiskoi Federatsii i Verkhovnogo Soveta Rossiiskoi Federatsii,* no. 26, p. 324. See also, V.P. Popov, "Krest'ianskii vzgliad na kolkhoznuiu real'nost'," *Sotsiologicheskie issledovaniia,* no. 7, 1992, pp. 107–10; and V. Khannonov, "Pravovoe obespechenie ustoichivosti agrarnogo proizvodstva," *Gosudarstvo i pravo,* no. 5, 1992, pp. 91–102. For an excellent structural assessment of the decollectivization process, see Steven Wegren, "Private Farming and Agrarian Reform in Russia," *Problems of Communism,* May/June 1992, pp. 107–21.

29. *Moscow News,* 21 June 1992, p. 9.

30. See T.I. Zaslavskaia and Z.V. Kupriianova, eds., *Sotsial'no-ekonomicheskoe razvitie Sibirskogo sela* (Novosibirsk, 1987).

Water Wars

Siberian Rivers, Central Asian Deserts, and the Structural Sources of a Policy Debate

Michael L. Bressler

Siberia is defined by its size, its northern climate, and its copious store of natural resources. This last element especially influenced the fate of the region during the final quarter century of Soviet rule. Under Brezhnev, the Communist Party sought to tap Siberia's vast oil and gas reserves and to exploit further its rich mineral resources and seemingly endless stands of timber. Nor were Siberia's immense water resources overlooked. The region possesses well over half of the former Soviet Union's mean annual river flow and worldwide is ranked second only to Amazonia. The economic potential of these resources is so great that many believed Siberia's rivers held the key to resolving a quandary that plagued every Soviet leader since the October Revolution, namely agriculture.

There was a problem, however, in tapping these resources. Instead of flowing south to densely populated, agriculturally promising, but water-deficient Soviet Central Asia, the mighty rivers of Siberia snaked north, emptying into the Arctic Ocean. If not for this "accident" of nature, Soviet water resources experts argued, the problem of agriculture could be solved. Their proposed solution was an ambitious interbasin diversion of Siberian water from a point near the confluence of the Ob and Irtysh rivers south to Central Asia over a distance of some 1,550 miles. At the same time, they advised that a much less severe water resources "imbalance" west of the Urals should be corrected through the transfer of Arctic-bound water from the Russian European North to southern European Russia.

Proponents of the Siberian and northern (European) diversions promised that these undertakings would allow the Soviet Union to achieve what its leadership and people so desperately wanted and needed, self-sufficiency in agriculture. The Siberian project on its own would have expanded the amount of irrigated land in Central Asia by more than 50 percent. It would have provided jobs for a growing Uzbek population, and in its later stages would have revived the dying Aral Sea, a symbol of Central Asia's heritage. For its part, the northern diversion would have ensured the continued development of two of the country's richest and most promising agricultural areas, the southern Volga region and the Kuban. The northern project, its proponents argued, would also stabilize and eventually restore the then shrinking Caspian Sea and help resuscitate the heavily polluted Sea of Azov.[1]

The Siberian project, the larger and technically more challenging of the two, called for an initial diversion of 27.2 cubic kilometers (km^3) per year from western Siberia to Central Asia and the construction of a 1,550-mile-long main diversion canal (roughly equal to two-thirds the length of the Mississippi, and longer than the Colorado River). In its second stage, up to 60 km^3 would be diverted each year to the fields of Uzbekistan and Kazakhstan. At the same time, the northern project, though calling for only 5.8 km^3/year in its first stage, envisioned the eventual transfer of 67 km^3/year. To put these flow figures in perspective, the amount of water diverted by the Siberian project's second stage would have been slightly more than the average annual discharge of the Tennessee River, the United States's seventh largest, and compared to other large-scale reclamation projects would have been more than twice the size of California's impressive Central Valley system. The Siberian diversion's first stage alone would have equaled ten Central Arizona Projects.

The diversions' proponents believed that these two great attempts to transform nature represented the height of scientific progress. For their critics, however, the projects were symbolic of everything that was wrong with the Soviet Union under Brezhnev: a political system dominated by Moscow-based bureaucracies that sought only to attain their relatively narrow organizational goals. In so doing, they were unresponsive to the people, disinterested in the common good, and all too willing to sacrifice the interests of the country as a whole. A number of individuals, including such noted writers as Yurii Bondarev, Vasilii Belov, Sergei Zalygin, and Valentin Rasputin, believed that the large-scale diversion of water from the Russian North would lay waste to the environment and inundate numerous historical monuments. For them, the northern diversion was nothing less than an attack on Russian culture and the heart of Old Russia.[2]

Critics of the Siberian diversion also anticipated the worst. Given the scale of the project, its potential environmental effects were not fully known. Where the project's proponents saw the beneficial draining of waterlogged fields in northern and central west Siberia, opponents saw the destruction of wetlands and the endangering of countless species of flora and fauna. And whereas the diversion's supporters contended that the effects of a decrease in the flow of freshwater from the Ob River into the Arctic Ocean would be limited, critics believed that its impact was underestimated by water resources experts, who had great personal and organizational stakes in the Siberian project's implementation.

Figure 15.1. **The Mean Flow of Soviet Rivers ***

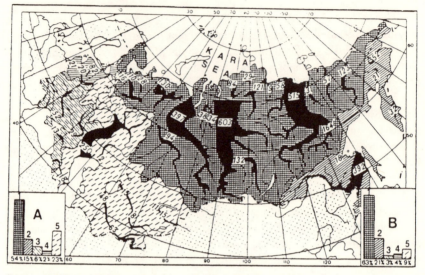

Source: Phillip P. Micklin, *Soviet Geography*, 27 (1986), p. 292.
Inset A: Percentage of Soviet territory draining into particular sea and ocean basins.
Inset B: Percentage of mean annual river flow discharging into particular sea and ocean basins.
Key to sea and ocean basins:
    1. Arctic Ocean
    2. Pacific Ocean
    3. Black Sea and Sea of Azov
    4. Baltic Sea
    5. Caspian Sea and Aral Sea
*In cubic kilometers per year.

    Some opponents also questioned the economic necessity of such grandiose undertakings, while others feared that the Siberian diversion would hinder the development of agriculture in the southern oblasts of western Siberia. Indeed, many argued that Central Asia did not really need *Siberian* water. If the Uzbeks and Kazakhs would only make more efficient use of their *own* resources, the Siberian diversion would be unnecessary and the dangers that such a project posed to Siberia's environment and economy would be averted.[3] For Central Asians and their supporters in Moscow, on the other hand, the future of the Aral Sea basin depended upon the delivery of Siberian water. With this project, they believed, Central Asia would witness the revival of its struggling land, culture, and society.[4] The political conflict over the projects was intensely bitter and, with respect to the Siberian diversion, at times contained racial undertones.

    Both projects reached the party's policy agenda in 1976 at its Twenty-fifth Congress. In spite of objections raised by the diversions' critics, the Politburo

Figure 15.2. **The Proposed Northern and Siberian Rivers Diversion Projects**

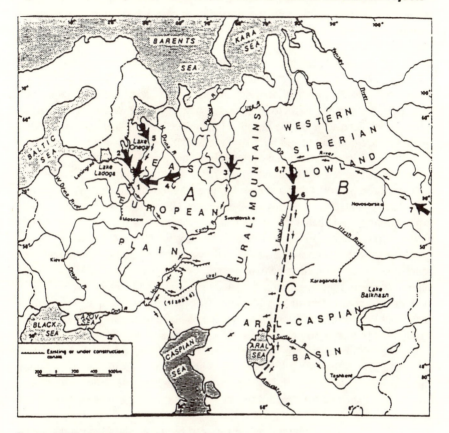

Source: Phillip P. Micklin, *Soviet Geography*, 27 (1986), p. 297.

A. Northern Divisions

    Phase I

    1. First stage (Lakes Lacha, Vozhe, and Kubena and upper Sukhona River)

    2. Second stage (Lake Onega)

    3. Third stage (upper Perchora River)

        Phase II

    4. First stage (lower Sukhona and Malaya Northern Division Dvina Rivers)

    5. Second Stage (Onega Gulf Reservoir)

B. Siberian Diversions

    Phase I

    6. Irtysh River and middle and upper Ob River

    Phase II

    7. Middle and upper Ob River and Enisei River

C. Main diversion canal from Siberia to Aral Sea region

authorized the implementation of the northern project's first stage in 1982. Two years later, the party took steps that appeared to ensure the Siberian diversion's eventual approval. By 1986, digging had already begun on the northern diversion, and teams from Central Asia were in the field building the infrastructure necessary to support the imminent construction of the Siberian project.[5] At this point, however, the projects were defeated and pushed off the policy agenda by a new Soviet leader, Mikhail Gorbachev. Although the decision to halt the projects seemingly brought the issue to a close, the battles fought over these grandiose schemes left deep scars on the political landscape that continue to be felt, especially in the region that would have benefited most, Central Asia.

Policy decisions in which the evaluation of "nontechnical" criteria were either neglected or ignored were, as we know now, routine during the Soviet era. A number of recent works that examine resource (mis)management, environmental degradation, and their legacies in the former USSR have sought to provide explanations for this behavior on the part of Soviet policy makers. Much of this literature focuses on the impact of an ideology which saw the Soviet state's relationship with nature as an adversarial one and held as its central tenet the belief that "nature existed to be exploited, to be wrestled into submission."[6] The main mechanism for exploiting nature was the country's planned economy.

A critical component of this ideology was the assumption that the environment could be "improved" and that "accidents" of nature could be "corrected" through the power of Soviet science. The ideology also carried with it the belief that bigger was by definition "better." Such thinking underlay Stalin's attempts to transform nature after World War II, Khrushchev's Virgin Lands program, and Brezhnev's decision to build the Baikal-Amur Mainline. In so doing, each Soviet leader showed little regard for the social and ecological aspects of development.

The developmental ideology was reinforced by the Soviet planned economy. In theory, the planned economy should have prevented, or at least lessened the impact of, the negative externalities associated with economic development, but a growing body of research shows that its effect on Soviet society and the environment was quite the opposite. Several characteristics of the planned economy, including the priorities set by the Soviet state (which favored gross output above all else), the absence of a reliable way to establish price (natural resources were, by and large, available free of charge), and "departmentalism" on the part of government agencies, combined to wreak havoc on the environment.[7]

In considering the Communist Party's decisions with respect to the Siberian and northern rivers diversion projects during the 1970s and early 1980s, there is little doubt that they were in part the products of a development ideology that encouraged grandiose efforts to transform nature, as well as of a planned economy run amok. At the same time, however, these decisions were also the result of policy-making structures and processes that existed *outside* the context of the pathologies associated with the planned economy and the Soviet state's approach to development. For a more complete understanding of the party's decisions concerning the use and management of the vast water resources of the Russian North and Siberia, it is necessary to examine the character of the policy-making process under Brezhnev.[8]

Exploring the conflict over the control and management of Siberian and northern water, this essay will show how an effort on the part of the Brezhnev leadership to create a more "rational" policy process (driven by a desire to avoid repeating Khrushchev's policy mistakes) created its own problems in that it allowed a self-interested water resources policy community to manipulate the process and promote an agenda that did not initially correspond with that of the Soviet leadership.[9] In this way, it becomes possible to explain how the USSR came as close as it did to carrying out two such grandiose water diversion projects in spite of the fact that their possible environmental, socioeconomic, and cultural effects on Siberia and the Russian North were little known, let alone fully understood.

The essay argues that while Brezhnev and the Politburo established the basic direction of land reclamation and water resources development policy, the structure of the decision-making process ensured that specialists who were proponents of the rivers diversion projects were in a position not only to influence the specific shape of the Politburo's agenda but also to dominate the development of policy alternatives. The result was that these experts were able to obtain the policy outcomes they desired. In achieving their aims, however, they potentially placed the natural environment of Siberia and the Russian North at risk, and with it, the social, economic, and cultural foundations of these regions.

Policy Making During the Brezhnev Era

The nature of the policy process under Brezhnev was shaped by two separate, though closely related, elements. First, the Soviet leadership's great respect for and faith in science ensured that technical experts would be given a leading role in the policy process. Brezhnev and many of his Politburo colleagues were convinced that the problem of Soviet agriculture could be solved once and for all through the power of science. Second, the Brezhnev leadership was determined not to repeat the process-generated policy mistakes of the Khrushchev era. While it is true that Khrushchev often sought the advice of specialists, his impetuous nature frequently led him to turn to such notable charlatans as T.D. Lysenko, an individual of questionable scientific talent, whose policy proposals in agriculture and their promise of quick results at little cost gained the Soviet leader's support. The effects of such policy processes were often disastrous and ultimately contributed to Khrushchev's removal in October 1964.[10]

In response, the Brezhnev leadership sought to rationalize the policy process. Decisions would no longer be taken in a haphazard manner. Instead, the party would pay close attention to "objective" conditions. This primarily meant relying heavily on the expertise and advice of well-respected specialists within the scientific community, in addition to approaching important policy decisions in a deliberate manner. Through such a strategy the new leaders believed they could take the best that Soviet science had to offer and at the same time avoid the "harebrained schemes" they believed had marked the Khrushchev era.[11]

There were weaknesses in the Brezhnev strategy, however. The most notable was a compartmentalization of the policy process. If Khrushchev erred in turning too often to specialists outside the mainstream of the scientific establishment, Brezhnev's mistake was to rely too heavily on expert "insiders." Almost from the beginning of the Brezhnev era, the new policy process was structured so that those whose expertise fell outside the narrowly defined boundaries of a given policy realm had great difficulty in penetrating the process. From the moment Brezhnev decided to launch the USSR's first large-scale reclamation program, he relied almost exclusively on the counsel of experts from the Soviet water resources community, especially the talented and energetic engineers of the USSR Ministry of Land Reclamation and Water Resources (Minvodkhoz). They were the experts and could be counted upon, Brezhnev believed, to provide an objective assessment of the country's reclamation needs.[12] Given this assumption, the party leadership rarely turned to others for advice, and as a result, gave the Minvodkhoz-led policy community a commanding position in the decision-making process.[13]

A key consequence of this policy structure was that once Brezhnev and the party established guidelines in a particular policy area and were committed to investing the financial resources necessary to support their overall policy aims, government technocrats had the latitude, and indeed "permission" from the Politburo, to influence the *boundaries* and *specific content* of party policy. Certainly, Minvodkhoz did not have the power or freedom to launch major projects on its own. It lacked the political, material, and financial resources to do so. However, the Soviet leadership's dependence on Minvodkhoz's advice and expertise during the Brezhnev era repeatedly created opportunities for the ministry to advance its own agenda and to manipulate the policy process.

Minvodkhoz's first opportunity to stretch the limits of party policy came in March 1965 (more than a decade before the rivers diversion projects reached the CPSU's policy agenda), when the USSR State Production Committee for Irrigated Farming and Water Resources was asked to examine thoroughly the potential role of land reclamation in the development of Soviet agriculture. After careful scientific study, the organization was then to work out a large-scale reclamation program that would encompass the entire country.[14] The party's aim was nothing less than the creation of a robust and vibrant Soviet agricultural sector. The task of water resources experts was to give content to the party's broad policy goals.

The state production committee, soon to be reorganized as Minvodkhoz,[15] took full advantage of this opportunity by including in its report to the Central

Committee projections of the potential impact of the northern and Siberian rivers diversion projects on Soviet agriculture.[16] Although the party chose not to include either of the projects in the reclamation program approved at the Central Committee's May 1966 plenum, Minvodkhoz's behavior set the tone for interactions between the party leadership and the ministry for years to come. The party had not specifically asked Minvodkhoz to examine the question of the large-scale interbasin transfer of water resources, but it was apparently not displeased that the ministry had taken the initiative to do so. In fact, under the new decision-making regime established by the Brezhnev leadership, this is exactly what Minvodkhoz was supposed to do. Thus, despite the ministry's failure to achieve its policy aims at the May plenum, the structure of the policy process itself, and the central role Minvodkhoz played in it, meant that the ministry would have several more opportunities in the years ahead to lobby the Soviet leadership.

Minvodkhoz's best chance to help push the projects onto the policy agenda came on the eve of the party's Twenty-fifth Congress, scheduled to convene in late February 1976. As the government's planners prepared the new five-year plan, the country found itself reeling from the effects of a series of severe droughts that had exposed the continuing underlying frailty of Soviet agriculture.[17] Taking advantage of the policy crisis created by drought, and mindful of the Soviet leaders' ambitious goals in agriculture as well as their bias toward large projects—although the projected cost of the diversions, large even by Soviet standards, gave the Brezhnev leadership much reason to hesitate—Minvodkhoz, in the words of one observer, "bombarded" the Central Committee and Council of Ministers with information in the months and weeks leading up to the party congress in an attempt to generate support for the projects.[18]

It was at this point that the structure of the policy process played a decisive role in influencing the party's thinking. The rivers diversion projects were not the only alternatives potentially available to the Soviet leadership, but Minvodkhoz's position in the policy process allowed it to filter out other possible solutions, chief of which was the more efficient use of local water resources in the Soviet South.[19] The Brezhnev leadership's heavy reliance on Minvodkhoz and the water resources community ensured that the rivers diversion projects would surface as the only "viable" long-term solutions to the country's water resources problems. Given the compartmentalized nature of the policy process, the Brezhnev leadership would be in no position to challenge the soundness of the ministry's proposals. Nor were the Soviet leaders inclined to do so anyway, because they had such great respect for Minvodkhoz's engineers.[20] In the end, the ministry's patience and persistence would be rewarded as the party included provisions in the new five-year plan (1976–80) for a large-scale research and design effort on the proposed rivers diversion projects. After more than a decade of lobbying, the projects had finally reached the party's policy agenda.[21]

As the water resources community knew, however, getting the diversions on the agenda was but the first step. There was no guarantee the projects would be implemented. Indeed, within a year of the party's decision to place the projects on the agenda, Soviet agricultural policy appeared to be on the verge of taking off in a new direction. No longer content with simply pouring huge sums of the state's resources into agriculture, Brezhnev began to demand that capital investment be utilized much more efficiently and that the state receive a higher return on its investment. This turn toward efficiency did not bode well for the eventual implementation of such capital-intensive programs as the rivers diversion projects.

Even so, at least two unrelated forces were working in Minvodkhoz's favor. First, in spite of the Soviet leaders' desire that the ministry become more efficient in its work, they also called for further rapid expansion of the amount of land under irrigation. In a political system that rewarded high volume over increases in efficiency, there could be little doubt about which imperative Minvodkhoz would follow. In the same tenor, the Politburo continued to support research and design work on the rivers diversion projects. Second, a new crisis in agriculture in the early 1980s also gave the ministry's fortunes a boost. More bad weather during the last half of the 1970s, followed by a disastrous harvest in 1981 (brought on again by severe drought), prompted the Communist Party to launch the so-called "Food Program" in May 1982. It would be the party's most ambitious effort to strengthen the flagging agroindustrial sector. Much to Minvodkhoz's delight, the program included provisions for the implementation of the northern diversion.[22]

Brezhnev's conflicting policy priorities and the USSR's inhospitable climate, however, were not the only factors that accounted for Minvodkhoz's policy victory. One other critical element was again the ministry's dominant position in the policy process. Minvodkhoz and its organizational allies could not dictate policy, yet their control over the shaping of policy alternatives (in which they continued to argue that small-scale, efficiency-oriented projects, on their own, were not a solution to the South's water problems) ultimately left the Politburo with little choice but to push ahead with the rivers diversion projects.

Indeed, it was at this point in the process (policy development and review) that structure became the water resources community's greatest ally. As a consequence of Brezhnev's compartmentalization of the process, policy development was conducted virtually in the absence of independent high-level review. Of the many expert commissions organized by Gosplan and the State Committee on Science and Technology (GKNT) to examine the proposed diversion projects, none as wholly independent of the water resources community. Although the composition of these bodies was not chosen by Minvodkhoz, these commissions were nevertheless made up of, and often chaired by, prominent members of the water resources community.

In the early 1980s, for instance, Grigorii Voropaev, then director of the USSR Academy of Sciences's Institute of Water Problems, was the chair of Gosplan's State Expert Commission (GEK) subcommission on the "Technical and Economic Substantiation of the First Stage of the Siberian Rivers Diversion Project."

One of Voropaev's deputies on the subcommission was I.A. Shiklomanov, at the time director of the State Hydrology Institute. In the late 1970s, Voropaev served as the deputy chair of a second Gosplan subcommission that also investigated the Siberian project. That body was lead by D.Ia. Ratkovich, a colleague of Voropaev's at the Institute of Water Problems. A few years later, Voropaev would also head the USSR Academy of Sciences/GKNT Scientific Council on Comprehensive Problems of the Caspian Sea. Given its focus, this council's findings would have implications for the future of the northern diversion project. Finally, at about this same time, Polad Polad-Zade, then First Deputy Minister of Land Reclamation and Water Resources, served as chair of a GKNT scientific-technical commission on the territorial redistribution of water resources.

The problem posed by such assignments was that although the ministry and its organizational allies acknowledged the importance and necessity of making more efficient use of available water resources in the Soviet South, Minvodkhoz's overriding concern remained the final approval of the rivers diversion projects.[23] In addition, even though the Institute of Water Problems, for instance, prodded Minvodkhoz to develop plans that would limit the potential negative environmental and socioeconomic impact of the diversions, it too had much at stake in the projects' eventual approval. In light of these strong organizational interests, and the policy community's conviction that only grandiose projects could solve the problem of Soviet agriculture anyway, the likelihood that efficiency would be identified as a viable solution to the South's water deficit was slight.[24]

From the Soviet leadership's perspective, the logic of such a policy-making structure, in spite of these shortcomings, was clear. The water resources community's scientists and engineers were, after all, the experts. That they might allow organizational goals to interfere in the development of policy alternatives and in the shaping of the policy agenda does not appear to have occurred to anyone within the Soviet leadership, including the reform-minded Mikhail Gorbachev, who from 1978 through 1985 served as party secretary for agriculture.

It is misleading, however, to say that the policy-review process was the *exclusive* domain of those who favored the implementation of the diversion projects. All told, more than 150 organizations participated in the research and design effort at one point or another. Experts from the water resources community were the most important players in the policy process, but a number of organizations that stood to lose as a result of the projects' implementation were also invited to participate. Indeed, the diversions' critics were even allowed to voice some of their objections against the proposed projects.

This "legitimate" criticism, however, was limited to marginal issues. Critiques that threatened to weaken the projects' underlying justification were rarely tolerated. In short, even if a few policy outsiders were allowed to participate in the policy process, there could be little doubt that Minvodkhoz and its allies remained the most important players. Consequently, although the diversions' critics could affect policy on the fringes during this stage of the process, the specific direction and shape of policy were ultimately established by the water resources community.

Given the policy community's influence over the process, and the support that rivers diversion eventually gained within the Soviet leadership, few articles critical of the projects appeared in the mass media before glasnost. For the handful that were published, commentary was limited to specific features of the planned diversions. Broad attacks on the projects were prohibited.[25] As a consequence, the proposed diversions were rarely challenged in a public forum. In fact, in the years before Gorbachev came to power, only one such article appeared in the Soviet press, a piece by economist and demographer Viktor Perevedentsev. That this article was published at all was something of a fluke.

Perevedentsev reported that a high-ranking water resources expert, I.A. Gerardi (chief design engineer of the Siberian project), told him personally in the fall of 1979 that the water resources establishment would not allow the publication of negative articles about the diversions. Perevedentsev submitted his critique anyway in November of that year to the widely read weekly *Literaturnaia gazeta,* but to no avail. The article was published more than two years later, but only, Perevedentsev believes, because Gerardi's declining health had by that time confined him to a hospital bed. With the projects' most ardent defender out of the way, the article could now make its way past the censors.

Perevedentsev's experience, however, remained an isolated case. Even so, his article's publication shattered the image of consensus that the Soviet press had attempted to create.[26] Indeed, water resources specialists had been engaged in a lively debate with policy outsiders over the wisdom of the diversions since at least the early 1970s, long before the projects reached the party policy agenda. The arena for this conflict was not in the pages of the Soviet press, but rather in the meeting rooms of scientific conferences, far removed from the view of the Soviet public.

Disagreements among supporters and critics of the projects touched on a number of issues, including the diversions' possible environmental and socioeconomic effects, the role of Siberian scholars in the policy process, anxiety on the part of Siberians over "the fate of the water resources of the region, and of their wish to participate actively in the resolution of this difficult and complex problem," the methodology used by design organizations in evaluating the environmental impact of the diversions, complaints that design work was far ahead of the scientific research effort, other criticisms related to the work of design organizations, and a perceived lack of economic justification for the Siberian project.[27] Such criticism hindered Minvodkhoz's efforts to push the projects through, but the ministry's influence over the policy process ultimately prevailed. Ironically, for all of Brezhnev's efforts to rationalize decision making, he instead unwittingly created a policy process that prevented him from achieving that end.

Conclusion

If structure played a decisive role in the Soviet leadership's decisions to support the Siberian and northern diversions in the early 1980s, so too was it largely responsible for the projects' demise a few years later as a consequence of Gorbachev's efforts to open up the Soviet bureaucracy to public scrutiny through glasnost. Though Gorbachev had not consciously intended to target Minvodkhoz or the rivers diversion projects, the effect of glasnost, by opening up the policy process to actors who before had been prohibited from making meaningful contributions, was to wrench control of the process out of the hands of the Minvodkhoz-led water resources community. In contrast to their experiences under Brezhnev, the ministry's critics found that they could now attack Minvodkhoz and its allies with impunity.

Gorbachev had not opposed the projects when he came to power in March 1985 (and indeed, he seemed to favor them), but the debate that ensued as a result of glasnost prompted the party leadership to order a full policy review during the summer of 1986. Based on that review's findings, the party and the Soviet government decided to halt the construction of the northern project and to scrap plans for the implementation of the Siberian diversion. Scientific research on the question of rivers diversion was to continue, but the new, more open political climate ensured that the possibility of reviving either project was remote.[28]

Although the USSR has since collapsed, the lessons learned from the rivers diversion experience are of continuing relevance to post-Soviet Russia. This essay demonstrates how an effort on the part of the Brezhnev leadership to create a more rational policy process produced something quite different. By assigning a leading role to the water resources community, and at the same time limiting the access of non–water resources specialists, the Soviet leaders created a policy environment in which Minvodkhoz and its organizational allies could easily slant their advice in ways that were beneficial to the policy community but not necessarily to the country at large (though they appear to have sincerely believed that the diversions were in the USSR's best interests). If not for Gorbachev's restructuring of the policy process, there is little doubt that the projects would have been further implemented.

The close connections between policy structures and policy outcomes found in this essay are neither unique to the cases nor to the country studied, whether one considers other policy areas (such as the Baikal-Amur Mainline) or other authoritarian systems (for instance, China).[29] Examples of how structure can play a critical role in agenda setting and policy development can be identified in Western democracies as well. The American experience with respect to water resources management and development, for instance, shows a number of points in common with this study's findings.

As was true in the Soviet case, the American water resources establishment (led by the U.S. Army Corps of Engineers and the U.S. Bureau of Reclamation) found itself in a position where it too could control the policy process. The policy community's expertise was reason enough in the eyes of the U.S. Congress to turn the process over to the Corps' and Bureau's talented and well-regarded engineers. Not until the late 1960s, with the entrance of environmentalists into the process (and the institutionalization of their participation through the National Environmental Protection Act of 1969), were the Corps of Engineers and the Bureau of Reclamation forced to address the environmental and social concerns of those who had previously been shut out of the decision making.[30]

This essay ends, appropriately, on a cautionary note. The development and survival of democratic institutions in Russia alone will not ensure the protection of Siberia's fragile environment or its rich resources. Whether a political system is authoritarian or democratic, policy structures in both can produce outcomes that have the potential to exact a high price on nature and a region. As other essays in this volume suggest, throughout Russian and Soviet history central authorities have tended to view Siberia as a colony to be exploited. The critical decisions concerning economic development in the region were made in St. Petersburg and Moscow, not in Novosibirsk and Irkutsk.[31]

But the structure of the process helps determine the level of control any given actors might have over policy making and the degree to which their values and goals will predominate, whether they are bureaucrats, politicians, scientists, or members of Russia's new business elite. As Russia develops both economically and politically, there is little doubt that Siberia's vast resources will continue to be at the center of policy debates over their use, management, and protection. The character of these clashes and their outcomes will be shaped by the policy process's structure. Those who dominate the process will be in a position to control the destiny of the region and indeed, perhaps, all of Russia.

Notes

1. For arguments in favor of the diversions, see "Severnye vody—iugu" (an interview with I.A. Gerardi), *Pravda*, 2 July 1971, p. 6; N. Nekrasov and N. Razin, "Vody severa pomogut iugu," *Pravda*, 11 June 1978, p. 3; and S. Ziiadullaev, "Dlia polivnogo zemledeliia," *Ekonomicheskaia gazeta*, no. 5 (1981), p. 7.

2. See their speeches at the Sixth Congress of the Russian Republic Writers' Union, *Literaturnaia gazeta*, 18 December 1985, pp. 4, 6–7; and at the Eighth Congress of the USSR Writers Union, *Literaturnaia gazeta*, 2 July 1986, pp. 3–4, 9–10.

3. See, for example, M. Lemeshev, "Protiv techeniia," *Sovetskaia Rossiia*, 20 December 1985, p. 3; and A. Aganbegian et al., "Zemlia—glavnoe bogatstvo," *Pravda*, 12 February 1986, p. 3; and M. Volkov et al., *Pravda*, 29 July 1987, p. 3. On the anticipated economic losses of one southern Siberian region, see S. Maniankin (at the time CPSU committee first secretary of Omsk oblast), *Izvestiia*, 16 April 1985, p. 2.

4. See for instance, speeches by M.Kh. Khudaibergenov (then party first secretary of Khorezm oblast) and A.S. Sadykov (then president of the Uzbek Academy of Sciences) at the Twentieth Congress of the Communist Party of Uzbekistan, in *Pravda vostoka*, 5

February 1981, p. 4; and "Sibaral—kanal veka" (an interview with G.V. Voropaev), *Sovetskaia Kirgiziia,* 5 April 1985, p. 2.

5. On the northern diversion's progress, see the text of Iurii Bondarev's speech in *Literaturnaia gazeta,* 2 July 1986, p. 4. On the Siberian project, see "Nachali!: sdelan novyi shag v rabote po perebroske chasti stoka Sibirskikh rek v Sredniuiu Aziiu," *Pravda vostoka,* 9 January 1985, p. 1. For a discussion of the projects' removal from the policy agenda, see Michael Lee Bressler, "Agenda Setting and the Development of Soviet Water Resources Policy, 1965–1990: Structures and Processes" (Ph.D. dissertation, University of Michigan, 1992), ch. 5.

6. Murray Feshbach and Alfred Friendly, Jr., *Ecocide in the USSR: Health and Nature Under Siege* (New York: Basic Books, 1992), p. 43.

7. For a discussion of these and other issues, see Feshbach and Friendly, *Ecocide in the USSR;* John Massey Stewart, ed., *The Soviet Environment: Problems, Policies, and Politics* (Cambridge: Cambridge University Press, 1992); and Joan DeBardeleben, "Economic Reform and Environmental Protection in the USSR," *Soviet Geography,* vol. 31 (1990), pp. 237–56.

8. Two recent works on environmental degradation in the USSR reflect a growing appreciation of the potential impact of structure on policy. See Barbara Jancar, *Environmental Management in the Soviet Union and Yugoslavia* (Durham, NC: Duke University Press, 1987); and D.J. Peterson, *Troubled Lands: The Legacy of Soviet Environmental Destruction* (Boulder, CO: Westview Press, 1993).

9. This essay is based in part on research the author conducted in Moscow during the fall of 1990. Sources include articles from the Soviet press, scientific works, CPSU and government documents, internal documents of Gosplan and other organizations, as well as interviews with participants in the policy process (including academics, scientists, engineers, journalists, writers, editors, and highly placed officials within the Soviet bureaucracy).

10. See Roy A. Medvedev and Zhores A. Medvedev, *Khrushchev: The Years in Power* (New York: Columbia University Press, 1976).

11. For criticisms of Khrushchev's "subjectivism," see *Plenum Tsentral'nogo Komiteta Kommunisticheskoi Partii Sovetskogo Soiuza, 24–26 marta 1965 goda,* stenographic record (Moscow, 1965), passim. For Brezhnev's views on the role of specialists in the policy process, see his *Ob osnovnykh voprosakh ekonomicheskoi politiki KPSS na sovremennom etape: Rechi i doklady,* vol. 1 (Moscow, 1979), 2d ed., pp. 185, 202, 224, 279, 287, 336–37.

12. See Brezhnev, *Ob osnovnykh voprosakh ekonomicheskoi politiki KPSS na sovremennom etape,* p. 201.

13. In addition to Minvodkhoz and its associated research institutes, the water resources community included such prominent organizations as the USSR Academy of Sciences's Institute of Water Problems, sections of the Academy's Institute of Geography, the USSR Ministry of Energy and Electrification's research institute Gidroproekt, as well as a number of institutes located at the periphery in both the Russian Federation and the non-Russian republics. For a detailed examination of the policy community, see Bressler, "Agenda Setting and the Development of Soviet Water Resources Policy, 1965–1990," pp. 49–65.

14. For a discussion of this early phase in the policy process, see the memoirs of the first Minister of Land Reclamation and Water Resources, E.E. Alekseevskii, *Ia liubliu etu zemliu* (Moscow, 1988), pp. 176–81.

15. This reorganization occurred in September 1965. See *Resheniia partii i pravitel'stva po khoziaistvennym voprosam,* vol. 5 (Moscow, 1968), pp. 651, 655.

16. See Alekseevskii's speech to the CPSU Central Committee plenum, "O shirokom razvitii melioratsii zemel' dlia polucheniia vysokikh i ustoichivykh urozhaev zernovykh i drugikh sel'skokhoziaistvennykh kul'tur," *Pravda,* 28 May 1966, p. 3.

17. Brezhnev himself commented in a speech to the Twenty-fifth CPSU Congress that "never in a single five-year plan has our land encountered such unfavorable circumstances." Brezhnev, *Ob osnovnykh voprosakh ekonomicheskoi politiki KPSS na sovremennom etape,* vol. 2, p. 306.

18. Author interview, N.I. Koronkevich (Doctor of Geographical Sciences, Institute of Geography), 31 October 1990.

19. For an example of the policy community's views, see A.N. Voznesenskii, G.G. Gangardt, and I.A. Gerardi, "Principal Trends and Prospects of the Use of Water Resources in the USSR," *Soviet Geography,* vol. 16 (1975), pp. 291–301. Article originally published in *Vodnye resursy,* no. 3 (1974), pp. 3–14.

20. For Brezhnev's views on Minvodkhoz, see his *Ob osnovnykh voprosakh ekonomicheskoi politiki KPSS na sovremennom etape,* vol. 1, p. 201, and vol. 2, pp. 102, 172.

21. See *KPSS v rezoliutsiiakh i resheniiakh s''ezdov, konferentsii i plenumov TsK,* vol. 13. (Moscow, 1987), p. 54.

22. See *KPSS v rezoliutsiiakh,* vol. 14, p. 296.

23. For evidence of this, see Otakhon Latifi, *Pravda,* 26 November 1984, p. 2.

24. In fact, as early as April 1975 (nearly a year before the rivers diversion projects reached the CPSU policy agenda), the participants of a conference hosted by the USSR Academy of Sciences's Scientific Council on Problems of the Biosphere, the Institute of Geography, and the Institute of Water Problems expressed the view that the more efficient use of southern water resources "could not be viewed as an alternative" to the diversion of northern water. See *Rekomendatsii vsesoiuznogo rabochego soveshchaniia po nauchnomu prognozu vliianiia mezhbasseinogo pereraspredeleniia rechnogo stoka na prirodnye usloviia evropeiskoi territorii i sredinnogo regiona SSSR* (Moscow, 1975), p. 4. See also a report of this conference in *Vodnye resursy,* no. 3 (1976), pp. 166–68.

25. For example, see V. Podoplelov and A. Bratsev, "Shestoe uslovie," *Literaturnaia gazeta,* 17 November 1976, p. 10; and I. Rusinov, "Proekt trebuet proverki," *Trud,* 6 December 1977, p. 3. See also author interviews, V.I. Perevedentsev (senior researcher, Institute of the International Workers Movement), 5 November 1990; and Koronkevich, 15 November 1990.

26. V. Perevedentsev, "Zamysel zamanchiv, no . . . ," *Literaturnaia gazeta,* 10 March 1982, p. 11. See also author's interview with Perevedentsev, 5 November 1990.

27. See A.A. Bostandzhoglo and B.G. Fedorov, "Vsesoiuznoe soveshchanie po kompleksnoi programme ekonomicheskogo sotsial'nogo razvitiia sredinnogo regiona v sviazi s territorial'nym pereraspredeleniem vodnykh resursov," *Vodnye resursy,* no. 6 (1982), pp. 178–79; A.Z. Amstsislavskii et al., "Simpozium po okhrane rechnykh vod Sibiri," *Vodnye resursy,* no. 1 (1979), pp. 199–201; N.I. Koronkevich et al., "Okhrana rechnykh vod Sibiri," *Izvestiia AN SSSR, seriia geograficheskaia,* no. 2 (1979), pp. 154–55; S.M. Kudriavtseva, "Soveshchanie po problemam i perspektivam vodnogo blagoustroistva territorii zapadnoi Sibiri," *Vodnye resursy,* no. 5 (1980), pp. 201–3; and Perevedentsev, "Zamysel zamanchiv, no . . . ," p. 11. According to Perevedentsev (in a conversation with the author), questions concerning the Siberian project's economic justification were raised during a fall 1979 conference by future Gorbachev economic advisor Abel Aganbegian.

28. A discussion of the factors that prompted Gorbachev's change of mind can be found in Michael L. Bressler, "Reform from Above, Innovation from Below," unpublished manuscript.

29. For a brief discussion of the BAM, see Philip Pryde, *Environmental Management in the Soviet Union* (Cambridge: Cambridge University Press, 1991), pp. 236–38. On the impact of structure and process on policy outcomes in China, see Kenneth Lieberthal and

Michael Oksenberg, *Policy Making in China: Leaders, Structures, and Processes* (Princeton: Princeton University Press, 1988). Of particular interest is their chapter on China's answer (if not in function, at least in scale) to the rivers diversion projects, the recently approved Three Gorges dam.

30. See Daniel McCool, *Command of the Waters: Iron Triangles, Federal Water Development, and Indian Water* (Berkeley: University of California Press, 1987); Marc Reisner, *Cadillac Desert: The American West and Its Disappearing Water* (New York: Penguin Books, 1986); John Ferejohn, *Pork Barrel Politics: Rivers and Harbors Legislation, 1947–1968* (Stanford: Stanford University Press, 1974); and Arthur Maass, *Muddy Waters: The Army Engineers and the Nation's Rivers* (Cambridge, MA: Harvard University Press, 1951).

31. Even now, as the locus of decision-making authority shifts from the center to the periphery within the Russian Federation, the results have been less than satisfactory. When forced to make a choice between much needed short-term economic growth versus environmental protection over the long haul, local decision makers have often favored the former over the latter. See Peterson, *Troubled Lands*, pp. 182–84.

Whose Environment?

A Case Study of Forestry Policy
in Russia's Maritime Province

Elizabeth Wishnick

Concern for the environment has always been a political statement in Russia. More than twenty years ago, when a small group of scientists and writers in Siberia spoke out to protect the unique ecosystem of Lake Baikal, they helped lay the groundwork for glasnost. In the 1980s, concern about the impact of nuclear power on the environment and public health fueled nationalist sentiment in Ukraine and the Baltic republics. Since the collapse of the USSR, control over the vast natural resources in Siberia and the Russian Far East has led to a power struggle between Moscow and the regions, and among competing interests within the regions themselves.

While the Yeltsin government has taken some important steps in the environmental area, the economic chaos and political decentralization that have accompanied the reform process have complicated efforts to protect the environment. Before the introduction of market mechanisms, vested interests often had a decisive influence on development strategies that totally disregarded costs to the environment. At the same time as federal enforcement authority has weakened since late 1991, however, the number of competing claims to control over resources has grown.

Although new laws have been passed to protect key resources such as forests, these laws have failed to untangle the overlapping responsibilities of the federal, regional, and local governments and have been unable to come to terms with the impact of the market on the protection and use of natural resources.

This essay presents a study of the political, economic, environmental, and foreign policy interests involved in forestry in Russia's Maritime province (*Primorskii krai*). The forestry sector was selected because the forests in this area constitute a unique ecosystem, which, although relatively unscathed, may be a prime target for exploitation in these difficult economic times.[1] Center–periphery conflict is not unique to forestry, however, as other essays in this volume on the struggle for economic and political control over coal and oil amply demonstrate.

A first section of this chapter explores what is at stake: the fragile forest ecosystem, problems facing foresters who try to protect it, and the difficult economic situation confronting the timber industry. Efforts to protect the environment through legislation are examined in a second section. While well intentioned, the new legislation has served to fuel the power struggle between regions and the center about control over natural resources. A third section examines the impact of these tensions on the protection of forest resources, while a fourth section presents a case study of a forestry joint venture between Hyundai and the Maritime province timber industry to illustrate the conflicts of political, economic, and environmental interests found in the forestry sector. A final section offers some general points about center–periphery relations and regionalism in the Maritime province, particularly concerning the different interests of the center and the region in foreign economic relations with Northeast Asia.

Uneasy Coexistence: Forests, Foresters, and Loggers

Siberia contains more than half of the world's coniferous forests and two-fifths of its temperate forests. Spanning an area the size of the continental United States, Siberian forests amount to one-fifth of the world's total forested area. The Maritime province, located in the southern part of the Russian Far East, hosts a mixed conifer/broad-leaved forest that is unique to the region. A wealth of plant species from both the northern taiga and southern subtropics can be found in the southern half of the Maritime province, including a large number that grow only in this area and many species that date back 65 million years ago to the Tertiary period.[2] The region is also home to an exotic mixture of rare fauna that came from the forests of East and Southeast Asia to escape glaciation.[3] Several endangered species, such as the Siberian tiger and the Amur leopard, are among the fauna. In an effort to protect these species, five state nature reserves (zapovedniki) are located in the Maritime province.[4]

In addition to maintaining biodiversity and a habitat for endangered species, the forests of the Maritime province provide a home for native peoples and a place for recreation and food gathering for all the local inhabitants. The forests also help prevent soil erosion and mitigate global warming. Despite the scientific, economic, and social importance of forests, in recent years the mounting economic crisis and growing political confusion have hampered efforts to protect the Maritime province's unique ecosystem.

The economic crisis has hit the forestry sector in the Maritime province very hard. Resources for forest fire prevention and day-to-day management have dried up. Every year several million acres of forest land in Russia burn because of fires started by people.[5] Foresters lack the aviation and ground equipment necessary to fight fires.[6] Underpaid and understaffed, they are fighting a losing battle against common problems such as safeguarding the forests from harmful insects, a particular concern in the Far East, and preventing poaching.[7] Some game wardens have been known to hunt the animals they were supposed to protect and then sell the skins for several thousand dollars—a real temptation, considering their salaries often come to less than $20 per month.[8] A skin from the endangered Amur tiger can bring in $10,000, while the fine for poaching is only 4 million rubles (about $1,300).[9] Aleksei Iablokov, chairman of the Ecological Commission of the Russian Security Council, noted that "poaching has today reached unprecedented scales. Sometimes it is easier to halt the implementation of broad-scale ecologically harmful projects . . . than to collar one person setting off on a hunt."[10]

Many of the most aggressive poachers are Chinese traders interested in glands from various rare animals, such as the Himalayan brown bear, for use in traditional medicines.[11] Chinese involvement in poaching has exacerbated Russian-Chinese relations in the Maritime province, where the growing number of Chinese traders has already led to considerable dissatisfaction. The local newspapers have been publishing articles decrying the Chinese "economic siege" in the region and alleging that most of the Chinese traders "contrive by any means, legal or illegal, to fill their purses by engaging in free trade in our markets."[12] The local population feels exploited by the tendency of officials and businesses to trade natural resources such as timber for cheap Chinese consumer goods. Moreover, industrial production in the Maritime province has been falling in all sectors since 1991, in part because local enterprises are unable to obtain needed raw materials.[13]

The turndown in the timber industry is symptomatic of the depressed state of the local economy. Since timber production is no longer under the control of the federal Forestry Service, which is now only responsible for forest management and protection, the newly created private forestry interests are experiencing a severe shortage of capital for investment in processing technology and infrastructure.[14] As a consequence, they mainly supply raw logs, mostly for foreign markets, while local areas experience shortages of processed wood products. In 1992, timber processing in Russia was down by 20 percent and overall wood exports fell by 11 percent.[15]

An impoverished timber industry does not necessarily mean a reprieve for the environment, however, since many ecological problems are actually caused by inefficient and wasteful processing methods that the timber companies lack the funds to correct. Because processed timber is in greater demand overseas and attracts a higher price, improved processing techniques would be beneficial for both the timber industry and the health of the forests.

According to a Russian government official, approximately 50 percent of the volume of timber harvested in Russian forests is wasted during felling, processing, shipping, and transportation. Improvements in these areas would mean cutting fewer trees and reducing Russia's dependence on foreign processing.[16] As the Minister for Environmental Protection and Natural Resources, Viktor Danilov-Danil'ian, stated, "the most effective and economical means of protecting the environment is the rational and sustainable use of each of the resources."[17]

The boreal forests are slow growing, and maintaining a stable level of forest cover through replanting is particularly important. Valerii Shubin, head of the Forestry Service, admits that forest regeneration has been given scant attention in recent years.[18] Things were no better under centralized planning, however. When replanting efforts were made in the past, at times they were completely counterproductive. For example, seeds for pine trees from western Russia were planted in the Khabarovsk region, where this species does not grow.[19]

New Legislation and Environmental Protection

Beginning in the late 1980s, a series of attempts have been made to include incentives for environmental protection in legislation. The 1987 Law on State Enterprises, for example, mandated that enterprises pay for the natural resources they use and reimburse localities for damage to the environment.[20] The 1992 Law on the Protection of the Environment further defined the payment of fees for resource use and fines for violations, required that environmental impact statements (*ekspertizy*) be conducted, and provided financial incentives for the use of "clean" technology.[21]

A new Forestry Law was passed in March 1993 to enhance the protection of Russian forests.[22] Like the Law on Environmental Protection, the Forestry Law purports to introduce market elements into forest management. Russian and foreign commercial loggers must be licensed by local authorities and pay fees for short- or long-term leases up to fifty years. The new law also specifically prohibits monopolistic practices and advocates equal access to forest resources. Timber companies are responsible for the environmental health of the forests they contract to use and may be fined for violations.[23]

Despite its good intentions, the new Forestry Law's hesitancy to fully embrace market mechanisms limits its ability to set incentives for forest protection.[24] Without the ability to purchase forest lands, timber companies would have little incentive to invest in regeneration, for example, since they would not reap any of the benefits of replanting before their fifty-year lease expired.

The law's inadequate delineation of the responsibilities of the federal, regional, and local authorities creates equally serious problems.[25] All three levels of government are supposed to manage the forests jointly, but local authorities are in charge of granting logging licenses and the federal and regional governments have no right to intervene. Local authorities also have the right to set the fines for violators of the Forestry Law. Given the dire state of the economy, cash-poor local governments may set unreasonably low fines to maintain logging activities or be easily bribed by foreign companies.[26]

Although the new Forestry Law applies in its entirety to foreign companies, the economic situation gives them an unfair advantage in certain areas. For example, Article Thirty specifically forbids monopolistic practices in forest use, but it would be difficult for a local timber company to outbid a foreign company because of the low value of the ruble.[27]

The Struggle for Control Over Forest Resources

The vast resources of Siberia and the Russian Far East and their great distance from the central government have led to pressures for autonomy since the early nineteenth century.[28] In recent years, local authorities in Siberia and the Russian Far East have taken advantage of the center's loss of control over political and economic activities in the regions to demand a greater say in the management and use of their resources. In Aleksei Iablokov's view, parochialism represents a very serious threat to environmental protection efforts. He contended that "local soviets appear not as guarantors of the preservation of nature but initiators of its destruction. The cause of such a situation is the . . . lack of a strong state authority capable of organizing inexhaustible use of nature in the interests of the entire society."[29]

Control over natural resources is a political issue in Siberia and the Russian Far East because of the structure of the region's economy. In Michael Bradshaw's view, "Siberia and the Far East exhibit all the characteristics of the classical 'resources frontier region.' "[30] In 1989, Siberia and the Far East accounted for almost 70 percent of the total output of Russia's resource-producing and processing industries.[31] These resources are then shipped either to European Russia or abroad, in exchange for machines to aid western Russia's manufacturing base.

According to Gennadii Alekseitsev, a forestry specialist on the presidential staff, there is strong disagreement between the Russian government's vision of forestry management and the desire of local and regional authorities to assume greater control over forest resources. Local and regional governments think that the federal authorities should restrict their involvement to protection efforts and infrastructure maintenance.[32] This is a reaction to the previous system of federal management whereby the center both paid for forestry protection and collected all the revenues from local forestry use.[33] The excessive devolution of control to the regions, however, could adversely affect the resolution of problems with inter-regional implications, such as the privatization of forested land, forestry research, and the system of protection networks.[34]

Conflicts over forestry issues do not always stem from a clear dispute between federal and regional policy makers. In the neighboring Khabarovsk and Amur regions, for example, the operation of North Korean logging camps has pitted local deputies against Foreign Ministry officials and human rights advocates. According to a joint venture agreement between Russia and North Korea signed in 1968, the 20,000 North Koreans working in the logging camps are subject to North Korean labor regulations. Although officially volunteers, the workers are in effect held captive by North Korean security agents based in the camps, who confiscate their passports. Due to the deplorable conditions in the camps, some of the North Korean workers have tried to escape or have become involved in poaching, and North Korean security agents have been allowed to apprehend them. While there has been some public opposition to the camps and a few local deputies have opposed the renewal of the agreement on human rights grounds, thus far economic arguments have been more persuasive, since Russia receives two-thirds of the wood cut by the North Koreans. According to the head of the Khabarovsk regional administration, Petr Titkov, without the North Korean loggers the forestry sector would collapse.[35]

Moreover, the regional authorities believe that human rights issues are the Foreign Ministry's responsibility, not theirs.[36] The joint venture agreement expired at the end of 1993 but was extended to allow the two countries to work out a new agreement.[37] In recent rounds of negotiations, the Russian Foreign Ministry has addressed the human rights issue, arguing that the North Koreans should have the same legal rights as Russian workers.[38]

Conflicts of Interest: Hyundai's Joint Venture at Svetlaia and Bikin

Greater economic autonomy for the regions may have unintended social and environmental consequences. The case study described below examines the conflicts of interest that may arise among federal environmental authorities, regional and local officials, native peoples, and foreign investors over forestry issues.

In 1991, the Hyundai Corporation of South Korea entered into a joint venture with the Maritime province State Timber Industry (*Primorlesprom*). The joint venture was awarded a thirty-year concession to cut one million cubic meters of roundwood a year for thirty years on 600,000 acres on the Bikin River, on the east side of the Sikhote-Alin mountain range near the city of Svetlaia. The Svetlaia venture was originally supposed to cut only dead and dying trees from the old-growth forest, which contains protected species such as Korean pine, but it has reportedly proceeded to clear-cut the area.[39] Svetlaia's logging concession also overlaps with the northern range of the Amur tiger, an endangered species. Only 250 to 500 of the animals are left in the Russian Far East, and habitat loss due to logging has contributed to the decline in their numbers.[40]

The Russian government has proven powerless to regulate Svetlaia's activities. The joint venture went ahead with logging before the Maritime province and federal Russian environmental impact statements were carried out.[41] Even though the environmental impact statements were negative, the logging continued with the support of local and regional authorities, who welcome the revenues it brings in.[42] By some accounts, Hyundai bribed local officials, giving them new jeeps, for example, to garner support for local timber operations.[43] Since the South Korean conglomerate is unwilling to invest in timber-processing infrastructure in the region, preferring to export raw logs to Japan and other countries, the Maritime province could only expect to reap short-term profits from the venture.[44]

In the spring of 1992, Hyundai tried to expand its operations into the Pozharskii district, near the Bikin watershed, which is reserved for the native Udege people as a hunting ground. The Udeges, related to descendants of the Manchus, are hunters who have traditionally lived in the Sikhote-Alin mountains and along the coast of the Sea of Japan.[45] Although the local government in Pozharskii district and the Udege were opposed to logging in the Bikin valley, on 21 July 1992 the governor of Vladivostok at the time, Vladimir Kuznetsov, gave Hyundai permission to move its operations there and log 500,000 cubic meters of timber along the Bikin River annually.[46]

The governor was acting on shaky legal ground, however. An April 1992 decree on the protection of the traditional homelands of the small peoples of the North stipulated that the Bikin valley, a traditional hunting and fishing area for Udege people, could not be developed without their consent.[47] The Udege were prepared to put up a fight. In August 1992, when Hyundai trucks reached the boundary of the Udege lands, they were met by a group of armed Udege hunters and Cossacks who were protesting the logging.[48] The Udeges picketed the Maritime province governor's office and sent a representative to then Vice President Rutskoi to protest the governor's decision to go ahead with logging without their consent.[49]

The Udege, joined by the Nanai people and the Socio-Ecological Union, protested against the governor's decision.[50] As a result of their efforts, the Maritime province soviet passed a law overturning the governor's decision on 2 September 1992. The Svetlaia joint venture protested, and later that month the Maritime province court ruled that the soviet had exceeded its powers in overturning the governor's order.[51] Then the Maritime province soviet appealed to the Russian Federation court, which also upheld the order. Finally, they appealed to the Supreme Court of the Russian Federation.[52] On 27 November 1992, the Supreme Court ruled against Hyundai's bid to log in the Bikin valley and held that the Maritime province soviet had the right to overturn the governor's decree granting the joint venture logging rights in this area.[53]

In 1992, the Svetlaia joint venture cut only 190,000 cubic meters of roundwood, down from one million in 1991—Hyundai had hoped to extend its logging operations in the Bikin valley to make the joint venture more profitable by expanding the yield. The Hyundai Corporation, contending that its losses have reached $7 million, may file a claim for compensation with a commercial mediation agency in London. Maritime province officials, for their part, fear that the controversy over Bikin will put a brake on foreign investment in the timber industry in the region.[54] Some environmentalists have been concerned that regional officials would allow logging to go on in the Bikin valley despite the Supreme Court ruling. In early 1993, however, a Supreme Soviet commission came to Maritime province to examine the Bikin case and affirmed that logging should not take place in the valley.[55] Nonetheless, during a recent inspection visit, Greenpeace reported that harmful logging practices continue at the original Svetlaia site.[56]

The Supreme Court ruling in favor of the Udege will not solve the problem of conflicts of interest and overlapping responsibilities in forestry law, since the decisions of the courts cannot create new laws or regulations.[57] What the Bikin case shows, however, is that another check exists against environmental violations—the watchful eye of the public. While the Forestry Law did not allow for public participation in forest management, the Udege used other laws to make their voice heard.

How interested is the public in environmental issues? According to a 1992 poll, the state of the environment ranked fifth for citizens of Vladivostok and seventh for residents of the Far East as a whole. Not surprisingly, price increases and the lack of goods were the top concerns in all the areas surveyed.[58] According to Mikhail Kozeltsev, an economist at Moscow State University, the environmental movement was successful in closing plants that were harmful to the environment, only to realize later that the sole producer of a necessary good had just been eliminated. As a result, shortages worsened, particularly in the pharmaceutical sector.[59]

In addition, analysts who have followed the development of environmental movements in the former Soviet Union and the former Soviet bloc see the relative decline in public interest in the environment as a phase in the political development in these countries. While environmental movements in east Central Europe and the former Soviet Union were an effective component of the opposition forces that ended Communist rule, since the collapse of Communism environmentalists involved in political life are having difficulty adjusting to new tasks, such as governing and building democratic institutions.[60]

Environmentalists argue, however, that the public would be more concerned about environmental issues if people had greater access to information and more involvement in decisions that affect their local environment. Aleksandr Lobiakin, a biologist and head of the Far Eastern air base in charge of putting out forest fires, claims that the Russian environmental protection system does not perform as well as the American one only because it lacks one fundamental component: input from environmental organizations and the public.[61] One of the main criticisms the Socio-Ecological Union expressed about the new Forestry Law, for example, was that unlike the earlier law, the new version failed to provide for public participation in the protection of forest resources.[62]

Some American non-governmental (NGOs) organizations have become involved with efforts to promote public participation in environmental protection. ISAR received funds from the Agency for International Development for partnerships between Russian and American NGOs that would encourage public participation in environmental protection.[63] Thanks to electronic mail links with their Russian counterparts, for example, American NGOs were able to publicize the controversy over Hyundai's effort to log the Bikin valley.[64]

Far from Moscow, Close to Asia

As the Bikin case demonstrated, many people in the Maritime province perceive foreign investment in the forestry sector as a lifeline for a struggling industry, but such activities have adverse environmental costs. Because the Maritime province borders on the Sea of Japan and shares riverine boundaries with China and North Korea, opportunities for joint ventures and participation in transnational economic development projects are likely to grow. In addition, due to the high transportation costs involved in trade with central Russia and other states of the former Soviet Union, the region has been pushed into greater cooperation with neighboring Asian states.

While foreign economic relations with Northeast Asian states lower transportation costs, they have not been problem free. Traders in the Maritime province appreciate the higher quality of the goods from Japan, South Korea, and Taiwan but often lack the hard currency to purchase them. China, on the other hand, has been willing to conduct trade on a barter basis, but increasingly the goods that are brought in from the northern provinces are perceived in the Maritime province as being goods of last resort, that is, worth buying only if the higher-quality goods from the other Asian states are beyond reach. Popular attitudes regarding trade with China also have been colored by problems with illegal immigration and crime (including wildlife poaching) associated with the influx of Chinese "shuttle-traders," who enter Russia on tourist visas to sell their wares.[65]

Because important natural resources often are located in border regions in Northeast Asia, economic and environmental issues are tightly linked. Environmental problems have led to friction between Russia and its neighbors over maintaining shared resources such as the Amur River, Russia's river boundary with China, and the Sea of Japan. Residents of the Maritime province are concerned over water pollution generated by the much larger population on the Chinese side of the Amur, while Japan has protested the Russian Pacific Fleet's dumping of nuclear waste in the Sea of Japan.

As friction has developed between the Maritime province and its neighbors over a range of issues, residents in the region have been quick to criticize Moscow's foreign policy toward Northeast Asia as being insensitive to regional problems. Inadequate information about the Russian-Chinese border talks, for example, led to an outcry in the Maritime province administration in the summer of 1993 over Moscow's purported intention to hand over some of the region's territory to the Chinese. Now Foreign Ministry officials grant interviews to the regional press to explain Russia's positions at the border talks and raise regional concerns such as crime and illegal immigration in meetings with their Chinese counterparts. In other areas, however, the region has been less successful in influencing Moscow's policies. To reduce Russian dumping of nuclear waste in the Sea of Japan, the Japanese proposed cooperating on a project to store the waste. While Vladivostok has shown interest in the idea, Moscow has expressed little enthusiasm for it.[66]

Despite new legislative efforts to protect the environment, the chaotic political and economic climate makes environmental protection more difficult. Federal enforcement mechanisms are weak, and local leaders are often more concerned with short-term economic gain and political advantage in their struggle with the center about control over natural resources. Many regions in the Russian Far East, such as the Maritime province, feel increasingly cut off from Moscow due to high transportation costs and divergent interests and seek instead to expand economic ties with their neighbors in Northeast Asia. Increased foreign investment and trade may boost the local economy, but they also leave the region's resources open to exploitation by foreign companies and unscrupulous traders. Local populations, such as the Udege in the Bikin case, however, have learned to publicize their concerns and will help remind their leaders that control over fragile resources such as forests involves responsibilities as well as rights.

Notes

1. In 1992, lumber accounted for the second largest share of the region's hard currency export earnings. Fish products took the largest share. Center for Russia in Asia, *RA Report*, July 1993, p. 43.
2. Algirdas Knystautas, *The Natural History of the USSR* (New York: McGraw-Hill, 1987), pp. 25, 116–19.
3. Ibid., pp. 119–34.
4. *Zapovedniki* are biological preserves and research areas which do not allow tourism. The largest in the Maritime province, Sikhote-Alin (347,532 hectares), has been designated a world biosphere reserve according to the UN's Man and the Biosphere Program. Philip R. Pryde and Victor L. Mote, "Environmental Constraints and Biosphere Protection in the Russian Far East," in Allan Rodgers, ed., *The Soviet Far East* (London, New York: Routledge, 1990), pp. 47–51.
5. Liubov' Latypova, "Na Dal'nem Vostoke ozhidaetsia rekordnoe chislo pozharov," *Izvestiia*, 16 April 1993, p. 4; Carl Reidel, "Back to the Future in the Land of Ghenghis Khan," *American Forests*, May–June 1992, p. 22.
6. Interview with Valerii Aleksandrovich Shubin, RSFSR Ministry of Forestry (now called Forest Service), by Konstantin Klimenko, editor in chief of *Ekologicheskaia gazeta*, no. 11–12, 1991, p. 6, in JPRS-TEN–92–008, 5 May 1992, p. 75.
7. Roza Budrina, "Les gubiat—ne shchepki letiat," *Rossiiskie vesti*, 4 May 1993, p. 3.
8. Suzanne Possehl, "Russia and America Team Up to Save Endangered Tiger," *The New York Times*, 31 August 1993.

9. B.J. Chisholm, "Cooperation in the Taiga: The Key to Saving the Amur Tiger," *Surviving Together,* Spring 1994, p. 36.

10. Interview with Aleksei Iablokov, "In Rescuing We Are Rescued!" *Kul'tura,* 24 April 1993, p. 3; in JPRS-TEN-93-014, 28 May 1993, p. 62.

11. Dorinda Elliott and Daniel Glick, "The Wasteland," *Newsweek,* 26 July 1993, p. 28.

12. Vladimir Shcherbakov, " 'Velikii brat' k nam tianet ruki: Kitaiskaia ekspansiia v Primorskom krae Rossii," *Vladivostok,* 1 September 1993, pp. 1, 5.

13. Center for Russia in Asia, *RA Report,* July 1993, p. 35.

14. Leonid Zavarskii, "Lesopromyshlenniki obsuzhdali svoe budushchee," *Kommersant,* no. 44, 11 March 1993; interview with Peter Voronkov, Chief Forestry Economist at the All-Russian Scientific Research Institute of Silviculture and Forest Mechanization, October 1992, in Paul Soler-Sala, "Institutions and Trends in the Russian Forestry Sector During a Time of Great Transition: A Set of Interviews with Russian Foresters, September 1992–March 1993," report prepared for the Office of International Forestry, USDA-Forest Service, Washington, DC, p. 24.

15. O. Borisov, "Tendentsii neuteshitel'ny," *Lesnaia gazeta,* 21 January 1993, p. 1.

16. Interview with Aleksandr Eremeev, Deputy Chief of the Russian Federation's Department of Nature Use, Ecology, and Health Protection, 11 December 1992, in Soler-Sala, p. 118. On transportation problems, see P. Dubynin, "Kak by ne sgnila," *Lesnaia gazeta,* 27 April 1993, p. 3.

17. V.I. Danilov-Danil'ian, "Okhrane prirody—edinuiu politiku," *Lesnaia gazeta,* 13 April 1993, p. 2.

18. Speech by V. Shubin to Presidium of Council of Ministers, "Gosudarstvennaia programma lesovosstanovleniia v Rossii," *Lesnaia gazeta,* 14 August 1993, p. 1.

19. A. Khoroshilov, "Za byloe velichie taigi," *Lesnaia gazeta,* 14 August 1993, p. 2.

20. Law of the USSR on the State Enterprise (Association), *Pravda* and *Izvestiia,* 1 July 1987, pp. 1–4; in *Current Digest of the Soviet Press,* vol. 39, no. 31, 1987, p. 17.

21. Law on Protection of the Environment, *Rossiiskaia gazeta,* 3 March 1992, pp. 3–6; in JPRS-TEN-92-007, 15 April 1992, pp. 57–79. Enforcement is likely to be a problem. On this point, see Andrew R. Bond and Matthew J. Sagers, "Some Observations on the Russian Federation Environmental Protection Law," *Post-Soviet Geography,* September 1992, p. 472.

22. "Osnovy lesnogo zakonodatel'stva Rossiiskoi Federatsii [Forestry Law]," *Rossiiskaia gazeta,* 17 April 1993, pp. 10–12. For an analysis of the law, see Julia Levin, "Russian Forest Laws—Scant Protection During Troubled Times," *Ecology Law Quarterly,* vol. 19, 1992, pp. 688–89, 712–14.

23. Forestry Law, p. 11. Enforcing the forestry law is likely to be difficult since it does not include criminal penalties or make officials personally liable. See Levin, p. 713.

24. Interview with Peoples' Deputy Vladimir Ageevich Tikhonov, "Snova vremenshchiki?" *Lesnaia gazeta,* 11 February 1993, p. 1; L. Bolodina, "Zakon—taiga, kto khoziain?" *Spasenie,* no. 4, January 1993, p. 1.

25. For a discussion of this problem, see Iu. Kukuev, "Novyi zakon—novye zaboty," *Lesnaia gazeta,* 15 May 1993, p. 1; L. Mazurova, "Sovety mogut vse," *Lesnaia gazeta,* 26 January 1993, p. 1. On the legal confusion, see Iablokov interview in *Kul'tura,* p. 61.

26. Alexei Grigoriev, "Russia's New Forestry Act," *Surviving Together,* Summer 1993, pp. 19–21. Grigoriev is a forestry specialist with the Socio-Ecological Union.

27. Interviews with two of the authors of the Forestry Law, Olga Krirodagova and Yurii Kukuev, in Soler-Sala, p. 111; and Alexey Grigoriev, "Critique of Proposed Basis for Russian Forestry Law," in Soler-Sala, p. 234.

28. "Panel on Siberia: Economic and Territorial Issues," *Soviet Geography,* June 1991, p. 368.

29. Iablokov interview in Kul'tura, p. 61.

30. Michael Bradshaw, "Siberia Poses a Challege to Russian Federalism," RFE/RL Research Report, 16 October 1992, p. 8.

31. Ibid., p. 9. For example, Siberia and the Russian Far East produced 30.6 percent of Russia's timber, wood, and paper in 1990. The share of the Russian Far East (of which the Maritime province is a part) was 7.4 percent.

32. Interview with Gennadii Alekseistev, in Soler-Sala, p. 10.

33. Interview with Aleksandr Eremeev, Deputy Chief of the Russian Federation's Department of Nature Use, Ecology, and Health Protection of the Population, in Soler-Sala, p. 117. Eremeev argues that the current trend is to develop a system whereby local governments pay for a substantial portion of forest protection and management activities but reap the benefits from their area's forest resources. The federal government's main role is in forestry protection enforcement and management policy.

34. Interview with Yurii Kukuev, Assistant Director of the Forest Fund Department of the Russian Forestry Committee, in Soler-Sala, p. 111.

35. Mikhail Kozhykhov, "Drovoseki Kim Il Sena [Kim Il Sung] vse-taki ostanutsia v Sibiri, iz kotoroi pri zhelanii mozhno sbezhat' v Iuzhnuiu Koreiu," Izvestiia, 12 May 1994, p. 3. The timber cut by the North Korean workers is 25 percent cheaper than timber cut by Russians. Most of the logs are then sold abroad for badly needed hard currency. On the North Korean logging camps, see Jeff Lilley, "Great Leader's Gulag," Far Eastern Economic Review, 9 September 1993, pp. 21–22; O. Borisov, "Lesozagotovki: Rossiia-KNDR," Lesnaia gazeta, 18 March 1993.

36. Boris Reznik, "Strogo sekretnye koreiskie ob'ekty v russkoi taige," Izvestiia, 26 March 1994, p. 4.

37. Russian Far East Update, May 1994, p. 11.

38. Kozhykhov, p. 3.

39. Hokkaido Shimbun, 8 November 1992, in RA Report, January 1993, p. 85; David Gordon and Antony Scott, "The Russian Timber Rush," Amicus, Fall 1992, p. 15; "Foreign Logging Threatens Siberian Tiger and Its Forests," Surviving Together, Spring 1992, p. 13; "Bikin Valley Forest Preservation Becomes International Issue," Surviving Together, Fall/Winter 1992, p. 19.

40. Possehl, p. C4.

41. Interview with Alexei Grigoriev, January 1993, in Soler-Sala, p. 124.

42. Levin, p. 692; Gordon and Scott, p. 15.

43. Elliott and Glick, p. 30.

44. Grigoriev interview in Soler-Sala, p. 123.

45. James Forsyth, A History of the Peoples of Siberia: Russia's North Asian Colony, 1581–1990 (Cambridge: Cambridge University Press, 1992), p. 211. The 1989 census reported that there were 2,011 Udege. Utro Rossii, 20 August 1993, cited in RA Report, January 1994, p. 143.

46. "Bikin Valley Forest Preservation . . . ," p. 19; "Russian Supreme Court Rules Against Hyundai Logging Operation," Surviving Together, Spring 1993, p. 32. According to Alexei Grigoriev, Hyundai wanted to expand to an area in the Bikin valley that has an extremely high forest fire risk. In his view, if urgent measures are not taken to protect the area from fires, Hyundai's proposal to harvest the trees may be the lesser of the two evils. Personal communication, January 1994, and interview in Soler-Sala, p. 123.

47. The decree also stipulates that the small peoples of the North have the right to conclude agreements and licenses for the use of renewable resources. Ukaz Prezidenta Rossiiskoi Federatsii, "O neotlozhnykh merakh po zashchite mest prozhivaniia i khoziaistvennoi deiatel'nosti malochislennykh narodov Severa," Rossiiskie vesti, 24 April 1992, p. 4. Also see "Native Peoples Gain Power," Far East Update, December 1992, p. 7.

48. Elliot and Glick, p. 30; "Bikin Valley Forest Preservation . . . ," p. 19.

49. *Far East Update,* September 1992, p. 10.

50. The Nanai, like the Udege, are descendents of the Manchus. They live along the Amur River in neighboring Khabarovsk krai. Forsyth, p. 9.

51. "Russian Supreme Court Rules . . . ," p. 32.

52. Ibid., December 1992, p. 9. Seoul YONHAP in English, 26 November 1992, in JPRS-TEN-93-001, p. 64.

53. "Russian Supreme Court Rules . . . ," p. 32.

54. *Far East Update,* February 1993, p. 4; and *Hokkaido Shimbun,* op. cit.

55. *Taiga News,* March 1993, p. 4.

56. Natal'ia Ostrovksaia, "Kontsern 'Hyundai' unichtozhaet ussuriiskuiu taigu," *Izvestiia,* 28 June 1994, p. 5.

57. Tatiana Zakharchenko, "The Environmental Movement and Ecological Law in the Soviet Union: The Process of Transformation," *Ecology Law Journal,* vol. 17, p. 467.

58. May 1992 poll results published in *Tikhookeanskaia zvezda,* 3 July 1992, cited in *RA Report,* January 1993, p. 20.

59. Michael Kozeltsev, "Old and New in the Environmental Policy of the Former Soviet Union," in Barbara Jancar-Webster, ed., *Environmental Action in Eastern Europe* (Armonk, NY: M.E. Sharpe, 1993), p. 71.

60. Barbara Jancar-Webster, "Introduction," in ibid., pp. 6–8.

61. In Liubov' Latypova, "Na Dal'nem Vostoke ozhidaetsia rekordnoe chislo pozharov," *Izvestiia,* 16 April 1993, p. 4.

62. Alexei Grigoriev, "Russia's New Forestry Act," p. 19.

63. ISAR was formerly known as the Institute for Soviet-American Relations.

64. "Bikin Valley Forest Preservation . . . ," p. 19.

65. See, for example, Vasilii Khramtsov, "Zapovednik dlia brakon'erov," *Utro Rossii,* 28 August 1993, p. 2.

66. Andrey Kholenko, "Moskva namerena pogret' ruki na radiatsionnoi opasnosti v Primor'e," *Vladivostok,* 31 March 1994, pp. 1, 3.

Part V

Northeast Asia: Re-emergence of a Transnational Region

What we are calling Northeast Asia is sometimes treated as the North Pacific, encompassing coastal northern China, the Russian Far East, the Korean peninsula, Japan, and the upper western seaboard of North America (Alaska, Canada, and the state of Washington). In this view, the possibilities afforded by the great ocean take on a larger significance. When seen more in continental terms, and therefore as including Mongolia and Siberia, the emphasis tends to fall on the land linkages among steppe, forest, and tundra zones, as well as the shared coastline opening onto the Okhotsk and Japan Seas. In either case, the area is viewed as a transnational region with a common history, and potentially, a common future.

Considerable coherence has been imparted to a continental Northeast Asia by different factors across various time periods. Among these influences have been the early spread of Chinese culture northward and the subsequent rise of a Chinese empire, Russian expansion and Russian imperial ambitions (enlarged in British and American projections of Russian influence), and Japanese imperial adventures.[1] Throughout, cross-border trade has been prominent. Not even the divisions brought on by Communism and anti-Communism could erase or even fully impede these historical ties. With the end of Soviet Communism, Northeast Asia's experience as a multicultural frontier zone where interethnic contacts have been prominent shows signs of considerable strengthening, as new kinds of cultural, political, and economic interaction become possible. For the Russian Far East, renewed openness to the outside world has been the most important consequence of the tumultuous last decade. Contemporary trends in Northeast Asia form the final section of this volume.

Gilbert Rozman, a sociologist at Princeton and a widely published scholar on the interactions among Russia, China, and Japan, analyzes the competing scenarios now emerging for regional cooperation. He shows that what had been a sharply divided tension spot, and before that a contentious arena for the ambitions and grievances of adversarial states, is on its way to becoming the setting for a different kind of competition, one generated primarily from within and directed toward some form of welcome interdependence. Rozman also takes note of the many obstacles to regional integration, especially mutual misperceptions and persistent territorial disputes. He remains cautiously optimistic about the possibilities for integration.

* * *

Political borders in Northeast Asia have been imposed and reversed many times in the last century and a half, leaving a legacy of great ambiguity. Despite determined Japanese and Chinese irredentism, prospects for a peaceable redrawing of the current map, which would necessarily involve Russian concessions, seem dim. But beneath the surface of official pronouncements, processes bearing on matters of long-term territorial control are under way, particularly in the Sino-Soviet case.

"For all of Siberia," Stuart Kirby has written, "the overwhelming, close-looming, gigantic fact . . . written with huge letters across the base line of the map is China. . . . The Soviets have left the whole region, by Chinese standards, almost empty of people and almost unutilized."[2] Recently, with the reopening of the frontiers, the number of Chinese living legally and illegally in Russia has skyrocketed, provoking fears of an imminent "takeover." Viktor Larin, director of the Academy of Sciences Far Eastern Institute of History, Archaeology, and Ethnography in Vladivostok and a specialist on modern China, examines the many-sided reverberations of present-day Chinese "penetration" into Russian territory.

Russia's first "Yellow Peril" scare took place before the revolution.[3] Chinese settlers began to move into northern Manchuria in the late eighteenth and early nineteenth centuries, some making it as far as the fertile plain north of the Amur River not long before Russia's N.N. Murav′ev (later, Murav′ev-Amurskii) undertook his expeditions down the Amur, hoping to transform the Amur valley into a food base for eastern Siberia by bringing in Cossack and peasant settlers from the Transbaikal region. Despite official recognition by China of Russia's incorporation of the Amur, after Murav′ev's departure in 1861 many of the Chinese streaming into Manchuria advanced into Russia's Ussuri region.[4]

The tsarist government encouraged Russian settlement, tried to restrict further non-Russian immigration, and even expelled large numbers of Chinese peasants, but the Chinese population inside Russia continued to grow. "By 1900," Lewis Siegelbaum has written, "all the towns between Chita and Vladivostok contained Chinese quarters with a numerous population of shopkeepers and workmen." In fact, given the shortage of Russian laborers, laws prohibiting the hiring of Chinese laborers were routinely flouted. Chinese construction workers, diggers, porters, merchants, and peasants proved indispensable to the construction of the Trans-Siberian—a situation fraught with irony, since one of the principal aims of the railroad's construction was to forestall Chinese penetration.[5]

Not long after the civil war was concluded, Soviet Russia's borders in the Far East were closed. If the total number of Chinese in all of Russia prior to 1917 was perhaps 300,000, that number had declined to 81,000 by the time of the 1926 census. It rose briefly in 1932, when the Japanese took control of Northern Manchuria, only to drop precipitously in 1937–38, when the NKVD cleared the Russian Far East of all ethnicities among which Japanese spies might be hiding. Throughout the Soviet period, the number of permanent Chinese residents in the USSR remained negligible. But this circumstance has been sharply reversed since 1991. No one knows for sure how many Chinese are living inside the Russian Federation, but the fear, racism, and talk of turnover have been revived. Larin provides a firsthand, almost alarmist report.

* * *

Koreans, too, have migrated into Russian territory (since at least the 1860s), establishing large permanent settlements before the revolution. Korean-Russian relations have not always been warm (Koreans were targeted by the same laws against hiring as were the Chinese), but no doubt because of the differences in overall population size there has been far less of the anxiety that has characterized Sino-Soviet relations. Koreans remained a presence inside the USSR during the entire Soviet period. And yet, in the years since 1985, for Koreans no less than the Chinese, eastern Russia has come to represent a kind of "new frontier," a theme explored by Kim Hakjoon, a professor of political science and former chief press spokesman for the president of South Korea.

Reviewing the vicissitudes of the Korean experience inside Russia and the USSR, Kim reminds us that during the post–World War II Soviet occupation of North Korea and the subsequent formation of a North Korean state, many Soviet Koreans served as key administrative staff. And following Russia's establishment of diplomatic relations with South Korea in 1992, Soviet Koreans once again were called upon to play a prominent role in fostering ties. What the future will bring is of course impossible to predict, especially given the prospect of the unification of North and South. But as Kim argues, the widening relations between the Korean peninsula and Russia make sense geographically as well as historically.

* * *

In the mid–nineteenth century, Russia's Aleksandr Herzen, among others, presciently called the Pacific Ocean "the Mediterranean of the future."[6] Today, though, most of Northeast Asia remains peripheral to the twentieth-century Trans-Pacific economic boom, which continues to be most visible in Southeast Asia (southern China, Hong Kong, Taiwan, Singapore, Malaysia, Indonesia, and Australia), as well as Japan, South Korea, and the western United States. Just such a broad-based comparison of Southeast Asia and Northeast Asia forms the final essay in this section, written by Hamashita Takeshi, a leading sinologist at Tokyo University.

Beginning with the demise of the tribute-trade system presided over by the Chinese Imperial Court, Hamashita traces the outlines of a traditional regionalism, where the rhetoric of bilateral, tributary ties was belied by a network of multilateral trade relations. With the opening of China to the West, new configurations formed within Asia, not in "response" to the European impact, as the standard historiography reads, but to take advantage of the new trade opportunities no longer prohibited by a central government weakened in battle with the West and the Taiping Rebellion.[7]

As Hamashita argues, this heightened subnational regionalism within China, usually condemned as the prelude to warlordism, can also be seen as a sponsor of growing transnational contact in East Asia. In particular, the strengthening of an intermediary identity for Chinese as either "northerners" or "southerners" corresponded to cross-border migration to and integration with Northeast and Southeast Asia, respectively. Hamashita goes on to trace the implications of this seesawing balance of power between regionalism and the state for Sino-Japanese relations, possibly the most important issue in twentieth-century East Asia.

One key to the experience of Southeast Asia has been the Chinese diaspora, especially the roles played by "foreign" Chinese capital in setting up businesses in southern China and of "naturalized" Chinese capital in Singapore, Indonesia, and elsewhere. Another key has been Japanese willingness to invest in manufacturing and to permit at least limited technology transfers. Whether similar large-scale cooperation will work in Northeast Asia remains to be seen. At least one proposal, the Tumen River project—reviewed by Rozman—has attracted wide attention, but it remains largely unrealized.

If, as Hamashita suggests, it seems unlikely that Northeast Asia can undergo the same kind of boom that has overtaken Southeast Asia, this does not mean the maintenance of the status quo. On the contrary, the Tumen River project is but one demonstration of the drawing power of the new regionalism. Looking for an identity to replace their pejorative status as a "periphery," Japanese on the Sea of Japan coast, Chinese in the northern interior and on the coast, Koreans (at least in the southern half of the peninsula), and Russians from the Maritime province to the Urals have all been speaking vociferously of "their" regional interests, whatever the concerns and policies of Tokyo, Beijing, Seoul/Pyongyang, and Moscow. The trend toward decentralization means that what were chiefly center–periphery relationships are giving way to regional ties across national boundaries. The surest sign of this outbreak of regionalism is that everyone wants to become a "bridge": Mongolia, a bridge between China and Russia; Korea, between Japan and Russia; China, between Asians and Europeans (Slavs)—not to mention Alaska, between America and the entire North Pacific. In such a climate, open trade might become an engine, bringing along transport and communications infrastructure, that could make a reality out of some of the dreams for the integration of a demilitarized and developed Northeast Asia. Whether the crippling legacies of the past can be so easily overcome, however, remains to be seen.[8]

Notes

1. The coherence of Northeast Asia in the Pleistocene period is argued by Chester Chard, *Northeast Asia in Prehistory* (Madison: University of Wisconsin, 1974), p. xv.

2. E. Stuart Kirby, "The Pattern of Siberian Development: Actual and Potential," in *Exploration of Siberia's Natural Resources* (Brussels: NATO, 1974), as cited in Allen Whiting, *Siberian Development and East Asia:Threat or Promise?*, (Stanford: Stanford University Press, 1981) p. 2.

3. Lewis Siegelbaum, "Another 'Yellow Peril': Chinese Migrants in the Russian Far East and the Russian Reaction Before 1917," *Modern Asian Studies,* 12 (2), 1978, pp. 307–29. For a more general treatment of "Yellow Peril," including a short chapter on "Russian voices," see Heinz Gollwitzer, *Die gelber Gefahr: Geschichte eines Schlagworts* (Göttingen: Vandenhöck, 1962).

4. Owen Lattimore, *The Inner Asian Frontiers of China* (Boston: Little, Brown, 1962); R.H.G. Lee, *The Manchurian Frontier in Ching History* (Cambridge, MA: Harvard University Press, 1970), pp. 78–115; F.V. Solov'ev, *Kitaiskoe otkhodnichestvo na Dal'nem Vostoke Rossii v epokhu kapitalizma, 1861–1917* (Moscow, 1989). The latter work was originally produced as a "closed" candidate dissertation, but perestroika made it possible to transfer it into the public domain. Although most studies in the "closed" category are of little scholarly value, the exceptions can be spectacularly exceptional because of the special access to "closed" sources enjoyed by those with appropriate clearance and no expectation of open publication.

5. Siegelbaum, "Another 'Yellow Peril'," pp. 314–17; V.V. Grave, *Kitaitsy, koreitsy, i iapontsy v Priamur'e* (St. Petersburg, 1912). In the heyday of Russian imperialism, the Chinese Eastern Railway (CER) was viewed as an exporter of Russian influence, but after the Russo-Japanese War, when defensive considerations became of paramount importance, it became clear that railroads were a two-way street. Discussions of Russian divestiture of the CER were ultimately fruitless, because even though the line through Chinese territory was no longer needed by Russia, it would be too dangerous in enemy hands. The Siberian Intervention would prove the truth of this argument, when the Japanese advance into Siberia was preceded by securing control of the CER. See B.A. Romanov, *Russia in Manuchuria (1802–1906)* (Ann Arbor: J.W. Edwards, 1952); original Russian ed. 1928; and George Lensen, *The Damned Inheritance: The Soviet Union and the Manchurian Crises, 1924–1935* (Tallahassee, FL: Diplomatic Press, 1974).

6. Aleksandr Herzen, *Polnoe sobranie sochinenii* (Petrograd/Leningrad, 1917–25), vol. XII, p. 275, as cited in David Dallin, *The Rise of Russia in Asia,* p. 23.

7. For a persuasive English-language critique of the West-centered history of the East (sometimes labeled the "Fairbank school"), see Paul Cohen, *Discovering History in China: American Historical Writing on the Recent Chinese Past* (New York: Columbia University Press, 1984).

8. A sobering picture of the historical burdens that are still felt in the Russian Far East can be found in John J. Stephan, *The Russian Far East: A History* (Stanford: Stanford University Press, 1994).

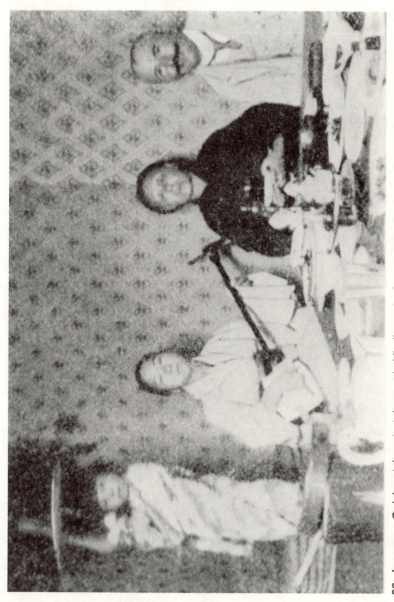

23. Japanese Geisha-style entertainment in Vladivostok. *Source: Wirt Gerrare, Greater Russia: The Continental Empire of the Old World* (New York, 1903).

24. Russian tourists accompanied by their Chinese servant arriving at the Japanese port of Otaru on Hokkaido, 1890s. *Source:* Annette Meakin, *A Ribbon of Iron* (New York: Arno Press, 1970).

25. The Russian fleet firing a salvo upon arriving at winter quarters in Nagasaki, Japan, 1890s. *Source: Das Russland der Zaren: Photographien von 1839 bis zur Oktoberrevolution* (Moscow, 1989).

26. Stiff Soviet resistance to Japanese incursions at Lake Khasan in 1938 helped discourage the Japanese army from its northern strategy, in favor of a southern thrust toward Indonesia and an attack on the United States at Pearl Harbor. 1938 poster by the artist V. Efimov. *Source: Forpost geroev: Geroicheskie povestvovaniia o podvigakh dal'nevostochnikov* (Khabarovsk, 1973).

27. The Soviet (Red) Army arrives in Dairen (Dalian, Dal'nii), 1945, forty-one years after eviction by Japanese troops. *Source:* N.P. Suntsov, *Krasnoznamennyi dal'nevostochnyi: Istoriia krasnoznamennogo voennogo okruga* (Moscow, 1971).

28. At Suifenhe where the Chinese Eastern Railway crosses into Russia's Maritime province, an obelisk in front of the station commemorates the Soviet invasion/liberation of August 1945. *Photo by David Wolff.*

29. The plaque reads: "Glory to the Red Army, having liberated Manchuria from the Japanese yoke." The Chinese version replaces "Manchuria" with "us." *Photo by David Wolff.*

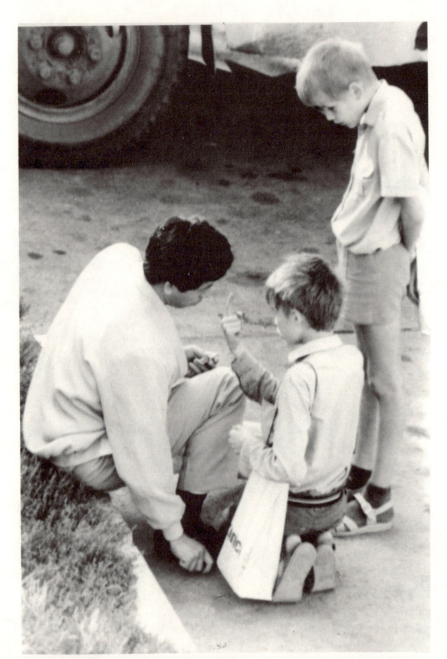

30. Russian boys in Khabarovsk bargaining with a Chinese merchant, who is stockpiling Soviet-era coins. The hammer-and-sickle are no longer in circulation. *Photo by David Wolff.*

31. Shanghai visitors display their imported Siberian foxes purchased at Suifenhe. *Photo by David Wolff.*

32. Russian "tourist-merchants," some of them traveling thousands of miles, are accommodated by Russo-Chinese tourist agency joint-ventures. Widely known as *chelnoki*, meaning those who shuttle to and fro, the merchants are sometimes also called *kamazy*, because of their truck-like stature. *Photo by David Wolff.*

33. Contemporary Ethnographic Museum in Iuzhno-Sakhalinsk, capital of Sakhalin, originally built by the Japanese during the period when they controlled Southern Sakhalin. *Source:* V.D. Uspenskii, *Dal'nie reisy* (Moscow, 1969).

KHABAROVSK INTERNATIONAL SCHEDULE

FROM	TO	FLIGHT N°	DAYS	ACFT	STOP	DEPARTURE
KHABAROVSK	ANCHORAGE	SU 327	7	IL-62	0	22-15
ANCHORAGE	KHABAROVSK	SU 328	7		0	21-40
KHABAROVSK	SAN FRANCISCO	SU 327	7	IL-62	1	22-10
SAN FRANCISCO	KHABAROVSK	SU 328	7		1	16-50
KHABAROVSK	NIIGATA	SU 811	1 5	TU-154	0	14-10
NIIGATA	KHABAROVSK	SU 812	1 5		0	15-30
KHABAROVSK	NIIGATA	SU 815	6	TU-154	0	13-25
NIIGATA	KHABAROVSK	SU 816	6		0	14-30
KHABAROVSK	HARBIN	SU 815	3	TU-154	0	12-30
HARBIN	KHABAROVSK	SU 816	3		0	12-15
KHABAROVSK	HARBIN	SU 815	5	TU-154	0	21-45
HARBIN	KHABAROVSK	SU 816	5		0	21-00
KHABAROVSK	PYONGYANG	SU 813	4	TU-154	0	10-10
PYONGYANG	KHABAROVSK	SU 814	4		0	12-05
KHABAROVSK	SEOUL	SU 817	7	IL-62	0	11-30
SEOUL	KHABAROVSK	SU 818	7		0	13-40
KHABAROVSK	HARBIN	CJ 902	2 4	MD-82	0	19-00
HARBIN	KHABAROVSK	CJ 901	2 4		0	13-45
KHABAROVSK	NIIGATA	JL 994	2	B-7	0	17-10
NIIGATA	KHABAROVSK	JL 993	2		0	

34. Direct flights to the United States, Japan, China, North Korea and South Korea leave from the Khabarovsk International Airport. *Photo by David Wolff.*

Spontaneity and Direction Along the Russo-Chinese Border

Gilbert Rozman

In the eyes of the world, the Sino-Soviet border—now reduced to the Sino-Russian border, but still the longest between any two countries—long symbolized a fortress mentality. It was closed to virtually all traffic and heavily militarized on both sides, and even neighboring towns were unable to gain comparative advantage through trade. The promise of earlier openings at the beginning of this century and in the 1950s was snuffed out. As measured by the ratio of military buildup to civilian prosperity, or of state mobilization of local resources for protectionist goals to material incentives for open commerce with the outside, this area represents how far the world remained only a short time ago from the ideals of free trade, open borders, and peaceful coexistence.

Suddenly this border has opened its gates and again become a source of opportunities and dreams. The end of the cold war, the normalization of relations between Beijing and Moscow, and the synchronization of economic reform in China and Russia have brought about a remarkable transformation. The details of expanding trade and joint ventures are becoming well known, but the nature of the new relationship is still a matter of controversy. In an effort to determine what type of cross-national community is taking shape, this essay examines forces drawing Northeast China and the Russian Far East together and reviews the various options under discussion within the region.

The new community that is forming is significant not only because it represents a radical departure from past tensions in the area but because it is a test, with very high stakes, for a world in transition. Nowhere more significantly than in Russia and China is the world struggling with the consequences of transition from cold war geopolitical reasoning, traditional Communist social organization, and nationalist assumptions about economic interests. Beyond analogies to other budding regional associations, the Sino-Russian relationship is a test for cooperation between great powers facing an unknown future. The dismantling of communism in the two countries where it reached its purest form continues; thus this is also a test of how much the present can break with the past.

With community ties taking shape from below as much as from above, and from "civilizational" forces as well as economic ones, the sprouts of Northeast Asian regionalism pose a challenge to social science understanding of the alternative forms that regionalism may take. Discussions of the evolving European Community and of NAFTA seem far removed from the developments in this far corner of Asia. What is happening along the Sino-Russian border does not easily fit into past notions of international relations, economic development, or regional cooperation. Thus it offers us an opportunity, in a time of transition, to find meaning with potentially far-reaching theoretical ramifications from events that are still unfolding.

At least eight types of regional communities figure into discussions centering on the emerging ties in Northeast Asia:

1. a *Macroregion,* which functions as a super-region dotted with megaprojects launched jointly by two or more great powers and capable of supplying a vast area of the globe;[1]
2. a variety of *Microregions,* originating from spontaneous localism or borderlessness and taking the form of small subregions linked by barter or other microlevel ties;[2]
3. a small number of *Regional Nuclei* of free economic zones, provided incentives from above as the chosen spearheads of growth to attract joint ventures and international firms;
4. a *Power Region* formed by a shared military-industrial complex, in which old state enterprises in the midst of convergence re-establish links dating from the 1950s;
5. a *Criminal Region* of illegal or semilegal syndicates, reliant on smuggling and privileged access to the extent that they connive to control the main channels of cross-border relations;[3]
6. an *Imperial Region* of blatant or disguised expansionism, whereby one country gains effective control over territories beyond its border;
7. a *Closed Region,* in which countries working together claim and defend a stake that they have carved within a world of intense regional competition; and
8. a *Melting Pot* region, in which a genuine community develops based on large-scale migration, cultural interaction, and assimilation.

Changing economic structures, public consciousness, and administrative policies present us with evidence to judge the prospects for each of these types of community as a new region is taking shape in Northeast Asia.

The fact that all eight of these images of regionalism can be found, directly or indirectly, in the literature on Northeast Asia demonstrates that we are not dealing with some kind of pure case. Diverse forces are pulling the new region in different directions. At present, various embryonic forms of community coexist. Although there are signs of sequential changes from one type of community to another, at this early stage of cross-national community building there is no definite answer as to which type or, more likely, combination of types will prevail. That will be decided, in part, by the balance of power in each country among national capitals, large territories in the Far East of Russia and the Northeast of China, existing provincial-level units (sheng, oblast, and krai), and smaller cities and local areas.

At the start of 1994, as Russians warily anticipate an economic renaissance following the consolidation of power under Boris Yeltsin and Chinese nervously await a generational change in the top leadership that would not interrupt a remarkable period of economic growth, we cannot expect to find a clear-cut plan for regionalism, only the possibility of detecting some of the unfolding trends. These trends will increasingly tie the hands of future leaders and limit their economic options. The course of regionalism is being set even before national and international eyes have focused clearly on what is happening.

The options for regionalism differ primarily along three dimensions: centralization, openness, and type of authority. In contrast to the earlier overcentralization in Moscow and Beijing, much decision making now occurs locally. Yet, the eventual balance remains in doubt among five levels: the large cross-national region, the nation, the domestic regional association, the province, and the local city or cluster of counties. Cross-border ties can be decided at each of these levels, with varying implications for regional identity. Types of regionalism also can be compared according to their degree of openness internally and externally. Narrowly economic regional ties raise different implications for regional identity from multifunctional ties across porous borders. Ultimately power can remain in the hands of old socialist elites, gravitate toward new capitalist ones, or slip into the clutches of groups deemed criminal by both of the above. The eight options described below reflect different patterns of centralization, openness, and type of authority.

Macroregion

Regionalism in Northeast Asia is one of the grandest of the post–cold war dreams that aroused interest at the start of the 1990s. Unlike either the "new world order" championed in the United States for nation-states of a new type or the "global community" that inspired cosmopolitan thinkers in Moscow, the ideal of regionalism stirred a different sort of alliance—an alliance in favor of localism while also supporting internationalism.[4] For a corps of local boosters in cities such as Changchun, Harbin, Vladivostok, Khabarovsk, Niigata, and Kanazawa, this ideal takes the form of a grandiose vision: the birth of a mighty economic area born of macroprojects combining boundless Russian raw materials and land, virtually unlimited Chinese labor and entrepreneurship, and vast Japanese capital and technology.[5]

This program should result, according to its backers, in nothing less than a new Hong Kong at Tumenjiang, where Russia and North Korea meet and China is separated by only about fifteen kilometers from the sea.[6] At the same time, an extended loop of thousands of kilometers of pipelines fueling Japan as well as both sides of the Sino-Russian border should also come into being.[7] Finally, the program envisions the advent of cross-national technology transfers, agricultural showcases, and "projects of the future" on a scale scarcely imagined elsewhere on the globe. The dreamers fit their own home areas into central locations on these blueprints, winning support from local governments to launch sister-city relations, host international conferences, establish think tanks, and issue a stream of publications sketching the outlines of what promises to be a harmonious and prosperous future.[8]

Some Chinese in the major universities and institutes of the Northeast share in these dreams. Especially at conferences on the Tumenjiang project and in a host of new journals on Northeast Asian regionalism,[9] Chinese have taken an upbeat position on the future of their region. They cannot avoid looking to South China for inspiration as to what economic reform and the open door have wrought in barely a decade. Yet, apart from Dalian, which opened as a development zone beckoning to foreign firms first in 1984 but is located on the Yellow Sea far from Russia, Northeast China is short on "dragon's heads" that can pull a vast hinterland out of poverty or of macroprojects that will lead the way into a new century. To make shared dreams for regionalism come true, the role of Russia is indispensable, and Chinese pin their hopes on cooperation, even as Russia's opinion shapers remain more cautious.

Russian reluctance to picture a megaregion of the future stems from lack of confidence in their own country's role in the coming division of labor. Exploitation of the natural resources of Siberia is as likely as not to be equated with other countries stealing what is rightfully Russia's, with little thought that large earnings will contribute to development or increased living standards within Russia. The tone in local newspapers of the Russian Far East is decidedly more negative than in papers of the Chinese Northeast and the Sea of Japan coastal area of Japan. Public-opinion polling in the Vladivostok area confirms the existence of a mood of suspicion resistant to bold steps toward regionalism. No doubt repeated disappointments over much ballyhooed Soviet megaprojects, including the Baikal-Amur rail line through the Far East that was supposed to usher in a new age in the 1980s, leave a residue of skepticism.

Microregion

Even as a regionalism capable of rivaling plans for the European Community, NAFTA, or the South China Sea glittered in the headlines of local brochures, a less obtrusive form of regional cooperation was taking shape through the pragmatic strategies of separate communities and businesses. Actual steps far removed from central controls were advancing from the grassroots level. Of these, arguably the most important are microlevel contacts elicited by border trade between the Russian Far East and the Chinese Northeast, which have over a span better measured in months than in years changed the geography of the area. Since the spring 1988 decision in Beijing to delegate cross-border trade permission to the provincial level, burgeoning cross-border trade at dozens of points has become the driving force for a new regionalism.

Koreans were for a time expected to become active too in the budding cross-border trade. But the growing isolation of North Korea and the problems preventing a return to the Far East by large numbers of Koreans whose families were expelled by Stalin and now reside primarily in Central Asia have slowed the evolution of what may eventually become a network forged by one ethnic group that joins the many parts of the region together. In the meantime, Sino-Russian border ties had by 1992 become the most dynamic force for regionalism.

From Manzhouli in Inner Mongolia to Hunchun in Jilin province, Chinese local areas have competed to record the largest volume of trade with their Russian counterparts just across the border. The province of Heilongjiang is in the forefront; in 1992–93 a "Russia fever" was raging in its media. Closest of all areas in China to Russia's three large border cities—Vladivostok, Khabarovsk, and Blagoveshchensk—Heilongjiang is comfortable with the dispersed microregion pattern along its extended 3,000-kilometer border. In this way, many parts of the province, from Heihe in the north to Suifenhe in the east—both remote from commercial routes—are able to join in the national economic boom.

If the macroregion option means a limited number of huge investments under state sponsorship, the microregion approach draws driblets of small investments distant from state oversight and often skirting state regulations. It means the empowerment of local governments. Simultaneously, it accelerates opposition to the legacy of centralization in China and Russia. Localism does not, however, mean narrow visions of regionalism ahead. Amid the border trade fever, *People's Daily* described the construction of a bridge joining Heihe to Blagoveshchensk as turning the city of Heihe into an important Eurasian trade tunnel.[10]

Regional Nuclei

Dalian claims to be China's northeastern entrepôt, which deserves continued priority as its spillover effects reach further and further into a vast hinterland. In 1988, designation of the entire Liaodong peninsula as an export-processing zone demonstrated Dalian's reach. More investment in its superior port and auxiliary spending to buttress the new expressway leading north to the capital of Liaoning province at Shenyang and beyond will bring the greatest returns, argue the boosters of Dalian, who add that only one regional city on a par with Hong Kong is needed for China to achieve balance between the already booming Southeast and the newly developing Northeast. This viewpoint may seem plausible to many supporters of high technology and a Japan-centered strategy of export-oriented growth, but it leaves backers of cities to the north alarmed that trickle-down development will be long in reaching their communities.

Dalian is being challenged by Jilin province's insistence that Tumenjiang be established as a comparable center (which would then help Changchun, the provincial capital, become the railroad center of the region) and Heilongjiang's parallel effort to restore to its capital at Harbin the function of China's crossroads for transportation ties to Russia from all sides and an identity as the center of the Northeast Asian economic area.[11] Even within Liaoning province, the capital at Shenyang, which has long enjoyed the status as the premier city in Northeast China, is anxious to continue to capitalize on its location as the juncture linking Dalian to the south, Beijing to the southwest, and the bulk of the cities in China's three northeastern provinces. Chinese of diverse background agree on the need for nuclei. Provinces and cities compete to rise in the urban hierarchy. In August 1992, Harbin and Changchun were named border-economy open zones, giving a boost to their hopes only five months after four border cities in the Northeast were among the first to be so named.

Vladivostok and Khabarovsk also have pretensions to widen their range as regional centers. Long rivals for top billing in Russia east of Irkutsk, they recognize that the terms of competition are changing. Since January 1992, Vladivostok has been an open city. It now has its own direct air link to Japan. To the extent that the Sea of Japan becomes the center of regional growth, as anticipated both in Japan and by the planners of the Tumenjiang project, the seaport of Vladivostok will gain an advantage. Already joint ventures and foreign consulates (the Japanese consulate relocated from nearby Nakhodka) are showing a new preference for Vladivostok, although some remain in Khabarovsk.

The urban hierarchy of Northeast Asia is still in flux. Will one city clearly emerge on top, steadily drawing under its umbrella rival centers? Will several nuclei in cities of more than 600,000 population compete for a time while no one of them is dominant? At the very least, what have been self-contained urban networks are being transformed into interstate networks. If Russia's development continues to lag and most of the cross-border commerce stays in the hands of Chinese, then the outcome may be that the smaller Russian cities become integrated into the hierarchies of China's major cities, topped by several with populations of 3 to 6 million. Aware of this danger, leaders in Russia's Maritime province have developed a plan for Greater Vladivostok, that appears to some to represent a form of protectionist resistance to the three-country Tumenjiang proposal, with a hinterland covering much or all of the same territory.[12]

Power Region

Small-scale trade may be flourishing at border crossings, and administrators may be lobbying for special status and national benefits to their cities to duplicate the achievements of Shenzhen and other cities designated as special economic zones, but the economies of the Russian Far East and China's Northeast remain heavily skewed toward large state-owned industries that continue to operate. Fearful of unemployment, both sides cater to the military-industrial lobbies. Multitiered price systems and the lack of economic accountability for money-losing enterprises leave controls over many enterprises incomplete. In circumstances of declining state salaries relative to the private sector and rising open market prices for goods still controlled by the state enterprises, the potential for corruption is enormous.

Old ties have been renewed between state enterprises on both sides of the border. China has sought Russian military equipment and technology. In addition to formal bilateral agreements on sales, sightings of a stream of Russian experts and officials in China have fueled rumors that all manner of deals are being made with or without the knowledge of the Russian government. In other words, should there be a change of political direction in Moscow, the re-established military-industrial connections in Northeast Asia may become further cemented.

Changes in 1993 in the governors of Russia's Maritime province and Sakhalin oblast strengthened the hand of the industrial establishment. The consolidation of power by Prime Minister Viktor Chernomyrdin following the December 1993 elections led to the departure of market reformers in favor of what one reformer called "red managers." Meanwhile, China's continued assertion that it is a socialist state, its willingness to export arms technology that the United States views as destabilizing to world peace, and the importance of its military in the leadership succession that is not far off all keep the old guard in the spotlight.

The major boulevard of Changchun is named after Stalin. Large statues of Mao Zedong stand outside military buildings in Harbin and elsewhere. Prior to the failure of the August 1991 coup in Moscow, talks between the plotters and the Chinese establishment apparently led to a degree of understanding that hinted at a new friendship aimed against American hegemony and what the Chinese leadership decry as the "strategy of peaceful evolution." The possibility remains that the stronghold of the military-industrial complex in Northeast China and the heavily militarized Far East of Russia will again find common interests.

On both sides of the border critics warned against the tendency to use political power to conduct commerce (known as *guandao* in China). They charged that there was excessive control from above and insufficient reliance on laws.[13] What had been a rallying cry in 1989 was appearing again in internal circulation journals in 1992,[14] and then in 1993 burst into China's open press as the focus for a massive attack on excessive state intervention in the economy. In the

Russian Far East, too, there were warnings that local administrations and new businessmen had so few contacts and that a psychology born of poverty was so pervasive that Russian authorities insisted on subsidizing costly homegrown food rather than depend on plentiful Chinese supplies.[15]

Criminal Region

Barter and small-scale transactions have attracted "shuttle traders" of a sort not customarily visible in international commerce. Until recently, cheap transport made it possible for former Soviet citizens to come to China from far away and, even with a tiny amount of capital, to purchase amounts of goods that they could take back in their luggage and resell to earn a sizable profit. After surcharges on extra weight made it harder to bring back a lot of luggage, there was still some profit in wearing many layers of clothing and lugging a few bags. Chinese traders were often, in fact, peasants from nearby provinces. Established trading organizations played a lesser role. No wonder that accusations of improper business practices piled one on top of the other, especially charges that Chinese dealers were peddling shoddy goods.

The Russian press charged that Chinese criminal gangs were fighting in Russian cities among themselves and that a powerful criminal group based in Harbin was trying to control all of the Chinese dealers.[16] It warned that Russian business partners were being deceived, and when they pursued the culprits in China, they sometimes ran up against army connections protecting the wrongdoers.[17] Russians called the Chinese traders swindlers (*zhuliki*) and reacted to the "typhoon" of Chinese joint ventures in 1992, after registration procedures had been decentralized and simplified, as a means to avoid customs duties through short-lived operations without bringing much investment into Russia.[18] The Chinese conceded some of these problems, insisting that they needed to tighten controls to ensure that good-quality products were exported.

For the Russians, the problem of criminality in cross-border relations was at least as much a homegrown phenomenon. One newspaper reported on a battle for control of Vladivostok between the ex-convicts who had been released from the region's many labor camps and the upstart "Mafia" groups, who got their start in the lucrative racket of Japanese secondhand car imports.[19] Another report described double contracts for the export of Russian raw materials, with only the foreign partners having a record of the actual prices. The resulting outflow of foreign currency was described as a second Niagara Falls.[20] Outside criminals from the Caucasus (southerners), battling for control in the port of Nakhodka, were blamed too.[21]

Criminals and operators in business for a quick killing seized the opportunities in border trade. Ordinary citizens felt helpless before the "wild" (*dikii*) atmosphere around them. They were embarrassed by the stories about Russian sailors in Japan, stealing and smuggling and making their compatriots unwelcome visitors too.[22] In search of a different sort of regionalism with benefits for all, people feared that the only result would be a region run by crime.

Imperial Region

Conspiracy theorists in Russia feared either that Japan with its vast capital would buy control over the Far East or that China with its demographic dominance would flood the area with migrants. Lacking self-confidence or trust in their own leaders, Russians in the Far East doubt that cross-border relations will be to their benefit. One article written under a pseudonym by local academics in Vladivostok charged that ties between China and Russia are an uneven match. Beijing has a strategy, while Moscow looks the other way as local forces do as they please. Chinese businessmen are prepared, while Russian counterparts lack coordination. The authors warned that China's real aim is to reverse what it regards as unequal treaties from the past.[23]

When Russia agreed in 1992 to fulfill its earlier treaty obligation to grant China access to the Sea of Japan, some commentators charged that Russian interests were being sold out. Permission for China to build a railroad to the port of Zarubino near Tumenjiang drew warnings that this would be only the first step to a Chinese takeover of the area. A Vladivostok newspaper objected that local governments had been bypassed in the decision and accused Moscow of ignoring the fact that Russia and China have "completely different intentions, plans and concrete actions."[24]

Polls in the Far East confirm that leaders and ordinary citizens alike are more willing to accept American or Japanese joint ventures or other regional ties than Chinese ones. In a sample of one hundred leaders of the southern Maritime province (including Vladivostok) who were asked in early 1993 with which collective(s) they prefer to work, 64 percent answered American, 44 percent Japanese, 16 percent South Korean, and only 4 percent Chinese.[25]

By the fall of 1993, the central press was expressing its alarm at the "flood" of Chinese, the "invasion" that had begun, and the vulnerability of the Far East.[26] Warning that a million Chinese may be living without registration in Siberia and the Far East, an article in *Izvestiia* linked the foreign presence with the source of banditry and with the syndrome of a besieged fortress under the heading "Siberia—Only for Russians?"[27] Parts of the local press were even verging on hysteria, as in one series of articles on the "Chinese gambit" in the Maritime province warning of plans to colonize the area.[28]

Chinese sources insist that any region in which their country participates will be a model for equality. China will resist hegemonism, of which the Soviet Union was long accused. Economic ties will set an example for North–South relations; balanced trade, technological sharing, and direct investment will all serve to raise the level of developing countries. Of course, it is China that is seen as a developing country. This outlook does not go far to reassure some Russians

that China has abandoned the view "which regards Siberia as its own historical territory, only temporarily belonging to the Russian nation."[29] The long-
smoldering border dispute has not completely gone away. A 1991 agreement to
demarcate the border, which began to be implemented in 1993, is said to be
making the border "civilized,"[30] but it has not transformed the psychology of all
Russians.

Closed Region

If the world is entering an age of strong regional associations, then Northeast
Asia must be prepared to build its own region capable of defending its interests
against protectionism abroad. China's interest in regional ties increased noticeably in the aftermath of the Tiananmen crackdown in opposition to pressure from
the United States. Ties with the Soviet Union—not only economic but other
types of networks, too—were reinvigorated.[31] Under the impact of recurrent
tensions with the United States, Chinese continue to discuss the need for regional
support, including dependable ties with Russia.

In Russia, a backlash in 1992 against leaning too closely on the West also
heightened interest in regional partners. It was said that Russia is more than a
European country, that it has a Eurasian identity. Ties to China came to be seen
as a means to balance ties to the West, helping simultaneously to preserve
national security and culture.[32] On the whole, however, there was little appeal
for the Yeltsin camp to join a regional group with a socialist and confident China
aimed at linking Asian countries closely together in resistance to the West.

This idea could only appeal to desperate opponents of Yeltsin with harsh
words against Russia's increasing dependency on the West and praise for
China's alternative path to "reform with dignity." Such reasoning was usually
Moscow-centered, just as those in China who were worried about the United
States or Japan often preferred to group Northeast and North China together into
one formidable area centered in Beijing and capable of defending national interests within a new cross-national regionalism.

Melting Pot Region

Internationally minded policy makers and officials in Moscow, in the face of a
rising tide of xenophobic nationalism in 1992, suggested that nationalism not be
ceded completely to forces hostile to the global community. It would be better to
deflect their appeal by finding a different form of state-centered thinking consistent with an open posture toward the outside world.[33]

Through the censorship of Chinese writings there also seemed to appear a
reform outlook open to a more far-reaching form of regional interaction than
Beijing advocated.

It was primarily Japanese sources, arguing for a region reaching beyond Russia and China to include Japan as well as the Koreas, that stood behind open regionalism. Yet, these, too, hesitated to discuss intermarriage, intercultural sharing beyond exchange visits, long-term migration, and other measures of close interaction between nations. Local boosters in Niigata, Kanazawa, and other cities along the Sea of Japan blamed Tokyo for stifling initiatives toward regionalism, but like supporters of economic regionalism in the local cities of China and Russia, they found it difficult to move from the stage of conceptualization to that of concrete action.

The Path of Regionalism

Regionalism is a state of mind as well as a set of conditions. The conditions can materialize in diverse spheres: economically, in the interdependence of supply and demand across national frontiers; strategically, in the loss of concern about armed forces or potential military threats from neighboring countries; territorially, in porous borders that lose significance for keeping people in or out; and organizationally, in the web of interlocking networks that bind the fate of diverse nations. Conditions in each of these spheres ordinarily influence the way people think about regionalism, but there are other factors related to attitudes about nationalism, internationalism, and localism that affect the psychology of regionalism.

Sino-Russian and Sino-Soviet relations have long been viewed as both a matter of national interests (geopolitics, strategic balances, territorial disputes, and rivalry for leadership in a global movement) and a question of clashing perceptions and pride (sensitivity to national differences, tolerance of different stages of socialist development, mutual respect between leaders accustomed to unrivaled domestic authority, and coexistence of differing ideological claims where legitimacy is assumed to be based on them). Even as national interests have been redefined and ideology has fallen into disrepute, bilateral ties still rest on a combination of interests based on actual conditions and psychology rooted in perceptions.

In the first stage of the new regionalism in Northeast Asia there was a dual response. On the one hand, the macroregion ideal represented the high road of what a glorious future may lie ahead. On the other hand, fear of a criminal region or an imperial region accompanied the low road of changes under way and was deeply worrisome. Intellectuals looking from a distance, for example, from the Sea of Japan coast, had the luxury of ruminating about the high road that might someday be, while pensioners and others whose security was in jeopardy in the midst of little-understood change all around had trouble seeing beyond the low road.

As Vladimir Zhdanov explains in his essay in this volume, Siberian regionalism is a force for bargaining with Moscow but does not threaten to split Russia, especially after the consolidation of power in the final months of 1993 following the storming of the parliament. In the Far East there has been frequent disappointment toward Moscow's inaction and its economic disincentives, but on the whole, local areas are looking for more leadership from the center, not separatism that would put them face-to-face with a much more populous and better-organized China. Representative of this outlook, Viktor Larin in his essay contrasts Moscow's weak China policy, which enables China to arrange ties to the Russian Far East to its own advantage, to the unified state policy in support of the policies of Northeast China. And as Hamashita Takeshi notes in his essay, the role played by Greater China and overseas Chinese in forming the Southeast Asian region is not likely to be repeated in Northeast Asia, at least if Russian alarmists have their way.

As events unfolded, planners and on-site observers saw before them two immediate choices: accept the momentum of microregions taking shape spontaneously from below, or steer the process through the development of regional nuclei with heavy investment from outside. A battle was taking shape between territorial authorities. Beijing and Moscow were distant but important players in resolving the differences. Even if they were slow to arbitrate competing claims (Yeltsin would not approve the Greater Vladivostok plan although local boosters fought for it, and Deng Xiaoping in 1990 chose Pudong in Shanghai as the next priority in development without, to the consternation of local boosters, making a similar choice in the Northeast), the urban hierarchy was sorting itself out.

The urban hierarchy in the region is being transformed from below. Border trade points are multiplying in size, in some cases climbing to 100,000 or more population. Larger cities are attempting to balance the loss of traditional state-sector jobs with jobs in joint ventures and in "open door" commerce to the outside. Through foreign trade, cities are becoming realigned as steps in a ladder dominated by regional centers, some beyond the national border. Long-established provincial capitals face new risks. On the one hand, loss of their monopoly position in the command economy may cause them to fall on the urban ladder, as smaller cities shift their transactions elsewhere. On the other hand, if they ride the wave of change, their provincial base might be extended to a regional one. In 1992–93, many Northeast Chinese cities were showing vitality in this transition, but the cities of the Russian Far East were not faring nearly as well. Russians show insufficient trust in the authorities and business groups in Harbin to accept a second-rung status for Vladivostok or Khabarovsk.

In the coming years, the fate of Northeast Asia will be decided on different playing fields. Success in the GATT talks in December 1993 and continued cooperation in great power relations are two factors shaping the course of regionalism around the globe. Power struggles and policy choices in Moscow and Beijing are other factors that continue to set limits on localism and, at the same time, regionalism. Three major alternatives are present: a power region suspicious of the outside world and reminiscent of the Sino-Soviet alliance of the 1950s; a closed region robust in its own economic integration but defensive of its interests in a world marked by regional competition; or a melting pot region within a world of decreasing barriers. Japan's role is crucial in deciding among these alternatives. In a power region, Japan would be excluded. In a closed region, it would be an indispensable partner. Finally, in a melting pot region, it, along with the United States and South Korea, would no doubt play a leading role.

Japanese view the expansion of ties between China and Russia as merely a prelude to regionalism. As one of their leading analysts of the region asserted, there will be no region without Japan.[34] They take for granted the need for "open regionalism."[35] At the same time, they are careful in their search for principles on which Northeast Asian regionalism may be based and yet not impose Western values. All of the countries must move patiently toward the gradual and stable evolution of multiethnic identities. Taga Hidetoshi labels the new person at the end of this process a "Japan Sea rim person" (*Kannihonkaijin*).[36] This is an idealistic notion whose time is not near. So far the first steps toward regionalism centering on border areas of China and Russia are far away from producing such a multiethnic identity, but they leave little doubt that a new era is dawning as some sort of regionalism takes shape.

The two options highest on openness and normal international business authority are the macroregion with heavy Japanese investment in Russia and the melting pot region in which nationalism fades in importance. Neither Russia, wary of foreign encroachments, nor China, defensive about socialism, is ready to accept so much openness. The two options that thrive in conditions of decentralization and loss of control from above are the microregions resulting from border-trade fever and the criminal region beyond the control of normal channels of authority. In 1992 and 1993 these options rose to prominence, but given the Russian outcry against criminal control and the readiness at both the central and provincial levels in China to reassert control as needed, it is doubtful that they will be as important in the coming years.

The two options that best signify a reversion to old authority—a variant of the old Sino-Soviet alliance involving the cooperation of the military-industrial sector—are the power region and the closed region preparing to counter the West and, perhaps, Japan as well. If we wager on the state as the force that will ultimately prevail, allowing some openness without threatening internationalism and some decentralization without worrisome challenges from newly empowered elites, we need not assume that the outcome will favor either a power or an imperial region. If the imbalance continues between a self-destructing Russia and a confident China, the result may be, through indirect and unplanned consequences more than conscious strategy, the imperial region under Chinese dominance. Alternatively, if the prime movers are the provinces, then we can expect considerable openness (in Russia by default to meet economic needs) and sustained, if only partial, decentralization, both fully consistent with the regional nuclei approach. Competition to outdo one's neighbor in development holds the best hope for a natural transition toward regionalism in which market economics prevails over power politics.

Most writings on Northeast Asian regionalism advocate provincial-level interests battling against centralization. In Russia, concern has shifted, as well, toward excessive openness that leads to Chinese dominance. There is little likelihood that the center will recover much of its earlier power at the expense of local economic initiative. In the foreseeable future, local advocates will continue to press for their home area's interests, adding to the competition that serves the regional nuclei model.

Notes

1. Toma Takeo, *Ugoki hajimeta kan Nihonkai keizai ken* (Tokyo, 1990), pp. 73–76.
2. Taga Hidetoshi, "Kan Nihonkai ken no sode," in idem, *Kokkyō o koeru jikken: kan Nihonkai sōsho 1* (Tokyo, 1992), pp. 9–11.
3. Sergei Agafonov, "Tokyo vstrevozhen rasshireniem Rossiisko-Iaponskikh mafioznykh kontaktov," *Izvestiia*, 20 November 1992, p. 4.
4. Taga, "Kan Nihonkai ken no sosde," pp. 4–11.
5. Ren Wenxia, "Lun Dongbeiya quyi jingji hezuo yu fengong," in Dongbeiya yanjiu congshu bianjibu, ed., *Dongbeiya jingji quan de meili* (Dalian: Dalian ligong daxue chubanshe, 1992), p. 23.
6. Yasuhiro Mori, "Watching the Development Flow: Tumen River Projects Chart Changes in Northeast Asia," *The Japan Times Weekly International Edition,* 15–21 February 1993, p. 17.
7. Asako Murakami, "Natural Gas Pipeline in Asia Involving Fifty-one Companies Touted," *The Japan Times Weekly International Edition,* 28 June–4 July 1993, p. 13.
8. Japanese publications are the most substantial. For example, see Nihonkai ken keizai kenkyūkai, *Kan Nihonkai kōryū jiten '93* (Tokyo: Sochisha, 1993). Chinese publications are the most numerous. Along with many journals focused on the region, there are books such as Jin Zhenji, *Dongbeiya jingji quan yu Zhongguo de xuanze* (Beijing: Zhonggong zhongyang dangxiao chubanshe, 1992). In Russia there are many pertinent newspaper articles and some reports as well as the journal *Rossiia i ATR,* which began in 1992 and, unlike most publications in China and Japan, focuses on history rather than the future.
9. *Dongbeiya luntan* [Northeast Asia Forum], issued by Jilin University, and *Dongbeiya yanjiu* [Northeast Asia Studies], of the Center for Northeast Asia Studies in Jilin, are two examples.
10. "Zhongguo Eluosi jian Heilongjiang daqiao," *Renmin ribao,* 19 March 1993, p. 4.
11. Press Office of Harbin Municipal People's Government, "Environment for Investment in Harbin" (Harbin, 1993).
12. G. Christoffersen, "The Greater Vladivostok Project: Transnational Linkages in Regional Economic Planning," paper delivered at the annual meeting of the American Association for the Advancement of Slavic Studies, November 1993.
13. Gan Chengzhong, "Qanmian shenhua gaige yu youhua," *Heihe xuebao,* no. 1, 1989, pp. 1–4.
14. Jin Weike, "Guanyu jinyibu fazhan Zhonge bianjie maoyi de jidian jianyi," *Neibu wengao,* no. 19, 1992, pp. 17–20.
15. E. Panasenko, "Kazhdomu svoe," *Tihookeanskaia zvezda,* 3 March 1993, p. 2.
16. " 'Zubnaia bol' pogranichnoi militsii," *Utro Rossii,* 19 February 1993, p. 3.
17. "Vo Vladivostok pribyli nechistoplotnye Kitaitsy," *Konkurent,* 2–9 March 1993, p. 5.

18. A. Ivanchikov, "Kitaiskii bum," *Tikhookeanskaia zvezda,* 2 March 1993, p. 2.
19. Vladimir Semenov, "Mafiia: ot razborok k voine," *Utro Rossii,* 6 February 1993, pp. 1–2.
20. Vladimir Oshchenko, "Vlast' liubopytstvuet," *Vladivostok,* 27 February 1993, p. 3.
21. "Kavkaztsy v Nakhodke," *Krasnoe znamia,* 2 February 1993, p. 4.
22. "Rossisskim turistam v'ezd zapreshchen," *Krasnoe znamia,* 27 February 1993, p. 3.
23. A. Setarov, "Rossiiskie vorota dlia Kitaia," *Utro Rossii,* 31 July 1992.
24. O. Kul'gin, "Zarubino prodali?" *Krasnoe znamia,* 13 February 1993, p. 1.
25. E. Plaksen, "Mnenie rukovoditelei Iuzhnogo Primor'ia o vkhozhdenii v ekonomicheskuiu struktury ATR i proektakh 'Tumangan' i 'Bol'shoi Vladivostok'," unpublished report, Far Eastern Division of the Russian Academy of Sciences, Institute of History, Archaeology, Ethnography, Vladivostok, 1993.
26. Valerii Sharov, "Kitaiskaia karta," *Literaturnaia gazeta,* 27 October 1993, p. 13.
27. Aleksei Tarasov, "Sibir'—tol'ko dlia russkikh?" *Izvestiia,* 2 November 1993, pp. 4–5.
28. "Kitaiskii gambit v Primor'e: Chem dlia nas obernetsia?" *Novosti: gazeta o Vladivostoke,* 12 October 1993.
29. Aleksei Tarasov, "Prizrak kommunizma voskresaet v kraiu Stalinskikh lagerei," *Izvestiia,* 25 February 1993, p. 4.
30. "Granitsa stanet tsivilizovannoi," *Tikhookeanskaia zvezda,* 5 March 1993, p. 1.
31. *Kitaiskaia Narodnaia Respublika v 1990 godu: politika, ekonomika, kul'tura* (Moscow, 1992), pp. 154–69.
32. A. Muradian, " 'Evraziiskaia' kontseptsiia—model' obshchestvennogo razvitiia Rossii?" *Problemy Dal'nego Vostoka,* nos. 1–3, 1992, pp. 49–56.
33. Aleksei Bogaturov, Mikhail Kozhokin, and Konstantin Pleshakov, "Posle imperii: demokratizm i derzhavnost' vo vneshnei politike Rossii," *RNF—Rossiiskii—RNF nauchnye doklady no. 8* (Moscow, 1992).
34. Kanamori Hisao, "Jobun," in Toma Takeo, *Ugoki hajimeta kan Nihonkai keizaiken,* p. 3.
35. Ogawa Kazuo, *Saigo no niu-furontia: Kan Nihonkai keizaiken* (Tokyo, 1993), p. 54.
36. Taga Hidetoshi, "Kokkyō o koeru jikken no genjō," in Hokuriku kokusai mondai gakkai, ed., *Nihonkai-taian o nao hedateru mono wa nani ka* (Toyama, 1993), pp. 8–20.

"Yellow Peril" Again?

The Chinese and the Russian Far East

Viktor Larin

During the last three and a half centuries, relations between two neighbors, Russia and China, have been characterized by both cooperation and competition. At the present time, these same contradictory elements continue to mark relations between the two great powers in the political, economic, and ideological spheres, as well as in informal contacts among their citizens. Rivalry in geopolitics and the competitive desires of both Russia and China for political and military leadership are offset, to some extent, by the shared aspiration to maintain a balance of power in Asia.

At the same time, however, the potential for integrating complementary economies has been placed in jeopardy by the moves on both sides toward the protection of home industries. Meanwhile, the long-standing similarity in political cultures is not matched in the areas of material, mass, and intellectual cultures. As a result, considerable differences have appeared between the two nations in behavior and mutual understanding. The treatment of the past, often mobilized to rationalize and explain the present, also exhibits ambivalent tendencies. Military expeditions, mutually beneficial trade, unequal treaties, territorial disputes, and so-called "fraternal assistance," all these and more are retained in the historical memory of Russo-Chinese interaction.

At the present time, this duality seriously impedes any analysis of the present or prognosis for the future of Russo-Chinese relations. According to many specialists, Russia is seeking to become closer to China because of geopolitical interests, namely, the desire to ensure national security and favorable outside conditions for carrying out its reforms. China, aside from the security of its northern borders, is especially interested in obtaining modern Russian equipment at reasonable prices.[1] Chinese purchases of weapons will provide much-needed assistance for Russia's struggling defense industries, and in this way will supposedly strengthen the Russian economy. China is already on the path to becoming a major military power in the Asia–Pacific region, and Russian arms purchases will facilitate this process.[2]

Thus, on the state level, both sides are greatly interested in developing good neighborly relations, primarily through economic cooperation. The Russian and Chinese economies are very similar in quality, structure, culture of consumption, and technological level. Hundreds of Chinese factories are still using Soviet equipment in need of retooling. The possibilities exist for Russia to sell China a wide range of industrial products, including energy equipment, aircraft and heli-copters, trucks, ships, fertilizers, wood, machine tools, and so on. The Russian market is capable of digesting practically the entire range of goods produced for export in the industrial and agricultural sectors of the Chinese economy.[3]

About all this there exists little disagreement. The question is whether eco-nomic cooperation will correspond to the national interests of Russia and China and the interests of Asia as a whole, especially those areas closest to the two powers. The reality of these rapidly developing relations indicates that the interests of Asia more broadly do not always coincide with Russo-Chinese interests. Moreover, both countries have to confront numerous factors working against bringing them together. Under these conditions it is particularly import-ant to be flexible in making decisions. Both sides should properly appraise the situation and consistently uphold their national and regional interests. They must consider the development of relations and their aftereffects and use them for the public interest. It must be admitted that today the Chinese government is more farsighted and understands its own national interest better than does the Russian government.

As Bonny Glaser has written, "while the Chinese view Russia as preoccupied with its own problems and unable to expand abroad, they do not rule out the eventual economic reinvigoration of the former Soviet Union, which they con-tend could pose a threat to Chinese security in several ways."[4] Chinese fear that, in the long run, an economically rejuvenated Russia could become a fierce economic competitor, vying with Beijing for markets for commodities, goods, construction contracts, joint ventures, foreign investment, and technology. Some Chinese also raise the specter of a revival of Russian "traditional great-nation chauvinism" as posing an expansionist threat to China, citing some imprudent statements by Moscow bureaucrats.[5] The Chinese government has evidently de-cided that it is not going to cooperate in the restoration and reform of the Russian economy but instead will exploit the current situation to its own advantage.

At the same time, the Russian government, preoccupied with present eco-nomic difficulties and searching for foreign-currency income, shuts its eyes to those negative side effects that are the result of a sharp increase in Russo-Chinese economic cooperation. It acts in this manner because it neither under-stands nor is interested in its regional interests. Such a situation poses serious long-term risks for Russia but is hard to alter in the short term.

Within this context of the general tendencies and current state of Russo-Chinese relations, it remains to analyze the specific role played by the Russian Far East and northeastern China and the strains that recent developments have reintroduced into one of the world's most important bilateral relationships.

The Russian Far East and Northeast China in Russo-Chinese Relations

In the 1990s, geopolitical contradictions and ideological disagreements have yielded the foreground of public opinion to economic cooperation. Various forms of inter-relationship such as trade, industrial, and agricultural cooperation have begun to play a leading role, not only on the national level but also on a regional level. At the same time, people-to-people contacts have become increasingly utilitarian, as exemplified by the mass training of Chinese-language interpreters throughout the Russian Far East (hereafter RFE). Nowadays, not only the universities but also many scientific institutes, technical colleges, private companies, and cooperative societies have taken up this work. Cultural and political contacts have also acquired a trade or industrial color, especially with the breakdown of administrative structures in the former USSR.

The collapse of the Soviet economy in 1991–92, a break in economic relations among regions, and high transport costs practically cut the RFE off from industrial centers in European Russia. Instead of the Russian and European commodities traditionally consumed in the region, the Russian Far East has had to import most of its goods from Asian countries. This turn to foreign economic relations has become the most important factor for stability in the social and economic situation in the regions of the RFE. Take the case of the Russian Maritime province (*Primorskii krai*). In 1992, its foreign trade turnover tripled compared to 1990, reaching $721 million.[6] This remarkable result was achieved despite strict quotas, the licensing of export goods, and a high rate of export duties taken even on goods with state licenses.

China's share in the foreign trade of Russia's various Far Eastern regions has depended on their geographical proximity and the state of their economy. Chinese participation is most important for the Amur oblast, the main center for re-export of goods from Russia and other parts of the former Soviet Union to China. In 1992, 87 percent of the total exports from and 98 percent of the imports into the Amur oblast were connected with China. In the foreign trade turnover of Khabarovsk krai, China's share was 84 percent; in the Maritime province, 57.3 percent; but in Magadan oblast, only 13.5 percent.[7]

Nonetheless, the potential for regional economic exchange between the two countries is limited. The development of the RFE as a source of raw materials, coupled with Russia's military advance onto the Pacific, favored mining and other industries related to the military. At the same time, Northeast China followed a similar path, encouraging heavy industry with a secondary emphasis on agriculture.[8] So far, neither the funding nor the will has been available to realize the RFE's desire for fundamental economic restructuring.

On paper, at least, all existing projects reject an orientation toward raw material production and labor-intensive industries. The development of labor-saving technologies in the Russian Far East is especially important due to a lack of labor power in the region. But the notion of further cooperation based upon the complementary requirements of the Russian Far East for labor power and the Chinese for raw materials has not shown itself to be a viable alternative, despite the inherent promise.

The Chinese attempt since the late 1980s to capture a Russian market with cheap, low-quality goods has also proved detrimental to real economic cooperation. Chinese goods, especially those from the Chinese Northeast, have acquired a certain uncomplimentary notoriety, so Russian consumers now prefer to purchase more expensive, but superior, goods from Japan, South Korea, Singapore, and other countries. As a result, China's share in the trade turnover of the Maritime province has dropped from 57.3 percent in 1992 to 43.5 present in 1993.[9]

Thus, the first and simplest stage of Russo-Chinese economic cooperation at the regional level, which was conducted mostly by barter agreements, cannot become a model for economic relations. Several factors will inhibit development along these lines. First, the Russian Far East's population of eight million represents a relatively small market, and its downward demographic trend does not encourage optimistic projections. Second, the poor quality and limited range of goods offered by the Chinese works against trade expansion. Trade potential on the Russian side is also limited. Sea products, timber, and fertilizer are the main export items from the Maritime province. In 1992, the first item accounted for 75 percent of total export volume. The corresponding figures for timber and fertilizer were 10.4 percent and 9.6 percent, respectively. Thus, exports of these three commodities equaled 95.2 percent of the total.[10]

At the same time, All-Russian legislation on foreign economic relations and the mentality of local officials and businessmen prevent the RFE, despite its favorable geographic position, from assuming a go-between role in trade relations between the countries of the former Soviet Union and the more distant parts of China. On the Russian side, thousands of enterprises and companies are now trading with China. In most cases, they operate on a small scale, utilizing the barter system. They compete mercilessly with each other, often selling goods at a loss. There is no reason to believe that these activities benefit the overall economic objectives of the RFE.

At first glance, China's unified state policy on the development of Russo-Chinese relations seems to have already brought some good results. Consequently, Chinese investment and the Chinese themselves have flowed into the RFE in ever greater numbers. This was particularly noticeable in the southern part of the region, where trade ties quickly metamorphosed into financial relations. Immediately following Yeltsin's visit to China, January 1993 became a boom month for Chinese investment in the Maritime province. Of 747.5 million rubles invested throughout the Russian economy by foreign companies during this month, 459.36 million rubles were accounted for by six joint ventures between companies in the Chinese Northeast and counterparts in Vladivostok.[11] Unfortunately, this represented only a short-term rise in Chinese investment and did not result in any large-scale projects. Moreover, the profile of Chinese projects is narrow, aiming only at the immediate production and distribution of deficit goods on the Russian market. Minimization of both start-up capital and recoupment time are the dominant criteria. The conflict between this short-sighted approach and the region's long-term developmental interests will surely limit investment opportunities as much as the lack of complementarities discussed above.

Let us step back for a moment to clarify the basic interests and priorities of both sides. A list of the RFE's desiderata would include: (1) satisfaction of internal market demand to escape dependence on the central parts of Russia; (2) establishment of a regional foreign currency reserve based on trade surpluses and transit fees; (3) elimination of chronic labor shortages in construction and agriculture by the employment of Chinese; (4) sponsorship of Russian commodity producers capable of competing on the Chinese market; and (5) learning Chinese agricultural technologies more suitable to the shared geography and climate of the region than those techniques brought with them by migrants from European Russia.

A comparable Chinese list might consist of the following items: (1) production and sale of goods made in Northeast China to the Russian Far East to promote local Chinese industry; (2) the ability to purchase necessary energy resources and raw materials; (3) establishment and consolidation of an economic position in Russia; (4) acquisition of advanced technologies both from Russian industries and scientific centers in the Far East; (5) utilization of the southern part of the RFE as a transit center for export goods; (6) collection of fees for middleman services to firms in the countries of the former Soviet Union and southern China; and (7) relief of domestic demographic pressures through out-migration.

Although incomplete, these lists of basic priorities make clear the unequal conditions and aspirations under which the neighboring regions of Russia and China are now operating. In addition, there are several objective obstacles that limit the possibilities for trade and cooperation. Among the more important obstacles are the limited assortment of goods available from both sides; the lack of communications; transportation and border control infrastructure (a problem endlessly discussed but never acted upon); ambiguous and ineffective Russian legislation on economic issues; a shortage of specialists capable of realizing regional projects; the absence of a mutually advantageous model of regional cooperation for bilateral development; a language barrier, as well as ethnic and cultural perceptions and misperceptions.

With regard to the final point, it may be interesting to consider the results of polls taken in the southern part of the Maritime province in September 1992 and February 1993 by the Institute of History in Vladivostok. According to these polls, 45 percent of officials and 10 percent of the general population set their economic hopes on integration with China. But only 4 percent of officials and only 2 percent of the population would prefer to work together with Chinese, as opposed to representatives of other nationalities (all other conditions being equal). Preferences stood at 44 percent of officials and 33 percent of the general population for the Japanese, while 16 percent and 6 percent chose the South Koreans. When asked which positive characteristics they associated with the Chinese, 50 percent replied diligence, but no other redeeming features garnered strong votes. Only 9 percent found the Chinese polite (34 percent for Japanese); fewer still found the Chinese responsible (8 percent, versus 37 percent for Japanese) or honest (5 percent, versus 7 percent for Japanese).[12]

Alongside the impediment to strengthened relations presented by the Russian perception that the trade-off of Chinese population and cash for Russian space and resources is unfair, further inequalities arise in the administrative realm, where a unified Chinese state policy must be contrasted with official Moscow, whose interest in the RFE appears slight. Since guiding principles are based on "global categories" defined by the Ministry of Foreign Affairs together with concerned lobbies and bureaucrats who profit from the grant of import–export licenses, it is no surprise that from the RFE's perspective, Moscow has allowed China to arrange things to its own advantage.

This callous disregard for regional interests is at the root of the deterioration of relations between Moscow and the RFE. Too many differences exist in their conceptions of Russo-Chinese cooperation. For example, the employment of Chinese workers on a large scale in the RFE is seen in Moscow as the simplest way for the Russian government to eliminate the labor shortage in the region, but it does not take into account the experience of tsarist Russia. For the region itself, Chinese in-migration is a source of serious political and social problems and, from this point of view, the movement of the Chinese to the RFE is treated as expansionism.

Another example concerns the recent Soviet-Chinese agreement of 16 November 1991 regarding border demarcation in the Far East. According to this agreement, two islands in the Amur River, located just opposite Khabarovsk, as well as 960 hectares of rich forests in the Ussuri region, are to become Chinese territory. This decision was made without informing either the local authorities or the residents. The flood of negative reactions is thoroughly understandable. The regional mass media have characterized this decision by the president and the Russian government as "servility to the Chinese."[13]

Correctly assessing Moscow's weaknesses, China appears to have begun a policy aimed at penetrating Siberia and the RFE and strengthening its position there. The goals of such a policy seem to be a market expansion for Chinese goods; access to natural resources in exchange for the labor used to extract them; an improved position as construction contractors on the Russian market; and increased investment in production, trade, and services, mostly in the form of joint ventures. One Russian source claims that Beijing has created a state program funded at 5 billion yuan (more than $600 million) to support Chinese investment in the Russian Far East.[14]

While the Chinese on balance appear to be pursuing nothing less than a shift in surplus population from Northeast China to the RFE to form a Chinese diaspora with secure property rights, the Russian government has no comprehensive, long-term plan for dealing with this threat. Nor is it evident that the Far East is high on Moscow's priority list. Keeping this sense of abandonment in mind is extremely important in considering the revival of "Yellow Peril" sentiments after years of quiescence on that score.

"Yellow Peril"

Before the incorporation of the Maritime province into Russia and the beginning of its development by the Russians, there were virtually no Chinese in the region. One reason for this was the Manchu prohibition against Chinese settlement in Manchuria, leaving a large wilderness buffer between the RFE and China proper.[15] A second reason was the absence of any demand for Chinese labor or goods.

The assimilation of the right bank of the Ussuri by Russia in the second half of the nineteenth century brought with it an influx of Chinese into the area, primarily as seasonal laborers and manufacturers. The great majority of them, utilizing the absence of a strong border control, slipped across the border illegally and in this "nonlegal" status began to engage in various enterprises: the procurement of antlers and ginseng, the gathering of fur, the search for gold and pearls.[16] Many found a demand for their labor in the new cities founded by the Russians.

At the end of the nineteenth and beginning of the twentieth centuries, the region developed very quickly, and its labor power requirements were mainly satisfied by newcomers. These workers came from European Russia, Siberia, China, and Korea. They were concentrated in the construction, timber, mining, fishing, and transportation industries. The region needed unskilled workers, and since the Chinese and Koreans were paid considerably less than the European residents of the region, local employers preferred to hire what was then known as Oriental labor.[17]

In the period from 1905 to 1910, Chinese in the Ussuri region numbered roughly 345,000, including 130,000 industrial workers and traders, as well as 200,000 farmers who rented land from Russian peasants. Nonagricultural seasonal workers made up the difference, with ginseng gatherers being one of the largest subgroups.[18] Only about 80,000 to 90,000 Chinese lived permanently in the region. The others usually returned to China in the winter. In contrast to the Chinese, many Korean families migrated to the RFE without looking back. Most of them worked on the land. As of February 1916, there were about 145,000 foreigners living in the region, of whom 95 percent were either Chinese (78,000) or Korean (60,800).[19]

From the beginning, Russian authorities treated the Chinese well, seeing in them a source of cheap labor. Along with the emigrants to the RFE, however, came a whole host of problems, from banditry and opium use, the sale of narcotics, and the spread of opium dens to the establishment of gambling houses and brothels, smuggling, spying, and secret societies. The Russian government, aiming to secure its Far Eastern borders, took measures to exclude Asian (mainly Chinese) workers from the regional labor market. By a government decree on 12 June 1910, it was forbidden to employ foreigners in public enterprises and work opportunities in private companies were also restricted. Statistics suggest that these measures were effective, but the manpower demands of World War I reversed the trend. Whereas by 1903 foreign workers made up 51 percent of the RFE labor market, by 1913 this number shrank to 11 percent, only to rise to 33 percent in 1915.[20]

In the 1920s, the flow of Chinese into the RFE continued. At the beginning of 1923, there were close to 150,000 Chinese living in the RFE, of whom 20 percent were in the Maritime province.[21] This number remained almost constant for the next decade, but in the middle of the 1930s, an expulsion of the Chinese began, reaching its climax in 1938, when the last Chinese were repatriated or deported to Central Asia.[22] Strong-handed measures eliminated the large Chinese presence in Russia for the next half century.

The issue resurfaced in 1992 in connection with the evaluation of the use of foreign labor in the region. In 1990 and 1991, the tenor of the press on the question of Chinese labor had been more or less cordial. The Chinese had demonstrated greater cost-effectiveness than local labor in construction and agricultural jobs. In addition, Chinese consumer goods were in constant demand, filling the empty shelves of stores throughout the RFE. Even though trade was still conducted by disadvantageous barter (for metal, cement, wood, fertilizer, and technology), many contracts were signed in the heat of the moment, often at the ultimate expense of the Russian side.

In late 1992, however, the Chinese labor question reached a critical juncture. On discovering that the "shuttle trade" was more profitable than routine labor, the Chinese "universally switched to business."[23] Even though Russian enterprises and bureaucrats were ready to pay exorbitant amounts in scarce goods, fertilizer, and advanced technology, Chinese workers were unavailable. When officials from Krasnoiarsk looked into the possibility of inviting Chinese to cultivate vegetables, Chinese authorities demanded an up-front per person charge of five tons of aluminum.[24]

With a host of opportunities to choose from and ready employers everywhere,

Chinese, once inside the border, gained complete freedom of movement. Post–Soviet Russia's policing mechanisms proved insufficient for the task. Under the Russo-Chinese intergovernmental agreement on "visa-free" exchange, Chinese citizens needed only an invitation from a person or group with juridical status in order to come to Russia. Since such invitations were readily available, the Russians had effectively relinquished control of entry rights to the Chinese authorities, who could still refuse their citizens exit visas. The consequences for the Russian side were extremely unsettling. Toward the end of 1992, Chinese mass migration to Siberia and the Russian Far East began to be implemented, as some well-informed sources claimed, on the basis of a Beijing program for resettlement of surplus population from the Chinese Northeast to the RFE.[25]

The Chinese make use of a wide range of methods to cross into Russian territory. The most prevalent include labor contracts and "business trip" invitations, frequently originating in Central Asia. Another method involves working for one of the many joint ventures already in existence or joining a "tourist group." Once in Russia, many of these so-called "tourists," "scientists," and "businessmen" make all possible efforts to stay indefinitely. Those with contracts avoid returning home even after the contract's expiration. For the second time in this century, Russian Asia has run up against the "Yellow Peril."

In the summer of 1992 in the Maritime province, 6,000 of a total 7,076 foreign workers were Chinese.[26] For 1993, there were no exact statistics, but estimates fluctuate between 40,000 and 150,000. The number of those who remain for longer than three months is not known, since the police lack the powers necessary to monitor the situation.[27] According to an assertion made by the executive director of the Siberian Association, V. Ivankov, there are now close to 1 million Chinese living illegally in Siberia and the RFE.[28]

At the close of 1993, not only the local press, but even central news agencies, began to discuss the threat of Chinese expansion, the essence of which appears to be the peaceful settlement and economic assimilation of the RFE. Eventually, the Russians will be squeezed out. The economic and social damage caused by the euphoria of blind friendship is a common theme.[29] The Chinese migrational flood, it is noted, includes not only ordinary merchants but also drug dealers, thieves, murderers, and other criminal elements. This aggravates the already serious crime situation in the Russian Far East and in Russia as a whole. Certain crimes are directed exclusively at Chinese, and conflicts between Russian and Chinese gangs have increased. The Chinese, it is claimed, also actively attempt to monopolize markets and to undermine the financial system of Russia. In 1993 alone, according to unofficial data, the total value of hard currency transferred from Russia to China was almost $50 million.[30] Russian currency in Chinese hands is often spent on the purchase of invitations, passports, and forged documents allowing free entry into and movement within Russia. Funds are also used to bribe officials to issue export licenses.[31] Certain areas of the Russian taiga have been virtually cleaned out by Chinese poachers.

Violations, it is argued, take place in areas other than economics, too. For example, the Chinese at the border are often in breach of visa laws, sanitary regulations, and customs rules. Smuggling of goods, including narcotics, is rife. In 1992, the Maritime province deported only ten Chinese for the violation of local laws.[32] This low figure is an indication of weakened police powers, not the absence of crime. The increasingly common perception in the RFE that the Chinese are taking advantage of the current situation to obtain strategic supplies inspires strong anti-Chinese sentiments. The more Chinese are present to remind people of this state of affairs, the more likely the chances of violent conflict and tragedy.

Local authorities no longer believe that Moscow will solve the urgent problems of the region. In the second half of 1993 they began themselves to take activist measures, implementing various local regulations to stop and control Chinese penetration and influence. Krasnoiarsk has begun to issue its own licenses to enterprises wishing to bring in foreign workers. Siberia and the RFE have implemented a strict registration system. In October–November 1993, regional leaders met in Khabarovsk and Vladivostok to discuss the adoption of further measures.[33] In June 1993, the Cossacks of the Maritime province were given permission to establish guard stations along the border to counteract smuggling and poaching, while in September *Izvestiia* reported on an initiative to prevent Chinese from rooting out ginseng on the Russian side.[34]

Conclusion

China will always be an important neighbor for Russia, both for security and economic reasons. The Russian Far East knows this at least as well as Moscow does and is therefore deeply interested in the development of relations. The character of recent contacts, however, fosters a series of serious problems that must be resolved in the near future. The different interpretations that each side places on the phrase "mutually beneficial cooperation" is the proximate cause of friction, but the deeper sources include diverging economic agendas and the internal difficulties both Russia and China are experiencing as they reform. Of even longer duration are the reasons that lie in the overlapping, but not always identical, historical memories of the two peoples and the tension between national and regional Russian interests.

At present, cooperation is creating an unequal partnership. Chinese actions are more calculated, regulated, goal-oriented, and active. Russia, which is passing through an epoch of crisis in the power structure, an economic breakdown accompanied by self-enrichment by unprincipled entrepreneurs, and a legal vacuum in which local regulations do little to disentangle disorder, presents a different picture altogether. This disparity, and especially the mass migration of Chinese to the eastern regions of Russia, creates serious dangers against which Moscow is either unable or unwilling to take concrete countermeasures. The long road to agreement between two great powers, their peoples, and their regions lies ahead.

Notes

1. A.V. Gavrilov, "Rossiia i Kitai: sblizhenie ili protivostoianie?" in *Obshchestvo i gosudarstvo v Kitae: Tezisy dokladov*, vol. 2 (Moscow, 1993), pp. 161–63.

2. Leszek Buszynski, "Russia's Priorities in the Pacific," *Pacific Review*, vol. 6, no. 3, 1993, p. 288.

3. Alexander B. Parkansky, *The Disintegration Trends in Eastern Russia and the Russian Economic Opportunities in the Northern Pacific Area: New Order in Post-Communist Eurasia* (Sapporo, 1993), p. 133.

4. Bonny S. Glaser, "China's Security Perceptions: Interests and Ambitions," *Asia Survey*, vol. 33, no. 3, March 1993, p. 256.

5. Wang Bingyin, "Eluosi yatai zhengqiede diaozheng he womende duiqie," *Dongbeiya yanjiu*, no. 2, 1993, pp. 32–33.

6. "Primorskoe kraevoe upravlenie statistiki," *Utro Rossii*, 3 February 1993.

7. Goskomstat RFSFR. Amurskoe oblastnoe upravlenie statistiki. Magadanskoe oblastnoe upravlenie statistiki. Primorskoe kraevoe upravlenie statistiki. *Statisticheskie materialy za 1992 g.*

8. Wang Shengjin and An Jingchun, "Zhongguo Dongbei Sansheng jiu shi niandaide kaifa chanye yu Dongbeiya quyu Jingji," in *Dongbeiya jingji fazhan yanjiu (guoji xueshu taolunhui wenji* (Changchun: Jilin renmin chubanshe, 1993), pp. 118–26.

9. *Utro Rossii*, 3 February 1994.

10. *Utro Rossii*, 3 February 1993.

11. *Vladivostok*, 6 March 1992.

12. V.L. Larin and E.A. Plaksen, "Primor'e: perspektivy razvitiia cherez prizmu obshchestvennogo mneniia," in *Rossiia i ATR*, 1, 1993, p. 11; E.A. Plaksen, "Mnenie rukovoditelei Iuzhnogo Primor'ia o vkhozhdenii v ekonomicheskuiu strukturu ATR i proektakh 'Tumangan' i 'Bol'shoi Vladivostok' (po materialam sotsiologicheskogo oprosa)," unpublished manuscript, Vladivostok, 1993.

13. P. Ivashov, "Ugrozhaet li rossiiskomu Dal'nemu Vostoku 'kitaiskii sindrom'," in *Dal'nevostochnyi uchenyi*, no. 30, 1993, p. 4.

14. V. Shcherbakov, "Velikii brat k nam tianet ruki," *Vladivostok*, 1 September 1993, p. 5.

15. For more on Chinese migration to Manchuria, see M.A. Patrusheva and G.A. Sukhacheva, *Ekonomicheskoe razvitie Man'chzhurii* (Moscow, 1985).

16. F.V. Solov'ev, *Kitaiskie otkhodniki i ikh geograficheskie nazvaniia v Primor'e* (Vladivostok, 1973).

17. D.V. Murzaev, *K voprosu ob ekonomicheskom sostoianii Amurskoi oblasti za poslednee desiatiletie* (Blagoveshchensk, 1914), p. 96.

18. V.K. Arsen'ev, *Kitaitsy v Ussuriiskom krae* (Khabarovsk, 1914).

19. A.I. Alekseev and B.N. Morozov, *Osvoenie russkogo Dal'nego Vostoka (konets XIX–1917g)* (Moscow, 1989), p. 13.

20. L.I. Galiamova, *Ocherki istorii formirovaniia rabochego klassa Dal'nego Vostoka Rossii (1860–fevral' 1917g.)* (Vladivostok, 1984), p. 47.

21. G.A. Sukhacheva, "Bich strany: khunkhuzy v Man'chzhurii i Primor'e v 20-e gody XX v.," *Rossiia i ATR*, no.1, 1992, p. 95.

22. E.N. Chernolutskaia, "Russkii s kitaitsem brat'ia navek? (neizvestnye stranitsy deportatsii kitaitsev iz Primor'ia)," *Komsomol'skaia pravda*, 20 March 1993.

23. *Vladivostok,* 21 April 1993.
24. *Izvestiia,* 2 November 1993.
25. V. Shcherbakov, "Velikii brat," p. 5.
26. *Vladivostok,* 22 September 1992.
27. V. Shcherbakov, "Velikii brat," p. 5.
28. *Izvestiia,* 2 November 1993.
29. V. Medvedev, "Pukhovik iz Pekina: miagko steletsia, da zhestko spat'," in *Komsomol'skaia pravda,* 30 October 1993; A. Tarasov, "Sibir'—tol'ko dlia russkikh?" in *Izvestiia,* 2 November 1993.
30. V. Shcherbakov, "Velikii brat," p. 5.
31. P. Ivashov, "Ugrozhaet li," p. 3.
32. *Utro Rossii,* 23 January 1993.
33. *Vladivostok,* 6 November 1993.
34. *Rossiiskaia gazeta,* 13 August 1993; *Izvestiia,* 14 September 1993.

The Emergence of Siberia and the Russian Far East as a "New Frontier" for Koreans

Kim Hakjoon

Siberia and the Russian Far East have been important areas for Koreans since the period of prehistory. Some parts of these territories belonged to the early Korean political entities known as Kochoson ("Old Korea" or "Ancient Korea"), Koguryo, and Parhae (Pohai in Chinese). Although Siberia and the Russian Far East were separated from later Korean state forms, the region served as a key sanctuary for Korean independence fighters engaged in efforts to overthrow Japanese colonial rule. The Korean Communist movement began there as well. Today, a sizable body of Koreans with Russian citizenship live in the region.

Notwithstanding these historical ties, Siberia and the Russian Far East were until recently forbidden and forgotten in South Korea. But in 1988, the South Korean government adopted a "Northern Policy" aimed at expanding diplomatic relations with then socialist countries, the result of which was that Siberia and the Russian Far East, as well as Manchuria, emerged as objects of active public discussion and even as a prospective "new frontier" for Koreans into the next century. The subsequent rapprochement between Russia and South Korea has only served to strengthen these tendencies. The following essay will be devoted to elucidating the current and past ties between the Korean people and the eastern parts of Russia.

Pre–World War II

Leading scholars of the ancient history of Korea generally concur that the progenitors of the present Korean people founded Kochoson ("Old Korea") as "confederated kingdoms" during the fifth and fourth centuries B.C. in territories encompassing Manchuria and parts of northern China. At that time, the Russian

Far East formed part of Manchuria.[1] Although it is unclear whether Kochoson's borders included the present Russian Far East, some South Korean historians maintain that the Dong-I tribe, ("eastern barbarian") of Kochoson, forerunners of the Korean people, did in fact rule over that area.[2]

Within the territory claimed by Kochoson, mainly in southern Manchuria and northern Korea, the political entity of Koguryo was founded around 37 B.C. Along with Paekche in southwestern Korea and Silla in southeastern Korea, the appearance of Koguryo marked the emergence of the "three kingdoms period." By the fifth century A.D., Koguryo had become the dominant kingdom, covering at its peak large swaths of Siberia and what would become Russia's Maritime province.[3] By the late seventh century, Koguryo declined, but within thirty years of its demise arose a new kingdom, Parhae, whose patrimony has been the subject of controversy but which can be viewed as the successor to Koguryo.[4] At its height, around the ninth century, Parhae occupied a vast area stretching from the present Russian Maritime province in the east to the Amur River in the north.[5]

The history of these seemingly remote kingdoms was recovered in the twentieth century. Chang To-bin, a young Korean exiled to Vladivostok in 1912 for anti-Japanese activities, prompted by his discoveries of Parhae relics in Ussuriisk (north of Vladivostok), published an article in Korean asserting that Parhae's territory had encompassed Russia's Maritime province. In 1954, N.N. Zhabelina, a Soviet archaeologist living in Ussuriisk, without knowledge of Chang's publication, found the same Parhae relics in the same place. Today, even Chinese archaeologists accept the view that Parhae had encompassed parts of present-day Russia.[6]

With the dissolution of Parhae in 926, the Korean nation forever lost the territories of Siberia and the Russian Far East, as well as Manchuria. More than that, the kingdom of Parhae itself was "lost," as Korean writers became enamored of China and accepted Chinese claims that Manchuria had always been, simply, home to China's "eastern barbarians." It took centuries for this sinocentric view on Korea's past to change.

In the seventeenth century, Koreans dispatched an expeditionary force to aid the Ching Chinese in repelling an apparent invasion from the north across the Amur River. At the time, the Koreans did not know that the foreign troops they faced were Russian; rather, they surmised that the invaders belonged to a Manchurian tribe called the Rason. For their part, the Russians appear to have been preoccupied with the Chinese and failed to take note of their first encounter with Koreans. Both people, it seems, were transfixed, albeit in different ways, by the civilization of China.[7]

Finally, in the eighteenth century, when Korean studies rather than Chinese studies found favor among certain Korean scholars, a few historians began to study Parhae, arguing that "Parhae should be included as an integral part of Korean history."[8] Observing the weakening Manchu Ching dynasty, these scholars warned of the possibility that the Manchus would be forced northward, putting pressure on the Korean peninsula. They therefore suggested studying the history of Manchuria, especially in the period of Parhae, to re-establish a sense of Korea's "lost territory." (No mention was made of Russia's Maritime province, then still a part of China.)

In 1861, Russia acquired most of the Russian Far East, including the Maritime province, from China and began offering incentives to attract immigrants. Within two years, farmers from thirteen households in northeastern Korea crossed the Tuman River (Tumen, in Chinese) into Russia's Pos'et district. Spurred by famine and other natural calamities, this first exodus became a mass flight by the 1870s. Within another few years, the number of Korean immigrants reached approximately 12,000; by 1910, the year of the demise of the Yi Kingdom, the number grew to perhaps 80,000.[9]

Japanese annexation of the Korean peninsula in 1910 encouraged another mass exodus into Siberia and the Russian Far East, which provided a critically important sanctuary for an anti-Japanese movement. Some Korean immigrants established political organizations, such as the New Korean Community (Shinhanchon) on the outskirts of Vladivostok and in Vladivostok proper, the Korean People's Association (Haninminhoe). Bands of anti-Japanese guerrillas were also formed, notably in Nikolsk-Ussuriisk and Vladivostok. In 1916, the Korean National Council, a kind of Korean government in exile, was organized, instantly becoming the largest and most influential Korean émigré organization up to that time. At the same time, about half of the Koreans in Russia were naturalized, and during World War I many were drafted into the tsarist army (to avoid service, many fled to Manchuria).

Koreans could not help but participate in the revolutionary events of 1917–22, engaging in partisan warfare and joining with the Bolsheviks to expel the Japanese from Soviet soil. In January 1918, one group of Russian Koreans who had settled around Irkutsk formed a separate section of the Irkutsk Communist Party (it was later renamed the All-Russian Korean Communist Party, or Chonrohaninkongsantang). Also in 1918, Lee Tong-hui established the Korean Socialist Party (Haninsahoetang), with Bolshevik assistance, in Khabarovsk.[10] By 1923, Koreans made up 20 percent of the Soviet Communist Party in the Maritime province.

In Korea, the failure of the March First Independence Movement of 1919 resulted in another mass exodus to Siberia and the Russian Far East. Some independence fighters sought to establish a unified Korean government in exile, with its own army in Russia, but the Korean provisional government was instead founded in Shanghai in April 1919. In 1921, Korean guerrilla forces in Siberia united with their counterparts in Manchuria under the banner of the Korean Volunteer Army (Taehanuiyonggun), headquartered in Alekseevsk, to fight the Japanese occupation force in Siberia. Soviet authorities, however, soon disbanded these units, fearing factional fighting.[11]

During the Russian Civil War, the Japanese expeditionary forces, in a sign of growing concern about the Korean presence in Soviet Russia, conducted raids on Korean communities. More decisive measures were forthcoming. With the Soviet-Japanese treaty of 1925, whereby Japan recognized the Soviet state, the Soviet government pledged to eliminate anti-Japanese activities, thereby dashing the hopes of the Korean nationalists. Still, the presence of so many Koreans inside the USSR remained a matter of concern in Japan throughout the interwar period.[12]

With the demand for labor encouraging steady immigration, the number of Koreans inside Siberia and the Russian Far East continued to grow. By 1929, the population of Koreans in the USSR was estimated at more than 200,000. Koreans constituted the third largest ethnic group in eastern Siberia (after the Russians and Ukrainians). Koreans were granted voting rights, allowed to print newspapers, and operate schools, and generally to develop Korean language and culture.[13] A nominally self-governing Korean national district was established around Pos'et in the 1920s, although proposals in 1929 to create a Far Eastern Korean People's Republic inside the Russian Federation were rejected.

In the 1930s, the Korean community inside the USSR was severely jolted, first by collectivization, which encouraged class tensions as well as out-migration, and then by repressive measures undertaken in the wake of Japanese aggression in Manchuria. After further Korean immigration had been restricted and efforts were made to naturalize all those already in the country, in the late 1930s the entire Korean population of the Soviet Far East—at least 180,000 people—was deported over two months' time to Soviet Central Asia, a measure directed at countering Japanese espionage.[14] Survivors have reported that the police authorities simply left the deported Koreans in the middle of nowhere; casualty figures from this operation remain unknown.[15]

Soviet Koreans survived these ordeals, however, forming large and vibrant communities in Central Asia. Many Koreans were able to attain high posts in the Soviet administration.[16] Second- and third-generation Koreans proved particularly valuable to the Soviet state, when in August 1945 it occupied the northern half of Korea. Indeed, Koreans who had lived and trained inside the USSR became the leaders of the Korean Communist state, among them Kim Il-song, recently deceased ruler of North Korea.

Kim's record as an anti-Japanese partisan can be traced to a Chinese Communist–controlled guerrilla army known as the Northeast Anti-Japan United Army in Manchuria. When Japanese military operations in Manchuria intensified, Kim retreated in 1941 to Khabarovsk with the remnants of his forces (Kim's son, Kim Jong-il, was born in the city the following year). Although Kim Il-song's activities inside the USSR have never been clarified fully in North Korean publications, some sources have acknowledged that he received Soviet military training and served as an officer in the Soviet army.[17]

Whatever his training, Kim returned to Korea with the Soviet occupation force following Japan's surrender in August 1945. With the apparent blessing of his Soviet benefactors, he began a series of maneuvers that culminated in his seizure of power in the soon-to be-formed North Korean state. It was this strong connection between North Korea and the USSR that led the South Korea government into a resolute policy of prohibiting all interaction, including cultural exchange and scholarly inquiry, with territories that had played a large role in Korean history.

Re-establishment of Ties: South Korea and the Russian Far East

With the division of the peninsula following the creation in August and September 1948 of the South Korean and then the North Korean states, and with the outbreak of the Korean War in 1950, Korea became a focal point of the cold war. The USSR came to be regarded in South Korea as a "hostile country"; South Korea, in the eyes of the north and its benefactors, was viewed as nothing other than "a colony of American imperialism in Northeast Asia."

As anti-Communism became the hallmark of South Korean politics and identity, it became taboo to teach about the Soviet Union in meaningful detail. In particular, the history of the Korean Communist movement in Siberia and the Russian Far East could not be taught in Korean schools. Even the story of the Korean nationalist movement in Siberia and the Russian Far East, despite its anti-Communist orientation, was studiously avoided, lest discussion shade off into references to the Korean Communist movement. Neither South Korea nor the USSR permitted its citizens to travel to the other country.

In the 1970s, a certain relaxation came to be felt in association with the policy of détente that affected U.S.-Soviet relations. South Korea sought an improvement in its relationship with the USSR and showed interest in proposals then being discussed to develop Siberia with international assistance. In any event, the USSR showed itself to be unappreciative of South Korea's overtures, which came to naught.[18]

The chilly political environment manifested itself indirectly in South Korean historiography. North Korean historians became immersed in research on Kochoson, Koguryo, and Parhae, emphasizing that these political formations encompassed eastern Siberia, the Russian Far East, Manchuria, and even northern China, with the corollary that the North Korean state was their successor (the South was seen as the successor to one of the "three kingdoms," Silla, infamous for betraying Korea through its alliance with the Chinese Tang dynasty). South Korean historians, meanwhile, paid little attention to these questions.[19]

During the 1980s in South Korea, there arose a body of fiction devoted to Kochoson, Koguryo, and Parhae. This literature, exemplified by a series of *Dan* writings by an anonymous "prophet," forecast the unification of the entire Korean nation and its rise to preeminence in East Asia. Against the background of the rigid policies of the Fifth Republic (a "civilian" version of military rule), escapist fantasies about past Korean glory and the re-establishment of Korean rule over eastern Russia and Manchuria won a certain following. In such ways did the psychological pressure for national reunification grow.

Even to imagine the eventual reunification of Korea meant that South Korea had to renew diplomatic ties with the USSR and the People's Republic of China. In such a way would North Korea's position—insistence on unification only on its terms—be softened. And so, in February 1988, in his inauguration speech, South Korean President Roh Tae-woo formally announced the new "Northern Policy." Promising the normalization of relations with all socialist countries, President Roh pursued the Northern Policy energetically and successfully. The hosting of the Seoul Olympics in 1988, the radical changes in socialist countries in 1989–90, and the subsequent end of the cold war helped pave the way for the promised renewal of diplomatic ties with East European countries (1988–89), the USSR (1990), and China (1992).[20]

Not surprisingly, the renewal of diplomatic ties with the USSR has permitted a South Korean rediscovery of Siberia and the Russian Far East. Tourist visits have increased, as has bilateral trade. A fair number of organizations have emerged in South Korea dedicated to cultivating ties with eastern Russia. And academic seminars on Kochoson, Koguryo, and Parhae have become popular. Some journalists have termed this new interest "the resurrection of Siberia and the Russian Far East," as well as the ancient kingdoms, in the daily lives of South Koreans.

A warm nostalgia for "ancient lands" has become visible. "The Russian Maritime province and Manchuria are our *Heimat*," wrote one South Korean historian in 1993. "Whenever we think of those areas, they make us feel something moving."[21] A former congressman went a step further, arguing that as in the past, the Russian Far East could become an integral part of a Korean commonwealth in the future. Naturally, he stressed the study of Kochoson, Koguryo, and Parhae. Participants at a historical roundtable, which along with the congressman included several professors and a businessman, heartily agreed.[22]

Similarly, a leading anthropologist in South Korea argued in 1993 that a Korean Autonomous Region ought to be established in the Russian Far East, a cause for which the Korean government should campaign. Along with the present Korean Autonomous Region in Yenbien, Manchuria, such a turn of events would help an (eventually) unified Korea become "a powerful state," assisting Russia and China while checking Japan.[23] He based his argument on the trend indicating that Koreans in Uzbekistan and Kazakhstan have been steadily returning to the settlements they inhabited prior to the 1937 deportation. Following Yeltsin's apology for Stalin's ill-treatment of Soviet Koreans and the promulgation of a law in March 1993 exonerating Soviet Koreans from charges of spying, the migration of Koreans from Central Asia to the Russian Far East has accelerated. Perhaps as many as 100,000 of the 500,000 Koreans in territories of the former USSR have migrated back.

Champions of reconstituting Korea's ties with eastern Russia stop short of advocating the recovery of "lost territory," something they acknowledge to be neither desirable nor feasible in the current international situation. Rather, they are content to call for "the natural formation of a common cultural and economic sphere among the Korean nation" within the Korean peninsula and adjacent areas where there have been historical ties.

Occasionally, however, the vague notion of a "common cultural and economic sphere" will become a greater "Korean Commonwealth," part of a borderless world that is allegedly coming to Northeast Asia. In such a view, South Korea ought to encourage not only the formation of a Korean Autonomous Region in Russia to parallel the one in Manchuria but also immigration en masse to these territories.[24] Chang Chi-hyok, chairman of the Koryo Synthetic Fiber Group (Kohap) in South Korea, has boldly predicted that as a result of immigration, "within fifty years, in the Russia Far East and Manchuria there will be about ten million Koreans."[25]

Despite assurances that no moves are afoot to recover lost territory, Russians and Chinese remain suspicious of South Korea's newfound interest in their countries. These suspicions have been duly recognized in South Korea. The same businessman who predicted a mass migration has cautioned Koreans, no doubt in light of his extensive interests in the Russian Far East, not to irritate either the Russians or the Chinese, arguing against the organization of a Korean Autonomous Region and for the need to curb Korean nationalism.[26] The possibility of serious disputes arising out of Korean nationalism remain real.

Beyond notions of historical ties and a common Korean cultural and economic sphere, many South Korean businessmen have shown increasing concrete interest in eastern Russia's underground resources, no doubt the greatest in the world.[27] The champion of eastern Russia among Koreans, Chang Chi-hyok, has written that because of its resources the Russian Far East will become the central area of a "Northeast Asia and Pan-East Sea [Sea of Japan] Economic Cooperation Sphere" in the not-too-distant future. He strongly advises his Korean colleagues to invest there too.[28]

Chang takes comfort in his view that Korea's position in eastern Russia remains superior to Japan's. He points to the two Russo-Japanese wars of the twentieth century, as well as to Japan's enduring hesitancy to strengthen its traditional adversary through large-scale investment.[29] "Some Russians," Chang has written, "entertained the fond hope that Korean investment would reduce the Far East's reliance on Japanese capital and thus free regional development from being hostage to the Northern Territories [Kuriles] dispute."[30] Moreover, according to Chang, Russia's reception to an increased Korean presence contrasts sharply with fears of a "Chinese rush" into its territories that threatens to upset the demographic balance of the region in China's favor.

Alongside Chang's Kohap, Samsung and Hyundai have also opened branches in Vladivostok (Kohap's remains the largest). Smaller Seoul-based firms have built a casino, distributed Bibles in Khabarovsk, sold electric billy clubs in Blagoveshchensk, and imported reindeer horns from Chukotsk.[31] In 1992 the South Korean government opened a branch of its Trade Promotion Corporation and in 1993 a consulate general, both in Vladivostok. The Trade Promotion Corporation sponsored meetings to discuss programs for the joint development of the Russian Far East, including the construction of infrastructure.[32]

No doubt the most ambitious joint development proposal is the so-called Tumen River Project, first raised in 1990 at an international conference in Changchun, China, co-hosted by the Asia–Pacific Research Institute of Jilin Province and the East–West Center of Hawaii. In 1991, the United Nations Development Project Regional Bureau for Asia and the Pacific held a conference on Northeast Asian regional cooperation in Ulan Bator, Mongolia. Priority for the development of the Tumen River delta was accorded to all six of the countries concerned: China, North Korea, South Korea, Japan, Russia, and Mongolia. A series of follow-up conferences have been held in Seoul, Pyongyang, Vladivostok, and Beijing. Driving these discussions is a vision of the Tumen delta's multinational complementarity as permitting the rise of a kind of Northeast Asian Hong Kong or Singapore.[33]

Russia recognizes the need for regional cooperation and foreign assistance in the development of its eastern territories, given that most of the factories in the area are military-related and have thus suffered irreparably from the curtailment in defense spending. South Korea, for its part, is also bullish on regional cooperation, hoping thereby to open up North Korean society and promote reunification. A potential expansion of South Korea's export market also inclines that country in the direction of the new regionalism.[34]

Conclusion

Although the Korean peninsula is small (about the size of Minnesota or Japan's Honshu), its total population exceeds 80 million. Koreans need a "new frontier" to absorb emigration, and in Siberia and the Russian Far East they seem to have found one. To be sure, at present, economic and political uncertainties in Russia have proved to be a serious psychological impediment to massive migration. At the same time, the lack of infrastructure, high fixed costs, labor shortages, and severe climatic conditions have combined to restrict Korean investment. But should Russia become more stable, this situation is liable to change, and the attractiveness of the "new frontier" will grow.

Meanwhile, in 1991 North Korea declared that a free-trade zone would be introduced in the part of its country bordering on Russia and China, around the cities of Rajin and Sonbong. The opening up of that society would appear to be inevitable. This would in turn have enormous consequences for the unification question, the most important national agenda in South Korea and North Korea in the coming years. In that context, the South's "rediscovery" of Siberia and the

Russian Far East looms large indeed. The pursuit of regional cooperation across national boundaries can only strengthen South Korea's economic and geopolitical position, serving in addition as a strategic lever in its relationship with North Korea and its policies to open that country.

Notes

1. Lee Ki-baik, *A New History of Korea,* trans. Edward W. Wagner with Edward J. Schultz (Cambridge, MA: Harvard University Press, 1984), pp. 13–22.

2. For example, Ahn Ho-sang, *Dong-I-jokui yetyoksa* (An Ancient History of the Dong-I Tribe) (Seoul, 1971).

3. Andrew C. Nahm, *Korea: Tradition and Transformation* (Elizabeth, NJ: Hollym International, 1988), pp. 29–31.

4. Chinese historians have maintained that Parhae was founded by the Malagals, a seminomadic Tungusic people who had been scattered in many tribes over a wide expanse of Manchuria, southern Siberia, and northeast Korea, and that the history of Parhae is best understood as the story of China's "northeastern barbarians." See, for example, Wang Chong-ri, *A Brief History of Parhae* [in Chinese] (Beijing, 1984); Korean translation published in Chunchon, 1987. By contrast, both North Korean and South Korean scholars have claimed that Parhae was founded by the Koguryo people with the help of the Malagals, arguing that the predominantly Koguryo ruling class regarded the kingdom as a revival of Koguryo, as evidenced by surviving communications with the forerunners of the Japanese. Lee, *A New History,* p. 72.

5. Lee, *A New History,* p. 73.

6. Song Ki-ho, *Parhae-rul Chajaso* (In Search of Parhae) (Seoul, 1993), pp. 136–67.

7. Kang Chujin, "Diplomatic Relations Between Korea and the Soviet Union" [in Korean], in *Korea and the Soviet Union* (Seoul, 1979), pp. 14–25.

8. See the publication prepared by the Korean National Commission of UNESCO, Sohn Paw-key et al., *The History of Korea* (Seoul, 1970), p. 172.

9. Suh Dae-sook, *The Korean Communist Movement, 1918–1948* (Princeton: Princeton University Press, 1967), p. 4; Lee Chong-sik and Oh Ki-wan, "The Russian Faction in North Korea," *Asian Survey,* 8 (4), April 1968, pp. 270–71.

10. Suh, *The Korean Communist Movement,* p. 8.

11. Lee Chong-sik, *The Politics of Korean Nationalism* (Berkeley: University of California Press, 1963), pp. 101–26, 130–36; Suh, *The Korean Communist Movement,* p. 11–29.

12. Hara Teruyuki, "The Korean Movement in the Russian Maritime province, 1905–1922," in Dae-Suk Suh, ed., *Koreans in the Soviet Union* (Honolulu: University of Hawaii Press, 1987), pp. 1–23; S. Anosov, *Koreitsy v Ussuriiskom krae* (Khabarovsk, 1928); Ivan Gozhenskii, "Uchastie koreiskoi emigratsii v revoliutsionnom dvizhenii na Dal'nem Vostoke," in *Revoliutsiia na Dal'nem Vostoke* (Moscow-Leningrad, 1923), vyp. 1.

13. Lee and Oh, "The Russian Faction," pp. 271–72.

14. Wada Haruki, "Koreans in the Soviet Far East, 1917–1937," in Suh, ed., *Koreans in the Soviet Union,* pp. 24–59.

15. Lee and Oh, "The Russian Faction," pp. 273–74.

16. Kim Syn Khva, *Ocherki po istorii Sovetskikh Koreitsev* (Alma-Ata, 1965).

17. Lee Chong-sik, "Kim Il-song of North Korea," *Asian Survey,* 7 (6), June 1967, p. 377; Yang Sung-chul, "The Kim Il-song Cult in North Korea," *Korea and World Affairs,* 4 (1), Spring 1980, pp. 161–86.

18. Kim Hakjoon, "The Soviet Union in American-Korean Relations," in Koo

Youngnok and Suh Dae-sook, eds., *Korea and the United States: A Century of Coopera-tion* (Honolulu: University of Hawaii Press, 1984), pp. 203–10.

19. An exception is Yun Nae-hyon's articles of 1984 and 1986, republished in his book, *Choson Kodaesa* (The Ancient History of Korea) (Seoul, 1989). The first North Korean book on Parhae was published in 1962; in the South, the first such book appeared in 1987.

20. Peggy Falkenheim Meyer, "Gorbachev and Post-Gorbachev Policy Toward the Korean Peninsula: The Impact of Changing Russian Perceptions," *Asian Survey,* 32 (8), August 1992, pp. 759–62.

21. Song, *In Search of Parhae,* pp. 7, 127.

22. Lee Yun-ki, preface to *Hanminjote kong dong chae* (The Korean Commonwealth) (Seoul, 1993), vol. 1, p. 17. For the agreement, see pp. 92–116.

23. Lee Kwang-kyu, "The Korean Autonomous Region Should Be Established" [in Korean], *Wolganchoson,* October 1993, pp. 606–9.

24. Lee Yun-ki, preface, pp. 16–18.

25. Chang Chi-hyok, "Advance into the Russian Maritime Province Rather Than into China" [in Korean], *Shindonga,* December 1992, p. 491.

26. Ibid., p. 494; and Chang Chi-hyok, "We Should Not Irritate Russia" [in Korean], *Wolganchoson,* September 1993, pp. 587–89.

27. Robert Rehbein, "The Japan–Soviet Far East Trade Relationship: A Case of the Cautious Buyer and the Overconfident Seller," *Journal of Northeast Asian Studies,* 8 (2), Summer 1989, p. 40; James Dorian et al., "Multi-lateral Resource Cooperation Among Northeast Asian Countries: Energy and Mineral Joint Venture Prospects," paper prepared for the Workshop on the Emergence of the Russian Far East: Implications for North Pacific Regional Institution Building, East–West Center, Honolulu, 19–21 August 1993, p. 5.

28. Chang, "Advance," p. 490.

29. Michael Kapitsa, "The Evolving Situation in Northeast Asia and the Korean Problem," *Korea and World Affairs,* 16 (3), Fall 1992, p. 498.

30. Chang, "We Should Not Irritate," p. 588.

31. John J. Stephan, "The Russian Far East," *Current History,* October 1993, p. 336.

32. *The Report of the First Joint Congress of the South Korean–Russian Far East Cooperation Committee* [in Korean] (Seoul, 1992); *The Report of the Second Joint Congress of the South Korean–Russian Far East Cooperation Committee* [in Korean] (Seoul, 1993).

33. Kim Euikon, "Political Economy of the Tumen River Basin Development: Problems and Prospects," *Journal of Northeast Asian Studies,* 11 (2), Summer 1992, p. 38; Ahn Choong-yong, "Search for New Approaches and Methods for Economic Cooperation in Northeast Asia," *The Korean Journal of International Studies,* 24 (3), Autumn 1993, p. 355; Mark Valencia, "Economic Cooperation in Northeast Asia: The Proposed Tumen River Delta Scheme," *Pacific Review,* 4 (3), 1993, pp. 263–71.

34. Kim Euikon, "Political Economy," pp. 39–40.

The Future of Northeast Asia

Southeast Asia?

Hamashita Takeshi

It has long been the practice to analyze modern Asia from the viewpoint of nations and international relationships. Through this framework, much historiographical labor has been expended examining the degree of so-called "nation building" and the acceptance of "international" law in Asian countries. This approach has also been understood to reveal the degree of "modernization" of Asian countries. After much controversy concerning the adaptability of this Western-oriented modernization model to Asia, however, it has also been argued that "areas" or "regions"—an intermediate category between the nation and the world generally—should be analyzed in their full historical meaning.

In fact, the region is a historical reality that encompasses a variety of social ties not adequately dealt with under the typical national-international framework. In studies of economic history, the regional economies that mediate among national and international economies should indeed be given much more weight. At the same time, scholars carrying out regional studies should avoid limiting themselves to local matters, which constitute only a part of the overall picture.[1]

Using a regional-studies approach, it is possible to reconceptualize the historical process of modern Asia. The history of modern Asia needs to be clarified, not in terms of the "stages of development" of the Western modernization model, but in terms of the complex of inter-relationships within the region itself, viewed in the light of Asian self-conceptions. Generally speaking, Asian history is the history of a unified system characterized by internal tribute/tribute-trade relations, with China at the center. This tribute system is the premise of "modern" Asia and is reflected in several aspects of contemporary Asian history.[2]

This essay will attempt to outline briefly the long-term structure of a China-centered tribute-trade system, indicating its fundamental implications for the Japan–China relationship, and to explore the respective roles of these two countries in Northeast Asia, by way of comparison with Southeast Asia.

The Structure of the Tribute System

In theory, the tribute "system" was a relationship between two countries, China and the tribute-paying country, with tribute and imperial "gifts" as the medium and the Chinese capital as the "center." Modifying this perspective, however, is the fact that the "system" did not function in this single dimension only, but instead involved several other lesser satellite tribute relationships not directly concerning China that together formed a considerably more complex system of reciprocal relations. The tribute system in reality embraced both inclusive and competitive relations extending in a web over a large area. The case of the Liuqiu Islands (Ryukyus), for example, shows China and Japan in a competitive relationship because the Liuqiu kings sent tribute missions to both Peking and Edo during the Qing period. In the case of Korea, too, we find that while it was most certainly a tributary of China, it also sent missions to Japan. And Vietnam required tribute missions from Laos. Thus all these countries maintained satellite tribute relations with each other and constituted links in a continuous chain.[3]

The other fundamental feature of the system that must be kept in mind is its basis in commercial transactions. The tribute system in fact paralleled or was in symbiosis with a network of commercial trade relations. For example, trade between Siam (Thailand), Japan, and South China had long been maintained on the basis of profits from the tribute missions, even when much of the non–tribute trade was barely remunerative. In the eighteenth century, when the rice trade from Siam to Guangdong and Xiamen became unprofitable, the traders shifted their interest to Liuqiu and Nagasaki in Japan, thus maintaining, and even strengthening, the general multilateral trade relationship.[4] The story of the commercial penetration of Chinese merchants into Southeast Asia and the emigration of "overseas Chinese" is of course historically intertwined with the building of this trade network. Commercial expansion and the tribute-trade network developed together. Trade relations in East and Southeast Asia expanded as tribute relations expanded.[5]

It should also be noted that this tribute trade functioned as an intermediary between Europe and the countries of East Asia. In the records of Dutch and Portuguese trade with China during the Kangxi period (1662–1722), we find cottons and woolens of European provenance. Similar European goods can also be found on lists of tribute articles from Sulu and Siam to China in 1727 and 1730, respectively.[6] Tribute relationships in fact constituted a multilateral network of tribute trade, absorbing commodities from outside as well as redistributing them within the system.

These aspects of the tribute-trade system were accentuated during the Ming–Qing transition in the sixteenth and seventeenth centuries, when the ideal of sinocentric unity was expanded and consolidated, with Korea, Japan, and Vietnam being particularly strongly affected. Tribute trade was expanded through the participation of European countries, and private trade expanded along with tribute trade. Trade-related institutions, such as trade settlement and tax collection, were simultaneously elaborated. Such were the foundations of a sinocentric international order in Asia.

Sinocentrism stimulated the emergence of nationalism among China's tributary countries. Vietnam, for example, began to require tribute from Laos, and Korea insisted on the continuation of orthodox sinocentrism under the Qing dynasty, which was initially seen as a "barbarian" dynasty by Korea. Vietnam criticized China when forced to change its national name from Nanyue to Yuenan merely because a Nanyue kingdom had previously existed in ancient China. These phenomena demonstrate how tributary countries began to take on national identities vis-à-vis China based on their own understandings of sinocentrism.[7] Thus, the notion of sinocentrism was not solely a preoccupation of China but was also felt throughout the tribute zone. A sense of separate national identity was born in Asia within the tribute system through the common ideals on which tributary relationships were based. Satellite tribute zones surrounding the Chinese-dominated core had a historical existence of their own that continued until their own modernization.

Europe and the Asian Tribute-Trade System

If we view the tribute-trade zone as a historical system functioning with its own integrating discipline, what implications does this have for our understanding of the relationship between East and West? And how should we view the long-term history of the Sino-Japanese relationship within this zone?

As was mentioned at the outset, generally speaking, the Western countries were not placed outside the tribute system but were instead included under the logic of tribute relations and geographically were located at some indeterminate distance beyond the frontiers of China. In Guangdong, for example, Great Britain was not even identified by Chinese officials as the same country that had sent an envoy to Tibet. Accordingly, when Western countries first dealt with Asia, they had little choice but to deal with the tribute relations that were the basis of all relations in the region. They could enter Asia only by participating in the tribute-trade network. Attempts to modify this state of affairs would have to follow the establishment of a working base within the system. From the viewpoint of Asian history, Asian countries never responded individually or separately to Western countries coming to Asia; they responded through the tribute-trade system to which all of them belonged as integral parts.

The history of relations between China and Siam provides an interesting example of how Asian countries viewed Western countries and utilized them for Asian purposes. In 1884, during the Sino-French war over Indochina, the governor-general of Guangdong and Guangxi, Peng Yulin, sent the self-strengthening movement entrepreneur Zheng Guanyin on a mission to Siam. His personal records contain the following section, which at first glance seems to contradict the image of an enlightened intellectual of the time: "On the 26th of May 1884, when Zheng Guanyin met Chen Jinzheng, the 'consul' of Siam in Singapore, Zheng said, (a) that it was a 'crime' for Siam to have stopped its tribute embassies to China and (b) that such a decision by Siam wasn't justified *even* under international law."[8] Although Zheng was supposedly an enlightened, Westernized Chinese, referring to international law and borrowing it as a standard of judgment, he did not in fact apply the Western concept of international relations to Siam but argued instead for maintaining the historical tribute relationship, a superior–subordinate relationship. In other words, he utilized international law only as an argument, not as a basis for equal relations. On the other hand, Chen counterattacked by saying that if China wanted to arrange a treaty with Siam, it should assure an invitation to negotiations in Guangdong or Tianjin.[9] Chen thus utilized the Western concepts of international law and treaty negotiations between equals to back his argument. At heart, however, both of them clearly saw the relationship between the two countries as tributary.

In general, we may say that the entrance of Western countries into the Asian tribute-trade zone started with their participation in intra-Asian trade. Portugal and Holland, for example, conducted intermediary trade within the Asian area to earn funds to purchase necessities in Europe. And Great Britain's penetration of Asia began in the seventeenth century on the strength of its superiority in shipping. British ships carried Asian products like rice, previously imported as a tribute-trade item, to China, where they bought Chinese products like tea and silk with the proceeds. Only in the nineteenth century did Western countries start to cultivate raw materials, such as rubber, in Asia to meet their own industrial needs and to sell their industrial products to Asia.

For this purpose, the Europeans had to link the intra-Asian trade with the international market by establishing appropriate places for the settlement of trade balances. Such sites played an intermediary role between two distinct markets. When Hong Kong and Singapore adopted this function, they absorbed huge funds from overseas Chinese.[10] Consequently, the Southeast Asian and southern China economies established close links, extending their joint influence into the Indian Ocean. And yet, despite this geographic extension, the marketing structure of Europe's colonies in Asia continued to display traits characteristic of the intra-Asian tribute-trade system. Elements of domestic, regional, and international markets were all to be found in Singapore and Hong Kong.[11]

The Basis of Modern Sino-Japanese Relations

Studies on the subject of modern Sino-Japanese relations have concentrated on comparative analysis of the differences in speed and direction of "modernization" following the "Western impact."[12] Japan's "success" was traced through self-strengthening to expansion following victory in the 1894 Sino-Japanese War. This is an obviously Eurocentric approach, focusing on the search for a "little West" in Asia.

From an Asian perspective, it would appear to be more logical to trace Sino-Japanese relations as they evolved from the tribute system. The main issue of Japanese modernization then becomes the means by which to displace China from the center of the tribute-trade structure, leaving Japan in the position of what would be the "Middle Kingdom." Economically, this was simply a way of coping with long-term Chinese dominance over commercial relations in Asia. But because of the political-economic linkages inherent in the tribute-trade system, this change required the complete reconfiguration of relations among Japan, China, Korea, and the Liuqiu Islands. This, in turn, would send tsunami-sized ripples throughout Northeast and Southeast Asia, wherever the tribute-trade system still held sway.

If we accept this interpretation of the Japanese initiative, which achieved fullest expression as the East Asian Co-Prosperity Sphere, there are important historiographic implications, in both the economic and political realms. Existing studies describe Japanese modernization in terms of the recovery of tariff autonomy and industrialization, that is, as matters of national sovereignty and the formation of a national economy. The goal was purportedly clarification of the process by which Japan realized "national wealth and power" (*fukoku kyōhei*), the great rallying cry of the Meiji period. Concentration on the "how," however, has led to neglect of the "why." Because of the Eurocentric focus on Japanese escape from subordination to the West, the importance of the historical relationship between Japan and China has been ignored. Japanese motivation for undertaking modernization after the opening of Japanese ports can only be understood from within the web woven by the tribute-trade system.

The main reason why Japan chose the direction of industrialization was its defeat in attempts to expand commercial relations with China. Japanese merchants faced the well-established power of overseas Chinese merchants built through the Dejima trade in Nagasaki during the Edo period. Chinese merchants monopolized the export business in seafoods and native commodities, and Japanese merchants were unable to break their competitors' grip on the market. When the Japanese consul in Hong Kong, Mr. Suzuki, emphasized the importance of the Hong Kong market in 1890 in a report he sent to the Japanese Ministry of Foreign Affairs commenting on the low spirits of Japanese merchants in Hong Kong, he pointed out that Chinese merchants were united and had a long-term strategy that could forgo short-term profits. He also noted that Japanese merchants lacked sufficient funds to weather even temporary losses and that there were indications that Japanese producers sold their products to Chinese merchants at cheaper rates than to Japanese merchants. In short, the consul was pessimistic about the possibility of Japanese merchants establishing themselves in the Hong Kong market.

But the power and knowledge possessed by Chinese merchants in Japan sometimes worked in favor of Japanese exports. For example, it was from China that Japanese manufacturers received the information necessary to produce cotton goods that could substitute for Western wares on the Chinese market. In 1887, Chinese merchants in Yokohama began to purchase cotton cloth in Saitama prefecture near Tokyo. The parties concerned pushed the authorities to promote exports to the Chinese market. When the Hong Kong consul was consulted, he in turn requested the advice of prominent Chinese merchants.[13] This case illustrates the general course of Japanese industrialization predicated on import substitution, not only on the domestic market but also for Asia as a whole.

Increased foreign trade with Western countries also provided motivation for industrialization through the development of new exports, such as silk and coal.[14] Although this tendency was the result of initiatives undertaken by Western firms, their main aim was not to export industrial goods from their own countries, but to import Asian products. Hence, trade relations in East Asia were not significantly altered by the opening of the Japanese market.

Political relations between Japan and China in the early Meiji period can now also be reinterpreted. Most previous studies of the Sino-Japanese treaty signed on 13 May 1871 conclude that the treaty gave expression to a new equality between the two nations, as demonstrated by the establishment of mutual consular jurisdictions. As such, the treaty is considered a milestone in the modern international relations of East Asia.[15] It is doubtful, however, that the Chinese truly regarded the Japanese side as equal. Underlying Chinese recognition of other states was the traditional idea of a hierarchy with the Chinese emperor at the top, a structure similar to the Chinese vision of domestic society. It was virtually impossible for the Chinese to conceive of "equality" with their emperor.

The Kiakhta Treaty of 1727 provides another example of this problem. Here, too, "equality" finds expression in Article Six, which provides for an exchange of letters between the Russian Senate and the Qing Office of Barbarian Control (*Lifanyuan*).[16] Compared with the one-sided nature of the tribute system, in which China was clearly dominant, the exchange of letters appears evenhanded. But China did not really see Russia in equal terms, as evidenced by the word "control" in the bureaucratic structure overseeing the Chinese side of the agreement. The treaty also opened trade on the border between the two empires, instead of limiting exchange to the Assembly Hall in Beijing. Nonetheless, trade at the new site was still conducted as a part of the tribute-trade relationship.

Given this historical experience with "equality," how should we reinterpret the Sino-Japanese Treaty of 1871? Although more influential than the Office of Barbarian Control had been, the Yamen of Foreign Affairs, which conducted the negotiations, was still limited in its powers. It could not bind governors and governors-general of provinces to implement the treaties it signed. In fact, since this office had been established under duress by Western powers, it seems unlikely that the treaties it brokered were accepted as tokens of equality throughout the Qing bureaucracy.[17] In the end it was the Japanese side that after 1871 took up this expression of "equality" as the basis for reorganizing international relations in East Asia in Japan's favor.

"Modernization" in Asia, then, was generated as a negative reaction to the all-inclusive superior–subordinate relations of the traditional tribute system. Mercantilist control over tribute by the Qing dynasty led overseas Chinese merchants to oppose the trade policy and expand their own private trade. As a result, the Qing state shifted roles from that of a monopolistic trader-merchant to that of a tax collector. European countries gained a toehold in Asia by first utilizing the tribute-trade system and then expanding their influence through investment in that system. Japan, using Westernization as a means of modernization, tried to remake the Asian system with Japan at the center, but found itself trapped between powerful sinocentric forces and an equally strong West. In the end, it proved fateful for Japan to confront in all its aspects a system that was still largely functioning in East Asia.

China and Japan in Northeast and Southeast Asia

The considerations discussed above should give a strong sense of the central importance of China and the Chinese to all historical events and processes in East Asia. It should also be clear that the way in which the patterns of relations were subsumed under the heading "tribute-trade system" prefigured modern Sino-Japanese interactions, to this day a crucial relationship for the understanding of East Asia, both north and south. These points, in turn, have important implications for questions regarding region formation and development in this century and the next.

As in so many other ways, China is also the demographic center of gravity in East Asia. Since the eighteenth century, accelerating population growth has become the most consequential social fact in Chinese history. From that point onward, all of Chinese history is colored by this motif. And in the same way that the ideal domestic social hierarchy was transformed into an international-relations hierarchy, so did this single tremendous social fact flow outward from the Middle Kingdom, taking with it millions of impoverished Chinese. External migration from South China, mainly Fujian and Guangdong provinces, to Southeast Asia led to the creation of a vast network of human and financial relations that underlies regional ties even today. This great mass changed local labor markets, making possible the rapid development of both new and old industries. In Southeast Asia these included tin mining, rubber plantations, and rice cultivation.

The peak of this southward movement started in the 1890s, at about the same time that the Qing government decided to foster the colonization of Manchuria to prevent Russian absorption of the Chinese northeast. Within a few years, massive out-migration from Shandong province had begun to transform a great wilderness into the world's most important source of soybeans. As intermediary ports for both the outflow of bodies and the inflow of remittances, Hong Kong and Tianjin grew rapidly. Other urban beneficiaries of this traffic were Singapore, Bangkok, and Manila in the south and Dalian, Harbin, and Vladivostok to the north.[18] Even though the northern variant was by land and the southern option was by sea, each was brought about by the same pressures and assisted in the gradual shift of Chinese economic activity outward toward the periphery.

For Chinese historians, this period in the late nineteenth and early twentieth centuries is usually seen as a prelude to the fall of the Qing dynasty, as centrifugal forces sapped the center of strength. The great trauma of the Taiping Rebellion, the bloodiest civil war in history, was finally ended by local armies nominally under Beijing's command, but who were in fact loyal to and paid by regional leaders. Simultaneously, Western powers steadily pressured the central government into opening even more of China to trade and travel. Between internal and external influences, the Qing government was forced to loosen its grip on the great ports already mentioned above and the revenue they generated. The lack of a unifying impulse from Beijing allowed the split between north and south noted above to develop further, as trade routes mirrored ever more closely the human and financial networks generated by migration.[19] The end of tribute and the loss of control over its "modern" equivalent, customs duties, effectively ended the central government's efforts at resource redistribution. Henceforth, regional inequality would increase, strengthening both objective differences between regions and the sense of divergent interests.

Once the Chinese government had lost the ability to project influence into the periphery, the vacuum was filled by foreign powers. In Manchuria, this meant Russia and Japan. Although these two powers originally began their encroachment in conflict, after 1905 they preferred to divide the spoils. Japanese commercial and financial activities developed rapidly, led by the South Manchurian Railway Company, whose main office was established in 1906, the Mitsui Bussan company (1904), and the Yokohama Specie Bank (1904). With three impressive edifices at Dairen, these state-sponsored companies expressed the durability of their commitment to the continent.[20]

These institutions laid the foundation for a Japanese role in Manchuria since Japanese banks provided Japanese companies with funds to do business there. To extend influence, loans for railways and the Chinese provincial government were also tendered.[21] Japan soon tried to turn her privileges into a monopoly. In 1905, her attempt to take over management of the Manchurian customs met with staunch opposition from the British and American ambassadors in Tokyo. In discussions with the Japanese Foreign Ministry, they presented evidence that Japanese goods were entering Manchuria duty free and that Japanese-owned railways offered lower carriage rates for Japanese products. Attempts by the Hong Kong and Shanghai Banking Corporation to get permission to issue local paper currency in Manchuria on a par with the Yokohama Specie Bank's silver notes were rejected. The point here is that as Japanese state-sponsored endeavors penetrated to the grassroots level, crushing local enterprise and excluding other competitors, the inevitable backlash grew in intensity and had only one target.

The backlash against the Japanese replacement of the Chinese as the center of

Asia only gathered in strength. The annexation of Korea (1910), the Twenty-One Demands (1915), the Siberian Intervention (1918–22), and the creation of Manchukuo (1932) spread anti-Japanese sentiments throughout the region. Economic tensions in the 1930s and military occupation in the 1940s provided a similar effect in Southeast Asia. Fifty years later, the legacy of these economic and military invasions is still with us.[22]

Japan remains extremely wary of any state-sponsored action in Asia that could be mistaken for a replay of the East Asian Co-Prosperity Sphere. This makes Japan cautious in Southeast Asia, but it represents a contradiction in Northeast Asia. In the latter, Japan also comes face-to-face with the Americans and the Russians, both of whom are interested in participating in a regional revival. Japan's diplomacy with these two countries is a "strong state" style, the exact opposite of her approach to Asian countries like Korea and China. This may be an insurmountable difficulty that will keep Japanese involvement in Northeast Asian cooperative international ventures to a minimum. Furthermore, without government support and guarantees it is unlikely that the private sector will undertake the monumental infrastructure projects presently under consideration.

There are also a number of differences that will make it difficult for Northeast Asia to follow the Southeast Asian model. The most important of these is the lack of an appropriate human network that could serve as a template for regional structures. In Southeast Asia, the overseas Chinese perform this function. The absence of such a network is extremely critical, since these networks serve as insurance against state interference in regional activities. Although there are overseas Chinese populations in Northeast Asia, they remain small, and studies suggest that family ties, the basis of commercial activity in South China, are in any case not as strong in North China.[23]

It is possible that the Korean diaspora, hundreds of thousands strong in Russia, China, Japan, and the United States, could provide this element, but this will become clear only after reunification on the Korean peninsula. If there is no common culture on which to base a core network, then Northeast Asian regionalism will simply become a cross-border urban network. It is difficult to imagine how such an entity could put down the deep local roots necessary for long-term survival.

Northeast and Southeast Asia are not simply two separate objects for comparison. They are also the two halves of a greater whole. And China remains at the center. Keeping in mind the ties between central government strength and regional cohesion, the coming decade promises several crucial junctures. In 1997, the reclamation of Hong Kong by mainland China will take place. Although the Basic Agreement between the People's Republic and Great Britain promises fifty years of parallel systems, it remains to be seen whether Beijing can digest this capitalist node by peaceful means. Observations from South China suggest that "infection" by Hong Kong has already pulled that region out of Beijing's orbit.

Meanwhile, increased activity along the Russo-Chinese and Sino-Korean borders is indicative of northward pulls from the periphery. Even the "Yellow Peril" paranoia that has seized the Russian Far East, though dangerous and condemnable, can be interpreted as an extreme reaction to powerful currents that are changing the ways people live. Not surprisingly, many feel threatened and have chosen a violent response. Although Beijing appears to be as commanding as ever, from the historical perspectives explored above, we know that stepped-up activity along the periphery often accompanies central weakness and hesitancy. The dynamism of Northeast and Southeast Asia betrays the unspoken geopolitical expectation that at the center in Beijing the mandate of heaven is about to change hands.

Nonetheless, if Northeast Asian integration gets off the ground, increasing economic interpenetration of the nations involved is certain to generate friction and require mediation. But by whom? Grassroots-level involvement of the state is undesirable, because that will endanger the whole endeavor. Only some kind of intraregional body committed to solving problems in the interests of future cooperation can handle this kind of situation. Such an association, combining Eastern and Western powers, might show the path to a new paradigm for Sino-Japanese relations and away from the sinocentric Asia we have inherited from the past.

Notes

1. This article is the outgrowth of the author's interest in the internal ties of the Asian area in the modern period. See also Hamashita Takeshi, "Tribute and Emigration: China's Foreign Relations and Japan," in T. Umesao and M. Matsubara, eds., *Control Systems and Culture* (Osaka: National Museum of Ethnology, 1989).
2. Although discussions of the world economic system stress the importance of nations in the Western world, the Asian tribute system will be described here as a complex of areas. See John W. Meyer, "World Policy and the Authority of the Nation-State," in Albert Bergeson, ed., *Studies of the Modern World-System* (New York: Academic Press, 1980).
3. Uehara Kaneyoshi, *Sakoku to Han Bōeki* (Naha, 1981); Nakamura Fusataka, *Nissen Kankeishi no Kenkyū* (Tokyo, 1969); and Takeda Ryōji, "Genchō shoki no shin to no kankei, 1802–1870," in Yamamoto Tatsuro, ed., *Betonamu-Chūgoku Kankeishi* (Tokyo, 1975).
4. Sarasin Viraphol, *Tribute and Profit: Sino-Siamese Trade, 1652–1853* (Cambridge, MA: Harvard University Press, 1977), ch. 4; Hayashi Harukatsu and Hayashi Nobuatsu, eds., *Ka-i hentai*, I, II, III (1958–59 edition).
5. Wada Hisanori, "Tōnan Ajia ni okeru shoki kakyō shakai," *Tōyō Gakuhō*, vol. 42–1 (1959); idem, "Jūgo-seiki no Jawa ni okeru Chūgokujin no tsūshō katsudō" in *Ronshū Kindai Chūgoku Kenkyū* (Tokyo, 1981).
6. In *Qinding daqing huidian shili* (Imperial Regulations of the Qing Period), vol. 503, and *Chaogong gongwu* (Tribute Articles) (Beijing, n.d.).
7. Pak Chi-won, *Yeol ha ilqi* (Seoul, 1732), p. 5; Takeda Ryōji, *Batabiajo nisshi*, vols. 1–3 (Tokyo, 1975); Zhang Zunwu, *Qinghan zongfang maoyi, 1847–1885* (Academica Sinica, 1978); Yoshiharu Tsuboi, *L'Empire Vietnamien face à la France et à la Chine, 1847–1885* (L'Harmattan, 1986).

8. Suzuki Chūsei, *Chibetto o meguru chūin kankeishi* (Tokyo, 1962), ch. 8.

9. Zheng Kuanyin, *Nanyou Riji* (Taibei, 1967), p. 26.

10. Ibid., p. 33.

11. Jiang Haiting, *A History of Straits Settlement Foreign Trade, 1870–1915* (Singapore: National Museum, 1978); K.N. Chaudhuri, *Trade and Civilization in the Indian Ocean* (Cambridge: Cambridge University Press, 1985); Wong Lin Ken, "The Trade of Singapore, 1819–69," *Journal of the Malayan Branch of the Royal Asiatic Society,* vol. 33, part 4, December 1960.

12. Frances V. Moulder, *Japan, China and the Modern World Economy* (Cambridge: Cambridge University Press, 1977), ch. 1.

13. Okuda Otojiro, *Meiji shonen ni okeru honkon nihonjin* (Taibei, 1937), pp. 275–81.

14. Ibid., pp. 244–47.

15. Ishii Kanji, *Kindai nihon to igirisu shihon—Jadine maseson shō*kai o chūshin ni (Tokyo: University of Tokyo Press, 1984), ch. 2.

16. Fujimura Michio, "Meiji shoki ni okeru nishin kōshō no ichi danmen—ryūkyū bunto joyaku o megute - (I)" in *Nagoya daigaku bungakubu kenkyu ronshu - shigaku,* 16, 1968; idem, "Meiji isshin gaikō no kyū kokusai kankei eno taiō—Nisshin shūkōjoki no seiritsu o megute," in Ibid., 14, 1966.

17. Yoshida Kinichi, *Kindai roshin kankeishi* (Tokyo, 1974), ch. 3; Eric Widmer, *The Russian Ecclesiastical Mission in Peking During the 18th Century* (Cambridge, MA: Harvard University Press, 1976).

18. All six cities are ports participating in international, overseas Chinese trade. Harbin is the only one located on freshwater, hundreds of miles from the sea. In this sense, Vladivostok outpaced its urban rival, Khabarovsk, thanks to the rapid growth of the Chinese community.

19. Possibly it is in this period that we should search for the origins of the intermediate identity by which Chinese place themselves as either Northerners (*beifangren*) or Southerners (*nanfangren*). Although these differences are usually described in almost anthropological terms, more recent migrations may have caused the new arrivals to choose a category larger than native place in order to find common ground with their new neighbors. It is also worth noting that historians of China have argued that the birth of modern Chinese nationalism also takes place in this period. For example, see Mary Rankin, *Elite Activism and Political Transformation in China: Zhejiang Province, 1865–1991* (Stanford, 1986).

20. Many of the Yokohama Specie Bank's functions in this cooperative triad were taken over a decade later by the Bank of Chosen (Korea). Dairen is the Japanese pronunciation for Dalian, meaning "great link," which was the Chinese transmutation for Russian Dal'nii, meaning "far"—from Moscow's perspective, it was indeed.

21. *Nihon gaikō* monjo (Diplomatic Documents of Japan), 40, 1908, no. 2, pp. 518–43, details a 1908 loan negotiation with Xu Shichang, governor-general of the Three Eastern Provinces and later president of the Chinese Republic.

22. The speculative reasoning and comparisons that follow practically assume the fortuitous removal of the two standing impediments to cooperation in Northeast Asia, the Northern Territories Problem and North Korea. Even given these unlikely events, there are still many problems to overcome.

23. Recent studies, however, have begun to argue the importance of family and lineage in North China. For example, see Prasenjit Duara, *Culture, Power and the State: Rural North China, 1900–42* (Stanford, CA: Stanford University Press, 1988), pp. 86 ff.

EPILOGUE

Regionalism, Russia, and Northeast Asia

An Agenda

David Wolff

Regions, like countries, are historical creations and not geographic givens. Siberia, the Russian Far East, and Northeast Asia are no exceptions. Neither are the fifteen new states that since 1991 have succeeded the USSR. Many of the dynamics of region formation and center–local tension within Russia run parallel to the state-building processes in newly sovereign states and the Commonwealth of Independent States negotiations. To understand these constitutive processes of state and region formation, especially the key dynamic of decentralization, it is necessary to forgo an exclusive emphasis on Moscow and incorporate new perspectives emerging locally.

The authors contributing to this volume are well positioned for gathering such local perspectives. Not only are they for the most part members of the last generation that will have personally experienced the Union of Soviet Socialist Republics, an exposure which gives them a certain intuition regarding change and continuity across the post-Soviet divide, but being young they are less overwhelmed by the collapse of the USSR and of Communism. More than that, however, they have been able to engage in the kind of fieldwork that previous generations could not. Never in this century has the training of a qualified cohort of specialists on Russian Asia coincided with open access to that myth-enshrouded land and its dust-covered archival treasures. The age of discovery returns. While this opportunity lasts, let us engage in Northeast Asian studies.[1]

But where is Northeast Asia? And what is a region anyway? The dictionary and the atlas lie close at hand, but they can provide formal parameters at best, good only for disposing of the questions when the lack of more convincing answers causes discomfort. When accompanied by twenty specialist articles, though, each carving out a feature of this larger portrait, one feels emboldened, even obliged, to try to explain the difficulties inherent in these seemingly simple definitions and to draw up a research agenda that will take us closer to clarity, both empirical and theoretical.

Let us start with "region." In the past, geographers used this word to imply natural arenas for human interaction and shared culture. The Amur River basin, for example, has served as the core of a region joining the Russian Far East, the Chinese Northeast, and Eastern Mongolia into a shared habitat and transportation network. If waterways, in general, become the great link, a focus on the Sea of Japan will add to the Amur basin much of Japan, Korea, and China's Shandong province. Here we are approaching the scope of what we call Northeast Asia, in common parlance, but are only one slippery, logical step away from including the whole North Pacific. It is to regional processes themselves, however, that we must look for the parameters of our subject matter, and in that sense, a region called Northeast Asia has once again shown definite signs of cohesion.

Recently, as scholars have become more sensitive to the "createdness" of many boundaries, both external and internal, geography and the history of ideas have combined to excavate once-influential mental maps. These visions, although often lacking a basis in physical geography, have gained wide currency, especially when in harmony with the geopolitical interests of powerful states.[2] In this volume, individuals from various disciplines attempt to define the region. Take, for example, the contributions of our Russian colleagues. Vladimir Zhdanov, the political scientist, sees the crucible for regionalism in the struggle for cooperation among local interests. Pavel Minakir, the economist, searches for the preconditions of regionalism in investment, production, and distribution policies. Viktor Larin focuses on recurring demographic trends; while Vladimir Shishkin probes center–periphery tensions through historical materials. Each of the processes examined has a somewhat different geographic range, and of course, the lines on the map move over time. The result brings to mind the story of the blind men and the elephant, but one hopes that disparate soundings will produce a fuller understanding.

This volume's organization provides a second example of the multiplicity of regional definitions. Although Siberia and the Russian Far East are treated separately in the second and third sections, the first and fourth demonstrate strong bonds between these areas in both the past and present. There is, in short, an organic quality, if you will, to "Russian Asia." Siberia sometimes serves as an intermediary, or buffer, between Moscow and the Far East, while the Russian Far East mediates between Siberia and the non-Russian Far East. And just as the Russian Far East is affected by transnationalism, so Siberia's southern tier centered on Irkutsk has interacted throughout modern history with Buriatia and Mongolia, while western Siberia makes its presence strongly felt in Central Asia. Taking a wide-angle view, we can see that circulatory processes have helped to synchronize and unify the history of the greater Russo-Chinese borderland.

So, the region is a cohesive unit of imaginary geography, the boundaries of which will be traced by different disciplines and research objectives according to their own lights. But how big a unit? In this volume, as in the literature at large, the sense of region follows two tracks at once, although the two overlap. To simplify, Siberia and the Russian Far East (as well as Russian Asia) are subnational entities; Northeast Asia is transnational. In Russian, too, we find that an unqualified *dal'nii vostok* could refer to either the Russian Far East or the much larger transnational Far East, depending on context. Both variants of regional boundaries struggle with the political realities of national states. In fact, the concept "region" acquires maximum heuristic value by "leaving the state out." For that is exactly what regionalism does.

The subnational variant by its very nature poses a threat to central control every time it affirms its identity. For straightforward reasons of geographic continuity, subnational regions are often borderlands whose historical uniqueness is based on ties across the borderline. This emphasis stands in opposition to a nationalizing history and ideology in which ties and similarities to the center are highlighted.

In the Chinese Northeast, the tension between national state and region has rendered problematic the execution of a nationally sponsored movement to publish local gazetteers. It has also led to an ongoing public and official debate regarding the appropriateness of celebrating the centennial of Harbin in 1998, a hundred years from the day when the Russians began construction of a modern railway hub at the site of a fishing village. Strong, probably unstanchable, political and business pressures have built up in support of the idea that celebrating should be done while the celebrating is good. After all, in 1948 all local events paled into insignificance beside the great contemporary national drama of the civil war. Other voices, however, warn against endorsing past acts of imperialist aggression.[3]

In similar fashion, the Russian Far East and central historical studies have also gone their separate ways. Volumes on the history of the short-lived Far Eastern Republic (1920–22) are appearing with minimal participation by scholars from St. Petersburg and Moscow. The high costs of publication are held responsible, but the print runs are so minuscule that circulation to European Russia becomes impossible. Scholarly meetings exhibit like tendencies. The theses (*tezisy*) for an October 1992 conference in Vladivostok contains sixty-nine reports, one each from St. Petersburg and Moscow. Local scholars, for their part, feel marginalized in national institutions (which is nothing new). Increasing difficulties in and costs of communication and travel have been blamed for this state of affairs, yet such problems have not in fact prevented new initiatives between Moscow and Beijing.[4]

It is, to be sure, a long and rarely successful road from the subregional idea to significant regional autonomy, but there are many shortcuts from local difference to central paranoia and repression. Stalin's regional ethnic cleansing of 1937–38 swept away many of the demographic telltales of the Far Eastern borderland.

Koreans, Chinese, and Harbinites were followed into death and deportation by the cadres who had arrested them. This cohort from the party, military, and security organs had served long enough in the Russian Far East to catch the taint, if not the spirit, of the place.[5] Charges of collusion, espionage, and criminal venality have also struck at Chinese officials in the Northeast, while expulsion of the Russians from that region was at the heart of Chinese official policy in both Beijing and Nanjing from the 1897 occupation by the tsarist navy of Port Arthur until the 1955 withdrawal of the Red Army from that same base. In the Chinese historiography, this has been subsumed under the general category of coping with many-headed imperialism, in Chinese traditionally referred to as Rights Recovery (*huishou quanli*).

No less than the subnational one, the transnational variant also carries uncomfortable implications for the state. A transnational region encompasses subnational units and complete countries. For the former, belonging to a potent organization extending beyond the borders of the home country strengthens the subnational ability to make claims on the center. As Hamashita Takeshi's essay shows, there are clear two-way linkages between and among effective central power, local autonomy, and cross-border integration. Although throughout this volume transnational regionalism has generally been interpreted optimistically as concomitant with peaceful cooperation and joint development, it is also important to keep in mind the phenomenon's implications for weakening central authority. In contemporary China, for example, that scenario inspires hope and fear in equal measure.

The danger to the state posed by a transnational region is susceptible to paranoid exaggeration, since the cross-border ties that bind the region together often emanate from foreign soil, beyond influence or even detailed observation. Such a constellation of forces acting across state lines has much in common with the popular "transnational agenda," which includes such problems as migration, pollution, technology transfer, terrorism, and trade. Like these phenomena, the multiplicity of regionalism's sources, impacts, and local meanings makes it particularly resistant to state-sponsored social engineering, even when interstate rivalry does not proscribe international concert. In the face of this predicament, state responses may be extreme, even Draconian. A sealed border not only fends off the external enemy but also isolates potential internal opponents from cross-border bases of support. The 1930s' purges in the Russian Far East were accompanied by fortification of the border and a widespread cult of the borderguard.

Some of the same difficulties that confront states trying to find measured, but effective, solutions to waxing regionalism also complicate the scholarly study of these problems. Subnational ambitions are well aware that state capitals are hostile to their aspirations and make strong efforts to cover their tracks, often well enough to make research at the grass roots the only effective way of gathering information. By the same line of reasoning, central statistics regarding cross-border contacts are suspect. The center's assertion that it is fully aware of all significant processes under way in the regions rings loud but inspires little confidence. By extension, researchers who rely exclusively on "authoritative" state-sponsored information and informants are seriously handicapped.

Although the lack of distinctive language to separate the two kinds of regionalism—subnational and transnational—makes conceptual conflation understandable, a closer examination suggests three related contrasts for us to consider. First, there is a hierarchical dimension. Transnational regions are a larger unit containing subnational parts. "Nesting regionalisms" as a phrase suggests a research strategy by which the summing of the parts is a necessary prelude for comprehending the whole. Second, experience with one kind of regionalism can provide a repertoire for the other. For example, long years of barter along the Russo-Chinese border are finally being superseded by more sophisticated financial arrangements, but barter has meanwhile undergone a resurgence throughout Siberia and the Russian Far East as a means of evading the Moscow tax authorities.[6]

Third, and finally, there is a causative, interactive link between the two varieties of region. Autonomous behavior by subnational regions often sponsors transnational contacts, in turn reinforcing both psychological and economic differentiation from the center at the subnational level. For an unwary state, this can turn into an escalating cycle of regionalisms, as vicious as the international tit for tat by which borders are closed, sealed, and militarized. Although the guns are pointed across the borderline, we should keep in mind that the imposition of autarkic isolation is also an attack on the prosperity of the regions that feed on cross-border contact.

At such moments, borderlines appear to be as firm as the dark lines on the political map, as concrete as the reinforced blockhouses on both sides, and as unalterable as the conflicting assertions of the respective foreign ministries. For scholars, however, borders are shifting lines of variable weight. This is equally true in outlining states and regions. But when state borders shift, creating a zone in which subjects/citizens of two or more countries have lived, that space takes on a shared social history belonging to none of the national histories involved. Such a place is a borderland, where the same sites have different names, different histories, and different meanings for both the people who call it home today and those who gaze longingly across the borderline with irredentist intent.

This definition can be illustrated by examining the question of Japan's "Northern Territories" (*hoppō ryōdo*), which now refers exclusively to the fate of three islands and an island grouplet, the Habomais, but once had a larger range of connotations. For starters, the Kurile Islands and Sakhalin have been traded back and forth several times in the last century, both by treaty and invasion. Gravesites of both Japanese and Russian peoples dot the islands. Further afield, the Japanese have established their presence in Russian Asia several times, whether by invitation, intervention, or internment. This, too, has become an aspect of the "Northern problem," as the full repertoire of Russo-Japanese contacts is often called. Finally, it should be noted that even Hokkaido, Japan's northernmost island, falls into this category, with its late-nineteenth-century colonization and choice of landlocked capital at Sapporo driven by fears of Russian invasion. It is appropriate that the special collection within the Hokkaido University library known as the Northern Materials Repository (*Hoppo shiryoshitsu*) gathers together rich holdings about Hokkaido, the Russian mainland, and everywhere in-between. This, in brief, suggests the historically elastic nature of the Russo-Japanese borderland, where two nations' geographic identities overlap.[7]

The borderland, by its multicultural nature, is the logical core for a transnational region. The motion necessary to create a regional core, however, can take the form of human motion rather than geopolitical shifts with attendant border adjustments: The essential ingredient is the shared social history. In Southeast Asia, for example, it can be argued that the Chinese diaspora is the glue that holds the region together. Studies that focus on contemporary political economy pay particular attention to the rise and impact of the "Four Little Dragons." This moves Southeast Asia's center of gravity northward and eastward into the South China Sea, where mainland China looms large on the northern and western horizons. Furthermore, "the dragon" traditionally implies China. Might not the millions-strong Chinese and Korean communities sprinkled all along the Pacific Rim also serve as "developmental diasporas" bringing regional cohesion and prosperity to Northeast Asia? It is hoped that this volume will provide some food for thought about a few aspects of this fundamental question.

These, in brief, are some of the challenges of defining and studying regions, and Northeast Asia, in particular. As targets that move in time, space, and the eye of the beholder, they defy simple generalizations and casual acquaintance. Just as no state can grasp the full thrust of transnational phenomena, neither can individual scholars, regardless of linguistic and cultural training, encompass these complex wholes. Only collective regional knowledge and varied disciplinary approaches can bring us near the mark. This book may be considered as a step, however limited, to that end.

Notes

1. A series of Central Intelligence Agency maps issued in the 1980s make clear that, with the exception of a half-dozen cities, all of Asian Russia fell into three categories: "Formal closed," "de facto closed," and "remote or inaccessible."

2. On the constructedness of the line between Europe and Asia, European Russia and Asian Russia, see W.H. Parker, "Europe: How Far?" *Geographical Journal,* v. 126, 3 (Sept. 1960), pp. 278–97; and Mark Bassin, "Russia Between Europe and Asia: The Ideological Construction of Geographical Space," *Slavic Review,* v. 50, 1 (Spring 1991), pp. 1–17. Along the same lines, but for a different "great divide," see Larry Wolff, *Inventing Eastern Europe: The Map of Civilization on the Mind of the Enlightenment* (Stanford: Stanford University Press, 1994). A particularly vivid illustration of the fabrication process can be found on page 38 of Peter Sahlins, *Boundaries: The Making of France and Spain in the Pyrenees* (Berkeley: University of California Press, 1989), whereby

nonexistent mountains are drawn onto a map to provide a "natural" borderline. Finally, Pierre Bourdieu's work on "distinction" has led to sociological studies of "boundary work."

3. The only reasonable alternative date seems to be the Qing government's decision to organize a purely Chinese administrative office (*binjiang guandao*) at Harbin in 1905, or its actual establishment in 1906. Some of the most active scholarly figures in the debate over Harbin's birthday are Duan Guangda, Ji Fenghui, and Li Shuxiao, the first two espousing 1898 and the last against. Interestingly enough, Li is the only one of the three trained as a Russianist.

4. Recent works on the Far Eastern Republic include the document collection *Dal'nevostochnaia respublika: Stanovlenie. Bor'ba s interventsiei* (Vladivostok, 1993) and the article collection *Iz istorii dal'nevostochnoi respubliki* (Vladivostok, 1992). These were printed in 300-copy and 250-copy runs, respectively. The conference in question was "Grazhdanskaia voina na Dal'nem Vostoke Rossii: Itogi i uroki," 5–9 October 1992.

5. John Stephan, "Far Eastern Conspiracies? Russian Separatism on the Pacific," *Australian Slavonic and East European Studies,* vol. 4, nos. 1–2, 1990, pp. 135–52. The NKVD orders to deport the Koreans and arrest *kharbintsy* were issued by N.I. Ezhov on 29 August and 20 September 1937, respectively. For texts, see TsGASA, Central State (Archive of the Soviet Army), f. 33879, op. 1, d. 115, ll. 1–2; and the Bulletin of the Association of Emigrants from China in Israel, *Igud yotsei sin,* May–June 1994, pp. 36–37.

6. For a discussion of barter in Russia, see Caroline Humphrey, "'Icebergs', Barter and the Mafia in Provincial Russia," *Anthropology Today,* vol. 7, 2 (April 1991), pp. 8–13.

7. Hokkaido University strengthened its holdings on Northeast Asia by purchasing George Lensen's library and papers.

Selected Bibliography

The following bibliography includes materials cited in the notes and is intended to facilitate use of this volume. Further references can be found in many of the books listed. Comprehensive bibliographical work in all appropriate languages remains a pressing task in the study of Northeast Asia. Nothing has yet replaced the now much-dated multi-lingual bibliography published under Robert Kerner's name in 1939 (see below).

Archives

Gosudarstvennyi Arkhiv Novosibirskoi Oblasti (GANO)
Gosudarstvennyi Arkhiv Sakhalinskoi Oblasti (GASO)
Gosudarstvennyi Arkhiv Rossiiskoi Federatsii (GARF)
Hoover Institution Archives
Japanese Defense Ministry Archives (JDAA)
Japanese Foreign Ministry Archives (JFMA)
Nauchnyi Arkhiv Sibirskogo Otdeleniia AN SSSR (NASO)
Rossiiskii Gosudarstvennyi Istoricheskii Arkhiv (RGIA)
Sakhalinskii Tsentr Dokumentatsii Noveishei Istorii (STsDNI)
Tsentr Khraneniia Dokumentatsii Noveishei Istorii Krasnoiarskogo Kraia (TsKhDNIKK)
Tsentral'nyi Gosudarstvennyi Arkhiv Dal'nego Vostoka (TsGADV)

Newspapers (published in Moscow unless noted)

Afto-nom [Iakutsk]
Akademstroevets [Novosibirsk]
Dal'nevostochnye izvestiia [Khabarovsk]
Dal'nevostochnyi uchenyi [Vladivostok]
Dongbeiya luntan [Jilin]
Dongbeiya yanjiu [Jilin]
Ekologicheskaia gazeta
Ekonomicheskaia gazeta

Ekspress khronika
Heihe Xuebao [Heihe]
Hokkaido Shimbun [Sapporo]
Igud yotsei sin [Tel-Aviv]
Izvestiia
Izvestiia Eniseiskogo gubkoma RKP(b) [Krasnoiarsk]
Izvestiia Sibirskogo biuro TsK RKP(b) [Novosibirsk]
Izvestiia Sibirskogo revoliutsionnogo komiteta [Omsk]
Kommersant
Komsomol'skaia pravda
Konkurent [Vladivostok]
Krasnoe znamia [Vladivostok]
Krest'ianskie vedomosti
Kultura
Lesnaia gazeta
Literaturnaia gazeta
Literaturnaia Rossiia
Mezhdunarodnaia zhizn' [Novosibirsk]
Moskovskie novosti
Nasha gazeta [Kemerovo]
Nashe vremia
Neibu wengao [Beijing]
Nezavisimaia gazeta
Novosibirskie novosti [Novosibirsk]
Novosti: Gazeta o Vladivostoke [Vladivostok]
Pravda
Pravda vostoka [Tashkent]
RA Report [Honolulu]
Renmin ribao [Beijing]
Rossiiskaia gazeta
Rossiiskie vesti
Russian Far East Update [Seattle]
Sakhaada [Iakutsk]
Sel'skaia zhizn'
Sibirskaia gazeta [Novosibirsk]
Sotsialisticheskaia Iakutiia [Iakutsk]
Sovetskaia Kirgiziia
Sovetskaia kul'tura
Sovetskaia Rossiia
Sovetskaia Sibir' [Novosibirsk]
Sovety Iakutii [Iakutsk]
Stroitel'—Soiuz trudiashchikhsia Kuzbassa [Kemerovo]
Surviving Together
Tikhookeanskaia zvezda [Vladivostok]
Tiumenskie izvestiia [Tiumen]
Trud
Utro Rossii [Vladivostok]
V boi za ugol' [Kemerovo]
Vedomosti Novosibirskogo oblastnogo soveta narodnykh deputatov [Novosibirsk]
Vladivostok [Vladivostok]
Vlast' truda [Irkutsk]

Yakutiia [Iakutsk]
Za bol'shuiu khimiiu [Kemerovo]
Za Bolshevistskuiu putinu [Nogliki]
Za nauku v Sibiri [Novosibirsk]
Zapadnaia Sibir' [Omsk]
Zheleznodorozhnik Kuzbassa [Kemerovo]
Znamia truda [Lenin-Kuznetsk]

Books, Articles, Unpublished Manuscripts

Abov, A. "Oktiabr' v Vostochnoi Sibiri (otryvki vospominanii)," *Sibirskie ogni* 4, 1924.

Agalakov, V. T. *Podvig Tsentrosibiri (1917–1918): Sbornik dokumentov* (Irkutsk, 1986).

———. *Podvig Tsentrosibiri* (Irkutsk, 1968).

———. *Sovety Sibiri (1917–1918 gg.)* (Novosibirsk, 1978).

Ageev, Aleksandr. "Varvarskaia lira," *Znamia*, 2, 1991.

Ahn, Choong-yong. "Search for New Approaches and Methods for Economic Cooperation in Northeast Asia," *The Korean Journal of International Studies* 24 (3), Autumn 1993.

Ahn, Ho-sang. *An Ancient History of the Dong-I Tribe* [in Korean] (Seoul, 1971).

Alekseev A.I. and B.N. Morozov. *Osvoenie russkogo Dal'nego Vostoka (konets XIX - 1917g)* (Moscow, 1989).

Alekseev, V. V., ed. *Urbanizatsiia Sovetskoi Sibiri* (Novosibirsk, 1987).

Alekseevskii, E. E. *Ia liubliu etu zemliu* (Moscow, 1988).

Alpatov, Lev. *Sakhalin (putevye zapiski etnografa)* (Moscow, 1930).

Amburger, Erik. *Geschichte der Behördenorganisation Russlands von Peter dem Grossen bis 1917* (Leiden: E. J. Brill, 1966).

Amosenok, E. and V. Bazhanov. "Oboronnyi kompleks regiona," *EKO* [Novosibirsk], 9, 1993.

Amtsislavskii, A.Z. et al. "Simpozium po okhrane rechnykh vod Sibiri," *Vodnye resursy*, 1, 1979.

Anderson, Benedict. *Imagined Communities* (London: Verso, 1983).

Andriianov, V. "Gornyi udar," *Dialog*, 1, 1990.

Anosov, S. *Koreitsy v Ussuriiskom krae* (Khabarovsk, 1928).

Armstrong, Terence, ed. *Yermak's Campaign in Siberia* (London: Hakluyt Society, 1975).

Arsen'ev, V. K. *Kitaitsy v Ussuriiskom krae* (Khabarovsk, 1914).

Artemov, E. T. *Formirovanie i razvitie seti nauchnykh uchrezhdenii AN SSSR v Sibiri, 1944–1980 gg.* (Novosibirsk, 1990).

Artsimovich, L. A. "Sibirskii nauchnyi tsentr budet odnim iz krupneishikh nauchykh tsentrov strany," *Tekhnika -molodezhi*, 2, 1958.

Asmis, Rudolf. *Als Wirtschaftspionier in Russisch-Asien* (Berlin: G. Stilke, [ca. 1924]).

Azarkh, E.D. et al. "Osnovnye printsipy i napravleniia perestroiki upravleniia sferoi obsluzhivaniia naseleniia i reshenie zhilishchnoi problemy na sele," *I.E.O.P.P. Preprint* (Novosibirsk, 1987).

Aziatskaia Rossiia 4 vols. (St. Petersburg, 1914).

Bacon, Sir Francis. *Essays and New Atlantis*, Gordon S. Haight, ed. (Toronto: D. Van Nostrand, 1942).

Baddeley, John F. *Russia, Mongolia, and China, Being Some Record of the Relations Between Them from the Beginning of the XVIIth Century to the Death of the Tsar Alexei Mikhailovitch A.D. 1602–1672.* (London: Macmillan, 1919).

Bahry, Donna. *Outside Moscow: Power, Politics, and Budgetary Policy in the Soviet Republics* (New York: Columbia University Press, 1987).

Balzer, Marjorie Mandelstam. "Dilemmas of the Spirit: Religion and Atheism in the Yakut-Sakha Republic," in Sabrina Ramet, ed., *Religious Policy in the Soviet Union* (Cambridge: Cambridge University Press, 1992).

————. "From Ethnicity to Nationalism: Turmoil in the Russian Mini-Empire," in James Millar and Sharon Wolchik, eds., *The Social Legacy of Communism* (Cambridge: Cambridge University Press 1994).

————. "Nationalism in the Soviet Union: One Anthropological View," *Journal of Soviet Nationalities* 1, Fall 1990.

————. "Shamanism and the Politics of Culture" *Shamanism*, 1 (2), 1993.

Barratt, Glynn. *Russia in Pacific Waters, 1715–1825* (Vancouver: University of British Columbia Press, 1981).

Barth, Fredrik. *Ethnic Groups and Boundaries* (Boston: Little, Brown, 1969).

Bassin, Mark. "Inventing Siberia: Visions of the Russian East in the Early Nineteenth Century," *American Historical Review*, 96 (3), June 1991.

Berdyaev, Nikolas. *The Russian Idea*, trans. R.M. French (Boston: Beacon Press, 1962).

Berg, Raissa. *Acquired Traits*, trans. David Lowe (New York: Viking, 1988).

Billington, James. *The Icon and the Axe: An Interpretive History of Russian Culture* (New York: Vintage, 1970).

Böss, Otto. *Die Lehre der Eurasier: ein Beitrag zur russischen Ideengeschichte des 20. Jahrhunderts* (Wiesbaden: O. Harassowitz, 1961).

Bogaturov, Aleksei, Mikhail Kozhokin, and Konstantin Pleshakov. "Posle imperii: demokratizm i derzhavnost' vo vneshnei politike Rossii," *RNF—Rossiiskii—RNF nauchnye doklady no. 8* (Moscow, 1992).

Bogdarin, Siulbe. *Toponimika Iakutii* (Yakutsk, 1985).

Bogoras, W. [V. Bogoraz]. *The Chukchee* (New York: Stechert, 1909).

————. "O pervobytnykh plemenakh," *Zhizn' natsional'nostei*, 1, 1922.

————. "Ob izuchenii i okhrane okrainnykh narodov," *Zhizn' natsional'nostei*, 3–4, 1923.

Bol'sheviki zapadnoi Sibiri v bor'be za sotsialisticheskuiu revoliutsiiu (mart 1917 - mai 1918g.): Sbornik dokumentov i materialov (Novosibirsk, 1957).

Bond, Andrew R. and Matthew J. Sagers. "Some Observations on the Russian Federation Environmental Protection Law," *Post-Soviet Geography*, September 1992.

Bor'ba za vlast' sovetov v Irkutskoi gubernii: Sbornik dokumentov (Irkutsk, 1957).

Bostandzhoglo, A. A. and B. G. Fedorov. "Vsesouznoe soveshchanie po kompleksnoi programme ekonomicheskogo sotsial'nogo razvitiia sredinnogo regiona v sviazi s territorial'nym pererazpredeleniem vodnykh resursov," *Vodnye resursy*, 6, 1982.

Bradshaw, Michael. "Siberia Poses a Challege to Russian Federalism," *RFE/RL Research Report*, 16 October 1992.

Bragina, Daria G. *Sovremennye etnicheskie protsessy v Tsentral'noi Iakutii* (Yakutsk, 1985).

Bramall, C. "The Role of Decollectivization in China's Agricultural Miracle, 1978–1990," *Journal of Peasant Studies*, 20 (3), 1990.

Bressler, Michael L. "Agenda Setting and the Development of Soviet Water Resources Policy, 1965–1990: Structures and Processes," Ph.D. dissertation, University of Michigan, 1992.

————. "Reform from Above, Innovation from Below," unpublished manuscript.

Burawoy, Michael and Pavel Krotov. "The Economic Basis of Russia's Political Crisis," *New Left Review*, March/April, 1993.

Burleigh, Michael. *Germany Turns Eastward: A Study of Ostforschung in the Third Reich* (Cambridge: Cambridge University Press, 1988).

Chard, Chester. *Northeast Asia in Prehistory* (Madison: University of Wisconsin, 1974).

Chaudhuri, K. N. *Trade and Civilization in the Indian Ocean* (Cambridge: Cambridge University Press, 1985).

Chayanov, A. V. *Theory of Peasant Economy* (Madison: University of Wisconsin Press, 1986).

Chekhov, Anton. *Ostrov Sakhalin (iz putevykh zapisok)* (Moscow, 1895), translated as *A Journey to Sakhalin* (Cambridge: Ian Faulkner, 1993).

————. *The Island: A Journey to Sakhalin* (New York: Washington Square Press, 1967).

Cheng, Tien-fang. *A History of Sino-Russian Relations* (Washington, DC: Public Affairs Press, 1957).

Chevigny, Hector. *Russian America, 1764–1867* (New York: Viking Press, 1965).

Chisholm, B. J. "Cooperation in the Taiga: The Key to Saving the Amur Tiger," *Surviving Together*, Spring 1994.

Chislennost', sostav i dvizhenie naseleniia v RSFSR (Moscow, 1990).

Christoffersen, G. "The Greater Vladivostok Project: Transnational Linkages in Regional Economic Planning," paper delivered at the annual meeting of the American Association for the Advancement of Slavic Studies, November 1993.

Chivilikhin, Vladimir. "I. N. Zhukov," in *Doroga: Iz arkhiva pisatelia* (Moscow, 1989).

Clarke, Simon, et al., eds. *What About the Workers?* (London: Verso, 1993).

Cleinow, Georg. *Neu-Sibirien (Sibkrai): eine Studie zum Aufmarsch der Sowjetmacht in Asien* (Berlin: Hobbing, 1928).

Clubb, O. Edmund. *China and Russia: The Great Game* (New York: Columbia University Press, 1971).

Cohen, Paul. *Discovering History in China: American Historical Writing on the Recent Chinese Past* (New York: Columbia University Press, 1984).

Coleman, Frederic. *Japan or Germany: The Inside Story of the Struggle in Siberia* (New York: G.H. Doran, 1918).

Collins, David. "Russia's Conquest of Siberia: Evolving Russian and Soviet Historical Interpretations," *European Studies Review*, 12 (1), 1982.

Collins, David. *Siberia and the Russian Far East* (Santa Barbara: Clio Press, 1991).

Cook, Linda J. "Lessons of the Soviet Coal Miners' Strike of Summer 1989," *The Harriman Institute Forum*, 4 (3), March 1991.

Coquin, François-Xavier. *La Sibérie: Peuplement et immigration paysanne au XIXe siècle* (Paris: Institut d'études slaves, 1969).

Crowe, Barry. *Concise Dictionary of Soviet Terminology, Institutions and Abbreviations* (London: Pergamon, 1969).

Dallin, David. *Soviet Russia and the Far East* (New Haven: Yale University Press, 1948).

————. *The Rise of Russia in Asia* (New Haven: Yale University Press, 1949).

Danckwortt, P.W. *Sibirien und seine wirtschaftliche Zukunft; ein Rückblick und Ausblick auf Handel und Industrie Sibiriens* (Leipzig: Teubner, 1921).

Danilov, Victor and N. A. Ivnitskii. *Dokumenty svidetel'stvuiut: 1927–1929, 1929–1932* (Moscow, 1989).

Dediushina, N. A. and A. I. Shcherbakov. "O formirovanii nauchnykh kadrov Sibirskogo otdeleniia AN SSSR," in A.P. Okladnikov, ed., *Voprosy istorii nauki i professional'nogo obrazovaniia v Sibiri*, vol. 1 (Novosibirsk, 1968).

Dekrety Sovetskoi vlasti, vol. 2 (Moscow, 1959).

Dem'ianenko, V. N. "Pravovye problemy 'razgosudarstvleniia' kolkhozov," *Gosudarstvo i pravo*, 2, 1993.

de Souza, Peter. "Siberian Futures? Economic Perspectives," *Siberica* 1 (3), 1990.

DeBardeleben, Joan. "Economic Reform and Environmental Protection in the USSR," *Soviet Geography*, 31, 1990.

Dibb, Paul. *Siberia and the Pacific: A Study of Economic Development and Trade Prospects* (New York: Praeger, 1972).

Dienes, Leslie. "A Comment on the New Development Program for the Far Eastern Economic Region," *Soviet Geography*, 19 (4), 1988.

———. *Soviet Asia: Economic Development and National Policy Choices* (Boulder: Westview Press, 1987).

Dilks, David. *Curzon in India*, 2 vols. (New York: Taplinger Publishing Co., 1969).

Dimanshtein, S. I. "Sovetskaia vlast' i mel'kie natsional'nosti," *Zhizn' natsional'nostei*, 46, 1919.

Diment, Galya and Yuri Slezkine, eds. *Between Heaven and Hell: The Myth of Siberia in Russian Culture* (New York: St. Martin's, 1993).

Dmytryshyn, Basil. "Russian Expansion to the Pacific, 1580–1700: A Historiographical Review," *Siberica* 1 (1), Summer 1990.

Dmytryshyn, Basil, et al., eds. *To Siberia and Russian America: Three Centuries of Russian Eastward Expansion, 1558–1867* 3 vols. (Portland: Oregon Historical Society, 1985–1989).

Dong, Xiao-yuan and G. Dow. "Monitoring Costs in Chinese Agricultural Teams," *Journal of Political Economy*, 101 (3) , 1993.

Doolin, Dennis J. *Territorial Claims in the Sino-Soviet Conflict: Documents and Analysis* (Stanford: Stanford University Press, 1965).

Dorian, James et al. "Multi-lateral Resource Cooperation Among Northeast Asian Countries: Energy and Mineral Joint Venture Prospects," paper prepared for the "Workshop on the Emergence of the Russian Far East: Implications for North Pacific Regional Institution Building," East-West Center, Honolulu, 19–21 August 1993.

Dubie, Allain. *Frank A. Golder: An Adventure of a Historian in Quest of Russian History* (Boulder: East European Monographs, 1989).

Dubinin, N. P. *Vechnoe dvizhenie*, 3rd edition (Moscow, 1989).

Dukhovskoi, S. M. *Vsepoddaneishii otchet priamurskogo general-gubernatora Generala-Leitenanta Dukhovskogo, 1896–1897* (St. Petersburg, 1898).

Edmonds, Richard Louis. "Siberian Resource Development and the Japanese Economy: The Japanese Perspective," in Robert Jensen, et al., eds., *Soviet Natural Resources in the World Economy* (Chicago: University of Chicago Press, 1983).

Ekonomicheskoe polozhenie Rossii nakanune Velikoi Oktiabr'skoi sotsialisticheskoi revoliutsii (Moscow-Leningrad, 1967).

Emmons, Terrence and Bertrand Patenaude. *War, Revolution, and Peace in Russia: The Passages of Frank Golder, 1914–1927* (Stanford: Hoover Institute, 1992).

Ericson, Richard. "Soviet Economic Structure and the National Question," in Alexander J. Motyl, *The Post-Soviet Nations* (New York: Columbia University Press, 1992).

Ershov, Iu. "Noveishaia ekonomicheskaia istoriia: Kratkaia kharakteristika ekonomicheskoi dinamiki na obshcherespublikanskom fone," *EKO*, 9, 1993.

Esakov, V. A. *Geografiia v Rossii v XIX-nachale XX veka* (Moscow, 1978).

Euikon, Kim. "Political Economy of the Tuman River Basin Development: Problems and Prospects," *Journal of Northeast Asian Studies*, 11 (2), Summer 1992.

Faust, Wolfgang. *Russlands goldener Boden: der sibirische Regionalismus in der zweiten Hälfte des 19. Jahrhunderts* (Cologne, Vienna: Bohlau, 1980).

Ferejohn, John. *Pork Barrel Politics: Rivers and Harbors Legislation, 1947–1968* (Stanford: Stanford University Press, 1974).

Feshbach, Murray and Alfred Friendly, Jr. *Ecocide in the USSR: Health and Nature Under Siege* (New York: Basic Books, 1992).

Fisher, Harold A. "Frank A. Golder, 1877–1929," *Journal of Modern History*, 1 (2), June 1929.

Fisher, Raymond H. *Bering's Voyages: Whither and Why?* (Seattle: University of Washington Press, 1977).

———. *The Russian Fur Trade 1550–1700* (Berkeley: University of California, 1943).

Fleischhauer, Ingeborg. *Die Deutschen in Zarenreich* (Stuttgart: Deutsche Verlags-Anstalt, 1986).

Ford, Harold. "Russian Far Eastern Diplomacy, Count Witte, and the Penetration of China, 1895–1904," Ph.D. dissertation, University of Chicago, 1950.

Forsyth, James. *A History of the Peoples of Siberia: Russia's North Asian Colony, 1581–1990* (Cambridge: Cambridge University Press, 1992).

Fuller, William C. *Civil-Military Conflict in Late Imperial Russia, 1881–1914* (Princeton: Princeton University Press, 1985).

Galiamova, L. I. *Ocherki istorii formirovaniia rabochego klassa Dal'nego Vostoka Rossii (1860-fevral' 1917g.)* (Vladivostok, 1984).

Gavrilov, A. V. "Rossiia i Kitai: sblizhenie ili protivostoianie?" in *Obshchestvo i gosudarstvo v Kitae: Tezisy dokladov* vol. 2 (Moscow, 1993).

Geller, Mikhail and Aleksandr Nekrich, *Utopiia u vlasti: Istoriia Sovetskogo Soiuza s 1917 goda do nashikh dnei*, 2nd ed. (London: Overseas Publications Exchange, 1986).

Geyer, Dietrich *Russian Imperialism* (New Haven: Yale University Press, 1987).

Gibson, James. "The Significance of Siberia to Tsarist Russia," *Canadian Slavonic Papers*, 14 (3), 1972.

Gibson, James. *Feeding the Russian Fur Trade* (Madison: University of Wisconsin Press, 1969).

———. *Imperial Russia in Frontier America* (New York: Oxford University Press, 1976).

Gladyshev, A. I., ed. *Administrativno-territorial'noe delenie Sakhalinskoi oblasti* (Iuzhno-Sakhalinsk, 1986).

Glaser, Bonny S. "China's Security Perceptions: Interests and Ambitions," *Asia Survey*, 33 (3), March 1993.

Gogolev, A. I. "Cultural History of the Yakut (Sakha) People: The Work of A. I. Gogolev," *Anthropology and Archeology of Eurasia*, 31 (2), Fall 1992.

———. *Istoricheskaia etnografiia Iakutov* (Yakutsk, 1986).

Golder, Frank. *Russian Expansion on the Pacific 1641–1850* (Cleveland: A. Clark, 1914).

Goldman, Marshall I. *The Spoils of Progress: Environmental Pollution in the Soviet Union* (Cambridge, Mass.: MIT Press, 1972).

Goldstein, S. and A. Goldstein. "Population Mobility in the People's Republic of China," *Papers of the East-West Population Institute*, no. 95 (Honolulu: East West Center, 1985).

Gollwitzer, Heinz. *Die gelbe Gefahr: Geschichte eines Schlagworts* (Göttingen: Vandenhoeck, 1962).

———. *Europe in the Age of Imperialism, 1880–1914*, trans. David Adam and Stanley Baron (New York: Harcourt, Brace, and World, 1969).

Golovnin, P. N. *The End of Russian America: Captain P. N. Golovnin's Last Report*, translated by Basil Dmytryshyn and E. A. P. Crownhart-Vaughan (Portland: Oregon Historical Society, 1979).

Gorechenko, E. E. "Sotsial'nye problemy razvitiia malykh sel'skikh poselenii," *I.E.O.P.P. Preprint* (Novosibirsk, 1986).

Gurvich, I. S. *Etnicheskoe razvitie narodnostei severa v Sovetskii period* (Moscow, 1987).

Gustafson, Thane. *Crisis Amid Plenty: The Politics of Soviet Energy under Brezhnev and Gorbachev* (Princeton: Princeton University Press, 1989).

Hamashita, Takeshi. "Tribute and Emigration: China's Foreign Relations and Japan," in T. Umesao and M. Matsubara, eds., *Control Systems and Culture* (Osaka: National Museum of Ethnology, 1989).

Hara, Teruyuki. "The Korean Movement in the Russian Maritime Province, 1905–1922," in Dae-Sook Suh, ed., *Koreans in the Soviet Union* (Honolulu: University of Hawaii Press, 1987).

———. *Indeigirka gono higeki* (The Tragedy of the Indigirka) (Tokyo, 1993).

———. *Shiberia shuppei* (The Siberian Intervention) (Tokyo, 1989).

Harrison, J. F. C. "The Victorian Gospel of Success," in *Victorian Studies*, 1 (2), December 1957.

Harrison, John A. *"Kito Yezo Zusetsu* or a Description of the Island of Northern Yezo by Mamiya Rinzo," *Proceedings of the American Philosophical Society*, 99 (2), 1955.

———. *Japan's Northern Frontier: A Preliminary Study in Colonization and Expansion with Special Reference to the Relations of Japan and Russia* (Gainesville: University of Florida Press, 1953).

———. *The Founding of the Russian Empire in Asia and America* (Coral Gables: University of Miami Press, 1971).

Hauner, Milan. *What is Asia to Us? Russia's Asian Heartland Yesterday and Today* (Boston: Unwin Hyman, 1990).

Hausladen, Gary. "Recent Trends in Siberian Urban Growth," *Soviet Geography*, 28 (2), 1987.

Hewett, E. *Reforming the Soviet Economy: Equality versus Efficiency* (Washington, DC: Brookings, 1989).

Hinton, W. *The Privatization of China*, (New York: Monthly Review Press, 1990).

Hiraoka, Mashide. "Nihon Roshiagaku-shi ko," *Tōyō*, 31 (4), 1928.

Hoetzsch, Otto. *Russland in Asien: Geschichte einer Expansion* (Stuttgart: Deutsche Verlags-Anstalt, 1966).

Hosking, Geoffrey. *The Awakening of the Soviet Union* (Cambridge, MA: Harvard University Press, 1990).

Hosoya, Chihiro. "Kitasaharinno sekiyu shigen o meguru nichi-ei-bei no keizai funsō," in Hosoya, ed., *The History of International Economic Conflicts in Pacific-Asian Regions* (Tokyo, 1983).

Huang, Phillip. *The Peasant Family and Rural Development in the Yangzi Delta, 1350–1988*, (Stanford: Stanford University Press, 1990).

Humphrey, Caroline. *Karl Marx Collective: Economy, Society and Religion in a Siberian Collective Farm* (Cambridge: Cambridge University Press, 1983).

Huntington, Samuel. *The Third Wave* (Norman: University of Oklahoma Press, 1991).

Iamskov, A. N., ed. *Sovremennye problemy i veroiatnye napravleniia razvitiia natsional'no-gosudarstvennogo ustroistva Rossiiskoi Federatsii* (Moscow, 1992).

Ibragimova, Z. and N. Pritvits, *"Treugol'nik" Lavrent'eva* (Moscow, 1989).

Ignat'ev, A. V. *Vneshnaia politika vremennogo pravitel'stva* (Moscow, 1974).

International Energy Agency. *Oil and Gas Information 1992* (Paris: International Energy Agency, 1992).

Istoriia Sibiri. 5 vols. (Leningrad, 1968).

Jackson, W. A. Douglas. *The Russo-Chinese Borderlands* (Princeton: D. Van Nostrand, 1962).

Jancar, Barbara. *Environmental Management in the Soviet Union and Yugoslavia* (Durham, NC: Duke University Press, 1987).

Jeff Lilley. "Great Leader's Gulag," *Far Eastern Economic Review*, 9 September 1993.

Jiang, Haiting. *A History of Straits Settlement Foreign Trade, 1870–1915* (Singapore: National Museum, 1978).

Jin, Zhenji. *Dongbeiya jingji quan yu Zhongguo de xuanze* (Beijing: Zhonggong zhongyang dangxiao chubanshe, 1992).

Jochelson, Waldemar [Vladimir Iokhelson]. *Peoples of Asiatic Russia* (New York: Museum of Natural History, 1928).

Josephson, Paul. "Rockets, Reactors and Soviet Culture," in Loren Graham, ed., *Science and the Soviet Social Order* (Cambridge: Harvard University Press, 1990).

————. *Physics and Politics in Revolutionary Russia* (Berkeley: University of California, 1991).

Kabuzan, V. M. *Dal'nevostochnyi krai v XVII-nachale XX vv., 1640–1917* (Moscow, 1985).

Kagarlitsky, Boris. *The Disintegration of the Monolith* (London: Verso, 1992).

Kalugina, Z. I. *Lichnoe podsobnoe khoziaistvo v SSSR* (Novosibirsk, 1991).

Kameda, Jiro. "Rokoku sokan Nichi-Ro jiten oyobi sono hensan mono," *Kokugaku-in zasshi*, 39 (11).

Kang, Chujin. "Diplomatic Relations Between Korea and the Soviet Union" [in Korean], in *Korea and the Soviet Union* (Seoul, 1979).

Kapitsa, P. L. "Osnovnuiu stavku delat' na molodezh'," *Tekhnika-molodezhi*, 2, 1958.

Kappeler, Andreas. *Russland als Vielvölkerreich* (Munich: Verlag C. H. Beck, 1992).

Kassianow, N. *La Sibérie et la poussée allemande vers l'Orient* (Bern: P. Haupt, 1918).

Kempe, Frederick. *Siberian Odyssey: A Voyage into the Russian Soul* (New York: Putnam, 1992).

Kennan, George. *Siberia and the Exile System*, 2 vols. (New York: Century, 1891).

Kerner, Robert. *The Urge to the Sea: The Course of Russian History. The Role of Rivers, Portages, Ostrogs, Monasteries, and Furs* (Berkeley: University of California Press, 1942).

————. "A Northeastern Asia Seminar," *Pacific Affairs*, 5, December 1932.

————. "The Russian Eastward Movement: Some Observations on its Historical Significance," *Pacific Historical Review*, 17, May 1948.

Kerner, Robert, ed. *Northeastern Asia, a Selected Bibliography*, 2 vols. (Berkeley: University of California Press, 1939).

Khannonov, V. "Pravovoe obespechenie ustoichivosti agrarnogo proizvodstva," *Gosudarstvo i pravo*, 5, 1992.

Khisamutdinov, Amir. *The Russian Far East: Historical Essays* (Honolulu: Center for Russia in Asia, 1993).

Khorvat, D.L. "Memoirs" (manuscript held in Hoover Institution Archives).

Khrushchev, N. S. *Khrushchev Remembers*, translated by Strobe Talbott, (Boston: Little, Brown, 1974).

Kim, Hakjoon. "The Soviet Union in American-Korean Relations," in Koo, Youngnok and Suh, Dae-sook, eds., *Korea and the United States: A Century of Cooperation* (Honolulu: University of Hawaii Press, 1984).

Kim, Syn Khva. *Ocherki po istorii Sovetskikh Koreitsev* (Alma-Ata, 1965).

Kirby, E. Stuart. "The Pattern of Siberian Development: Actual and Potential," in *Exploration of Siberia's Natural Resources* (Brussels: NATO, 1974).

————. *Russian Studies of China: Progress and Problems of Soviet Sinology* (London: Macmillan, 1975).

————. *Russian Studies of Japan: An Exploratory Survey* (New York: St. Martin's, 1981).

Kitanina, T. M. "Russko-Aziatskii bank i kontsern I. Stakheev," in M. P. Viatkin, ed., *Monopolii i inostrannyi kapital v Rossii* (Moscow-Leningrad, 1962).

Knystautas, Algirdas. *The Natural History of the USSR*, (New York: McGraw-Hill, 1987).

Kolarz, Walter. *The Peoples of the Soviet Far East* (New York: Praeger, 1954).

Komarov, Boris [pseudonym]. *The Destruction of Nature in the Soviet Union* (White Plains, NY: M.E. Sharpe, 1980).

Kondrat'ev, N. D. *Rynok khlebov i ego regulirovanie vo vremia voiny i revoliutsii* (Moscow, 1991).

Koronkevich, N. I. et al. "Okhrana rechnykh vod Sibiri," *Izvestiia AN SSSR, seriia geograficheskaia*, 2, 1979.

Kozeltsev, Michael. "Old and New in the Environmental Policy of the Former Soviet Union," in Barbara Jancar-Webster, ed., *Environmental Action in Eastern Europe* (Armonk: M.E. Sharpe, 1993).

Krahmer, Gustav. *Russland in Asien* (Leipzig: Verlag von Zuckschwerdt, 1899–1904).

Krauss, Rosalind. "Poststructuralism and the Paraliterary," in *The Originality of the Avant-Garde and Other Modernist Myths* (Cambridge: MIT Press, 1985).

Krausse, Alexis. *Russia in Asia: A Record and a Study, 1588–1899* (London: G. Richards, 1899).

Kriukov, V. and A. Sevastianova. "Tiumenskaia oblast' v perekhodnyi period," in *Vserossiiskaia konferentsiia po ekonomicheskomu razvitiiu Sibiri* (Novosibirsk, 1993).

Krupinski, Kurt *Japan und Russland: Ihre Beziehungen bis zum Frieden von Portsmouth* (Königsberg and Berlin: Ost-Europa, 1940).

Krushanov, A. I., ed. *Stranitsy istorii rybnoi promyshlennosti Sakhalinskoi oblasti (1925–1987 gg.)* (Iuzhno-Sakhalinsk, 1989).

Kudriavtseva, S. M. "Soveshchanie po problemam i perspektivam vodnogo blagoustroistva territorii zapadnoi Sibiri," *Vodnye resursy*, 5, 1980.

Kulakovskii, A. E. *Nauchnye trudy* (Yakutsk, 1979).

Kulikov, A. "Gorod bol'shoi nauki," *Sibirskie ogni*, 3, 1958.

Kuno, Yoshi. *Japanese Expansion on the Asiatic Continent: A Study in the History of Japan with Special Reference to Her International Relations with China, Korea, and Russia*, 2 vols. (Berkeley: University of California Press, 1937–1940).

Kushner, Howard I. *Conflict on the Northwest Coast: American-Russian Rivalry in the Pacific Northwest, 1790–1867* (Westport, Conn.: Greenwood Press, 1975).

L'vov, A. K. "Kul'turnye bazy na severe," *Sovetskaia Aziia*, 3, 1926.

Lantzeff, George V. *Eastward to Empire* (Berkeley: University of California, 1973).

———. *Siberia in the Seventeenth Century* (Berkeley: University of California, 1943).

Lapin, Boris. in Lapin and Nadezhda Tenditnik. "Deti Arbata ili Deti Rossii? Dialog pisatelia i kritika o massovoi kul'ture v sovremennoi proze," *Sibir'*, 3, 1989.

Larebo, Haile M. *The Building of an Empire: Italian Land Policy and Practice in Ethiopia, 1935–1941* (Oxford: Clarendon Press, 1994).

Larin, V. L. and E. A. Plaksen. "Primor'e: perspektivy razvitiia cherez prizmu obshchestvennogo mneniia," in *Rossiia i ATR*, 1, 1993.

Lattimore, Owen. "The Gold Tribe, 'Fishskin Tatars' of the Lower Sungari," in idem., *Studies in Frontier History: Collected Papers, 1929–58* (London: Oxford University Press, 1962).

———. *The Inner Asian Frontiers of China* (Boston: Little Brown, 1962).

Laue, Theodore von. *Sergei Witte and the Industrialization of Russia* (New York: Columbia University Press, 1963).

Lee, Chong-sik and Ki-wan Oh. "The Russian Faction in North Korea," *Asian Survey*, 8 (4), April 1968.

———. "Kim Il-song of North Korea," *Asian Survey* 7 (6), June 1967.

Lee, Ki-baik. *A New History of Korea*, translated by Edward W. Wagner with Edward J. Schultz (Cambridge, Mass.: Harvard University Press, 1984).

Lee, Robert H. G. *The Manchurian Frontier in Ch'ing History* (Cambridge, MA: Harvard University Press, 1970).

Lembergskaia, V., ed. "Dvizhenie v voiskakh na Dal'nem Vostoke," *Krasnyi arkhiv*, 11–12, 1925.

Lenin, V. I. *Polnoe sobranie sochinenii*, vol. 50.

Lensen, George. "Japan and Tsarist Russia: the Changing Relationships, 1875–1917," *Jahrbücher für Geschichte Osteuropas*, 10, October 1962.

————. "The Importance of Tsarist Russia to Japan," *Contemporary Japan*, 24 (10–12), April 1957.

————. *Balance of Intrigue: International Rivalry in Korea and Manchuria, 1884–1899* 2 vols. (Tallahassee: University Presses of Florida, 1982).

————. *Japanese Recognition of the USSR: Soviet-Japanese Relations, 1921–1930* (Tokyo: Sophia University, 1970).

————. *Korea and Manchuria between Russia and Japan* (Tallahassee: Diplomatic Press, 1966).

————. *Report from Hokkaido: The Remains of Russian Culture in Northern Japan* (Hakodate: Hakodate Municipal Library, 1954).

————. *Russia's Japan Expedition, 1852–1855* (Gainesville: University of Florida Press, 1955).

————. *The Russian Push for Japan: Russo-Japanese Relations, 1697–1875* (Princeton: Princeton University Press, 1959).

Levin, Julia. "Russian Forest Laws—Scant Protection during Troubled Times," *Ecology Law Quarterly*, 19, 1992.

Levin, M. G. and L. P. Potapov, eds. *The Peoples of Siberia* (Chicago: University of Chicago Press, 1964).

Lieberthal, Kenneth and Michael Oksenberg, *Policy Making in China: Leaders, Structures, and Processes* (Princeton: Princeton University Press, 1988).

Liebow, E. *Tally's Corner*, (Boston: Little Brown, 1967).

Lieven, Dominic. *Russia's Rulers Under the Old Regime* (New Haven: Yale University Press, 1989).

Liubomudrov, Mark. "Izvlechem li uroki? O russkom teatre i ne tol'ko o nem," *Nash sovremennik*, 2, 1989.

Lobanov-Rostovsky, Andrei. *Russia and Asia* (New York: Macmillan, 1933).

Lonsdale, Richard. "Siberian Industry Before 1917: the Example of Tomsk Guberniya," *Annals of the Association of American Geographers*, 53, 1963.

Maass, Arthur. *Muddy Waters: The Army Engineers and the Nation's Rivers* (Cambridge, MA: Harvard University Press, 1951).

Macey, David A. J. *Government and Peasant in Russia, 1861–1906: The Prehistory of the Stolypin Reforms* (DeKalb, IL: University of Northern Illinois Press, 1987).

McCool, Daniel. *Command of the Waters: Iron Triangles, Federal Water Development, and Indian Water* (Berkeley: University of California Press, 1987).

MacKinder, Harold. "The Geographical Pivot of History," *The Geographical Journal*, 23 (4), 1904.

McKinnon, Ronald. *The Order of Economic Liberalization: Financial Control of the Transition to a Market Economy* (Baltimore: the John Hopkins University Press, 1991).

Maksimov, P. S. *Mezhnatsional'nye otnosheniia v regione (po materialam Iakutskoi ASSR)* (Yakutsk, 1990).

Malozemoff, Andrew. *Russian Far Eastern Policy, 1881–1904, with Special Emphasis on the Causes of the Russo-Japanese War* (Berkeley: University of California Press, 1958).

Mancall, Mark. *China and Russia: Their Diplomatic Relations to 1728* (Cambridge, MA: Harvard University Press, 1971).

Marks, Steven G. *Road to Power: The Trans-Siberian Railroad and the Colonization of Asian Russia, 1850–1917* (Ithaca, N.Y.: Cornell University Press, 1991).

Martin, Rudolf. *Die Zukunft Russlands und Japans; die deutschen Milliarden in Gefahr* (Berlin: C. Heymann, 1905).

Mathieson, Raymond. *Japan's Role in Soviet Economic Growth: Transfer of Technology Since 1965* (New York: Praeger, 1979).

Masutaka, Kidosaki et al. *In Search of Oil in Northern Sakhalin* [in Japanese] (Yokohama, 1983).

Mazour, Anatole. "Dmitrii Zavalishin: Dream of Russian-American Empire," *Pacific Historical Review*, 5 (2), 1936.

Medvedev, Roy A. and Zhores A. Medvedev. *Khrushchev: The Years in Power* (New York: Columbia University Press, 1976).

Medvedev, Zhores. *Soviet Agriculture* (New York: Norton, 1987).

Mehnert, Klaus. "The Russians in Hawaii, 1804–1819," University of Hawaii, Occasional papers, no. 38, Honolulu, 1939.

————. *Ein Deutscher in der Welt: Erinnerungen 1906–1981* (Stuttgart: Deutsche-Verlags-Anstalt, 1981).

Merk, Frederick. *History of the Westward Movement* (New York: Alfred A. Knopf, 1978).

Meyer, John W. "World Policy and the Authority of the Nation-state," in Albert Bergeson, ed., *Studies of the Modern World-System* (New York: Academic Press, 1980).

Meyer, Peggy Falkenheim. "Gorbachev and Post-Gorbachev Policy toward the Korean Peninsula: The Impact of Changing Russian Perceptions," *Asian Survey* 32 (8), August 1992.

Migirenko, G. S., ed. *Novosibirskii nauchnyi tsentr* (Novosibirsk, 1962).

Mikkelson, Gerald and Margaret Winchell. "Valentin Rasputin and His Siberia," in idem., transl. and ed., *Siberia on Fire: Stories and Essays by Valentin Rasputin* (DeKalb, IL: Illinois University Press, 1989).

Minakir, P. A. , ed. *Dal'nii Vostok Rossii: Ekonomicheskoe obozrenie*, 2 vols. (Moscow, 1993).

————. Gregory L. Freeze, ed. and trans., *The Russian Far East: An Economic Handbook* (Armonk, NY: M.E. Sharpe, 1994).

Moletotov, I. A. "Problema kadrov Sibirskogo nauchnogo tsentra i ee reshenie (1957–1964 gg.)," in B. M. Shchereshevskii, ed., *Voprosy istorii Sovetskoi Sibiri* (Novosibirsk, 1967).

Moskoff, W. *Labour and Leisure in the Soviet Union: The Conflict between Private and Public Decision Making in a Planned Economy* (London: Macmillian, 1984).

Mosse, Robert, ed. *The Soviet Far East and Pacific Northwest* (Seattle: University of Washington Press, 1944).

Mote, Victor. "The Cheliabinsk Grain Tariff and the Rise of the Siberian Butter Industry," *Slavic Review*, 35 (2), 1976.

Moulder, Frances V. *Japan, China and the Modern World Economy* (Cambridge: Cambridge University Press, 1977).

Muradian, A. " 'Evraziiskaia' kontseptsiia—model' obshchestvennogo razvitiia Rossii?" *Problemy Dal'nego Vostoka*, 1–3, 1992.

Murzaev, D. V. *K voprosu ob ekonomicheskom sostoianii Amurskoi oblasti za poslednee desiatiletie* (Blagoveshchensk, 1914).

Nansen, Fridjof. *Through Siberia, the Land of the Future* (New York: Frederick Stokes, 1914).

Nederlander, Munin. *Kitezh: The Russian Grail Legends*, translated by Tony Langham (London: Aquarian Press, 1991).

Neverov, Valerii and Alexander Igolkin. "Kon'iunkturnyi obzor," *Ekonomika i zhizn'*, December 1991.

Nihonkai ken keizai kenkyūkai. *Kan Nihonkai kōryū jiten '93* (Tokyo: Sochisha, 1993).

Nikolaev, I. I. and I. P. Ushnitskii. *Tsentral'noe delo: Khronika Stalinskikh repressii v Iakutii* (Yakutsk, 1990).

Nikolaev, Ivan. *Zagadka Mikhaila Nikolaeva* (Yakutsk, 1992).

Nilus, E. Kh. "Upravlenie dorogi kak tsentral'nyi organ tekhnicheskogo i administrativnogo nadzora" (manuscript held in Hoover Institution Archives).

1990 Energy Statistics Handbook, (New York: United Nations, 1992).

Nish, Ian. *The Origins of the Russo-Japanese War* (London: Longman, 1985).

Oka, Sakae. *Kita karafuto* (Tokyo, 1942).

Okada, Kenzo. *Hakodate kaiko shiwa* (Hakodate, 1946).

Okun, S. B. *The Russian-American Company*, ed. by B. D. Grekov, translated by Carl Ginsburg (Cambridge, 1951).

Olcott, Martha Brill. *The Kazakhs* (Stanford: Hoover Institution Press, 1987).

Ose, Keishi. *Nichi-Ro bunka sōdan* (Tokyo, 1942).

"Osushchestvlenie leninskoi natsional'noi politiki u narodov Krainego Severa SSSR," *Sovetskaia etnografiia*, 1, 1970.

Ota, Saburo. *Nichiro karafuto gaikōsen* (Tokyo, 1941).

Palma, Giuseppe Di. *To Craft Democracies* (Berkeley: University of California Press, 1990).

Palsson, Gisli. *Beyond Boundaries: Understanding, Translation and Anthropological Discourse* (London: Berg, 1993).

Parkansky, Alexander B. *The Disintegration Trends in the Eastern Russia and the Russian Economic Opportunities in the Northern Pacific Area: New Order in Post-Communist Eurasia* (Sapporo, 1993).

Parker, W. H. "Europe: How far?" *Geographical Journal*, 120 (1960).

Parthé, Kathleen. *Russian Village Prose: The Radiant Past* (Princeton University Press, 1992).

Patrusheva M. A. and G. A. Sukhacheva. *Ekonomicheskoe razvitie Man'chzhurii* (Moscow, 1985).

Pavlovsky, Michael. *Chinese-Russian Relations* (New York: Philosophical Library, 1949).

Pereira, Norman. "Regional Consciousness in Siberia Before and After October 1917," *Canadian Slavonic Papers*, 30 (1), 1988.

Pertsik, Ye. N. *Gorod v Sibiri* (Moscow, 1980).

"Pervye shagi russkogo imperializma na Dal'nem Vostoke," *Krasnyi arkhiv*, 52, 1932.

Peterson, D. J. *Troubled Lands: The Legacy of Soviet Environmental Destruction* (Boulder, CO: Westview Press, 1993).

Pevzner, A. M. "Sovremennoe sostoianie narodnogo Sibirskogo khoziaistva i perspektivy ego razvitiia," in *Pervyi Sibirskii kraevoi nauchno-issledovatel'skii s"ezd*, vol. 5 (Novosibirsk, 1928).

Pierce, Richard. *Russia's Hawaii Adventure, 1815–1817* (Berkeley: University of California Press, 1965).

Pika, Aleksandr. "Malye narody severa: iz pervobytnogo kommunizma v real'nyi sotsializm," in *Perestroika, glasnost', demokratiia, sotsializm: V chelovecheskom izmerenii* (Moscow, 1989).

Polansky, Patricia. "The Russians and Soviets in Asia," *International Library Review*, 14, 1982.

Popkin, Cathy. "Chekhov as Ethnographer: Epistemological Crisis on Sakhalin Island," *Slavic Review*, 51 (1), 1992.

Popov, V. P. "Krest'ianskii vzgliad na kolkhoznuiu real'nost'," *Sotsiologicheskie issledovaniia*, 7, 1992.

Poppe, Nikolaus. "The Economic and Cultural Development of Siberia," in Erwin Oberlaender et al., eds., *Russia Enters the Twentieth Century, 1894–1917* (London: Temple Smith, 1971).

Pozdneev, Dmitrii. *Opisanie Man'chzhurii*, 2 vols. (St. Petersburg, 1897).

Poznanskii, V. S. *V. I. Lenin i sovety Sibiri (1917 - 1918): Rukovodstvo voenno-politicheskoi deiatel'nost'iu sovetov v bor'be s kontrrevoliutsiei* (Novosibirsk, 1977).

Priamur'e: fakty, tsifry, nabliudeniia (Moscow, 1909).

Price, Ernest. *The Russo-Japanese Treaties of 1907–16 Concerning Manchuria and Mongolia* (Baltimore: Johns Hopkins University Press, 1933).

Proffer, C. and E. Proffer. *Contemporary Russian Prose* (Ann Arbor: Ardis, 1982).

Pryde, Philip R. and Victor L. Mote. "Environmental Constraints and Biosphere Protection in the Russian Far East," in Allan Rodgers, ed., *The Soviet Far East* (London: Routledge, 1990).

————. *Environmental Management in the Soviet Union* (Cambridge: Cambridge University Press, 1991).

Przeworski, Adam. "Democracy as a Contingent Outcome of Conflicts," in Jon Elster and Rune Slagstad, eds., *Constitutionalism and Democracy* (Cambridge: Cambridge University Press, 1988).

Quadflieg, Franz. *Russische Expansionspolitik von 1774 bis 1914* (Berlin: F. Dummler, 1914).

Quested, R.K.I. *"Matey" Imperialists?* (Hong Kong: Hong Kong University Press, 1982).

————. *Sino-Russian Relations: A Short History* (Boston: Allen and Unwin, 1984).

Raeff, Marc. *The Well-Ordered Police State: Social and Institutional Change Through Law in the Germanies and Russia, 1600–1800* (New Haven: Yale University Press, 1983).

Rasputin, Valentin. "Vniz i vverkh po techeniiu," in *Vniz i vverkh po techeniiu* (Moscow, 1972).

Razvitie narodnogo khoziaistva Sibiri (Novosibirsk, 1978).

Razymov, A. A. "Pomozhet li rynok vozrodit' derevniu?" *Sotsiologicheskie issledovaniia*, 3, 1991.

Ramos, Alcida. "From Eden to Limbo: The Construction of Indigenism in Brazil" in George Bond and Angela Gilliam, eds., *The Social Construction of the Past: Representation As Power* (London, New York: Routledge, 1994).

Rehbein, Robert. "The Japan-Soviet Far East Trade Relationship: A Case of the Cautious Buyer and the Overconfident Seller," *Journal of Northeast Asian Studies* 8 (2), Summer 1989.

Reichman, Henry. *Railwaymen and Revolution: Russia, 1905* (Berkeley: University of California Press, 1987).

Reidel, Carl. "Back to the Future in the Land of Ghenghis Khan," *American Forests*, May-June 1992.

Reisner, Marc. *Cadillac Desert: The American West and Its Disappearing Water* (New York: Penguin Books, 1986).

Remnev, A. V. *Upravlenie Sibir'iu i Dal'nim Vostokom v XIX-nachale XX vv.: Uchebnoe posobie* (Omsk: Izdanie Omskii Gosudarstvennyi Universitet, 1991).

Ren, Wenxia. "Lun Dongbeiya quyu jingji hezuo yu fengong," in Dongbeiya yanjiu congshu bianjibu, ed., *Dongbeiya jingji quan de meili* (Dalian: Dalian ligong daxue chubanshe, 1992).

Riabikov, V. V. *Tsentrosibir'* (Novosibirsk, 1949).

Riasanovsky, Nicholas V. "The Emergence of Eurasianism," *California Slavic Studies* (4), 1967.

Romanov, B. A. *Rossiia v Man'chzhurii* (Leningrad, 1928).

Romanova, G. N. *Ekonomicheskoe otnoshenie Rossii i Kitaia na Dal'nem Vostoke : XIX - nachalo XX v.* (Moscow, 1987).

Rosenberg, Michael. *Die Schwerindustrie in Russisch-Asien: eine Studie über das Ural-Kusnezker-Kombinat* (Berlin: Volk und Reich, 1938).

Rotberg, Robert I. *The Founder: Cecil Rhodes and the Pursuit of Power* (New York: Oxford University Press, 1988).

Roziner, Feliks. *Nekto Finkelmaier* (London: Overseas Publication Interchange, 1981) *A Certain Finkelmeyer*, translated by Michael Heim (NY: W.W. Norton, 1991).

Rozman, Gilbert. *Japan's Response to the Gorbachev Era, 1985–1991: A Rising Super-power Views a Declining One* (Princeton: Princeton University Press, 1991).

———. *The Chinese Debate about Soviet Socialism, 1978–1985* (Princeton: Princeton University Press, 1987).

Rumer, Boris. "Current Problems in the Industrialization of Siberia," *Berichte des Bundesinstituts für Ostwissenschaftliche und Internationale Studien*, no. 48, Cologne, 1984.

———. "Panel on Siberia: Economic and Territorial Issues," *Soviet Geography*, 32 (6), 1991.

Saeki, Kiichi. "Towards Japanese Cooperation in Siberian Development," *Problems of Communism*, 21 (3), May-June 1972.

Sahlins, Peter. *Boundaries: The Making of France and Spain in the Pyrenees* (Berkeley : University of California Press, 1989).

Satow, Ernest Mason. *Korea and Manchuria Between Russia and Japan, 1895–1904* (Tallahassee: Diplomatic Press, 1966).

Scheinpflug, Alfons. *Die japanische Kolonisation in Hokkaido* (Leipzig: Firttlirt and Sohn, 1935).

Schiffer, Jonathan. *Soviet Regional Economic Policy: East-West Debate on Pacific-Siberian Development* (Basingbroke: Macmillan, 1989).

Scott, James. *Weapons of the Weak*, (New Haven: Yale University Press, 1985).

Serebrennikov, I. I. "The Siberian Autonomous Movement and its Future," *Pacific Historical Review*, 3 (3), September 1934.

Sergeev, M. A. *Nekapitalisticheskii put' razvitiia malykh narodnostei Severa (Trudy Instituta Etnografii, Novaia Seriia, Tom XXVII)* (Moscow-Leningrad, 1955).

Seton-Watson, Hugh. *The Russian Empire, 1801–1917* (Oxford: Clarendon Press, 1967).

Share, Donald. *The Making of Spanish Democracy* (New York: Praeger, 1986).

Shchereshevskii, B. M., ed. *Voprosy istorii Sovetskoi Sibiri* (Novosibirsk, 1967).

Shishkin, V. I. *Revoliutsionnye komitety Sibiri v gody grazhdanskoi voiny (avgust 1919 - mart 1921)* (Novosibirsk, 1978).

Shreider, D. I. *Nash Dal'nii Vostok: Tri goda v Ussuriiskom krae* (St. Petersburg, 1897).

Shumiatskii, B. Z. *Sibir' na putiakh k Oktiabriu: Vospominaniia pervogo predsedatelia Tsentrosibiri* (Irkutsk, 1989).

Siegelbaum, Lewis. "Another 'Yellow Peril': Chinese Migrants in the Russian Far East and the Russian Reaction Before 1917," *Modern Asian Studies*, 12 (2), April 1978.

Siniukov, V. N. "O forme federatsii v Rossii", *Gosudarstvo i pravo*, 5, 1993.

Skorik, P. "Kul'turnyi shturm taigi i tundry," *Prosveshchenie natsional'nostei*, 10, 1932.

Skrine, F. H. *The Expansion of Russia, 1815–1900* (Cambridge: Cambridge University Press, 1903).

———. and Alexander Ular. *A Russo-Chinese Empire* (Westminster: A. Constable, 1904; French edition 1902).

Slezkine, Yuri. "Russia's Small Peoples: The Policies and Attitudes Towards the Native Northerners, 17th Century –1938," Ph.D. dissertation, University of Texas at Austin, May 1989.

———. *Arctic Mirrors: Russia and the Small Peoples of the North* (Ithaca: Cornell University Press, 1994).

Smith, Anthony D. *The Ethnic Origins of Nations* (London: Blackwell, 1986).

Sohn, Paw-key et al. *The History of Korea* (Seoul: Korean National Commission for UNESCO, 1970).

Solov'ev F. V. *Kitaiskoe otkhodnichestvo na Dal'nem Vostoke Rossii v epokhu kapitalizma, 1861–1917* (Moscow, 1989).

———. *Kitaiskie otkhodniki i ikh geograficheskie nazvaniia v Primor'e* (Vladivostok, 1973).

Solzhenitsyn, Aleksandr. *Letter to the Soviet Leaders*, translated by Hilary Sternberg (NY: Harper and Row, 1974).

Starr, S. Frederick. "Tsarist Government: The Imperial Dimension" in J. Azrael, ed., *Soviet Nationality Policies and Practices* (New York: Praeger, 1978).

————. *Decentralization and Self-Government in Russia, 1830–1870* (Princeton: Princeton University Press, 1972).

————, ed. *Russia's American Colony* (Durham, NC: Duke University Press, 1986).

Statisticheskii ezhegodnik Rossii 1913 g. (St. Petersburg, 1914).

Stepan, Alfred. "Paths toward Redemocratization: Theoretical and Comparative Considerations," in Guillermo O'Donnell et al. *Transitions from Authoritarian Rule* (Baltimore and London: The Johns Hopkins University Press, 1986).

Stephan, John J. "Far Eastern Conspiracies? Russian Separatism on the Pacific," *Australian Slavonic and East European Studies*, 4 (1–2), 1990.

————. "Hawaii's Russian Connection in Asian and Pacific Studies: Tradition and Prospects," *Center for Asian and Pacific Studies (CAPS) Newsletter*, 1 (4), October-December 1982.

————. "The Political and Economic Landscape of the Russian Far East," in Tsuyoshi Hasegawa et al., eds., *Russia and Japan: An Unresolved Dilemma Between Distant Neighbors* (Berkeley: University of California Center for International and Area Studies, 1993).

————. *Sakhalin: A History* (Oxford: Clarendon, 1971).

————. *The Kuril Islands: Russo-Japanese Frontier in the Pacific* (Oxford: Clarendon, 1974).

————. *The Russian Far East: A History* (Stanford: Stanford University Press, 1994).

————. *The Russian Fascists: Tragedy and Farce in Exile, 1925–45* (New York: Harper and Row, 1978).

Stephan, John J. and V. P. Chichkanov, eds. *Soviet-American Horizons on the Pacific* (Honolulu: University of Hawaii Press, 1986).

Suh, Dae-sook. *The Korean Communist Movement, 1918–1948* (Princeton: Princeton University Press, 1967).

Sukhacheva, G. A. "Bich strany: khunkhuzy v Man'chzhurii i Primor'e v 20-e gody XX v.," *Rossiia i ATR*, 1, 1992.

Suny, Ronald Grigor *The Making of the Georgian Nation* (Indiana: Indiana University Press, 1988).

Suslov, V. I. "Predotvratim li raspad?" *Eko*, 5, 1993.

Suslova, V. E. *Ugol' Kuzbassa*, (Moscow, 1984).

Sviatikov, E. G. *Rossiia i Sibir': Ocherki po istorii Sibirskogo oblastnichestva v XIX veke* (Prague: Obshchestvo Sibiriakov v ChSR, 1930).

Swearingen, Rodger, ed. *The Soviet Far East: Strategic Dimensions in Multinational Perspective* (Stanford: Hoover Institute, 1987).

Syun, Seung Kwon. *The Russo-Japanese Rivalry over Korea, 1876–1914* (Seoul: Yuk Phub SA, 1981).

Tamir, Yael. *Liberal Nationalism* (Princeton: Princeton University Press, 1993).

Tang, Peter S. H. *Russian and Soviet Policy in Manchuria and Outer Mongolia, 1911–1931* (Durham, N.C.: Duke University Press, 1959).

Teague, Elizabeth. "Miners' Strike in Siberia Winds Down, Strike in Ukraine Spreads to Other Areas: A Status Report," *RL 334/89*, 20 July 1989.

Tikhvinsky, S. L. *Chapters from the History of Russo-Chinese Relations* (Moscow, Progress Publishers, 1985).

Tolz, Vera. "Regionalism in Russia: The Case of Siberia," *Radio Free Europe/Radio Liberty Research Report*, 2 (9), 26 February 1993.

Toma, Takeo. *Ugokihajimeta kan Nihonkai keizai ken* (Tokyo, 1990).

Treadgold, Donald. *Soviet and Chinese Communism: Similarities and Differences* (Seattle: University of Washington Press, 1967).

Treadgold, Donald. *The Great Siberian Migration* (Princeton: Princeton University Press, 1957).

Umov, V. "Rossiiskii srednii klass: Sotsial'naia real'nost' i politicheskii fantom," *Polis (Politicheskie issledovaniia)*, 4, 1993.

Ustinov, V. S. and G. S. Shirokalova. "Krizis sel'skogo khoziastva i sovremennoe agrarnoe zakonodatel'stvo," *Gosudarstvo i pravo*, 3, 1993.

Ustiugov, P. "Zadachi natsional'noi raboty na krainem severe," *Revoliutsiia i natsional'nosti*, 1, 1931.

Valencia, Mark. "Economic Cooperation in Northeast Asia: The Proposed Tumen River Delta Scheme," *Pacific Review* 4 (3), 1993.

Valliant, Robert. "Japan and the Trans-Siberian Railroad, 1885–1905," Ph.D. dissertation, University of Hawaii, 1974.

Vanderlip, Washington. *In Search of a Siberian Klondike* (New York: Century and Co., 1903).

Varneck, Elena and H.H. Fisher, eds. *The Testimony of Kolchak and other Siberian Materials* (Stanford: Hoover Institute, 1935).

Veksman, A. M. et al., *Stroitel'stvo goroda nauki* (Novosibirsk, 1963).

Velkoff, V. and K. Kinsella. *Aging in Eastern Europe and the Former Soviet Union* (Washington, D.C.: Center for International Research, Bureau of the Census, 1993), report no. 93/1.

Verdery, Katherine. *National Ideology Under Socialism: Identity and Cultural Politics in Ceausescu's Romania* (Berkeley: University of California Press, 1991).

Vil'chek, Liliia. "Vniz po techeniiu derevenskoi prozy," *Voprosy literatury*, 6, 1985.

Vinogradov, Vladimir. "Sibirskii tsentr nauki," *Sibirskie ogni*, 5, 1967.

Vinokurova, Uliana A. *Bihigi Sakhalar* (Yakutsk, 1992).

———. *Tsennostnye orientatsii Iakutov v usloviiakh urbanizatsii* (Novosibirsk, 1992).

Viraphol, Sarasin. *Tribute and Profit: Sino-Siamese Trade, 1652–1853* (Cambridge, Mass.: Harvard University Press, 1977).

Vladimir [Zenone Volpicelli]. *Russia on the Pacific and the Siberian Railway* (London: S. Low, Marston, 1899).

Vladivostok: Sbornik istoricheskikh dokumentov, 1860–1907 gg. (Vladivostok, 1960).

Volkov G. N. "Etnopedagogicheskaia kontseptsiia national'noi shkoly," in *Mezhdunarodnaia konferentsiia natsional'naia shkola: konsteptsiia i technologiia razvitiia* (Yakutsk, 1993).

Vsepoddaneishii otchet Shtats-Sekretaria Kulomzina po poezdke v Sibir' dlia oznakomleniia s polozheniem pereselencheskogo dela, 2 vols. (St. Petersburg, 1896).

Vucinich, Wayne, ed. *Russia and Asia: Essays on the Influence of Russia on the Asian Peoples* (Stanford: Hoover Institute, 1972).

Wachold, Allen Glen. "Frank A. Golder: An Adventure in Russian History," Ph.D. dissertation, University of California, Santa Barbara, 1984.

Wang, Shengjin and Jingchun An. "Economic Development of the Northeastern Three Provinces of China and the Northeast Asia Economic Area," paper presented at the International Conference on Northeast Asia Economic and Trade Cooperation and the Strategy of Jilin Province Economic Development, Changchun, July 1993.

Watrous, Stephen. "Russia's Land of the Future: Regionalism and the Awakening of Siberia," Ph.D. dissertation, University of Washington, 1970.

Wegren, Steven. "Private Farming and Agrarian Reform in Russia," *Problems of Communism*, May/June 1992.

Weiser, Adele. *Die Völker Nordsiberiens: unter Sowjetischer Herrschaft von 1917 bis 1936* (Munich: Klaus Renner, 1989).

White, John. *Transition to Global Rivalry: Alliance Diplomacy and the Quadruple Entente, 1895–1907* (Cambridge: Cambridge University Press, forthcoming 1996).

————. *The Diplomacy of the Russo-Japanese War* (Princeton: Princeton University Press, 1964).

————. *The Siberian Intervention* (Princeton: Princeton University Press, 1950).

Whiting, Allen. *Siberian Development and East Asia: Threat or Promise?* (Stanford: Stanford University Press, 1981).

Widmer, Eric. *The Russian Ecclesiastical Mission in Peking During the 18th Century* (Cambridge, MA: Harvard University Press, 1976).

Wishnick, Elisabeth. *Mending Fences with China: The Evolution of Moscow's China Policy, 1969–1992* (forthcoming).

Wolf, Eric. *Europe and the People Without History* (Berkeley: University of California Press, 1982).

Wolff, David. *To the Harbin Station: The Liberal Alternative in Russian Manchuria, 1898–1914* (Berkeley: University of California Press, forthcoming).

Wolff, Larry. *Inventing Eastern Europe: The Map of Civilization on the Mind of the Enlightenment* (Stanford: Stanford University Press, 1994).

Wood, Alan. "Siberian Exile in the Eighteenth Century," *Sibirica*, 1 (1), 1990.

————, ed. *Siberia: Problems and Prospects for Regional Development* (New York: Croom Helm, 1987).

————, ed. *The History of Siberia: From Russian Conquest to Revolution* (New York: Routledge, 1991).

Wood, Alan and R. A. French, eds., *The Development of Siberia: Peoples and Resources* (New York: St. Martin's, 1989).

Wong, Lin Ken. "The Trade of Singapore, 1819–69," *Journal of the Malayan Branch of the Royal Asiatic Society*, 33 (4), December 1960.

Yakhtonoff, Victor. *Russia and the Soviet Union in the Far East* (New York: Coward-McCann, 1931).

Yang, Sung-chul. "The Kim Il-Song Cult in North Korea," *Korea and World Affairs* 4 (1), Spring 1980.

Yergin, Daniel. *The Prize: The Epic Quest for Oil, Money and Power* (New York: Simon and Schuster, 1991).

Yoshimura, Michio. "Nihongunno kitakarafuto senryō to nissō mondai," *Seiji Keizai Shigaku*, 132, 1977.

Yun, Nae-hyon. *The Ancient History of Korea* [in Korean] (Seoul, 1989).

Zaharchenko, Tatiana. "The Environmental Movement and Ecological Law in the Soviet Union: The Process of Transformation," *Ecology Law Journal*, vol. 17.

Zaslavskaia T. I. and Z. V. Kupriianova, eds., *Sotsial'no-ekonomicheskoe razvitie Sibirskogo sela* (Novosibirsk, 1987).

Zhirkov, Egor P. "Obrazovanie i razvitie: natsional'naia strategiia na podstupakh k XXI veku," in *Mezhdunarodnaia konferentsiia natsional'naia shkola: konsteptsiia i technologiia razvitiia* (Yakutsk, 1993).

Index

Academic freedom, 89–105
Academy of Sciences, 10, 89, 92, 94, 97, 161, 195, 228
Agriculture, 69–70, 151, 172, 188–189, 224–239, 278. *See also* Collectivization
    khutor, 31
    policy, 77, 93, 240–249, 278
    private farming, 188, 224–239
    trade with China, 291–294, 297
    yields, 82, 177, 188, 224–225
Akademgorodok, 70–71, 89–105, *photo 17. See also* Lavrent'ev
    social clubs, 91, 101–104
Alaska, 8, 18, 147, 269, 273
Aleksandrovsk, 56–61, 63–65, 163
Alekseev, Admiral E.I., 50
Alekseevsk, 304
Alexander II (Romanov), 25
Alexander III (Romanov), 25, 42
Altai region, 123
Amalrik, Andrei, 110
Americans, 5, 57, 283. *See also* United States
American West, 70
Amur basin, 4, 18, 69, 135, 324
    Amur oblast, 10, 27, 41–43, 172, 260, 292
    Amur River, 6, 19, 40, 44, 59, 161–162, 270, 295, 303, *photos 3, 16*
Asia. *See* Northeast Asia, Southeast Asia, other countries
Asian identity, 160–161
Astaf'ev, Viktor, 110–111
Autonomy. *See* Center-periphery relations

Baikal, Lake, 6, 18, 91, 101, 114, 144, 154, 189, 256
Baikal-Amur Mainline (BAM), 101, 150, 244, 251, 278
Bikin River, 261–264
Blagoveshchensk, 40, 57, 279, 309
Bolsheviks. *See also* CPSU
    civil war, 49, 59–60, 70, 76–84
    1920s and 1930s, 163–165, 304
Borders, 23–27, 325–327
    bordertrade, 264, 275–289, *photos 31, 32*
    constructed, 270
    Russo-Japanese, 3, 19, 63
    Sino-Korean, 302–311, 320–321
    Sino-Russian, 19, 40–52, 52*n.1*, 134, 136, 270, 275–298, 320–321
Borodin, Leonid, 111
Brezhnev era, 100–101, 108, 168, 189, 195–196, 241, 244–251
Bureaucracy. *See* Central planning
Buriats, 27, 33–34, 133, 141, 144, 152, 324

Capital. *See* Investment
Catherine the Great (Romanov), 29
Center-periphery relations, 17, 41, 136, 323–324. *See also* Central authority, local authority, regionalism
    autonomy, 72, 77, 91, 122–130, 134, 139, 199, 260
    Russian Far East, 140–155, 174, 256–257
    Siberia, 5, 189, 193–205, 205*n.1*, 207–220, 224

Central authority, 24, 101, 175, 179,
   225
nomenklatura elites, 195, 210
vs. regional authority. *See*
   Center-periphery relations
Central Executive Committee of the
   Soviets of Siberia. *See* Tsentrosibir'
Central government and bureaucracy,
   75–78, 134, 178, 241
Central planning, 210, 212, 216, 244
Centralization, 75–88, 98, 126, 277
Cheliabinsk, 18, 30
Chernenok, Mikhail, 111
China, 3–10, 136, 147, 180, 203–204, 225,
   251, 254–255*n.29*, 264, 269–273,
   275–288, 306–309, 324–326. *See*
   also International relations, overseas
   Chinese
Chinese in Russia, 43, 166, 258, 275–302,
   photos 5, 30–32
   pre-Soviet, 18, 24, 43–49
   post-Soviet, 169
   Soviet, 19–20, 187
Chinese Eastern Railway (CER), 18,
   40–54, 56, 273*n.5*, *photos 4, 28*
Chivilikhin, Vladimir, 110
Civil society, 210. *See also*
   Democratization
Civil vs. military power, 40–49, 275
Civil war. *See* Russian Civil War
Cities, 42, 51, 70, 279–282. *See also*
   Urban population
Coal, 69–70, 149–150, 177, *photo 22*
   as a social service, 227, 234–235
   extraction, 187–188. *See also* Extractive
   industries
   trade, 317. *See also* Trade
   unionism, 196, 207–220. *See also*
   Labor
Collectivization, 109, 121, 150, 165,
   170*n.13*, 227
   decollectivization, 188, 224,
   227–228. *See also* Cooperatives
   recollectivization, 189, 233
Colonialism, 23, 36, 49, 75, 120, 195, 269,
   283
Colonization, 3–4, 17, 20, 23, 25,
   36, 45. *See also* Demography,
   migration
Committee of the Siberian Railroad, 25,
   30, 32, 35

Communist Party of the Soviet Union
   (CPSU), 71. *See also* Bolsheviks
civil war and 1920s, 77–86, 162–164, 304
local and regional organs, 77–86,
   91–104, 143,
   1930s–1989, 90–104, 210–214,
   240–250, 254*n.24*
   post-1989, 122, 153, 193, 203, 205
Construction industry, 95, 226. *See also*
   Housing
Cooperatives, 189, 229, 232–233. *See*
   also Decollectivization
Corruption, 5, 202, 211, 262, 281. *See*
   also Crime
Crime, 28, 134, 180, 264, 276, 282,
   298–299, 325–326. *See also*
   Smuggling, pilfering, poaching
Culture and identity, 28, 139–155, 218
Culture Base (1929), 164–165. *See also*
   Sakhalin
   Nivkh, 161
   Sakha cultural revival, 145. *See also*
   Sakha
   Siberian, 71, 108–117, 207

Dalian (Dairen, Dal'nii), 19, 47, 64,
   278–280, 318, *photo 27*
Decentralization, 92, 188–207, 256,
   323. *See also* Center-periphery
   relations, local authority, regionalism
Democratization, 122, 188, 207–220,
   252. *See also* Civil society, political
   freedom
Demography, 24–27, 142, 152, 283,
   293–295, 318, 324–325. *See also*
   Korean migration, migration,
   overseas Chinese, Yellow Peril
De-Stalinization, 71, 89, 92, 98, 102. *See*
   also Khrushchev era
Development, 109
   colonization policy, 3
   Siberia, 23, 26
   economic, 172–185, 193, 199, 280
   economic policy, 90, 114, 122–123, 187,
   197, 205, 242–245, 306
   rural, 227
Diamonds, 137*n.3*, 149–151, 174

Economy. *See* Labor, prices, privatization,
   productivity, property rights,
   stagnation, trade, wages

Efficiency. *See* Productivity
Elderly, 226–227, 230, 233–234
Energy, 148, 294. *See also* Coal, gas, oil
Enisei gubernia, 78, 81
    River, 26
Environment, 189, 202, 241, 244, 249,
    252, 256–265, 326
Ethnicity, 153, 199, 305. *See also* Culture
    and identity
European identity, 160
Exile, 42, 69, 79
    political and criminal in Siberia, 4–5, 17,
        28, 75
    Sakhalin, 135, 162
Expansionism, 276, 295. *See also*
    Colonization
Exports, 124–125, 176, 189, 281,
    316–317. *See also* Free economic
    zone, imports, trade
    of raw materials, 184, 196–197, 208,
        258–262
    to Asian countries, 42, 179–182, 262
    to the Soviet Union/Russia, 291–297, 309
Extractive industry, 121, 123, 173–176,
    183, 187. *See also* Coal, diamonds,
    gas, oil, timber

Far Eastern Republic (1920–22), 65, 83,
    153, 163, 325, *photo 10*
    People's Revolutionary Army of the, 80
February Revolution (1917), 7, 57, 134
Federalism, 24, 77, 122, 152, 189, 219,
    259
Fengtian province, 45
First All-Siberian Congress of Soviets, 76
Fish, 58, 177
    domestic consumption, 162–163, 183
    export, 182, 187, 265*n.1*, 293
    foreign, 169
    processing, 70, 174, 183
Forestry. *See* Timber
Free economic zone, 42, 182, 218, 276,
    280, 309
Fujiadian, 45–46

Gamovskii miatezh (1918), 57
Gas. *See also* Extractive industries, natural
    resources
    in the Russian Far East, 130*n.3*, 149,
    in Siberia, 70, 121–122, 187, 193–204,
        240

General Agreement on Trade and Tariffs
    (GATT), 286
Giliaks. *See* Nivkhi
Glasnost, 189, 211, 250–251, 256
Golder, Frank (1877–1929), 7–8, 13*n.19*
Great Britain, 6–7, 17, 315
Grigor'ev, Leonid, 59
Grossman, Vasilii, 110
Gulag, 110, 135–136, 187

Harbin, 56, 277, 280–282, 318, 325–326,
    photo 6
    Russians in, 6, 18–19, 40–54, 325–326
Heavy industry, 35, 70, 121, 172, 292
Heihe, 279
Heilongjiang (Amur) province, 279–280
Higher education, 89–105
Hokkaido, 10, 19–20, 55, 137*n.4*,
    327–328, *photo 24*
Hong Kong, 315–318, 320
Housing, 200, 226–227. *See also*
    Construction industry

Iadrintsev, Nikolai (1842–1894), 5,
    72*n.2*
Imports, 176, 179–180, 184, 292,
    295. *See also* Exports, trade
Industrialization, 70, 85
Industry 25, 51, 95, 185, 196, 225, 292,
    294. *See also* Construction industry,
    extractive industry, heavy industry
Inflation, 199, 213, 232–233. *See also*
    Prices
Infrastructure, 25–27, 278–279, *photo
    34*. *See also* Railroads
    in Siberia, 77, 195, 226–228, 244
    in the Russian Far East, 40, 166, 172,
        175, 179, 184–185, 258, 260, 294
Institutions, 197, 209, 211, 252
Integration, regional, 180, 270
Interethnic. *See* Multiethnic
International Relations, 312, 318
    Korean-Russian, 271, *photo 34*
    Russo-Chinese, 3, 7, 19, 40, 42,
        270–301, 320, *photo 34*
    Russo-Chinese Defense Treaty (1896),
        44
    Russo-Japanese, 3, 7, 19, 22*n.10*, 55, 63,
        photos 25–27, 29, 34
    Joint Soviet-Japanese Development
        Scheme (1965), 187

International Relations *(continued)*
  Portsmouth Treaty (1905), 49, 55–56,
    162
  Russo-Japanese Treaty (1907), 51
  Russo-Japanese Treaty of Alliance
    (1916), 57
  Russo-Japanese War (1904–1905), 3, 19,
    46, 49, 55–56, 134, 273*n.5*, *photo 7*
  Soviet-Japanese Basic Convention
    (1925), 65, 305
  Sino-Japanese, 312–316
  Sino-Japanese Treaty (1887), 317
  Sino-Japanese War (1894–1895), 18, 24
Investment, 136
  in Siberia, 121, 125, 130*n.3*, 193–199,
    201, 203–204, 225, 231, 248
  in the Russian Far East, 173–174, 179,
    258, 262–265, 279, 283, 291–296,
    309, 324
  foreign, 125, 179, 182–185, 187–190,
    262–265. *See also* Joint ventures
  Chinese, 279, 283, 291–296
  Japanese 278
  Korean, 262–265, 309
  Western, 203–204
  private
    in Siberia, 201
    in the Russian Far East, 179, 182, 185,
      258, 279
  state, 248
    in Siberia, 121, 125, 130*n.3*, 193–199,
      225, 231, 248
    in the Russian Far East, 173–174, 179,
      279
Irkutsk, 30, 76, 112, 115, 324, *photo 9*
  gubernia, 81
  University, 10

Japan. *See also* International relations,
    Northern Territories dispute
  economic power and investor, 150, 169,
    180, 185, 187, 203–204, 262–264,
    293–295, 324
  Japanese Expeditionary Army for
    Sakhalin, 62–63
  Japanization, 63
  pre-World War II, 3–10, 19–20, 24, 43,
    48–52, 302–304, 312–321, *photo 10*
  post-World War II, 136, 147, 269–271,
    282–287, 307, 309
  Sakhalin, 55–68, 135, 142, 162–166

Jews, 29, 46–48, 51, 134, 172
Jilin province, 45, 279–280, 309
Joint ventures, 182, 200–204, 280–291,
    294. *See also* Investment
  with Chinese, 280–291
  with Japanese,63. *See also* Polar Star
    Association, Staakhev & Company
  with Koreans,190, 257–264,
  with Westerners, 201

Kazakhs, 33, 189
Kemerov oblast, 121, 123, 228–229
Kemerovo city, 228
Kerner, Robert (1887–1956), 8–11, 13*n.21*
Khabarovsk, 18, 40–45, 136, 172,
    277–280, 286, 292–299, 304–305,
    309, *photos 30, 34*
Khanti-Mansiisk, 199–200
Khorvat, Colonel Dmitrii L., 43–45
Khrushchev era, 93–99, 167–168, 244–246
Kim, Il-Song, 305
Kolchak, Admiral Aleksandr V., 58–59, 80
Korea, 3–4
  Korean migration, 51, 271, 304–305, 320
  North Korea, 169, 203, 264, 271,
    278–279, 305–307
    labor, 187, 260–261,
  pre-Korean War, 6, 19, 43, 56, 166,
    296–297, 302–305, 313–314,
    319–320, 326
  post-Korean War, 10, 147, 269, 273,
    279, 285, 305–310
  South Korea, 271, 287,
    as investor, 150, 169, 180, 185, 190,
      203–204, 261–264, 283, 293,
      295, 306–308
Krasnoiarsk, 123, 297, 299
  krai, 125, 127
Kuhara Mining Company, 57, 63
Kulomzin, Anatolii N. (1838–1924), 17,
    20, 23–36, *photo 1*
Kunaev, Stanislav, 113
Kuzbas, 207–220, *photo 21*

Labor, 77, 177, 193, 207–220
  strike, 47, 121, 196, 205, 211–215,
    photo 21
  supply, 226, 293–296, 305
Land as a natural resource, 188, 224–225,
    278, 295
Language, 145, 162

Lantzeff, George (1892–1955), 8, 14*n.24*
Lavrent'ev, Mikhail A., 89, 92, 94,
  98–100, 104, *photo 17*
Lenin, Vladimir I., 78, 81, 164, 168
Liaodong Peninsula, 47–49, 279
Lipatov, Vil, 111
Literacy, 165–166, *photo 13*
Lobanov-Rostovsky, Prince Andrei
  (1892–1979), 8, 14*n.26*
Local authority, 26, 79, 189, 193,
  259–260, 279, 323–324. *See also*
  Center-periphery relations,
  regionalism
Long-Term State Program on the
  Economic Development of the Far
  Eastern Economic Region until the
  year 2000, 179. *See also*
  Development

Manchuria, 3, 56, 162, *photos 6, 26, 29*
  Chinese in, 270–271, 296, 318–319
  Japanese in, 271
  Koreans in, 302–308,
  Russians in, 6, 18–20, 40–54. *See also*
    Harbin
Maritime province (*Primorskii krai*), 172,
  303–304, 307, *photo 28*
  development of, 280–283, 292–299
  inhabitants, 27, 41–43, 272
  natural resources, 189, 256–265
Market transformation, 180–181, 194,
  197, 199, 204, 210, 224, 236,
  256. *See also* Privatization
Mehnert, Klaus (1906–1984), 8–9, 14*n.32*
Migration, 17, 20, 23, 30, 178, 225, 228,
  272, 276, 298–299, 309, 318, 326,
  photos 2, 3. *See also* Colonization,
  demography
Military, 41, 46, 50, 128, 136, 187, 194,
  291–292, 327. *See also* Civil
  Army 24, 41, 60, *photos 27, 29*
  conversion of, 125, 183–184
  industry, 121, 130*n.1*, 174, 276, 281,
    290, 292
  Navy 46, 56–60, 64, 136, *photo 25*
Minerals, 69, 134, 148–149, 197–198, 240
Mongolia, 3–4, 34, 147, 269
  between China and Russia, 273
  Mongol-Buriats, 18, 144
  revolution, 20, 83
  and Siberia, 324

Mozhaev, Boris, 111
Multicultural. *See* Multiethnic
Multiethnic, 27, 34, 40, 43, 142–144,
  148–149, 154, 269, 328
  multiethnic conflict, 142, 150, 175, 215,
    219
  multiethnic populations, 24, 32, 42
Multiracial. *See* Multiethnic
Murav'ev, Nikolai N. (1809–1881), 18,
  28, 270

Nagasaki, 313, 316, *photo 25*
Nakhodka, 182, 280, 282
Nationalism, 215, 256, 284, 308
  Russian, 122
  Sakha, 144–146, 152–153. *See also*
    Sakha
  Siberian, 5–6
Native and aboriginal peoples, *photos 12,
  14–16*. *See also* Nivkhi, Sakha,
  Udege
  Russian Far East, 133–136, 139–155,
    160–169, 257, 265
  Siberia, 5, 18, 23, 33–35, 44, 190
Natural resources, 187–189, 202. *See also*
  Diamonds, extractive industries, fish,
  gas, land, minerals, oil, timber, water
  control over, 56, 64, 134, 210–218
  development, 89–95
  domestic consumption, 83, 173, 224,
    240–244
  export, 187–189, 195, 278
  Russian Far East, 182–184, 264–265,
    294–296
  Siberia, 252
Nature, managed, 189, 240–252
New Economic Policy, 82
Nicholas II (Romanov), 25, 42–43, 168
Nikolaev, Mikhail, 140, 142, 147, 151–152
Nikolaevsk Incident, 55–62
Nikolaevsk-na-Amure, 40, 55–60
Nikolsk-Ussuriisk, 40
Nivkhi, 133–135, 160–169, *photos 11, 13*
Nizhnevartovsk, 200–202
NKVD (People's Commisariat of Internal
  Affairs), 80–81, 167, 271
Non-governmental organizations (NGOs),
  263–264
Northeast Asia, 190, 193–194, 203–205,
  257, 264–265, 269–329
Northern Sakhalin Oil Company, 65

Northern Territories dispute, 308, 322n.22, 327
Novosibirsk, 96, 98, 100, 123–124, 126, 225, 228
oblast, 121, 123, 229
State University, 99

October Revolution (1917), 134–135, 146, 161
Oil, 240, *photos 18, 19. See also* Extractive industries, natural resources
export and foreign interests, 169
Russian Far East, 177
Sakha, 149
Sakhalin, 55–70, 187
Siberia, 240
Tiumen, 76, 121–122, 130n.2, 188, 193–204
Omsk, 58, 64, 80, 113
gubernia, 81–82
Output. *See* Productivity
Overseas Chinese,
in Asia, 272, 313–320
in Russia, 270–271, 322n.18

Pacific Rim, 150, 161, 179–181
Parliament, dissolution of Russian (October 1993), 72, 125–128, 151, 207
Party, the. *See* Communist Party of the Soviet Union
Pensions. *See* Elderly
Perestroika, 72, 104, 121, 143, 160, 168, 189, 210–213, 273n.4
Peter the Great (Romanov), 111
Pilfering, 229–231, 238n.25. *See also* Poaching
Planning. *See* Central Planning
Poaching, 258, 261, 264, 298. *See also* Pilfering
Polar Star Association (*Hokushinkai*), 58–59, 61, 63
Political freedom, 102
Political power, 207
Population. *See* Demography
Port Arthur, 19, 47, 326, *photo 7*
Prices, 124, 175–176, 179, 195–197, 199, 219, 231, 263. *See also* Inflation
Private Property, 31, 210. *See also* Property rights

Privatization, 148, 180. *See also* Market transformation
asset distribution, 229, 231, 233, 236
industrial, 188–190, 200–202, 205
rural, 150, 188–189, 224–237, 258
Productivity, 188, 224–226, 229–230, 236, 238n.20, 248–249, 297
Property rights, 136, 207–209, 296. *See also* Private property

Railroads, 57, *photos 5, 6. See also* Baikal-Amur Mainline, Chinese Eastern Railroad, South-Manchurian Railroad, Trans-Siberian Railroad, Ussuri Railroad
Rasputin, Valentin, 71, 108–117, 241
Raw materials. *See* Natural resources
Regionalism, 147, 323–328
Russian Far East, 139–155, 178, 259–260, 275–288
Siberia, 6, 23, 71–72, 75–88, 98, 120–138, 224, 189. *See also* Nationalism
Resource sharing, 150–151
River diversion, 91, 189, 240–252
Roziner, Feliks, 113
Rural population, 156n.8, 167, 224–226
Russian Civil War, 70, 79, 134, 217, 305, *photo 9*
Russian Revolution of 1905, 49, 134
Russification, 24, 33, 143, 147, 150, 161–163
linguistic, 32, 145
Russo-Chinese Bank, 44
Rybakov, Anatolii, 110

Sakha, 134–135, 137n.3, 139–155, 187. *See also* Nationalism, cultural identity
Sakha Keskile (Sakha Popular Front), 142, 147–148
Sakha Omuk (Sakha People), 142, 148–149
Sakha Republic, 139–155, 172
Sakhalin, 281, *photos 11, 33*
free economic zone, 182
native peoples, 135, 160–172
oil, 187
Russo-Japanese relations, 19–20, 55–68, 142, 204, 327. *See also* International relations

Science, 70–71, 89–105, 125, 175, 189, 198, 240–252 *See also* Academy of Sciences, technology
Second All-Siberian Congress of Soviets (1918), 77
Self-government, 133
Separatism,
  Far Eastern economic, 153
  Siberian, 122, 126
Settlement, *photos 1, 3. See also* China, colonization
  pre-Soviet, 17–18, 25–35, 36*n.5*, 41, 133–134, 159*n.30*, 270
  Soviet, 23, 142, 167–168, 178, 225
Shukshin, Vasilii, 111
Siberian Agreement (*Sibirskoe soglashenie*), 123–130
Siberian Division of the Academy of Sciences. *See* Academy of Sciences
Siberian Intervention (1918–1922), 9, 19, 55–62, 320 *photo 8*
Siberian krai-level Executive Committee of Soviets. *See* Sibkraiispolkom
Siberian Revolutionary Committee. *See* Sibrevkom
Sibkraiispolkom, 83–85
Sibrevkom, 79–82
Singapore, 272, 293, 315, 318
Siniavskii, Andrei, 110
Smuggling, 297–299 *See also* Crime
Social experiments, 23–36, 40–52, 160–169, 224–237. *See also* Literacy
Social services, 235–237, 238*n.19*
Solzhenitsyn, Aleksandr, 110, 115, 118*n.8*
Southeast Asia, 19, 136, 272, 312, 318, 320–321, 328
South-Manchurian Railway, 51, 319
Soviet identity, 160
Sovnarkom, 78, 81, 84
Special Commission for Siberian Economic Aid (*Rinji Shiberia Keizai Enjo Iinkai*), 58
Sputnik, 93
Stagnation, 174–175
Stakheev, Ivan & Company, 57–63
Stalin, Joseph V., 164, 168, 187, 244, 279, 307, 325
State Ownership, 31, 210. *See also* Investment, privatization
Stephan, John, 9, 56, 63

Strike. *See* Labor
Sungari river, 40, 43, 45

Taxes,
  agricultural tax, 82
  budget, 85
  collection, 30, 235–236, 313, 318
  control over (central vs. local), 123–124, 149–151, 178–181, 193–202, 327
Technology, 44, 92–93, 175, 248, 258. *See also* Science
  import of, 182–187, 196, 204, 278–283, 291–297, 326
Timber, 57–58, 174–177, 184, 240, *photo 20*
  export, 169, 182, 187–190, 291–297
  Maritime province, 256–265
Tiumen oblast, 82–83, 121, 123, 130*n.3*, 188, 193–201,
  city, 198
Tomsk, 5, 30, 43, 48, 115, 123, 125
  Siberian Duma, 77
  University, 10
Tourism, 183–184, 307, *photo 24*
Trade, 161, 265, 275, 283, 292–293, 297, 309, 312–313, 317, 326. *See also* Exports, imports
  with China, 291–297
Trans-Siberian Railroad, 7, 17–18, 24–32, 35, 42, 65, 120, 271, *photos 1, 3*
  auxiliary enterprises, 25, 35
  colonization, 150
Transition, 209, 218, 237, 275. *See also* Democratization, market transformation
Transport. *See* Infrastructure
Tribute, 135, 272, 312–318
Tsentrosibir', 76–77
Tumen river, 272, 275–288, 304, 309

Udege, 262–263
Unions. *See* Labor
United States, 23, 28, 78, 169, 180, 281, 284, 287, 320
Urban population, 27, 42, 70, 156*n.8*
Ussuri Railroad, 42–43
Ussuri region, 56, 270, 295–296
Ussuri River, 296

Vampilov, Aleksandr, 111
Village Prose, 71, 108–117

Vladivostok, *photos 4, 14*
  Japanese in, 49, *photos 8, 23*
  pre-Soviet, 6, 18, 40–42, 45, 271,
    303–304, 318
  post-Soviet, 153, 263–265, 277–278,
    282–286, 294, 299, 308–309
  Soviet, 10, 59
Vologda, 112, 115

Wages, 196, 226, 228, 230–232,
    238*n.20*. *See also* Prices
War. *See* International relations
Washington Conference (1921–22), 63
Water, 240–252. *See also* River diversion

Western business practices, 202
White, John, 9
Witte, Sergei, 24–36, 44, 46–50
Wood. *See* Timber

Yakut Union, 134
Yakutian Autonomous Republic, 134
Yakuts, 22*n.11*, 133–134. *See also* Sakha
Yakutsk, 135, 143, 154
Yamal-Nenetsky, 199
Yellow Peril, 27, 31, 270, 290–300, 321

Zalygin, Sergei, 111, 241
Zemstvo, 26, 59